FINDING
AND
BUYING
YOUR
PLACE
IN
THE
COUNTRY

FINDING AND BUYING YOUR PLACE IN THE COUNTRY

Les Scher

Artwork by Roger Bayless

Text Illustrations by Carol Wilcox

COLLIER BOOKS
A Division of Macmillan Publishing Co., Inc.
New York

COLLIER MACMILLAN PUBLISHERS
London

The purpose of this book is to give general guidance in the purchase of real estate and not to provide legal advice. In dealing with legal problems the reader should obtain the advice of a lawyer.

Macmillan
Publishing Co., Inc.
866 Third Avenue
New York, N.Y. 10022
Collier Macmillan
Canada, Ltd.

Library of Congress
Catalog Card Number: 72–12959

First Collier Books
Edition 1974
Fifth Printing 1978

*Finding and Buying
Your Place in the Country*
is published in a
hardcover edition
by Macmillan
Publishing Co., Inc.

Printed in the
United States
of America

To my parents,
Hannah and Meyer Scher,
in gratitude
for taking me to the country
at an early age
and for making
this book possible

ACKNOWLEDGMENTS

Early in 1971 Paul Kleyman, editor of the *Intersection Newsletter* in San Francisco, urged me to write an article as a prelude to a book that would contain everything a person needed to know to realize his or her dream of owning a place in the country. I spent the next two years putting together this information. I am indebted to Paul for getting me started.

During those years I was greatly aided in my task by the hospitality of Stu Miller, Gillian Wilson, Steve and Gayle Chase, Bill Leifer, Stanley Shell, Phil and Toni Jones, and Roy Palmer; by the inspirational black classical music of Rahsaan Roland Kirk; and by the encouragement I had previously received from Thomas Clayton, Christopher Grose, Buck and Claude Delventhal, and Paul and Judy deBarros.

Thanks also to Clement Alexandre of Macmillan Publishing Co., Inc., for his patience, faith, and good humor.

Finally there is one person who worked as hard as I did to realize this book. To Carol Wilcox go my love and gratitude for editing, typing, illustrating, researching, and remaining by my side throughout the many months we worked together.

LES SCHER

Contents

Part IV

Deciding on a Fair Price

Part V

Financing Your Purchase

Part VI

The Contract of Sale

Part VII

Going Through Escrow

Part VIII

Using a Lawyer

Appendix

Illustrations

MODEL FORMS

Introduction

My father told me when I was very young the first thing a man must do is to own a piece of land. When you go into a store and you buy something it's chattel, but when you own a piece of land, that's real. And that's where the words "real estate" originated.

—Chuck Berry

This book is meant to be a tool that you should carry with you as you go through the processes of finding and buying your place in the country. You will have to read parts of it more than once in order to absorb all of the information. Many of the things I discuss will become much clearer when you actually get out and start dealing with real estate agents, looking at land, and delving into the public records at the local City Hall. If you have the time and inclination to follow the course of in-

vestigation I outline, you will be protected with the minimal need for a lawyer. Even when you retain counsel for some aspect of the purchase, such as inspecting the final draft of your Contract of Sale, the legal fees will be far less than if the attorney drew up the contract himself. After your purchase, you will continue to find this book useful for such contingencies as fighting an increase in property taxes, confronting the Building Inspector, or appropriating water from a stream.

The chapters in this book are divided into eight parts with an Appendix at the end. Part I, *Looking for Land,* should be used in conjunction with the Appendix. This first section gives basic information on how to find out about land for sale, and it teaches you how to protect yourself when dealing with real estate agents by explaining the role they play and the sales tactics they use. Part II, *Checking Out the Land,* outlines in detail the factors you should consider when choosing the general location of the land and evaluating the various aspects of a specific parcel, especially the soil, the water, and the condition of the structures. Part III, *The Land and the Law,* explains in an easy-to-follow manner the legal protections you need and how to investigate them. Part IV, *Deciding on a Fair Price,* will help you evaluate the fair market value of the land and bargain skillfully with the seller to get his asking price down to a figure you consider reasonable. Part V, *Financing Your Purchase,* explores the types of financing, the sources of loans, and available government programs. Because the financial world has a language all its own, a glossary of terms is also included. Part VI, *The Contract of Sale,* presents a model form which you can copy from the book, modify for your own transaction, and thus help insure that you will be adequately protected in your purchase. This is the heart of the book and the most important section. Part VII, *Going Through Escrow,* demystifies the escrow process and explains title searches, abstracts of title, and title insurance. The various forms of co-ownership are outlined and a Model Owners Agreement is included. Different types of deeds are then described. Part VIII concludes the book with a discussion of lawyers and some final words to the reader.

USEFUL RESOURCES AND HOW TO ORDER THEM

Throughout the book you will find lists of Useful Resources containing hundreds of available publications and sources of information which supplement the material included in the chapters. Most of the resource literature is available at no cost, and the few items that are not free

cost less than a dollar. Even if you order only the free publications you will acquire a personal library that will be invaluable as you proceed to find and buy your land, and it will continue to be useful long after your purchase.

When ordering any materials give the complete title and order number, and list the publications in alphabetical and numerical order. Where an order number is not given, the full title will be sufficient. Always include your return address in detail, including the zip code.

In ordering free publications, you will receive them faster if you send the information on a post card. You should never order more than one copy each of ten publications at one time from the same source.

Those resources that must be purchased should be ordered by sending a postal money order, an express order, or personal check. Send the exact amount specified for each item and specify in your order the form and amount of remittance. You do not have to pay for postage even if you live in Canada. There is no limit to the number of items you can purchase at one time.

If you are ordering literature from government agencies, you might have to wait as long as six months before receiving it. It is usually much faster to go to the various government agencies yourself and pick up what you want, since most offices maintain a large stock of available material. The addresses of all Government Printing Office bookstores are given at the end of the book in Appendix J.

It is nice to receive maps and photographs rolled up in a cardboard tube rather than unprotected in an envelope where they can get bent or torn. There is no extra charge for this service but you must specifically request that your order be mailed in a tube

FINDING
AND
BUYING
YOUR
PLACE
IN
THE
COUNTRY

I

LOOKING
FOR
LAND

chapter 1

How to Start Your Search

Purchasing land should be done as carefully as selecting the person you will share it with. The more land you see, the more you will learn about differences in value and about your expectations. Try to keep an open mind when land hunting. Many people find that, after seeing many kinds of places, they choose a different type of environment than they had originally sought. Take your time and approach your search with a relaxed but probing attitude. Even if you are not ready to actually buy land at the present time you should begin looking, since it takes time to find the right place and you want to find out as much information as you can about country property before you buy.

Take your outdoor camping equipment, or your trailer if you have one, when you go land hunting. Most real estate agents and sellers will allow you to stay on the land for a day or two so that you can get a sense of what it is like. (The aspects of the land that you can explore while camping there are discussed in Part II, *Checking Out the Land*.) You can't begin to get an idea of whether the property will be right for you unless you spend some time on it. You should stay at least several days on the land, preferably during different seasons.

You want to see the property at its best and at its worst. Most land is sold in the spring and early summer, from April through July.

This is usually the most beautiful time of year. The weather is getting warm, the wildflowers are in bloom, the grass is green, and water is plentiful. People are beginning to think of getting a place to spend the approaching summer and those to follow. Sales usually drop a little during the driest summer months but increase again in the early fall, from September through October. Land prices are highest during these seasons because the demand is greatest. (The effect of the number of interested buyers on the price of a piece of property is discussed in Chapter 20: *Bargaining to Get the Seller's Asking Price Down.*) The best time to buy is in the late fall and winter when the number of buyers diminishes and prices are at an annual low level. Few people will venture forth to look at land in the dead of winter when many country roads are impassable. If you see some land you like in the spring, try to wait until December or January to buy it. Not only will you probably get it for a much better price at that time but you will also be able to see it under both good and bad conditions. If you still like it when the roads are muddy and rutted and the skies are overcast, you know you will be happy with your purchase. However, if you see some land for the first time in the middle of winter when it is covered with snow, do not buy it until you see it after the snow melts. A beautiful covering of snow can disguise a poor piece of land.

If possible, try to live in the area in which you want to buy before actually making your purchase. You may find that you do not like the area as well as you imagined you would. It is usually easy to find a house or cabin to rent for a few weeks or months. If you ask around you might be able to find a job as caretaker on someone's property. This is an economical way to live in the country while looking for your own piece of land. If you are a resident, you will probably hear about places for sale that an outsider would not find out about. Many people do not sell their land through real estate agents in order to avoid paying an agent's commission. Some do not even advertise in the local paper or post signs but simply rely on friends passing the word. There are several common ways to find out about property for sale without living in the area, however.

Most real estate agencies print up listings of "available properties" which they will send to you on request. Go to the main branch of your local library or telephone company and ask to see the Yellow Pages of the directory for the area in which you are interested in purchasing land. You can then send letters to all the real estate agents there asking for their listings and telling them what you want. They will send you the current listings and let you know when something comes into their offices that might interest you.

Large real estate agencies publish land catalogues listing various pieces of property they have for sale. In the Appendix at the end of the book, I list the catalogues now available free from major real estate companies that have local franchises throughout the rural areas of the United States. The two most famous companies are Strout Realty and United Farm Real Estate Agency. These catalogues will give you an idea of prices in the various areas of the country.

When reading any real estate advertisement, notice what is excluded as well as what is included. Any piece of land can be written up to sound good or can look beautiful in a tiny photograph. An ad will always refer to a parcel's good qualities. For example, if no mention is made of water availability, there is probably not a good water supply.

Another common advertising technique used by many real estate agencies is illustrated by the following quote from a major catalogue:

From this catalog select the property or section that suits you best and see it now! Delay might mean that someone else might beat you to the bargain you have chosen. The catalog will be in the hands of thousands of other people in every corner of the U.S., and the first person on the ground with the necessary deposit is the one who gets the place of his choice!

Don't let such ads scare you into thinking that you must buy land immediately because nothing will be left if you don't. Lots of land is still available and more becomes available every day as large ranches and farms split up. Although land prices continue to rise, good deals are constantly coming up, and if you know what you are doing, you will be able to get a good piece of land at a reasonable price for many years in the future.

Another common way to locate land for sale is to look in the local papers in the area and in the classified ads of major newspapers of a nearby city. The Sunday edition of large newspapers carries the most real estate advertisements.

When you go to an area you should prepare index cards containing a description of the type of land you want and hang them on the local bulletin boards with an address at which you can be reached. You can also place an ad in the local paper for a small fee.

It is possible to purchase land other than from a private party. The federal and state governments sell and lease land to the general public. Although homesteading is no longer possible in this country, it might become a reality again in some areas at a later date. Mining claims have been used to obtain land on a short-term basis. A program exists whereby summer homes can be leased in the national forests. Information on how to obtain all the available literature on the above subjects is given in the Appendix. Also included therein is resource information on land in Alaska and Canada for the heartier land buyers and the addresses of land agencies in each state that sells state-owned land.

Land can also be purchased at tax sales held when property taxes have not been paid by the owner. This land seems to be a bargain, but many technical aspects are involved and I do not recommend that you buy such land without consulting an attorney. In most cases, you must pay cash for the land and after you buy it the owner still has a legally specified period of time to pay the back taxes and redeem the land. If this happens, you will get your money back with interest, but you will lose the land. Tax sales are discussed in Chapter 17: *Taxes and Assessments.* You can get all the facts on the local laws in your area from the county Tax Collector.

A variation on buying land at a tax sale is to look in the Tax Collector's public file in the county Tax Collector's office to find parcels that have back taxes due on them. You can then contact the owners and ask them if they would like to sell. You might find an owner who is desperate and willing to sell his place at a bargain price.

Buying land at a foreclosure or trustee sale also involves technical legal problems and should not be attempted without hiring an attorney.

You will not have any problems finding land for sale. Your main concerns will be the quality of the land, the price you will pay for it, the inclusion in your Contract of Sale of all the necessary legal protections, and the method of financing your purchase. The remainder of the book is devoted to these things.

FOR SALE
40 ACRES
JET REALTY
324-1862

chapter 2

Real Estate Agents, Realtors, and Salesmen

Real estate agents are a foul breed, though one in twenty is all right and can help you.

—Stewart Brand, founder and editor of *The Whole Earth Catalog*

HOW TO DEAL WITH THE OTHER NINETEEN

When Stewart Brand made the above statement in the last issue of *The Whole Earth Catalog,* he was undoubtedly speaking from experience. The odds are against finding the one agent in twenty who will be completely open and honest in his dealings with you. This book will tell you what you need to know to deal with the other nineteen you are likely to confront.

When you drive into the country, it seems as if the main industry is selling land. It takes virtually no training or education to become a land hustler, and most real estate agencies are operated on the level of a used car lot. The manner in which they promote themselves with large gaudy signs proclaiming nothing but good deals is a good indication of the ethics of their operations.

THE DIFFERENCES BETWEEN THE REAL ESTATE AGENT, THE REALTOR, AND THE SALESMAN

A person who is licensed by the state to sell land will be either a real estate "agent" or "broker," a "realtor," or a real estate "salesman." The terms "agent" and "broker" are used interchangeably.

The Real Estate Agent or Broker

States generally require that a person aspiring to become a real estate agent serve as an apprentice to an already licensed agent for a specified period of time, that he take a few college courses, and that he pass an examination on basic real estate law. However, brokerage laws are not very detailed, and licenses are easy to obtain. The real estate agent acts as a middleman throughout the negotiations between you and the owner who is selling his land. For example, if you want to make an offer to buy some land, you will give your offer to the broker to deliver to the seller. The seller then gives his response to the agent, who delivers it to you. The agent cannot legally refuse to inform the seller of any facts involving a possible sale, even if the amount of money or terms you offer seem outrageous. Usually an agent can accept a deposit from you on behalf of the owner, although he rarely has the power to actually accept your offer and sign a final Contract of Sale on the seller's behalf. Some states permit real estate agents to write certain documents, such as Deposit Receipts and Contracts of Sale, although many areas consider contract drafting to be an illegal practicing of law. (See Chapter 28: *The Model Contract of Sale*.)

The Realtor

In an attempt to create an aura of "professionalism" for the land-selling industry, the National Association of Real Estate Boards (NAREB), consisting of 1,500 local boards, established a code of ethics by which its members swear to abide. A "realtor" is any real estate agent who has been accepted as a member into one of the local real estate boards. In my experience, realtors generally seem more anxious than the average real estate agent to comply with state and local real estate laws. Because of the extra status they enjoy, they are usually cautious to avoid doing anything that would cause them to lose their membership in NAREB. An agent or salesman working

under a realtor is kept under close supervision by that realtor. Although you will encounter few realtors in small towns, you can always identify an agent who is a realtor by a sign in his window displaying the round emblem and initials of NAREB.

The Real Estate Salesman

To become a real estate salesman only requires passing a very simple examination. No apprenticeship is required and no experience is necessary. For this reason, most people you will meet selling land will be salesmen. Salesmen must work under a licensed real estate agent and can show land only under the agent's authority. A salesman cannot sign any documents or receive any money in his own name, but he can do so in the agent's name. The average salesman knows very little about land, real estate laws, or the property he is showing. His knowledge about the parcels he is instructed to show comes solely from his employer, the real estate agent. Although an agent is legally responsible for the acts and words of his salesman, some agents deliberately misinform their salesmen so as to mislead potential buyers.

The following story is an excellent example of how a salesman can be used by an agent for the purpose of defrauding a purchaser. I know the principals involved in this case and saw how the buyer was taken. A salesman convinced a buyer to purchase some land by assuring him that a beautiful creek ran across the property. The buyer, without double-checking anything the salesman told him, signed a contract, paid the purchase price, and had his deed recorded. Then he decided to get a survey done before beginning to build his house to be sure that it would be on the property. He should have demanded that a survey be taken before he bought the land. The survey showed, to the buyer's surprise, that the creek was not on his property. Since the land was worthless without water from the creek, he went to the former owner to try to get his money back but was unsuccessful. The former owner had never promised him that the creek was on the property and, in fact, had never even met him. The buyer then tried to locate the salesman, but he had since left the agent's employment. The agent claimed he had never told his salesman that the creek was on the property. But he did admit that when the salesman asked if the creek was on the property, he said that he thought it might be but that he could not be sure without a survey. Getting nowhere, the buyer then filed a complaint with the District Attorney against the salesman and real estate agent for land fraud. The District Attorney found the salesman and brought him in for questioning, at which time he stated that the agent did tell him the creek was on the land and that he knew nothing about the property other than what he had been told by the agent. In rural areas close ties develop among politicians, businessmen, and law enforcers. Therefore, it was no surprise that the District Attorney refused to take any action, whitewashing the fraud for lack of evidence; after all, the buyer had nothing in writing to prove he had been told the creek came with the land. The buyer then retained a lawyer to sue the parties involved, but the outcome is uncertain. The only sure thing is that the buyer did not get what he paid for, and will have to pay much more in legal fees to try to get his money back, with no assurance of success.

When a salesman misinforms a buyer, by the time the buyer realizes something is wrong, the salesman is often long gone. There is a huge turnover in salesmen because the requirements are so easy and because many people become salesmen in order to find a good deal on a piece of land and then drop out of selling. Few salesmen are paid a regular salary. Usually they get a fraction of the agent's commission for a sale they work on, so there is little incentive to work regularly and they come and go as they please. Unless a salesman intends to apply for a license to become a real estate agent, there is no pressure on him to be well informed or particularly honest. Though a buyer who has been defrauded can always sue the seller, the agent, and the salesman, going to court is easier said than done.

Even if you are positive that you have the law on your side and that you will have no problem proving your case, you still have to hire an attorney, pay court costs, and follow through with a lengthy and costly litigation. And if the defendant agrees to settle the matter out of court, you will still have legal fees to pay. In many areas, the courts are jammed with cases and a year or two may pass before you can even get into court. If you do not have evidence in writing you will have a difficult time proving your case.

Never depend on your ability to bring a successful case against someone should he defraud you. Your goal is to investigate the property so thoroughly before you buy that you will not have any reason to bring a court action later. As a safety factor, make sure your Contract of Sale specifies all the terms and conditions of the deal so that you will have a good case if those terms are not met.

THE REAL ESTATE AGENT WORKS FOR THE SELLER

A basic fact to remember when dealing with the real estate agent is that he is working for the seller.* Although he is a middleman, he is not an independent person who simply tries to find a buyer for a piece of property. Usually the seller has signed a form of Listing Contract, making the agent an "employee," and when the agent finds an acceptable buyer the seller will pay him a commission. Thus the agent is directly responsible, and owes complete loyalty, to the seller. Since the agent's commission is based on a percentage of the selling price, it is in his interest to get the highest price possible for the land. Commissions usually start at 6 percent of the selling price and often go as high as 10 percent. The agent's role in setting the asking price for the property is explained in Chapter 20: *Bargaining to Get the Seller's Asking Price Down.*

A seller usually gives his property to an agent under one of the following common types of Listing Contracts. The most desirable contract for an agent is an "exclusive right to sell" the property, which means that he is the only person allowed to sell the land during the period the contract is in force. No other agent can show the land, and if the seller finds a buyer on his own, a commission must still be paid to the agent under contract.

* Throughout the remainder of this book, I will refer to the owner of land as the seller and the person who sells his land for him as the broker or real estate agent. It is implied that the "agent" could be a realtor or a salesman.

Under an "exclusive agency" contract, no other agent can show the land, but the seller reserves the right to sell the land himself without being obligated to pay a commission to the agent.

The third type of contract is the "open listing," in which the seller will list his land with several different brokers. The first one to find a satisfactory buyer gets the commission. The seller can also sell the land himself and not pay anyone a commission. Most brokers dislike this type of listing and will only show open-listed land after showing their exclusive listings.

If you see land that is listed by several brokers under an open listing, you can choose the broker you like best or you can locate the seller and buy directly from him. The agent who is named on a "For Sale" sign on a piece of property does not necessarily have an "exclusive right to sell" the land. If the sign does not state that the agent has an "exclusive right to sell," you should contact the owner first because if you buy directly from him you can save the amount of the commission.

Since most sellers figure the price of the commission into their asking price in order to pass the expense on to the buyer, if you do not buy through an agent you can use that fact when bargaining to get the price reduced. If a broker shows you the land and then you go and deal directly with the seller, the broker might claim he is responsible for making the sale and may ask for a commission. However, a broker is not usually given credit for a sale unless he gets the buyer to sign the Contract of Sale or give a deposit.

Many sellers of rural land, particularly if it is underdeveloped or used only as a second home, will not live in the area. But you can identify the parcel on a map and go to the Tax Assessor's office to obtain the owner's name and address. (This is explained in Chapter 17: *Taxes and Assessments*.)

A Real Estate Agent Will Try to Sell Anything While Promising Nothing

An agent makes money only if he sells some property, and competition for listings in rural areas is extremely tough. Most real estate agents will take any listing they can get, regardless of the condition of the property. It might be lacking in adequate water, legal access rights, well-drained soil, or other features of good land, but that won't stop an agent from taking the listing. He has nothing to lose by trying to sell such land. Eventually someone will buy it.

The agent is not going to mention the bad points of a piece of property. Only by asking the right questions and demanding specific answers do you stand any chance of learning the true facts. Don't be satisfied with equivocal statements, such as "I think so," "I don't think there's been a problem in the past," or "Nobody can make a guarantee about that in this area." This type of statement is meaningless. The ancient rule of *caveat emptor*, (let the buyer beware) applies: it is up to you to clarify all the facts of the situation. By giving an equivocal answer to a question, the agent is not committing himself to anything. Even if he makes a definite statement, unless you get it in writing, it is worthless. You must receive more than equivocal, worthless statements when preparing to lay down thousands of dollars.

GORDO   BY GUS ARRIOLA

Work Out Everything Before the Deal Is Closed

Never buy land on the agent's promise or assurance that a problem can be worked out after the deal is closed. For example, if you are supposed to share a well with adjoining landowners but no agreement has been drawn up as to what the arrangement will be, the agent might tell you that your neighbors are great people and that you will have no problem working out an arrangement after you buy the land. This is a common and dangerous sales hustling technique. Once you pay your money and take title, the agent is out of the picture. If your neighbors don't turn out to be so nice, you can be in real trouble. Don't assume the agent is going to help you with problems once he gets his commission. If he can't arrange all the details in writing before you buy the land, he certainly won't do so afterwards.

These Lines Are Always Good for a Laugh

"I'll let you in on a secret about the seller."

"I'm going to show you something nobody else has seen."

"The land is really worth more than the seller is asking."

"So far, nobody else has seen this property."

"If I had the money, I'd buy this piece myself."

"Look, a lot of people are interested in this property, so you better make up your mind quickly."

THE BROKER'S PSYCHOLOGY

After dealing with countless real estate agents I have found two standard psychological approaches used in selling country property. The first I call the "Welcome to the country, smile, and don't worry about a thing" approach and the second is the "Why are you trying to complicate the deal by asking all those questions?" approach.

"Welcome to the Country, Smile, and Don't Worry About a Thing"

The rural land dealer exudes this attitude. The first thing you notice is his informal, unbusinesslike appearance. But don't let the absence of a necktie mislead you into thinking he is necessarily more "down-home" and honest than slick, high-pressure city agents. Coming from the city, you will be easily soothed by the country vibrations. The agent will try to make you feel completely at ease and will assure you he can help you find a nice piece of land. If he can convince you that he has nothing but your interests in mind, he hopes that you won't question anything he tells you.

An interesting new touch to the land sales business is the use of young "hip" salesmen employed by many brokers to "relate to" young people who come in looking for land. They have long hair and some will try to get you stoned, with the expectation that then you will automatically trust them. Be extremely careful of these "house hippies." The worst land I have seen was shown to me by "hip" young salesmen who knew absolutely nothing about real estate.

Similar tactics are used on a larger scale by developers who fly customers to their subdivisions for the weekend, provide free meals and drinks, let them ride horses and go swimming, and then make a big sales pitch. These sales gimmicks are part of the same approach, which could also be called "buttering up the buyer."

"Why Are You Trying to Complicate the Deal by Asking All Those Questions?"

This approach is extremely effective, particularly when used with buyers who know little about what they are doing. Nobody wants to sound stupid. Thus when a buyer asks too many questions, the real estate agent gives him a look that implies: "What's the matter, are you stupid or something?" Agents dislike anyone who asks a lot of questions, especially lawyers who "complicate deals with all kinds of trivial conditions." The broker would have you believe that buying land is simply a process of finding a parcel that looks good to you and paying your money. The rest is just "paperwork." This is exemplified by the common statement made by brokers that the Deposit Receipt is just a receipt for some money and only one of many forms the buyer will get. Little does the buyer know that once the Deposit Receipt is signed by both parties, it becomes the binding contract for the land purchase. (See Chapter 28: *The Model Contract of Sale*.)

An experienced agent knows very quickly whether a buyer is going to be an "easy sale." He bases his judgment on how much knowledge you appear to have about real estate, how much money you intend to spend, and whether you have "buyer's fever." Thus, when a buyer starts asking questions about extremely important legal matters, such as title insurance, easements, water rights, building permits, and financing, the broker passes them off as if they are merely secondary to the deal. They are secondary to the broker. His goal is to sell the land. He cannot get a commission, regardless of how large or small, unless he sells the property. Anything that delays the sale he will avoid. For example, if you ask to have the land surveyed or to be shown the wording of easements that are to be contained in your deed, he will give you the impression that you are imposing on his valuable time, and getting on his nerves—because you will be.

Once you have read this book, you will have many questions to ask the agent selling the property about every aspect of your purchase, and you will probably sound like a lawyer to him. Never let a broker's comments that you are "paranoid," "uptight," or concerned with "minor points" embarrass or impede you when investigating your prospective purchase. A broker has nothing to lose when he takes your money. You are the only one who can lose anything.

MANY AGENTS WILL CUT INTO THEIR COMMISSIONS TO MAKE A SALE

A real estate agent must sell a piece of property before he can make a commission. Depending on the circumstances, a broker might personally pay to clear up a problem which a seller won't pay for in order to make a sale. For example, a client of mine wanted to buy some land that had not been surveyed, and one of our conditions was that a legal survey be completed with all boundary lines marked on the ground. (Every buyer should have the basic protection of knowing what he is buying.) The seller absolutely refused to spend the $800 for a survey, and I would not let my client go ahead with the deal until he was certain where the boundary lines were. Everything else was satisfactory and we made it clear to the broker that the only thing holding up the sale was the seller's refusal to conduct a survey.

The broker stood to make about a $1,500 commission on the sale. His Listing Contract was about to terminate and he was afraid that if he did not sell the property by the final date, the seller would go to a different broker and he would lose the right to sell the land. Therefore, he decided to personally hire a licensed surveyor to conduct a survey, after which my client purchased the property. The broker cut his commission by more than half, but $700 is better than nothing.

If a seller is intransigent on a condition of your purchase, such as getting a survey, a test drilling for water, an easement or water right, or structural and pest inspection, ask the broker to pay for it. If he is desperate for a sale or is worried about the seller taking the property to someone else, he might be willing to give you what you want.

BROKERS ALSO NEGOTIATE LOANS

A broker might tell you that he can get you the loan you need. Brokers often have very close ties with local banks and savings and loan associations. But you have to be careful of two things. The first is that a broker will probably charge you for this service. Second, the loan he will get for you might have a higher interest rate, origination fee, and other costs than you can get elsewhere. This is because of a kickback to the broker. (See Chapter 25: *Borrowing from Third Party Lenders*.)

DESTROYING THE MYTH THAT A REAL ESTATE AGENT MUST PROTECT HIS REPUTATION

A common misconception perpetrated by the rural real estate business is that a broker would not dare to harm his reputation by misleading buyers. However, the country land broker who makes a living selling land primarily to city dwellers does not have to worry much about his reputation, since the stranger who drives into town and stops at the first broker's office he comes to does not know anything about the person he will be dealing with. In a town near my home, a few defrauded purchasers printed and distributed leaflets protesting the dishonesty of the broker who had sold them their property and warning prospective buyers not to do business with this man. This protest did not affect the broker's income in the slightest. He is still the most successful real estate agent in town despite the fact that he is held in very low esteem by a large part of the community.

The fact that a broker shows you a piece of land does not commit you to continue to patronize him. If you hear that a particular broker has lost his license or is being investigated by the District Attorney or local Real Estate Board, find out if this is true before buying land from him. Write to your state Department of Real Estate and ask what the current status of the broker is and whether he has been charged with fraudulent sales practices. It is illegal for a person to claim he is a broker if he is not.

PREPARING TO DEAL WITH AN AGENT

Many real estate agents prefer that you write or call to make an appointment to view land rather than just drop in. Go to the phone company or to the public library to get a copy of the phone book for the area you want to investigate. Look under "Real Estate" in the Yellow Pages, write down the addresses of all the brokers in town, and send duplicate letters to every agency telling them when you will be in the area and requesting an appointment to view their property. Most brokers will send you pamphlets describing what they have for sale. If some of the described properties are already sold, the honest broker will have marked them with a "sold" stamp.

The broker will want to know what kind of place you are looking for and how much money you have to spend. If you are restricting your search to land with electricity that is not more than fifteen minutes from the nearest town and has a year-round creek running through it, the broker will immediately know if he has anything that will interest you. But you should always try to get him to show you everything he has. Never tell the broker the actual amount of money you have to spend so you will be in a better position to bargain to get the purchase price down later. (See Chapter 20: *Bargaining to Get the Seller's Asking Price Down.*) Simply tell him the price range of property you can afford. But always act like a serious customer or the broker might not show you the best of what he has, particularly if it is far from his office.

If you do not like any of the property a broker shows you, you can leave your name with him and tell him to write you a card if something comes up that meets the description of what you want. This does not mean that he is working for you and he should not charge you for his service. It is possible to hire a broker to find property for you, but I don't think the expense is worth it.

Don't Worry—You Will Know How to Protect Yourself

After you read and study all the material in this book, it will make little difference which real estate agent you go to because you will know enough to protect yourself by investigating the land using the Model Contract of Sale (See Chapter 28.) Whether a broker is completely honest or not will be irrelevant, so you can go to any broker in town: nobody will be able to cheat you.

II

CHECKING OUT THE LAND

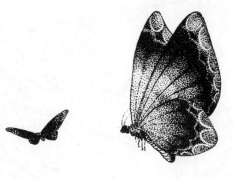

chapter 3

Climate

DO YOU KNOW WHAT TO EXPECT?

The first thing that the person who moves from the city to the country notices is the weather. As a resident or worker in the city you probably spend most of the day indoors under artificial lighting, insulated from the climate by permanently sealed and tinted windows and air-conditioning. You imagine that when you move to the wide open spaces you will delight in the smell of the earth after a light rain and the warmth of the early morning sun shining on fields and trees. But getting in and out of an isolated area on a slippery, rutted dirt road in the snow and rain, trying to start your car in sub-freezing weather, using a cold, damp out-house, having your water pipes freeze, and keeping yourself and your animals warm are also part of country life.

Urban expatriates often make the mistake of moving to an area of the country where the weather is completely different from what they are used to, and then often find they are unable to adjust to the new climatic conditions. I strongly recommend that you spend part of each of the four seasons, and preferably a whole year, in the area where you intend to buy land in order to assure yourself that you are willing and able to keep yourself happily alive in that area's climate.

CLIMATE REGIONS MAP

The basic elements of climate that you should consider and research when land-hunting are temperature, humidity, rain and snow, drought, floods, winds, frost, sunshine, fog, cloudiness, hurricanes, cyclones, tornadoes, and dust-storms. The best general climate guide available is the United States Department of Agriculture Climate Regions Map, which divides the country into thirty-two separate climate regions. It is reprinted here as Illustration 1, followed by a description of each region.

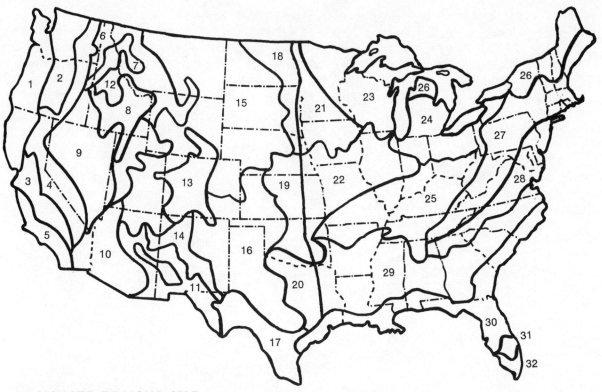

1. CLIMATE REGIONS MAP

Region 1 comprises the Pacific Coast west of the Coast Range from Santa Cruz Bay to the Canadian line. Its characteristics are cool, dry summers with frequent fogs and heavy winter rainfall with lowest temperatures 8 to 10 degrees below freezing in the north to about freezing in the south.

Region 2 includes the Willamette Valley in Oregon and the region of similar climate north of it in Washington, including the shores of Puget Sound. The summers are warmer and drier than in Region 1, and the average lowest temperatures are from 10° to 20°F.

Region 3 includes the Sacramento and San Joaquin valley in California. This region has hot, dry summers and mild winters with 10 to 20 inches of rainfall. The temperature drops to 8 or 10 degrees below freezing on the valley floor, with slightly higher temperatures on the hillsides.

Region 4 includes the Sierra Nevada and Cascade mountain ranges. This region has hot, dry summers except for occasional scattered showers in the mountains. Most of the winter precipitation, from 20 to over 50 inches, falls on the western slopes, where winters are moderate to cold. East of the mountains, wide variations in temperatures occur frequently. The Sierra Nevadas have snow annually as low as 2,000 feet. Throughout this entire area, conditions vary considerably according to elevation.

Region 5 comprises the coast west of the Coast Range from Santa Cruz to Santa Barbara, thence to San Diego, Redlands, and Riverside, including what is popularly known as "Southern California." The summers are dry, cool on the coast and warm inland; the winters are moderately rainy, from 30 inches in the mountains to 10 inches in the valleys, being nearly free from frost on the coast and in the foothills.

Region 6 is the Columbia River Valley in eastern Washington. The summers are warm; the winters have ordinary temperatures of 10° to 15°F., with extremes occasionally of zero.

The annual rainfall varies from 7 to 20 inches, mostly in winter and spring.

Region 7 includes the plateau of the eastern part of the state of Washington and the valleys of northern Idaho and western Montana. The summers are warm, and the lowest winter temperatures range from zero to 15°F., with an annual rainfall of 10 to 20 inches.

Region 8 is the Snake River Plains and the Utah Valley. It is a semi-arid country with water available for irrigation. The summers are hot, and the winters often have minimum temperatures of zero to −10° F. with a rainfall of 9 to 15 inches, mostly in winter.

Region 9 is the northern part of the great arid interior plateau included in the states of Oregon, Nevada, and Utah. Its characteristics are hot days and occasional frosty nights in summer with cold winters and about 10 inches of rainfall annually.

Region 10 includes all the Southwestern Desert, including portions of California, Arizona, and a corner of Nevada. The climate is hot to scorching, with a rainfall of 3 to 10 inches.

Region 11 comprises the southern part of the great arid interior plateau included in New Mexico and Arizona. Its characteristics are the same as the plateau farther north (Region 9), except that the temperatures are higher.

Region 12 is that part of the Rocky Mountains included in Idaho, Montana, Wyoming, Washington, and Oregon. The temperature and rainfall vary greatly, depending on elevation and exposure.

Region 13 includes the Rocky Mountains of Utah and Colorado. It is similar to the region farther north, except that the temperatures for the same elevation are about 7 degrees warmer.

Region 14 includes the Rocky Mountains of Arizona and New Mexico. It is similar to the region farther north, except that temperatures for the same elevation average about 6 degrees warmer than Region 13 and 13 degrees warmer than Region 12.

Region 15 is the northern Great Plains area south to Kansas and Colorado, extending from about the 5,500-foot contour on the west to the black soils on the east. It is extremely cold in winter in the northeastern portions, usually dropping to −30° or −40°F., while close to the mountains it is 20 degrees warmer. The summers are moderately warm. It is generally recognized as the northern part of the dry-farming area, with a rainfall of about 15 inches.

Region 16 is the central portion of the Great Plains including the plains portions of Kansas, Oklahoma, and New Mexico; also portions of the plains in Colorado and Texas. It extends eastward from about the 6,500-foot contour on the west to the black soils on the east. The rainfall varies from 12 to 22 inches. The climate is warmer and has greater evaporation than Region 15. It is the southern portion of the dry-farming area.

Region 17 is the dry, hot portion of southwestern Texas, with 12 to 22 inches of rainfall, but excessive evaporation.

Region 18 is the sub-humid black-soils country lying east of the dry-farming area of the northern Great Plains and is intermediate as to moisture between Region 15 and the more humid area to the east of it. The winters are very cold and dry.

Region 19 is the sub-humid black-soils area of Kansas, southern Nebraska, and much of Oklahoma. There is more moisture than in the dry-farming country to the west of it and less than in the area farther east. It is a locality of sudden variation in winter temperatures and of hot winds in summer.

Region 20 is the sub-humid or transition region of central Texas with black and chocolate-colored soils. In moisture conditions it is intermediate between the dry-farming regions farther west and the humid climate of eastern Texas.

Region 21 is in the northern part of the prairie country with frequent droughts of more than thirty days in the western portion and cold winters with drying winds. The rainfall is 20 to 30 inches, occurring mostly in the summer season.

Region 22 is that portion of the prairie country having higher temperatures than Region 21, but subject to similar cold drying winds in winter. The rainfall is 30 to 40 inches.

Region 23 is the western part of the Great Lakes forest area. The eastern portion is slightly warmer and more humid than the western portion, the latter much resembling Region 21.

Region 24 is largely that part of the country influenced by the Great Lakes, lying east of Lake Michigan, extending south into Ohio and eastward to Lake Ontario. There is considerable moisture in the atmosphere in addition to a rainfall of 30 to 40 inches rather well distributed through the year. The winter temperatures are more moderate than in Region 23.

Region 25 includes the Ohio and lower Tennessee River valleys and the Ozark Mountain region. The winter temperatures are rather moderate with much alternate freezing and thawing, while the summer is warm with a thirty-day drought often occurring near its close. The rainfall is 40 to 50 inches.

Region 26 includes the colder sections of the eastern United States, comprising much of Maine, New Hampshire, and Vermont, the mountainous portions of New York, and a portion of northern Michigan. It is characterized by cold winters with heavy snowfall and short summers of long days and cool nights.

Region 27 is the Appalachian Mountain country, including much of New England and New York, most of Pennsylvania, and the mountainous portion of the states southward. The rainfall is abundant, usually from 35 to 50 inches, and is well distributed through the season. In the colder parts the snowfall is abundant.

Region 28 lies just east of Region 27 and includes the Piedmont and some adjoining sections with similar growing conditions. It extends from northern Alabama northeastward across the Carolinas and Virginia to New Jersey and the coast of Massachusetts. It is warmer than Region 27, with abundant rainfall except in late summer, when thirty-day droughts often occur. The winters are open, with much freezing and thawing, and there is but little snow protection to be relied upon.

Region 29 includes most of the cotton country, extending from what is known as East Texas eastward and northward to the Atlantic Ocean in North Carolina and Virginia. It lies between the Piedmont region and the swampy lower Coastal Plain that borders the Gulf of Mexico and the Atlantic Ocean. The rainfall is abundant, being from 45 to 60 inches, and is well distributed, except toward the last of the rather warm summer, when a long drought frequently occurs, particularly in the western portion.

Region 30 is the swampy Coastal Plain from Wilmington, North Carolina, southward along the Atlantic Ocean and westward along the Gulf of Mexico. It has moderate summer temperatures with hot sunshine, short winters, an abundance of rainfall (50 to 60 inches), except in the Texas portion, and is almost subtropical.

Region 31 is southern Florida, with the exception of the sub-tropical fringe. It is subject to annual frosts, often becoming sufficiently cold to kill the tops of tender plants without killing their roots, and has rather warm summers and a rainfall of about 50 inches.

Region 32 is the tropical coast of southern Florida. It has slight range of temperature with no killing frosts and a rainfall of 50 to 60 inches.

GEOGRAPHICAL DIFFERENCES BETWEEN EAST AND WEST

The East is less mountainous than the West, and geographical changes are relatively gradual from one section to another. (See Illustration 2.) Likewise temperatures generally increase slowly as you go from north to south. The West, on the other hand, contains large rugged mountain ranges with great differences in elevation over short distances. For example, Mount Whitney, one of the highest peaks in the United States (14,495 feet), and Death Valley, a desert wasteland containing the lowest point in the United States (276 feet below sea level), are less than 85 miles apart. This extreme topography causes the climate to be much more diverse throughout the West than in the East. Temperature differences tend to be based on elevation and can vary greatly within a small area. When looking for land, especially in the West, don't assume that the climate of your prospective homestead is the same as the climate of the nearest town 20 miles away. For instance, the areas all around us often get fog in the mornings and afternoons whereas our valley, protected from the ocean on one side and the river valley on the other by two mountain ranges, gets almost no fog throughout the year.

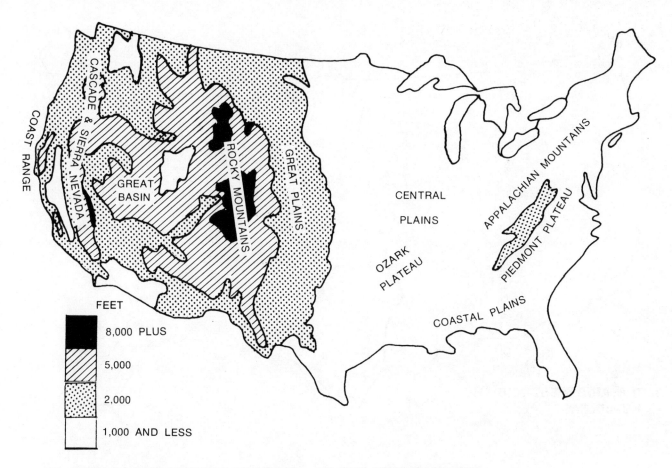

2. PROMINENT PHYSICAL FEATURES OF THE UNITED STATES

Legend (FEET):
- 8,000 PLUS
- 5,000
- 2,000
- 1,000 AND LESS

RAIN AND SNOW—THE HUMID EAST AND THE ARID WEST

An average of 30 inches of water falls as rain or snow in the United States each year, but this precipitation is not divided evenly over the country. Illustration 3 indicates the dividing line between the humid East and the arid West.

Although the heaviest mean annual rainfall is over 100 inches near the north Pacific Coast, and several other locations in the West have a mean annual precipitation in excess of 40 inches, most of the West, from Texas north to Montana and the Dakotas through the Great Plains area, averages less than 20 inches of rainfall annually, and much of the Southwest averages less than 10 inches a year.

The East gets considerably more rain because of the mixing of Arctic air with the semi-tropical air masses from the South. The warm southern air flow curves across the Gulf of Mexico, up the Mississippi, and then turns east over the Appalachians to the Atlantic. The Arctic air mass from the north pushes the warm air upward, which lowers the temperature, resulting in heavy rains in both summer and winter. Illustration 4, the Average Annual Precipitation, and Illustration 5, the Average Summer Precipitation, show the great difference in precipitation between the humid East and the arid West. The eastern half of the United States, which contains about 40 percent of the country's total land area, gets 75 percent of the rain and snow. It is because of this excessive water that most of the floods occur in that part of the country.

19

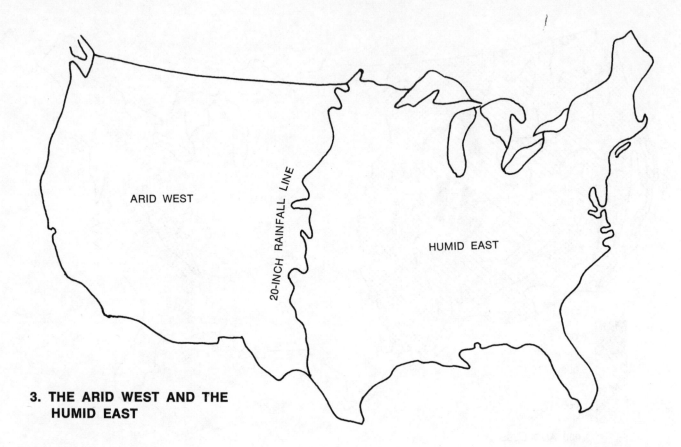

ARID WEST

20-INCH RAINFALL LINE

HUMID EAST

3. THE ARID WEST AND THE HUMID EAST

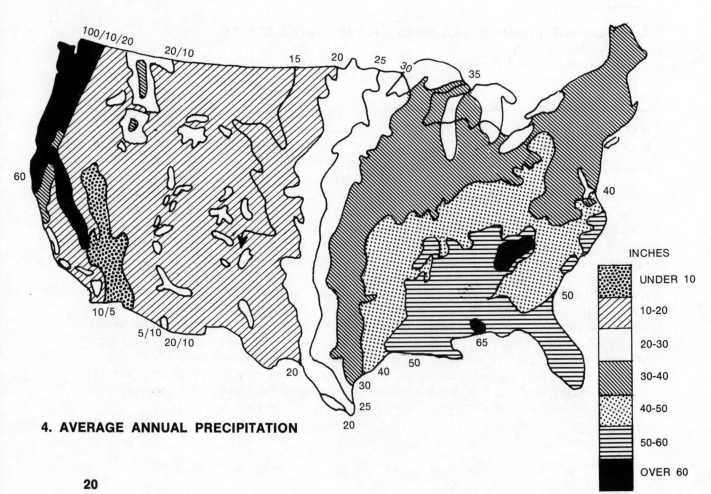

4. AVERAGE ANNUAL PRECIPITATION

INCHES

UNDER 10

10-20

20-30

30-40

40-50

50-60

OVER 60

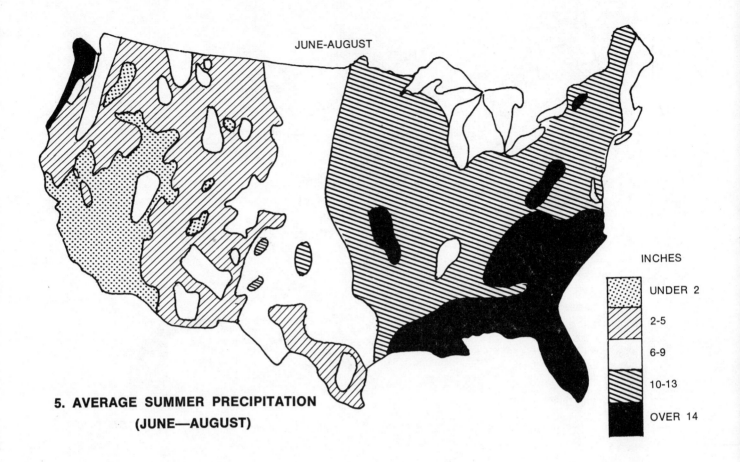

JUNE-AUGUST

INCHES

UNDER 2

2-5

6-9

10-13

OVER 14

**5. AVERAGE SUMMER PRECIPITATION
(JUNE—AUGUST)**

FLOODS

In whichever part of the country you are looking, if the land is next to a river or stream you should seriously consider the possibility of a flood. (See Illustration 6 to find the season in which floods generally occur in your area.) In our area, a devastating flood wiped out several towns along our main river in 1964. I have met a few people who bought land since then along that river. They all know about the 1964 flood but none have actually studied the history of flood damage or the likelihood of future floods occurring. They only know that their homesteads might be wiped out some winter and have accepted perennial anxiety.

Most county libraries maintain a local history section which contains a large collection of information on past floods including photos, newspaper and magazine articles, and maps indicating where the worst damage occurred. They also have information on flood-control measures subsequently taken by the county.

Unfortunately some of the finest land is located in vulnerable flood-plain areas along large rivers, but most rural areas are developing flood-control projects, which lessen potential hazards. You should examine the progress of local flood-control plans if you are looking for land along a watercourse. Be especially cautious when buying land along a river that has had a forest fire or extensive logging operations conducted on its banks. Removing the trees increases the amount of surface water runoff and greatly increases the potential for floods where none have occurred in the past. Heavy grazing and farming also help to cause floods by destroying the natural ground cover.

The size of a stream does not indicate its propensity to flood. Even the smallest streams have sent several feet of water into living rooms during heavy storms. Carefully balance your desire to live in a "flood area" with the potential dangers to your homestead.

21

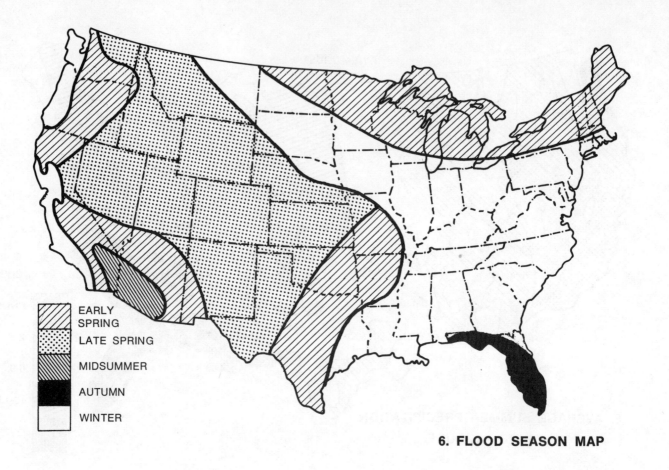

EARLY SPRING

LATE SPRING

MIDSUMMER

AUTUMN

WINTER

6. FLOOD SEASON MAP

Flash Floods

In many parts of the United States flash floods are a chance threat. These are local floods of great volume and short duration, generally resulting from heavy rainfall, and are often the most damaging floods because they occur on short notice and are highly unpredictable. During a recent flash flood in the James River basin in Virginia, 27 inches of rain fell in about eight hours, drowning 153 people and destroying everything in the area. Some of the states most seriously affected by flash floods are Maine, New Jersey, North and South Carolina, Ohio, Virginia, and West Virginia. However, flash floods are not limited to the East. In May of 1972, the Guadalupe River in Texas overflowed in a flash flood when 12 inches of rain fell in one day raising the river 9 feet above flood level. The National Weather Service is setting up automatic alarm systems in flash-flood areas throughout the East. If an alarm system has been installed in your area

the price of the land may increase slightly, but the added cost will be worthwhile.

Storms of flash-flood proportion occur in the Great Plains states when moist tropical air moves in and collides with dry polar air, causing heavy rains, thunder, and lightning. In these storms, one-third of the average annual precipitation can fall in twenty-four hours; occasionally one-fifth of the annual supply falls in one hour, and then four months pass without any rain at all.

DROUGHT

Too little rain and snow can be as bad as too much. Drought is a serious threat to many areas of the country. The usual problems in the arid West have already been mentioned earlier and will be described in great detail in Chapter 4: *Is There Enough Water on the Land?* Recurring droughts are a normal feature of the climate in southern parts of the

Great Plains, which have had four major droughts since 1880. The most severe occurred during the 1930s throughout the "Dustbowl" and caused many farmers to lose their land. The latest drought in that area lasted for four years in the 1950s.

Major water supply crises also occur in other parts of the country. Between 1961 and 1966 most of the fourteen Northeastern states suffered a serious lack of water. The areas most affected extended from eastern Massachusetts to eastern Pennsylvania. Many rural inhabitants found their wells completely dry during most of the year and trees, grass, flowers, and crops showed the serious effects of the long water shortage. In addition, wells along the Atlantic Coast were contaminated by seawater seeping into the ground as large amounts of freshwater were withdrawn during dry periods. Other parts of the humid East suffered major droughts in the 1930s and 1949 as well as through the 60s.

A thorough study of the drought history of an area, and the community's ability to meet future crises, will give you the best indication of what might be in store for you if you buy property there.

FROST AND SUNSHINE—
THE LENGTH OF THE
GROWING SEASON

If you are interested in growing your own food you will want to know the number of frost-free days the area has since many fruits and vegetables cannot tolerate freezing weather. Illustrations 7 and 8 together indicate the average frost-free periods throughout the country. These maps are very general but can aid you in determining where the best areas are for what you intend to grow. You should check local conditions, visit farms and nurseries in the area, and talk to long-time residents about the weather, the length of the growing season, and the crops that are grown there.

7. AVERAGE DATES OF THE LAST KILLING FROST IN THE SPRING

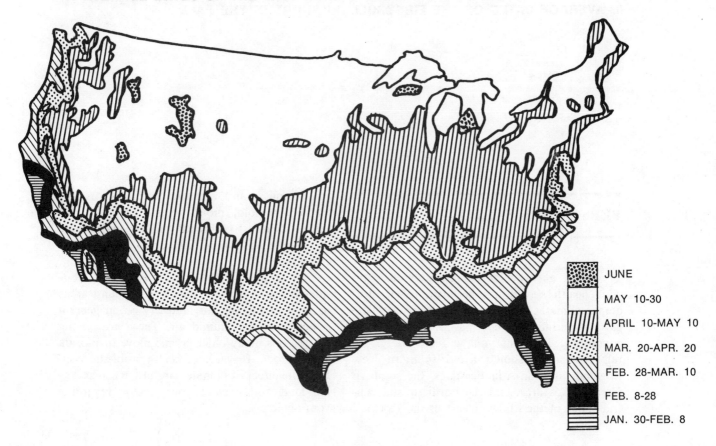

JUNE
MAY 10-30
APRIL 10-MAY 10
MAR. 20-APR. 20
FEB. 28-MAR. 10
FEB. 8-28
JAN. 30-FEB. 8

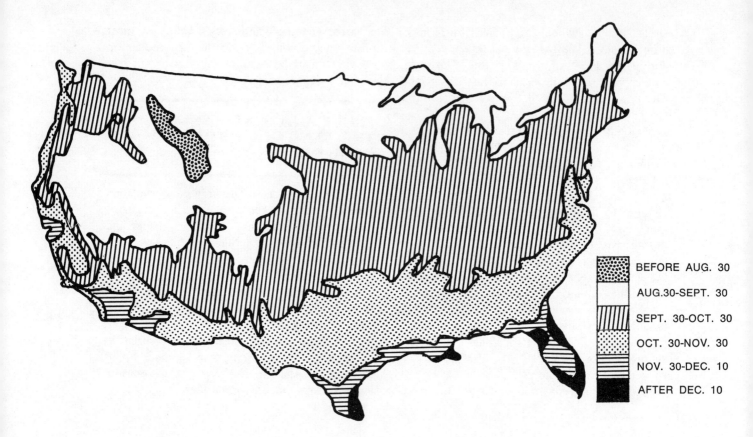

	BEFORE AUG. 30
	AUG. 30-SEPT. 30
	SEPT. 30-OCT. 30
	OCT. 30-NOV. 30
	NOV. 30-DEC. 10
	AFTER DEC. 10

8. AVERAGE DATES OF THE FIRST KILLING FROST IN THE FALL

PERSONAL HEALTH

The effect a particular climate may have on your health should not be overlooked. Hot, humid climates often aggravate asthma, allergies, hyperhidrosis, eczema, and other skin conditions. Those of you who are allergic to ragweed pollen should avoid southern New England, the Mid-Atlantic states, the southern Great Lakes area, and the northern and central states of the Midwest east of the Rockies.

Rheumatic and arthritic problems are increased in cold, moist areas. High altitudes causes shortness of breath and are undesirable for people with lung difficulties and cardiac conditions.

The rainfall in the coastal regions is considered healthier than that in the inland areas because of the salt air, and dry air in general is healthier than humid air. These are among the reasons many older people move to Florida and Arizona. If you have health problems, consider the effect of climate carefully when selecting land and consult your doctor regarding your choice.

A FINAL WORD

I have discussed only a few of the major problems caused by weather but there are many others. If you stay in an area awhile and study its climate history, you will know if you want to live there permanently. The most desirable areas of the country are those with the most temperate climatic conditions, and land prices there are much higher than elsewhere. Land costs generally decrease in proportion to the harshness of the winters. Do not be attracted to cheap land unless you are prepared to meet the exigencies of its climate. I have found that weather and its attendant problems have been the major factor in causing people to leave their newly purchased land and return to areas with a more familiar climate.

USEFUL RESOURCES

Climate Maps

Plant Hardiness Zone Map, Catalog No. A 1.38:814/2, indicating the approximate range of average annual minimum temperatures throughout the United States, is available for 25¢ from:

> The Superintendent of Documents
> Government Printing Office
> Washington, D.C. 20402

The Federal Government has detailed climate booklets for the twenty-four states listed below. Each booklet includes maps showing the mean length of freeze-free period, the maximum and minimum temperatures for January and July, and the annual precipitation. Written summaries discuss the state's geography, topography, air circulation, precipitation, snowfall, temperature, growing season, winds, waterways, relative humidity, thunderstorms, tornadoes, hurricanes, floods, droughts, and water supply. Also included are sources of more detailed information. Send the specified amount of money to the Government Printing Office at the address listed above.

Catalog No. C 30.71/3:2	Arizona	15¢
„ :3	Arkansas	20¢
„ :4	California	60¢
„ :5	Colorado	15¢
„ :8	Florida	15¢
„ :9	Georgia	20¢
„ :11	Illinois	20¢
„ :13	Iowa	15¢
C 55.221:17 S/N 0319-0016	Maine	35¢
C30.71/3:18	Maryland	15¢
„ :19	Massachusetts	20¢
„ :20	Michigan	20¢
C 55.221:21 S/N 0319-0018	Minnesota	20¢
C30.71/3:23	Missouri	20¢
„ :28	New Jersey	10¢
C 55.221:30 S/N 0319-0017	New York	25¢
C30.71/3:23	N. Carolina	30¢
„ :32	N. Dakota	10¢
„ :34	Oklahoma	30¢
„ :35	Oregon	20¢
„ :38	S. Carolina	30¢
„ :41	Texas	40¢
„ :49	Alaska	20¢
„ :51	Hawaii	20¢

Weather Bureau and Department of Commerce

In each state the United States Department of Commerce has a local Weather Bureau office with complete weather information for each county. You can get the local number from the telephone book or by writing the United States Department of Commerce (Main Office):

> U.S. Department of Commerce
> Weather Bureau, Climatological Section
> National Records Section
> Asheville, North Carolina 28801

Further information is available from:

> U.S. Department of Commerce
> Environmental Science Services
>   Administration
> Environmental Data Service
> Silver Spring, Maryland 20900

Local Sources of Information

Local and county libraries have weather statistics, including information on disasters, such as floods and droughts. The county agriculture agent has weather charts and data on the variations of the growing seasons in your area.

The Chamber of Commerce has brochures containing local climate information. The local airport and fire department will have a weather station with a thorough record of the area's climate. They can be very helpful and often have the most accurate local statistics. The local Board of Health or county Health Department has pollen count statistics and other climate data that relate to health problems.

chapter 4

Is There Enough Water on the Land?

Of all our natural resources, water has become the most precious.

—Rachel Carson in *Silent Spring*

DRY LAND ISN'T ALWAYS IN THE DESERT

Most people buy land in the spring and early summer when creeks are full, springwater is bursting from the hills, and the meadows are green. In late August and September, the early buyer is often shocked to find that all of his water has dried up. If you have lived primarily in urban areas where water has always been just a turn of the tap away, you don't realize the work and expense involved in bringing water where you want it. Just to get running water into your house might involve installing a generator, pump, pipeline, holding tank, and well. You might see land with a beautiful creek and not realize that it is too far away from the nicest building site to be of any use.

If there is no water visible on the land, you will be told that everyone in the area uses wells and that if you dig deep enough you will find water. The facts are that not all land has underground water, finding any is often difficult, and drilling a well is expensive. A big creek or a good well on a neighboring property does not mean there is water on your land. Do not be fooled by such misconceptions.

To get a complete picture of the general pattern of water distribution throughout the United States you should read Chapter 3:

Climate. Even if you have a year-round creek running through your land, you will be restricted in taking water from it by your state's water laws. A complete discussion of water rights is contained in Chapter 10: *Water Rights.*

TYPES OF WATER SOURCES

Water sources are either on the surface or underground. Surface waters include rivers, streams, creeks, lakes, ponds, bogs, marshes, mudflats, springs, and cisterns. Water is trapped underground in two types of areas: in aquifers, loose water-bearing materials like gravel, sand, and clay, or in consolidated water-bearing rocks, notably limestone, basalt, and sandstone. In many cases, surface water sources are excellent for irrigation, livestock, firefighting, ponds, and other uses, but cannot be utilized for drinking. Therefore, a well is often a necessity regardless of the presence of surface water.

The following sections cover the various aspects of each type of water source that you can have on land you buy.

SURFACE WATERS

Rivers, Streams, and Creeks

Rivers, streams, and creeks differ primarily in size and length. Rivers are large watercourses that are often navigable and public. Although you should have enough water available for your use, you may find that you have to share your river with motorboats, waterskiers, and swimmers, although swimming may be unpleasant because of the film of gas and oil left on top of the water by motorboats. Look upriver to see if there are factories, lumbermills, or other pollutors that might make the river unpleasant to swim in and dangerous to drink. If you are interested in fishing, ask the local bait shop about the fishing potential of the river.

How much logging has occurred upstream? According to the Environmental Protection Agency, streams in logged areas contain up to seven thousand times more sediment after logging. The resulting siltation kills mature fish, smothers spawning beds, destroys stream vegetation, and clogs smaller creeks.

Check to be sure there are no plans to build dams on the river that will flood your land. Get a copy of the Master Water Plan for your area from your state Water Resources Department. In an area 15 miles from us, people have been buying land along a small river at very cheap prices. I couldn't figure out why they were getting such a good deal until I got a copy of our county's *Study of Water Requirements and Water Resources,* which shows plans to construct two dams on that river. One dam is to be 160 feet high with a storage capacity of 35,000 acre-feet of water. When this dam is built, many new homesteads along the river will be condemned by the government and will become the bottom of a new lake. (See Chapter 15: *Eminent Domain and Condemnation.*)

Streams and creeks are much smaller than rivers, and often do not flow continuously throughout the dry season, especially in the arid West. The only way you can tell if your stream or creek will flow year round is to see it flowing during the driest part of the summer, usually August and September. Don't accept the word of a real estate agent that a creek never goes dry. Even if he is not deliberately misleading you, he probably has never lived on the land and has no idea how much the flow decreases. If a creek is your only year-round source of water, your activities will be limited by the amount of water in it during its lowest period.

Check with the local Farm Advisor, Health Department, or U.S. Geological Survey office to see if the stream has ever been "gauged," or measured. Talk to other people who live along the creek or stream to see what their experience has been. Look at their crops and those on the land you want to buy, if there are any, to get some idea of what the stream can support. If you are buying land that has never been lived on and nobody knows the performance of the stream, you should definitely see the stream at its lowest point to determine if it will support your homestead.

You will probably want to know if you can fish in your stream. Many streams are classified as spawning grounds where fishing is prohibited. You can check the state Fish and Game Code, which is usually obtainable in the local bait shop, to find out how your stream is classified. Often extremely heavy penalties are levied for fishing in spawning areas.

A unique problem along the coasts is the flow of saltwater into inland streams and creeks. If you buy land near the ocean, be sure your stream does not have this problem. Saltwater is bad for crops and drinking.

Lakes and Ponds

If you purchase land on a lake you will have many of the same problems you would on river land in terms of recreational disturbances and polluted water. Lakeside land is a very desirable place to live, but before you buy you should consider how crowded yours will become in the summer. Illustration 9 indicates the location of each type of "lake property."

You might be lucky and find a parcel of land with a pond on it. If you do, find out the source of the water that feeds it. If a creek or spring feeds the pond, make sure the flow is sufficient to keep the pond full year round. The presence of fish in the water is a good sign of a healthy pond. If they can live there, it probably doesn't get stagnant in the summer, but you should test the water before assuming you can swim in it safely. Ask about the mosquito problem in the summer. This is often an undesirable sidelight of a pond. If the pond is a

good one it is worth the extra money you will pay for the land.

It is much more likely a real estate agent will show you a possible "pond site" rather than a pond. He might show you some springs or creeks that could be used to feed a man-made pond and tell you that the site has already been researched. Never assume a pond can be built unless a reliable source, such as a geologist, your local Farm Advisor, or Soil Conservation Service agent, investigates the site and determines its feasibility as a pond site. Ponds depend on the soil's ability to retain water, an adequate and continuous water flow, and proper geographical conditions. I have seen ugly mudholes where hopeful new landowners put a lot of energy into creating beautiful ponds only to find that their soil wouldn't hold water. Building a pond requires heavy-duty equipment, expensive building materials, and possibly a system to divert water to the pond from a water source. The mere presence of an "excellent pond site" should never be your primary reason for buying a piece of land. A "pond site" is a common sales gimmick used to make land seem more attractive and justify a high selling price. Don't be swayed by such tactics. I could go on any piece of land and point out a possible "pond site." So could you.

Bogs, Marshes, and Mudflats

The presence of bogs, marshes, and large mudflats can present advantages or disadvantages. Occasionally geographical layout will be such that you can build a dam and create a pond. Usually, however, these areas will be nonproductive, unusable breeding grounds for mosquitos and other pests. When they exist on the property, you are paying for land that cannot be used. Use this as one of your arguments when bargaining to lower the selling price.

Springs

In many areas, springs are the primary source of water. A spring occurs where water seeps to the surface from a crack in the rock formation or where a road cuts through a water vein. Artesian wells are like springs, except that

9. LOCATION OF TYPES OF LAKE PROPERTIES

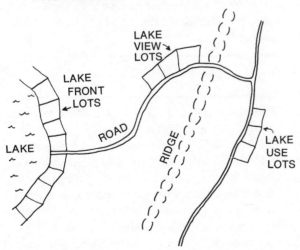

the water is forced up by underground pressure.

Often a spring will be only a tiny trickle of water coming out of a hillside. Don't underestimate its value until you measure its rate of flow. If a spring produces 1 gallon of water a minute, which looks like a trickle, it produces 1,440 gallons every twenty-four hours. If you have a large holding tank to collect the water as it flows to the surface, this amount could support a small homestead. When you are looking at land with springs, take along a gallon jar and measure the flow per minute using a watch with a second hand. Multiply this amount by 60 to get the flow per hour, then multiply that result by 24 to get the flow per day. Of course, you will have to see the spring during the driest part of the year to be certain that the flow is still sufficient for your needs. (See "How Much Water Will You Need?" later in this chapter.) The rate of flow can often be increased if a spring is properly dug out and "opened up." Never attempt to do this without the advice of an expert, because you might cut open too much and cause the spring to go underground.

If you want to locate a spring on some land, maps are available that indicate springs and groundwater sources. These can be good quadrangle maps or special water maps. You may obtain maps of your area from the local Soil Conservation Service or Farm Advisor. The United States Geological Survey and the Army Corps of Engineers might also have results of water studies done in your area. (See "Useful Resources" at the end of this chapter.) Even if you can't locate a water source on a map, you should go over the land on foot searching for new or undiscovered springs. Look under the brush for wet spots. Remember that the presence of springs on neighboring lands does not mean that any exist on your land. Water may flow out of one side of a mountain and not the other.

Cisterns

Cisterns are large circular or rectangular storage tanks either completely open at the top to collect rainwater or open only enough to allow a pipe to enter and bring in water from roofs or fields. They are made of cement, wood, or metal. The collected water is rarely used for drinking due to the possibility of contamination. However, it can be used for swimming and irrigation.

Examine any cisterns on the land for leaks, holding capacity, connections to the water sources, and general condition of the structures and their enclosures.

UNDERGROUND WATER

Wells

Eighty percent of rural water in the United States comes from underground sources and is pumped to the surface through wells. Underground water, or "groundwater," is preferred for drinking because it is purer than surface water. Groundwater can be brought up at any point and thus obtained close to where you need to use it. Because surface water flows away swiftly and is subject to tremendous evaporation, the fluctuation in a stream or creek varies more than the steady supply of groundwater. The primary difficulty with a well is the high cost of digging, casing, and sealing it and the necessity for a pump to bring the water to the surface.

If electricity is not available, you will have to use a generator to run your well-pump. You might have a motor running several hours every day. This is a noisy, polluting, and expensive operation, and mechanical breakdowns can be frequent. If you can use a windmill or wind generator your life on the land might be more pleasant. You can receive specifications for windmills and other pumps from the sources listed in "Useful Resources" at the end of this chapter.

Problems

If you are going to use a well, find out the history of water problems in the area before you buy. When large quantities of water are pumped, a "cone of depression" forms which lowers the water table underlying the land (see Illustration 10). Sometimes too much water is pumped out to allow an adequate rate of water replenishment and the shallower wells in an area may dry up as the water table gets lower.

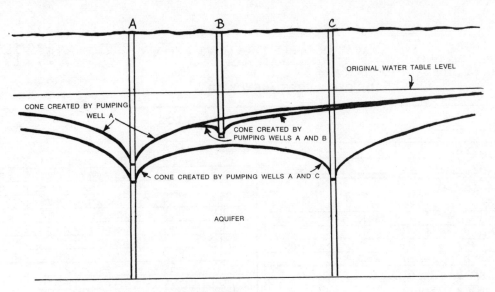

10. CONES OF DEPRESSION

Once the water table is lowered it might take several years for it to be replenished and all the wells in the area will have to be dug deeper, at great expense to the landowners. Surprisingly, this has been more of a problem in the eastern half of the United States, although it has occurred in some areas of the West. A farming area near us experienced a very bad underground water exhaustion problem for several years until a tremendous flood replenished the underground water basin eight years ago. Since then equilibrium has been maintained and there has been no serious water shortage.

A common problem in areas near saltwater, especially on the East Coast, is saltwater seepage into wells, often caused by too many wells or faulty wells. Be very careful of this when looking at land near a body of saltwater.

Wells Already on the Land

If you look at land that has a well on it, you should ask the seller to show you any records he has indicating the amount of water pumped at various times of the year. Examine his pumping setup to see if it is in good condition. Does it need a new pump or motor? Ask him to start up his pump and watch it operate for a few hours. Does the well need to be dug deeper to get a larger flow to meet your intended needs? Remember that the depth and size of a well does not necessarily coincide with its capacity to yield water. A well must have a watertight pump-mounting surface seal around the top of it to prevent contamination from the entry of foreign matter into the well casing. This sanitary seal consists of a 12-inch concrete base above the surface of the ground and a 30-inch concrete casing that goes at least 30 inches below the ground level. Is the casing cracked or leaking?

A well must be located a safe minimum distance from any sewage disposal system before it will be approved by the county Health Department. If the well does not meet these requirements you may be prohibited from using it after you buy the land. Has the seller had his well approved and does he have the Certificate of Approval? (See Chapter 13: *Building and Health Codes.*)

The well "casing" is a tube inserted into the well to prevent the sides from collapsing. Can you tell what condition it is in? Ask the seller what brand of pump he is using and what its capacity is. How old is the equipment and when was it installed? When was the well drilled and has it had to be drilled deeper since it was first installed? Who drilled the well? Go to the well-driller and ask to see the Drilling Log or Driller's Report to read what information he has regarding the quality of the well and its capacity. Sometimes a driller will not show you this document without the owner's permission. If the seller will not grant you permission to inspect the report, you should be suspicious of the quality of the well. Illustration 11 is an example of such a report.

ORIGINAL
File Original, Duplicate and Triplicate with the
REGIONAL WATER POLLUTION
CONTROL BOARD No._____
(Insert appropriate number)

WATER WELL DRILLER'S REPORT
(Sections 7076, 7077, 7078, Water Code)

THE RESOURCES AGENCY OF

Do Not Fill In

N⁰ 117312

State Well No._____

Other Well No._____

(1) OWNER:

Name   Gabriel Stern

Address   Anywhere

U.S.A.

(2) LOCATION OF WELL:

County   Somewhere   Owner's number, if any—

R. F. D. or Street No.   Section 21, Township 4 South, Range 2, East
10 miles west of Eugene on south side of Hwy. 135
Riverside Ranch

(3) TYPE OF WORK (check):

New well ☒   Deepening ☐   Reconditioning ☐   Abandon ☐

If abandonment, describe material and procedure in Item 11.

(4) PROPOSED USE (check):

Domestic ☒ Industrial ☐ Municipal ☐
Irrigation ☐ Test Well ☐ Other ☐

(5) EQUIPMENT:

Rotary ☒
Cable ☐
Dug Well ☐

(6) CASING INSTALLED:

SINGLE ☒ DOUBLE ☐

From	ft. to	ft.	Diam.	Gage or Wall	If gravel packed Diameter of Bore	from ft.	to ft.
" 0	" 184		6 5/8	10	9	0	184
"	"			"		"	"
"	"			"		"	"
"	"			"		"	"
"	"			"		"	"

Type and size of shoe or well ring

Describe joint   Welded

Size of gravel: 1/2"

(7) PERFORATIONS:

Type of perforator used   Torch

Size of perforations   6   in., length, by   3/16   in.

From	ft. to	ft.	Perf. per row	Rows per ft.
" 164	" 184	"	2	1
" 124	" 164	"	4	1
"	"	"		
"	"	"		

(8) CONSTRUCTION:

Was a surface sanitary seal provided? ☒ Yes ☐ No   To what depth   20   ft.

Were any strata sealed against pollution? ☐ Yes ☒ No   If yes, note depth of strata

From   ft. to   ft.

Method of Sealing   Cement on pack

(9) WATER LEVELS:

Depth at which water was first found   ft.

Standing level before perforating   ft.

Standing level after perforating   114   ft.

(10) WELL TESTS:

Was a pump test made? ☐ Yes ☒ No   If yes, by whom?   Bail

Yield: 25   gal./min. with   30   ft. draw down after   1   hrs.

Temperature of water   Cool   Was a chemical analysis made? ☐ Yes ☒ No

Was electric log made of well? ☐ Yes ☒ No

(11) WELL LOG:

Total depth   184   ft.   Depth of completed well   184   ft.

Formation: Describe by color, character, size of material, and structure.

From	to		Description
0	ft. to 13	ft.	Brown clays
13	34	"	Clayee brn. & yellow sand (very soft)
34	44	"	Brown clays
44	45	"	Brown sandstone
45	49	"	Sandy grey clay
49	65	"	Fractured blue rock
65	67	"	Hard blue rock
67	69	"	Grey clay
69	90	"	Blue fractured rock w/streaks of clay
90	103	"	Brown rock w/streaks of brown clay
103	107	"	Brown clay w/rock
107	109	"	Fract. brn. rock w/stks. of clay
109	129	"	Fract. hard rusty grey rock
129	138	"	Very hard fractured greywackie
138	145	"	Blue and grey rock
145	151	"	Hard grey clay with rock streaks
151	157	"	Grey rock (rough)
157	162	"	Hard grey clay with rock streaks
162	167	"	Hard black and grey rock with fractures
167	174	"	Hard grey clay with rock streaks
174	176	"	Hard black rock
176	181	"	Hard grey clay with rock streaks
181	183	"	Hard black rock
183	184	"	Hard grey clay with rock streaks

Work started   9/20   19 73   Completed   9/28   19 73

WELL DRILLER'S STATEMENT:

This well was drilled under my jurisdiction and this report is true to the best of my knowledge and belief.

NAME   Wilcox Drilling & Pump Company
(Person, firm, or corporation)   *(Typed or printed)*

Address   Anywhere

U.S.A.

[SIGNED]_____

Well Driller

License No.   32890   Dated   October 2, 19 73

11. SAMPLE WELL DRILLER'S REPORT

ANALYZING LAND WITH NO VISIBLE WATER

If there is no surface water on the land before you buy it, you must know whether you will hit a decent supply if you dig a well. Ninety percent of all water beneath the surface of the ground occurs in the top 200 feet, and the average depth of all domestic water wells in the United States is slightly less than 50 feet.

Groundwater exists only in the area called the "zone of saturation." This is the area beneath the ground in which all the openings and pores in the soil, sand, gravel, or rock are filled with water. Developing a well involves drilling a hole into the zone of saturation, which allows water to drain by gravity from the saturated earth into the well, where it is pumped up to the surface, only to be replaced by other water flowing toward the well. (See Illustration 12.) The rate at which this new water moves into the well, its "recharge rate," determines the amount that can be withdrawn at any one time. Thus you will want to know not only if there is underground water present but also its quantity and rate of flow. The total groundwater in an area is replenished every year by new precipitation, which controls the amount of water present in the zone of saturation.

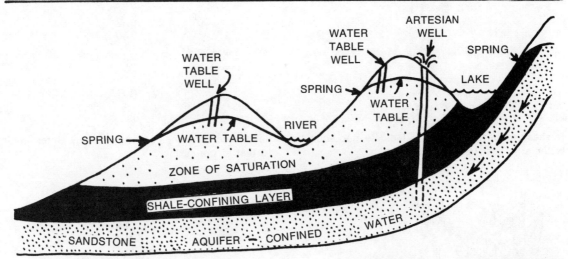

12. SOURCES OF GROUNDWATER

LOCATING UNDERGROUND WATER

Plants as Indicators of Groundwater (Phreatophytes)

One method used to locate underground water is to find those plants, called phreatophytes, that exist only when their root systems can reach the water table. (The name "phreatophyte" is derived from two Greek words meaning "well plant.") Some phreatophytes not only indicate the presence of groundwater but also the quality and approximate depth of the water below the surface. For instance, in arid regions willow or cottonwood trees usually mean that good-quality water is available within 20 feet of the surface. Some species of birch, sycamore, alder, bay, and live oak also indicate groundwater at shallow depths. Unfortunately, the value of these plants as indicators is reduced in humid regions where there is an abundance of water in the soil. Some of the principal plants that indicate groundwater in arid regions are shown and briefly described in Illustration 13. Each area of the country has its own phreatophytes. Your local well-driller, Farm Advisor, Agriculture Experiment Station, or other advisory agency (see "Useful Resources") will know the ones to look for in your area.

Rushes, sedges, and cattails indicate good-quality water at or just below the surface.

Reeds and cane indicate good-quality water within 10 feet of the surface.

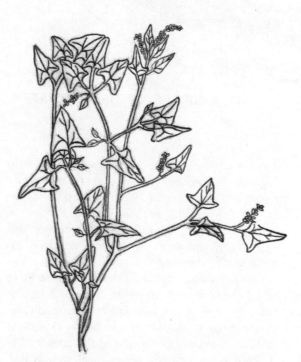

Salt bush is a reliable indicator of variable-quality water near the surface. It usually grows along the margins of salt flats.

Pickleweed indicates mineralized water near the surface. It usually grows on salt flats in soil that has between 1 and 2 percent salt content.

13. PHREATOPHYTE EXAMPLES

34

Arrow weed indicates good-quality water 10 to 20 feet below the surface.

Elderberry shrubs and small trees indicate water within 10 feet of the surface.

Rabbit brush indicates water within 15 feet of the surface.

Black greasewood indicates mineralized water 10 to 40 feet below the surface.

Mesquite indicates good quality water 10 to 50 feet below the surface.

Witching, Dowsing, and Divining to Find Groundwater

An ancient method used to find water that is still used today is witching or dowsing for water with a divining stick or rod. As far back as the sixteenth century farmers walked across their land carrying a forked branch in front of them waiting for it to point down to the ground over a water source. A forked or straight twig from a peach, willow, hickory, dogwood, or cherry tree is the most common tool used by diviners. The twig is held between both hands facing out and up and is supposed to roll down or spin around when held over water. Almost every rural area has its well-known diviners. Some work for free and others charge a fee for their "divining" services. Some claim to be able to tell which way the water flows and how deep it is by the movement of the divining rod. If the fee is reasonable you might take advantage of their powers. I would not buy land solely on the basis of their findings, but they might confirm some other appraisals made by a well-digger or Farm Advisor.

Well-Driller's Appraisal of Groundwater

The local well-driller will probably give you the most complete and accurate appraisal of the availability of water on your land and the cost of pumping it. Get the appraisal from the driller you intend to hire to drill the well because all or part of his appraisal fee will be refunded when you finally hire the company to do the drilling. In our area, the appraisal fee is $18.50 an hour and there is a 50 percent refund if the well is put in within a year. The appraiser will compare your land to other property in the area where his company has drilled wells. Each company keeps accurate logs of drilling depths, and the quantity and quality of water that is finally pumped. They also examine the soil, vegetation, and geography to estimate the location of water.

Unfortunately, a company generally won't guarantee its appraisal but a test drilling can be done for a smaller charge than a complete well. If your decision to buy land is solely contingent on whether water is found, should a test drilling produce water you can go ahead and drill the final well. When selecting the company to do the drilling, compare appraisal fees and refund provisions and the costs for drilling, sealing, and casing the well. Also compare the drilling methods and the grade of casing to be used. Ask for recommendations from the local Health Department and people living in the area. Hire the driller with the best reputation regardless of price. When it comes to well construction, like anything else, you get what you pay for.

TYPES OF WELLS

The following basic introduction to the types of wells should help you estimate the costs of putting in a well on land you intend to buy and evaluate wells already on the land.

Dug Well

The oldest type of well is the dug well. It is dug with a pick and shovel, usually 3 to 4 feet in diameter, to a maximum depth of 50 feet.

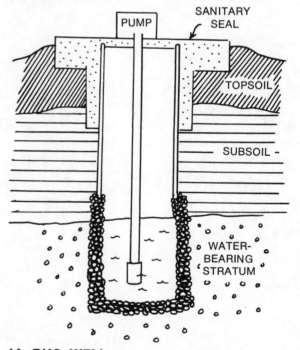

14. DUG WELL

These wells are dangerous and painstaking to dig, and often go dry because they are so shallow. Their main advantage is the large storage area, but this permits contamination more easily than other wells because of seepage through the well walls and from the large opening on top. Dug wells are probably more common in Canada these days than in the United States. (See Illustration 14.)

Bored Well

Bored wells are similar to dug wells except that they are often deeper and smaller in diameter. An auger-bucket, either power or hand operated, is used to dig these wells, which often run to 100 feet and are cased all along the inside wall. The bored well is practically obsolete today because of the more efficient driven and drilled wells.

Jetted or Hydraulic Well

This type of drilling can be done only in soft sandy soils as are found in some coastal areas. The well is drilled by applying a high-pressure stream of water which cuts through the earth and washes it out of the hole. As this is done, a 1½-inch pointed jetting tool is shoved down into the loose sand as far as it will go, and when it stops the well is complete. If you take a garden hose and "jet" the water into the ground you do the same thing. This method is useless if rock or clay is reached.

"Churn," "Spud," or Percussion-Tool Drilled Well

To drill this type of well a large chisel-shaped bit is pounded into the ground over and over again by lifting it high into the air and dropping it. With each fall the bit digs deeper into the ground. During this process, water is poured into the developing hole to transform the loosened dirt into mud, which is then drawn out of the hole. It takes a long time to drill a well in this manner, but it is still effectively done by commercial drillers.

Drilled Well

Drilled wells are the most common type of wells being used today. The method was first used when oil drillers built special power equipment to drill oil wells. The type of drill used is the "rotary" tool, which rotates like a drill into the earth rather than pounding the surface as the percussion tool does. The drill has a sharp cutting bit on the end and the shaft is hollow. As the drill turns into the earth, water is forced down into the drill stem, and the pressure of the water sends the cut dirt and rock to the top of the hole. As the drill goes deeper into the ground, additional sections of stem are screwed on to increase the length of the drill. (See Illustration 15.)

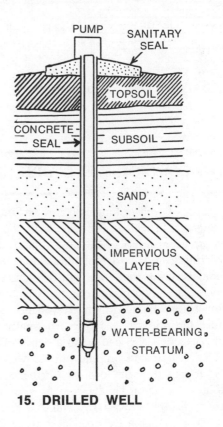

15. DRILLED WELL

Driven Well

A driven well is usually cheaper to construct than a drilled well. Pipe sections several feet long are screwed together with a sharp wellpoint and screen on one end. The pointed end is pounded into the ground until it reaches below the water table level and a sufficient amount of water can enter the well through the screen. The ground must be soft enough to take a driven well since hard rock and clay cannot be penetrated. The depth is limited to a maximum of 50 feet and only a small flow of water will be attained. Occasionally several driven wells are joined together with a single pump to get a greatly increased flow. As with all wells a driven well may be cut into the earth horizontally or vertically. (See Illustration 16.)

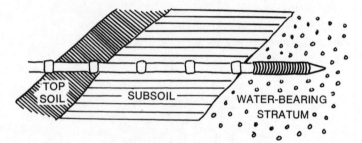

16. DRIVEN WELL (Horizontal)

THE COST OF WELL DRILLING

The cost of well drilling is based on the depth of the well in feet, the toughness of the earth, and the accessibility of the area. The usual cost for drilling into hard rock under normal conditions is $10 a foot, although this figure could vary greatly depending on the area and the competition among drillers. If you reach water before hitting rock, the price is usually cut in half. A drilled well can go to a depth of 1,000 feet. You can find out the normal well depth in your area from the local well-driller and thus estimate the approximate cost to you. In our area, wells are between 150 and 300 feet deep. At $10 per foot a well can cost from $1,500 to $3,000. Drilled well construction includes lining the inside of the well with a steel casing to protect it from contamination and collapse, and pouring a concrete or grout seal around the top.

There is always a chance you will not hit water. No driller is going to guarantee water when he starts drilling. He just tells you his price per foot and then drills until he hits water or you can't afford to pay for another foot. You can pay several thousand dollars for a dry hole, and that is one of the biggest risks of buying country land. Even in areas where water is plentiful, drilling is successful only about 85 percent of the time. The people representing the other 15 percent are simply out of luck and money. You must be certain there is water before you buy.

IS THE WATER DRINKABLE?

If water is declared "potable" by the county Health Department it is safe to drink. The safety is determined by examining the water at your source and the conditions around it. You will probably not be surprised to know that animal manure and soil bacteria are usually harmful to a water supply. Human sewage and poisonous sprays are the primary causes of contaminated water.

Drinking, tasting, or smelling water will tell you nothing about its potability since even clear, good-tasting water may be contaminated. However, your local county Health or Sanitation Department will gladly conduct a free or inexpensive water analysis for you. A Health Inspector will come out to collect the sample and to examine the source and surrounding area. He will determine if an existing or intended septic tank, outhouse, or cesspool is too close to the water source. If the water flows through farm land or irrigated land, it can be tested for the presence of insecticides. If your land is very isolated, the Health Inspector will give you a sanitized bottle and tell you how to properly collect a water sample for testing. The basic water test includes a coliform bacterial count, which reflects the amount of human and other warm-blooded-animal excreta in it. If you want a more complete mineral and bacterial analysis, which is not usually necessary, you will have to pay to have it done by a commercial laboratory.

Underground well or spring water is usually safer than surface water. Underground water has been sifted through the porous earth, which purifies it, whereas contaminated surface water must travel a long distance to get the cleansing effect of underground sifting.

I recommend that you always get the basic water test done no matter what the history of the drinking water on the land is. The family living there may have been drinking the water for fifty years, but pollution can occur virtually overnight. Polluted water can cause cholera, typhoid fever, amoebic dysentery, infectious hepatitis, and possibly polio. Don't take any chances.

Minerals in the Water

The quality of water is also affected by an excessive amount of calcium and magnesium, which causes it to become "hard." Try to work up a lather with a bar of soap and a dish of the water. The harder the water, the less suds you'll get. Hard water is less desirable for washing, cooking, and heating, but is generally not a serious detriment. Water-softening equipment can be purchased and installed at any time.

Other minerals may affect the quality and taste of the water. Iron in water affects the flavor of cooked vegetables, coffee, and tea. It stains clothes and water pipes, and causes a reddish-brown sediment or oily scum to appear on the surface. Hydrogen sulfide gas and sulfate give water a "rotten egg" odor and taste which you will find highly objectionable. The water may also have silt suspended in it, which gives it a muddy or cloudy effect. These and other mineral problems can be corrected through the use of chlorination and filtration equipment, which will be an added expense to you and good cause for demanding a reduction in the purchase price.

HOW MUCH WATER WILL YOU NEED?

Without water you cannot cook, grow vegetables, flowers, and orchards, raise animals, bathe, wash, swim, fight fires or quench your thirst. Although water needs differ depending on various factors, the United States Department of Agriculture lists the following daily water requirements:

Needed by:	Gallons Per Day
Each person (including use of flush toilet and shower)	30–70
Each milk cow	35
Each horse	6–12
25 chickens	1–3
Each hog	2–4
Each sheep	2
Garden (1,000 sq. ft., say 50 x 20 ft.)	70 (or 700 every 10 days) minimum

If you intend to have a large garden or plant an orchard, berries, and flowers, you will need a much greater supply of water than you need for animals. If you must pump your water, you will not want to run your pump for twenty-four hours, even if it is electric. Be sure that both the well and the pump have the capacity to deliver the amount of water you will need in the time you want it.

Always overestimate your water needs because after buying your land, your ability to develop it will be limited by the amount of water available.

THE WATER SUPPLY SYSTEM

If you are looking at undeveloped land, you must determine its suitability for a water supply system. The water supply system is the means by which you get the water from its source to your house, garden, trees, fields, and animals. The standard equipment includes pipe or hose, one or more holding tanks, a pump and motor or generator, a pump house, and various pieces of hardware such as valves and faucets. If you are looking at land that already has a developed water system you will want to know if it was well designed and built and if it is still working properly.

The purpose of the following sections is not to tell you how to develop a water system but to give you an idea of what to look for and think about in terms of developing or repairing a water system on land you might buy. Each type of water system has its own maintenance problems. Setting up an adequate water system can cost thousands of dollars. Before you buy a piece of land, estimate the costs required to develop a new water system or repair an existing one. If the expense is beyond your means, do not purchase that land.

Gravity-Flow System

The cheapest and easiest way to bring water where you need it is by using the force of gravity. To do this the water source must be higher in elevation than the place you want to bring the water to so that when you lay your hose or pipe the water will flow freely of its own accord to the lower point. However, because air is lighter than water, the hose between the two points must drop steadily downhill or air bubbles will collect in the high spots of the hose and slow down or stop the flow of water. If you cannot avoid laying the hose over a high spot, you can prevent air from entering it by putting in the proper valves or by keeping both ends of the hose constantly submerged in water.

If a hill is situated above a building site but you cannot find a spring or other water source in it, you might consider drilling a horizontal well into the side of the hill to get water to flow out without using a pump. Ask a well-driller to appraise the possibility of finding water this way on land you might buy. It is difficult to determine different elevations over a long distance on a piece of land with the naked eye and special meters are needed. The well-digger has this equipment or you can rent it from a local surveying rental service and run your own test.

The only materials needed to set up a gravity-flow water system are a holding tank, which might be a springbox, lake, pond, or dammed up portion of a creek, the necessary pipe or hose, and various valves, faucets, and other hardware. This system is the cheapest and easiest to maintain because no pump is necessary.

Siphon System

The siphon system is similar to the gravity-flow system in that the source must be higher in elevation than the point to which you eventually want to bring the water. However, any rise in the ground that is higher than the source requires siphoning to get the water to flow over it. This is done by sucking the water up over the rise and down far enough the other side so that it begins to flow of its own accord. As long as you don't lose the siphon, the water will continue to flow. Every time the siphon is broken by air getting in the hose, you must suck the water to get it going again. You can use the same methods to prevent air from entering the hose as you would use in the gravity-flow system. The difference between these two systems is that in a pure gravity-flow system, none of the high spots in the hose are higher than the source so no sucking is required to start the system.

If the rise is too high or the distance too great to begin the siphon by sucking with your mouth, you will need a pump to get it going. Otherwise, the siphon water system requires the same equipment as a gravity-flow system and costs the same to install and maintain.

Pumping Your Water Using Gas, Electricity, or the Wind

Unless you are fortunate enough to have a source positioned so that the water will flow by a gravity or siphon system, you will need a pump. The most common pump used for shallow wells and surface water sources is the gasoline-powered centrifugal pump which sucks water up and pushes it out with great force. A 2-horsepower pump of this type can only suck the water to a height of about 20 feet. However, if you can place the pump at the source, say along a stream or pond, it can push the water several hundred feet up a bank or hill.

If your source of water is a deep well, you will need an electric pump. The 1-horsepower electric jet-pump can suck up water from a maximum depth of 110 feet. However, the electric submersible well-pump is more commonly used today. It is a long cylindrical pump that is placed at the bottom of the well, and can push water up 450 feet. A 1-horsepower submersible pump can push up 10.2 gallons of water per minute from 220 feet down.

Since these pumps require electricity, you will either have to bring it in or supply it by means of a generator. The most common generators are powered by gasoline or diesel fuel. There are also wind generators that look like windmills, and they produce electricity that recharges a set of storage batteries. If wind conditions are suitable, you can run an electric pump using this system without the noise and pollution of a gas or diesel generator.

You can also use a windmill directly to pump water from a source straight down, like a well. It is cheap, nonpolluting, and quiet compared to a gasoline-powered pump or generator. Today windmills are still widely used in place of the combustion engine or electric pumps in the southernmost parts of the country, notably Texas, and in parts of Pennsylvania. If one already exists on the land, find out if it still functions and what its capacity is. You will be fortunate if there is one on your land but don't let its quaint but magnificent beauty persuade you to purchase land that is otherwise not what you want or to pay a higher price for the land than it's really worth.

If you will need a pump and possibly a generator, find out the cost of buying and installing equipment sufficient to meet your needs before you buy the land. Since you can't do anything on the land until you have water, you should figure the cost of a motor and pump into the purchase price as part of your initial investment.

If a pump is set up on the land, ask the owner or real estate agent to start it up so you can see how well it works and how much water is pumped. Watch it pump for at least a half-hour to be sure it operates well. Get the brand names and numbers of the motor or generator and pump so you can check with the local dealer to see how much they're worth and what their specifications are. Find out how long the owner has used the equipment and if he has had any problems with it. Does he have any repair bills, and does he still have a valid warranty for the equipment? (See "Useful Resources" at the end of this chapter for available pump information.)

Holding Tanks

Unless you have a lake, pond, or other large natural body of water situated higher than your homestead area, you will need at least one holding tank in your water system to keep a large quantity of water available. The greater your water needs, the larger the tank will have to be. If you want to irrigate an orchard and garden or grazing fields for your animals, you will need a large tank. For instance, if you plan to have a half-acre garden, it will require the equivalent of 1 inch of rain every ten days or about 11,350 gallons. If you want to water once every five days, you will need a tank that holds at least 5,675 gallons just to water your garden. Fruit trees need to be watered less frequently than smaller plants, but they need a large amount of water when irrigated because their roots go extremely deep.

If there is a holding tank on the land, determine its capacity to be sure it is large enough for your intended needs. To figure out the volume in cubic feet of a cylindrical tank, multiply the area of the base in feet by its height in feet. (To refresh your memory, the formula is $3.1416 \times r^2h$, where r is the radius of the base and h is the height of the tank.) The volume in cubic feet of a square or rectangular tank is figured by multiplying the length times the width times the height in feet. Once you get the volume in cubic feet, you have to transform the result into gallons. To do this, multiply the number of cubic feet by 7.4805, which is the number of gallons in 1 cubic foot. For example, assume you have a cylindrical tank with the following dimensions: the height is 10 feet and the radius of the base is 4 feet. Plugging these numbers into the formula, we get $3.1416 \times 4^2 \times 10 = 3.1416 \times 160 = 502.66$ cubic feet. To translate this figure into gallons of water, multiply $502.66 \times 7.4805 = 3,760.15$ gallons.

If the tank is large enough, check it to be sure it doesn't leak. Examine the structure that supports it to see if it is sturdy. The tank might be inside of a well house. If so, is that in good shape? Holding tanks are extremely expensive and repairing a damaged one could be costly. Mention any necessary repair work to the owner, and either have him fix it before you buy the land or use this as another reason why he should lower his asking price. Price the tank on the land at the local supply house. Wooden tanks are always more expensive than metal ones. If you have to develop your own water system, figure in the cost of purchasing and installing a holding tank and its supporting structure.

Pipes and Fixtures

Check the pipeworks on the land to see if there are sufficient domestic and irrigation works to suit your needs. Look for leaks or evidence of recent repair. Has steel, concrete, or plastic pipe been used? Is it constructed so that the water does not freeze in the winter? Each type of pipe has its own value.

The water system, if one exists, will be included in the selling price of the land so you should evaluate its quality and value before buying. Often the system has been used for many years and the owner underestimates the depreciation in its value. Look for things that need improvement or parts that need replacement, and point these out when bargaining to get the price down.

An Example to Help You Visualize Your Water System

Illustration 17 shows the present and future water systems possible on our land. It is included to help you visualize how to look at a piece of land and consider its possibilities for water development. The three systems shown all use a large holding tank (5,000 gallons) situated on a high point of the land above the house, garden, orchard, and animals, so that a gravity flow can be used.

System ① carries water from a holding box built around a spring that was exposed when a road was cut into the side of the hill. Since the spring is higher in elevation than the holding tank, a gravity flow brings a continuous flow to the tank. The spring only produces about 700 gallons a day, which is not enough to support our needs. Our garden alone requires 600 gallons a day. Since the young fruit trees, berries, flowers, animals, and ourselves also need water, we must develop another method of getting more water.

System ② illustrates the most inexpensive and logical next choice, which is to pump water from the nearest creek up to the holding tank.

System ③, which might be cheaper in the long run, requires drilling a well above the

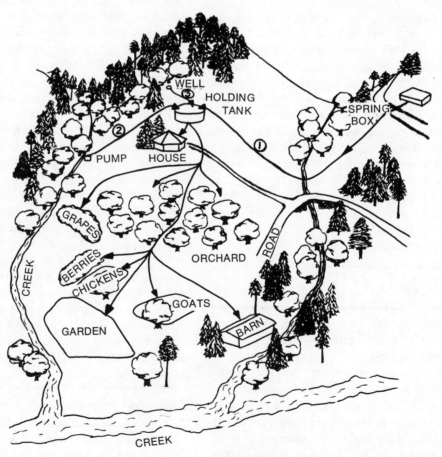

17. POSSIBLE WAYS TO DEVELOP WATER

holding tank. A row of bay trees is growing up the side of the hill behind the holding tank, which indicates underground water. Since this is on the side of a hill, we could drill a horizontal well, which would enable us to get a gravity flow into the holding tank. Although this system would not require a pump, we don't know how much water this source would produce. After spending the money to drill a well, we might find that the rate of flow is not sufficient to meet our needs.

The three year-round creeks alone insure us that we have a more than adequate water supply. If you plan your purchase carefully, you should always have enough water for your needs.

OUTSIDE WATER SUPPLY— PUBLIC UTILITY COMPANIES, PRIVATE WATER COMPANIES, AND PUBLIC WATER DISTRICTS

Some rural areas, especially those containing large farms in arid regions, have established irrigation companies, mutual water companies, and public or private utility companies that handle the task of supplying water within their service districts. The legal and operational setup is different for different agencies. If you have to purchase water from a private profit-oriented water company or a public utility company, you will pay rates regulated by the Public Utilities Commission. If you are supplied by a mutual water or irrigation company, you will have to join a private, nonprofit association of landowners who have organized to supply water to themselves.

Real estate ads will usually indicate if water is supplied by a private water company. The following are statements made in recent ads for land in Colorado: "good water shares available," "water line goes by property, irrigation dependent on classification by water users," "ditch irrigation, 500 water shares," and "35 tillable acres now ditch irrigated, 35 water shares with land."

The right to receive water is often based on ownership of shares of stock in the company. Instead of receiving monetary dividends, the shareholder receives water according to the amount of stock he owns. The price of stock can be quite high in areas where water is scarce. For instance, if you are buying land on which you intend to irrigate 1 acre and five shares of stock are needed to get enough water to irrigate that acre, you will have to buy those shares, either from the seller at the time of purchase or from the company after you own the land. If each share is worth $100 on the current market, it's going to cost you an extra $500 to get water on your land. If the owner includes shares of stock with the land, make sure you are not being overcharged for the water since he will undoubtedly add the cost of the shares onto his asking price.

You should check with the company to find out how dependable it is, how many of your neighbors belong to it, and what the value of the shares is.

It is always better to buy the owner's water shares with the land, because sometimes they are not easy to obtain. There may not be any surplus water available to a new farmer or, since these companies are private, the members may not like your life-style and may refuse to sell shares to you under some pretext. The ad that says "irrigation dependent on classification by water users" means that the members of the water company have control over how much water, if any, will be sold to the landowner. Also an ad that says "water shares available" doesn't mean that you will be able to get them. If shares do not come with the land, you had better be sure that you can purchase some or lease some before you buy, or have the seller buy what you need and then add the cost onto the price of the land. Don't buy on an assurance that you can get shares after the deal is closed. You might be left high and dry.

Public water or irrigation districts are formed by state and local legislatures to provide water to their inhabitants. Each district has definite boundaries, local control, and, most importantly, the power to tax and assess property within the district. You are familiar with the idea of paying property taxes for school districts. Water districts operate the same way.

If your land is within the boundaries of a water district, you will want to know how you can get water and what the present and future tax assessment will be. Generally the value of land within such a district increases even if the land has its own independent source of water. Whether or not you use district water you will have to pay the assessments, just as you pay school taxes even if you don't have children. If you want to buy land but need to obtain your water from a district, you should be sure the land is within the district. Many districts will extend their services to land not previously within their boundaries if circumstances so warrant this action. To obtain this service you will have to go before the county Planning Commission, Board of Supervisors, or Water District Board and petition them to allow your land into the service area. It will be easier to have the seller of the land do this before you buy and you can accompany him to the hearings. If you cannot get serviced from the district and water is unavailable from any other source, the land is worthless and you had better start looking somewhere else.

THE WATER PROTECTION CLAUSE IN THE CONTRACT OF SALE

Never buy land without a written guarantee that a year-round source of water exists that is sufficient to meet your needs. Two guarantees are provided in the Model Contract of Sale in Chapter 28. Clause 18(c) is a warranty by the seller that a visible water source delivers a specified minimum amount of water throughout the year. If the water dries up after you buy the property, the seller will be liable for a breach of this warranty. The fact that he makes this warranty, however, does not relieve you of the responsibility of examining the water situation during the critical dry months before you buy the land.

Clause 19(f) is a condition to the sale that should be used if no water source presently exists on the land. You want to have at least a test drilling and preferably a completed, productive well drilled before, not after, you finalize your purchase. The ideal situation is to have the seller pay to drill the well. If he locates a good water supply, he can add the price of the well to the purchase price. If he cannot locate water, you will not have to proceed with the purchase, the contract will be rescinded, and your money will be returned to you. If the seller resists such a condition, you can offer a compromise by agreeing to pay for

half the drilling costs even if no water is found on the land. You should not agree to pay the entire costs if no water is found, since, if you do, you could spend a few thousand dollars drilling a dry well on land you do not own.

You do not want to make your land purchase on promises alone. If the seller is not willing to guarantee that there is water on the land, he does not care if he cheats you. You should never buy dry land without a condition in the contract, unless you like gambling with very high stakes.

USEFUL RESOURCES

Publications on Water, Wells, Pumps, and Ponds

All of the following are free from:

U.S. Department of Agriculture
Office of Information
Washington, D.C. 20250

Irrigation of Western Farms—AB 199
Snow Surveys—AB 302
Your Water Supply and Forests—AB 305
Conservation Irrigation in Humid Areas —AH 107
Guide for Surveying Phreatophyte Vegetation—AH 266
Ponds for Water Supply and Recreation— AH 387
Water Supply Sources for the Farmstead and Rural Home—F 2237
Treating Farmstead and Rural Home Water Systems—F 2248
Trout Ponds for Recreation—F 2249
Electric Water Pumps on the Farm— L 436
Replenishing Underground Water Supplies on the Farm—L 452
Planning the Electric Water System and Plumbing for Your Homestead—M 674
Distribution, Control and Measurement of Irrigation Water on the Farm—M 926
Farmstead Water Supply System, Plan No. 5963—M 1100
What Is a Watershed—PA 420
30,000 Communities Without Water—PA 653

Development of a Procedure for Estimating the Effects of Land and Watershed Treatment on Stream Flow—T 1352

SCS National Engineering Handbook, 1964 "Soil-Plant-Water Relationships," Chapter 1, Irrigation, Section 15

SCS National Engineering Handbook, 1959 "Irrigation Pumping Plants," Chapter 8, Irrigation, Section 15

The following is free from:

State Water Resources Control Board
Room 1140
Resources Building
1416 Ninth Street
Sacramento, California 95814

Water Well Standards: State of California

The following are free from:

California Agricultural Extension Service
90 University Hall
University of California
Berkeley, California 94720

Small Earth Dams—Circular 467
Soil and Water Management for Home Gardens—AXT-111
What Does Water Analysis Tell You?—AXT-118

The following are available free from:

U.S. Geological Survey
Department of the Interior
Washington, D.C. 20242
  or from any Public Inquiry Office listed in "Useful Resources" for Chapter 5.

What is Water?
The Hydrologic Cycle
Real Estate Lakes, U.S.G.S. Circular 601-G
Estimated Use of Water in the United States in 1970, U.S.G.S. Circular 676
River Surveys Index
Index to Surface Water Section, edition 1970, 1970
Index to Water Quality Section, edition 1970, 1970
Index to Ground Water Stations, edition 1968, 1969
Index to Areal Investigation and Miscellaneous Water Data Activities, edition 1970, 1971

National Water Resources Data Network
U.S. Geological Survey Publications on Floods
The Hydrologic Data Network of the U.S.G.S.

The following are available for the specified cost from the the same address given above:

U.S.G.S. Water Supply Paper 416 (History of Witching) 30¢
A Primer on Water Quality 30¢
A Primer on Water 35¢
A Primer on Ground Water 25¢
Outline of Methods for Estimating Ground Water Supplies 20¢

The following is free from:

The American Association for Agricultural Engineering and Vocational Agriculture
Coordinator's Office
Agricultural Engineering Building
Athens, Georgia 30601

Planning Water Systems for Farm and Home

The following is free from:

Department of National Health and Welfare
Ottawa, Ontario, Canada

Sanitation Manual for Isolated Regions

The following is free from:

Committee to End Radiological Hazards
Box 148
150 Christopher Street
New York, N.Y. 10014

The Pollution of Waterways by Atomic Wastes, including a list of U.S. and Canadian nuclear projects, showing size, pollution areas, and cities and population endangered.

The following are available for the specified cost from:

The Superintendent of Documents
Government Printing Office
Washington, D.C. 20402

Military Water Supply, Catalog No. D 101.11:5-295, $1

Wells, Catalog No. D 101.11:5-297/2, $1
Fish Kills Caused by Pollution in 1971,
Catalog No. EP 2.24:971 S/N 5501-00410, 75¢
Manual of Individual Water Supply Systems, Catalog No. FS 2.6/2:W 29/2, 40¢

The following are commercial companies involved in manufacturing and selling drilling equipment, hydraulic rams, pumps, windmills, and water- and wind-driven electric plants. The literature that comes with their advertisements contains useful information. I do not endorse these products in any way.

Gas motor drills:
Deeprock Manufacturing Company
Box 870
Opelika, Alabama 36801
Request their pamphlet:
How to Drill Your Own Well

Mechanical pumps and rams:
Rife Hydraulic Engine Manufacturing Company
Box 367
Milburn, New Jersey 17041

Windmills and pumps:
Aeromotor Windmills
Broken Arrow, Oklahoma 74012

Baker Pump Manufacturing Company
Evansville, Wisconsin 53536

Dempster Windmills and Pumps
P.O. Box 848
Beatrice, Nebraska 68310

Heller-Aller Windmills and Pumps
Corner Perry and Oakwood
Napolean, Ohio 43545

Water-driven electric plants:
Leffel Hydraulic Turbines
The James Leffel Company
Springfield, Ohio 45501

Wind-driven electrical plants:
Bucknell Engineering Company
10717 E. Rush Street
South El Monte, California 91731

Dyna Technology, Inc.
P.O. Box 3263
Sioux City, Iowa 51102

Le Jay Manufacturing Company
Belle Plaine, Minnesota 56011

Quirk's Victory Light Company
33 Fairweather Street
Bellevue Hill
N.S.W. 2023
Australia

Solar Wind Company
RFD 2, Happytown Road
East Holden, Maine 04429

Get a *Suburban, Farm, and Ranch Catalog* from your local Sears store for pictures, specifications, and prices of pumps, tanks, and well equipment.

Information on dowsing can be requested from:

American Society of Dowsers, Inc.
30 Day Street
South Portland, Maine 04106

Aquatometer Accurate Electronic Water Location, Inc.
Department ME
Route 376
Poughkeepsie, New York 12603

United States Geological Survey Water Resources Division

This federal agency is under the U.S. Department of the Interior. It has offices in every state conducting research on surface and underground water supplies. Their information is available free to the public and you should always write to your state USGS Water Resources District Office and ask for any information they have on the area you are interested in. You can obtain the address of your local office by writing the main office or the regional office covering your state. These offices and the states within their regions are:

U.S. Geological Survey
Water Resources Division
National Office
Department of the Interior
Washington, D.C. 20240

Western Region Office
U.S. Geological Survey
Water Resources Division
345 Middlefield Road
Menlo Park, California 94025

(Alaska, Arizona, California, Hawaii, Idaho, Nevada, Oregon, Washington)

Central Region Office
U.S. Geological Survey
Water Resources Division
Building 25
Denver Federal Center
Lakewood, Colorado 80225

(Arkansas, Colorado, Iowa, Kansas, Louisiana, Missouri, Montana, Nebraska, New Mexico, North Dakota, Oklahoma, South Dakota, Texas, Utah, Wyoming)

Southeastern Region Office
U.S. Geological Survey
Water Resources Division
1459 Peachtree Street NE
Suite 200
Atlanta, Georgia 30309

(Alabama, Florida, Georgia, Kentucky, Mississippi, North Carolina, South Carolina, Tennessee)

Northeastern Region Office
U.S. Geological Survey
Water Resources Division
George Washington Building
Arlington Towers
1011 Arlington Boulevard
Arlington, Virginia 22209

(Connecticut, Delaware, District of Columbia, Illinois, Indiana, Maine, Maryland, Massachusetts, Michigan, Minnesota, New Hampshire, New Jersey, New York, Ohio, Pennsylvania, Rhode Island, Vermont, Virginia, West Virginia, Wisconsin)

In addition to the above offices, you might be able to find the information you desire at any of the United States Geological Offices listed under "Useful Resources" at the end of Chapter 5: *The Earth—Soil, Vegetation, Topography.*

United States Topographic Maps

The United States Geological Survey Topographic Maps indicate the following water features: perennial and intermittent seasonal streams, wells and springs, intermittent lakes, marshes, inundated areas, dry lake beds, watertanks, dams, bridges, rivers, and perennial lakes.

Most real estate brokers keep such maps in their office. However, you can purchase the map for your area by following the instructions given in Chapter 5.

The Local Well-Drilling Companies

If you look in your Yellow Pages in the area of the land and its surrounding communities you will find one or more well-drilling companies. They are extremely helpful in determining the availability of water on your land. For a small fee they will do a test drilling or surface appraisal. They can show you any available Drilling Logs and Reports for wells already on the land or on neighboring land. The log indicates the depth of the well, the type of water-bearing material that has been drilled through, and the capacity and output of the well. Get the opinion of more than one company as to the possibility of water on your land. Ask them a lot of questions.

Local Board of Health

You can locate the nearest Health Department through the telephone directory. They will have brochures on water testing and potability. You can arrange to have them test your water for you and give you a chemical analysis as well as a bacterial and coliform count. They have minimum standards for contamination of water and will tell you if your water is safe to drink. They do all of this as a public service, or, in some cases, for a slight fee.

Local Water, Irrigation or Reclamation Districts, and Water Agencies

It is possible that your land will be within an area that is provided with water by a public or private water company, agency, or district. You should be able to find out if this is the case by asking the real estate broker or seller. Then go to the offices of the water facility and find out what their services are, how much water you can receive, and how much it will cost you. Even if your land is not covered by their operation they might be able to give you information regarding the availability of water on your land.

Other Sources of Water Information

County Agriculture Agent or Farm Advisor

Local Agricultural Experiment Station
(See "Useful Resources" at the end of Chapter 5.)

Forest and Range Experiment Stations
(See "Useful Resources" at the end of Chapter 5.)

Soil Conservation Service
(See "Useful Resources" at the end of Chapter 5.)

Army Corps of Engineers

The State Department of Water Resources or State Engineer
(Address requests for information and inquiries, using this title, to your state capital, or get the address from the Farm Advisor.)

Local Universities and Colleges
Various departments, such as the Department of Geology, conduct water surveys and investigations, and they might have some useful information.

The County Engineer
Most counties have a civil engineer who is responsible for investigating and documenting water and flood conditions, drainage and other geological problems. He might have some data you can use.

Research Centers Directory
Lists all agencies in each state involved in water research. (See "Useful Resources" at the end of Chapter 5.)

chapter 5

The Earth—Soil, Vegetation, Topography

What then of the man who hears these words of mine and acts upon them? He is like a man who had the sense to build his house upon rock. The rain came down, the floods rose, the wind blew, and beat upon that house; but it did not fall, because its foundations were on rock.

—*The Gospel of St. Matthew,*
Chapter 7: 24–26

When a real estate agent shows you property, he always emphasizes its best features. He is not going to walk you across the acre-long gully or tell you how the land turns into a giant undrained mud puddle for six months during the rainy season. He won't explain to you that the property is on a north slope and gets no sun all winter. He will show you some beautiful "home sites," but it will be up to you to determine if they can actually support buildings and gardens. Finding answers to questions about the condition of the soil, its drainage patterns, and ability to grow things is essential in analyzing the land you intend to buy. If the soil is good, you will have abundant vegetation and few problems with erosion, drainage, slipping foundations, and flooding. You should inspect the geography, seek advice from experts, and study maps and photographs.

TOPSOIL

Topsoil is the loose upper layer of the soil. It is usually richer and darker than the subsoil because it contains humus, or decayed vegetable matter, which is almost black in color and rich in plant nutrients. A dark, thick topsoil rich in humus indicates high fertility. (See Illustration 18.)

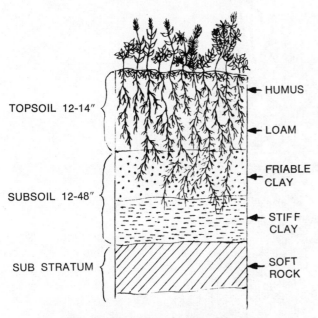

TOPSOIL 12-14″

HUMUS

LOAM

SUBSOIL 12-48″

FRIABLE CLAY

STIFF CLAY

SUB STRATUM

SOFT ROCK

18. MINIMUM SOIL THICKNESSES FOR GOOD LAND

Almost 60 percent of the topsoil in the United States has been lost or destroyed by poor management. Heavy farming has depleted valuable nutrients from the soil, and heavy grazing, logging, and fires have destroyed much of the cover vegetation that held the topsoil together. With the vegetation gone, erosion began. The action of water and winds removed the surface soil, washing it into the rivers and oceans. To get an idea of how much earth is carried off in a storm, fill a jar with water from the nearest creek the next time it rains and let the dirt settle to the bottom.

Good land should have at least 10 to 14 inches of loose topsoil. Ground that is rocky and hard lacks topsoil. If the earth is soft enough to poke a stick into easily, it has some topsoil. Generally, land near the ocean tends to be rocky and barren. The health and abundance of either natural or planted vegetation gives a good and simple indication of the soil quality. Land with too much vegetation on it is often better than land with not enough. Undesirable brush and weeds can be cleared quite easily with the right equipment, but bringing in lost topsoil that has been washed away because of poor ground cover is an enormous task. Uncleared brushy land will probably be cheaper to buy than land that has been cleared and is ready to build on. Ten of our eighty acres is flat land that is completely overgrown with thorny brush which could be cleared to make another home site area. However, because this area can't be used as it is, instead of increasing the value of the land as flat land usually does, it did not affect the purchase price.

Although erosion is one of the easiest things to spot, it is difficult to repair. In an eroded gully that has lost its topsoil, plant roots will have a difficult time getting started in the hard subsoil. The gully makes a natural channel for excess rainwater to run off the land so that baby plants that do get a foothold quickly drown or are swept away by the force of the water.

Sandy soils, steep slopes with little vegetation, and land that has been logged by the clear-cut method are particularly susceptible to erosion. Not all land that has been logged is bad, however. If enough trees were left to hold most of the soil in place, you can purchase some beautiful land at a much lower price than virgin timber land. You must carefully inspect the land for signs of erosion, though, and never buy land that has been "stripped."

If you are planning to farm for a living, you should carefully choose land with highly fertile soil. However, if you just plan to have a family vegetable and flower garden and perhaps a small orchard, you might consider buying less fertile land with the idea of building up a rich topsoil. The process is a slow one and requires that you cart in loads of organic matter, such as spoiled hay, grass clippings, leaves, wet garbage, and dirt, but it is a rewarding one.

SOIL TEXTURE

The texture of the soil is important for healthy plants, good drainage, and building construction. There are four basic soil textures: gravel, sand, loam, and clay. Gravel and sand are made up of large particles whereas clay consists of very tiny particles. Loam, the most common soil in the United States, consists of about equal parts of clay and sand. Because gravel and sandy soils are very loose, they quickly lose valuable nutrients, which are leached out in the water, and gain and lose heat rapidly, causing quick thawing and freezing. On the other hand, compact clay soil becomes mushy and sticky when wet, cutting off oxygen to the plant roots and making cultivation difficult. A loamy soil is preferred by most plants since it contains the best aspects of both sand and clay. To correct either a highly sandy soil or a heavy clay soil, you will have to build up the amount of humus in the soil.

The best way to determine the texture of the soil is to rub some in your hand and between your fingers. How does it feel? Sand is loose and gritty; clay is heavy and compact when dry and sticky and doughy when wet. It is usually gray or yellow. Loam will crumble in your hand and is black.

Dig some holes at different points of the land. Is it hard to dig? How soon do you hit rock? If you dig for several feet and still find a good loam and loose earth that is not too sandy, you have fine soil. If the whole area is rocky and hard, you will have problems. If a road has been put in, look at and feel the various layers of soil exposed where the road cuts into the earth.

DRAINAGE

Drainage refers to the amount of water that can be absorbed by the soil before it becomes saturated. At the saturation point, the water collects on the surface or "runs off" into the nearest creek or drainage ditch. Most plants will not grow where drainage is poor because their roots cannot tolerate being in more water than they can absorb. These plants actually "drown."

A layer of rock or other impervious material, such as hardpan or claypan, near the surface or a high water table can make drainage poor. A few types of soils, like adobe, have very poor drainage. When adobe gets wet, it swells up and prevents water from draining through it to deeper ground. Generally land in the humid eastern United States and in the

northern central states is most likely to have drainage problems.

Water-loving plants covering a meadow could indicate poor drainage, although those same plants located in a row or in a small clump would probably indicate the presence of an underground stream or spring.

Hardpan and Claypan

Hardpan (a compacted layer that is impenetrable by roots) and claypan (a hardpan consisting mainly of clay) occur naturally in the soil or result from years of intensive plowing. Poor plowing practices ruin the soil structure. The fine soil particles are compacted tightly together, which destroys the pore spaces in the subsoil and forms a dense, stonelike layer that cuts off the topsoil from the subsoil. These hard layers are usually impenetrable by plant roots or water. Plants trying to grow in the soil above the hardpan or claypan will have shallow roots that are easily injured by drowning and drought. The plant roots drown because water collects around them without being able to sink into the ground, and they dry up because they are so close to the surface that they cannot escape the hot sun by penetrating deeper into cooler, moist ground.

Drainage Tests

If little is growing on land that was once heavily farmed, be careful. Look at the land during and after a rainstorm. If the area becomes a huge mud puddle or the water runs off the surface without penetrating into the ground more than a few inches, the drainage is obviously bad and the subsoil might be an impervious material.

A dry test involves digging six or more holes 4 to 12 inches in diameter and at least 3 feet deep at various places on the land, especially where your house and garden will be. Does the ground feel as if you are chopping into rocks? If so, you have an indication that the soil is bad. When you have finished digging, take a knife and scratch the sides of each hole. If the dirt crumbles easily, the soil is not im-

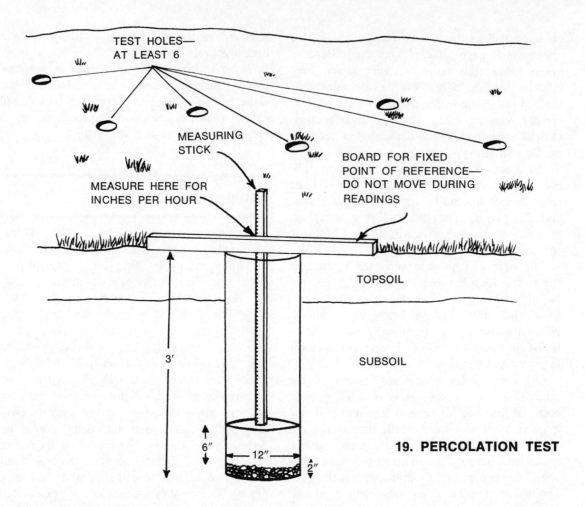

TEST HOLES—
AT LEAST 6

MEASURING
STICK

MEASURE HERE FOR
INCHES PER HOUR

BOARD FOR FIXED
POINT OF REFERENCE—
DO NOT MOVE DURING
READINGS

TOPSOIL

3'

SUBSOIL

6" 12" 2"

19. PERCOLATION TEST

pervious, but if the dirt is tightly compacted and hard to crumble, some kind of hardpan exists.

After you have examined the sides of the dry holes, you are ready to do a "percolation test." (See Illustration 19.) A percolation test determines how quickly and effectively water drains through a porous substance. First roughen the sides of each hole so that water can enter the soil easily, remove any loose dirt from the bottom, and add 2 inches of gravel to prevent sealing. Fill each hole with at least 12 inches of water. Keep the water level 12 inches above the gravel for four hours or more by adding water when needed. If you are doing this test during the dry season, keep the hole filled for at least twelve hours. The ground must simulate its condition during the wettest season of the year. When the dirt is thoroughly wetted, let the water level reach 6 inches above the gravel. Measure the drop in the water level every thirty minutes for four hours if the water

drains out slowly. If the water drains out quickly, measure the drop in the water level every ten minutes for one hour. Add water after taking each measurement to bring the level back up to 6 inches above the gravel. Multiply the last measurement of the drop in the water level by 2 if you are measuring every thirty minutes or by 6 if you are measuring every ten minutes to get the percolation rate in inches per hour. If the percolation rate is less than 2½ inches per hour, the permeability of the soil is insufficient for good plant growth and sanitation. Water will collect after a heavy rain, drowning your plants and flooding your septic tank.

A faster test involves pouring several gallons of water on dry ground. Wait a few minutes and dig into the soil to see how far the water has penetrated. If the soil is still dry a few inches beneath the ground, the drainage could be a problem.

Ask your local Health Inspector if you can

get a professional percolation test done. You may have to pay to have this test done by a licensed soil engineer or geologist in some places. For more information on drainage problems in your area and on how to test the soil, go to the state Agricultural Experiment Station or local office of the Soil Conservation Service. A Soil Map will also state the drainage qualities of each soil in the area. (See "Useful Resources" at the end of this chapter.)

Poor Drainage Affects Septic Tanks, Cesspools, Basements, and Building Foundations

Poor drainage often causes flooding in basements and septic tank systems. If there is a house with a basement on the property, go down and look at it carefully. Are there signs that it floods? Do the owners have a "sump pump" in the basement for pumping water out?

If you are planning to build a house on land with drainage problems, you can dispense with a basement but not a sewage disposal system. If your soil will not allow proper drainage, Building and Health Inspectors will not allow you to construct a dwelling if the building codes require the installation of a septic tank with a house. (See Chapter 13: *Building and Health Codes*.) If water will not drain properly, the water and sewage flushed into the septic tank and drained out by leach lines will float to the surface of the ground during a rainstorm. I have seen this happen in areas where drainage was poor, and it makes living conditions very unpleasant. The soil must be deep and permeable to effectively absorb the effluent, or discharge, from a septic tank. A rock layer or seasonal high water table in the upper 4 feet of the ground could make the area unsuitable for sewage disposal.

Where drainage is poor, you will also be required to construct special building foundations with extra stability. If water stands for a long period of time under a house, it will cause wood rot and mildew, which greatly decrease the value and the life of the house. It is important that you have the Building and Health Inspectors view the land before you buy so that you know you will have no problem obtaining permits afterward.

Correcting Drainage Problems

Correcting poor drainage is an expensive operation, requiring the construction of artificial drainage ditches or the laying of drainage tiles. Drainage tiles are pieces of tube with holes in them, spaced closely together directly above the impervious layer of soil, which collect and carry excess water out to a drainage area. (See Illustration 20.) If the land has already been laid with tiles, be sure they are in perfect condition because finding and correcting broken or separated tiles are expensive and time-consuming jobs. You should see the drainage system in full operation under the most arduous water conditions before buying. The owner should show you a complete diagram of the tile pattern so that you can conduct a thorough investigation. Drainage ditches are usually made of concrete and are spaced farther apart than tiles. The ditches are above the ground and water is carried in them to a creek or channel. They are also expensive to construct.

If proper drainage of land you want to buy requires a runoff system to deliver the water into a nearby creek or drainage ditch, you need a legal easement to cross neighboring lands. (See Chapter 9: *Easement Rights*.) If you want to divert water from your land onto adjoining lands, you can be held liable for damages. (See Chapter 10: *Water Rights*.)

In areas where drainage is a problem, your land might be within a drainage district that

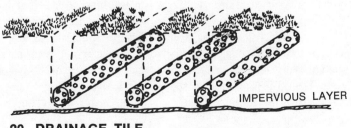

IMPERVIOUS LAYER

20. DRAINAGE TILE

was established to take water from all the lands through a common system of canals. Membership in a drainage district is similar to membership in an irrigation district, except that the purpose of the organization is different. (See *Chapter 4: Is There Enough Water on the Land?* to see how an irrigation district operates.) You should find out whether your land is within such a district and, if so, whether the seller is already a member. How much are the assessments on the land? Before you buy, speak to the Drainage District Advisor about any drainage problems and about what will be involved in bringing the land within the district if it is currently excluded.

If you plan to buy land that will require the laying of drainage tiles or construction of ditches, you should add this cost into the purchase price because it is something that must be done before you can live on the land. If you buy land that has a drainage system already installed, the price will be higher because of this improvement. You should consider whether the added expense is really worthwhile since it might be possible to find land in the area with good drainage for much less money. Occasionally the physical conditions of a particular parcel of land prevent good drainage regardless of what is attempted to alleviate the problem.

ACIDITY AND ALKALINITY

The acidity or alkalinity of the soil has a tremendous effect on the vegetation. They are measured on a pH scale which goes from 0 to 14, 0 being extremely acid and 14 being extremely alkaline. A soil with a pH factor of 7.0 is neutral. Nearly neutral soils, testing in the range of 6.5–7.0, are best for most fruits, vegetables, field crops, and flowers. (See Illustration 21.) Too much acid or alkali locks valuable nutrients into the soil, making them unavailable for plant use. An extremely acid or alkaline soil may be difficult to remedy. To correct an acid soil requires the annual application of quantities of lime. An alkaline soil requires sulfur or gypsum. If you cannot correct the soil deficiency, you will be limited to growing only certain items. For example, the only crops that will grow on a heavily acid

21. pH SCALE

BEST pH RANGE FOR MOST FRUITS, VEGETABLES, AND FLOWERS

soil are berries, potatoes, peanuts, radishes, and watermelon.

For centuries farmers used to taste their soil to test for acidity or alkalinity. If the soil tasted sour, it was too acid, if it tasted bitter, it was too alkaline, but if it tasted sweet it was good for raising crops. Today there are two other simple ways you can test your soil to determine "sweetness." One uses reagents; the other uses litmus paper. For both tests you should collect moist soil samples from a depth of about 6 inches (where plant roots are) from various parts of the land, since different areas may have different pH factors.

The reagent test requires that you purchase an inexpensive soil test kit. You can get one at any gardening supply house. Put a bit of the sample earth into a test tube or small clean container and mix in some of the liquid reagent that comes in the kit. The reagent is a chemical that changes color according to the pH factor. Look at the color that results from the mix and compare it with a color chart that comes with the kit to determine the acidity or alkalinity.

The cheaper test is done with litmus paper. You can purchase neutral litmus paper with a pH factor of 7.0 at a drug store or garden supply center. Press a piece of litmus paper into the moist soil sample. If the paper remains the same color and just gets wet the soil is neutral. If it turns blue it's alkaline, if pink it's acid.

After testing the soil, test the water source on the land to see if it is acid or alkaline. The water you use to irrigate your plants will affect them as much as the soil will.

You can get a more thorough test done by the local Farm Advisor, Soil Conservation Service, or college agricultural or soil department. After analyzing your soil, they will tell you what kind of things you can grow on the land.

PESTICIDES IN THE SOIL

You may want to know if pesticides, herbicides, or other poisons have been used on the land or on neighboring land since many of these poisons are very long-lived and can be carried by rainwater and irrigation water seeping through the soil to surrounding water supplies. If you are interested in organic gardening, you will want "pure" soil. Ask the owner what he has used on his plants. Look for poisons and spray containers in the barn, garage, basement, or greenhouse. The best insurance that you are getting unpoisoned soil is to buy land that has never been cultivated or lived on.

THE "BUILDING SITE"

Every real estate ad makes a point of mentioning that there is a building site on the land being sold. "Numerous building sites," "pretty building sites," "site to build a cabin or home," "excellent view home site," and "many-level building sites" are examples of how this is advertised. When you evaluate so-called building sites, remember my warning about "pond sites" in Chapter 4: *Is There Enough Water on the Land?* Just as anybody can point out a pond site, it is easy to call an area a "building site." But it takes careful analysis to determine whether a place is truly suitable for the construction of a home. A favorite tactic used in selling rural land is to take prospective buyers to a spot on the property where there is a nice "view" or fairly level clearing and call it a "home site." The site looks beautiful and its view overlooking the valley or lake captures the buyer. The person who buys this parcel may discover too late that the land is too steep to build on, that it is impossible to construct a road into the site, or that the drainage is insufficient for a septic tank.

Many considerations that don't apply to a city lot are necessary to determine the suitability of a country home site. The two most important of these are the feasibility of build-

ing a road into the site and of getting water to it easily. For instance, if a home site is on a ridge high above a creek, which is the only source of water, you might find it impossible or very costly to bring water there, especially if no electricity is available. (Refer to Chapter 4: *Is There Enough Water on the Land?* for the problems involved in getting water to the home site and garden areas.) If no road presently exists, you must get an estimate of the costs of constructing one before you buy. The terrain or the soil might make building a solid road to the site an impossible task. If an access road does exist but it is dirt, find out what the annual maintenance costs generally are to keep the road in good condition. You may find that the road becomes impassable in the winter, especially in snow country, which may mean a long walk from the county road with groceries. You might want to use a large propane fuel storage tank for heating, cooking, and lighting, which must be filled periodically by a large tanker truck. Your road must be kept in good enough condition for the truck to get in and out, and your home site must have an area for the tank that will be accessible to the truck.

Consider the site's exposure to the elements. A house on a southern or southeastern slope will always be warmer because it gets the winter sun. A building site at the bottom of a hill facing north, on the other hand, will probably be cold and damp all winter long. (See Illustration 22.) Another major decision is whether

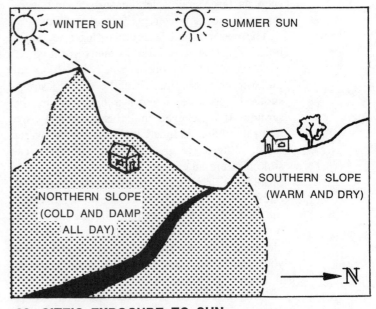

22. SITE'S EXPOSURE TO SUN

to buy on a mountaintop with a view or in a valley. On a ridge, you will probably be more exposed to high winds, a hot sun all day, and all the noises from the valley below. Valleys tend to be cooler, quieter, and closer to water sources. If you have your heart set on a spectacular view, consider all the other aspects of the location too.

The ground on which you build your house is very important. You will have problems if it is either extremely hard or soft. A rocky surface won't enable you to anchor your foundation well and water runoff may be a problem. Soft dirt will be unstable and incapable of supporting a heavy structure.

A major problem in areas of silty clay soil, commonly called adobe, is soil "creep." This occurs when the earth slowly oozes downhill in wet-weather months. During the dry summer months, the soil shrinks as the water content decreases, and huge cracks may open up in the ground. When the winter rains come, the unstable soil slips under the force of gravity until the particles settle into more stable positions. The greatest amount of soil movement occurs at the onset of the winter rains. Soil creep varies with the soil depth and pitch of the slope. Tests have shown that on a slope of only 8 degrees, soil 5 feet deep can move an average of half an inch each year at the surface. Soil creep can cause serious damage to foundations and walls. When examining an area, look for indications of poor soil stability, such as large cracks in the surface and leaning fence posts, power poles, and structures.

The possibility of land collapsing into "sinkholes" must be considered in many areas of the country. Sinkholes occur when the roofs of underground caverns, usually of limestone, suddenly collapse, leaving a huge pit in the ground. It is believed that this is caused by a natural or man-induced lowering of the water table. Where the necessary conditions exist, sinkholes are an extremely serious and frequent problem. For example, in Shelby County, Alabama, over 1,000 sinkholes have occurred in the past fifteen years. In fact, all of central and northern Alabama has soil that is very susceptible to cave-ins of this type. When investigating your soil, always ask about the occurrence of sinkholes and other regional soil problems.

With increasing frequency large areas of swamp and marshland, river beds, and flooded areas are being filled in with dirt in an attempt to gain more land on which to develop housing and make a larger profit. Do not buy real estate where the building sites consist of landfill. You will have no end of troubles. Before buying, find out if the ground will support a house and other structures without creating excessive settling or cracking of the foundation.

Excellent illustrations, photos, and discussion of these problems are contained in a Soil Conservation Service pamphlet entitled *Know the Soil You Build On.* (See "Useful Resources" at the end of this chapter.) The most common building problems are slipping and cracking foundations and walls, sliding hillsides, and flooded basements. The best ground to build on has soil at least 5 feet deep, allows good seepage of water, does not flood or lie over a high water table, and is level or moderately sloping. Steep slopes are generally poor building sites because they can slide and erode. The steeper the building site the more difficult it will be to construct a solid foundation.

A level home site is an asset to a piece of property and always raises the land's value. (See Chapter 19: *Evaluating the Price of the Property.*) If you plan to have only a house, garden, and small family orchard, you really only need a few level acres. Large stock animals, such as a cow or horses, need at least 1 acre per animal for grazing. One way to get level land cheap is to buy an area covered thickly with brush, since it is worth less than land that has already been cleared. Although considerable work may be required to clear the area, the soil is likely to be very rich, having been protected and fed by the brush for years. Be careful to protect the newly uncovered earth from erosion and you will have some valuable land for very little money.

NATIVE BUILDING MATERIALS AND FUEL ON THE LAND

You will be very lucky if you find land at a reasonable price in this country with enough trees on it to construct a house from them. Such abundance is found mostly in Canada where many people still construct their homes from standing timber on the land. Here, you will probably have to rely on such natural materials as rock and adobe rather than trees if you want to build from available resources.

In many areas where land has been logged, enough wood will be lying on the ground to use as fuel for cooking and heating your house for several years. Also, brush that must be cleared or dying trees that should be cut can be used for fuel. If you are buying in isolated country, wood fuel on the land is practically a necessity.

POISON OAK, POISON IVY, AND OTHER ALLERGIES

If you are sensitive to poison oak, ivy, or sumac, don't buy land that is covered with it. These prolific plants are very difficult to get rid of. They have to be dug up by the roots or continually sprayed with poisons. If you are allergic to them, you cannot do this yourself. Goats and donkeys will eat the stuff, but you will need quite a herd to make a dent.

Other allergies to plants, such as hay fever, can also make life in the country unpleasant. Try to avoid those plants that are particularly irritating to you. Visit the land in the worst season for your allergies, and if you start to wheeze and sniffle, look somewhere else. Ask a local Health Department official for information on local plant and pollen conditions.

EARTHQUAKE AND FAULT LINES

Although California and Alaska are most noted for their earthquakes, faults do exist in other regions of the country. A few major quakes have been recorded in New England, in South Carolina, in the Mississippi Valley region, and in the western mountain region of Montana, Wyoming, Utah, northern Arizona, and New Mexico. In most areas of the country, earthquakes are a minor problem. Even if a major quake occurs you will be safer in the country away from toppling buildings and the chaos of panicking people. Make sure that you don't build your house or access road on top of a fault line since minor shifting of the earth will cause you endless problems. Check with your state Division of Mines and Geology or your local Farm Advisor to determine whether fault lines exist in your area. They have maps showing where all the earthquake areas are located. Further information can be obtained from the National Center for Earthquake Research, U.S. Geological Survey Field Center, 800 Menlo Avenue, Menlo Park, California 94025.

MINERALS

I explain the importance of mineral rights and how to investigate them later in Chapter 11: *Mineral, Oil, Gas, Timber, Soil, and Other Rights.* You may be shown land that does not have mineral rights. These rights will be in the possession of the seller, another party, or the United States Government. Try to find out why the party in possession is holding onto the rights and investigate the geology of the area to determine the possibility of their ever wanting to exercise these rights.

You can do this by finding out what minerals are known to be on the land and in the general area. The same agencies that have earthquake information will have studies of the area's geology and facts on past and present mineral explorations in every part of the state. If it appears that the land does not have any minerals currently being used or sought after, you will probably be safe in buying it without mineral rights. Often the government or individuals will hold onto mineral rights without ever intending to use them. Sometimes the government will keep the mineral rights to a piece of land it sells as a matter of policy.

MAPS AND AERIAL PHOTOGRAPHS

When requesting information on the following maps and photos, include a description of the property you want covered. If it is within an area described by the United States Rectangular Survey, give the base and meridian, section, township, range, county, and state in which the parcel is located. (See Chapter 8: *Land Descriptions and Surveys.*) If the land is in another area, describe its location as precisely as possible under the particular survey system used.

Whenever ordering a map or photograph, ask for the most recent one available, since older maps and photos will not include new roads, highways, and buildings. In order to receive your map or photo in good condition, you must specifically request that it be sent in a mailing tube, so that it will not be folded by the sender or post office.

Soil Maps and Other Soil Information

Every state is represented by a Regional Field Office of the United States Forest Service (see "Useful Resources" at the end of this chapter), which has soil maps available to the public at little or no charge. A soil map, which breaks down the soil types throughout a given area, gives much information regarding the soil itself and what is growing on it (as you can see in Illustration 23). Each map has an accompanying chart and leaflet explaining how to read the symbols. Before buying land, you should get all the maps you can find to help you really know the geography of the area. Soil information can be obtained from most of the resources listed at the end of this chapter.

Illustration 23 is a portion of a USDA Forest Service Soil Map, which covers our land. It is based on aerial photos and on-site inspection and classification. Each symbol details important aspects of the soil and vegetation of the area. For example, the symbols D, T, M, 812/5, III represent the following information: D = Douglas fir, will not usually sprout if top is killed by fire, negligible browsing value for horses, cattle, sheep, goats, and deer; T = tan oak tree, will sprout following a fire, negligible browsing value for horses, cattle, sheep, goats, and deer; M = madrone tree, will sprout following a fire, negligible browsing value for horses and cattle and poor to negligible value for sheep, goats, and deer; 812/5 = Hugo soil series, over 4 feet deep, loam texture, slightly acid, light grayish-brown in color, rolling to steep uplands topography, good permeability for movement of water, air, and roots through the soil, drainage good, no toxins present, annual rainfall is 65-75 inches, good to very good for commercial timber, and fair for grasses; III = the height that the average Douglas fir tree reaches at the age of a hundred years on this soil is 140 feet.

Another source of soil maps and descriptions is the Soil Conservation Service (see "Useful Resources" at the end of this chapter), which publishes soil surveys for each state.

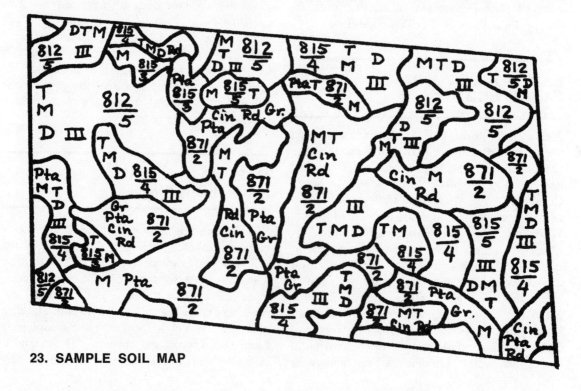

23. SAMPLE SOIL MAP

Included in the map and survey are soil land capability groupings, productivity ratings for trees, farm, and horticultural crops, soil ratings and limitations, soil morphology, the relation of soils to their environment, principles of soil classification, and a general description of the climate and other features significant to soil problems of the area.

Vegetation and Timber Stand Maps

These maps are similar in style to soil maps. If an agency, such as the Forest Service, has soil maps for your area, it will probably also have timber stand and vegetation maps. "Useful Resources," at the end of this chapter, contains information on where to get these maps.

Topographical Maps

The topographical map is an essential aid to understanding the lay of the land. The unique aspect of the "topo" map is the use of contour lines to indicate elevation. The distance between contour lines is usually 40 feet on the ground. Thus, the closer the lines are, the steeper is the terrain. These maps also show roads, railroads, cities, towns, and water features. By comparing aerial photographs of each area with actual ground inspections, the United States Geological Survey has prepared topographical maps for the entire United States.

Topographical maps are also called "quadrangle" maps because each unit of area surveyed is a quadrangle. You can get either 7½-minute or 15-minute quadrangle maps. Chapter 8: *Land Descriptions and Surveys* explains how an area is broken into quadranges. The 7½-minute quadrangle map is drawn to a scale of 1:24,000, which means that 1 inch on the map equals 24,000 inches or 2,000 feet, on the ground. Thus, 2 inches on the map equals approximately 1 mile. The 15-minute quadrangle map is drawn to the scale of 1:62,500, which makes 1 inch equal to about 1 mile on the ground. Thus, the 7½-minute maps give much greater detail.

The United States Geological Survey publishes an *Index to Topographic Maps* for each state, which you can obtain free by writing the main office or visiting your nearest USGS of-fice. Each index lists the map for each specific geographical region, or quadrangle, within the state by name and the year in which it was charted. The index also lists special maps available, the addresses of local map reference libraries, local map dealers, and federal map distribution centers. Order blanks and a list of prices are included. When you write for your state's index, also ask for the free booklet describing topographical maps and symbols.

Because of the popularity and importance of topographical maps, local sport shops, stationery stores, and dealers in civil engineering equipment usually sell them.

Aerial Photographs and Status Maps

Aerial photographs are taken with special automatic cameras that are held vertically while an airplane flies at a constant altitude above sea level along carefully laid out sky-trails. Each snap of the camera's shutter captures an area of ground which overlaps the ground covered in the last photograph by about 60 percent. Each strip of film covers a certain strip of ground. When the plane flies down the adjoining parallel strip of ground, the overlap between strips is from 30 to 50 percent. These photo strips are then laid out side by side to form a "photo index" showing the entire area.

Although aerial photography did not begin on a national basis until 1930, most areas of the United States have been covered. Some areas have been covered by more than one agency and the quality of reproductions tends to vary according to who took the pictures and the date they were taken. A good photo can help you study the geography of the land, including the extent of erosion, vegetation, and timber growth.

An aerial photo can also be used to get an idea of the location of a parcel's boundaries if they have not been marked on the ground or if only the corners have been marked by a surveyor. Draw in the boundaries according to the description of the land on a topographical map and compare it to an aerial photo done to the same scale. Since topographical maps are drawn using aerial photos, you should be able to locate and draw in the boundaries on the aerial photo quite easily. From the features shown in the photograph, you can then locate the boundaries on the ground fairly accurately.

The best way to look at an aerial photograph is with a set of paired stereoscopic prints. Placing two consecutive overlapping photos next to each other and using a stereoviewer or lens stereoscope, you can see the photo in 3-D. The effect is beautiful and each feature sticks right at you as if you were hovering over the land in a helicopter. If you have ever looked at a 3-D movie or comic book using a red and green viewer, you know the effect. You can use a stereoviewer, or similar device, at any of the agencies listed at the end of this chapter. You can buy one at stores that sell surveying or engineering equipment or from the Forest Service (Division of Engineering, Forest Service, U.S. Department of Agriculture, Washington, D.C. 20250). Also army surplus stores occasionally have them for sale. The folding pocket type is the least expensive.

Each agency that sells aerial photos issues free status maps showing what photos are available for your area. Each map indicates the area photographed, the date the photos were taken, the various sizes of photos available, the prices, and order blanks.

USEFUL RESOURCES

Below is a list of sources for aerial photos and the names of the status maps you can order from them at no cost. (The addresses for the agencies can be found in the lists on the following pages.)

United States Forest Service
Ask for *Status of Aerial Photography Coverage* for the state you are interested in. Photos are only available for areas where National Forests are located. Order from the regional office for your state.

United States Geological Survey
Ask for *Status of Aerial Photography in the United States* and *Status of Aerial Mosaics*. These publications list the government agencies that have photographed each area of the country and the commercial aerial photographers who sell prints of their photos, and they tell how you can order the photos. Order these publications from the Photographic Library and Distribution Service or Map Information Office.

Soil Conservation Service
Ask for *Status of Aerial Photography* and *Aerial Photography Mosaic Status Maps*. Order from the Cartographic Division.

Agricultural Stabilization and Conservation Service
Ask for *ASCS Aerial Photography Status Maps*. Order from any of their three offices.

United States Coast and Geodetic Survey
Ask for *Status of Aerial Photography*. This publication lists the photos of coastal areas and navigable rivers that you can order from them.

Local Commercial Aerial Photographers
Most areas have private businesses that engage in aerial photography. The cost of hiring a plane and photographer would be prohibitive, but in many cases they have already photographed your land, and, for a small fee, you can purchase a copy of a picture of your land. Inquire at local photography stores and airports, and look in the telephone directory under "Photographers-Aerial."

City Hall or County Courthouse
Many cities and counties have photographed large areas within their borders. Ask the Planning Commission if they have commissioned any aerial photographs of your area.

United States Forest Service Regional Field Offices (under the U.S. Department of Agriculture)*

Region 1:
Northern Region (northern Idaho, Montana, North Dakota, northwestern South Dakota, Washington)
Federal Building
Missoula, Montana 59801

Region 2:
Rocky Mountain Region (Colorado, Kansas, Nebraska, South Dakota, Wyoming)
Denver Federal Center
Building 85
Denver, Colorado 80225

* See Illustration 24.

Region 3:
Southwestern Region (Arizona, New Mexico)
Federal Building
517 Gold Avenue SW
Albuquerque, New Mexico 87101

Region 4:
Intermountain Region (southern Idaho, Nevada, Utah, western Wyoming)
Federal Building
324 25th Street
Ogden, Utah 84401

Region 5:
California Region (California, Hawaii)
630 Sansome Street
San Francisco, California 94111

Region 6:
Pacific Northwest Region (Oregon, Washington)
319 SW Pine Street
P.O. Box 3623
Portland, Oregon 97208

Region 8:
Southern Region (Alabama, Arkansas, Florida, Georgia, Kentucky, Louisiana, Mississippi, North Carolina, Oklahoma, South Carolina, Tennessee, Texas, Virginia)
1720 Peachtree Road NW
Atlanta, Georgia 30309

Region 9:
Eastern Region (Connecticut, Delaware, Illinois, Indiana, Iowa, Maine, Maryland, Massachusetts, Michigan, Minnesota, Missouri, New Hampshire, New Jersey, New York, Ohio, Pennsylvania, Rhode Island, Vermont, West Virginia, Wisconsin)
633 West Wisconsin Avenue
Milwaukee, Wisconsin 53203

Region 10:
Alaska Region (Alaska)
Federal Office Building
P.O. Box 1628
Juneau, Alaska 99801

Forest and Range Experiment Stations (under the U.S. Forest Service) *

Intermountain
507 25th Street
Ogden, Utah 84401

* See Illustration 25.

North Central
Forest Service USDA
Folwell Avenue
St. Paul, Minnesota 55101

Northeastern
6816 Market Street
Upper Darby, Pennsylvania 19082

Pacific Northwest
809 NE Sixth Avenue
P.O. Box 3141
Portland, Oregon 97208

Pacific Southwest
1960 Addison Street
P.O. Box 245
Berkeley, California 94701

Rocky Mountain
240 West Prospect Street
Fort Collins, Colorado 80521

Southeastern
Post Office Building
P.O. Box 2570
Asheville, North Carolina 28802

Southern
Federal Building
701 Loyola Avenue
New Orleans, Louisiana 70113

State and Private Forestry Offices

The state and private forestry offices are located in the same buildings as the United States Forest Service Regional Field Offices (see above) with the exception of the following area:

Northeastern Area (Connecticut, Delaware, Illinois, Indiana, Iowa, Maine, Maryland, Massachusetts, Michigan, Minnesota, Missouri, New Hampshire, New Jersey, New York, Ohio, Pennsylvania, Rhode Island, Vermont, West Virginia, Wisconsin)
6816 Market Street
Upper Darby, Pennsylvania 19082

State Agricultural Experiment Stations

Mail all inquiries regarding land-related subjects such as soil conditions, water availability, and erosion problems to the local Agricultural Experiment Station listed below. Always re-

24. UNITED STATES FOREST SERVICE REGIONAL FIELD OFFICES

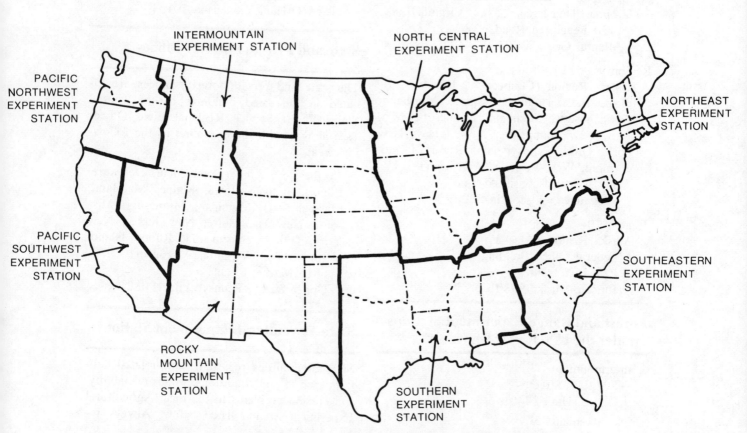

25. UNITED STATES FOREST AND RANGE EXPERIMENT STATIONS

quest a list of available publications. The first line of each address is: State Agricultural Experiment Station.

Auburn University
South College Street
Auburn, Alabama 36830

University of Alaska
P.O. Box AE
Palmer, Alaska 99645

University of Arizona
Tucson, Arizona 85721

University of Arkansas
Fayetteville, Arkansas 72701

University of California at Berkeley
2200 University Avenue
Berkeley, California 94720

University of California at Davis
205 Horticulture Building
College of Agriculture
Davis, California 95616

University of California at Los Angeles
280 Kinsey Hall
Los Angeles, California 90024

Colorado State University
Fort Collins, Colorado 80521

Connecticut Agricultural Experiment Station
123 Huntington Street
New Haven, Connecticut 06504

University of Connecticut
Storrs, Connecticut 06268

University of Delaware
Newark, Delaware 19711

Delaware State College
Dover, Delaware 19901

District of Columbia
Agricultural Experiment Station
Federal City College
425 2d Street N.W.
Washington, D.C. 20001

University of Florida
Gainesville, Florida 32601

University of Georgia
Athens, Georgia 30601

University of Georgia
Experiment, Georgia 30212

Universiy of Hawaii
2525 Varney Circle
Honolulu, Hawaii 96822

University of Idaho
Agricultural Science Building
Moscow, Idaho 83843

University of Illinois
Urbana, Illinois 61801

Indiana Agricultural Experiment Station
Purdue University
Lafayette, Indiana 47901

Iowa State University
Ames, Iowa 50010

Kansas State University
Manhattan, Kansas 66502

University of Kentucky
Agricultural Science Building
Lexington, Kentucky 40506

Louisiana State University
Drawer A-E, University Station
Baton Rouge, Louisiana 70803

University of Maine
Orono, Maine 04473

University of Maryland
College Park, Maryland 20742

University of Massachusetts
Stockbridge Hall
Amherst, Massachusetts 01002

Michigan State University
East Lansing, Michigan 48823

University of Minnesota
St. Paul Campus
St. Paul, Minnesota 55101

Mississippi State University
State College, Mississippi 39762

University of Missouri
2-69 Agricultural Building
Columbia, Missouri 65201

Montana State University
Bozeman, Montana 59715

University of Nebraska
Lincoln, Nebraska 68503

University of Nevada
Reno, Nevada 89507

University of New Hampshire
Durham, New Hampshire 03824

Rutgers, The State University
New Brunswick, New Jersey 08903

New Mexico State University
University Park, New Mexico 88070

Cornell University
Geneva, New York 14456

State University of New York
Geneva, New York 14456

New York State College of Agriculture
Cornell University
294 Roberts Hall
Ithaca, New York 14850

North Carolina State University
Box 5847, College Station
Raleigh, North Carolina 27607

North Dakota State University
State University Station
Fargo, North Dakota 58102

Ohio State University
Wooster, Ohio 44691

Oklahoma State University
Stillwater, Oklahoma 74075

Oregon State University
Corvallis, Oregon 97331

Pennsylvania State University
106 Armsby Building
University Park, Pennsylvania 16802

University of Rhode Island
Kingston, Rhode Island 02881

Clemson University
Clemson, South Carolina 29631

South Dakota State University
Brookings, South Dakota 57006

University of Tennessee
P.O. Box 1071
Knoxville, Tennessee 37901

Texas A&M University
College Station, Texas 77843

Utah State University
College Hill
Logan, Utah 84321

University of Vermont
Morrill Hall
Burlington, Vermont 05401

Virginia Polytechnic Institute
Blacksburg, Virginia 34061

Washington State University
College of Agricultural Research Center
Pullman, Washington 99163

Western Washington Research and
    Extension Center
Puyallup, Washington 98371

West Virginia University
Evansdale Campus
Morgantown, West Virginia 26506

University of Wisconsin
136 Agricultural Hall,
Madison, Wisconsin 53706

University of Wyoming
P.O. Box 3354, University Station
Laramie, Wyoming 82070

Soil Conservation Service (under the U.S. Department of Agriculture)

This federal agency works with local soil and water conservation districts. Most rural areas contain one or more conservation districts and a local Soil Conservation Service. They have maps and aerial photos and conduct on-site inspections and evaluations of soil quality and water resources. To locate your local office look in the telephone book under "U.S. Government," subheading "U.S. Dept. of Agriculture, Soil Conservation District," or ask the local Farm Advisor.

You should request a list of published soil maps and surveys and other information for your state from the main office:

Soil Conservation Service
U.S. Department of Agriculture
Washington, D.C., 20250

There is a main office for aerial photos and status maps:

Cartographic Division
Soil Conservation Service
Federal Center Building
Hyattsville, Maryland 20781

Agricultural Stabilization and Conservation Service (ASCS)

This federal agency is under the U.S. Department of Agriculture. To locate the local office in your area write:

Agricultural Stabilization and
Conservation Service
U.S. Department of Agriculture
Washington, D.C. 20250

Your local Farm Advisor will know where the office is located. The ASCS offices supply aerial photos, status maps, and indexes. The main office is:

Agricultural Stabilization and
Conservation Service
Aerial Photography Branch
Washington, D.C. 20250

The offices covering the following states are:

Western Aerial Photography Laboratory
Program Performance Division
Agriculture Stabilization and
Conservation Service—United States
Department of Agriculture
2205 Parley's Way
Salt Lake City, Utah 84109
(Arizona, Arkansas, California, Colorado, Hawaii, Idaho, Kansas, Louisiana, Montana, Nebraska, Nevada, New Mexico, North Dakota, Oklahoma, Oregon, Texas, Utah, Washington, Wyoming.)

Eastern Aerial Photography Laboratory
Program Performance Division
Agricultural Stabilization and
Conservation Service—United States
Department of Agriculture
45 South French Broad Avenue
Asheville, North Carolina 28801
(Alabama, Connecticut, Delaware, Florida, Georgia, Illinois, Indiana, Iowa, Kentucky, Maine, Maryland, Massachusetts, Michigan, Minnesota, Mississippi, Missouri, New Hampshire, New Jersey, New York, North Carolina, Ohio, Pennsylvania, Rhode Island, South Carolina, South Dakota, Tennessee, Virginia, West Virginia, Wisconsin.)

United States Geological Survey (under Department of the Interior)

Indexes of available topographic maps for each state are free from the main office or appropriate survey distribution office. In addition to the following sources, topographic maps are also sold by sports shops, stationery stores, and dealers in civil engineering equipment.

The following is a list of all United States Geological Survey (USGS) offices and the services provided by each of them:

Main Office of USGS

Includes Divisions of Topography, Geology, Water Resources, and Conservation; Survey Information Office, Map Information Office; Survey Library (open to public).

Located in:
General Services Administration Building
F Street between 18th and 19th Streets
Northwest
Washington, D.C. 20242

Mailing Address:
U.S. Geological Survey
Department of the Interior
Washington, D.C. 20242

Branch Offices of USGS

Includes same services as the main office. Each office has a large branch library open to the public.

United States Geological Survey
345 Middlefield Road
Menlo Park, California 94025

United States Geological Survey
Federal Center
Building 25
Denver, Colorado 80225

Photographic Library and Distribution Office

Distributes aerial photos.

United States Geological Survey
Federal Center
Building 41
Denver, Colorado 80225

Sell maps over-the-counter and by mail.

Maps of Alaska:
Distribution Section
United States Geological Survey
310 First Avenue
Fairbanks, Alaska 99701

Maps for areas west of the Mississippi River:
Distribution Section
United States Geological Survey
Federal Center
Building 41
Denver, Colorado 80225

Maps for areas east of the Mississippi River:
Distribution Section
United States Geological Survey
1200 South Eads Street
Arlington, Virginia 22202

Public Inquiry Offices

Have public libraries, distribute free literature, and sell all USGS topographical and geological maps over-the-counter.

108 Skyline Building
508 2nd Avenue
Anchorage, Alaska 99501

7638 Federal Building
300 North Los Angeles Street
Los Angeles, California 90012

504 Custom House
555 Battery Street
San Francisco, California 94111

1012 Federal Building
1961 Stout Street
Denver, Colorado 80202

602 Thomas Building
1314 Wood Street
Dallas, Texas 75202

8102 Federal Building
125 South State Street
Salt Lake City, Utah 84111

678 U.S. Court House
West 920 Riverside Avenue
Spokane, Washington 99201

Map Information Office (under the USGS)

This federal agency was established for the specific purpose of gathering together all the map and survey data compiled by all other federal agencies. If you want to know about any type of map, survey, or aerial photo available for a piece of land you can write the MIO and ask them what they have. Send all inquiries to:

Map Information Office
U.S. Geological Survey
Department of Interior
Washington, D.C. 20242

United States Coast and Geodetic Society (under the Department of Commerce)

This agency specializes in research of coastal areas and regions around navigable rivers. Send all inquiries regarding aerial photos to:

Director, Coast and Geodetic Survey
Attn: Photogrammetry Division
Washington Science Center
Rockville, Maryland 20852

Other Sources of Soil Information

Local Board of Health or County Health Department
Will test the soil for its suitability for septic tanks or other type of sewage system. Some land is unsuited for sewage systems because of the poor drainage and the health department will not issue the necessary permits, so get the soil checked before you buy.

Local Building Inspector
Has information on soil types, drainage, and erosion as they pertain to the suitability for construction of a dwelling. Get the inspector to look at your land before you buy and tell you if you will be able to get a permit for your intended construction.

Local Universities and Colleges
Various departments study local soil and vegetation conditions. Check for information at

such departments as the Department of Forestry, Department of Soils, Department of Plant Nutrition, Department of Geology, Mining Department.

State Mineral Agencies

Every state has its agency in charge of mineral and geology studies within the state. For example, South Dakota has a state Geological Survey, Oregon has a Department of Geology and Mineral Industries, California has a Division of Mines and Geology, and Texas has a Bureau of Economic Geology. You can get the address of your state mineral agency from your local Farm Advisor, your nearest USGS office, or the *Research Centers Directory.*

Research Centers Directory

The reference section of most libraries will have a publication entitled, *Research Centers Directory,* edited by Archie M. Palmer and published by the Gale Research Company. This book lists every agency involved in agricultural research and services in each state. By looking under your state in the *Research Centers Directory* you can find all the available sources of information and assistance in the evaluation of the land you are investigating.

Publications on Soil, Maps, and Aerial Photographs

The following are free from:

U.S. Department of Agriculture
Office of Information
Washington, D.C. 20250

Soils Suitable for Septic Tank Filter Fields: A Soil Map Can Help—AB 243
That Land Down There—AB 255
Know Your Soil—AB 267
Farmstead Sewage and Refuse Disposal—AB 274
Airphoto Use in Resource Management—AB 336
Soils and Septic Tanks—AB 349
Predicting Rainfall–Erosion Losses from Cropland East of the Rocky Mountains—AH 282
Forester's Guide to Aerial Photo Interpretation—AH 308

Flow and Retention of Water in Layered Soils—CRR 13
How to Control Soil Blowing—F 2169
How to Control a Gully—F 2171
Keep Your Tile Drains Working—L 347
Facts about Wind Erosion and Duststorms on the Great Plains—L 394
Soil and Water Conservation Research in the Pacific Coast Region—M 900
Water Intake by Soil, Experiments for High School Students—M 925
Got a Forestry Problem? Extension Foresters Can Help—PA 955
SCS National Engineering Handbook 1961, "Principles of Drainage," Chapter 1, Drainage, Section 16

The following are free from:

California Agricultural Extension Service
90 University Hall
University of California
Berkeley, California 94720

Soil and Water Management for Home Gardeners—AXT-111
Soil Analysis—OSA-98
Control of Erosion on Banks and Slopes around the Home—OSA-175
Soil Management on Hardpans and Claypans—OSA-191
Managing Layered and Compacted Soils—OSA-192
Permeability Problems Associated with Changing Water Supplies—OSA-236

The following are free from:

The U.S. Geological Survey Main Office, Survey Distribution Offices, or Public Inquiry Offices (see addresses above).

Publications of the Geological Survey, 1962–1970
Publications of the Geological Survey, 1971
Publications of the Geological Survey, 1972
New Publications of the Geological Survey (ask to be put on the list for future monthly mailings)
Popular Publications of the U.S.G.S.
Information Sources and Services
The U.S. Geological Survey
Tools for Planning—Topographic Maps

Topographic Maps
United States Geological Survey Library
Public Inquiry Offices of the U.S. Geological Survey
Photographic Library of the Geological Survey
Pacific Coast Center
Geologic Maps, Portraits of the Earth
Active Faults of California
Elevations and Distances in the United States

The following is free from:

Agriculture Stabilization and Conservation Service
Aerial Photography Branch
Washington, D.C. 20250

Aerial Photo-Maps of Your Farm—A Bonus for You

The following are available for the specified cost from:

The Superintendent of Documents
Government Printing Office
Washington, D.C. 20402

Maintaining Subsurface Drains, Catalog No. A 1.35:557 S/N 0100-02666, 15¢

Soil and Water Research on Claypan Soil (Midwest), Catalog No. A 1.36:1379, 35¢

Surface Drainage of Flatlands, Catalog No. A 1.38:1062, 10¢

Soil Erosion: The Work of Uncontrolled Water, Catalog No. A 1.75:260/2 S/N 0100-1550, 10¢

Know the Soil You Build On, Catalog No. A 1.75:320 S/N 0100-0655, 15¢

Controlling Erosion on Construction Sites, Catalog No. A 1.75:347 S/N 0100-1158, 25¢

Land-Capability Classification, Catalog No. A 1.76:210, 15¢

Uses of Airphotos for Rural and Urban Planning, Catalog No. A 1.76:315, 30¢

Wind Erosion Forces in the United States and Their Use in Predicting Soil Loss, Catalog No. A 1.76:346 S/N 0100-1041, 25¢

The Look of Our Land, An Airphoto Atlas of the Rural United States, the Far West, Catalog No. A 1.76:372, 60¢

Earthquake Investigations in the United States, Catalog No. C 4.19:282/6, 35¢

Earthquakes, Catalog No. C 55.2Ea 7/2/971 S/N 0317-0058, 30¢

chapter 6

Evaluating the House and Other Structures

But what of the man who hears these words of mine and does not act upon them? He is like a man who was foolish enough to build his house on sand. The rain came down, the floods rose, the wind blew and beat upon that house; down it fell with a great crash.

—*The Gospel of St. Matthew,*
Chapter 7: 26–27.

Whether you want to find land with a house already on it or to build your own house is a basic decision. An existing house adds a considerable amount to the price of land. If you are willing to put in the necessary labor, building your own can be fairly cheap and you can realize your dream house. Even if you hire a professional builder, you might save money in the long run buying undeveloped land and building the kind of house you want.

However, if you find a good piece of land with a house on it that is within your price range, you must be able to inspect the house to be sure it is soundly built and will be safe and comfortable to live in. If you want to refurbish an older house, you must determine how much work will have to be done and how much it will cost; the house might be too dilapidated to bring up to current building code standards. Faults in the structure that you find during your inspection can be used later in bargaining to get the purchase price down. (See Chapter 19: *Evaluating the Price of the Property* and Chapter 20: *Bargaining to Get the Seller's Asking Price Down.*)

This chapter will take you through every part of the house and tell you what to look for. Each item is listed to make it easier to refer to. Take this book with you on your inspection, along with a pencil, pad, flashlight, pocketknife, and some old clothes. Look at the house several times under good and bad weather conditions, in the daytime and at night, and you will have a good idea of how livable it will be for your family.

THE NEIGHBORHOOD

If the property is in a populated area, the first thing you will notice is how the house looks in comparison to other houses in the neighborhood. If it looks shabbier than surrounding homes, the price might reflect the value of the community while the actual worth of the house may be much less.

PLACEMENT OF THE HOUSE

Before examining the structure itself, study the placement of the house in relation to both the surrounding area and the environment as a whole.

Is the house placed so you have the privacy you desire? Can you see other houses, and can you be seen by neighbors and passers-by? If so, is the situation disagreeable to you and can it be easily remedied by constructing a fence or planting shrubs and trees?

What kind of a view is there from the most frequently used rooms in the house? Is the view appealing to you? A good view increases the price of a house, but makes life much more enjoyable.

Is the house placed so it receives the maximum amount of winter sun? The south side of the house should have the most windows and be where the most frequently used rooms are located. It should also have an overhanging roof or some other means of shading the inside of the house from direct sunlight in the summer. (See Illustration 26.)

Does the vegetation around the house allow enough sunlight in or is the house usually dark and damp? Many homes in the woods have a serious dampness problem because they are too well shaded by large trees. Some types of forests, such as redwood forests, are much damper than others. If you see the structure in the dry season, imagine what the conditions are like in the winter.

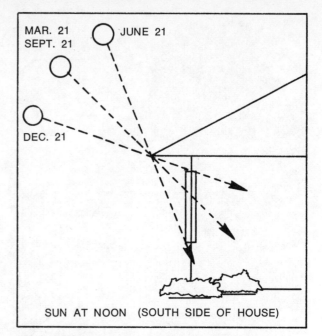

26. EXPOSURE OF THE HOUSE TO SUMMER AND WINTER SUN

Is the house conveniently situated in relation to the rest of the property? For example, are the gardening and recreational areas near the dwelling? Are the outbuildings and other structures, such as the pumphouse, storage tank, and generator, nearby? Climbing up a steep and distant hill to fix the water pump in a pouring rain or snowstorm can be miserable.

Many of the above factors are given little consideration by builders despite their importance.

BLUEPRINTS AND ORIGINAL BUILDING CONTRACT

—Find out if the original blueprints of the house and other specifications are available for inspection.

—If the house was built by a contractor or someone hired to do the job, ask the seller if he has the original contract, which might have warranties in it that guarantee against any defects in construction, including labor and materials.

FLOORS

—Do the floors slope? A tilting floor indicates serious foundation problems.

—Loose and noisy floorboards also indicate foundation problems. Walk over the floor slowly to feel if there is any sagging or give.

—Are the wooden floors nicely sanded and finished?

—Look where the floors meet the walls. Are the joints tight with no evidence of warping?

—If the floor is concrete covered with asphalt tile or wood flooring, are there any cracks in the covering?

—If the kitchen and bathroom floors are covered with linoleum or tile, look for cracks and chipped areas where water has entered and rotted the floor underneath. Is the tile or linoleum well laid and properly fitted around fixtures and along the walls? Has any of the covering come loose from the floor?

INTERIOR WALLS

Dry walls are wood, fiberboard, or gypsum wallboard nailed or taped onto the frame. Plastered walls are lath and plaster. Both types of walls might be painted or papered.

—Do the walls bulge or buckle?

—Is the plaster or paint cracking, or the paper peeling? Moisture, vapor, and condensation could cause these things to happen.

—Is a new paint job or wallpapering needed?

—Have the walls recently been painted or papered? If so, a defect may be hidden. Feel the walls and examine them closely. Wallpaper placed over the old covering might later peel.

—If you don't like the wall colors, you will have to figure in the cost of repainting or repapering.

—If there are water stains on the walls, the plumbing is deteriorating or the roof leaks.

CEILINGS

—Water stains on the ceiling indicate a leaky roof or bad plumbing.

—Look for recent plastering, taping, or painting as a warning that the roof leaks or the ceiling is in weak condition. It may have already begun to collapse in these places.

—Check the ceiling of the room directly underneath the bathroom for leaks.

DOORS

—Open and close all the doors. Are they snug without sticking? Is any warping evident? Examine the walls around the door, particularly over the top of the door. Cracks indicate a lack of proper bracing over and around the door opening.

—Is there weatherstripping on the doors leading outside? Is it in good condition or are there large cracks between the door and the door frame? Do you feel a draft when the doors are closed?

—Do all the doors latch properly?

—Are there screen doors? How is the screening?

—Are storm doors necessary?

—Do the doors need refinishing or painting?

—Are the doorways large enough for you to fit your furniture through?

WINDOWS

—Open and close all the windows to see if they are snugly installed. Is there a draft when they are closed?

—Is weatherstripping around the frame in good condition?

—Is there any broken or cracked glass?

—Are there warped sashes? (The sash is the frame holding the pane of glass.) Are windows loose or is putty chipping badly?

—If any of the windows have been painted or nailed shut, find out why.

—Are storm windows or shutters needed?

—Is there screening on all the windows? Are there any holes in the screens?

—Are there shades or blinds?

—If any windows are covered by shades or curtains, look behind the coverings.

—Is there enough light in the house from properly sized and placed windows? Pay special attention to lighting in the kitchen.

—Are there any skylights? Look for evidence of leaking around the edges.

THE BATHROOM

—Is the bathroom conveniently located?

—Inspect floor and wall tiling for leaks, cracks, looseness, and sloppy workmanship.

—Is there any indication that water leaks from the shower, bathtub, sink, or toilet? Is caulking chapped or cracked?

—Is there a shower and is it a good solid tiled or ceramic one, or is it a cheap metal semi-portable type?

—See "Plumbing" below.

THE KITCHEN

—Is the kitchen large enough for your needs and well laid out?

—If you are bringing in your own appliances, will they fit easily? If not, you will have to change the layout or buy a new appliance.

—An older kitchen might be less adaptable to modern conveniences, and this decreases the value of the house.

—Are appliances in the kitchen going to be included in the sale? For example, a stove, refrigerator, freezer, dishwasher, washing machine, clothes dryer, and blender. See that each item is in good working order. Check the age, brand name, and original cost of each item. Have any been repaired or overhauled recently? If so, get a receipt of payment for the overhaul which indicates what work was done and whether there is a guarantee on it.

—All appliances included with the home must be itemized in writing and included in the Contract of Sale.

WATER HEATER

—There are two kinds of water heaters: the instantaneous tankless type, and the storage tank type.

—The instantaneous type heats the water as it passes through small tubes in a combustion chamber, such as a firebox, and goes directly to the faucet.

—The storage tank type heats the water in an insulated tank and the water remains in the tank until it is used. When the tank is emptied it takes time to heat up a new tank of water. Most houses use the tank type water heater.

—Examine the water heater. If it bears the label of the National Board of Fire Underwriters, it meets normal safety requirements.

—The manufacturer's label on the tank gives the size of the tank in gallons.

—If the heater operates on gas or oil, a family of four needs a tank with a capacity of 30 gallons.

—Electrical water heaters take longer to heat up and a minimum size of 50 gallons is recommended.

—A full load of clothes in an automatic washer takes 25–40 gallons of hot water; dishwashing and rinsing averages 2–4 gallons; a tub bath takes 10–15 gallons, and a shower uses 9–12 gallons.

—Any evidence of leaks in the heating system? How old is it? Does the hot water appear rusty? This indicates a rusting heating system that needs replacing.

PLUMBING

—Faulty plumbing is the most expensive thing to repair in a home.

—Good water pressure is very important. Turn on all the faucets individually. Is there good pressure at each faucet? Turn on two or three faucets at the same time. With the water running at full force in the kitchen, is there adequate pressure in the bathroom? How is the pressure on the second floor?

—With the faucets on, flush the toilet and see if the water flow is affected. Poor plumbing will cause bursts of hot or cold water from a faucet when the toilet is flushed. This can be dangerous or unpleasant when taking a shower or washing.

—Is the pressure sufficient to permit you to install additional outlets or water facilities, such as another bathroom or a dishwasher?

—Do the faucets drip or leak? Look for water stains in the bathtub and sinks.

—Fill the sink and bathtub with water. Is the water rusty or clear? Old pipes or water heaters produce rusty water.

—Watch the water drain out. Is there good drainage or are some drains plugged?

—Drop a fistful of toilet paper or a cigarette into the toilet and flush it. Does it flush well, refill quietly and shut off completely?

—Do you like the fixtures: the sinks, tub,

shower, toilet, faucets, etc? The older they are, the less value they add to the house. In older houses, the hot and cold faucets are separate units, which makes it difficult to wash.

—Are any of the fixtures chipped or scratched?

—Find out the cost of installing modern fixtures and figure it into the other expenses of bringing the house up to contemporary standards.

—Does a plumbing diagram exist showing where all the pipes are in the house?

—Is there a problem with freezing pipes in the winter? The building inspector will know the depth at which pipes should be buried in the area to prevent freezing under local winter conditions. Determine from blueprints, questioning the seller, and physical inspection that the pipes are situated to prevent freezing.

—How easy is it to make repairs on the system? There should be a main valve which shuts off the water supply to the house. Is it conveniently located? In addition, does each faucet have its own shutoff valve so that you can repair one outlet without shutting off all the water to the house?

—Is there a water softener or filtration system for improving the quality of the water? If so, does it serve its purpose well? Get the brand name and price it. How old a unit is it and what is its service history? When was the last time a plumber was called to make repairs? Get his name and talk to him about the condition of the plumbing.

—See Chapter 4: *Is There Enough Water on the Land?* for a discussion of wells, pumps, and other aspects of the plumbing system.

SEWAGE DISPOSAL SYSTEM

—If the house is connected to public sewage lines, is there any indication of broken pipes or bad connections?

—Does the house use a septic tank system installed on the property? A septic tank is a large wooden or concrete box with a filtration system in it that is buried underground. Leach lines carry the strained effluent from the tank through an underground absorption field where the fluid drains into the earth.

—Is the septic tank an old wooden kind or a new single-unit concrete one? When was it installed and by whom?

—Where is the tank located and which way do the leach lines run? The owner should show you a diagram of the entire sanitation system. (See Illustration 27). There should not be any vehicles moving over this area, or vegetation growing there. If it appears this has occurred, the tank or leach lines might be damaged. You should not smell any sewage in the area.

—A septic tank should be cleaned every two years to remove the unfiltered material. This is done by a cleaning service that uses a tank truck, pump, and hose to pump the material from the septic tank. When was the tank last cleaned? Get the name and number of the cleaning company. Ask them to show you their service history of the tank and give you their opinion of its condition. Normal

27. SEPTIC TANK SYSTEM ARRANGEMENTS

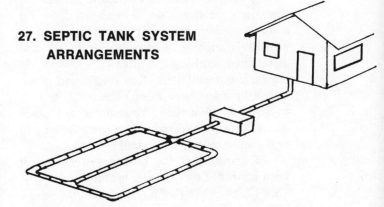

Closed or continuous tile septic tank system arrangement for level ground.

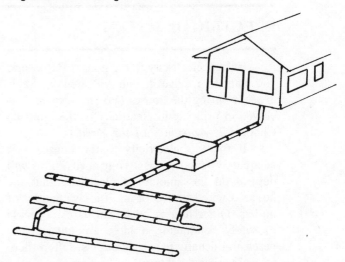

Serial distribution septic tank system arrangement for sloping ground.

maintenance requires the tank be inspected once a year.

—The tank has a cover on it which is lifted off to pump it out. Find the cover and see if it is easy to remove. If it is covered over with vegetation, that is a good indication that the tank has not been properly maintained.

—What is the liquid capacity of the septic tank? The proper size is based on the number of people living in the house and the number of facilities hooked to the tank. If you have more people in your family than the previous owners or you intend to add more water-using equipment to the house, you must be sure the septic system can absorb the extra load. Get advice on this from the dealer who installed the tank or presently services it. The local Health Department also has this information.

—A cesspool is a hole or tank in the ground that simply collects the sewage. It does not contain a filter system or leach lines and is grossly inferior to a properly installed and maintained septic tank. Although a cesspool is regularly pumped, it is often smelly and prone to overflow in heavy rains because of its lack of an absorption field. You should not place much value on a cesspool. Figure in the cost of replacing it with a septic tank.

—Regardless of the sewage system, has it been approved by the local health department? (See Chapter 15: *Building and Health Codes*.)

ELECTRICAL SYSTEM

—Is there electricity to the house? If not, and you want to receive it, you will incur a major expense wiring the house. (For the expense involved in bringing in electricity to the land see Chapter 7: *Amenities of the Area*.)

—If there is electricity to the house, is it adequately wired to meet your needs? This will depend on the amount of electricity that the house is wired to accept and the availability of outlets. Older houses have thin wire incapable of safely conducting a large amount of amperes and usually have few outlets. Often there is no overhead lighting.

—Does each room have outlets? The kitchen is the most important room to check. Are

there enough outlets for your appliances? If not, the wiring will probably not be sufficient because you should not overload the outlets.

—Are any wires loose or frayed?

—How many electrical appliances are presently being used around the house?

—The electrical system uses either a circuit breaker or fuse box. If a fuse blows or the current breaker is tripped, the electrical outlets on that line go dead. This often occurs when the system is overloaded or short-circuited. Does the house use fuses or a current breaker? Current breakers are used in modern systems.

—The local electric company can tell you how much load the present system can carry. Does the present system meet building codes and has it been approved?

—If the house has to be rewired to bring it up to current building code standards or to meet your needs, you should get an estimate of the costs involved from a local contractor. It is an expensive undertaking.

HEATING SYSTEM

Many different kinds of heating units are in use today. A central heating system warms the entire house from one source either by blowing hot air through outlets, vents, and ducts in each room or by circulating hot water through pipes in the walls, floors, or ceilings of each room. The former is called conductive heating, the latter is called radiant heating. Instead of central heating, each room might have its own space heater such as a radiator, wall heater, fireplace, or other type of unit. The heating system might use electricity, oil, gas, coal, or wood fuel. The best way to eliminate drafts is to locate heating units along outside walls, under the windows. Baseboard heating is the most efficient draft eliminator. See Insulation below.

—What heating system does the house have? Where are the individual outlets located?

—How much does it cost to run in the winter?

—Is heat supplied to each room in the house?

—Turn the heating units on to see how rapidly and effectively the house is heated.

—Does the heater make a lot of noise during operation?

—How old is the heating unit? What is its service history? Ask the local dealer what the life expectancy of such a unit is. Most heaters run trouble-free for only seven or eight winters.

—Look on the heater for the specifications. The "B.T.U. Output" is the amount of heat a furnace will emit. Write down the figure and see if its capacity is normal for the area.

—If the furnace is gas-fired, do you smell gas around it? The local gas company will inspect it free and tell you about its efficiency and cost of operation.

FIREPLACE AND CHIMNEY

—Your winter heating bills can be lowered considerably if you have an efficient fireplace.

—A good one is worth paying a little more for. However, fireplaces are often poorly designed or improperly maintained and can cause many problems. Inspect it carefully.

—When was it last cleaned and by whom?

—Are the walls and floor around the fireplace adequately protected? Do you see any smoke marks on the walls? There might be draft problems.

—Have the owner show you how to operate the damper. Does it work easily? Does it open all the way?

—Are the bricks in good condition?

—A metal fireplace is worth less than a brick or stone unit.

—Does the fireplace have vents on the side for extra heating efficiency?

—Is it large enough for good-size logs?

—Is it in a good location?

—Look where the chimney goes through the ceiling. Is it well protected? Any evidence of burning?

—When you go outside, examine the chimney. Any cracks or missing bricks? Does the top extend far enough above the roof to be safe and to create a good draft? When you go up on the roof, examine the top of the chimney. Is the opening protected so that sparks don't escape? Does it need cleaning?

—The Building Inspector can tell you if the fireplace is in good condition or what has to be done to bring it up to code.

—The best way to evaluate a fireplace is to see it in action. Ask the owner to light a fire for you.

INSULATION

The house must have good insulation as well as heating. A house is insulated to prevent heat loss by conduction and radiation in the winter and to keep out heat in the summer. This is done by placing a layer of material between the inside and outside wall of the house. Often an air space between the walls is the only insulation. Common types of insulating materials include foil, fill, slab, or board.

—Ask if there is any place in the house where you can see the insulating material. What kind is used? Older houses may have sawdust or newspaper, which are fire hazards.

—When the temperature outside falls, the inside surfaces of windows and exterior walls get colder. As the air within the house comes into contact with the cold windows and walls, it chills and settles to the floor, creating a draft as it moves across the floor. (As you walk through the house, does it feel well insulated? Is it uniformly warm? Do you feel cold drafts, especially on the floor?)

—If there is snow on the roof, how much of it is melted? Compare it with other houses in the area. Rapidly melting snow indicates heat is escaping through the roof because of poor insulation. (See Illustration 28.)

—Extremely cold climates require up to 6 inches of insulation whereas temperate areas need only a thin layer. Ask the local Building Inspector or building supply store about the standards for the area.

—The roof, attic, basement, and crawl space are areas that affect insulation. (See below.)

WELL INSULATED

28. INSULATION

POORLY INSULATED

VENTILATION

—As you walk through the house does the temperature seem too warm or too cold? Is the air clammy or stuffy? The first problem is caused by poor insulation, the second by improper ventilation.

—Proper ventilation allows good air circulation and is usually accomplished by opening windows on opposite sides of the house to create a slight breeze. If the openings on the cooler side of the house, usually the north side, are low and small and the openings on the hot side of the house, usually the south side, are high and large, the ventilation will be improved.

—Is the house comfortable in the summer?

—Ventilation in the winter when all the windows are closed is very important. In a properly constructed house the air will flow by its own conduction currents.

AIR CONDITIONING

In most areas of the country, air conditioning is a must for comfort. If the house you are looking at does not have air conditioning, beware if you are told that it will be simple to install by using the existing forced warm air or other heating system. An efficient heating system will have ducts or vents near the floor because heated air rises. But because cooled air falls, if you use the heating ducts also for air conditioning all the cool air will remain on the floor. Also, cool air needs larger vents, and if small heating vents are used, the cold air won't come into the room fast enough for comfort.

—For maximum efficiency, there should be separate, overhead air conditioning properly sized for the house in which it is installed.

—If there is air conditioning, what kind of a system is it?

—Where are the individual outlets located?

—How much does it cost to run in the hot months?

—Is cool air supplied to each room in the house?

—Turn the system on to see how rapidly and efficiently the house is cooled.

—Does the system make a lot of noise during operation?

—How old is the unit? What is its service history? Ask the local dealer what the life expectancy of such a unit is.

—If no air conditioning system presently exists, will you want one? If so, what will be the cost of installing an adequate system?

TERMITES AND OTHER DESTRUCTIVE INSECTS

Regardless of the age of the house or the type of construction used, it can be infested by termites and other damaging insects. The most common and serious troublemaker is the subterranean termite. A heavily infested house can have 250,000 termites constantly eating away at it. Even if the seller has had the house fumigated recently, termites can return within a short time. The problem may be so serious that further fumigation is worthless. Although termites are found throughout the United States, they are particularly numerous in the South Atlantic and Gulf Coast states and California. (See Illustration 29.) Termites inhabit over 200 million homes and cause $500 million damage a year.

Termites need two things to survive: wood and water. A termite will die in twenty-four hours if deprived of moisture. Good ventilation and dry ground under the house are essential in preventing termites. In heavily infested areas, a chemical barrier in the ground around the home is necessary.

There are several ways to detect termites:

The first is the presence of "termite highways." Termites live in underground nests and burrow into the foundation and the rest of the structure. You can see paths along the foundation where they burrow up the wood. Look for veins or streaks along the wood.

The second is the termite "tube" or "tunnel." These flattened tubes are made of mud suspended directly from underneath the floor to the earth. The termites travel through these tunnels to get from their nests in the moist ground to the wood. You will see these tubes in crawl spaces and basements. They are also built up the sides of the foundation, the walls, the water and drain pipes, and the chimney.

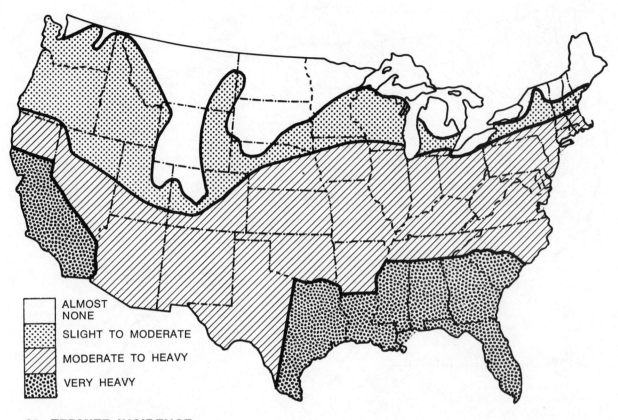

ALMOST NONE

SLIGHT TO MODERATE

MODERATE TO HEAVY

VERY HEAVY

29. TERMITE INCIDENCE

The third way to find termites is with a knife or screwdriver. Usually termite activity occurs inside wood that looks fine from the outside. Take your tool and make jabs at different parts of the house. If the wood is soft, you have termites or wood rot.

During your inspection, look for termites and discarded termite wings around anything that touches, or is near, the ground, including the foundation, basement walls, floor joists, the underside of the floor, house beams and posts, window frames, porches, drain and water pipes, along chimneys, on the attic walls, roof beams, and the underside of the roof.

There are other insects that can seriously damage a building. Some of these include the powder-post beetles which occur throughout the United States, the house borers found in the eastern United States from Florida through Massachusetts, the carpenter ants and bees, and two other types of termites. Your county Building Inspector can give you information on local

pest problems and how to examine a structure for pest damage.

WOOD ROT (DRY ROT)

Wood rot is more damaging than termites. It is a major problem in the North. (See Illustration 30.) When wood becomes wet, either from direct contact with water or by condensation, a fungus grows, causing the wood to decay. When this occurs, the wood takes on the appearance of being dried out. This is why wet wood is often called "dry rot." Once wood rot sets in, the entire structure can become dangerously weakened and the value of the house is greatly diminished. To prevent dry rot, the house must be dry and well ventilated. Wood rot commonly occurs in attics, basements, crawl spaces, and under porches. As you inspect the house, maintain constant vigilance

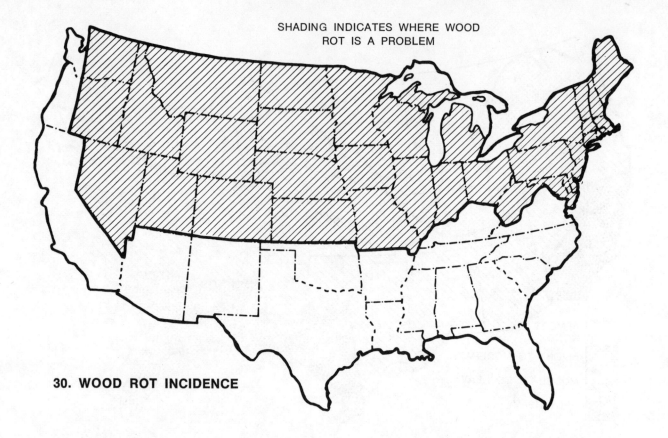

SHADING INDICATES WHERE WOOD
ROT IS A PROBLEM

30. WOOD ROT INCIDENCE

for wood rot. Use your flashlight to inspect every dark corner.

—When you see an area that looks rotten, take your pocketknife or screwdriver and scratch the wood. How easily does it break down? Stick the tool into the wood. If it sinks in easily, the condition is severe and probably too costly to repair.

THE ATTIC

Eighty percent of the heat lost from a house escapes through the roof. Therefore, an attic is very good for improving insulation because it creates an air pocket between the ceiling and the roof. The floor of the attic should also contain insulation.

—Is there an attic?

—Is it insulated on the floor and under the roof?

—An attic must have good ventilation and air circulation. There should be louvered openings on the sides of the attic. A louver is a slatted opening with screen wire on the inside

that aids ventilation. These vents should always remain open. If closed or if none exist, condensation occurs and the moisture deteriorates the ceiling, walls, and roof.

—Does any light shine through the roof? If so, that could be a leaky spot.

—Take out your flashlight and look for water stains on the attic floor, walls, and underside of the roof. If you see any, the roof leaks or ventilation is poor.

—Look for dry rot and termite damage.

—Does the roof sag? Does the ceiling (the attic floor) look solid?

—Are there windows in the attic?

—Does it seem possible to convert the attic into another room? If not, it is a good storage area. It is always the hottest place in the house because heat rises. If it has already been converted into a room, how is the quality of the workmanship?

THE BASEMENT

Many rural houses have a basement or cellar. It serves as an insulator for the house, and it

78

may be used as a workroom, storage area, food and wine cellar, or recreation room. The most severe problem in basements is flooding and dampness.

—A sump pump is turned on automatically or manually to pump water from a flooded basement. If you see one in the house, you know there are problems. Ask the owner why it is there, how often it is used, and why the basement floods. The problem might be corrected by placing drainage pipes or ditches around the house. It is more severe if the slope of the land itself is at fault. Talk to the Building Inspector about the problem and get an estimate of what has to be done to correct the problem.

—Other evidence of dampness is water stains on the walls and floors. Are there drainage holes in the floor? Are there signs of mud anywhere? Use your flashlight to inspect the basement carefully.

—If there is a drain, the floor should slope toward it.

—Even if the basement doesn't flood, it might have poor ventilation. Condensation causes moisture to form on basement walls unless there are open windows or vents where the weather is cool and dry. Are there sufficient vents or windows? Damp spots on walls or the floor could be due to condensation rather than water leaking in from outside.

—Are the basement walls and floor cement, wood, or dirt? A cement basement floor is the best kind. Do you see cracks in the walls or floor? Cracks cause water leaks and indicate structural defects. Has any kind of waterproofing been used on the walls and floors?

—If the basement is damp, it might require the installation of a dehumidifier. Is there one already installed? How old is it and what is its service history?

—In the basement you can inspect the foundation and look for evidence of termite infestation and wood rot.

STAIRWAYS, BALCONIES, AND TERRACES

—Check the condition of all stairways in the house.

—Are they brick, wood, concrete, or steel?

—Do they have sufficiently safe railings? This is very important if you have young children or older people in the family who could fall easily.

—Are there any loose boards or cracks in the concrete?

—Examine the condition of the balconies and terraces.

—Are there good railings?

—Is the flooring solid?

—Are there any leaks in the protective coverings against the rain and sun?

CLOSETS, CABINETS, BUILT-INS, AND STORAGE AREAS

—As you go from room to room, look in the closets and other compartments.

—Does each bedroom have a closet?

—Are the closets numerous enough and sufficiently roomy to meet the needs of your family?

—Well-designed built-ins are always used to impress a buyer and increase the value of a house, particularly built-in kitchens, where appliances are placed into the woodwork.

—Notice the quality of the design and construction of shelves, cupboards, and cabinets.

—Do they have glass, metal, or wooden doors that open and close easily?

—Are the joints solid?

A PORCH AND EXTRA ROOMS

An enclosed porch in some areas is an essential feature and will add value to the house.

—Check the condition and construction of both the inside and outside of the porch.

—Is the porch supported as well as the house itself?

—Is the crawl space underneath the porch well ventilated and dry?

—Check for termites and wood rot.

—Are the screens in good condition?

Any additional rooms, such as recreational and rumpus rooms, a laundry, workshop, darkroom, or storeroom are going to increase the cost of the house and you should evaluate their worth to you. If you plan to add on a room or two, is it feasible to do so? It might be cheaper to get a bigger house.

CRAWL SPACE

The crawl space is the area under a house between the ground and the bottom of the house. The bottom of the house must be a minimum of 6 inches from the ground. Walk around the house looking for vent openings into the crawl space. If none or an insufficient number exist, there will be excessive moisture from condensation under the house. This deteriorates the floors, foundation, and other parts of the structure. Vents are also necessary for safety if heating units are located within the crawl space and if gas and sewer lines run under the house.

You have to crawl into this space to see the foundation and the underside of the floor. (This is why you should wear old clothes.) Find the opening, take your flashlight, and crawl in.

—Has ground-cover paper or roofing been laid over the surface of the ground under the crawl space? This helps ventilation and insulation. What kind of condition is it in? Where this paper is used, vents are usually smaller. If the paper has deteriorated, the vents might be too small to prevent excessive moisture from forming.

—Is the heating unit located under the house? If so, inspect it as outlined above in "Heating System."

—Look at all visible pipes. Any leaks or corrosion?

—Look at the wiring. Do you see loose, frayed, or broken wires?

—Inspect the foundation in the manner specified below.

FOUNDATION

The foundation is the supporting structure of the house. The house might be built on poles, on posts and concrete, or on a concrete slab.

Pole construction is used primarily where the building site is not level. Huge poles are sunk deep into the ground and the house is built around them up in the air.

—If the poles are wooden, at least the buried part should be chemically treated to prevent them from rotting.

—Have they been treated against wood rot and termites? If so, when and by whom? Talk to the termite service that did the job and ask them what they know about the house.

—Has there been a chemical coating applied to prevent dampness? If so, how long ago was this done? Are there any cracks in the dampproof coating? Does water ever stand under the house?

If the house is built on posts sunk in concrete, the concrete might just be under each post or it might be under the entire perimeter of the house.

—Examine the concrete, either from the basement or from the crawl space, with your flashlight to see if there are any cracks.

—The concrete should show above the posts and not be completely buried under the earth since the concrete protects the wood from rotting.

—Is the foundation sinking into the ground?

—Do the floor joists, or supports, sag?

—Have the posts separated from the floor at any point?

—Are there any irregularities in the foundation that you can see?

—Check for wood rot and termites. Has the foundation ever been chemically treated against termites? When and by whom? Talk to the termite service that did the job and ask them what they know about the house.

—Has a chemical coating been applied to the foundation to prevent dampness and water from getting beneath the house? When was it applied? Are there any cracks in the dampproof coating?

If the entire house is set on a concrete slab, examine it at all visible points. This kind of construction is often difficult to inspect.

—Does the slab appear to be tilting or sinking into the ground at any point?

—Has the floor become separated from the slab at any point?

—Can you see any cracks in the cement?

—Check for termites and wood rot.

—Slab construction offers greater protection to termites once they have invaded the wood. Is there any termite shielding around the house? Has the concrete been chemically treated? When and by whom? Talk to the termite service that did the job for information about the condition of the house.

SIDING, EXTERIOR WALLS, AND TRIM

—Siding is the external covering of the house, whether boards, shingles, or some other material. How does it look? Are there any holes, cracks, or signs of patch jobs?

—Is any paint peeling? This can be caused by water getting into the walls or by condensation forming on the back of the siding due to moisture in the house and poor ventilation. Paint will also peel if it is an inferior or improper type or if too much repainting has been done. Talk to the local paint dealer about possible causes and the expense of correcting the condition. Find out when the house was last painted, what kind of paint was used, who did the job, and how much it cost.

—Examine the exterior trim for signs of wood rot or termites. Has it been painted recently? Is it fitted evenly?

—Do all the walls square with each other or is there sagging or sloping? These are signs of major structural defects.

ROOF GUTTERS, AND DRAIN PIPES (LEADERS)

—Get up on the roof. What kind of roofing is used: shingles, tar paper, gravel, plywood, etc.? Are any shingles missing, curling, or broken? If any are distinctly lighter in color, they are newer. Ask when they were put on and why. Is the roof material fireproof?

—Is the tar paper ripping or cracking?

—When was the roof last worked on, what was done to it, and who did the work?

—Look where the roof joins the chimney, at pipes, and at the connection where two roof slopes meet. Is there metal flashing installed in these places? Flashing is used to weatherproof joints and edges. Is it rusted and corroded? Are there cracks at any of these points?

—Is there any evidence of roof leaks?

—Does the roof extend out from the house sufficiently to prevent rain or snow water from running down the walls of the house? If it extends out far enough and you see water stains on the external walls, the roof might be leaking.

—Is there a complete gutter system around the roof? Any rust or corrosion?

—Are there drain pipes coming down from the roof? Are they in good condition and unclogged? Clogged pipes can cause water to back up and leak through the roof.

DRAINAGE

—Where does the water drain off the roof? If water stands around the house, it can seep through the foundation and cause wood rot and basement flooding.

—Look at the slope of the ground around the house. The ground should be graded so that water runs away from the house.

—Are there any drainage ditches or other drainage devices in the ground? Are they in good condition? (See Chapter 5: *The Earth— Soil, Vegetation, Topography.*)

WALKS AND DRIVEWAY

—Are the walkways in good condition? If they are cement, are there cracks anywhere?

—If there is a driveway, is it in good condition?

Information on access roads is included in Chapter 9: *Easement Rights.*

FENCING

—If the house or garden area has a fence around it, is it beginning to lean to one side and fall apart in places or does it look strong?

—Does it need a paint job?

—When was it built?

—If there is no fence and one is needed, what would it cost to erect one? Figure this into the house cost.

OUTBUILDINGS

The most common outbuildings in the country are garages, barns, and workshops. Often these buildings will be included in the deal at much less than their actual worth because they are used as extra selling points by the owner. Generally, these structures are not in as good condition as the house. The greater the emphasis the seller places on these buildings to justify his asking price, the more you should inspect them for defects.

Examine the Garage
—Is there any evidence that the roof leaks?
—Is is big enough to hold your car? Does it have a workshop or tool space in it?
—If it is connected to the house, give it as thorough an inspection as you give the house.
Examine the barn. Many barns have not been maintained well and will be in poor condition.
—Is there any evidence that the roof leaks?
—Is the foundation sound?
—Is the wood rotting? Is there any evidence of termites?
—If you want horses, cows, or goats, is it big enough for them?
—Is it insulated? Heated? Are any utilities supplied to it?
—Does it have potential as a human dwelling?
—What has it been used for in the past?
There might be any number of other assorted buildings on the land, including poultry houses, pig pens, rabbit hutches, feed storage sheds, and silos, granaries, game rooms, water tank housing, a tool and tack house, wellhouses, greenhouses, and generator houses.
—What utilities are supplied to the buildings?
—Are these buildings worth whatever additional value the seller places on them? Find out how the seller breaks down the total asking price, what he thinks the house is worth, what the other buildings are worth. You should not hesitate to ask this question. Find out how the Tax Assessor has assessed the value of these buildings for tax purposes. (See Chapter 17: *Taxes and Assessments.*)

LANDSCAPING

Landscaping is always emphasized in real estate ads. Such things as "spacious lawns," "plenty of shade trees around house," and "numerous ornamental paintings in a beautifully landscaped setting" can raise the price of land considerably. You must decide whether these things are important enough to you to warrant the extra cost.

If the land is a small parcel and you have neighbors close by, trees and shrubs might afford needed privacy. Orchards and other land improvements that take many years to develop before producing are valuable assets if they are free from disease and have been well cared for. An orchard that has been neglected for many years, however, will take time and work to bring back to productivity, and you should not have to pay extra for it. Flowers and vegetables are nice but their value is minimal. You can produce your own garden in one season. It is easy to be swayed by a lovely garden and pay an inflated price for the property. If you are buying land that is carefully landscaped, be sure you estimate its true value by placing most of the emphasis on the house and land itself rather than the frills.

ADDED ATTRACTIONS—DON'T LET THEM BLIND YOU

The seller might try to entice buyers with many extras, such as animals, animal feed and maintenance equipment, a television antenna, carpets, drapes, furniture, air-conditioning, appliances of all kinds, tractors, compost shredders, plows, lawn mowers, gasoline pumps and generators, lawn and patio furniture, and almost anything else you can think of. Be very careful about letting these extras attract you to a deal which otherwise might not be what you want. I have heard people talk more about the extras that come with a home than about the home and land itself. Real estate agents often exploit this tendency by placing great emphasis on these added features to keep the buyer's mind off the important things.

If extras are included, note the condition of

the items, their age and service history, and their brand names if applicable. Price the items yourself and then ask the seller how he computes their value in the total asking price. Have the seller operate each item for you. Is he overpricing these frills?

FINAL CONSIDERATION

Now that you have seen the house, the other buildings on the land, and the extras that come with the deal, think about the house again.

—How is the general quality of workmanship and materials?

—Would you feel comfortable living in it?

—Is it your idea of a relaxed home in the country?

—Does it blend in well with the land?

—Do you like the size of the rooms and the way they are laid out?

—Will your furniture fit in well?

—Is the house large enough for your present and future family needs?

—Will it lend itself well to any additions you might want to make to it? Can you get a building permit to construct additional rooms?

—Can the house be securely locked and sealed while you are away?

—If you are buying an old house and want to refurbish it, can you get the proper permits? Is it economically feasible to rebuild the structure?

—No house is perfect. There may be many things wrong with the house that can be fixed for only a few hundred dollars. Get estimates on the costs of repairing deficiencies. Armed with these figures you have three choices:

(1) Have the seller make the repairs before you buy the house.

(2) Bargain to get the price reduced at least by the amount needed to make the essential repairs.

(3) Do not buy the house because it is too dilapidated and the seller is not willing to cooperate with you.

USING A PROFESSIONAL INSPECTOR'S SERVICE

If you have decided that the land and house are definitely what you want, you might like to get a professional evaluation of the house done to double-check your evaluation. Within the last ten years, real estate inspector services have sprung up around the country to inspect and evaluate the present physical condition of a structure and estimate the current cost of making necessary repairs. (An inspector does not estimate the value of the house; that is done by an appraiser.) You can accompany the inspector when he goes over the house, and he will point out the defects to you. He will write up a detailed report which you can use when bargaining with the seller.

Shop around and compare inspection fees. The fee can be based on one or more of the following: where the house is located, how large it is, what the selling price is, and how long it takes to complete the inspection. The charge can be from $50 to $150. House inspector services are an unregulated business, so you must carefully check reputations and qualifications before you hire one. Never hire an inspector who also makes home repairs because he may exaggerate the defects with the hope that he will be paid to fix them. Do not hire anyone recommended by the seller or real estate agent, but you should get recommendations from the county Building Inspector. Inspection services will be listed in the phone book under "Real Estate Inspection." A registered civil engineer is also qualified to inspect structures.

Rather than get a complete structural inspection, you can get a termite and wood rot evaluation. This type of damage is the most destructive to a home and the most expensive to repair. A pest and fungus inspection costs less than a complete evaluation of the house and is considered essential by most lawyers.

My Model Contract of Sale (see Chapter 28) contains a warranty that the house is free of termite infestation and wood rot. (See Clause 18 (e) and the accompanying explanation.) You can also condition the purchase on your approval of a complete or partial structural report. Clause 19 (b) can be used for a complete inspection and Clause 19 (d) specifically provides for a pest and fungus report. You can thus sign a contract to buy the property but the deal cannot be closed unless you approve the results of a structural and termite report. If you receive an unfavorable report, you can terminate the agreement to purchase or have the price reduced by the amount needed to make the repairs. (See Clause 19 (a).)

If the seller is unwilling to warrant the condition of the house or allow the inclusion of these conditions, he might have something to hide. Actually, he should pay the inspection costs. You can compromise and pay half if you want. Sometimes if you demand a report, the real estate agent will pay for it if it will help him make the sale.

You can include other warranties of the condition of the property you are buying; for example, that the house is structurally sound, that all the appliances and machinery are in perfect working order, and that the livestock is in excellent health.

USEFUL RESOURCES

Publications to Help You Inspect a Home's Physical Condition

The following are free from:

U.S. Department of Agriculture
Office of Information
Washington, D.C. 20250

Foundations for Farm Buildings—F 1869
Fireplaces and Chimneys—F 1889
Simple Plumbing Repairs for the Home and Farmstead—F 2202
Plumbing for the Home and Farmstead—F 2213
Home Heating Systems—F 2235
Wood Decay in Houses: How to Prevent and Control It—G 73
Equipment for Cooling Your Home—G 100
Making Basements Dry—G 115
The Old House Borer—L 501
An Economical and Efficient Heating System for Homes—PRR 99
Building Decay Associated with Rain Seepage—T 1356

The following is free from:

The Department of Housing and Urban Development (HUD)
(See addresses in "Useful Resources" at the end of Chapter 26: *FHA and VA Loans.*)

Wise Home Buying HUD—267-F

The following is free from:

Veteran's Administration (VA)
(See addresses in "Useful Resources" at the end of Chapter 26: *FHA and VA Loans.*)

Pointers for the Veteran Homeowner: VA Pamphlet 26-5, Revised

The following is free from:

Nationwide Real Estate Inspector's Service, Inc.
6 East 39th Street
New York, New York 10016

Free Information Kit on house inspection services, including the article on termites entitled *Look Who's Coming to Dinner.*

The following are free from:

Consumer Product Information
Public Documents Distribution Center
Pueblo, Colorado 81009

Room Air Conditioners, Consumer Information Series No. 6
Protecting Your Home Against Termites, 151 A
How to Prevent and Remove Mildew, 176 A

The following is free from:

Canadian Central Mortgage and Housing Corporation
650 Lawrence Avenue West
Toronto, 7, Ontario, Canada

Canadian Wood-Frame House Construction

The following is free from:

Southern Forest Experiment Station
701 Loyola Avenue
New Orleans, Louisiana 70113

Finding and Keeping a Healthy House

The following are available for 15¢ each from:

> Small Homes Council–Building Research
> Council
> One East Saint Mary's Road
> University of Illinois
> Champaign, Illinois 61820

Insulation—F 6.0
Moisture Condensation—F 6.2
Heating the Home—G 3.1
Plumbing—G 5.0
Septic Tank Systems—G 5.5

The following are available for the specified cost from:

> Superintendent of Documents
> Government Printing Office
> Washington, D.C. 20402

Fire Resistant Construction of the Home and Farm Buildings, Catalog No. A 1.9:2227, 15¢

Controlling Wood-Destroying Beetles in Buildings and Furniture, Catalog No. A 1.35:558, 10¢

Low Cost Wood Homes for Rural America-Construction Manual, Catalog No. A 1.76:364, $1

Subterranean Termites, Catalog No. A 1.77:64/4, 20¢

Manual of Septic Tank Practice, Public Health Service Bulletin, Catalog No. FS 2.6/2:Se6/967, 50¢

Septic Tank Care, Catalog No. FS 2.50:96/3, 5¢

Room Air Conditioners, Catalog No. GS 1.19:6 S/N 2200-0074, 45¢

The following are available for the specified cost from:

> American Wood Preservers Institute
> 1651 Old Meadow Road
> McLean, Virginia 22101

PBB-FHA Pole House Construction, 50¢

PBH-Don't Touch That Site: Pole House Construction, 35¢

PBK-Bad Is Good: Pole House Construction, 35¢

chapter 7

Amenities of the Area

Amenities is a term often used by real estate agents to describe those aspects of an area that make it a satisfactory and enjoyable place to live. Whether you are buying a permanent country residence or a second home for seasonal use, you want a place that meets your needs. The factors that might influence your choice of location are discussed in this chapter.

A good way to find out about an area is to talk to everyone you meet while visiting there. However, if you can rent a house or get a job as a caretaker, you will get a much deeper insight into whether you want to live there permanently.

HOW MANY PEOPLE IN THE AREA?

Be careful if you choose land in an area that is presently, or soon likely to be, experiencing a land boom. A few states and most small towns fairly near cities are gaining population rapidly. Watch for ads for recreational subdivisions or residential developments as indications that an area is being "developed." Unless you are interested mainly in investing in a rapid growth area, you may not be prepared for some of the drastic changes your sleepy little town will undergo adjusting to its new growth. You may not recognize the place a few years after you buy. The area will be bustling with activity, taxes will go up, and zoning and building codes will be more stringently enforced.

On the other hand, if the population of an area is on the decline, land prices and taxes will be lower than in a developing area. However, it may be harder to find a job or open a business, and there may be a deficiency in available services.

According to government statistics, towns with 10,000 to 100,000 people are the fastest growing population centers in America. If you want to live in a place that will retain its rural qualities for a while, choose an area with less than 10,000 inhabitants and avoid areas in which packaged recreational or permanent-home subdivisions are being promoted. These developments are like small cities in the country.

The best source for statistical information about an area's population is the local field office of the Bureau of Census. These offices are listed in the "Useful Resources" section at the end of this chapter. Also see Illustrations 32 through 42 at the end of the chapter.

WHO ARE YOUR NEIGHBORS?

If you find a nice piece of land, meet your prospective neighbors and talk to them about your plans. They will probably be happy to meet you and proud to show you what they have done with their place. Spend an afternoon with them, and you will learn a lot about the community. You will want to be able to call on them occasionally to look after your place while you are away, to feed your animals or water your garden, and they will want the same from you. If you are moving to an isolated area, your neighbors might be more important to you than if you are living close to town.

If you have children, you will probably want neighbors with children in the same age group, particularly if you plan to live there permanently. On the other hand, if you don't have children, you many not want any children nearby who will climb your apple trees or adolescents who will race their cars. If most of your neighbors are young couples, you should expect an increase in the number of children in the area.

A unique problem with neighbors occurs in some areas where ranching is practiced. Many states still observe the "open range" law, which permits animal owners to let their livestock roam free. The burden of fencing in land is on the landowner who does not want the wandering herds to enter his property. Thus, if you buy a place next to a cattle ranch and you don't want cows wandering through your land, you will have to build a fence to keep them out. This is a costly project and should be figured into your purchase price.

EMPLOYMENT

Unless you are independently wealthy or interested in a vacation home only, you will have to decide how you want to support yourself. You may want to live near enough to the city so that you can continue to work at your present job or you may intend to work in the country, either near or on your land. Your decision will depend to a great extent on what you do to make money and what area you pick to live in. Many artists and craftsmen have no trouble working in their homes in the country and traveling to the city occasionally to sell their wares. Some craftsmen set up their studios in nearby towns that have a tourist trade.

Since we bought our land several years ago, many individuals have opened successful businesses in town, including a health food store, a book store, an art studio, a movie house, a Volkswagen repair shop, a veterinarian office, two restaurants, an ice cream parlor, two real estate agencies, two bars, and a grocery store. As rural areas become more populated with residents and tourists, business opportunities will increase.

If you are thinking of opening a business in your area, consider the demand for your kind of service, the competition, and anticipated trends in the area before you decide. Does the area attract an ample tourist trade to support your business? If there are other businesses similar to yours already in existence, is there enough demand to support another one? If the community is growing rapidly, what new facilities are wanted and needed by the newer residents?

Talk to other businessmen in the community, ask questions at the local Chamber of Commerce, read the newspapers thoroughly, look in the Yellow Pages to see what businesses are already established, and keep your eyes and ears open to the needs of the business and residential community. Check the local taxes, zoning, and building codes, and talk with the supervisors from the Small Business Administration, a federal agency specializing in loans to businessmen. (See "Useful Resources" at the end of this chapter.) and the Farmer's Home Administration. These agencies will have information on how to start a business, what the chances of success are based on past results, and how to get financial assistance. If you intend to buy an existing country business, thoroughly investigate it before purchasing, and find out why it's being sold. You may need the advice of a lawyer and an accountant to be safe.

Many people make part or all of their income in the country from home businesses such as raising animals, selling homemade clothing, furniture, or jewelry, running repair shops and other services, painting signs, selling antiques, and selling home-grown produce. The greater your imagination and abilities, the more likely you will think of a lucrative home business. You might have to buy property on a well-traveled road if you want to operate a business from your home.

Some of you are probably thinking about farming as a means of survival. The problems of setting up such an operation are far beyond the scope of this book, but the following government statistics reveal much about the current farm situation. The number of United States farms has been halved since 1940 to 2.8 million. The number of farm failures is more than six times that of small-business failures. Small farms supply less than 8 percent of farm sales, whereas less than 1 percent of United States farms make almost 25 percent of all sales. The number of Americans living on farms has decreased from 16 million in 1960 to 9 million in the early 1970s; only one person in twenty lives on a farm now as opposed to one in three in 1920.

Despite these gloomy figures, I believe it is possible to survive by operating a small farm business. The most informative and inspirational literature on setting up such an operation is published regularly in *The Mother Earth News, Lifestyles,* and *The Organic Gardening and Farming Magazine.* The addresses and subscription rates of these publications are given in Appendix A at the end of the book.

Other information is available in the "Useful Resources" section at the end of this chapter.

If you want to find employment in the country, try the small businesses, the farms and ranches, and the local industrial employers to see if anyone is hiring. Most rural areas have a high rate of unemployment so you must be realistic. However, those with special skills or credentials, such as teachers, nurses, doctors, lawyers, surveyors, and engineers, are usually in demand. Consult the publication put out by the federal government entitled *County Business Patterns* for the state and county you are interested in. It gives information for civilian jobs based on Social Security statistics, and lists what businesses are in the county, where they are located, what wages are paid, and how many people are employed. A new report for each state is issued every May. (See "Useful Resources" at the end of this Chapter.)

Each state and county also operates its own employment research agency, which keeps vital statistics on employment within the state. In "Useful Resources" at the end of the chapter, I list agencies in each state you can write to for statistical information and answers to any questions on employment. You can get more detailed information about local conditions from the nearest Department of Human Resources Development (HRD) or employment agency.

If you want to live in a rural area and continue to commute to a city job, you can do so in most parts of the country. Most cities are relatively compact and the country is not far away. Figure out how long it would take to get home from your place of employment in the city. It may take a half-hour to go the first 5 miles, but then once you are out of the city, you may be able to go another 30 miles in the next half-hour. Decide how much time you are willing to spend commuting each day, get a map of your area, pinpoint your place of work, and draw a circle around that point which covers those areas within a commuting distance within your desired time limit. You then have a large area to choose from. Don't make your circle too small. If you become too concerned about your commuting time you might end up looking at suburban property instead of real country land. Another ten minutes and you might find yourself in the heart of the backwoods. It's much closer than you think. Illus-

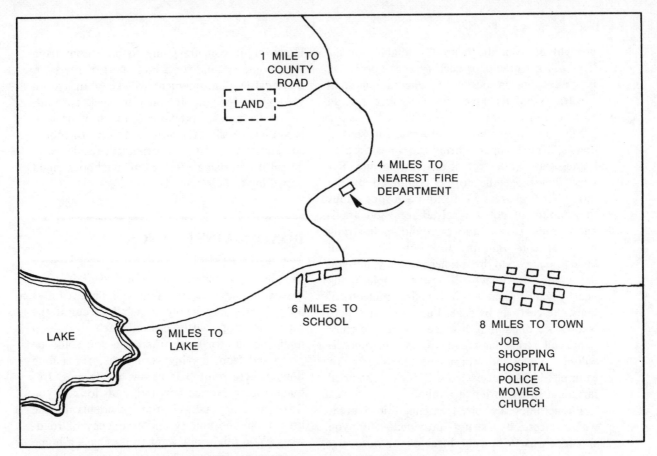

31. DISTANCES FROM LAND TO PLACES IMPORTANT TO YOU

tration 31 is an example of how to plot the distances from the land to the places that are important to you.

UTILITIES—WATER, SEWAGE, GAS, GARBAGE, ELECTRICITY, PHONE, AND MAIL DELIVERY

In most areas of the country, you will have to take care of your own utility provisions. The local town will not furnish water and other services beyond its limits.

Setting up a water system and a sewage disposal system are standard country procedures and you must determine the costs involved before buying your land. (See Chapter 4: *Is There Enough Water on the Land?* and Chapter 13: *Building and Health Codes*) If you want gas, most rural areas will rent portable refillable butane or propane tanks or will install a large tank behind your house which is refilled periodically by a tanker truck. Talk to the local propane dealer about charges for set-

ting up and servicing the system. You will have to get gas appliances.

Do not expect a garbage man to come by your home unless you are living in town. Most people use county and town dumps, for which there may be a small fee. In the country, you will probably recycle most of your garbage anyway.

Electricity seems to be the one thing most people can't do without. If you think you don't need it, try living without any for a while before buying land. Can you do without electric lights, a record player, television, and modern appliances, including power tools? If not, you will need land near existing electric lines. Electricity is extremely expensive to bring in from far away, and a gas generator is too expensive, noisy, and polluting to be practical for full-time use. Before you buy, be sure you have an easement to bring in utility lines and check into the costs involved. Only the electric company office nearest to the land can give you a complete estimate. Electric rates are determined by the number of appliances you have and the number of feet of line that will have to be brought in from the nearest available source. You will get credit for each type of appliance. For example, in our area, Pacific Gas and Electric (PG&E) gives 75 free feet for an electric refrigerator, 150 feet for an electric range, etc. These credits are cut for second homes. The company brings in lines free to homes within 800 feet of an existing line. Beyond that range the cost is computed by the foot. PG&E charges $1.40 for each foot minus the amount of credit received for each appliance. This is for above-ground pole-strung wires. If you want the line buried, you will have to pay two to three times more, even if you dig your own trench. If other people living nearby want to join you in bringing in electrical lines, the cost can be shared among you. There is always a maximum distance the electric company will string lines even if the customer is willing to pay the entire costs involved. For example, in Maine service will not be extended farther than a quarter of a mile.

Phone lines are often extended into areas where electricity is not provided. But you should check with your local phone company to see where service is given.

Mail is usually delivered to mailboxes along the public county roads so that should not be a problem. Ask about the mail service at the nearest post office.

FIRE AND POLICE PROTECTION

Many small towns do not have their own Fire and Police Departments. Often fire protection is maintained on a community volunteer basis. The greatest danger of fire exists in western mountainous areas where forest fires are an annual disaster. If you intend to buy forest land you should learn something of the history of forest fires in your area and how quickly and successfully they were contained. The local Forest Ranger station or Farm Advisor, as well as old-time residents, will have this information. In most areas, fire stations are only manned during the critical summer months. If possible, you should have a large reserve water supply and pump, if necessary, on your land if your area is susceptible to fires.

You shouldn't have much cause to call the police if you live outside the cities and suburbs.

However, if you are going to be absent from your home or land for a large part of the year, the local law enforcement will keep an eye on your place for you. If you want to keep hunters or trespassers off your land, or your land is too inaccessible for normal police protection, sometimes you can hire permanent residents, to patrol it for a small fee. Your neighbors might be willing to help you also.

ROAD MAINTENANCE

Frequent maintenance of public roads is a necessity in the country. You will have endless difficulties where heavy snowfalls occur if the roads are not swiftly cleared each day. You might be late for work often and you could be prevented from leaving your house for a long time. Where rainfall is heavy, roads need frequent repair. Notice how the roads look as you drive around. Ask old-time residents in the area about the quality and frequency of roadwork. You might not want to purchase a home so far away that it is the last area to be cleared each day. Consider the problems involved if you live off the main road, particularly if you only have a dirt access road. Check with your local Department of Roads to see what kind of service is provided for private roads. Usually a fee is charged for private road maintenance.

EDUCATIONAL FACILITIES AND CULTURAL ATTRACTIONS

If you have children, you will want to know about the schools in the area. Most children in the country are bused to a centrally located public school several miles away and you will want to buy near a bus pickup point. Usually the schools are small and have fewer facilities and teachers than city schools, but that does not necessarily mean they are not as good. Many country schools are excellent. A few private schools and "free schools" are appearing in the country, but aside from parochial schools, they have not been very successful yet. Never depend on such a school unless you determine its stability and cost. The Chamber of Commerce and local Board of Education can tell you the location of the schools in your area and the busing routes. Visit the school, talk to the teachers, and see what facilities they have. Take your children with you.

If you are interested in going to school yourself, many colleges sponsor basic extension courses in rural secondary schools. If you want an extensive variety of courses, or you want to attend concerts, movies, or amateur theatrical and sports events, you might buy in an area near a college or university. Excellent new colleges are being built annually in rural towns. Visit the college to see what it offers before you buy in the area. Land is usually more expensive in areas and towns where the school system has an excellent reputation.

MEDICAL FACILITIES

Local doctors, hospitals, and veterinarians are always an asset in the country. If you are in need of on-going medical treatment, you must be sure that good service is available in your area from doctors you can trust. Ask your present doctor if he knows a good area in which to settle where the medical facilities are reputable and not overly expensive. Don't be surprised at the informal, relaxed atmosphere in a country clinic. This does not necessarily mean the treatment is inadequate.

SHOPPING AREA

If you have a large family, a nearby shopping center or general store may be a requirement. Check out the shopping facilities in your area, particularly grocery and drug stores and Laundromats. How are the prices? Remember that prices for nearly everything will be higher in the country.

If you are 15 miles away from the nearest store, it is a 30-mile drive to pick up groceries. In the winter this can seem like a very long distance.

CHURCHES AND OTHER SOCIAL ORGANIZATIONS

Many of you will want to have the church of your choice in your new community. Look in the phone book for local churches. Attend a religious service and talk to the religious and lay leaders and members of the congregation.

If you are interested in social groups, ask the Chamber of Commerce about clubs in the area, such as bridge, gardening, and service groups. Your children may want to know about local scouting groups, agricultural clubs, and athletic teams. You can visit meetings and functions of such organizations to get a feeling of the kind of things they are doing and their receptivity to newcomers.

RECREATIONAL FACILITIES

If you intend to buy a vacation home, the recreational facilities of the area will be a major consideration. The local Chamber of Commerce will have maps and brochures detailing the area's vacation resources. If you are interested in water sports, like fishing, boating, and swimming, be sure you buy where public water facilities are available. Whether you are interested in hunting, golfing, skiing, mountain climbing, horseback riding, bowling, hot baths, movies, or good restaurants, recreational facilities are rapidly expanding in rural areas, particularly where the number of seasonal residents is increasing. You do not have to buy land in a massive, expensive, planned "recreational development" in order to satisfy your needs. Buy yourself a piece of land centrally located to the facilities you want. You will save a lot of money and have a true feeling of living in the country. For more on the disadvantages of "package-deal" subdivisions, see Chapter 14: *Subdivisions*.

THE GOVERNMENT AS A NEIGHBOR

Many real estate agents use the fact that land is located next to federal or state land as a selling point. You will frequently see ads stating that: "property borders National Forest," "property sits next to U.S. Government land," and "adjoining BLM land will provide thousands of acres of recreation." Be very careful when buying such land. Any federal land under

Bureau of Land Management (BLM) control can be used for grazing, logging, mining and removal of oil and gas, and industrial and recreational development under the "Multiple Use Classification" system.

The Bureau of Land Management, an agency of the United States Department of the Interior, controls the use of 465 million acres of public lands. Before buying property adjoining any of these holdings, go to the local BLM office. (See Appendix B or addresses.) or office of the Department of the Interior and ask for a full report on the present and intended future use of that government land. They will have a map indicating all uses planned for the land for the next five years. You should examine it thoroughly. What kind of activities are planned in the area near your land? Logging, mining, or a large influx of tourists can destroy your peace and quiet. But if the land is to be preserved and presents no problems as a neighbor, you may actually find yourself with a backyard of thousands of acres in which to play.

The same problems exist if your land adjoins a national park or other public lands. You must be extremely careful in investigating privately-owned land for sale within the boundaries of federally- or state-owned land. The government may have offered to buy or trade the property for government land located elsewhere in order to unify its holdings. Eventually the owners of that land could be forced to sell through condemnation. (See Chapter 15: *Eminent Domain and Condemnation.*)

LOCAL POLITICS

You can get a good sense of the political climate in a community by reading the local newspaper, listening to the nearest radio station, and by attending a Board of Supervisor's meeting. These meetings are open to the public and announced in advance in the local paper and at the local courthouse or city hall. They are informative and often entertaining in their change of pace from big-city politics. The board legislates and approves the county budget, local improvements, and appeals for zoning changes and variances. The governing bodies and local media are better indicators of

the flavor of life in the community than anything else.

A SAMPLE REPORT ON THE AREA

See the sample Final Subdivision Public Report (Illustration 62) in Chapter 14: *Subdivisions* to get an idea of what kind of information on the location of the land you should look for. The report includes facts on geological conditions, water, fire protection, electricity, gas, telephone service, sewage disposal, streets and roads, public transportation, schools, and shopping facilities.

NOISE

Many people buy land without realizing they are near enough to a road to pick up the sound of every car and truck that passes by all night. Heavy trucks, particularly industrial or logging trucks, often run only on weekdays or late at night, so if you look for land on holidays and weekends and don't spend at least one night on the property before you buy, you may not realize the full impact of the traffic.

Every sound in the country is greatly magnified—it comes out of the silence like a roar. If you live near a steep grade, the big trucks will be downshifting as they crawl up the hill. If your house is on the inside of a curve in a road, it might be directly in the path of oncoming headlights. When you look at property, stop to listen for sounds and see how the place is situated in relation to nearby roads.

If you live on a mountaintop, you will hear everything that goes on for miles around: traffic, chain saws, and construction noises. Valleys, by comparison, are relatively quiet because the mountains or hills on either side muffle the sounds. The noise factor is a major disadvantage to living on top of a ridge in a populous rural area.

Even if no road is close enough to bother your sleep now, one may be planned for the near future. Most areas have official county and city maps which indicate future street and road development. Talk to the Planning Department and the Department of Public Roads in your county or the state Highway Commission to determine where new construction will take place. With the increasing rural population, new road construction is proceeding at a rapid pace and represents a threat to the land buyer in terms of greater noise and possible condemnation. (See Chapter 13: *Eminent Domain and Condemnation.*)

Living in snow country exposes you to the new menace of the snowmobile's roar. Unless you intend to have one, you probably will not want to be anywhere near a snowmobile road. Many such roads are being developed throughout the country, officially and unofficially, and you might want to determine if any will be in the neighborhood of your new home.

Not until I spent some time as a caretaker on a large ranch did I realize the importance of avoiding a home under an airplane flight path. Every evening as I was quietly enjoying the beautiful sunset, a jet would roar directly overhead and spread its dirty exhaust across the sky. I made certain when we bought our land that no flight paths existed overhead. Most maps will tell you where military bases and public and private airports are located. You will have to determine how their presence affects your land.

You should also be aware of private landing strips on nearby farms and ranches. Many wealthy landowners now have their own planes and runways. Don't think this isn't much of a problem. An airplane is a toy in the hands of many private pilots. Even when used only for business, a low-flying plane that is flown directly over your place several times a day could make your life miserable. Ask your future neighbors if planes or jets are a problem.

SMELLS AND SMOKE

Lumber mills, paper mills, pulp mills, factories of all kinds, garbage dumps, and rendering plants are some of the air polluters that you do not want as country neighbors. Legislation controlling air pollution is slow in coming, so don't buy land under the false hope that the local mill will be forced to close down. I have seen rural areas with worse smog than any city I have been in. When we bought our land, we

made certain that the two local lumber mills that had recently closed down had no intention of reopening. During the period when they were going full blast, a clear blue sky was rarely seen.

Look at local maps to determine where such polluting agents exist in your community. Find out from the Chamber of Commerce or Planning Commission where new industries intend to locate, and check the zoning to see if industrial development is permitted in the area. (See Chapter 12: *Zoning Laws.*)

CROPDUSTING

Cropdusting is a method of spraying insecticides from small planes flying low over field crops. The poisons are easily carried in the wind to neighboring lands and can be a threat to the health of members of your family, particularly the very young, the very old, and the ill.

USEFUL RESOURCES

Publications on Choosing a Place to Live and Making a Living

The following are free from:

U.S. Department of Agriculture
Office of Information
Washington, D.C. 20250

Rural Recreation Enterprises for Profit— AB 277
Special Forest Products for Profit—AB 278
Farm Costs and Returns—AB 230
Poverty in Rural Areas of the U.S.— AER 169
Part-Time Farming—F 2178
Facts for Prospective Farmers—F 2221
Could Trout Farming Be Profitable for You?—L 552
Where and How to Get a Farm: Questions and Answers—L 432
Rural Recreation, New Opportunities on Private Land—M 930

So You're Planning a Vacation Farm Business—PA 604

Rental and Co-Op Housing in Rural Areas—PA 800

The following are available for the specified cost from:

The Superintendent of Documents
Government Printing Office
Washington, D.C. 20402

Rural Recreation: A New Family-Farm Business, Catalog No. A 1.2: R24 25¢
Managing the Family Forest, Catalog No. A 1.9:2187/2 S/N 0100-01366, 45¢
Catfish Farming, a New Farm Crop, Catalog No. A 1.9:2244, 15¢
Income Opportunities for Rural Families from Outdoor Recreation Enterprises, Catalog No. A 93.28:68, 25¢
Employment Outlook, Agriculture, Catalog No. L 2.3:1650-106, 20¢

The following is free from:

Consumer Product Information
Public Documents Distribution Center
Pueblo, Colorado 81009

Fair Housing U.S.A.—The Fair Housing Law 131A

Annual reports are issued for each state that give the county and city breakdown of employment and rate of pay by industry and trade groups. The statistics are based on Social Security sources, which include 90 percent of paid civilian employment. The report, called *County Business Patterns,* is issued annually in May at a cost of $1 for each state's report. Ask for your state's report of *County Business Patterns* and mail $1 to:

The Superintendent of Documents
Government Printing Office
Washington, D.C. 20402

Other Sources of Information on the Area and Its Facilities

Chamber of Commerce or Visitors Bureau

The county or city agency in charge of promoting the area's assets is one of the first places you should visit for information on employ-ment, recreational facilities, schools, cultural and social activities, shopping and medical facilities, and churches. Take a bunch of their free brochures.

Local Newspapers and the Yellow Pages

These will give you an idea of the type of businesses in the area and a feel for what the local attitudes and social life are like.

Utility Company

Only the local power company can give you accurate information on the availability and cost of supplying electricity and gas. They also have their own studies of population growth in the area and can give you some predictions on where the future growth is to occur and how soon.

Telephone Company

Information on available installation and costs.

Board of Education

Information on educational facilities and busing service of public and private schools.

Forest Ranger Station and Farm Advisor

Information on available fire protection service.

Department of Roads

The county, city, and state road departments have information on when roads are cleared and whether private roads can be cleared by the public road crews.

Small Business Administration

This is a federal agency in charge of providing information on how to commence and operate a small business. It also makes loans available for this purpose. Write for the address of your local office. Almost any type of business you can think of is covered in their pamphlets. Write and request a list of available pamphlets in the following series:

Small Business Bulletins
Small Business Management Series
Management Research Summaries
Starting and Managing Series Aids Annuals

Address all requests and inquiries to:
Small Business Administration
Washington 25, D.C.

Bureau of Census (U.S. Department of Commerce Field Offices)

You can get any information about the results of census activities in each state from any of the following offices of the Department of Commerce. They also have resources which you can use in the office or purchase that will give you just about any kind of information you desire from the history of the population growth to the age of the residents.

908 South 20th Street
Birmingham, Alabama 35205

412 Hill Building
Anchorage, Alaska 99501

230 North First Avenue
Phoenix, Arizona 85025

11000 Wilshire Boulevard
Los Angeles, California 90024

450 Golden Gate Avenue
San Francisco, California 94102

Room 161, New Customhouse
Denver, Colorado 80202

450 Main Street
Hartford, Connecticut 06103

400 West Bay Street
Jacksonville, Florida 32202

25 West Flagler Street
Miami, Florida 33130

75 Forsyth Street N.W.
Atlanta, Georgia 30303

125-29 Bull Street
Savannah, Georgia 31402

1015 Bishop Street
Honolulu, Hawaii 96813

219 South Dearborn Street
Chicago, Illinois 60604

210 Walnut Street
Des Moines, Iowa 50309

610 South Street
New Orleans, Louisiana 70130

U.S. Customhouse
Baltimore, Maryland 21202

John F. Kennedy Federal Building
Boston, Massachusetts 02203

Federal Building
Detroit, Michigan 48226

110 South Fourth Street
Minneapolis, Minnesota 55401

601 East 12th Street
Kansas City, Missouri 64106

1520 Market Street
St. Louis, Missouri 63103

300 Booth Street
Reno, Nevada 89502

U.S. Courthouse
Albuquerque, New Mexico 87101

117 Ellicott Street
Buffalo, New York 14203

26 Federal Plaza
Foley Square, New York, New York 10007

Federal Building
Greensboro, North Carolina 27402

550 Main Street
Cincinnati, Ohio 45202

666 Euclid Avenue
Cleveland, Ohio 44114

520 S. W. Morrison Street
Portland, Oregon 97204

1015 Chestnut Street
Philadelphia, Pennsylvania 19107

1000 Liberty Avenue
Pittsburgh, Pennsylvania 15222

334 Meeting Street
Charleston, South Carolina 29403

147 Jefferson Avenue
Memphis, Tennessee 38103

1114 Commerce Street
Dallas, Texas 75202

515 Rusk Avenue
Houston, Texas 77002

125 South State Street
Salt Lake City, Utah 84111

400 North 8th Street
Richmond, Virginia 23240

909 First Avenue
Seattle, Washington 98104

500 Quarrier Street
Charleston, West Virginia 25301

238 West Wisconsin Avenue
Milwaukee, Wisconsin 53203

2120 Capitol Avenue
Cheyenne, Wyoming 82001

State Agencies with Employment Statistics

The following state offices will send you available studies and charts on employment conditions within the state. You should ask specifically about the type of employment you are interested in.

Alabama—Department of Industrial Relations, Montgomery 36104

Alaska—Employment Security Division, Department of Labor, Juneau 99801

Arizona—Unemployment Compensation Division, Employment Security Commission, Phoenix 85005

Arkansas—Employment Security Commission, Department of Labor, Little Rock 72203

California—Division of Labor Statistics and Research, Department of Industrial Relations, San Francisco 94101

Colorado—Department of Employment, Denver 80203

Connecticut—Employment Security Division, Department of Labor, Hartford 06115

Delaware—Employment Security Commission, Wilmington 19801

District of Columbia—U.S. Employment Service for D. C., Washington 20212

Florida—Industrial Commission, Tallahassee 32304

Georgia—Employment Security Agency, Department of Labor, Atlanta 30303

Hawaii—Department of Labor and Industrial Relations, Honolulu 96811

Idaho—Department of Employment, Boise 83707

Illinois—Division of Research and Statistics, Department of Labor, Chicago 60606

Indiana—Employment Security Division, Indianapolis 46204

Iowa—Employment Security Commission, Des Moines 50319

Kansas—Employment Security Division, Department of Labor, Topeka 66603

Kentucky—Bureau of Employment Security, Department of Economic Security, Frankfort 40601

Louisiana—Division of Employment Security, Department of Labor, Baton Rouge 70804

Maine—Employment Security Commission, Augusta 04330

Maryland—Department of Employment Security, Baltimore 21201

Massachusetts—Division of Statistics, Department of Labor and Industries, Boston 02202

Michigan—Employment Security Commission, Detroit 48202

Minnesota—Department of Employment Security, St. Paul 55101

Mississippi—Employment Security Commission, Jackson 39205

Missouri—Division of Employment Security, Jefferson City 65102

Montana—Unemployment Compensation Commission, Helena 59601

Nebraska—Division of Employment, Department of Labor, Lincoln 68501

Nevada—Employment Security Department, Carson City 89701

New Hampshire—Department of Employment Security, Concord 03301

New Jersey—Department of Labor and Industry, Bureau of Statistics and Records, Trenton 08625

New Mexico—Employment Security Commission, Albuquerque 87103

New York—Research and Statistics Office, Division of Employment, N. Y. State Department of Labor, State Campus Building 12, Albany 12201

North Carolina—Division of Statistics, Department of Labor, Raleigh 27602

North Dakota—Unemployment Compensation Division, Workmen's Compensation Bureau, Bismarck 58502

Ohio—Division of Research and Statistics, Bureau of Employment Services, 145 S. Front Street, Columbus 43216

Oklahoma—Employment Security Commission, Oklahoma City 73105

Oregon—Department of Employment, Salem 97310

Pennsylvania—Bureau of Employment Security, Department of Labor and Industry, Harrisburg 17121

Rhode Island—Division of Statistics and Census, Department of Labor, Providence 02908

South Carolina—Employment Security Commission, Columbia 20202

South Dakota—Employment Security Department, Aberdeen 57401

Tennessee—Department of Employment Security, Nashville 37219

Texas—Employment Commission, Austin 78701

Utah—Department of Employment Security, Salt Lake City 84111

Vermont—Department of Employment Security, Montpelier 05602

Virginia—Division of Research and Statistics, Department of Labor and Industry, Richmond 23214

Washington—Employment Security Department, Olympia 98501

West Virginia—Department of Employment Security, Charleston 25305

Wisconsin—Unemployment Compensation Department, Madison 53701

Wyoming—Employment Security Commission, Casper 82601

32. STATES RANKED BY TOTAL POPULATION :1970

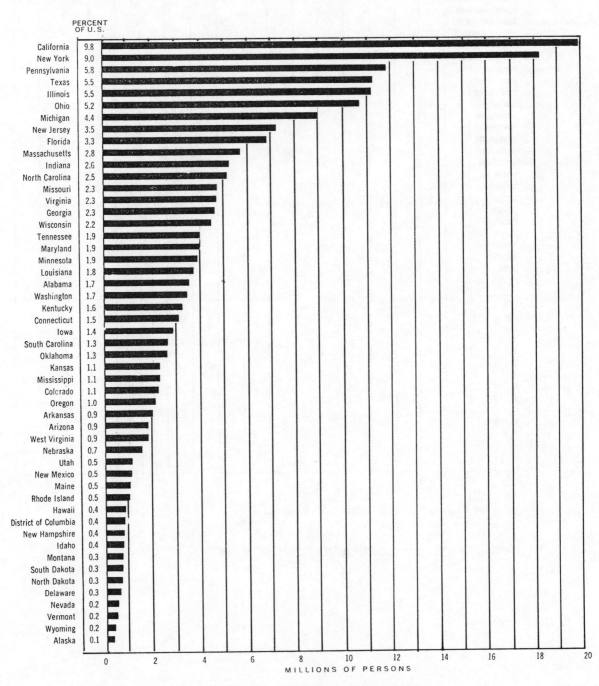

1970 U.S. CENSUS OF POPULATION, U.S. Department of Commerce, Bureau of the Census

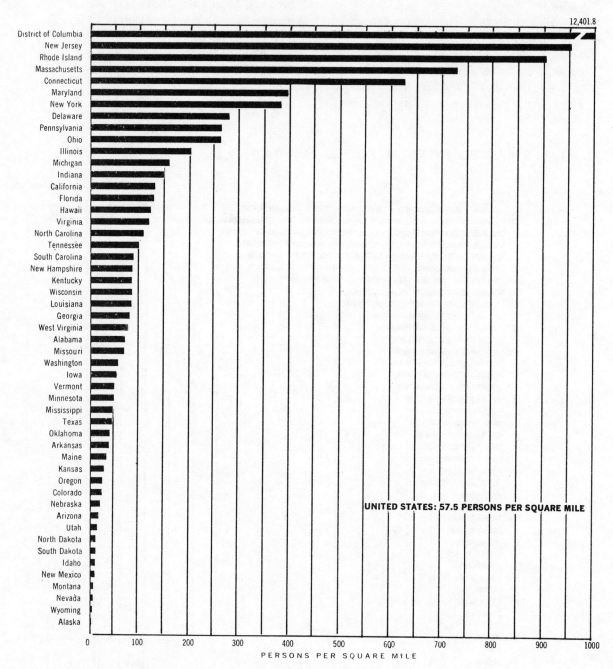

12,401.8

	PERSONS PER SQUARE MILE
District of Columbia	
New Jersey	
Rhode Island	
Massachusetts	
Connecticut	
Maryland	
New York	
Delaware	
Pennsylvania	
Ohio	
Illinois	
Michigan	
Indiana	
California	
Florida	
Hawaii	
Virginia	
North Carolina	
Tennessee	
South Carolina	
New Hampshire	
Kentucky	
Wisconsin	
Louisiana	
Georgia	
West Virginia	
Alabama	
Missouri	
Washington	
Iowa	
Vermont	
Minnesota	
Mississippi	
Texas	
Oklahoma	
Arkansas	
Maine	
Kansas	
Oregon	
Colorado	
Nebraska	
Arizona	
Utah	
North Dakota	
South Dakota	
Idaho	
New Mexico	
Montana	
Nevada	
Wyoming	
Alaska	

UNITED STATES: 57.5 PERSONS PER SQUARE MILE

0   100   200   300   400   500   600   700   800   900   1000

PERSONS PER SQUARE MILE

1970 U.S. CENSUS OF POPULATION, U.S. Department of Commerce, Bureau of the Census

33. STATES RANKED BY POPULATION DENSITY :1970

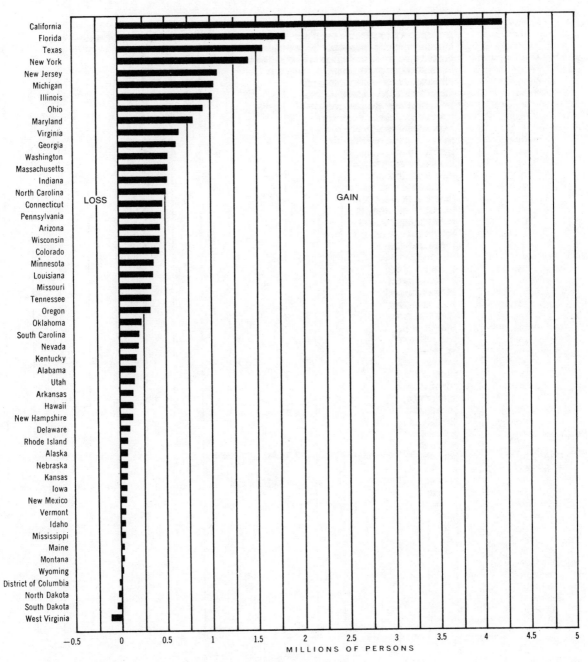

California
Florida
Texas
New York
New Jersey
Michigan
Illinois
Ohio
Maryland
Virginia
Georgia
Washington
Massachusetts
Indiana
North Carolina
Connecticut
Pennsylvania
Arizona
Wisconsin
Colorado
Minnesota
Louisiana
Missouri
Tennessee
Oregon
Oklahoma
South Carolina
Nevada
Kentucky
Alabama
Utah
Arkansas
Hawaii
New Hampshire
Delaware
Rhode Island
Alaska
Nebraska
Kansas
Iowa
New Mexico
Vermont
Idaho
Mississippi
Maine
Montana
Wyoming
District of Columbia
North Dakota
South Dakota
West Virginia

LOSS   GAIN

-0.5   0   0.5   1   1.5   2   2.5   3   3.5   4   4.5   5

MILLIONS OF PERSONS

1970 U.S. CENSUS OF POPULATION, U.S. Department of Commerce Bureau of the Census

34. STATES RANKED BY AMOUNT OF POPULATION CHANGE :1960–1970

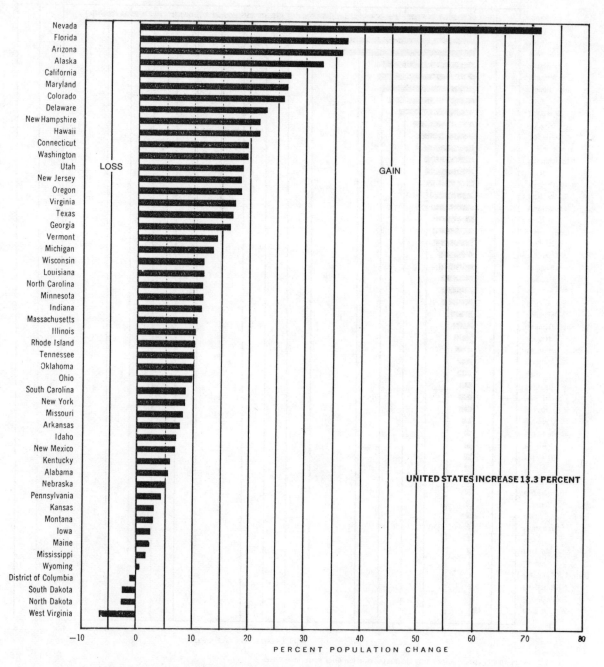

LOSS

GAIN

UNITED STATES INCREASE 13.3 PERCENT

PERCENT POPULATION CHANGE

1970 U.S. CENSUS OF POPULATION, U.S. Department of Commerce, Bureau of the Census

35. STATES RANKED BY PERCENT OF POPULATION CHANGE :1960–1970

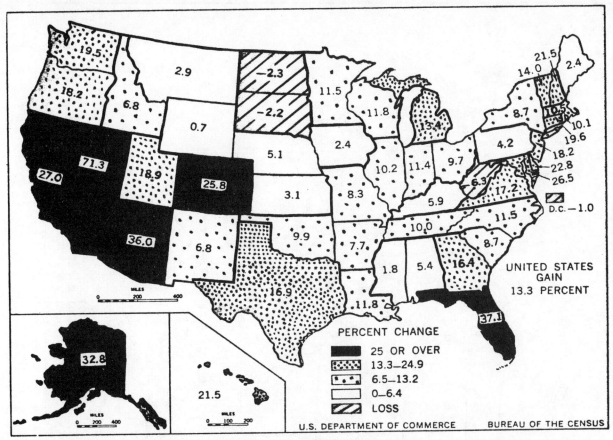

36. PERCENT OF CHANGE IN TOTAL POPULATION BY STATES : 1960–1970

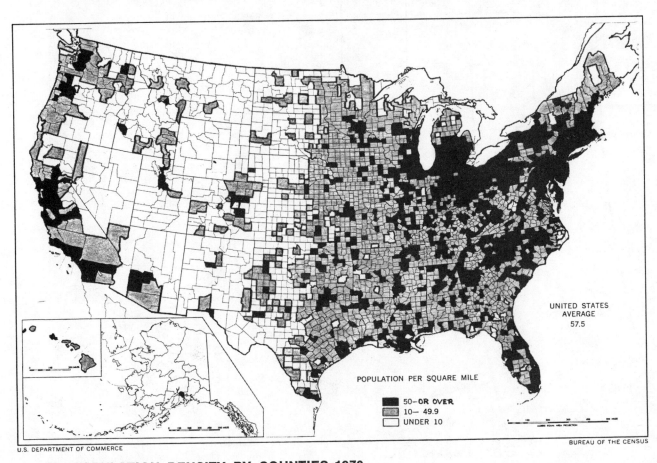

37. POPULATION DENSITY BY COUNTIES : 1970

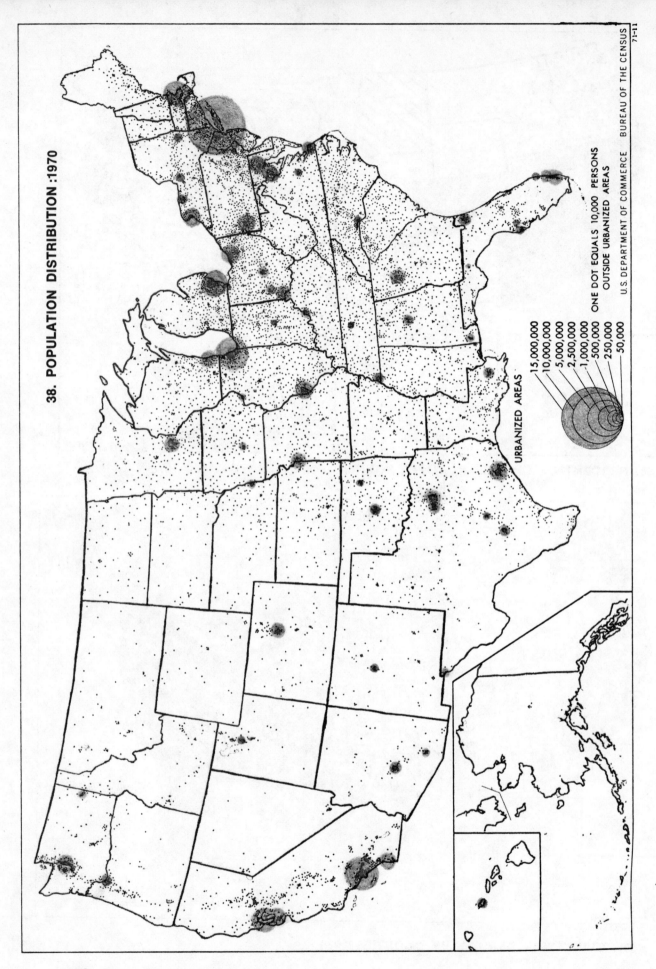

38. POPULATION DISTRIBUTION : 1970

URBANIZED AREAS

15,000,000
10,000,000
5,000,000
2,500,000
1,000,000
500,000
250,000
50,000

ONE DOT EQUALS 10,000 PERSONS
OUTSIDE URBANIZED AREAS

U.S. DEPARTMENT OF COMMERCE   BUREAU OF THE CENSUS

71-11

102

Regions Divisions States	Total	Population								
		Less than 1,000	1,000 to 5,000	5,000 to 10,000	10,000 to 20,000	20,000 to 30,000	30,000 to 40,000	40,000 to 50,000	50,000 to 100,000	100,000 or more
United States	3,141	26	299	554	794	400	249	140	3 2	347
REGIONS										
Northeast	217	-	4	4	12	16	18	17	52	91
North Central	1,056	7	112	201	276	139	92	44	90	95
South	1,423	5	81	267	419	217	125	56	151	102
West	445	14	102	82	87	28	14	23	39	56
NORTHEAST										
New England	67	-	2	2	4	10	6	5	14	24
Middle Atlantic	150	-	2	2	8	6	12	12	38	70
NORTH CENTRAL										
East North Central	437	-	7	40	93	69	62	28	65	73
West North Central	619	7	105	161	183	70	30	16	25	22
SOUTH										
South Atlantic	589	-	22	120	147	85	54	24	79	58
East South Central	364	-	7	56	135	69	32	16	33	16
West South Central	470	5	52	91	137	63	39	16	39	28
WEST										
Mountain	279	12	74	64	62	14	8	11	18	16
Pacific	166	2	28	18	25	14	6	12	21	40
NEW ENGLAND										
Maine	16	-	-	-	1	6	1	2	3	3
New Hampshire	10	-	-	-	1	-	3	-	4	2
Vermont	14	-	1	1	2	4	2	2	2	-
Massachusetts	14	-	1	1	-	-	-	-	2	10
Rhode Island	5	-	-	-	-	-	-	1	2	2
Connecticut	8	-	-	-	-	-	-	-	1	7
MIDDLE ATLANTIC										
New York	62	-	1	-	2	2	5	7	19	26
New Jersey	21	-	-	-	-	-	-	-	5	16
Pennsylvania	67	-	1	2	6	4	7	5	14	28
EAST NORTH CENTRAL										
Ohio	88	-	-	1	8	15	15	6	24	19
Indiana	92	-	1	5	22	22	15	4	12	11
Illinois	102	-	2	14	29	13	12	7	8	17
Michigan	83	-	2	13	16	8	12	6	9	17
Wisconsin	72	-	2	7	18	11	8	5	12	9
WEST NORTH CENTRAL										
Minnesota	87	-	2	10	33	20	8	5	4	5
Iowa	99	-	-	15	47	19	2	6	5	5
Missouri	115	-	5	31	42	14	9	2	6	6
North Dakota	53	-	19	19	9	2	-	1	3	-
South Dakota	67	-	25	25	12	2	1	-	2	-
Nebraska	93	7	23	31	20	4	4	1	1	2
Kansas	105	-	31	30	20	9	6	1	4	4
SOUTH ATLANTIC										
Delaware	3	-	-	-	-	-	-	-	2	1
Maryland	24	-	-	-	4	5	-	2	6	7
District of Columbia	1	-	-	-	-	-	-	-	-	1
Virginia	134	-	3	35	39	21	12	6	7	11
West Virginia	55	-	1	13	11	11	7	2	8	2
North Carolina	100	-	1	12	19	16	10	8	25	9
South Carolina	46	-	-	2	9	8	7	4	11	5
Georgia	159	-	12	50	49	18	10	2	11	7
Florida	67	-	5	8	16	6	8	-	9	15
EAST SOUTH CENTRAL										
Kentucky	120	-	3	31	50	14	10	1	8	3
Tennessee	95	-	3	16	26	24	9	4	8	5
Alabama	67	-	-	-	21	16	8	4	12	6
Mississippi	82	-	1	9	38	15	5	7	5	2
WEST SOUTH CENTRAL										
Arkansas	75	-	-	16	30	12	6	3	7	1
Louisiana	64	-	-	5	17	11	10	2	11	8
Oklahoma	77	-	2	19	23	15	7	4	4	3
Texas	254	5	50	51	67	25	16	7	17	16
MOUNTAIN										
Montana	57	3	19	15	13	-	3	1	3	-
Idaho	44	2	10	12	11	2	2	1	3	1
Wyoming	23	-	5	7	7	2	-	-	2	-
Colorado	63	3	22	14	11	3	-	-	3	7
New Mexico	32	-	7	4	7	3	1	6	3	1
Arizona	14	-	-	-	3	2	2	2	3	2
Utah	29	1	8	7	6	2	-	1	.	3
Nevada	17	3	3	5	4	-	-	-	-	2
PACIFIC										
Washington	39	-	5	3	7	5	2	4	6	7
Oregon	36	-	4	6	5	5	3	2	6	5
California	58	1	2	3	10	3	1	4	8	26
Alaska	29	1	17	6	3	-	-	1	-	1
Hawaii	4	-	-	-	-	1	-	1	1	1

39. NUMBER OF COUNTIES BY SIZE : 1970

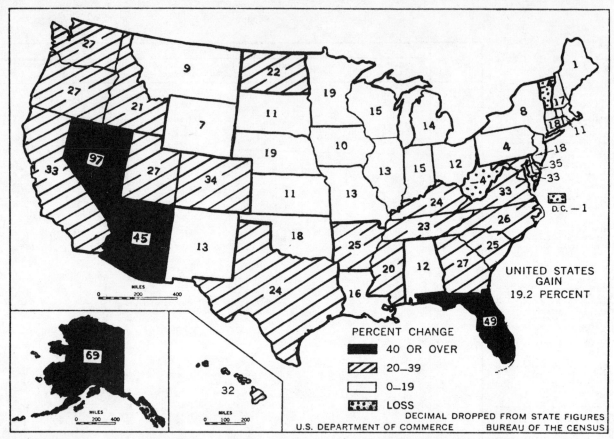

40. PERCENT OF CHANGE IN URBAN POPULATION BY STATES:1960–1970

PERCENT CHANGE

- 40 OR OVER
- 20–39
- 0–19
- LOSS

UNITED STATES GAIN 19.2 PERCENT

DECIMAL DROPPED FROM STATE FIGURES

U.S. DEPARTMENT OF COMMERCE BUREAU OF THE CENSUS

41. PERCENT OF CHANGE IN RURAL POPULATION BY STATES:1960–1970

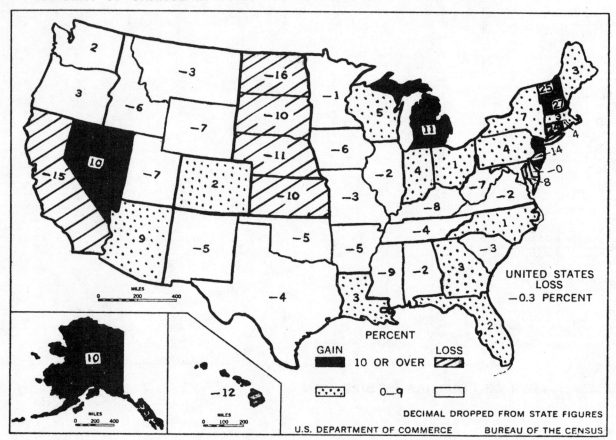

PERCENT

GAIN — 10 OR OVER — LOSS

0–9

UNITED STATES LOSS —0.3 PERCENT

DECIMAL DROPPED FROM STATE FIGURES

U.S. DEPARTMENT OF COMMERCE BUREAU OF THE CENSUS

42. AREA, 1970, AND POPULATION PER SQUARE MILE, 1920-1970

States	Area in square miles, 1970 Total	Land[1]	Inland water[2]	Population per square mile of land area 1970	1960[3]	1950	1940	1930[4]	1920	Rank according to— Total area, 1970	Land area, 1970	Population per square mile of land area 1970	1960[3]	1950	1940	1930[4]	1920
United States........	3,615,122	3,536,855	78,267	57.5	50.6	42.6	37.2	34.7	29.9	...	...	...	...	...	...	...	...
NEW ENGLAND																	
Maine...................	33,215	30,920	2,295	32.1	31.3	29.4	27.3	25.7	25.7	39	39	37	37	36	35	35	33
New Hampshire...........	9,304	9,027	277	81.7	67.2	59.1	54.5	51.6	49.1	44	44	21	26	25	24	24	22
Vermont.................	9,609	9,267	342	47.9	42.0	40.7	38.7	38.8	38.6	43	43	32	33	31	30	29	29
Massachusetts...........	8,257	7,826	431	727.0	657.3	396.2	545.9	537.4	479.2	45	45	4	4	4	4	3	3
Rhode Island...........	1,214	1,049	165	902.5	819.3	748.5	674.2	649.8	566.4	50	50	3	2	2	2	2	2
Connecticut.............	5,009	4,862	147	623.6	520.6	409.7	348.9	328.0	286.4	48	48	5	5	5	5	5	5
MIDDLE ATLANTIC																	
New York...............	49,576	47,831	1,745	381.3	350.6	309.3	281.2	262.6	217.9	30	30	7	6	6	6	6	6
New Jersey.............	7,836	7,521	315	953.1	805.5	642.8	553.1	537.3	420.0	46	46	2	3	3	3	4	4
Pennsylvania...........	45,333	44,966	367	262.3	251.4	233.1	219.8	213.8	194.5	33	33	9	8	8	7	7	7
EAST NORTH CENTRAL																	
Ohio...................	41,222	40,975	247	260.0	236.6	193.8	168.0	161.6	141.4	35	35	10	9	9	9	9	9
Indiana................	36,291	36,097	194	143.9	128.8	108.7	94.7	89.4	81.3	38	38	13	13	13	12	12	12
Illinois...............	56,400	55,748	652	199.4	180.4	155.8	141.2	136.4	115.7	24	24	11	11	11	10	10	10
Michigan...............	58,216	56,817	1,399	156.2	137.7	111.7	92.2	84.9	63.8	23	22	12	12	12	13	13	13
Wisconsin..............	56,154	54,464	1,690	81.1	72.6	62.8	57.3	53.7	47.6	26	25	23	23	22	21	21	23
WEST NORTH CENTRAL																	
Minnesota..............	84,068	79,289	4,779	48.0	43.1	37.3	34.9	32.0	29.5	12	14	31	31	32	33	33	31
Iowa...................	56,290	55,941	349	50.5	49.2	46.8	45.3	44.1	43.2	25	23	30	29	29	28	27	25
Missouri...............	69,686	68,995	691	67.8	62.6	57.1	54.6	52.4	49.5	19	18	28	28	27	23	22	20
North Dakota...........	70,665	69,273	1,392	8.9	9.1	8.8	9.2	9.7	9.2	17	17	44	44	42	42	42	40
South Dakota...........	77,047	75,955	1,092	8.8	9.0	8.5	8.4	9.1	8.3	16	16	45	45	43	43	43	42
Nebraska...............	77,227	76,483	744	19.4	18.4	17.3	17.2	18.0	16.9	15	15	41	39	39	39	39	39
Kansas.................	82,264	81,787	477	27.5	26.6	23.2	21.9	22.9	21.6	14	13	38	38	38	38	37	35
SOUTH ATLANTIC																	
Delaware...............	2,057	1,982	75	276.5	225.2	160.8	134.7	120.5	113.5	49	49	8	10	10	11	11	11
Maryland...............	10,577	9,891	686	396.6	313.5	237.1	184.2	165.0	145.8	42	42	6	7	7	8	8	8
District of Columbia......	67	61	6	12,401.8	12,523.9	13,150.5	10,870.3	7,981.5	7,292.9	51	51	1	1	1	1	1	1
Virginia...............	40,817	39,780	1,037	116.9	99.6	83.2	67.1	60.7	57.4	36	37	17	15	15	18	18	16
West Virginia..........	24,181	24,070	111	72.5	77.2	83.3	79.0	71.8	60.9	41	41	26	21	14	14	14	14
North Carolina.........	52,586	48,798	3,788	104.1	93.2	82.7	72.7	64.5	52.5	28	29	18	17	16	15	16	19
South Carolina.........	31,055	30,225	830	85.7	78.7	69.9	62.1	56.8	55.2	40	40	20	20	20	20	20	18
Georgia................	58,876	58,073	803	79.0	67.8	58.9	53.4	49.7	49.3	21	21	25	25	26	25	25	21
Florida................	58,560	54,090	4,470	125.5	91.5	51.1	35.0	27.1	17.7	22	26	15	18	28	32	34	38
EAST SOUTH CENTRAL																	
Kentucky...............	40,395	39,650	745	81.2	76.2	73.9	70.9	65.2	60.2	37	36	22	22	19	16	15	15
Tennessee..............	42,244	41,328	916	94.9	86.2	78.8	69.5	62.4	56.1	34	34	19	19	17	17	17	17
Alabama................	51,609	50,708	901	67.9	64.2	59.9	55.5	51.8	45.8	29	28	27	27	23	22	23	24
Mississippi............	47,716	47,296	420	46.9	46.0	46.1	46.1	42.4	38.6	32	31	33	30	30	27	28	28
WEST SOUTH CENTRAL																	
Arkansas...............	53,104	51,945	1,159	37.0	34.2	36.3	37.0	35.2	33.4	27	27	36	35	33	31	31	30
Louisiana..............	48,523	44,930	3,593	81.0	72.2	59.4	52.3	46.5	39.6	31	32	24	24	24	26	26	27
Oklahoma...............	69,919	68,782	1,137	37.2	33.8	32.4	33.7	34.6	29.2	18	19	35	36	35	34	32	32
Texas..................	267,338	262,134	5,204	42.7	36.4	29.3	24.3	22.1	17.8	2	2	34	34	37	37	38	37
MOUNTAIN																	
Montana................	147,138	145,587	1,551	4.8	4.6	4.1	3.8	3.7	3.8	4	4	48	48	48	48	47	46
Idaho..................	83,557	82,677	880	8.6	8.1	7.1	6.3	5.4	5.2	13	12	46	46	45	45	45	45
Wyoming................	97,914	97,203	711	3.4	3.4	3.0	2.6	2.3	2.0	9	9	50	49	49	49	49	47
Colorado...............	104,247	103,766	481	21.3	16.9	12.8	10.8	10.0	9.1	8	8	40	41	41	41	40	41
New Mexico.............	121,666	121,412	254	8.4	7.8	5.6	4.4	3.5	2.9	5	5	47	47	47	47	48	48
Arizona................	113,909	113,417	492	15.6	11.5	6.6	4.4	3.8	2.9	6	6	42	42	46	46	46	47
Utah...................	84,916	82,096	2,820	12.9	10.8	8.4	6.7	6.2	5.5	11	11	43	43	44	44	44	44
Nevada.................	110,540	109,889	651	4.4	2.6	1.5	1.0	0.8	0.7	7	7	49	50	50	50	50	50
PACIFIC																	
Washington.............	68,192	66,570	1,622	51.2	42.8	35.6	25.9	23.3	20.3	20	20	29	32	34	36	36	36
Oregon.................	96,981	96,184	797	21.7	18.4	15.8	11.3	9.9	8.2	10	10	39	40	40	40	41	43
California.............	158,693	156,361	2,332	127.6	100.4	67.5	44.1	36.2	22.0	3	3	14	14	21	29	30	34
Alaska.................	586,412	566,432	19,980	0.5	0.4	0.2	[5]0.1	0.1	0.1	1	1	51	51	51	51	51	51
Hawaii.................	6,450	6,425	25	119.6	98.5	78.0	66.0	57.5	39.9	47	47	16	16	18	19	19	26

[1] Dry land and land temporarily or partially covered by water, such as marshland, swamps, and river flood plains; streams, sloughs, estuaries, and canals less than 1/8 of a statute mile in width; and lakes, reservoirs, and ponds less than 40 acres of area. [2] Permanent inland water surface such as lakes, reservoirs, and ponds having 40 acres or more of area; streams, sloughs, estuaries, and canals 1/8 of a statute mile or more in width; deeply indented embayments and sounds, and other coastal waters behind or sheltered by headlands or islands separated by less than 1 nautical mile of water; and islands having less than 40 acres of area. Does not include water surface of the oceans, bays, the Gulf of Mexico, the Great Lakes, Long Island Sound, Puget Sound, and the Straits of Juan de Fuca and Georgia, lying within the jurisdiction of the United States but not defined as inland water. [3] Figures for 1960 based on area measurements; revised since publication of 1960 reports. [4] Figures for 1930 based on 1940 area measurements; revised since publication of Vol. I. 1930. [5] Census taken as of Oct. 1, 1939.

III

THE LAND
AND
THE LAW

chapter 8

Land Descriptions and Surveys

Throughout history most problems of land ownership have arisen from boundary disputes. Precise surveying was begun by the Egyptians nearly seven thousand years ago, but even today most land has not been accurately surveyed and boundary disputes continue to be a major problem for the landowner.

Laws require only that a deed contain a legal "description" of the land, which defines the parcel in such a way that it cannot be con-

fused with any other piece of land. However, this description does not tell you where the boundaries are precisely located on the ground. That is done by a survey, based on the land description. Because surveys are expensive, most rural parcels are sold without them, despite their importance to the buyer. I will explain why you should demand to have a survey taken on land before you buy after I explain the various descriptions used in deeds.

In the United States parcels are legally described in one of the following three ways:

1. By reference to a section, township, and range, which are part of the United States Government Survey or Rectangular Survey System.

2. By metes and bounds, also known as the Monument and Marker System.

109

3. By reference to a recorded map, plat, or tract system.

DESCRIPTIONS BY REFERENCE TO A SECTION, TOWNSHIP, AND RANGE

The United States Government, under the direction of the United States Surveyor General, began to survey its original public lands in 1784 using the Rectangular Survey System, dividing the lands into sections, townships, and ranges. Large portions of land were broken up into rectangles on a map and then located and marked on the ground by a survey team. By using these marked points, any parcel within a rectangle can be precisely described and located today.

The United States Rectangular Survey System is the most common form of land description used in the country today. Twenty-nine states use it, including all the states north of the Ohio River and west of the Mississippi except Texas, Alabama, Mississippi, and Florida. It was the form used when we purchased our land and I will use it throughout this book.

The description in our deed states that we own:

The South Half of the Northwest Quarter of Section 21, Township 4 South, Range 2 East, —— Meridian.

The government started its survey by dividing its land into portions, each of which was given a vertical line running north and south called the "principal meridian" and a horizontal line running east and west, perpendicular to the principal meridian, called its "base line." There are thirty-six principal meridians in different parts of the country. (See Illustration 43.) Each meridian is individually named; for example, the Mount Diablo Meridian, Indian Meridian, and Second Principal Meridian. You can see in our deed description above that there is a blank space where the name of the meridian should be. I have left this blank to keep my home anonymous. A description including the name of the principal meridian locates the area in which the land is situated. You then work backwards in the description.

On both sides of the principal meridian line, the land is cut into equal strips 6 miles wide called "ranges." (See Illustration 44.) On both sides of the base line, the land is cut into equal strips 6 miles wide called "townships." (See Illustration 45.) Together these strips form a "land checkerboard." Each square of the "checkerboard" is called a "township" and has

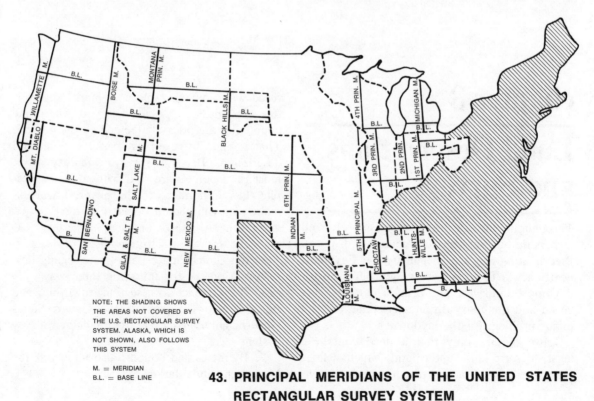

NOTE: THE SHADING SHOWS THE AREAS NOT COVERED BY THE U.S. RECTANGULAR SURVEY SYSTEM. ALASKA, WHICH IS NOT SHOWN, ALSO FOLLOWS THIS SYSTEM

M. = MERIDIAN
B.L. = BASE LINE

43. PRINCIPAL MERIDIANS OF THE UNITED STATES RECTANGULAR SURVEY SYSTEM

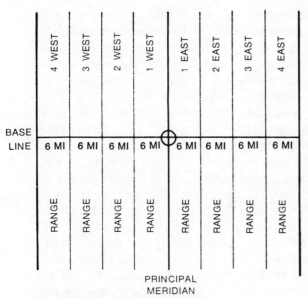

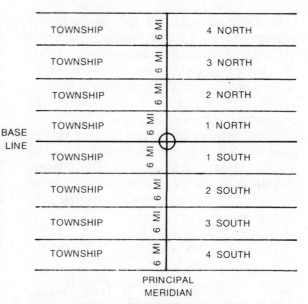

44. DIVIDING INTO RANGES

45. DIVIDING INTO TOWNSHIPS

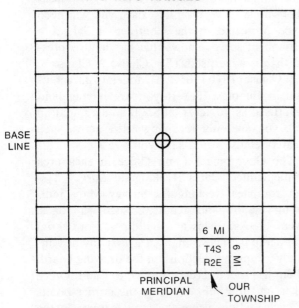

46. RESULTING TOWNSHIPS

TOWNSHIP 4 SOUTH, RANGE 2 EAST

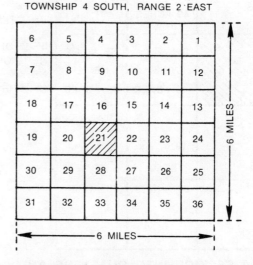

47. DIVIDING TOWNSHIPS INTO SECTIONS

boundary lines 6 miles long on all four sides. (See Illustration 46.) The range and township strips are numbered outward from the meridian and base lines and can be used in the same way as you use a highway map or atlas to find any township.

In Illustration 46, I indicate which township contains our land. It is a square located two ranges to the east of the principal meridian and four townships to the south of the base line. Thus, it is described as "Township 4 South, Range 2 East."

Since a township is a square 6 miles on a side, it contains 36 square miles. (Area

= length times width.) Thus, each township is divided into 36 square-mile "sections," each containing approximately 640 acres and having sides about 1 mile long. (See Illustration 47.) (An acre is a square approximately 208.71 feet long on each side with an area of 43,560 square feet or 4,840 square yards.) The sections in each township are numbered, starting in the northeast corner and moving alternately right and left, then left to right, concluding in the southeast corner. Illustration 47 indicates how Township 4 South, Range 2 East is divided into thirty-six sections. Section 21, in which our land is located, is shaded.

111

Each 640-acre section is then quartered into 160-acre parcels, called "quarter sections," which are designated as the northeast, southeast, northwest, and southwest quarters. Quarter sections are then quartered into parcels, called "40s" or "square forties," since each one contains approximately 40 acres. A square forty can then be quartered into four 10-acre parcels, which might be subdivided further into four 2½-acre parcels, and so forth. Illustration 48 indicates the possible subdivisions of section 21. The location of our 80 acres is the shaded portion of the section.

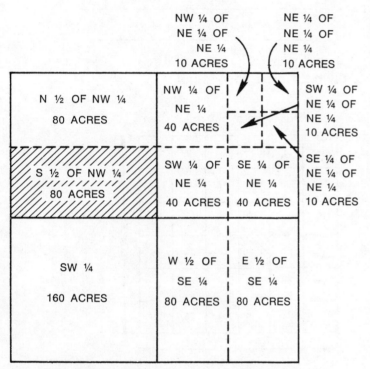

48. DIVIDING A SECTION INTO QUARTERS AND SMALLER PARCELS

When we found the land we wanted to buy, the real estate agent gave us a copy of its description as it would appear in our deed. Using a large quadrangle map, based on the United States Rectangular Survey that covered the proper meridian and township, we located Section 21. Taking a pencil, we quartered the section and then halved the northwest quarter horizontally. Thus, we located the south half of the northwest quarter of Section 21. The map depicted geographical land features and we could see what roads and creeks went through the land parcel. (Illustration 51 in Chapter 9: *Easement Rights* is a copy of what

we saw on the map.) Thus, without actually finding the corners and walking the boundaries, we got an approximate idea of what we would be buying. By superimposing the map over an aerial photograph of the same scale, we saw a more accurate picture of the land.

You will notice that Section 21 in Illustration 51 in Chapter 9 is not a perfect rectangle. Because of the curvature of the earth, the sections cannot be equal in acreage. For instance, our land seems to include 80 acres. In fact, on the ground the area covers only 78½ acres. Often more acreage will be advertised than you will actually receive. You can find out the true amount by referring to a legal survey of the land. A survey might already exist and be filed in a volume entitled *Record of Surveys* in the County Recorder's office, or the seller might have a copy of a survey. In cases where no survey presently exists, you will need to be protected in the Contract of Sale if a subsequent survey shows that less land is present than is advertised. (See Clause 2, Clause 3, and Clause 18(b) of the Model Contract of Sale in Chapter 28.) If you are buying land advertised as 40 acres, at $500 an acre, and, in fact, you are only receiving 38½ acres, such a safety clause could save you $750.

The Government Land Office in each area of the United States Rectangular Survey System compiles Rectangular Survey Maps indicating major land features, such as roads, rivers, creeks, towns and buildings, from aerial photographs. These maps are first divided into townships and sections on the drawing board. Then a ground crew from the Land Office hikes into the hills to locate the corner points of each section, using the land features in the aerial photographs as a guide. When a section is located, they usually bury permanent land markers, or monuments, in eight places: at each corner of the section and at the four points along the perimeter midway between the section corners.

These numbered and lettered markers are the starting points for private surveyors hired to locate subdivided parcels within the sections. The surveyors from the Government Land Office take thorough survey notes which are used by subsequent surveyors to find section corner markers.

You can get a copy of the original survey maps and notes indicating the location of section markers in your area from the General Land Office in the state. The location of the Land Office in each state is listed in Appendix G under *State Lands for Sale*. Records and maps are also kept at the headquarters of the Bureau of Land Management, and they may be available at the local BLM Land and District Office. (See Appendix B for addresses.) You might also be able to get a copy of these notes and maps from the county Tax Assessor or the real estate agent.

DESCRIPTIONS BY METES AND BOUNDS

Although most of the United States, and all of Canada, is within the United States Rectangular Survey System, many deeds describe land using the method of "metes and bounds." Metes are measures of length, such as inches, feet, and yards. Bounds are natural and artificial boundaries, such as rivers and roads. This system, which has been described as a treasure hunt, follows a course from a fixed point, called a monument or marker, to other fixed points until the area of land is entirely enclosed. Sometimes this method is called a Monument or Marker System.

In a description by metes and bounds, a fixed starting point is found on the ground that can be easily identified, such as an unusual tree, a pile of rocks, a road, a creek, the mouth of a stream, a bridge, or some other object. If a unique object cannot be found, the position is identified by its latitude and longitude, which can be found on a map of the area. Other similarly identified objects must be found at various points around the land so that a boundary line can be formed that encloses the area. Often the markers are highly variable, such as rivers or dirt roads, or impermanent, such as rock piles or trees. You may have heard stories of a landowner moving boundary markers to increase the size of his land. It is easy to get away with such tactics under this kind of a system. For this reason, a metes and bounds description should be used as a last resort. The system is usually used when irregular land shapes are sold and in areas that have not been laid out according to the United States Rectangular Survey.

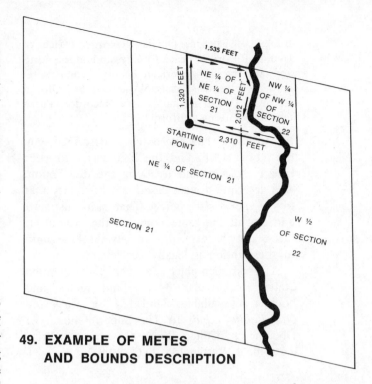

49. EXAMPLE OF METES AND BOUNDS DESCRIPTION

An example of metes and bounds description is shown in Illustration 49. Trace out the boundary line in the illustration by following the description. The parcel of land taking in the northeast quarter of the northeast quarter of Section 21 goes to the road, giving it an irregular shape. A description by metes and bounds of this land could read like this:

Beginning at the Southwest corner of the Northeast quarter of the Northeast quarter of Section 21, Township 4 South, Range 2 East, _____ Meridian; proceed a distance of 1,320 feet north along the western line of said Northeast quarter of the Northeast quarter of Section 21 to the Northwest corner of the Northeast quarter of the Northeast quarter of Section 21; thence east along the Northerly line of Section 21 a distance of 1,535 feet to the paved county road, the County Road; thence southerly along the road a distance of 2,012 feet to the southern line of the Northwest quarter of the Northwest quarter of Section 22; thence west along the southerly line of the Northwest quarter of the Northwest quarter of Section 22 a distance of 2,310 feet to the Point of Beginning.

Metes and bounds descriptions can take other forms than the one above. For example, land can be described with references to adjoining lands:

The land is bounded on the south and east by the land of Alys Mainhart as recorded in the deed at

Book 10, page 5, Official Records, Office of County Recorder, Peace County, and on the north and west by the American Beauty Ranch as recorded in the deed at Book 4, page 86, Official Records, Office of the County Recorder, Peace County, State of California.

Regardless of how the parcel is described, you must be able to find the boundaries to your land on the ground by using the description. The description must describe a boundary that totally encloses the parcel. That is, it must start and end at the same point on the ground. If this is not the case, do not buy the land until the description is legally perfected.

A good pamphlet describing the United States Rectangular Survey and metes and bounds is available. Send 15¢ for *Surveying Our Public Lands* to The Superintendent of Documents, United States Government Printing Office, Washington, D.C. 20402.

MAP, TRACT, OR PLAT SYSTEM

The third common method used to describe a parcel of land is by reference to another recorded instrument that identifies the land and usually contains a survey. You will probably not encounter this type of description unless you purchase land as part of a large rural or second-home subdivision. In that case, all the lots should already be surveyed and recorded with the county Recorder in a final parcel map, subdivision map, tract map, or plat. (Illustration 61 in Chapter 14: *Subdivisions* is an example of a parcel map.) Each parcel within the subdivision is described by referring to its location on the recorded map. For example:

The real property in the City of Goshen, County of Peace, State of Arkansas, described as Lot 80, Block D, Happy Home Subdivision (per map recorded July 2, 1972, Book 8, page 46 of Maps), Office of County Recorder of Peace County.

If you look up page 46 in Book 8 you will find a map of the subdivision divided into lots. Be sure the lot number on the map corresponds to the lot you think you are purchasing. The subdivision map will show the location of markers on the ground that delineate the boundaries of each parcel. Using the map, locate

the markers for your lot, and you will see what you are buying.

If your land is described by reference to another document, the document should be properly recorded with the county Recorder and must definitely identify your parcel of land.

LEGAL SURVEYS

A legal survey is made by a team of licensed surveyors or civil engineers who carefully lay out in bearings (angles) and distances the exact location of the property on the ground. The survey is based on the description of the parcel given in the deed. So that you will have no delusions as to where your boundaries lie, be sure that they are precisely surveyed and marked on the ground by a legal survey.

If the seller has a copy of a survey in his possession which he claims identifies the boundaries of the land for sale, check these points:

1. Was the survey conducted by a licensed surveyor or registered civil engineer?

2. Is it recorded in the County Records as an official survey of the land?

3. Does the county Recorder consider it to be legally binding, and what is his opinion of its accuracy based on current standards?

4. By using it, can you locate on the ground exactly where the boundaries are? Have permanent markers been placed in the ground by the surveyor?

In most cases, only the corners of the property are marked with permanent stakes. If you can locate all the corners, you might be able to estimate the boundary lines fairly accurately yourself with a compass, a tape, a flag on a tall post, and a friend or two. However, if an important part of the property you are buying, such as a spring, creek, road or house, appears to be close to a boundary line, you should definitely get a licensed surveyor to run the line between the two corner points before you buy.

If no survey of the land exists, you can only estimate from a map where the boundaries lie. When an inch on a map equals 1,000 feet on the ground, it only takes the thickness of a pencil lead to put a valuable stream either on or off the property.

Surveys are expensive. The average fee in our area is $100 a day per man working on the survey. The total cost depends on the amount of time it takes to find the corners, run the boundaries, and complete the technical details. If no surveys have been done in the area around the land and the locations of marked section corners or other starting points are far away, or if the last survey was done so long ago it is no longer recognized as legally binding, the job could take several weeks. Often large sections of land in rural areas have been sparsely or inaccurately surveyed. The job will also take longer if the terrain is rugged, if the parcel is large, or if you want the surveyors to run and mark the entire length of the boundary lines rather than just stake out the corners. Always go to the local surveyor and ask him what he knows about the land. He will give you an estimate of what a survey would cost and can tell you where he estimates the boundary lines to be.

If you want a guarantee that you are getting what you are paying for, you must demand a legal survey before you buy a parcel of land. The seller should pay to have a survey done if one does not already exist. Naturally, he will be reluctant to provide you with a survey if it will cost him any money. But often, he has already added the estimated cost of a survey into his asking price, anticipating that the buyer will demand a survey. Thus, in reality, you are already paying for it.

In many cases, the seller will state that the price will have to be increased if you want a legal survey. If you are certain that you want the land and the purchase price is otherwise satisfactory, you should insist on a survey and pay the seller the cost involved. You will get your money back when you sell the land, since property is more valuable when it is surveyed. It is also easier to sell. But don't give in to the seller without a fight. At least, try to get him to pay half of the survey cost.

I have encountered instances where the real estate agent paid for a survey in order to make a sale to a demanding buyer. An agent would rather make half a commission than none at all. If the seller is intransigent, never hesitate to ask the agent to get the survey done.

A few states have laws prohibiting a seller from conveying land without a legally recorded survey. Most subdivision laws require surveys of each parcel to be sold. My Model Contract of Sale has protective clauses in it that make the closing of the deal subject to the buyer's approval of a legal survey. See Clause 2, Clause 3, Clause 18(b), and Clause 19(b) of the Model Contract and the accompanying explanation in Chapter 28.

You will undoubtedly encounter real estate agents who will tell you that it is not customary to get land surveyed in the area and that your neighbors agree on where the property lines are. For such an agreement to be legally binding, there must be a recorded Boundary Line Agreement in the county Recorder's office. The agent will point out to you where the approximate boundaries of the property are. Unfortunately, many people who buy land on this basis find out later that the boundaries are not where the agent "thought they were." Recently in our area a highly publicized lawsuit was initiated against a well-established real estate agent in town who sold the same waterfall to three different land buyers. Each buyer thought the waterfall was on his property. Had the buyers demanded surveys before they bought, this could not have happened.

MEASUREMENTS

A List of Measurements Used in the Rectangular Surveys

Township = 36 square miles = 6 miles on each side.

Section = 1 square mile = 640 acres = 5,280 feet on a side.

Quarter section = 160 acres = 2,640 feet on a side.

A List of Measurements That Might Be Used in Any Type of Survey

1 link = 7.92 inches.

1 rod = 16.5 feet = 25 links = 5.5 yards.

1 chain = 66 feet = 4 rods.

1 pole = 1 rod

1 mile = 5,280 feet = 80 chains = 52.8 engineer's chains = 320 rods.

1 furlong = 40 rods.

1 acre = 10 square chains = 1/640 of a square mile = 43,560 square feet = 4,840 square yards = 160 square rods. If it is a square acre it will be 208.71 feet on a side.

These measurements are used in old surveys. Today surveys are conducted with a steel tape, rather than a chain. This tape, sometimes called an engineer's chain, is 100 feet long with links of 1 foot. Under this new method a mile would be 52.8 chains, or tapes. Be sure to determine whether the survey of the land is under the old or new system.

Measurements are taken on the ground without regard for height variations in the earth's surface. Thus if the measurement is a line 500 feet long it is taken as if the ground were flat, or measured in the air and then laid out on the ground.

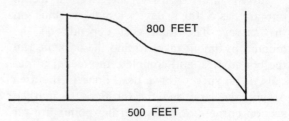

50. MEASUREMENTS TAKEN AS THOUGH GROUND WERE FLAT

In Illustration 50, the 800-foot walking distance is measured at 500 feet because the measurement is taken from the air. If it were not done this way, surveys and land descriptions would be even more ambiguous and fluctuating than they are at the present time.

chapter 9

Easement Rights

Most of the country land we looked at was located some distance away from a public road. Usually one or more people owned land between the property and the road. This is true of the land we bought, which is a mile in from the public county road with access to it by a single private dirt road. The dirt access road passes through three individually owned parcels. Before we signed any papers we wanted to be guaranteed that we would have a legal right to cross the private land from the county road to our place. In legal language, we wanted a *deeded easement*.

Easement conflicts frequently cause legal disputes in and out of court, but there is no reason why you should have any problems if you do a thorough job of investigating and negotiating before you buy. When you are shown a piece of land, the first thing you should do is ask the real estate agent if there is deeded ac-

cess to it. Ask him to show you a map that identifies all intervening parcels and their owners. If he tells you there are no existing easements to the land, then it is presently worthless. What value is land if you don't have a legal right to get to it? As foolish as it may seem, people have unknowingly bought such land in the past and will continue to do so.

ACQUIRING AN EASEMENT

In most cases, the seller will already have a proper easement. If he does not, then you should demand that he, or the real estate agent, get a legal right of way from each owner of the intervening properties. Once you have a recorded easement in your deed, it will last forever in your favor unless stated otherwise in its description. A landowner will probably charge for the right to cross his land with a vehicle. If the seller has to pay for the easement, he will undoubtedly add that cost into the total purchase price. Sometimes the real estate agent will urge you to buy the land, assuring you that he can get the right-of-way permission you need at a later date. However, you should buy only after you get the easement, not before.

HOW TO CHECK THE DEEDED ACCESS ON A MAP

You will understand the concept and importance of an easement if you study the following maps. I will use our own situation to show you how to check an easement description against a quadrangle map. Illustration 51 is a portion of the quadrangle map of our area and is the type of map found in any real estate agent's office. (If you read Chapter 8: *Land Descriptions and Surveys,* you will understand how this quadrangle map was created.) Illustration 52 shows the same area as Illustration 51, but land features, roads, and houses are indicated. The numbered areas in Illustration 52 are parcels of land owned by private parties. These parcels do not necessarily follow the regular section and quarter divisions in Illustration 51 since land parcels are split in many different ways. Before signing anything we asked the real estate agent to type up a description of the easement we were to get ex-

51. EASEMENT EXAMPLE

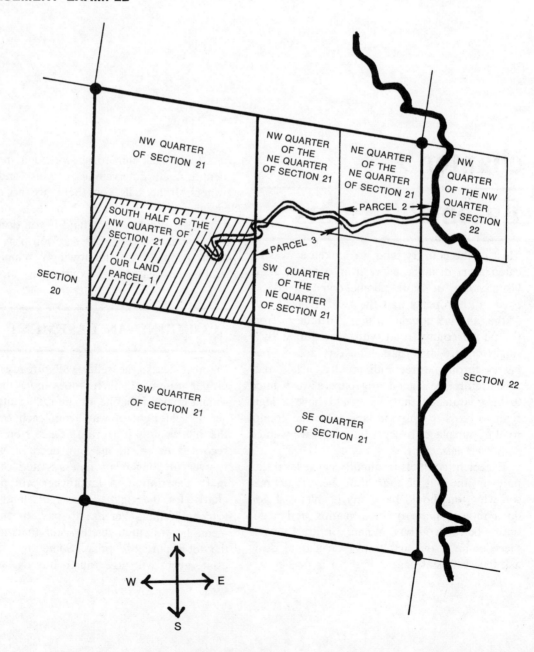

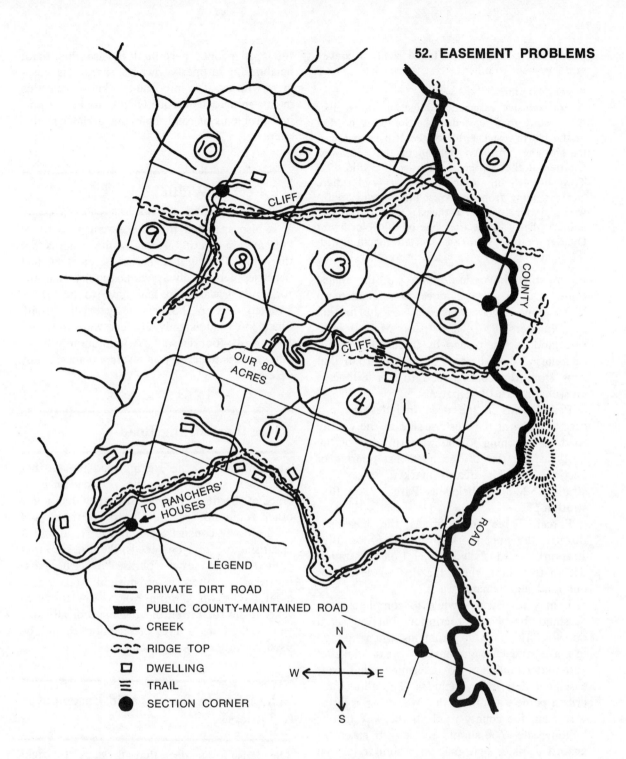

LEGEND

≡ PRIVATE DIRT ROAD

■ PUBLIC COUNTY-MAINTAINED ROAD

⌒ CREEK

〰 RIDGE TOP

▢ DWELLING

≡ TRAIL

● SECTION CORNER

actly as it would appear in our purchase contract and deed. According to what he typed we were purchasing:

That real property situated in the County of ——, State of California described as follows:

PARCEL ONE:
The South Half of the Northwest Quarter of Section 21, Township 4 South, Range 2 East, —— Meridian.

PARCEL TWO:
A nonexclusive easement 60 feet in width over the existing road located in the Southerly portion of the Northeast Quarter of the Northeast Quarter of Section 21 and in the Southerly portion of the Northwest Quarter of the Northwest Quarter of Section 22, in Township 4 South, Range 2 East, —— Meridian, and extending from the West line of said Northeast Quarter of the Northeast Quarter, Easterly to the West line of the

County Road, together with the right to convey said easement to others.

PARCEL THREE:

A nonexclusive easement 60 feet in width over the existing road located in the Southerly portion of the Northwest Quarter of the Northeast Quarter and the Northerly portion of the Southwest Quarter of the Northeast Quarter of Section 21, Township 4 South, Range 2 East, —— Meridian, and extending from the West line of said Southwest Quarter to the Northeast Quarter, Easterly and Northerly to the East line of said Northwest Quarter of the Northeast Quarter, together with the right to convey said easement to others.

Follow the above descriptions on the maps. Parcel One is our 80 acres. It is shaded on Illustration 51 and marked ① on Illustration 52. Numbers ②, ③, and ④ on Map B indicate land parcels owned by three different individuals. You can see that the dirt road that runs from the county road to our 80 acres crosses through these parcels.

Parcel Two in the deed includes the dirt road starting at the western side of the county road and running to the western edge of the northeast quarter of the northeast quarter of Section 21. This area is marked ② on Illustration 52, and labeled as Parcel 2 on Illustration 51.

Parcel Three then brings the easement through the area marked ③ and ④ on Illustration 52, and labeled Parcel 3 on Illustration 51, to the point where the dirt road touches our land and remains on it.

It may take you a while to completely understand the above description, but once you do, you will have no problems when you go to make your own purchase. It is essential that you understand how to determine what your easement description includes. The above-described parcels assure us that we own a right of way from the county road all the way to our building site. You should check your easement against a quadrangle map in a similar fashion to ensure that you are getting unquestionable access rights.

"Nonexclusive" Easement

You will notice in the preceding description of our easements that they are specified to be "nonexclusive." This means that we are not

the only people permitted to use this road; neighboring property owners share this easement with us. It is important to know what this means in actual practice. I talk about the mutual problems of road maintenance later in this chapter.

"60 Feet in Width"

It is also specified that the easement is to be "60 feet in width." Actually the road is not this wide. The right of access is set at 60 feet because there is always a possibility that the road might wash out and have to be reconstructed next to the previously existing road. Since the road is only 20 feet wide now, we have a 40-foot leeway. A minimum 60-foot allowance is necessary as a safety clause in any easement.

"Over the Existing Road"

The phrase "over the existing road" means that our access route follows the dirt road in existence at the time of purchase rather than some other route not yet developed. If there is a road already constructed into your land and it is satisfactory for your needs, then be sure that your deed includes the phrase "over the existing road" so there is no misunderstanding at a later date which route your easement is to take. If the road itself has been specifically surveyed, then the survey description should be used because of its preciseness.

"The Right to Convey Said Easement to Others"

The clause in our deed that allows us "the right to convey said easement to others" is important since we might wish to sell our 80 acres in the future. Although most courts have ruled that an easement that benefits the easement holder in the use of his land automatically goes with the land, the inclusion of the right to convey, in writing, makes it specific. It is always best to express the full intent of an agreement in the purchase contract and deed.

MAKE SURE YOUR ACCESS DESCRIPTION INCLUDES THE ENTIRE ROUTE

One land buyer I interviewed has a serious problem caused by his failure to examine his easement carefully enough before his purchase. He discovered too late that he did not have the access he thought he had. His parcel is indicated by ⑤ on Illustration 52. When he bought his land there was already a road running from the county road to his building site. In his deed, the easement was described as the road going through Parcels ⑥ and ⑦, leading to his boundary line. You can see that the dirt road hits his land just above the lower left corner of parcel ⑦. But notice that the access road then crosses through his land at the lower right corner, goes off his land, courses through three other people's property, ⑧ ⑨, ⑩, and then circles back onto his land, terminating at his house.

Because this road was already in existence when he purchased his land, he assumed that his easement covered the entire route. The real estate agent only told him that he had "deeded access to his land." The title company did a title search before closing and insured him for the access outlined in his deed, which only went from the County Road to his boundary line. But at the point where the road enters his land is a cliff, which makes it impossible for him to build a road from there to his house. This cliff is indicated on the map.

Thus he is now negotiating with the owners of ⑧, ⑨, ⑩ for easement rights across their property. He will probably have to pay a large sum of money for those rights should they decide to give them to him. They are not bound to do so. Our friend does not have a case against the agent or title company since they only guaranteed him access to his land, which he had. The easement just didn't go all the way to his house as he had assumed. It was our friend's fault because he failed to check his easement description against a map.

EASEMENTS WHERE NO ROAD EXISTS AT THE TIME OF PURCHASE

If you are buying land that does not have an access road already built, you must carefully examine the easement you are to be given in terms of its suitability for a road. Ideally you should get the seller to put in the road before you buy. He will probably add this cost to the selling price, but since constructing a road involves many problems, it is better to have the seller assume the risks.

If you wish to put the road in yourself you should insert the following condition, or safety clause for your protection in the Model Contract of Sale (see Chapter 28):

The Buyer shall make a diligent effort to construct a permanent access road along the route designated by the Easement in the Contract of Sale and the Deed. The road shall be no less than 20 (twenty) feet in width, and shall extend from the most accessible public road to the Buyer's building site. The road shall be adequate for ingress and egress of heavy-duty vehicles. The Buyer shall construct the road by any means of his choosing and the maximum cost the Buyer is willing to assume is $___. If the Buyer cannot locate and develop an adequate access road for his needs, as specified herein, and he has performed all of the conditions herein, then this Contract is rescinded immediately and the Buyer shall receive all money he has paid to the Seller, and the Buyer shall suffer no further liability under this Contract. Furthermore, the Seller shall reimburse the Buyer for the total amount the Buyer has expended in his attempt to construct an access road.

Have a local contractor, construction company, or road builder examine the area and determine the best route to your land before you purchase. They will probably do this for free, as well as give you an estimate of costs, because they anticipate being hired for the job. Give the contractor's written report to the seller, and tell him that you want an easement that covers every part of that route because it is the most feasible access route to your land. If he cannot deliver easement coverage over that area, then you should not buy the land. If you do not take the above precautions you might discover too late that you have been given an easement unfit for the construction of a low-cost permanent road.

KNOW WHERE YOUR ACCESS ENTERS YOUR PROPERTY

When you get an easement be sure it goes to the most desirable place for entry, usually your building site. A difficult situation developed for our neighbors because they failed to get an easement where they needed it. Their property is number ④ on Illustration 52. They use the same dirt road that we do. But notice where it hits their property line in the upper left hand corner of ④. Since their only good building sites were on the upper right hand side of their land, they built their house there, as indicated on the map. Directly below the house is a trail which the owners find much more convenient to use than coming up from the point where the access road meets their property. However, you can see that the trail leaves the access road and crosses part of the property belonging to ③. Thus they are trespassing at that point. Legally they need another easement to cross that small portion of their neighbor's land.

Instead of asking the owner of parcel ③ for an easement, our neighbors went ahead and built some steps up the cliff along the short trail to their house. When the woman who owns Parcel ③ made one of her rare visits to her land she was very upset about the trespassing and the steps across her property. She is now suing the owners of Parcel ④ for trespass and damage to property. She will probably win in court and the trespassers will be forced to enter their land far from their house where their right of way first touches their land. They may also have to pay some money for damages.

DETERMINING THE VALIDITY OF YOUR EASEMENT

Since an easement is a property right it should be documented in writing in any Contract of Sale and deed. This is very important. Easements should also be filed with the county Recorder. When you get a title search before closing, easement rights will be inspected only if they are to be included in your deed.

PRELIMINARY EASEMENT CHECK

You can do your own preliminary easement check. Find out from the real estate agent who owns each parcel between your land and the public road. If he doesn't have this informa-

tion you can get it from the local Tax Assessor. If possible find out the year each landowner, including the person you are buying your land from, purchased his property. Copies of all recorded deeds are kept in the county Recorder's office which is usually in the County Courthouse or local City Hall. Look in the Deed Index or Grantee Index, which is often filed by year, under the name of the present owner to see where to find a copy of his deed. In his deed you should find a description of an easement which either is exactly the same as, or includes, your easement. If you find this, you can then go back to the Deed, or Grantee, Index and look up the name of each person whose land your easement crosses over. In each of their deeds you should find a clause stating that the property is subject to an easement across it. The description of this easement should be the same as the one you will have in your deed. To do a complete easement check you should look in each person's deed who was a previous owner of your land. This is a very tedious and time-consuming job which you may want to leave to the title company. For a thorough discussion on searching the records, see Chapter 31: *The Title Search, Abstract of Title, and Title Insurance Policy.*

SHARING AND MAINTAINING AN EASEMENT

In the usual nonexclusive easement, where several people have the same easement rights over a single road to their respective properties, there is often no indication of who will be responsible for the upkeep of the access road. Usually this responsibility is shared by the people who hold the easement. Occasionally, someone does not accept his responsibility. Here is our situation.

You can see that three other landowners, numbered ②, ③, and ④ in Illustration 52, share the easement with us. The owners of ② and ③ help us repair the road each summer, but easement holder ④ refuses to join with us in this division of costs. He knows that since we live farther down the road than he does we will have to repair the road whether or not he helps us. We could bring a successful court action to force him to pay his share but we still hope he will do so voluntarily. Thus, two neighbors and ourselves share the $75 annual expenses.

When other people are using the same easement access that you are going to use, you should speak to some of them before you buy. Ask about the average cost of road repairs and who pays for them. If you find out this information before hand you may foresee future difficulties with noncooperative neighbors. The deed of each easement holder should state that he is responsible for a proportionate share of road maintenance according to his use.

If you are the only person who has an easement over a road, you alone will be responsible for maintenance. The landowner of the parcel through which your easement runs cannot interfere with your use of the road and does not have to maintain your access. If both of you use the same access, legally you are each responsible for upkeep. This maintenance cost will be greater the farther you are from the public road. Before you buy your land be sure you can afford your isolation.

When examining your access road, notice how much permanent improvement has been made which will decrease yearly maintenance expense. Look for culverts, which are steel or concrete pipes placed under the road surface to drain water away from the road. Culverts are essential in preventing a dirt road from becoming impassible due to large ruts and puddles resulting from winter rain or snow. They are expensive items and if other landowners use your road you will want all of them to cooperate when it comes to upkeep and improvement. One large culvert in our road cost $300. You can make your own culverts out of wood and place them underground yourself if you are willing to do a great deal of work.

GETTING THE COUNTY TO MAINTAIN YOUR EASEMENT

Real estate agents will sometimes tell a prospective buyer that the road he will be using will be taken over and maintained by the county after the buyer purchases the land. Be very skeptical of such claims. There are always stiff requirements that must be met before public tax money is spent on any road. For example, in California if a group of property owners want their road to be taken into the county system, they first must bring the road up to county standards at their own expense. This requires ditching, putting in culverts, and laying a minimum amount of surface gravel or asphalt, which is a very costly job. And once this work is done and the county takes over maintenance of the road, by law it becomes permanently open to the public.

DOES A NEIGHBOR HAVE AN EASEMENT OVER YOUR LAND?

Easement problems also occur if an access is owned across your land by other landowners. Then it is your land that is being crossed, and it is said to be "encumbered" by or subject to an easement. You can often determine if your land is subject to an easement by personally examining it. Obviously if a road runs through your place continuing onto another person's land and you can see that someone is using it, you should suspect that an easement exists.

UNRECORDED EASEMENTS

Easement by Necessity and Implication

Often a title search will uncover the existence of an easement. However, there are instances where easements are off the record and therefore not protected by a Policy of Title Insurance. For example, if one piece of land is divided into several parcels, those that are separated from the road can cross the intervening land without deeded access. (See Illustration 53) Assume A originally owned both

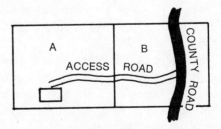

53. EASEMENT BY NECESSITY

Parcels A and B. He sells B and does not record an easement across it. He still has a legal right to cross B's land since he had been using the access road for many years and there is no other means by which he can get to the public road. The law says he has an easement by necessity and that he implicitly kept an easement for himself when he sold parcel B. You will not find this kind of easement in any public records, yet B cannot prevent A from crossing his land.

Easement by Prescription

There is another way an easement can be created without being recorded as part of a deed. If a person openly crosses someone else's land continuously for a prescribed number of years as if he has a right to do so, but, in fact, the owner has not given him permission, the user can get an easement by prescription, commonly called a prescriptive easement. This easement is as binding as if the holder had been given it in writing. The time period required before habitual use becomes a permanent right varies in each state. In California, it takes five years to establish a prescriptive easement, whereas it takes ten years in Oregon, fifteen years in Minnesota, and twenty years in Illinois.

IT IS YOUR DUTY TO INSPECT THE PARCEL

The implied easement and prescriptive easement will not appear in the County Records and will not be covered by your Policy of Title Insurance. For this reason it is very important that you personally walk over and examine your land in its entirety. Make a thorough investigation of any roads or paths that cross the land, whether or not they appear to be well traveled. Perhaps the road is only used at certain times of the year. The burden is placed on you to inspect the premises before you purchase in order to determine the existence of unrecorded easements. Once you have signed your contract you will have little chance in court of preventing someone from crossing

your land who possesses a legally sound unrecorded easement.

IS THE EASEMENT OVER YOUR LAND GOING TO BOTHER YOU?

When one or more landowners have the right to cross your land at any time, such activity could seriously interfere with your peace and quiet. The burden will be greater if the road runs next to your best building site than if it merely crosses the corner of the land far from the living area. Also your own access problems could be greater due to the number of people using the access road. If an encumbering easement breaks up the unity of some land you are interested in, you should use this point to get the price down. However, you should evaluate the situation carefully before you buy. The following story illustrates the importance of predicting the future impact of an easement on the enjoyment of your land.

Some communal neighbors, who live on the ridge above our valley, bought 40 acres which were originally part of a large ranch that now extends to the south and southwest of them. Their land is numbered ⑪ on Illustration 52. When the ranchers sold the 40 acres they reserved easement rights for themselves along the dirt road that crosses the commune's land. You can see the road running along the ridge of the mountain from the county road to the ranchers' houses. The only available building sites on the 40 acres are next to the dirt road, which is where the commune members built their dwellings. Now daily sunbathing is frequently interrupted by the spectre of a jeep-load of staring cowboys as they enter and leave their ranch.

In addition, the ranchers use heavy-duty vehicles on the road, which inevitably produce huge ruts during the winter rains. This prevents access by the commune, which has only lightweight two-wheel drive vehicles. When the ruts get too deep the members have to walk into their land, until the road can be repaired the following summer. Although the commune could find recourse in the courts since they are being prevented from using their legal access road, such action is costly and time consuming. So they have learned to live with this encumbering easement. But would you want to?

You cannot know the use patterns of an easement unless you spend some time on the land before buying it. I would never buy any land that has an easement within eyesight of the homestead area.

UTILITY LINE EASEMENT

Easements are not restricted solely to personal access. The right to bring utility lines along the easement route can be included. Your easement should provide for "ingress and egress and public utilities." Even if you don't want electricity brought in yourself, it is helpful to have this in your deed if you ever decide to sell your land. A future buyer might want his easement to specifically include utilities. When we bought our land this was not specified in our deed because we didn't want electricity ourselves. But now I think it would have been wise to have included it, as a future selling point.

You will also want to be aware of a utility easement across your land. Although you might be willing to see a car go by a few times a day, you might not enjoy the sight of telephone and electrical poles and wires strung across your property. But the cost of getting lines into an area farther than a couple of thousand feet is prohibitive for the average landowner, so even if there is a utility easement present the chances that it will be used are probably slight.

"THE LAND HAS FRONTAGE ON COUNTY ROAD"

You will frequently see the above phrase in real estate advertisements. Don't make the assumption that road frontage necessarily means direct road access. The side of the property

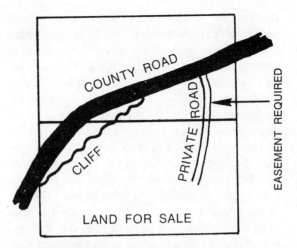

54. ROAD FRONTAGE DECEPTION

that borders the county road might be a cliff or a ravine. In such cases, entrance must be gained by crossing a neighbor's land. Illustration 54 shows road frontage with easement access required.

AN EASEMENT WARRANTY— YOUR BEST INSURANCE

An excellent means of obtaining extra easement protection is to include a warranty clause in the Contract of Sale. I have done so in the Model Contract of Sale which is in Chapter 28. Clause 18(a) states that the seller warrants the buyer that he will receive legal access, or easements, over the most accessible route between the public road and his building site. This warranty covers the problems discussed in this chapter and assures you of legal recourse against the seller if any undisclosed easement problems arise after the deal is closed. Clause 18(k) keeps the warranty binding even after you receive the deed to the property.

A FINAL WARNING

The importance of understanding easements and knowing when and where they are located cannot be overstressed. Beware of the real estate agent who tells you: "Don't worry about getting an easement. The former owner of this land has been using this road for years. Everybody is real friendly. Nobody around here ever gets easements." Tell him that if nobody cares if you use the road then he should have no problem getting the landowners to sign a piece of paper giving you written permission to do so.

Think about the future. The people who now own the land you will cross might not care whether you do so, but the next owner might not be so gratuitous. Or the present owner might not like your looks and decide that he's not going to treat you as he did the last owners. All he has to do is put up a gate and tell you not to cross his land if you don't have deeded access. These situations are very common in the history of real estate disputes.

You must also protect yourself against easements that could interfere with your use of the land. A thorough personal inspection of your prospective purchase is mandatory for uncovering evidence of easement. It is helpful to discuss the situation with the seller and his neighbors. Question the real estate agent thoroughly on the matter.

A deeded easement should be described as precisely as possible, in terms of location and purpose. Remember that an easement may not always be revealed by a title search. Thus a comprehensive general warranty is necessary. Finally, easements crossing the seller's land should be used to your advantage when negotiating the selling price.

chapter 10

Water Rights

The water right is a property right. It is a valuable right. And it is real estate. . . . The holder of a water right in an area in which the competition for water is keen needs to be constantly on guard to protect his right against infringement or loss. It is said that "Eternal vigilance is the price of a good water right."
—Wells A. Hutchins, leading water rights expert

The importance of having water on your land has been pointed out in great detail in an earlier chapter. The mere presence of water on your property, however, does not necessarily insure that you have unfettered rights to use it. Every state has specific and detailed laws regarding water rights and how they may be obtained and lost that apply to all users of the water. It is impossible for me to detail all of the water laws in each individual state, but I will explain basic theories and their applications to different types of water sources. Contact your state Department of Resources or your local Farm Advisor to find out how you can get a pamphlet detailing the water laws of the state where your land is located. For example, in California you can write to the state Water Resources Control Board in Sacramento for a pamphlet entitled *Regulations and Information Pertaining to Appropriation of Water*. (See "Useful Resources" at the end of this chapter.) Similar guides are put out in other states.

THE PURPOSE OF WATER LAWS

All water is classified as either surface water or underground water. These waters are regulated by different laws, as enacted by state legislatures and interpreted by the state and federal courts. The primary aim of the water laws is to prevent the waste of water and to use what is available in the most beneficial manner possible.

SURFACE WATERS

Surface waters include lakes, rivers, streams, springs, ponds, marshes, and any other visible water. Most rivers and lakes are considered to be "navigable" public waters and the federal government has control over them. If your land abuts on or includes navigable waters, you have water rights as long as they do not interfere with public use.

However, it is more likely that if your land has surface water on it, it will be a "nonnavigable" stream, spring, or pond. Whether navigable or not, all surface water in the United States is subject to either riparian laws, prior appropriation laws, or combinations of the two.

These two separate areas of water law, riparian rights and prior appropriation rights, developed because the water needs in the arid West are very different from those in the humid East. East of the 100th Meridian West Longitude line rainfall is abundant throughout the year, whereas west of that line rainfall is sparse and nearly all of it falls during the winter months. (See Chapter 3: *Climate*.) Illustration 55 shows the distribution of the types of water rights to surface water used by each state throughout the country.

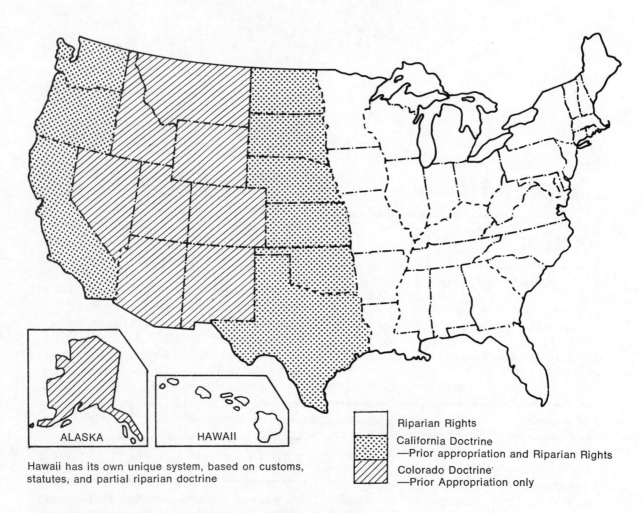

ALASKA   HAWAII

Hawaii has its own unique system, based on customs, statutes, and partial riparian doctrine

☐ Riparian Rights

▦ California Doctrine
—Prior appropriation and Riparian Rights

▨ Colorado Doctrine
—Prior Appropriation only

55. ACQUISITION OF SURFACE WATER RIGHTS

Riparian Rights

Water laws, like the rest of our laws, evolved from the English common law brought here by the early settlers. Since these settlers first established themselves in the humid eastern portion of the country where water is plentiful, the riparian laws of England, itself a humid country, were nicely suited to the region. Thus is was logical that we accepted them as our first water laws.

A riparian landowner is one whose land is directly adjacent to the water source. The amount of land actually touching the water is usually irrelevant. The majority of land for sale with surface water contains springs rather than a definable stream. If a spring does not pass beyond the boundary of the land on which it is located, the owner of the land has sole rights to use the water as he wishes. But if the spring is the source of a natural stream that flows across other lands, it falls within the laws of riparian rights. Where many riparian landowners have property adjacent to a single stream or lake, riparian laws are used to determine how much water each is allowed to use.

Originally this country followed the doctrine, inherited from English law, that required that each riparian landowner must let the stream flow in its "natural state" to lower lands. Thus, the flow could not be diminished in quantity or impaired in quality by a riparian user, and any water diverted must be returned to the stream before leaving the user's property. The purpose of this rule originally was to insure the free passage of water downstream from one mill wheel to the next. As of this writing, eight states still follow this "natural flow" method of allocating water. They are Georgia, Maine, Mississippi, Missouri, New Jersey, Pennsylvania, South Dakota, and West Virginia. Since this method results in the wasteful loss of much water into the sea, today the majority of state courts and legislatures more often follow the "reasonable use" rule in determining riparian rights.

Reasonable use is a priority system that follows the rule that a riparian landowner can use all the water he needs for "ordinary" or "domestic" purposes without regard to the effect of such use on the water flow to lower riparian landowners. Domestic uses include taking water for washing, cooking, drinking, and watering domestic stock animals and gardens. Often a state will fix a maximum quantity considered reasonable for domestic use. For example, California permits 18.5 gallons per day per 100 square feet for irrigation of home gardens. For a house with a sink and flush toilet, each person is permitted a maximum of 40 gallons per day. "Extraordinary" uses, often referred to as "artificial" uses, include taking water for irrigation of commercial crops, manufacturing, mining, and other commercial uses. All domestic uses by all riparian landowners on the stream must be fulfilled before any one of them can use the surplus water for artificial uses. Sometimes an upper riparian landowner in using water for domestic purposes only takes all the available water and none flows to lower riparian landowners. This is allowed as long as the use is "reasonable," you should be aware of use patterns upstream when buying land with the expectation of receiving a good steady flow of water.

In determining which artificial uses take priority after all domestic uses have been fulfilled, many facts are considered, including the length of the stream, the volume of water, the extent of riparian land ownership, and the purpose and extent of the use. Using water for aesthetic and recreational purposes, such as swimming and fishing, is far down on the list of preferred uses. Taking water out of a stream to store for use later is usually not allowed under riparian system. Only if every other riparian owner has enough for both domestic and artificial uses can water be taken and stored. Fortunately, the riparian system predominates mainly in the eastern half of the United States where water is plentiful and storage is not usually necessary. The states that follow the "reasonable use" riparian laws exclusively are: Alabama, Arkansas, Connecticut, Delaware, Florida, Illinois, Indiana, Iowa, Kentucky, Louisiana, Maryland, Massachusetts, Michigan, Minnesota, New Hampshire, New York, North Carolina, Ohio, Rhode Island, South Carolina, Tennessee, Vermont, Virginia, and Wisconsin.

Riparian rights go with the land itself and cannot be lost because of disuse. They always remain with the land adjoining the water unless specified otherwise. Illustration 56 shows an effect of a sale of riparian land.

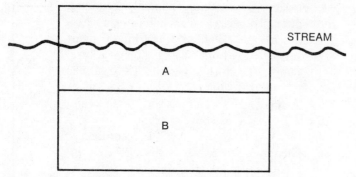

56. SALE OF A RIPARIAN RIGHT

Both parcels A and B were originally one unit of land owned totally by A. When parcel B was sold, the buyer did not automatically get riparian rights to the stream because his parcel does not adjoin the stream. However, if A included riparian rights and access rights in the deed to B, then B can use the stream. This is legal because B is in the watershed and was originally a part of the riparian land. The sale simply divided the riparian land into two parcels when previously it had all been owned by one person.

Once a riparian right is lost, however, the loss is permanent and can never be regained. If B, in the above example, did not get riparian rights reserved in his deed, parcel B can never regain those rights even if it is resold to A and reunited as one parcel of land adjoining the stream. If you are buying land that is being severed from a riparian piece of land, riparian rights will attach to your land only if expressly reserved in writing in your Deed.

If you buy land with a stream or other surface water on it, you will be paying for that water since it increases the value of the land. A seller who reserves riparian rights and easement rights for himself, or the buyer of another parcel he may sell, to cross your land and use the stream should greatly reduce his asking price since such a reservation means you must share the stream on your land with others. The seller may try to reserve these rights for other parcels he is selling because it makes any property not adjoining the water a better sales prospect. Carefully evaluate the effect on your home if other property owners have the right to come onto your land and run water lines to their property.

When you buy riparian land or land with riparian rights granted in the deed, you can be sold only those rights the seller possesses already. Therefore, you must find out what his rights include. Be certain that the seller has not previously granted his riparian rights to another user, leaving him with no rights to give you. Because this information may not show up in the deed, be sure that it is covered in your title search. Courts are destroying riparian rights in legal disputes where they cannot absolutely be shown to exist, so if there is any doubt about your rights, resolve them before taking title to the land.

As a riparian landowner your right to have an adequate water flow includes a right to pure water. Lawsuits between riparian owners over the issue of pollution are fairly common. However, a private action is not as effective as when a state agency acts to prevent pollution. If you want adequate relief you will have to file a complaint with the appropriate state agency as well as the court. Upstream polluters are also liable for damages and possible criminal charges. In some areas, pollution that occurs as a result of bathing or watering stock animals is permissible.

In many states, you are not free to stock and take fish from some streams or lakes that are riparian to your land. We cannot fish in our creek under any circumstances because it is classified as a "spawning creek" by the state Fish and Game Department. The fines for fishing illegally are often several hundred dollars. You should look up your stream's classification in the state Fish and Game Regulations before you buy your land if fishing is a major reason for moving to the country. You might also want to check the local rules regarding fish stocking. You generally need a permit to stock your stream or lake and the type of fish you can use is selected by state officials to protect nearby public waters.

As a riparian landowner you own the rocks in the stream bed and may remove them for use on your land as long as you do not disturb the flow of the water to lower riparian users.

Although the property line of land bordered by a nonnavigable stream generally extends to the middle of the stream, it is wise to have this written into your deed if a creek or stream is used as a boundary line of the land. The property line of land on a navigable stream or lake

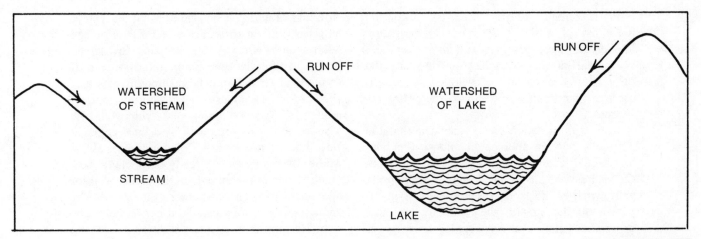

extends to the low-water mark. On a nonnavigable stream, as the course of the water gradually shifts through the years, the property lines shift with the stream. The soil that is slowly deposited on your land during the shifting process is your gain and your opposing neighbor's loss. This process is called "accretion." However, if the stream changes course as a result of a sudden storm or flood rather than by a gradual process of change, the rule of accretion does not apply and the boundary lines do not change.

All riparian owners are eligible to take and use the water only on land within the "watershed," which is that area that drains into the stream, river, or lake. (See Illustration 57.) If you buy a large piece of land on a stream and want to pump water from the stream over a hill to use on a section of your property that is in another watershed, you will be appropriating the water and thus subject to "appropriation laws" rather than riparian laws. Legal action could be taken against you by other riparian owners lower than you on the stream and by "prior appropriators" because you are illegally depriving them of stream water.

Prior Appropriation Rights (Alone or with Riparian Rights)

In 1849 gold was discovered in California, and people swarmed into the West. Mining towns, army camps, and trading posts grew up around major water routes. At first gold was mined directly from the streams in the Sierra Mountains by using the naturally flowing stream water to wash the sand out of the sifting pans, leaving the gold on the bottom. As gold processing became more advanced, however, long ditches were dug to create more water pressure to separate the gold, and tremendous amounts of water were required. It became necessary, also, to store huge quantities of water in large reservoirs so that mining could continue during the long dry summer months. New laws were needed to define who could use the limited supplies of water, and prior appropriation laws were adopted.

The basic principle involved in the law of prior appropriation is "first in time is first in right." The first user, often called the "prior" or "senior appropriator," is permitted to take all the water in the stream he can put to a reasonable and beneficial use to the exclusion of all other higher or lower on the stream who want to take water after him. This rule came into being to avoid wasting water and to better apportion water in dry periods. The feeling was that it was preferable to let one individual water user take all the available water needed in a drought rather than to distribute the water in amounts inadequate for each of several users.

As the amount of gold gradually dwindled, many miners and new settlers turned to farming. They began to construct ditches to divert water from streams for a new purpose, to carry it to their lands for irrigation. By 1880, the feasibility of raising large crops by irrigation had proven successful, and intensive land development in the West began. Many of the prior appropriation laws, developed by miners, carried over to this new use of the water resources.

Prior appropriation rights specified that the first settler in an area could choose the land he wanted and build irrigation ditches from the nearest stream to his fields. It was irrelevant whether his land was contiguous, or riparian, to the stream, since nobody else was using the water. The next settler to come to the area had second choice of the land and secondary rights to appropriate the available water to irrigate his land. This pattern was repeated with subsequent settlers.

Thus, because of the scarcity of water and the needs of mining and agriculture, the original riparian laws which the humid East had adopted from England gave way to the new doctrine of prior appropriation. Nine of the most arid western states now follow the "Colorado doctrine" which only recognizes prior appropriation laws and does not differentiate between riparian and nonriparian lands. These states are Alaska, Arizona, Colorado, Idaho, Montana, Nevada, New Mexico, Utah, and Wyoming.

The other nine western states follow the "California doctrine," which does distinguish riparian lands but also has coordinated the principle of prior appropriation into the laws. These states are California, Kansas, Nebraska, North Dakota, Oklahoma, Oregon, South Dakota, Texas, and Washington. In these states, appropriators are nonriparian users only. Riparian users always have priority over appropriators. (See Illustration 58 to see the relationship between riparian rights and appropriation rights.) Hawaii has a unique system derived from custom and ancient rights which are beyond the scope of this discussion.

The appropriator in every state except Montana must apply to the state for a permit and license to take water. The time of appropriation and priority to use the water dates from the time formal application is made to the state even though actual use may not begin until long after that date. When buying land in one of these states, you should investigate the history of water applications on your stream.

Not only should you determine what legal steps have been taken to secure water rights on the seller's land but you should also investigate similarly other lands adjoining the stream. If you intend to divert a large amount of water and expect to invest a substantial sum of money in diversion equipment, you would be wise to have a survey taken by a local engineer who knows the river. You should establish where diversions have already been made, how much water is taken out of the river by prior appropriators, and whether there will be enough left for your use. You can write to the state Resources Agency or state Engineer and ask if any permits have been sought or licenses issued to appropriate water on your stream or river.

This research for prior appropriators is difficult and often inconclusive, but at least make some preliminary investigations since the standard Policy of Title Insurance does not guarantee water rights. You do not want to find your stream dry in August because your upstream neighbor is pumping out all the water before it reaches your property line, and you can do nothing about it because he has a ten-year permit from the state to do so. If you are in an appropriation state that does not recognize riparian rights, you have no recourse. If you are in one of the nine appropriation states that do recognize riparian rights, you could force the appropriator to allow enough water through to meet your water requirements.

Obtaining a Permit

The procedure for obtaining an appropriate permit is similar in each state. I have reprinted a typical application form below. (See Illustration 59.) You can obtain the application forms and rules for filing in your state from your state Resources Agency or state Engineer in charge of water allocation. The procedure I describe below is only an example and may not be applicable in your state.

As you can see the application is quite detailed and specific. It calls for a description of the diversion works including location and amount of water to be diverted, a schedule of when the work is to be completed once you have your permit, a description of the proposed use, and information on the effect of the appro-

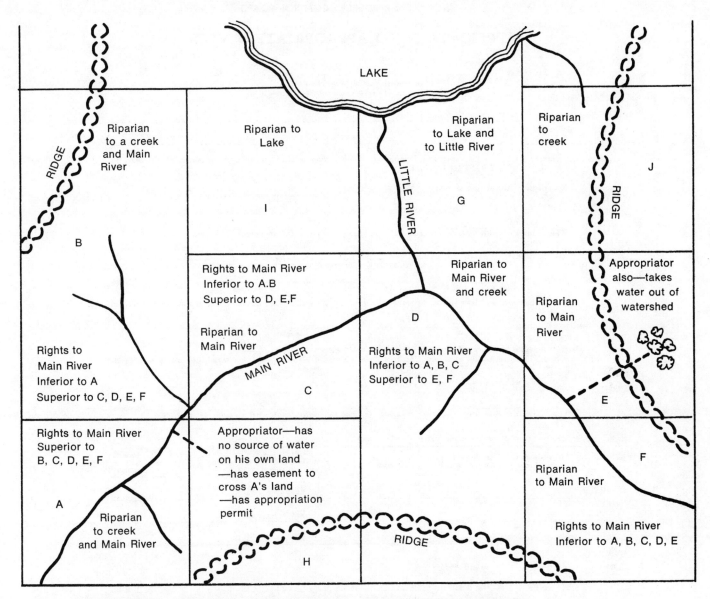

58. RELATION BETWEEN RIPARIAN AND APPROPRIATION RIGHTS

(LETTERS REFER TO INDIVIDUAL PARCELS)

priation on fish and wildlife and how you are prepared to deal with such effects. You are also required to pay filing fees and include copies of a project map.

You should file for a permit as soon as possible since the filing date is the one used to determine who is prior in time. After you have filed your application, notice of the filing is issued and posted in public places and at the stream so that anybody else who may be prior in time to you or who may have objections can protest. If anybody wishes to protest your application they have to submit written protest to the agency and to you, the applicant, within a specified time period. You then have fifteen days to answer the protest and must reply to the specific complaints. You must file this answer with the agency and send a copy to the complainant.

A hearing is then held before a division of the state Water Resources Agency, which has the authority to grant permits. At this time witnesses and any other evidence regarding the case is heard. If the agency feels the information is insufficient, it may order a field investigation at which you and the protester may be present. The data obtained from this investigation are used to help the agency make a final

APPLICATION TO APPROPRIATE WATER

Application No._____ Filed_____ at_____ M.

(Applicant must not fill in the above blanks.)
(This application must be typewritten or legibly written in ink.)

I, _____
    Name of applicant

_____
    Address   City or Town   State   Zip Code

do hereby make application for a permit to appropriate the following described unappropriated waters of the State of SUBJECT TO VESTED RIGHTS:

1. **The name of the source** at the point of diversion is_____
                                          If unnamed, state nature of source and that it is unnamed.

tributary to_____

2. **The amount of water** which applicant desires to appropriate under this application is as follows:

    (a) To be diverted directly to beneficial use_____ cubic feet per second
                                                                                                    gallons per day
        16,000 gallons per day is approximately 0.025 cubic foot per second. Use gallons per day if less than 0.025 c.f.s.

to be diverted from _____ to _____ of each year.
                              Beginning date   Closing date

    (b) To be stored and later applied to beneficial use_____ acre-feet per annum, to be collected

between _____ and _____ of each season.
              Beginning date   Closing date

If offstream storage is proposed, maximum rate of diversion to storage will be_____ c.f.s.

NOTE.—Neither the amount nor the season may be increased after the application is filed. If underground storage is proposed a special supplemental form will be supplied by the State Water Resources Control Board upon request.

3. **The use** to which the water is to be applied is_____

_____ purposes.
    Domestic, irrigation, power, municipal, mining, industrial, recreational, stockwatering, fish culture, etc. Describe more fully in paragraphs 13, 14, 15, 16 and/or 17.

4. **The points of diversion or rediversion** are to be located as follows:

List all points giving coordinate distances or bearing and distance from section corner or quarter section corner	40-acre subdivision of public land survey or projection thereof	Section	Township	Range	Base and Meridian
	¼ of ¼				
	¼ of ¼				
	¼ of ¼				

The points of diversion are located in_____ County.

5. **The main conduit** will terminate in_____ of Sec._____, T._____, R._____, _____ B. & M.
                                    State 40-acre subdivision of public land survey or projection thereof.

Description of Diversion Works

NOTE.—An application cannot be approved for an amount grossly in excess of the estimated capacity of the diversion works.

6. **Intake or headworks** (complete only those blanks which apply)

Complete (a) and/or (b) for direct diversion or diversion to offstream storage.

    (a) Diversion will be made by pumping from _____
                                                          Sump, offset well, unobstructed channel, etc.

    (b) Diversion will be by gravity, the diverting dam being _____ feet in height (stream bed to level

of overflow), _____ feet long on top, and constructed of_____
                                                                              Concrete, earth, brush, etc.

    (c) Complete for storage reservoirs only

Height of dam, ft. (streambed to spillway level)	Crest length of dam, ft.	Freeboard above spillway level, ft.	Material of construction

WRCB 1 (11-68)

59. APPLICATION FORM TO APPROPRIATE WATER

7. Storage Reservoirs

Name, if any	Sections flooded by reservoir. Also name 40-acre subdivisions unless shown on map	Surface area, acres	Capacity acre-feet

For any reservoir having a capacity of 25 acre-feet or more, complete the following:

Diameter of outlet pipe, inches	Length of outlet pipe, feet	Difference in elevation, spillway level to top of outlet pipe in reservoir, feet	Fall in outlet pipe, feet

8. Conduit system (describe diversion conduits and main distribution conduits only)

(a) Open channel_____; ditch_____; flume_____; canal_____. (check type to be used)

Width of top at water line, feet	Width at bottom, feet	Depth of water, feet	Length, feet	Grade, feet per 1,000 feet	Construction Materials: earth, rock, concrete, plastic, etc.

(b) Pipeline_____; sprinkler system_____; tunnel_____. (check type to be used)

Diameter, inches	Length, feet	Pump lift, feet	Gravity fall intake to outlet, feet	Construction Materials: steel, concrete, wood, etc.

9. (a) Estimated capacities of the pumping plants are _____; _____

(b) Estimated capacities of the diversion conduits are _____; _____

(c) Estimated total cost of the diversion works proposed is_____
Give only cost of intake, or headworks, pumps, storage reservoirs and main conduits.

Completion Schedule

10. (a) Construction work will begin on or before_____

(b) Construction work will be completed on or before_____

(c) Water will be completely applied to the proposed use on or before_____

(d) If complete, state year of completion_____

Description of Proposed Use

11. Place of use

Does applicant own the land where the water will be used?_____Jointly?_____

All joint owners should include their names as applicants and sign the application at bottom of page 4.

If applicant does not own land where the water will be used, give name and address of owner and state what arrangements have been made with him.

_____

_____

If area is unsurveyed state the location as if lines of the public land survey were projected. If space does not permit listing all 40-acre tracts, state sections, townships, and ranges and show detail on map.

40-acre tract	Section	Township	Range	Base and Meridian	If irrigation, state number of acres

12. Other rights. Describe all rights except other applications on file with the State Water Resources Control Board under which water is served to the above-named lands.

Nature of Rights (riparian, appropriative, purchased water, etc.)	Year of first use	Use made in recent years including amount, if known	Season of use	Source of other supply

13. Irrigation use. The total area to be irrigated is_____acres. Acreage of crops is as follows:

<small>Net acreage</small>

Rice_____acres; alfalfa_____acres; orchard_____acres; general crops_____acres; pasture_____acres.

Care should be taken that the various statements of acreage are consistent with each other, with the statement in Paragraph 11 and with the map.

The irrigation season will begin about_____and end about_____

<small>Beginning date</small>   <small>Closing date</small>

14. Power use. The total fall to be utilized is_____feet. The maximum amount of water to be used through

<small>Difference between nozzle or draft tube water level and first free water surface above.</small>

the penstock is _____cubic feet per second. The maximum theoretical horsepower capable of being generated by the

works is _____. The use to which the power is to be applied is _____.

<small>Second feet × fall ÷ 8.8</small>   <small>For distribution and sale or private use, etc.</small>

The nature of the works by means of which power is to be developed is _____. The size

<small>Turbine, Pelton wheel, etc.</small>

of the nozzle to be used is _____inches.

After use, the water will be discharged into_____in_____of

<small>Name of stream</small>   <small>State 40-acre subdivision</small>

Sec._____, T._____, R._____, _____B. & M.

15. Municipal use. The name of the city or town to be served is_____

having a present population of_____. The estimated water requirement per capita per day during the

month of maximum use is_____. The estimated average daily consumption during the month of maximum

use at the end of each five-year period until the full amount applied for is put to beneficial use is as follows:

_____

_____

_____

_____

16. Mining use. The name of the mining property to be served is_____

<small>Name of claim</small>

and the nature of the mine is_____. Mineral to be extracted is_____. The method of utilizing the

<small>Placer, lode, etc.</small>

water is_____. The estimated

ultimate water requirement for this project is_____

<small>Cubic feet per second, gallons per minute. State basis of estimate.</small>

will
The water will not be polluted by chemicals or otherwise. _____

<small>Explain nature of pollution, if any.</small>

After use the water will be discharged into_____in_____of

<small>Name of stream</small>   <small>State 40-acre subdivision</small>

Sec._____, T._____, R._____, _____B. & M.

17. Uses other than those described in Paragraphs 13 through 16. The nature of the use proposed is_____

_____

<small>Industrial, recreational, domestic, stockwatering, etc.</small>

State basis of determination of amount needed _____

<small>Number of persons, residences, area of domestic lawns and gardens,</small>

<small>number and kind of stock, type of industrial use, and unit requirements.</small>

_____

_____

136

18. If the required maps are not filed with the application, state the reasons for not filing them_____

_____

_____

I will need _____ (days) (months) within which to file the maps.

19. Does the applicant own the land at the proposed point of diversion?_____. If not, give name and address of

owner and state what steps have been taken to secure right of access._____

_____

20. What is the name of the post office most used by those living near the proposed point of diversion?_____

_____

21. What are the names and addresses of diverters of water from the source of supply downstream from the proposed

point of diversion?_____

_____

_____

22. (a) Have you investigated the effect of the proposed appropriation on fish and wildlife?_____

(b) Have you consulted with the State Department of Fish and Game concerning this proposed appropriation?_____

(c) Will your proposed diversion or impoundment of water beneficially or adversely affect fish and wildlife?_____

(d) State all data and information reasonably available to you or that can be obtained from the _____ Department of
Fish and Game concerning the extent, if any, to which fish and wildlife would be affected by the appropriation.

_____

_____

_____

_____

(e) Describe any measures you propose to take for the protection of fish and wildlife in connection with the appropriation.

_____

_____

_____

_____

Name of person filing application if other than applicant_____

Correspondence about this application should be sent to:

Name_____

Address_____ Telephone_____

	Mr.
Signature of applicant(s)	Mrs. _____
(Refer to Section 671 of the Board's regulations)	Miss
	Mr.
	Mrs. _____
	Miss

determination. If it approves your intended diversion, a permit is issued and you can begin to take the water. Approval by the agency does not insure water rights. It only indicates that you have been granted permission by the state to use water and this permission establishes a priority date for you. If others have prior permission and use up all the water, there is nothing you can do.

Once the permit is granted you must act with reasonable diligence to begin diverting and putting the water to good use. After you begin doing this, the agency grants you a license. You can keep this license forever so long as there are not three successive years in which no use is made of the diversionary works, in which case you would lose your appropriation rights. Whenever requested, you must report to the agency on what you are doing so that it can be sure the water resources are being put to "the best and most efficient use possible."

Dams and Reservoirs

If you wish to dam up your stream, you should be acquainted with any regulations in your state regarding dams. Generally, even though you are riparian to a stream, if you build a dam for the purpose of storing water for swimming, fishing, or irrigation, you are appropriating that water and must meet the regulations regarding water appropriation in your state. However, mere regulation of the flow of a stream is not an appropriation if it only detains, but does not reduce the flow of, the water. For instance, dams that are built to create enough head on a stream to drive a power plant do not diminish the actual flow.

Many states have standards set for dam and reservoir construction. Usually a dam must exceed certain specified limits before it qualifies for state control. For example, although California does regulate dams, it does not supervise any dams that are less than 6 feet high or hold less than 15 acre-feet of water. For any larger construction the builder must file for a permit and pay set fees. You can find out your state's requirements, if any, from the same agency that supervises the water uses described above. If an upstream user builds a dam that endangers your water supply, you should file a written complaint to the appropriate department in your county or state.

Thirteen states have enacted Mill Acts which permit a dam to be built by an upper riparian landowner for the purpose of supplying water power regardless of any detrimental effects on lower riparian users as long as they are compensated for damages. The states that have this stipulation for water are Connecticut, Georgia, Kentucky, Massachusetts, Minnesota, Mississippi, Nebraska, New Hampshire, North Carolina, North Dakota, Rhode Island, South Dakota, and Virginia.

Lakes

If you buy property on, or near, a lake, find out the rights and regulations regarding lakes in your state. A lake, like a river, can be navigable or nonnavigable but the same rules apply in most cases. In most states, the government owns the beds of navigable lakes and is prevented from selling them. Some states permit private ownership of navigable lake beds, but the owner cannot prevent the public from freely using the lake and taking water from it. In all states, the ownership of the shore goes with the adjoining property and the public may be prevented from using that part of the shoreline.

You may have more rights if you are on a nonnavigable lake. As a riparian landowner you own the bed of the lake along with all other riparian owners. You have the right to use the entire surface of the lake for recreation although your property may only adjoin the lake for a small distance along the shoreline. A minority of states, including Illinois, require that ownership of the lake bed must be specified in your deed before you may use the water, and some states restrict your use within the boundaries of your part of the lake bed.

If you are buying property that is not directly on a lake but the seller assures you that you have a right to use it, investigate his assurances. You will probably need an easement across someone's land to get to the lake, and you may need separate rights reserved in writing in your deed to use the lake. If you desire docking facilities for a boat, you will need written permission from the person who owns the docks. The permission should be permanent, otherwise you might be charged an excessive fee to renew the right at a later date.

All of these rights are valuable assets to the property and must be recorded in the public records and in your deed to be legally binding. Your title search should investigate your rights to use a lake if you expect to do so after you purchase your land.

UNDERGROUND WATERS

Wells capturing underground waters provide most rural landowners with their only water supply. Underground waters, usually called groundwater or percolating waters, form from the rain and snow runoff that drains beneath the surface rather than over it and is held in aquifers, porous earth formations such as gravel and sandstone. Some states divide underground waters into several categories, such as underground streams, underflow of streams, and percolating water, and apply different laws to each type of water.

Whereas numerous surface water laws had been enacted centuries ago, only a handful of laws relating to underground water had been passed prior to World War II. This was due to the fact that large-scale development of groundwater resources did not occur prior to that time. Underground water laws are extremely confusing, partly because legislation has not kept up with scientific research on the patterns of underground water movement. In this chapter I can only give you a general idea of the types of laws in force today. The variables are so great throughout the country that you must investigate your state's particular laws in order to gain a complete knowledge of your rights and liabilities.

As with surface waters, different types of water rights laws have developed for underground waters. These are the English common law doctrine of absolute ownership, the American rule of reasonable use, the California rule of correlative rights, and the prior appropriation doctrine.

The Doctrine of Absolute Ownership

The original rule established in England drew no distinction between underground water and the soil around it. Thus, no rights to groundwater as a separate entity were recognized. The owner of a parcel of land owned the water within it as part of the land. He could extract as much water as he desired, even if he drained all the water from the soil of adjoining landowners. This rule of unlimited withdrawals is now the prevailing doctrine in all the states of the humid Midwest and East, although statutes have been passed modifying the rule to various degrees in many of these states. The main reason for the lack of advancement in underground water laws in the East is that water shortages are not as much of a problem as in the states of the arid West. Texas is the only arid state that still follows the law of absolute ownership and unlimited withdrawal.

The Rule of Reasonable Use

A few arid states employ the American rule of reasonable use, which is simply a variation of the English rule of absolute ownership. It holds that a landowner can pump water from beneath his land, even if he draws water from a neighbor's land, so long as the amount he takes is reasonable in relation to the rights of surrounding landowners. Of course, this concept of "reasonableness" is difficult to determine, and, therefore, the reasonable use rule has not been applied in many states. Only Arizona, Nebraska, and Oklahoma continue to use it today.

The Rule of Correlative Rights

California is the only state that recognizes the rule of correlative rights. Under this rule, if two overlying landowners use their water reasonably and beneficially, they both must share a shortage according to their respective ownerships. No priorities exist between them. One landowner cannot use more than his share if the rights of another overlying landowner will be injured thereby. The purpose of this doctrine is to insure that all landowners get some water as long as any is available, regardless of how little.

The Prior Appropriation Doctrine

Priority between appropriators of underground water is based on the same "first in time is first in right" rule that is used for surface waters. All of the western states, except Nebraska, and Texas, have some form of prior appropriation law for underground water. Often this law is applied in combination with another doctrine for particular types of underground sources. The sixteen states that use prior appropriation are Alaska, Arizona, California, Colorado, Idaho, Kansas, Montana, Nevada, New Mexico, North Dakota, Oklahoma, Oregon, South Dakota, Utah, Washington, and Wyoming.

Thirteen of these states require a permit for all groundwater extractions, regardless of whether the appropriator is an overlying owner, unless the water is to be used only for domestic purposes or for watering stock, lawns, or gardens. The other three states, Arizona, California, and Montana, only require the landowner to apply for a permit to pump water in a few designated areas.

As with surface water prior appropriation, the date of issue of a permit determines one's priority in time of shortage. Once a permit is issued, it can be revoked if no water is used for a period of two to five years, depending on the state's requirements.

Investigating Potential Well Disputes

Even in areas of plentiful water, pumping can sometimes lower the water table sufficiently to cause problems. Many cases of water depletion due to an overabundance of wells in one water basin area have been recorded. When the basin dries up, all well owners suffer. Legal battles often arise between overlying owners because one of them causes the water level in the source to drop below the well depth of the adjacent user. For example, the first landowner pumps from a 100-foot well. A second landowner constructs a 200-foot well and pumps twice as much water as the first well owner. There is still water available for the latter's use, but he will have to extend his well deeper to get it. (See Illustration 10 in Chapter 4: *Is There Enough Water on the Land?*) The courts have arrived at various solutions to such problems. The second well owner may be ordered to diminish pumping in hopes that the water level will rise, or he may be required to pay the costs of lowering the first landowner's well to the new depth of the lowered water

table. A court might consider any use that lowers the natural water table to be unreasonable and enjoin such use. If the first user had a permit, the second user might be prohibited from drilling a well in the first place.

When you are looking for land, be sure enough water is available for your intended needs, because if you deplete the water source or lower its level, you could be liable for damages or enjoined from pumping. Ask adjacent landowners how much water they use and if they know the extent of the underground waters and the level of the water table. In prior appropriation states, check the county Recorder's office, state Engineer's office, or state Water Agency for permits that have been filed and approved that affect the extent of current pumping and the priorities of other well owners.

Many states regulate well drilling, and certain requirements must be met by both the landowner and the well driller. You might be required to file a Statement of Intent and file for a permit if you plan to dig a new well, dig one deeper, or repair an old one. The work may have to be inspected by a county or state official, and a permit fee may be demanded. The well driller might be required to file reports, or logs, with the state engineer, geologist, or surveyor. An analysis of the water's potability might have to meet certain legal standards. If you are buying land that already has a well on it and if the state or county has any ordinances governing wells, you will want to be sure the seller has complied with all the regulations. (See Chapter 13: *Building and Health Codes.*)

LOSING WATER RIGHTS BY PRESCRIPTION

The necessary elements for prescriptive water rights are the same as those for adverse possession. The prescriptive user must take and use the water in a hostile, actual, notorious, exclusive, and continuous manner under a claim of title. (These elements are explained in Chapter 16: *Adverse Possession.*) A prescriptive use of water can extinguish a riparian right in some states. For example, if a riparian user diverts more water than he is entitled to for the prescribed period of time, he can obtain a permanent right to take the water. Because of the difficulties involved in a water user knowing that an upstream user is taking more than his share and challenging his action before the prescribed period of time elapses, most states no longer recognize prescriptive water rights.

DIFFUSED SURFACE WATER

In some areas, "diffused" surface water, produced by rain, snow, or spring runoff, creates serious problems. Often a landowner will try to protect his land from flooding by diverting a large amount of runoff away from his house or fields and, in the process, damage neighboring property. If such a situation is likely to occur on land you might buy, find out the laws regarding diffused surface waters for your area.

A majority of states permit a landowner to pave or regrade his land in order to alter the flow of surface runoff only if he does so reasonably, with little danger of harm to adjoining lands.

Twelve states, Arizona, Arkansas, Hawaii, Indiana, Missouri, Nebraska, New York, North Dakota, Oklahoma, Virginia, West Virginia, and Wisconsin, follow the "common enemy" doctrine, which takes the view that flood and runoff waters are an enemy a landowner may combat by any means necessary even if his self-defense creates increased dangers for his neighbors. In other words, your neighbor can divert flood waters onto your land, you can divert them onto the next adjacent land, and so on. Although this may seem ridiculous and unreasonable, it was the original approach taken by the courts. If you are buying land in one of these twelve states, you must inspect the land for signs that it has been flooded or is in danger of being inundated by runoff from a neighbor's land. Since you will probably be a newcomer to the neighborhood, older residents might attempt to take advantage of you. Talk to them before you buy about the problems, if any, that result from excess water runoff. This is most important where your parcel is small and is surrounded by many other parcels.

A few states have formulated an approach to runoff surface water exactly opposite to the "common enemy" doctrine. This rule, called the "natural flow" doctrine, prohibits a landowner from interrupting or affecting the flow of water even if he is harmed by his inaction. The theory is that fewer people will be harmed this way. The states that follow this doctrine are Alabama, California, Georgia, Illinois, Kansas, Kentucky, Pennsylvania, and Tennessee.

Sometimes farmers approach drainage problems on a large scale with the combined help of many landowners. Since large areas of flat fertile land would be useless without adequate drainage or flood control, many areas have formed drainage districts. A drainage district is created when landowners in an area petition the state for permission to erect an extensive system of drains and ditches across large areas for the purpose of protecting valuable land. A vote is held in the affected area, and if the issue passes, a district is organized. Private lands can be purchased for easements to lay drainage title and ditches, and if the owners refuse to sell, their lands may be condemned and taken by the government's right of eminent domain. (See Chapter 15: *Eminent Domain and Condemnation*.) Tax assessments increase in the area because of the additional benefits afforded by the efficient large-scale drainage organization, and the price of land within the district generally increases. If your land is within a drainage district, find out what your assessments will be and how your land will be serviced by the district.

WATER SUPPLY DISTRICTS AND COMPANIES

Water companies and districts are organized to supply water to landowners where large areas need irrigation and the available water resources are inadequate.

Irrigation districts are organized in the same manner as drainage districts except that the irrigation district brings water to land rather than removing water from the land. Water costs in a district are regulated by the state Public Utilities Commission. Sometimes a special assessment will be levied by the district, on each property owner to pay for the water development.

Occasionally, instead of forming an irrigation district, farmers band together and organize their own mutual irrigation, or water, company. Each farmer owns shares in the company. The company purchases, stores, and distributes water to its shareholders. These private, nonprofit associations of landowners pool their separate water rights into the company and work together for the purpose of helping each other.

More common today are private commercial water companies that sell water as their "product." The amount of water to be received by a landowner is determined by a contract between the landowner and the company or by the amount of corporate stock bought by the purchaser. If the landowner has stock, his "dividends" are in water rather than money. In most cases, stock can be used only on the land for which it was issued. If you purchase land being serviced by a mutual or private water company, be sure you are to receive stock or a contract to get water as part of your purchase.

A public utility water company may be set up to sell water to anyone requesting it within its service area. This kind of water company operates like any other public utility company that serves a large city. You will be charged a rate established by state regulations according to the amount of water you use.

You now have a basic knowledge of the potential problems that can arise among water users. You can take steps before purchasing land to protect yourself. The seller may not be aware of many potential problems regarding the water on his land. He may never have used the water for the purposes you intend to use it for. He may have been appropriating water without getting a permit and you will fail to have seniority. You should understand what your rights will be before you buy the land, lest you be unable to get what you need when it's too late. You should also know the water problems explained in Chapter 4: *Is There Enough Water on the Land?*

If after you take title you ever do have a water problem that you can't settle by dealing with your fellow water users on a personal level, you may have to hire an attorney. He will probably initiate legal actions of quieting title and declaratory relief to settle boundary and water usage disputes. If immediate relief is sought, he will file a temporary restraining order (TRO) and a permanent injunction to prevent you from having your supply completely cut off. He might also file an action for damages. These expensive actions can be avoided by careful planning before you complete your purchase.

The various laws discussed throughout this chapter are subject to change at any time. Legislatures are constantly enacting new laws and eradicating old ones. Courts are always coming up with new decisions. It is your responsibility, unless you want to pay a lawyer to do the work, to investigate current water rights laws in your state and to determine the potential for future problems.

USEFUL RESOURCES

Local Farm Advisor, Agricultural Experiment Station, State Department of Resources, and State Engineer

Any of these sources should have information regarding your state's water laws and how the land you want to buy is affected by them. The addresses of the Experiment Stations is given in "Useful Resources" in Chapter 5: *The Earth —Soil, Vegetation, Topography*.

Every state has a Department of Resources. There is usually an agency within the department which has specific control over water resources, and which issues water regulations and oversees all water use. The director of this agency is usually called the state Engineer or Water Commissioner. If you write to your state's water agency, they will send you complete information on the laws for your state with an application form for a permit to appropriate where applicable.

The following are free from:

U.S. Geological Survey
Department of the Interior
Washington, D.C. 20240

or from any local office listed in "Useful Resources" for Chapter 5: *The Earth—Soil, Vegetation, Topography*.

Water Law with Special Reference to Ground Water—Circular 117

Water Rights in Areas of Ground Water Mining—Circular 347

Interpretation and Current Status of Ground Water Rights—Circular 432

Ground Water and the Law—Circular 446

Water Laws and Concepts—Circular 629

The pamphlet *Irrigation Water Rights in California*—Circular 452 is written specifically for California water users but it contains information that is useful for other states, including a glossary of water law terms. It is available free from:

California Agricultural Extension Service
90 University Hall
University of California
Berkeley, California 94720

The pamphlet *Regulations and Information Pertaining to Appropriation of Water* discusses how to apply for a permit and what information is required by the state. This pamphlet specifically applies to California but is a good example of these types of laws throughout the country. It is available free from:

State Water Resources Control Board
Room 1140
Resources Building
1416 Ninth Street
Sacramento, California 95814

chapter 11

Mineral, Oil, Gas, Timber, Soil, and Other Rights

When we decided on the property we wanted to buy we were surprised during our preliminary investigation to discover that our deed would include a reservation of mineral rights in favor of the federal government. The reservation read:

The Seller grants said land to the Buyer excepting therefrom all coal, oil, gas, and other hydrocarbon rights and mineral rights in said land together with the right to prospect for, mine, and remove the same as reserved by the United States of America in Patent recorded June 8, 1928, in Book 24, page 214 of Patents in the Office of the County Recorder of said County.

Mineral rights, oil and gas rights, timber rights, rights to take water, crops, and anything else in or on the earth can be reserved in a deed when the seller of a piece of land wants to keep a right to take these things. Once these rights have been legally reserved, they become encumbrances on the land title regardless of who buys the land. The right to take something from another's land is called a "profit." In our case, the federal government retained, or reserved, a profit to take oil and natural gas when it originally sold the land to a private buyer on June 8, 1928. The original deed was recorded in the Patents Books, which are on public file in the county Recorder's office, and thus it is binding on us and anyone else who buys the land after us.

INVESTIGATING A RESERVATION

You are probably wondering why we bought the land knowing that the government could come in and extract minerals at any time. Before we bought, we conducted a full-scale investigation of the history of mineral exploration in our area. We first went to our state Division of Mines and Geology, cornered an official, and spent the day with him going over technical mineral maps of our area and discussing the possibility of the government ever exercising its reservation rights. Tracing the history of oil exploration in our area, we found that in 1861 the first producing oil wells in California were drilled in a town just 20 miles north of us. The first shipment of oil came out of the area in 1865 when 100 gallons of oil were carried out of the hills in goatskin bags on the backs of mules. Drilling continued for only four months at that location and a total of 100 barrels of oil were pumped. In the late 1800s and early 1900s, oil rigs were put up in three other towns, which are all within 15 miles of our place. None of those derricks produced a substantial amount of oil and pumping was terminated. That activity was the sum total of oil drillings in our area. There was no evidence that large-scale mining of coal or other minerals had occurred. We also checked with the federal Office of Minerals and found nothing we did not already know.

Thus we knew that our land was not another Alaskan oil field and it was the unofficial opinion of the government official that the reservation would probably never be exercised. The federal government always reserves oil and mineral rights when it sells its land, and although it could always sell its profit to some enterprising company which might drill on pure speculation, we decided that the chances of that happening during our ownership of the land were not very high. We also took into consideration the fact that the government has held the profit since 1928 without using it. This reservation of oil and natural gas was the only defect or encumbrance on the title so we decided to buy the land since everything else about the deal was excellent.

In general I don't recommend buying land that has a reservation of a profit in the deed. However, after a thorough investigation, if you think that the reserved right will not be exercised during your ownership and if everything else in the deal is perfect, you might consider buying the land. I have told you about our investigation to give you an idea of the kind of detailed search you should conduct to ascertain the potential danger of a reservation of the right to remove something from the land. You should consider the length of time between the reservation and your purchase, and whether the profit has ever been exercised. Another important consideration is the potential damage that would be done to the land if the profit is ever used. For example, if oil is extracted, rigs would be used until all the oil was removed. They would then be removed. If the right to take gravel is reserved, a whole river bottom might be dug up. If timber rights are reserved, all the trees on your land can be cut. One of the most frequently reserved, and potentially most dangerous, rights is the right to cut and remove timber.

TIMBER RIGHTS

If your deed includes a reservation of timber rights, the owner of the profit can come onto the property to remove the trees at any time. When this reservation exists, the real estate agent or seller, might say that the land has already been logged once and that there cannot possibly be another cutting for a hundred years. Depending on how extensive the last cutting was and on how fast the trees grow, this may or may not be true. Even if it is, you will have a harder time selling the land to someone else as the time approaches for the trees to be cut, and you can never cut any of the trees yourself.

As with mineral rights, if the timber rights have previously been sold separately from the land, this sale is recorded in the county Recorder's office. You should be aware of the special meanings of the words used to reserve the right to cut timber. If the original seller reserved "timber rights," the holder of those rights could cut timber on the land at the time he received the right and at any later time. If the original sale specified only that "timber is reserved," the holder can only cut the timber growing at the time he received the profit. Thus, if trees have been cut once by the person who reserved the timber on your land and the cutting was done after the date of the reservation, that person no longer holds any right to cut trees. You will own the timber rights. If the timber was already cut, the land might look so bad that you wouldn't want it anyway.

Timber that has been cut and is lying on the ground does not automatically pass with the land. Once a tree is cut it becomes personal property, losing its status as real property. If trees have recently been cut on your land, you should be sure that your deed specifically states that you will acquire the fallen timber with the land and that the seller has not already sold the fallen timber to anyone else.

HOW TO FIND OUT IF THERE IS A RESERVATION IN THE DEED

Even if the seller or real estate agent does not inform you that you are not getting clear title to the entire land, you will know the truth when you receive an Abstract of Title, a Preliminary Title Search, or a Title Insurance Policy. Any profit given in a transaction prior to the sale to you will be recorded in the public records and thus will be uncovered by a title search. If it is not recorded, and you do not know about it, then it will not be legally binding on you. When you become aware of the presence of a prior reservation, you should go to the county Recorder's office and examine the original document that contains the reservation so you will know all the details of the encumbrance. This will help you conduct your investigation to determine the probabilities of the profit being exercised in the future. It is very easy to look up the document when you know the book and page number.

RIGHT OF ENTRY

If someone has been granted the right to extract something from your land, implied in that right is the right of entry unless it is specified otherwise. When the holder of a profit has the right of entry he can use the surface of the land in any reasonable manner to perform drilling or other operations for the purpose of extracting the materials that are the subject of the profit.

You will be in a much safer position regarding a reservation if it is specified that the holder does not have a right of entry. For example, the reservation in the deed might read like this:

The Seller grants the land to the Buyer reserving all oil, mineral, gas and other hydrocarbon substances below a depth of 500 feet under the real estate described in the deed, without the right of surface entry.

If the holder of the profit does not have the right of entry to your land, you can refuse him entrance to your property or you can charge him a fee for this privilege. In the above example, if you refuse entry, the holder of the profit can only dig on an adjoining parcel and take whatever is lower than 500 feet under your land. This type of reservation is used mainly for gas and oil, for which the right of entry is not essential because a well dug on someone else's land can pump the gas and oil that flows from beneath your land to the well.

RIGHT TO REMOVE CROPS

If you are buying farm land that has crops growing on it, you will want to ascertain whether the crops have been sold by the owner to another party before you buy the land. If that is the case, then the price of the land should be reduced accordingly. The crops on the land the season you buy might be all that have been sold or the owner might have a long-term contract with a buyer that will be binding on you if you purchase the land. Read any such contracts extremely carefully to ascertain their terms.

ROYALTY RIGHTS

If the title is subject to a profit that was sold by the present owner or someone prior to him, the person who sold the profit probably retained royalty rights to part of the income arising from a future taking of any materials. Try to determine from the recorded documents, the real estate agent, or the seller if any royalty arrangements have been made. If so, and you are considering buying the land, you should attempt to have such royalty rights transferred to you with the property. Then if the property is disturbed by oil drillers or anyone else, you will reap some benefit from the situation.

IF THE SELLER WANTS TO RESERVE A PROFIT

If the seller wishes to reserve the right to take something from the land after he sells it to you, then the situation is different from that which we confronted when we bought our land. It is one thing when the government reserved mineral rights as a matter of policy fifty years ago and has never exercised the right. But it is much different when your seller wants to hold onto some rights when he sells you the land. You should be extremely cautious in such a situation. Why does the seller want to reserve a profit? When he sells the land he should sell all of his rights in it. If he refuses to sell the land without reserving the right to remove something, I recommend that you start looking somewhere else.

GETTING A LOAN WHEN PROFITS ARE RESERVED

If you intend to borrow money with your land as collateral, some lending agencies might be reluctant to help you if it seems likely that excavations will occur on the land. They may feel that you and your land are not a very good risk because your ownership might be interfered with at a later date. You can determine the effect of any reservation in your deed on possible loans by talking to a few lending agencies before you buy. Obviously if a reservation prevents you from getting the loan you need to buy the land, you had better look for another piece of land.

PROFITS BY PRESCRIPTION (PRESCRIPTIVE PROFITS)

I have already talked about prescriptive easements in Chapter 9: *Easement Rights*. Profits can also be gained by prescription. The requirements are the same as for adverse possession

(see Chapter 16) except that the situation is different. To gain a prescriptive profit, the person who is claiming the right must have been removing the materials for the legally prescribed length of time, which is set by the statute of limitations. For example, if an adjoining landowner has been taking fruit from trees on the seller's land under the conditions required for adverse possession and he has done so for the required amount of time, he can claim a prescriptive profit to take the fruit for as long as he wants to continue to do so.

You can discover a prescriptive user only by inspecting the land. If you see evidence that rocks, soil, water, timber, crops, or other materials are being removed, find out what the situation is. A title search or Abstract of Title will not detect a prescriptive use.

RESERVATION OF PROFITS IN THE CONTRACT OF SALE

All reservations in the deed and against the title are to be written into Clause 4 of the Contract of Sale. (See Chapter 28.) You should have a copy of any reservations before you submit your offer so that you know what is not included in the title to the property. If you submit the contract to the seller and omit any reservations, he must write them into the clause that goes with the title. If a reservation not written into the contract is discovered to exist after the close of escrow, the seller will be liable in damages for a breach of contract and you can rescind the contract and get your money returned.

If you know a reservation exists but you want to make your offer to purchase include a condition that it must be removed before the close of escrow, you can do this under Clause 19. You can write the condition in the following manner:

(   ) The removal of the existing reservation which states that _____
_____

This reservation must be removed as an encumbrance on the title to said property, by an appropriate document recorded with the County Recorder, before the time scheduled for closing of escrow. If the condition is not satisfied, Buyer has the right at his election to terminate the agreement or waive the condition.

USEFUL RESOURCES

Federal Office of Minerals (Minerals Exploration Field Offices)

These offices can supply you with reports and maps covering the extent of mineral exploration in your area. The main office and four regional offices are under the direction of the United States Geological Survey. Their addresses are below.

Main Office
  Office of Minerals Exploration
  U.S. Geological Survey
  Washington, D.C. 20242

Region 1 (Idaho, Montana, Oregon, Washington)
  Office of Minerals Exploration
  Room 656
  West 920 Riverside Avenue
  Spokane, Washington 99201

Region 2 (Alaska, California, Nevada, Hawaii)

Office of Minerals Exploration
Building 2
345 Middlefield Road
Menlo Park, California 94025

Region 3 (Arizona, Colorado, Kansas, Nebraska, New Mexico, North Dakota, Oklahoma, South Dakota, Texas, Utah, Wyoming)
  Office of Minerals Exploration
  Room 203, Building 53
  Denver Federal Center
  Denver, Colorado 80225

Region 4 (All other states)
  Office of Minerals Exploration
  Room 11, Post Office Building
  Knoxville, Tennessee 37902

Information can also be obtained from the United States Geological Survey offices listed in Chapter 5: *The Earth—Soil, Vegetation, Topography.*

State Office of Minerals

Each state has its own Department of Minerals. Ask the local Farm Advisor, Agricultural Experiment Station, or Building Inspector, or write to the Federal Office (addresses given above) for your state and ask for the address of your state office.

chapter 12

Zoning Laws

Zoning is one of the public rights to regulate individual land use, without compensation to the owner, for the health, safety, and general welfare of everyone. Building and health codes and subdivision laws are also included in this public regulatory power. Depending on your reasons for buying land, zoning laws can be either excellent protection or a damper on your freedom. An investigation of the zoning in your area is an essential aspect of your purchase.

Over four-fifths of the three thousand counties in the United States have zoning power. Each county is first divided into districts, or zones, according to a master plan created by the local Planning, or Zoning, Commission. The basic zones are industrial, business, residential, and agricultural. But there can be many other types. The following list of some of the common types of zones is a good example of how land use can be broken down.

Zone Symbol	Description
A	Agriculture
A1	Agriculture; residential-agriculture; single-family
A2	Agriculture; poultry and rabbit raising
A3	Heavy agriculture; floriculture
AC	Arts and crafts
AE	Agriculture; agriculture-exclusive
AL	Limited agriculture
AR	Agriculture-residential; administrative-research
AV	Airport
B	Buffer
C	Business; commercial
C1	Limited commercial; retail
C1S	Shopping center

C2	General commercial; limited commercial; neighborhood shopping
C3	General commercial; regional shopping; community shopping
C4	Unlimited commercial; service stations
CA	Commercial-agriculture
CH	Highway commercial
CM	Commercial-manufacturing
CO	Commercial-office; professional office
CR	Restricted commercial; recreation-commercial; community reserve
D2	Desert-mountain
E2	One-family residence; estate; executive; small farms
E3	One-family residence; estate; mountain estate
FP	Flood plain
FR	Forestry-recreation
GA	General agriculture
GR	Guest ranch
H1	Highway
IA	Intermediate agriculture
IR	Industrial-recreational; industrial-administrative research
LI	Light industrial
M	Industrial; manufacturing
M1	Light manufacturing; residential-manufacturing
M3	Heavy industrial
O	Open space; official
P	Parking; parks
PC	Planned community
PF	Public facilities
PR	Park and recreation
Q	Quarries
R1	Single-family residential
R1H	Residential hillside
R2	Duplex; multiple-family
R3A	Multiple-family; mountain resort
R4	High-density multiple-family; suburban residential
R5	Tourist accommodations
R15	Single-family, low-density
RA	Residential-agriculture
RE	Residential estate
RF	Recreation-forestry
RR	Rural residential; resort-recreation; residential-resort
RRB	Restricted roadside business
RT	Recreational-tourist; residential transitional
RWY	Railway
SR	Recreation; scientific research
T	Trailer park
U	Unclassified; hog ranch
WA	Watercourse area
WR	Watershed-recreational

After the county has formed the zones, the specific regulations for each division limit the dimension of the buildings, the size of the building lots and subdivision limits, the density of the population and number of houses permitted, and the purposes for which the buildings and land can be used.

FIND OUT THE ZONING LAWS IN YOUR AREA BEFORE YOU BUY

Because zoning is not covered in an Abstract of Title or Title Insurance Policy, you will have to do some research on your own to insure that the land you want to buy is in an area that permits the specific activities you want and prohibits those you want to avoid.

All zoning regulations for a particular area are kept by the county Board of Supervisors, the Zoning Commission, the Planning Commission, or the Building Inspector. Ask to see the Master Plan of the entire area so you can determine the direction of future development. To determine the zoning for a specific parcel of land you should have its legal description, which you can get from the seller or real estate agent. You might then have to see the Tax Assessor and get the tax or parcel number for the land if that is how it is listed in the planning books for your community. If the area you are looking at has been incorporated into a town or city, it will be regulated by town or city ordinances; otherwise separate county ordinances will apply. In some areas, no zoning ordinance will exist at all.

If your area has not been zoned yet, you will have to exercise extreme care in the selection of your country home. After you purchase the land somebody might come along and construct a bar, junkyard, rendering plant, chicken farm, shopping center, recreation center, second-home subdivision, trailer park, or factory. You can't predict the future in an unzoned area. Don't assume that just because the land is far away from a town or city no ordinances exist. A piece of land can be very isolated and still be in an industrial zone where any big business can put up a factory and you might not be allowed to build a residence.

COMMON ZONING RESTRICTIONS TO WATCH FOR

Zoning law enforcement is usually carried out by the Building Inspector and Health Inspector. They will refuse to issue a permit if a proposed building or use of the land violates the zoning restrictions of the area. The penalties for violating these laws are very harsh, and enforcement in the more populated areas is relatively efficient. (See Chapter 13: *Building and Health Codes.*)

There are a few zoning restrictions that commonly hinder rural land buyers who want to live on their land. Among these are the following:

Seasonal Dwelling Restrictions

Many secluded areas are zoned for second-home summer use only. You will not be permitted to live on the land the entire year.

Number of Homes Permitted

Most rural areas restrict the number of homes that can be built in an area. For example, only one dwelling will be permitted for every 20 acres of land.

Minimum Size of Parcel for a Dwelling

No home can be built on a parcel of less than a specified minimum area.

Flood Plain Zoning

An area with a history of flooding might be zoned as a "flood plain" where all home construction is prohibited.

Trailers and Mobile Homes

Zoning laws often prohibit the use of mobile homes, trailers, buses, and vans for dwellings. Mobile homes and trailers, if permitted, are usually restricted to a specified area to prevent them from "cheapening" the value of surrounding houses.

VARIANCES AND USE PERMITS

If you want to use your land in a way prohibited by the zoning regulations, you must seek a "variance" or nonconforming "use permit." The purpose of issuing such permits is to retain flexibility in the zoning laws so that land may be used for activities that are compatible with the surrounding area or are only temporary. For example, if a trailer is prohibited as a dwelling, you could apply for a use permit to live in a trailer on your land while you are building a permanent residence.

An application must be made to the Board of Appeals, Board of Supervisors, or Planning Commission for a variance. The petition application must show that the intended use will not detrimentally affect the surrounding area or create problems for the regular uses permitted in the zone.

Variances are not issued automatically. If they were, the whole purpose of zoning would be defeated. If a real estate agent tells you to go ahead and buy the property because getting a variance will not be a problem, don't listen to him. Always get a necessary variance *before* you buy. Clause 19(c) of the Model Contract of Sale in Chapter 28 can be used to condition the closing of the deal on your ability to get a use permit. If the permit has not been granted by the close of escrow, you can either terminate the contract or extend the closing date.

ZONING WARRANTY

Clause 18(d) in the Model Contract of Sale is a warranty stating what the zoning is at the time the contract is signed and that it will continue to be so zoned at the close of escrow. This is to prevent the situation where a rezoning occurs before escrow closes that could prohibit your intended use of the land. If the zoning is changed, the contract can be terminated or you can sue the seller for breach of warranty.

Clause 18(f) is a warranty by the seller that there are no violations of any zoning ordinances resulting from any activity on his property at the time of sale, whether or not he has actually been cited by the county for a zoning violation.

USEFUL RESOURCES

The following pamphlet is available free from:

U.S. Department of Agriculture
Office of Information
Washington, D.C. 20250

Zoning for Rural Areas—L 510

The following are available for the specified price from:

The Superintendent of Documents
Government Printing Office
Washington, D.C. 20402

Why and How of Rural Zoning, Catalog No. A 1.75:196/2, 40¢
Zoning for Small Towns and Rural Counties, Catalog No. C 46.8:Z 7, 50¢

Free information is available from the following two national planning and zoning organizations:

American Society of Planning Officials
1313 East 60th Street
Chicago, Illinois 60637

American Institute of Planners
917 15th Street NW
Washington, D.C. 20005

Information on local zoning in your area can be obtained from the county Planning Commission, the county Zoning Commission, the Board of Supervisors, or the county Building Inspector.

chapter 13

Building and Health Codes

I sometimes think men do not act like reasonable creatures, when they build for themselves combustible dwellings in which they are every day obliged to use fire.

—Benjamin Franklin in his letter of 1787 entitled *Building Acts Anticipated*

Building and health codes, like zoning ordinances, are included in the right of the government to regulate individual land use for the health, safety, and general welfare of the people. The county may also regulate the construction of private roads that lead onto public county roads in order to protect those public roads. In this chapter I discuss building codes, permits, and enforcement; health codes and permits; road encroachment permits; and how to protect yourself to be sure no code violations exist on the property you are buying in the Contract of Sale.

BUILDING CODES

The first recorded building code was passed in New York (then called New Amsterdam) in 1625. The law specified types of roof coverings and locations of dwellings to prevent roof fires. In 1648, New York prohibited wooden or plastered chimneys, and inspections by firemasters were initiated. By 1656, straw and reed roofs were prohibited and ordered removed from all houses. Philadelphia went a step further in 1701 by passing a law providing that any person whose chimney caught on fire would be prosecuted and fined. From the very beginning building laws were enacted only after a disaster had occurred. Although fire prevention was the primary issue in the first building codes, today all aspects of construction are regulated.

Building laws are designed to protect people's financial investment as well as to insure their personal safety. Often the appearance of a structure will be regulated, and unusually designed houses will be discouraged. (I talk more about this later in this chapter.)

Today most building regulations throughout the United States are based on the Uniform

153

Building Code, which was established by the International Conference of Building Officials (ICBO) in 1927. The Uniform Building Code's stated purpose is to prevent people from being hurt physically or financially by providing minimum uniform standards of building construction.

The Uniform Building Code sets standards for: foundations, building materials, design, size and location of rooms, means of exits, windows and ventilation, fireproofing in construction, load and stress of materials for particular purposes, chimneys, stairways and guards, sanitary equipment, plumbing, and electricity. Reprinted here are some requirements from the Uniform Building Code which are a good example of the kind of details covered by the codes.

1. With each application for a building permit, two sets of plans for construction shall be submitted.
2. Plans shall be drawn to scale upon substantial paper and shall be of sufficient clarity to indicate the nature and extent of the work proposed and show in detail that it will conform to the provision of the uniform building codes.
3. Plans shall include a plot showing the location of the proposed building and of every existing building on the property.
4. Minimum room sizes:
   a. At least one room of 120 sq. ft.
   b. Rooms used for both cooking and living or living and sleeping at least 150 sq. ft.
   c. Rooms used for sleeping two persons—90 sq. ft. Each additional person—50 sq. ft.
   d. Kitchen at least 50 sq. ft.
5. Minimum horizontal dimension of any habitable room shall be 7'–0". Minimum ceiling height in habitable rooms, service rooms, and toilet rooms shall be 7'–6". Where sloping ceilings occur, the required ceiling height shall be provided in at least 50% of the room and no portion of any room having a ceiling height of less than 5' shall be considered as contributing to the minimum required areas. Minimum ceiling height in hallways, corridors, and closets shall be 7'–0".
6. No water closet (toilet) space shall be less than 2'–6" wide and shall have a minimum of 2'–0" clear space in front of the water closet.
7. Required window area and opening:
   a. Bathrooms and water closet compartments not less than 3 sq. ft. nor ⅛ of the floor area, ½ openable

b. Kitchens, rooms used for living, dining or sleeping purposes not less than 12 sq. ft. nor ⅛ of the floor area, ½ openable.
8. Every dwelling shall be provided with a kitchen. No kitchen shall be used for sleeping purposes.
9. Every dwelling shall have the following minimum sanitary facilities: water closet, lavatory, tub or shower and kitchen sink. All kitchen sinks shall be provided with hot and cold water. All of the above items shall be properly trapped, vented, and connected to an approved sewage disposal system.
10. There shall be no opening from a room in which a water closet is located into a room in which food is prepared or stored.
11. The specifications on this sheet are for conventionally framed dwellings and persons wanting unusual type construction should consult a professional designer.

Two thousand of the three thousand counties in the country follow the ICBO standards, although some areas make changes when necessitated by climatic or topographical conditions and local administrative procedures. The local Buildings Inspector's office will have copies available of the area's building requirements, including standards for building construction, electrical wiring, and plumbing.

PERMITS AND FEES

Before you can build or renovate a structure, you must submit your plans to the local Building Inspector for approval and pay the applicable permit fees. If the building is a standard-construction "conventionally framed dwelling" of stud wall or masonry construction, you can submit your own plans. The inspector will examine the plans for compliance with the codes. If they are suitable, they will be approved. Then you pay a permit fee based on the number of square feet in the building. There is a standard fee list for each area that you can see before paying a fee. At the time plans are approved, one-half of the stated building fee must be paid.

Other permits must be obtained for plumbing and electrical facilities and additional fees paid. These fees are based on the number of outlets to be built into the dwelling.

INSPECTIONS AND CERTIFICATION OF OCCUPATION

Once your plans are approved and a permit is issued you can build the house yourself. The law does not require you to hire professional builders. During construction many building departments make four inspections. The first is to look at the foundation before it is laid. The second is a frame inspection after the roof framing and basing are in place and pipes, chimneys, and vents are complete. The third is the wall inspection before plastering or siding is commenced. The fourth, and final, inspection comes after the building is completed and ready for occupancy. Many rural areas only require a single inspection after the house is completed.

Before a home can be lived in and after the final inspection, the building department will often be required to issue a Certificate of Occupancy. If you are buying a newly constructed house, be sure it has been certified properly.

GETTING AN UNCONVENTIONAL STRUCTURE APPROVED

If you intend to build an unusually designed dwelling, you will be required to write to the International Conference of Building Officials (see Useful Resources at the end of this chapter) to see if they have any approved plans for such a structure. They have approved standard plans for common unconventional designs, such as domes and round houses. In most areas, to get approval of an unconventional design, you must have specific plans drawn up by a licensed engineer or contractor.

TEST FOR STRUCTURAL STRENGTH

The Uniform Building Code provides that if a structure does not meet normal code requirements, the local Building Inspector may conduct a test for structural strength on the building before it can be approved. In many cases,

you will have to hire a structural engineer to conduct these tests to the satisfaction of the building department. Because of the growing popularity of domes, some companies have conducted strength tests on plywood domes. If you plan a dome, write for the results of tests undertaken by the following three companies:

> H. C. Nutting Company
> 4120 Airport Road
> Cincinnati, Ohio 45226
>
> Dyna Domes
> 22226 N. 23rd Avenue
> Phoenix, Arizona 85027
>
> Cathedralite Domes
> P.O. Box B
> Daly City, California 94015

Thus far, the ICBO has approved only the Cathedralite Dome design. Cathedralite sells a set of dome plans that will get automatic approval from any Building Inspector working under the Uniform Building Code. The reason for this is that the ICBO has already tested the design and approved it. (However, I do not endorse their designs in any way.) Most Building Inspectors have not had the experience of dealing with a dome and thus won't accept anything other than ICBO approved plans. But you must check with your local department to see what their attitude is. If you can convince an inspector you know what you are doing, you will be able to get approval for a dome or other unconventional design.

TEMPORARY DWELLINGS

If you want to buy land but don't have the money to put up a house right away, most counties allow you to live in temporary dwellings while building a permanent dwelling. In some areas, the Building Inspector does not have jurisdiction to regulate any "temporary dwellings" or canvas structures, such as tents or tepees. A tent usually means that 25 percent or more of the walls and roof are covered by canvas or other fabric.

If you have a bus, van, camper, or trailer, you can usually live in it on isolated land indefinitely except where zoning and building restrictions are strictly enforced.

LAND THAT HAS STRUCTURES ON IT

If you want to purchase land with a structure already on it, you should be sure that it has been approved and that it meets current building and health code standards.

Two problems can arise when you buy an older house. The first occurs if the structure was built to code but is now substandard because the code has since been revised. Fortunately new codes do not apply retroactively to buildings already approved in previous years. However, if it is determined that the structure is a fire or health hazard, or substandard under new code requirements, no permits will be issued for repairs, enlargements, or modernization of the building. The theory is that if you are unable to touch the house as it is, you will tear it down and rebuild according to contemporary standards. This situation is usually encountered in areas close to urban centers.

The more frequent problem in rural areas occurs if a house was built prior to the institution of building codes in that locality and thus was never built to any set standards. Whether you can live in it as is or must first have it brought up to code will depend on your local Building Inspector. I have encountered Inspectors who would take no pity in such a situation.

HOW TO FIND OUT IF A BUILDING IS UP TO CODE STANDARDS

To discover whether a building meets the current standards, you should visit the county Building Inspector and see what he has on file with regard to the structure. You will have to give him the name of the current owner and the location of the land. Don't tell him what you think is wrong with the place until you see what he has on it. He should have a paid permit with all approvals having been granted. If you are talking to the official who inspected the house, ask him what his opinion of the structure is. Then tell him what you are going to pay for it and see what his reaction is. He might reinforce your opinion or open your eyes to some defects in the property you had not considered.

APPEALING A DENIAL OF A BUILDING PERMIT

Every county that has building codes will have an established process for appealing decisions of Building Inspectors. The first level of appeal is often within the Building Codes Department itself where a Board of Appeals will hear your request for a modification of a specific ordinance. You must present your situation and explain why it is impractical for you to comply with the code. For example, you might have to completely rebuild an older house to meet the codes, or you might be located far from any other buildings and thus your structure will not decrease the value of surrounding buildings. In most cases, it will be difficult to convince the board why it is not practical for you to comply with the ordinance, but it is always worth a try if you feel you are being harassed. You should use the same method for preparing your case as that used for a tax appeal. (See Chapter 17: *Taxes and Assessments*.) If the appeal fails, you will probably have to go to court, which involves the expenditure of time and money.

Some people choose to ignore the codes and permit requirements altogether. I have been in many places where enforcement is insignificant. However, every area of the country is gradually becoming more efficiently regulated on all levels. Even if you manage to avoid the Building Inspector now, when you decide to sell your property in five or ten years, your buyers might not be willing to pay a good price for a structure that was not approved. Meeting code requirements in rural areas is often so easy that it is really only a matter of paying the fees.

PENALTIES

The Uniform Building Code establishes penalties for violation of the code in the following manner:

Any person, firm, or corporation violating any any of the provisions of this Code shall be deemed guilty of a misdemeanor and each such person shall be deemed guilty of a separate offense for each and every day or portion thereof during which any violation of any of the provisions of this Code is committed, continued, or permitted, and upon the conviction of any such violation such person shall be punishable by a fine of not more than $300, or by imprisonment for not more than 90 days, or by both such fine and imprisonment.

In addition:

Where work for which a permit is required by this Code is started or proceeded with prior to obtaining said permit, the fees required by said permit shall be doubled, but the payment of such double fee shall not relieve any persons from fully complying with the requirements of this Code in the execution of the work nor from any other penalties prescribed herein.

ENFORCEMENT

Most local laws permit an inspector to enter your property at any reasonable hour to enforce the provisions of the local ordinances. If you refuse him permission to enter, as some do, he may leave and return with a search warrant and an entire squadron of enforcers, including policemen, police dogs, sheriffs, and deputies. Sometimes the county agencies use small aircraft and helicopters which scan the countryside in search of new and illegal constructions. By checking the records they know if permits have been taken out on any new construction they spot from the air. If none have, they will pay the builder a visit.

Sometimes the Building Inspector will go to great lengths to enforce the regulations. In one place I visited, the Building Inspector used a helicopter to fly low over an area where many young people had recently immigrated and dropped smoke bombs over the sites of illegal structures. A crew on the ground then followed the smoke to the buildings and issued citations. Obviously every county is not this efficient. But when large numbers of new residents move in, the authorities usually keep an eye on their activities.

The salary of the Building Inspector is dependent on how much money he takes in for permits. If he manages to increase local revenue, he will not only have a better chance of keeping his job, but he also has a good argument for a salary increase. Much of the activity of Building Inspectors and other bureaucrats with a smattering of power is dependent on local politics.

HEALTH CODES AND PERMITS

Regardless of where you buy land, you will have to deal with the local health authorities. They are empowered to make sure that you have proper water and sewage facilities and to issue permits and collect fees. A small fee buys a permit for the construction of an outhouse and later installation of a septic tank. Contrary to popular belief, outhouses are not outlawed by many Health Departments. In many areas, if you do not have adequate running water under pressure to your house and the outhouse is not located within 200 feet of an adjacent residence, you are permitted to use a privy. The following are standard health requirements for outhouses:

1. It shall be unlawful to erect or maintain a privy or outhouse unless a suitable shelter be provided to afford privacy and protection from the elements. The door thereof shall be so constructed as to close automatically by means of a spring or other device.
2. The vault shall not be permitted to become filled with excreta nearer than two feet from the surface of the ground and such excreta shall be regularly and thoroughly disinfected.
3. The privy building shall be made flyproof.
4. The pit privy shall be at least 4 feet deep.
5. The pit privy shall be at least 75 feet from well or stream.
6. All privy buildings shall be kept in a clean and sanitary condition at all times.

Most areas today require that permanent septic tanks and leach lines be installed when a residence is constructed. This is often a costly venture requiring a machine operator to come in with a backhoe to dig your septic tank hole if you do not want to dig it yourself. The required minimum capacity of a septic tank is usually 750 gallons for a two-bedroom house. If you are purchasing land with a house already on it, be sure that the waste disposal system has been approved by the county and is functioning properly. You will save yourself a lot of trouble and expense if you discover inadequacies at an early stage in the proceedings. In most counties, cesspools and sewer wells are strictly prohibited, and even where they are allowed, they are an inferior method of waste disposal. Since these facilities are very common in many parts of the country, be sure the local regulations have not rendered such systems obsolete if they are in use on the land you are buying.

Health codes also regulate the construction of water facilities, particularly wells. Sanitary seals of concrete are required around the tops of wells to prevent seepage, and a coliform potability test is taken of all running water before it receives Health Department approval.

ROAD ENCROACHMENT PERMITS

Some counties are touchy about how private roads encroach, or lead onto, a county road since these adjoining roads, if not constructed and maintained properly, could cause damage to public roads. Problems include automobiles tracking mud from a dirt road onto a paved county road, washouts of dirt roads causing cave-ins and other problems for county roads, and dirt washing down onto paved roads.

Some counties regulate the construction of private roads and require permits and fees before road construction of a dirt road that will encroach onto a public road can be commenced. The private owner is required to bring his road up to the standards of the public road at the point where the two roads meet. To do this the costs vary but often run up to $150–$200, which includes grading materials, culvert pipe, and labor. If you are required to construct a road to get onto your land you should figure this cost into the purchase price and adjust the figures accordingly. If there is a good road into the property you will pay for this "extra."

Check on all road and encroachment requirements by talking to the local Department of Public Works. Often they will have a special office for roads called the Road Division. Find out if the seller has obtained the proper permits for his road and if it meets current county standards.

WARRANTY THAT NO CODE VIOLATIONS EXIST

Clause 18(f) of the Model Contract of Sale (see Chapter 28) is a warranty by the seller that no codes are being violated by his use of the property or by the construction of any improvement on it. This warranty means that no building, health, road encroachment, zoning, or other codes are being violated and that all permits have been issued and fully paid for. The fact that the seller signs this warranty as part of the contract should not relieve you of going to the local departments to determine if the seller has met the required statutes and codes.

CONDITION THE PURCHASE ON YOUR ABILITY TO OBTAIN NECESSARY PERMITS

If you intend to build a house on the land you are buying, you should speak to all the various inspectors about the local codes and have them look at the land to determine if there will be any problems with the building site that could prevent the issuance of the necessary permits. You should know before you buy that you can put a road in, build a house, and have adequate site conditions for sewage disposal. If there is any doubt about your ability to obtain a permit, you should insert the type of permit being sought in Clause 19(c) of the Model Contract of Sale. If you cannot get approval by the close of escrow, you can terminate the purchase and have your money returned or postpone the close of escrow. You must make a reasonable attempt to obtain the permit by submitting appropriate forms.

HOW ONE HOMEOWNER GOT RID OF THE BUILDING INSPECTOR

Many people in the country deal with the myriad bureaucratic hassles, permits, and fees by ignoring them and hoping they don't get caught. A good friend of mine named Paul chose the exact opposite tactic in dealing with his local Building Inspector, who was one of the toughest I have met. When Paul bought his place the largest structure on the land was a big beautiful red barn which he wanted to convert into his family dwelling. Because a barn in the eyes of the law is not meant to be a house, many problems were involved in meeting the requirements of the building codes.

Knowing in advance that he would meet the Building Inspector sooner or later, Paul went to his office and told him what he was going to do. He drew up some fairly sketchy but basic plans, submitted them for approval, and paid the first part of his fees. Then he began to modify the barn and make it his home. The inspector came to make an inspection and then began appearing on a regular basis. Each time he hassled Paul about some aspect of his remodeling job until he really got on Paul's nerves. So Paul decided to give him some of his own medicine.

Any time he began a new part of his remodeling, like a new wall, floor, beam, ceiling, or fireplace, he called up the Building Inspector and asked him what kind of materials he should use, how much he should buy, what kinds of nails or cement he should get, and how he should do the job. After several weeks of constant phone calls, the inspector had had enough. In complete exasperation he told Paul, "Goddammit, I'm not your architect or contractor. Stop calling and bothering me." Paul then sent in the rest of his fees and never saw the Building Inspector again.

As long as you know that your house is going to have to be built to code and be inspected by someone who's being paid with your fees, you might as well get your money's worth. Bug the inspector. Maybe he'll leave you alone. If you're way off in the hills, all he really cares about is getting those fees. As long as nobody is going to see your house and complain about it and his job will not be jeopardized, he will probably leave you alone. The most important element of his job is collecting the fees and that is his primary concern.

USEFUL RESOURCES

All local codes and sample plans can be obtained at your local inspector's office. Check with the Building Inspector, Department of Roads, and Health Inspector.

The three national organizations that make up the various codes will send you any information you want on any aspect of the requirements for house construction. Write to the following:

(Uniform Building Code)
International Conference of Building
  Officials (ICBO)
50 South Los Robles
Pasadena, California 91101

(Uniform Plumbing Code)
The Western Plumbing Officials
  Association
P.O. Box 247
Pasadena, California 91031

(The Electric Code)
The National Fire Protection Association
60 Batterymarch Street
Boston, Massachusetts 02110

Although local Building Inspectors usually distribute the required building regulations and sample construction plans, you can obtain a complete set of the Uniform Building Codes in an abridged version by sending $1.60 to the ICBO for the latest edition of Volume VI of *The Uniform Building Code.*

The following is available for the specified cost from:

The Superintendent of Documents
Government Printing Office
Washington, D.C. 20402

Local Land and Building Regulations: How Many Agencies, What Practices, How Much Personnel, National Commission on Urban Problems Research Report No. 6, Catalog No. Pr 36.8:Ur 1 2/R31/ No. 6, 55¢

chapter 14
Subdivisions

Friends, you are now in Cocoanut Manor, one of the finest cities in Florida. Of course, we still need a few finishing touches. But who doesn't? This is the heart of the residential district. Every lot is a stone's throw from the station. As soon as they throw enough stones, we're going to build a station. Eight hundred beautiful residences will be built right here. . . . You can have any kind of a home you want to. You can even get stucco —Oh, how you can get stucco. . . . And don't forget the guarantee—my personal guarantee. If these lots don't double in value in a year, I don't know what you can do about it.

—Groucho Marx portraying a land hustler in the movie *Cocoanuts*

BEWARE OF VACATION AND RECREATIONAL LAND DEVELOPMENTS

You have seen ads in periodicals and heard commercials on the radio and television about "planned recreational subdivisions." You are enticed with talk and photos of golf courses, swimming pools, other recreational activities of various types, and "modernly designed" homes in a country setting. Finally you are told that if you buy early you will make a small fortune when you sell in a few years. Do not fall for the Madison Avenue come-ons that offer you free vacations, traveling expenses, drinks, and other assorted sucker bait. Let them keep their presents, for they are borne by Trojan horses.

Here's how the developers make a fortune

off of you. A group of wealthy businessmen combine finances and organize themselves into a partnership or syndicate for the purpose of buying and subdividing land for a profit. They scout the country to locate a rural area they think is "ripe for development." When they find a large piece of undeveloped land, their eyes begin to see houses, streets, "Sold" signs, and dollar signs. They purchase the land for a mere pittance compared to what they will sell it for.

For example, recently in New Mexico, a land corporation bought 86,200 acres for $3 million and subdivided it into 86,176 lots. Without building any homes, they began reselling the land for ten times what they had paid for it. Profits from land sales and interest, by the time the last lot is sold, will be $112 million. Their expenses for advertising and meeting federal requirements are relatively minimal.

COMMON LAND FRAUDS

I have nothing against somebody making a profit, but not when it is done through fraudulent means, and particularly when the people who are defrauded are those who can least afford it. Buyers in subdivisions rely largely on what they are told through the media and by the real estate salesmen, and exercise little caution because they are not required to part with a large sum of money at once, but rather pay in low monthly installments. In most cases, the information is misleading because of what is left unsaid or because what is stated is a half-truth. Since this type of misrepresentation does not meet the legal requirements for fraud, it is often difficult to bring a developer to court.

The most common fraud is the failure of developers to construct promised amenities, such as lakes, recreation centers, swimming pools, golf courses, stables, and the like. In small print, the contract they use states that the developers do not have to construct these things until 90 percent of the lots have been sold. After they sell about 80 percent of the lots, more than enough to give them a healthy profit, they simply stop advertising and move their operation to a new development. Thus, they have not violated the terms of the contract, and

you are stuck with a lot in the middle of a thousand other lots with nothing to show for your $10,000 or more "investment."

Another scheme is the promise, which is never made in writing, that streets and other facilities will be installed by the county or municipality once the development gets built up. Most of these developments, however, are built in unincorporated areas outside of town boundaries. The lots are sold, and the streets, sidewalks, utility lines, and other expected facilities are never constructed. The average rural county cannot afford to build facilities for three thousand new homeowners, even with the initial tax gain from property taxes, and many rural areas do not welcome large subdivisions intruding into their quiet communities, destroying the ecology and the small-town mood of the area. In a recent example of a variation on on this scheme, developers truthfully told buyers that the water table under the development was enough to supply one million people for five hundred years. They forgot to mention that the utility company that was the only water supplier in the area had facilities for only eight thousand homes, whereas there were over sixty thousand lots for sale in the development.

Often subdivision lots are put up for sale before they have actually been surveyed into parcels and staked out on the ground, or if they have been surveyed, no roads have been put in. Salesmen will take prospective buyers to a hill overlooking the development and point out in the distance the lots that are for sale. The buyer never sets foot on the parcel he buys. When the time comes to put in a driveway and a house, the buyer discovers that his lot is steep, inaccessible, and without a decent building site. Never forget that the developers' idea of a "building site" might be a mountain goat's idea of heaven. A lot advertised as "readily accessible" might be reached only by foot or four-wheel drive.

Often salesmen will fail to mention that maps of a development are available and will get people to buy lots already earmarked for a future public road. Since this information is part of the public records, the buyer's ignorance is no defense. Anything that can be discovered from the records is held to be "constructive notice" to a land buyer.

Sometimes developers will try to create a

sense of urgency in prospective buyers by using two-way radio systems to give the impression that huge volumes of property are being sold, when actually this is not the case. Although these radios are also used for legitimate purposes of communication, be wary if you feel pressured.

Misleading advertising is rampant. A development might be advertised as "10 miles from town," which is true if you are a crow. For people, it's 40 miles by car. Phoney photographs and artist's "conceptions" of what a development will eventually look like are frequently used in ads. Small-print advertising is another common technique which, though legal, should be carefully scrutinized. My favorite example of this technique is a recent brochure distributed by the Lakeworld Corporation for its new "environmental project" called "Tahoe Donner" at Lake Tahoe, California. In large print, the colorful pamphlet states that "when the first snowfall comes, you'll head for Tahoe Donner's own private * ski resort, planned for family skiing. . . . Because Tahoe Donner is a private * ski resort, it's one of the few uncrowded places in the area." If you look for the asterisk, you will find it at the end of the brochure, where the following statement is printed in the smallest type used in the advertisement: "Lakeworld reserves the right to open the Tahoe Donner Ski Bowl to the public at any time."

The California Attorney General recently brought suits against eighty individuals and firms for a scheme involving "vacation certificates" given by companies in league with land promoters. California firms sell inexpensive tickets to Las Vegas, and while the "vacationers" are in Nevada, they are confronted by hard-sell land salesmen peddling desert and swampland worth a dollar or less an acre for $1,000 or more. Over two million vacation certificates have been sold for the undisclosed purpose of selling subdivisions in Nevada that would be illegal under California law.

The Federal Trade Commisssion recently clamped down on seven land sales companies because they were telling customers that their company's main interest was to provide real estate training when they were actually trying to sell land. These companies were also saying that adverse economic conditions don't affect land values.

Many subdivisions are sold that include a "Lot Owner's Association," which is supposed to maintain roads and other facilities in the development. These associations often sound better on paper than they work in actual practice. The administrator for HUD's Interstate Land Sales Full Disclosure Act (discussed later in this chapter) has stated: "Too often, the Lot Owner's Association is a smoke-screen established and controlled by the developer." You must read the conditions and agreements of any association before buying in a subdivision.

Many land promoters make a huge amount of money by selling land they don't have clear title to themselves. The promoter gets together enough cash to make a down payment on a large piece of land, and he gives the seller a mortgage for the rest. Then he subdivides the land and sells the parcels under Land Contracts whereby he doesn't have to deliver title for many years. He uses the payments from his buyers to make his own mortgage payments. This is a dangerous situation for the buyers because if for any reason the promoter's loan gets foreclosed on, they will never get title to the land. Other reasons why you should never buy under a Land Contract are discussed in Chapter 21: *Types of Financing: Land Contract, Mortgage, Deed of Trust.*

A point continually stressed by subdivision salesmen is the profits the buyer can anticipate when he resells the parcel. The buyer will be told that the developer will buy back the lot if it doesn't make a profit as an investment. Of course, this promise is never put in writing. It doesn't occur to the buyer that he can't resell at a profit until the developer has sold every single lot; otherwise he will be competing with the developer's own salesmen and prices. Even when the developer is out of the picture the buyer is in competition with thousands of other lot owners, all selling basically the same product. Look in the want ads of your local paper if you want an idea of how many people are trying to sell their lots. It's ridiculous. It has been estimated that the average minimum amount of time a lot owner must wait before he can make any profit on a resale is ten years.

Every lot buyer figures that all the other buyers will build houses on their lots and that this will increase the value of his lot, which he can leave undeveloped and sell at a profit when the surrounding land is built up. The trouble is every other buyer is thinking the same way. For example, in California the "build-out rate," the percentage of lots on which homes are actually erected, is only 1 percent in recreation land developments. For these reasons and because land in a development is so overpriced, you may find out too late that your "investment" has turned into a financial liability.

If you are interested in making a good land investment, you would be much better off buying a nice-sized piece of undeveloped land for the same price you would have paid for that tiny lot in a development. You can hold onto it for a few years and then sell it as a whole piece or subdivide it up yourself to make a larger profit. I guarantee you that you will always make more money reselling a 20-acre parcel that you buy for the same price you would pay for a 1-acre plot in a subdivision. The developer, not you, makes the profit on that land.

To buy land strictly as an investment and actually make any money you will have to spend a little more time planning your purchase than you would by simply sending a check to a large developer for one of his lots. It's not that easy to make money. You will have to research the local subdivision laws in your area to see if your scheme is possible and profitable. But if you are interested in making an investment you should be willing to spend some time and energy to make it a good one. This book is not about investments, but it is about spending your money wisely and getting what you expect to get in a land deal. You will always be better off buying a parcel of land in an area near the recreational facilities you want rather than in a planned "recreational community." Most areas in the country now have golf courses, swimming facilities, riding stables, bowling alleys, ski slopes, and the other amenities most people desire. In the country, 10 acres for $10,000 is almost always going to be a better investment than a 1-acre lot for $10,000 in a "recreational subdivision."

The above examples of fraudulent land sales techniques are only a few of the many that have been used by land promoters. You might think that a defrauded buyer always has the remedy available of suing the developer or salesman, but this is often impossible because the corporation or syndicate that sold the land has since disbanded or has gone bankrupt by means of slick legal maneuvering. Even if the developer is available to be sued, a lot of money is needed to hire a lawyer and proceed with a civil suit in court. Most lawyers require fairly large retainers, which the average land buyer can't afford since he has spent much of his money already on the land. Of course, developers usually have several experienced and slick lawyers ready at their defense. Since recourse in the courts is expensive and there is certainly no guarantee of success, your best insurance, if you insist on buying land in a promotional subdivision, is to use every resource and method of investigating subdivisions—which I will now discuss.

LAWS REGULATING SUBDIVISIONS

The first law regulating land subdivisions was passed in the late 1800s and required uniform land surveys. Then, in the 1920s, tremendous land swindles swept the country and more control was assumed by local governments. Many of the laws passed since then are full of loopholes, but the federal, state, and local governments are closing the loopholes and getting tougher as time goes on.

Generally the purpose of subdivision laws is to prevent the creation of lots of inadequate size and poor design, to prevent the creation of building sites in areas where the topography, floods, or other factors make safe and beneficial land use impossible, to prevent the creation of badly built roads, to prevent hazards from sewage effluent and inadequate drainage, to prevent the lowering of property values and loss of opportunity for a good overall development of neighborhoods caused by successive, uncontrolled, and haphazard land divisions, to prevent excessive cost to taxpayers of the county for providing services within the subdivision, and to prevent fraudulent land sales practices.

Not all subdivisions are large planned developments. Any land that is broken up into two or more parcels of any size is "subdivided." Many state and local laws apply to all types of subdivision—a 200-acre parcel being split into four pieces as well as a 2,000-acre parcel being split into four hundred lots. If you are planning to buy any land that has been subdivided for the purpose of reselling it, read this chapter carefully and check into all the laws that apply in your state and county.

THE FEDERAL INTERSTATE LAND SALES FULL DISCLOSURE ACT

In 1968, Congress passed a law regulating all land promoters who offer fifty or more undeveloped lots for sale through the mail or by advertising from one state to another in any kind of interstate commerce. The seller must first submit a Statement of Record with the Office of Interstate Land Sales Registration, an agency within the United States Department of Housing and Urban Development (HUD). The statement must include required information about the ownership of the land, the state of its title, its physical nature, the availability of roads and utilities, and other matters. All prospective buyers must receive a printed Property Report containing extracts from the Statement of Record at least forty-eight hours before signing a Contract of Sale. The Sample Final Subdivision Public Report later in this chapter is an example of the information that must be included in the Property Report. If a buyer is not shown the Property Report at least forty-eight hours before signing a contract, he has a "cooling off" period of forty-eight hours after signing in which to cancel the agreement and get out of the deal. There is talk of extending this period to seventy-two hours. If you want to receive a Public Report or any information on an interstate land promotion, write to the address given in "Useful Resources" at the end of this chapter.

THE BIG BUST OF 1972

In 1972, HUD came down on 450 land developers nationwide for alleged violations of the Interstate Land Sales and Full Disclosure Act. One of the biggest subdivision frauds attacked involved Lake Havasu Estates in Arizona. It all began in 1964, when the McCulloch Corporation developed Lake Havasu City in the Arizona desert on the edge of Lake Havasu, one of the rare lakes in the arid Southwest. Since that time, the subdivision has become a self-contained city of 10,000, famed for its purchase and reconstruction of the London Bridge.

This boom of Lake Havasu City prompted a group of unscrupulous investors to purchase 10,000 acres of desert 40 miles to the north, subdivide it, name it Lake Havasu Estates, and promote it in a national sales campaign. The sales brochures contained pictures of lake recreation and implied the land was near water and would soon have all types of facilities just like Lake Havasu City. The developers and salesmen did nothing to discourage confusion in buyers' minds between Lake Havasu Estates and Lake Havasu City. Potential buyers were shown a copy of the magazine *Arizona Highways*, which contained an article about the fine accomplishments at Lake Havasu City. Salesmen described Lake Havasu Estates as a great city of the future, although it has no known water supply, no electricity, telephone lines, or paved streets, no sewage disposal system, no garbage collection, no hospital, shopping areas, or schools. The only buildings it has are a large geodesic "dinesphere" that has never opened for dining and a portable sales office.

The developers of Lake Havasu Estates easily sold the plots sight unseen to buyers in other states by setting the price of each lot at $3,000 to $5,000 with a down payment of $165 and monthly payments of $57.29. Buyers were given a year to get a refund if desired. Although many buyers did request refunds, none were given.

In response to complaints by the victims of this white collar crime, a federal grand jury indicted nine of Lake Havasu Estate's officers and salesmen on charges of mail fraud, misrepresentation in selling and advertising, and failure to register lots and provide property records to purchasers as required by the Interstate Land Sales and Full Disclosure Act.

STATE AND LOCAL SUBDIVISION LAWS

State and local governments have authority founded in the Constitution to regulate and direct the future growth patterns of their communities. Therefore, they should shoulder their share of the responsibility to protect their land resources from profit-minded developers who not only bilk the buying public but devastate the land in the process.

—George K. Bernstein, Head of the Office of Interstate Land Sales Registration

Most state and local governments are also concerned with the regulation of land splits or subdivisions and have enacted their own laws, usually referred to as subdivision laws. Different laws are required for various types of subdivisions, which are distinguished on the basis of the size of the parcels and the number of parcels created. In some areas, the term "subdivision" may have a specific legal meaning. For instance, in California a "subdivision" is any split of land into five or more parcels which does not qualify as a "parcel division." A "parcel division" is a split of land into five or more parcels when each parcel is at least 20 acres and includes legal access to a public road. The legal requirements for land divisions vary among the states and areas within the states. However, these laws are becoming standardized, based on the federal laws. You will have to check with your local Planning Commission, Board of Supervisors, and Building Inspector to find out the laws that control your area. (See "Useful Resources" at the end of this chapter.)

Local governments usually control subdivisions in all stages of their development. Before a development can begin, the promoters must file a preliminary map or "plat" for approval by the public authorities. After the land is subdivided, they must get approval from the Building Inspector before construction can begin on dwellings, if any are to be built. Before the selling of land and homes can begin, a sales permit must be issued. Finally, before anyone can live in any houses on the land, a Certificate of Occupancy must be issued for each dwelling by the local authorities. (See Chapter 13: *Building and Health Codes*.) Some states also require that a bond be furnished as a guarantee that the developers will complete all the improvements promised to the buyers. The problem is that only the county can sue on the bond if the developers don't follow through on their promises. In general,

the more parcels there are, the more regulations apply to the development.

THE LOCAL PLANNING COMMISSION

The city and county Planning (or Zoning) Commissions throughout the country play a major role in what happens to real estate in their areas. The Planning Commission prepares a comprehensive long-term general plan for the development of land in the area of its jurisdiction. Once its conception of the area has been composed on paper, the group must approve all proposed land developments, using the plan as its guide.

The Planning Commission controls such matters as the location and extent of land use, the placement of roads, streets, and utilities, the density of the population and intensity of building construction, and zoning variances and use permits. When a plan for a subdivision is submitted to the Planning Commission for approval, in order to be approved, it is supposed to conform to the Master Plan. Since projected plans are never permanent, rezoning is often permitted for the purpose of allowing the proposed subdivision to go ahead with its plan.

You may become involved with the Planning Commission if you seek a variance of the zoning or a use permit to conduct certain activities on your land. If their meetings are open in your area you will learn much about the future plans and present attitudes of the local government by attending a commission hearing. More information on the Planning Commission is contained in Chapter 12: *Zoning Laws*.

PLATTING THE SUBDIVISION

Platting is the term used for the process of mapping out the planned development and plotting on paper the manner in which the land is to be divided. The plat must show the surveyor's layout of the parcels in relation to survey marks actually in the ground. Each lot must be numbered, its size indicated, and the length of all boundary lines and the location of all streets, easements, open areas, and facilities designated. Any aspect of the surrounding area affecting the subdivision must be shown.

Many states now require that a Preliminary Plat of a proposed subdivision be submitted and tentatively approved by the Planning Commission. Illustration 60 is an example of a Preliminary, or Tentative, Plat submitted for approval of a four-parcel land split, called a "minor division." Once the plat is approved, the subdivision will almost certainly progress to completion. The plat will include a separate document containing any protective restrictions and covenants that are part of the development, including the types of dwellings permitted in terms of style and quality and restrictions, if any, on businesses, fences, and maintenance of open space. The plat and any accompanying reports must indicate the extent of utilities, streets, curbs, gutters, sidewalks, storm and sanitary sewers, fire hydrants, street lighting, and other facilities to be provided.

Often, if the parcels are several acres or more in size, the developer is only required to indicate a few things on his plat. It must show that each parcel has been surveyed and laid

60. EXAMPLE OF A MINOR DIVISION TENTATIVE MAP

out on the ground. Easements from each parcel to the public road must be shown, a soil report indicating the adaptability of the area to proper installation of sewage facilities, usually septic tanks, must be included, and the available water supply must be located on the plat.

Plats may not be required for all land splits. For example, in California, only land splits in which any resulting parcel is less than 60 acres require complete surveying and the submission of a subdivision plat for approval by the Planning Commission and Board of Supervisors. Therefore, if a seller splits up a 130-acre piece of land into two parcels of 65 acres each, he will not have to file a plat for approval.

Those states that require the filing of a Preliminary Plat also require a Final Plat to be submitted after approval of the former. This second filing is really just a formality. After it is approved and recorded, the Building Inspector must give his approval of any proposed buildings. He investigates whether the proposed plans meet the present zoning regulations with regard to the size of the parcels and houses. If the plans do not meet these requirements, the Planning Commission will consider a request for rezoning or a variance for the development. Assuming the okay is given, the Building Inspector must then approve the buildings.

All required plats must be placed on file with the local Planning Commission and recorded with the county Recorder. There you can examine the submitted plats, if there are any, for the land you are interested in. You should be absolutely certain they have been approved and recorded since you can be refused building and health permits if your land is part of an unapproved subdivision. Always examine where your parcel will be in relation to the rest of the subdivision as indicated on the plat.

PARCEL MAPS

In some states, land splits containing fairly large parcels, usually 40 acres or more, require only "parcel maps," which are much less detailed than full-scale plats or subdivision maps.

The parcel map must be drawn up by a licensed surveyor or registered civil engineer and submitted to the county Surveyor or Engineer for approval before filing. Usually the map need indicate only the location of boundary lines for each parcel and easements from each parcel to the public road. Illustration 61 is an example of a parcel map submitted for a subdivision of ten parcels of approximately 44 acres each.

THE FINAL SUBDIVISION PUBLIC REPORT

Due to increasing fraudulent activities of large-scale land developers, several states now require promoters to submit a Public Report covering all the aspects of the planned subdivision. This is similar to the Federal Property Report required under the Federal Interstate Land Sales Full Disclosure Act.

I have included the entire contents of a Final Subdivision Public Report here (See Illustration 62). It indicates what a public report of this type must cover in order to meet the legal requirements of providing the buyer with essential information concerning his proposed purchase. If you are buying in a state that does not require such a report, it will be up to you to make your own report to satisfy yourself that your purchase is a wise one. You will see after examining this Final Subdivision Public Report that it covers exactly those questions about land that I am detailing throughout this book. Of course, you should double-check the contents of any report, but if you can get a Public Report, much of your work will already be done for you. All you will have to do is read and analyze the report to understand what is involved in your purchase.

Unfortunately, many land developers don't file these reports even when they are required. The state real estate enforcement agencies are usually understaffed and underfinanced and are unable to force the submission of such reports for many years until after much damage has already been done.

You must always demand a Public Report from the seller or real estate agent handling the sale of subdivided land. If he says there is none, then go to the county Planning Commission and find out if one is required. You might uncover an illegal subdivision in the process.

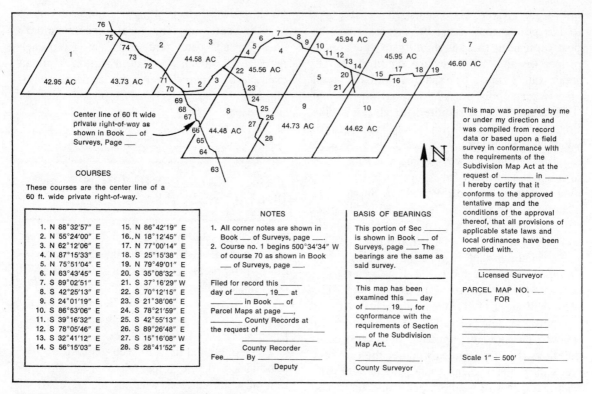

COURSES

These courses are the center line of a 60 ft. wide private right-of-way.

1. N 88°32′57″ E	15. N 86°42′19″ E
2. N 55°24′00″ E	16. N 18°12′45″ E
3. N 62°12′06″ E	17. N 77°00′14″ E
4. N 87°15′33″ E	18. S 25°15′38″ E
5. N 75°51′04″ E	19. N 79°49′01″ E
6. N 63°43′45″ E	20. S 35°08′32″ E
7. S 89°02′51″ E	21. S 37°16′29″ W
8. S 42°25′13″ E	22. S 70°12′15″ E
9. S 24°01′19″ E	23. S 21°38′06″ E
10. S 86°53′06″ E	24. S 78°21′59″ E
11. S 39°16′32″ E	25. S 42°55′13″ E
12. S 78°05′46″ E	26. S 89°26′48″ E
13. S 32°41′12″ E	27. S 15°16′08″ W
14. S 56°15′03″ E	28. S 28°41′52″ E

NOTES

1. All corner notes are shown in Book ___ of Surveys, page ___.
2. Course no. 1 begins S00°34′34″ W of course 70 as shown in Book ___ of Surveys, page ___.

Filed for record this ___ day of _____, 19___ at _____ in Book ___ of Parcel Maps at page ___, _____ County Records at the request of _____

_____

County Recorder

Fee_____ By _____

Deputy

BASIS OF BEARINGS

This portion of Sec ___ is shown in Book ___ of Surveys, page ___. The bearings are the same as said survey.

This map has been examined this ___ day of _____, 19___, for conformance with the requirements of Section ___ of the Subdivision Map Act.

_____

County Surveyor

This map was prepared by me or under my direction and was compiled from record data or based upon a field survey in conformance with the requirements of the Subdivision Map Act at the request of _____ in _____. I hereby certify that it conforms to the approved tentative map and the conditions of the approval thereof, that all provisions of applicable state laws and local ordinances have been complied with.

_____

Licensed Surveyor

PARCEL MAP NO. ___
FOR

_____
_____
_____
_____

Scale 1″ = 500′ _____

61. EXAMPLE OF A PARCEL MAP

DEPARTMENT OF REAL ESTATE

OF THE

STATE OF _____

_____, Real Estate Commissioner

In the matter of the application

(SELLER'S NAME)

for a final subdivision public report on
(NAME OF THE SUBDIVISION)
COUNTY,

FINAL SUBDIVISION
PUBLIC REPORT

FILE NO. _____

ISSUED: _____ (DATE)
EXPIRES: _____ (DATE)

THIS REPORT IS NOT A RECOMMENDATION OR ENDORSEMENT OF THE SUBDIVISION BUT IS INFORMATIVE ONLY.

BUYER OR LESSEE MUST SIGN THAT HE HAS RECEIVED AND READ THIS REPORT. THIS REPORT EXPIRES ON DATE SHOWN ABOVE OR UPON A MATERIAL CHANGE.

62. EXAMPLE OF A FINAL SUBDIVISION PUBLIC REPORT

SPECIAL NOTES

PROSPECTIVE PURCHASERS ARE URGED TO VISIT AND INSPECT THIS PROPERTY BEFORE ENTERING INTO AN AGREEMENT TO PURCHASE.

THIS TRACT IS BEING OFFERED FOR SPECULATION ONLY.

THIS MEANS THE SUBDIVIDER HAS NOT BEEN REQUIRED TO MAKE ANY SHOWING THAT THE LOTS MAY BE USED FOR ANY OTHER USE, SUCH AS RESIDENTIAL.

SINCE NO PROVISIONS HAVE BEEN MADE FOR ANY OTHER USE THAN SPECULATION OF RAW LAND, THE SUBDIVIDER HAS NOT MET REQUIREMENTS FOR WATER, ROADS, UTILITIES, SEWAGE DISPOSAL, OR OTHER USUAL REQUIREMENTS FOR A RESIDENTIAL SUBDIVISION.

PURCHASERS WHO MIGHT CONTEMPLATE THE EVENTUAL DEVELOPMENT OF THEIR LOTS SHOULD CONSIDER THAT SUBSTANTIAL COSTS COULD BE INCURRED TO MAKE THE PROPERTY SUITABLE FOR ANY PROPOSED USE.

PURCHASERS SHOULD ALSO UNDERSTAND THAT WITHOUT THE COOPERATION OF OTHER PROPERTY OWNERS, INDIVIDUAL LOT OWNERS MIGHT FIND IT DIFFICULT AND EXPENSIVE TO DEVELOP THE PROPERTY.

ANY PERSON WHO PURCHASES FIVE OR MORE LOTS IN A SUBDIVISION WITH THE INTENT OF OFFERING THE LOTS FOR RE-SALE MUST OBTAIN A SUBDIVISION FINAL PUBLIC REPORT FROM THE REAL ESTATE COMMISSIONER. IF THE LOTS ARE TO BE OFFERED FOR SALE FOR RESIDENTIAL OR OTHER USAGE, IT WILL BE NECESSARY THAT THEY BE SUITABLE FOR SUCH USE BEFORE THE COMMISSIONER CAN ISSUE SUCH A PUBLIC REPORT.

IN A SUBDIVISION SUCH AS THIS, THE SUBDIVIDER'S PROMOTIONAL AND SALES COSTS ARE GENERALLY GREATER THAN IN OTHER TYPES OF DEVELOPMENT. A PERSON CONTEMPLATING PURCHASE OF A PARCEL IN THIS SUBDIVISION WITH THE IDEA OF RESALE SHOULD CAREFULLY CONSIDER THE DIFFICULTIES OF RESELLING AT A PROFIT WITHOUT A PROMOTIONAL CAMPAIGN OR A SALES ORGANIZATION. HE SHOULD ALSO REALIZE THAT IN ATTEMPTING TO RESELL, HE MAY BE IN AN UNFAVORABLE COMPETITIVE POSITION WITH THE SUBDIVIDER AND OTHER PROSPECTIVE SELLERS OF PARCELS IN THE SUBDIVISION AND IN THE VICINITY.

PURCHASERS WHO WISH TO RE-SUBDIVIDE THEIR LAND INTO FOUR PARCELS FOR SALE OR LEASE, MAY BE REQUIRED TO COMPLY WITH THE SUBDIVISION MAP ACT PROVISIONS REGARDING ROADS AND SHOULD CONTACT THE COUNTY DEPARTMENT OF PUBLIC WORKS FOR THEIR REQUIREMENTS AND ESTIMATED COSTS OF FILING A PARCEL MAP.

THE ASSESSED VALUATION OF THIS LAND PRIOR TO SUBDIVIDING AND IMPROVING OF THE LAND IN CONNECTION WITH SUBDIVIDING IS $5.00 PER ACRE. ASSESSED VALUATION OF REAL PROPERTY IS 25% OF FULL CASH VALUE AS DETERMINED BY THE COUNTY ASSESSOR. THIS MEANS THAT THE FULL CASH VALUE OF A 20-ACRE PARCEL OF THE LAND BEFORE IMPROVEMENTS ACCORDING TO THE ASSESSOR IS $400. THE ONLY IMPROVEMENTS OF THE LAND TO BE MADE IN CONNECTION WITH THE SUBDIVIDING ARE DIRT-GRADED ROADS. THE SUBDIVIDER IS OFFERING 20-ACRE PARCELS OF THE LAND AT PRICES RANGING FROM $9,500 TO $17,500.

THERE IS LITTLE OR NO DEVELOPMENT IN THE SUBDIVISION TO DATE. THERE IS NO ASSURANCE OF SUBSTANTIAL DEVELOPMENT IN THE NEAR FUTURE.

THE SUBDIVIDER HAS NOT DEMONSTRATED TO THE DEPARTMENT OF REAL ESTATE THAT HIS PROPERTY AS SUBDIVIDED HAS INVESTMENT MERIT OR PROFIT POTENTIAL TO OWNERS OF PARCELS THEREOF.

LOCATION AND SIZE: In _____ County. Twelve (12) miles southwest of ___(TOWN)___, on County Road.

Approximately 400 acres divided into 20 lots or parcels.

TITLE: A title report shows title, among other things, to be subject to: A non-exclusive right of way for ingress and egress over the existing road lying within the North Half of the North Half of Section 24, and within the South Half of the Northeast Quarter and the Southeast Quarter of the Northwest Quarter of Section 13, Township 3 South, Range 2 East, _____ Meridian, as granted in the Deed dated January 4, 1971, executed by ___(GRANTOR'S NAME)___ to _____(GRANTEE'S NAME)_____, and recorded March 17, 1971, in Book 895, Page 60, Official Records, under Recorder's Serial No. 12663, in the Office of the County Recorder of said County.

The above referred to Deed also contains the following: "The above right of way is conveyed on the condition that it shall be used only for normal ranch use, and there shall be no commercial hauling over said right of way."

EASEMENTS: Easements for utilities, drainage, ingress and egress, roads, rights of way, pipelines, transmission lines and other purposes are shown on the title report and parcel map recorded in the Office of the _____ County Recorder, Case 5, Drawer 12, Page 68.

USES AND ZONING: Zoned for 20 acre minimum (Upland-Recreation).

RESTRICTIONS There are no recorded restrictions, however, this subdivision is subject to the provisions of all applicable county ordinances.

TAX ESTIMATES: If the subdivider is unable to give you the current tax information for your lot, you may approximate your taxes as follows:

Take 25% of the sales price, divide by 100, and then multiply by the total tax rate. The tax rate for the 19___-19___ fiscal year is $9.046. The tax rate and assessed valuation may change in subsequent years. For example, any bonded debt or special district assessment approved after the above tax rate had been set could increase the future rate.

MINERAL RIGHTS: You will not own the mineral, oil and gas rights of every nature and kind under your land. These have been reserved to previous owners in a deed recorded in Book 3 of Official Records, Page 104, and by Correction Deed under Recorder's File No. 3124, _____ County Records.

The right to surface entry has not been waived, and the owners of the mineral rights may enter upon the land at some future date to extract minerals, etc. This right could affect your ability to obtain financing for building on your property.

INTERESTS TO BE CONVEYED—CONDITIONS OF SALE: Grant deed will include non-exclusive right of way for ingress and egress, water pipe lines and public utilities.

PURCHASE MONEY HANDLING: The subdivider must impound all funds received from you in an escrow depository until legal title is delivered to you. (Refer Section 11013.2(a), Business and Professions Code.)

GEOLOGIC CONDITIONS: The State Division of Mines and Geology reports: "Some parts of this area are underlain by relatively soft rock formations. In this rural area we assume that development will be concentrated on the more favorable sites avoiding the steeper slopes. However, if construction is planned on steep terrain in the area, precautions should be taken during site development to minimize slope-stability problems."

WATER: The subdivider does not intend to install any water system or wells in this subdivision.

Existing springs and private water wells are the only source of water in this tract and you will be required to pay all costs to have a well installed.

The subdivider's well driller has submitted the following information:

"Ample water for domestic use should be obtained in this area by drilling small diameter deep wells or, in some cases, through the development of existing springs.

"The small diameter deep wells, in which rock will have to be penetrated, could cost between $3,000 and $5,000, with the pressure system costing between $1,000 and $1,500.

"Some existing springs could be developed with a cost of from $300 to $500. In most cases, a pressure system for this type of well would cost less than $500.

"Well depths will vary from area to area with the deep wells averaging from 150 to 300 feet. The springs should be able to be developed within 8 to 20 feet."

However, there is no guarantee of the quality or quantity or availability of water on each lot or parcel.

The State Water Code requires every person who digs, bores, or drills a water well to file a notice of intent prior to commencement of work and a report of completion within thirty days after the work has been completed. Said notice and report are to be filed with the district office of the Department of Water Resources administering the area in which the well is located. Forms will be furnished upon request by any district office of the Department of Water Resources.

FIRE PROTECTION: Furnished by Forestry Service if equipment is available, from May 15 to November 1. No fire protection is available from approximately November 1 to May 15 of each year.

ELECTRICITY: There are no electric facilities within the subdivision. The nearest Pacific Gas and Electric Company electric facilities are approximately 15,300 feet to the farthest parcel in the tract and the cost to reach that parcel would be approximately $153,000.

GAS: Natural gas service is not available.

TELEPHONE: The local Telephone Company reports that the extension of existing phone service lines to the farthest parcel in this tract (about 37,000 lineal feet) would be approximately $3,750, based on a cost of $10 per each 100 lineal feet of line (with no charge for the first 300 feet). A decrease in these amounts would be made in the event additional orders for service were received along this distribution route.

SEWAGE DISPOSAL: Septic tanks will be used for sewage disposal. You must pay for your septic tank. Prior to commencing construction, you should contact the local health department for specifications, requirements and any local problems.

A General Contractor estimates that the cost of septic tank installation would be $500 for a 2-bedroom, 1-bath home and $600 for a 3-bedroom, 2-bath home.

STREETS AND ROADS: The roads within this subdivision are private. No provision for their repair and maintenance has been made by the developer, and it is not contemplated that he will do so. All repair and maintenance of these private roads will be your responsibility and expense individually and collectively proportionately to the use of the road easement by you.

If you and your neighbor cannot agree on pro rata shares or upon the need or extent of repair and maintenance, it will be necessary for you to appeal to the proper superior court for the appointment of an impartial arbitrator or for the determination of the court as to the pro rata shares.

An engineer estimates it will cost lot owners $40,000 per mile to bring roads to county standards and that the annual cost for maintaining roads as existing at time of sale will be $350 per lineal foot.

Purchasers should be aware and should fully investigate the possibility that the development of the ground and roads in this subdivision may alter the terrain so as to affect access to the building site and the views for particular lots in the subdivision.

PUBLIC TRANSPORTATION: Bus service is approximately 12 miles from the subdivision at the nearest town.

SCHOOLS: County Unified School District. You should contact the school district for information concerning schools, class schedules, and bus service.

SHOPPING FACILITIES: In Wilco, 12½ miles southeast of the subdivision with limited facilities.

FHA AND VA APPROVAL

If a subdivider wants FHA and VA approval so that his market will be increased by prospective buyers who need FHA-insured and VA-guaranteed home loans, the subdivision must meet certain government standards. There are requirements on such things as housing design, taxes and assessments, restrictive covenants, physical plans for the area, housing needs, accessibility to public facilities, and other essentials of a good loan risk. For more information on this see "Useful Resources" at the end of this chapter.

GETTING AROUND SUBDIVISION LAWS

Of course, land developers have found ways of getting around existing subdivision laws. Some go ahead and subdivide without even attempting to comply with the laws, but there are legal ways to avoid them as well.

Let's assume that your state subdivision law applies only to land splits of more than four parcels. A seller wants to sell to eight separate buyers but he doesn't want to create eight parcels because then he would then be obligated to meet the standards of the subdivision laws, which would mean added expense and bother to him. So he makes four parcels and pairs the eight buyers, two to a parcel. Each member of a pair of buyers will own half of a parcel as specified in a contract between the two "partners" as drawn up by the seller. Since there are only four parcels, only four deeds will be issued, one for each pair of buyers. Thus, each buyer pays for his interest as if he were getting his own separate parcel, but in fact, each person is a tenant-in-common in relation to the others and will suffer the problems of such a relationship. The developer sells the land for as much as he would have made had he sold eight separate and independent parcels and he has legally avoided his legal responsibilities and the legal safeguards for the buyer.

A variation on this scheme is the creation of a "commune." A developer with a large piece of land advertises that each buyer will join with other buyers as tenants-in-common on a beautiful large piece of property and will have the right to construct a house on a building site of his choice on a first come, first served basis. Often a certain amount of land will be designated as open space. Thus, the buyer is one owner sharing his land with many other people under the pretext that he is buying into a "community," when, in fact, the developer has bought a large parcel of land at a reasonable price and resold it to many buyers at a tremendous profit. Regardless of how hip and relevant the terms are that describe the development in the promotional literature, there is no such thing as an "ecological, organic subdivision." A subdivision is a subdivision is a subdivision.

The above plan is not usually considered a "subdivision" under the legal definitions of most states, and therefore there are no regulations that must be met. In a few areas of the country state and local laws decree that where "five or more undivided interests" are sold, the development must comply with all normal subdivision requirements, such as plat approval and issuance of Public Reports.

A version of the above idea is the new condominium development, which includes an apartment arrangement surrounded by open land and recreational areas owned in common by all persons who buy the apartment units. The promotional literature emphasizes the ecological aspect of preserving open space. Aside from the fact that this "preserved" space includes golf courses, swimming pools, horse riding trails, and hundreds of people tramping across it, the investment is a poor one since the extremely high purchase price really only buys an apartment. The buyer could take his $20,000–$50,000, which is what one of these fancy apartments in the "country" costs, and get 50 or more beautiful acres of land near the recreational facilities he enjoys, and still have enough money left over to construct a comfortable house.

A GIANT IS SLAIN BY CLASS ACTIONS

In 1972, the Boise Cascade Corporation announced that it was getting out of the rural land sales business. For several years, this company had been the biggest land promoter in California and was nationally known for its high-pressure sales tactics. As a result of six California class action lawsuits charging it with false and misleading sales practices, Boise Cascade agreed to a $58.5 million out-of-court settlement which includes $24 million in refunds to dissatisfied land buyers. If a buyer chooses, he can file a claim for a refund of his money, though he will not see the profit he was promised when he bought the land.

Since few "buyer-investors" actually intended to live in the subdivisions, the buyer who decides to keep his land rather than seek a refund will own a tiny lot stuck in the middle of thousands of other empty parceled-out lots with streets and maybe a few extra facilities put in. As one newspaper analyzes it: ". . . the end of retail lot sales is expected to dishearten thousands of purchasers who expected to double or triple their money through what battalions of salesmen called investments backed by Boise Cascade's reputation." The company analyzes the situation in a less unfavorable manner: "This won't change anything for the present property owners in these projects. . . . It just means they won't get run over by salesmen."

USEFUL RESOURCES

The pamphlet *Real Estate Promotions* is available free if you send a stamped self-addressed envelope to:

National Better Business Bureau, Inc.
Chrysler Building
New York 17, New York

The Office of Interstate Land Sales Registration

This is under the U.S. Department of Housing and Urban Development (HUD). The addresses of the local HUD offices are given in "Useful Resources" at the end of Chapter 26: *FHA and VA Loans*. If you want any information on any subdivision you should also write to the main office:

Office of Interstate Land Sales
  Registration
Federal Housing Administration
U.S. Department of Housing and Urban
  Development
Washington, D.C. 20411

Send them the name and location of the subdivision you are interested in and ask them for any information they have on the project. They will also send you free the brochure, *Interstate Land Sales Can Be Risky*—HUD-15-F.

FHA and VA

The FHA and VA have information on their own specifications for a proper subdivision. They also have separate reports on projects which they have approved and you can ask for them at any local office. The addresses of regional offices of FHA and VA are given in "Useful Resources" at the end of Chapter 26: *FHA and VA Loans.*

You can get a free copy of *Neighborhood Standards* at any FHA office.

State Real Estate Commissioner

Your State Real Estate Commissioner has local offices throughout the state and they can give you any information they have on a subdivision. Ask any real estate agent or planning commissioner for the address of the Commissioner.

County Agencies

The best place to start any investigation about a land purchase, and particularly a subdivision development, is at the county offices overseeing land use in the area.

The following officials can give you the specified information:

Planning Commission (Director of Planning)—is the primary agency in charge of processing subdivision application, plats, and reports. It controls zoning and land use in general, and its information is available to the public.

Building Inspector—information on the use of the land as a "home site," specifically grading, stability, erosion, drainage, and building quality design for homes already constructed.

Health Officer or Department—information on water supply, sewage disposal, and health facilities.

Road Commissioner—information on the quality of road construction in the subdivision, specifically surface materials and grading, and easement provisions.

County Engineer—must approve geological, drainage, and flooding conditions of the subdivision.

County Surveyor—processes all surveys, plats, and maps submitted for a subdivision. You can copy any maps in his office.

Fire Officer—can give you information on fire protection in the area.

County or District School Superintendent—information on education facilities.

County Sheriff—home protection and public safety information.

chapter 15

Eminent Domain and Condemnation

Federal, state, city, and county governments, improvement districts, public utilities, and similar public and semi-public organzations have the power of "eminent domain." This right permits them to take private property for a "public benefit" by "condemning" it. Private lands have been condemned for such things as public irrigation systems, railroads, electric power plants, parks, government buildings, airports, streets, highways, and roads.

A TRUE CONDEMNATION STORY

The following story is condensed from an article originally published in *The Mother Earth News.*

In the spring of 1970, a young married couple purchased 760 acres of fine farm land which was bordered on two sides by federal land controlled by the Bureau of Land Management (BLM). The BLM is responsible for managing 400 million acres of government land. Like many land buyers, this couple falsely assumed that it was an advantage to buy next to government land.

One month after they moved onto their farm, a neighbor told them that the BLM was preparing to construct two logging roads across their land in order to reach the timber on the federal land bordering their farm. Although the couple found this hard to believe, they checked with the local BLM office and, much to their astonishment, found out the sad truth. One road was to run behind their house and right through the source of their water supply. The other road was to start at their driveway and continue on a path between their barn and house, cross over their pasture and enter the BLM land. (See Illustration 63.) Once constructed, these roads would be traveled by huge diesel trucks carrying cut logs from the BLM's "preserved" and "protected" woodlands.

The couple immediately registered a protest against the proposed plans and later prevented entry by a government surveying team which wanted to survey the exact location for the roads. The government was forced to go to federal court to formally request condemnation actions against that part of the property needed for the road. They argued that they had to cross the farm rather than choose an alternative route because "the proposed roads are the easiest and cheapest routes for the logging companies." The court granted the BLM "the right to enter, survey and mark on-the-ground the location of an easement in relation to established property corners, and to appraise the market value of such an easement." In addition, "the United States of America, acting through the Bureau of Land Management of the Department of the Interior, its representatives, agents, or contractors (is allowed) to remove, sell, or otherwise dispose of any trees necessary to such survey work."

The owners hired an attorney who forced the BLM to comply with some legal requirements they had ignored and this postponed immediate action on the road. But, after the government has complied with the regulations, the court will probably grant a permanent easement for the two logging roads. When this is done, the couple will be compensated an amount of money equal to the "appraised value" of the "condemned" land. But their farm will no longer be the quiet and private place they had longed for.

The previous owner who sold this farm probably knew of the proposed plans for the logging roads and was aware of the diminished value the land would have after their construction. He was not legally required to inform the buyers of this fact, and they, unfortunately, did an inadequate job of researching the land

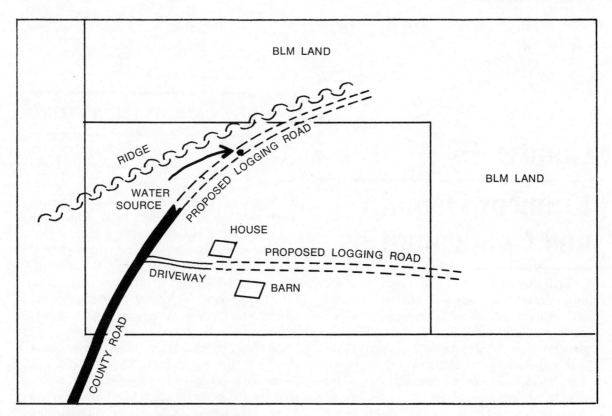

63. EXAMPLE OF CONDEMNATION

before they purchased it. Had they spent only an hour at the nearest BLM office they might have discovered what was in store for their land.

No private property is exempt from the government's power of eminent domain. However, the landowner can protest such action in court, in which case the government will have to bring a condemnation proceeding against him to prove that taking the land will benefit the general public and is required for public necessity. Since it is usually easy to prove to a court that the proposed action is for the "benefit of the public," the primary dispute in almost all condemnation or eminent domain cases is over the amount of "just compensation" to be paid the property owner.

"JUST COMPENSATION" UPON CONDEMNATION

If the entire property is condemned, the owner will be paid its "fair market value." (See Chapter 19: *Evaluating the Price of the Property*.) This is called the owner's "just compensation" for the taking of his property. The amount of just compensation does not include expenses involved in moving and relocation, personal inconvenience, the necessity to buy more expensive land if nothing else is available in the area, and loss of profits to any business conducted on the land. Generally the person whose property is condemned will not be happy about it, particularly when the entire parcel is not taken.

Most condemnations take only a part of a person's land. For example, in the condemnation story earlier, the government only took an easement for the logging roads across the couple's land. Therefore, the government only has to pay them the fair market value of the strips of land they condemn and an amount of money for "severance damages." Severance damages are the loss in value of the land as a whole caused by a condemnation and taking of only a portion of it. The damages are usually figured as the difference between the original market value of the entire parcel and its reduced market value after the roads are put in. Although this might be a large sum of money, it will not be enough to allow the couple to buy a comparable piece of land, and no amount

of money can make life satisfying in a home next to a logging road.

Even though none of your land is condemned, when property next to, or near, yours is condemned and you are injured in the process you can be compensated for noise, smoke, and loss of privacy. Since the value of such things is hard to determine, the affected person is rarely satisfied with his amount of "just compensation."

INVESTIGATING THE POSSIBILITY OF FUTURE CONDEMNATION OF YOUR LAND

When you are ready to buy some land, search out every possible plan for future construction and development in your area. If the land is bordered by public lands of any kind, check with the agency controlling those lands. (The addresses of the BLM offices in charge of federal lands and the state agencies in charge of state lands are located in Appendix B.) Look at their official maps and see what is planned for the land adjoining your property. City and county lands' offices will be located in the City Hall. The local Planning Commission and Road Department can give you much information and will show you the maps of proposed projects. The local and state Water Resources Agencies and the local office of the Soil Conservation Service will have information on proposed water and irrigation projects.

You should be looking for the most common causes of condemnation: roads, water and drainage canals, utilities, and dams. By doing a little investigating you can discover all the plans for the area that can affect your land. Look for proposals that have not yet been approved but can cause problems if they are.

Of course, there is nothing you can do to prevent future actions by the government that have not yet been discussed. Regardless of your thorough investigation, your land might someday be threatened by eminent domain. If this happens, you may have to retain an attorney to fight against the condemnation or for a just compensation.

THE WARRANTY FOR CONDEMNATION AND EMINENT DOMAIN

In many cases, long-time residents of rural areas will have inside information on future condemnation actions to be levied against their property, and they will sell out before this occurs. The unsuspecting buyer is left to suffer the consequences of eminent domain. The Model Contract of Sale in Chapter 28 has a warranty in Clause 18(h) to protect you in such a case. After you take title, if the land is condemned you can win a legal action against the seller by proving he had knowledge of the impending condemnation.

Clause 15 of the Model Contract of Sale deals with the possibility that the land may be taken by eminent domain after the signing of the contract and before the closing of escrow. If this occurs, the buyer can terminate the purchase or get the purchase price reduced by the amount its value is reduced by the condemnation.

If you are interested in reading more about the government's intentions to open up its lands for public and private uses, if necessary by means of eminent domain, you can get the pamphlet *Public Access to Public Domain Lands, Two Case Studies of Landowner-Sportsman Conflicts,* Catalog No. A 1.38:1122, for 65¢ from The Superintendent of Documents, Government Printing Office, Washington, D.C. 20402.

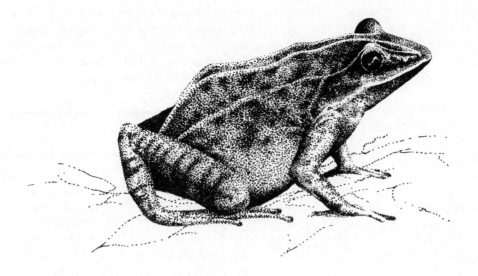

chapter 16
Adverse Possession

"SQUATTER'S RIGHTS"

Under certain circumstances you can lose title to part or all of your land by a legal device known as "adverse possession." This has been referred to as "squatter's rights" and is one of the legal traditions that gave rise to the expression "Possession is nine-tenths of the law." Buyers who purchase land as investors and never use it often don't keep track of their property and finally lose their title by adverse possession. The law was established to encourage use of land and to clear up confusing title conflicts arising most often between owners of adjoining land.

For a person to take your title away from you, his use of your land must be (1) hostile, (2) actual, (3) notorious, (4) exclusive, (5) continuous, and (6) under a claim of title for (7) a specified period of time. Each of these elements must be met by the person, or "squatter," who seeks to adversely possess your land.

(1) The possessor must use your land with-out your permission and must deny the fact that you are the true owner. Thus, if you give the person permission to, or specific orders not to, use the land, he can never gain title by adverse possession. His use must be "hostile" to you.

(2) The person must be making "actual" use of your land. He must be living or working on the land in some fashion. Some activities that have led to adverse possession of portions of land in the past include clearing brush, cutting trees, planting crops, putting in ditches, erecting a building, fencing off a section of the land, and living on the land.

(3) The user must be "notorious" in the manner in which he is on the land. He cannot sneak around the owner's property in such a manner that he could not be discovered and his activities must be visible to the owner if he were to examine his land.

(4) "Exclusive" possession means that the user must be on the land alone. If he is there with the owner or against the owner's specific orders, he cannot get title to the land.

(5) Use of the land must be "continuous" from the beginning of the prescribed time period to the end, although seasonal use for the prescribed number of years is generally permissible.

(6) The possessor must claim that he owns the land, even if he is wrong. His actions will

speak for themselves in this regard. If he is acting as if he believes he owns the land, he is taking the property under a "claim of title." If he ever admits that he knows he does not actually own the land, he cannot claim adverse possession.

(7) The time limit for acquiring adverse possession is called the "statute of limitations." All of the above elements must occur for a minimum length of time before adverse possession "ripens" into title. The minimum period varies among the states, from five years in California to twenty-one years in Pennsylvania. It runs from the time the possessor begins to use the property and continues running even if the property is sold by the actual owner.

ACQUIRING THE LAND

The most common instance of acquiring land by adverse possession occurs when a neighbor unknowingly puts up a fence that encloses a portion of an adjoining landowner's property. If he meets all the above requirements and has his fence up for the prescribed period of time, when he discovers that he has fenced in the neighboring land, he can go to court and get a court order, or declaratory judgment, stating that he now owns the land he has enclosed. Another common situation that leads to adverse possession is when a part of a building, a section of an orchard, or other improvement encroaches on a neighbor's land and this "mistake" is not discovered before the prescribed time period has elapsed.

The willingness of the courts to award title by adverse possession varies among the states. For example, some states require that the pos-

sessor have a document, such as a faulty deed, that appears to give good title but actually does not. Other states require that taxes be paid for the prescribed period by the user in order for him to gain legal possession.

PRECAUTIONS

A Title Report or Abstract of Title will not indicate that a person has met the requirements to adversely possess a piece of land, because the possessor's ownership will not be part of the public records until he makes a claim. A Standard Owner's Policy of Title Insurance will not insure the buyer against adverse possession because such activity can only be discovered by a correct legal survey and by inspection of the property. This shows the importance of having your land legally surveyed before you buy in order to discover where your boundaries are. (See Chapter 31: *The Title Search, Abstract of Title, and Title Insurance Policy.*)

If you buy land and discover that an adjoining landowner or anyone else is using the land, you must take immediate action to insure that you do not lose title to all or part of the property.

Adverse possession involves taking title to a piece of land. There is a similar legal right that can be gained to allow a person to take substances, such as water, minerals, and timber, from another person's land. This is called a prescriptive profit or prescriptive right. (See Chapter 10: *Water Rights,* and Chapter 11: *Mineral, Oil, Gas, Timber, Soil, and Other Rights.*) An individual can also gain a legal right to cross over another person's land by a method called a prescriptive easement or easement by prescription. (See Chapter 9: *Easement Rights.*)

chapter 17

Taxes and Assessments

YOU CAN'T LIVE ON THE LAND FOR FREE, EVEN IF IT'S PAID FOR

The tradition of taxing a person on the basis of the land he owns began toward the end of the Middle Ages. The idea was that taxes should be paid by those who could afford them. Up until the last one hundred years most people earned the greatest part of their income from agriculture, and the amount and quality of land a person owned was the most visible and reliable measurement of his wealth. Since land is difficult to hide, unlike stocks, bonds, money, and other personal property, it became an easy target for governments needing to raise money to run their operations.

REAL ESTATE TAXES ON LAND AND IMPROVEMENTS

The purpose of taxes is to pay for services provided to people living within the taxed area. The police and fire departments, hospitals, schools, libraries, street and sidewalk maintenance, recreational facilities, local government, and other public services are supported largely by property taxes. The Commerce Department's figures for 1972 show that property taxes brought in $38 billion, which was an increase of 18 percent over the previous year's total. There is no doubt that these taxes will continue to increase at an even greater rate in the future.

Fewer government services are provided the

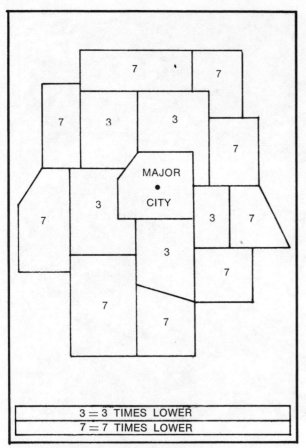

3 = 3 TIMES LOWER
7 = 7 TIMES LOWER

64. AMOUNT TAXES DROP IN COUNTIES SURROUNDING LARGE CITIES

farther away you are from large population centers, and the taxes drop accordingly. A recent study by the United States Department of Agriculture found that taxes on agricultural land in counties with a major city are three times higher than in the nearest neighboring counties and seven times higher than in the next group of counties. (See Illustration 64.)

Your local taxes may include a tax on real property (land and structures), a tax on personal property (appliances, machinery, etc.), special assessment liens, special district taxes, and possibly some others. There is no federal real property tax. The county Tax Assessor maintains all the tax records in each county and can give you information on all local taxes you will be responsible for. The assessor also determines the value of each parcel of property for taxes levied on it. The county Tax Collector, Treasurer, or other officer is responsible for collecting the tax. State laws specify when tax installments are due and what exemptions will be allowed.

APPRAISED VALUE (FAIR MARKET OR FULL CASH VALUE)

The Tax Assessor must appraise the "fair market value" or "full cash value" of land in his county each year for the purpose of levying taxes on it. This value is supposed to represent the amount of cash or its equivalent that the property would bring if it were put up for sale on the current market under conditions in which a willing buyer and seller knew all the facts of the situation. The assessor uses the same general standards for appraising the property as I outline in Chapter 19: *Evaluating the Price of the Property*. The basic method is the comparison analysis.

The assessor knows what property is sold each year by using the county Recorder's Deed Index. He determines the sale price from tax stamps and the amount of transfer taxes paid, questionnaires sent to new buyers, and personal interviews with real estate agents. If he knows what a parcel sells for, he knows what its fair market value is. Those parcels in the surrounding area that are not sold are compared to the land that is sold. If the property is similar, then it will be assumed that the unsold land has the same value as the sold land.

For example, if a 20-acre parcel with a $20,000 house on it sells in 1972 for $30,000, a similar 20-acre parcel with a $20,000 house on it that is located a half-mile away, and that has not changed hands in ten years, will be appraised at, or near, $30,000 under the comparison test. Of course, this is a very simple example, but it approximates the method used. Appraising property is not an exact science but uniformity is supposed to be the goal of every appraiser.

In areas where most of the land is undeveloped, the assessor looks at current market conditions and establishes a set market value for an acre of land. For instance, all land in a 100-square-mile area might be appraised at $50 per acre. Then the improvements on each parcel are examined and given separate appraisals. Conventional buildings are appraised higher than unusual structures, and older houses have a depreciated value placed on them. Since the assessor cannot look at all land each year, a parcel might have the same appraisal for several years regardless of improvements. But in many areas, the appraiser is notified every time a construction permit is issued and he makes a point to visit the land and reassess its value based on the new improvements being constructed.

After the Tax Assessor appraises the property, your final tax is determined according to the property's assessed value and the current tax rate.

ASSESSED VALUE

The assessed value is some percentage of the appraised value, usually 20–50 percent although it can be 100 percent. The percentage is called the "assessment ratio." For example, if a county bases its property tax on an assessment ratio of 25 percent, if the Tax Assessor determines that a piece of land has a fair market value of $20,000, the tax levied on it will be based on 25 percent of that figure, or $5,000.

THE TAX RATE

The "tax rate," or "mill rate," is the percentage of assessed value that is levied in taxes. It is usually described as the tax rate per $100 of assessed valuation.

The county government determines the tax rate each year by first drawing up a budget of proposed expenses for the coming year. Let's assume your county budget requires $30 million. The Treasurer then figures out how much money the county will receive from sources other than property taxes. Assume this income equals $6 million. This amount is subtracted from the total budget figure, and the remaining amount must be collected in the form of property taxes. This would be $24 million. The Tax Assessor adds up the appraised fair market value of all taxable land in the county and from this sum derives the total assessed value. Assume the fair market value of the land in your county is $2.4 billion. Assuming that the assessment ratio of assessed value to appraised value is 25 percent, the total assessed value of the land will be $600 million.

The $24 million needed by the county then is divided by the $600 million total assessed value. The result is the tax rate, which is .04 or 4 percent. Thus, your county will charge $4 on every $100 of assessed value. If your own property is appraised at $40,000 and then assessed at 25 percent of that, or $10,000, you will be charged $400 in taxes that year.

A Decrease in the Tax Rate Does Not Always Mean Lower Taxes

Be careful when the county declares it is lowering the tax rate. This does not automatically mean your taxes will be lowered. If the percentage used to determine assessed value increases at the same time the tax rate decreases, your taxes may actually be greater. This is a common tax ploy. Compare these two examples:

1. Tax rate in 1973   12% ($12 per $100 of assessed value)

   Assessment Ratio (assessed value to appraised value)   20%

   True value of property $20,000

   Assessed value (20%) $4,000

   Tax rate times assessed value ($4,000 × .12) $480 in taxes will be due

2. Tax rate (lowered) in 1974   10% ($10 per $100 of assessed value)

   Assessment Ratio (assessed value to appraised value)   25%

   True value of property $20,000

   Assessed value (25%) $5,000

   Tax rate times assessed value ($5,000 × .10) $500 in taxes will be due

Even though the tax rate is lowered, taxes increase by $20 because the assessment ratio is increased.

PROPERTY TAXES ON TIMBER, MINERALS, AND WATER RIGHTS

Your real property tax will be based on the value of the minerals, standing timber, water, and other permanent fixtures on the land as well as the land itself. The value of each of these things, however, is often determined separately and then added to the value of the bare land to find the overall worth of the property.

Standing Timber

To determine the value of standing timber on land for tax purposes, a survey, often called a "county cruise," is made of the trees on the property. Sometimes the survey will group several parcels together and evaluate the timber on a large geographical area. In that case, the timber tax assessment for each separate parcel is based on the value of the timber on the area as a whole, with no consideration given to the physical condition and accessibility of the timber. Usually, however, Tax Assessors rely on information supplied by the timber owners themselves, which is then corroborated by aerial photos and field sampling.

Only merchantable timber, mature trees capable of being cut and sold at the time of assessment, are considered. The definition of a mature tree varies, depending on the state's law. In California, a stand of trees can be declared mature forty years after the time of planting or removal of the original timber growth, or when its average quality and volume per acre are at least equal to the quality and volume of those timber stands in the area which are being converted into wood products. Values are usually determined by analyzing timber sales in the general area of the land.

Many landowners are forced to cut their trees to eliminate the excessive tax burden, which is the reason timber is taxed. If every rural landowner left his trees standing to provide beauty, preserve the soil, and maintain the water table, the lumber industry would have a diminished source of timber. Although lumber companies own much of their own land, once it is logged it is worthless to them for many years until the second or third growth develops sufficiently to be logged again. Often after their land is logged, they subdivide and sell it. Forty years later, when the trees are ready to be cut again, the government begins taxing for marketable timber, regardless of whether the owner is cutting the trees. If the landowner cannot afford to pay the increased

real property tax, the lumber companies are back in business with that same piece of land, or the subdivision developers take it over. The factors of taxation in this situation are analogous to those that are causing vast farm acreage to be sold to developers by farmers who can no longer pay the exorbitant taxes. This is the main reason some states have enacted preferential assessment systems, which I discuss later in this chapter. As timber supplies diminish further in the future, the value of timber will increase and many more property owners will be forced to log in order to be able to pay the increasing taxes on their land.

Ask the local Tax Assessor how timber is taxed in your county. He should show you a copy of the law regarding valuation of timber for tax purposes. Then find out if your state allows an Immature Forest Trees Exemption, which I discuss later in this chapter.

Fruit and nut trees are also assessed as part of the real property. If they are planted on a noncommercial basis, they increase the value of the property from the time they are planted. If they are part of a systematic planting in an orchard for commercial purposes, they may be exempt from taxation for a specified number of years. For example, in California fruit- and nut-bearing trees that have been planted less than four years are tax exempt.

Minerals

The value of minerals on your property will probably be slight and, therefore, have little effect on the real property tax. However, where the land has some proven mining value, the added tax assessment might be very high.

Water Rights

In states that recognize riparian rights, the real property tax assessment will usually include the value of any riparian rights that go with the land. In appropriation states the value of the right to take the water might be assessed differently. However it is done, the right of a landowner to take and use water on his land increases the value and, therefore, the property taxes. If water rights are shared with others, the value and taxes should be diminished somewhat. (See Chapter 10: *Water Rights.*)

PERSONAL PROPERTY TAXES

Over half of the states in the country levy a tax on personal property. Although this tax mainly affects businesses, certain household items and farm animals may be taxed in your area. However, most household furnishings and personal effects are exempt from the tax, as are automobiles. Although many states exempt intangible property such as stocks, bonds, and other "paper" assets, many areas do not exempt such intangibles as notes, deeds of trust, and mortgages.

SCHOOL TAXES

School taxes, like the general real property tax, are levied according to the value of your land. The tax rate may be different than the tax rate used for the general real property taxes, however. Every school district has its own methods but it is common to include school taxes within the general property tax bill. Check with the Tax Assessor's office for information on school taxes in your county.

These taxes support the schools in each district in the country and are levied regardless of whether the landowner has children in school. If the schools are old or inadequate for the growing rural population in your area, you can expect increased school taxes to finance new school construction.

SPECIAL TAX ASSESSMENTS

Property taxes pay the general expenses of running the local government and providing necessary services for the county's residents. Some services that are provided only to a particular group within the county are paid for by that group through another type of tax called a "special assessment." These usually include water and irrigation systems, drainage and sewer systems, road construction, and sidewalk and curb improvement. These projects can be initiated by the landowners who will benefit by the completion of such construction, or the city or county in which the area is located may have an election to set up a special improvement district. The cost of providing these services is usually split up among the landowners on the basis of the benefits to be received. A separate tax bill may be issued by the special district or the special assessment may be included as part of the county tax bill. If the tax is collected by the special district itself, you can go to the district office to determine the tax status of land you intend to buy.

Special assessments really hurt when your land is within a district that is providing sewers, water lines, new roads, and other improvements for a new, or soon-to-be-built, housing development. Your land may be several miles away from the development, but if you are within the district, you must pay for the subdivision's improvements. Check with the Tax Assessor's office to find out what properties are included in your district and what the district's boundary lines are.

Assessments are usually levied over a period of several years. For example, if a sewage district is installing sewer lines to replace septic tanks, each property owner's share in this improvement might be $300, payable over a period of three years at the rate of $100 annually.

Because special assessments support projects that increase the value of your land, you cannot deduct these taxes from your income tax as is possible with general property taxes. If you are thinking about buying in an area that is developing rapidly, you should expect future special assessments, which will be an added burden on your funds.

The Seller Should Pay the Entire Special Assessment Lien

A problem often arises when a seller has not completely paid off a special assessment tax, or lien, at the time he sells the property. For example, suppose the county has begun paving all the dirt roads in one section of the county. The value of this land increases immediately upon the announcement that the roads are to be paved, although the paving cannot be completed for three years. All the affected property has a special assessment levied against it. You want to buy land in this area and the seller is going to get a better price for his property than he could have gotten before the road paving began. Thus when you buy the land, you are, in effect, paying the assessment by paying a higher price. If you are also to assume payment of the assessment upon taking title to the land, you are paying for the improved roads twice. Therefore, a condition of the sale should be that the seller pay off all assessment liens before the closing of escrow.

The seller will probably resist this condition. A traditional solution of the conflict is that the seller pay for special assessments levied on work started before the buyer made his offer to buy. The buyer then pays for work started after he made his offer. I do not like this remedy. Rather I would insist that the seller pay the entire assessment before the close of escrow or subtract the amount due from the purchase price. Clause 11 of the Model Contract of Sale in Chapter 28 provides for this. But if the seller absolutely refuses to pay the entire assessment, of course, you will have to pay it after you purchase the property.

TAX LIENS

When taxes are declared each year, the county has a "lien," or claim, on the property until they are paid. Taxes are so important to the state and local governments that laws have been passed giving tax liens precedence over all other claims by creditors of the property owner. When property is foreclosed, taxes are always the first debts paid.

Each county has its own remedy for collecting unpaid taxes. The most common method is by a "tax sale." At the end of the year, if you have not paid your taxes, the county will sell your land at a tax sale to get its money. This is not usually as serious as it sounds. Often a municipality, and sometimes a private party or commercial investor, purchases a Certificate of Tax Sale which gives the buyer the right to take title and get a deed to your land if you do not pay the back taxes within a specified redemp-

tion period. The redemption period varies among the states but is usually up to a year. Occasionally no redemption period is allowed.

If you pay your taxes within this period, you will be charged penalty payments and interest on the unpaid taxes and the county will cancel the lien on your land. You will be issued a Redemption Certificate showing that payment has been made and that title has been redeemed. The person who "bought" your land at the tax sale then gets his money back, plus interest, and the county gets its taxes plus a penalty charge. If you fail to pay the back taxes within the redemption period, the purchaser of the land at the tax sale receives title to the property. Always keep the Redemption Certificate, and when you buy land, get any that may be in the possession of the seller before escrow closes.

Before the close of escrow you should examine the Tax Records book in the Tax Collector's office to see if any back taxes are due on the land. If so, find out if the seller can still redeem the property. If he can, he must pay the taxes before the close of escrow and thus clear the title to the land. This is stated in Clauses 4 and 11 of the Model Contract of Sale in Chapter 28. Never buy land with any tax lien on it other than the current year's. A seller should always be able to clear the record before escrow closes, using your deposit if necessary. If he needs your deposit and part of the down payment to pay back taxes, the escrow holder will pay them and obtain a Redemption Certificate before giving the seller his money. (See the Model Escrow Instructions in Chapter 30: *Opening and Closing of Escrow and the Role of the Escrow Holder.*)

PRORATION OF TAXES

Prorating taxes divides the obligation to pay them between yourself and the seller according to your respective periods of ownership during the tax year that you buy the land. The proration date is usually the close of escrow. However, any date you and the seller agree on may be used. Because the owner of the property at the time taxes become due will be responsible for paying the entire amount, provisions are made in the Contract of Sale to reimburse the party who pays the taxes for the period in which he does not own the property. (See Clause 9 in the Model Contract of Sale, Chapter 28.) Tax periods usually extend from January 1 to December 31 or from July 1 to June 30. However, the term used varies from state to state and you should check with the local Tax Assessor for the dates used in your area.

Here's an example of how a proration is figured. Assume the taxable year is from July 1 to June 30 and escrow is to close on February 15. The seller will own the property from July 1 to February 15, or seven and a half months of the taxable year. If the total taxes for the year are $396, the taxes each month will be $33. Figuring thirty days in a month, the taxes come to $1.11 per day. The seller will owe $231 for seven months and $16.65 for the fifteen days of February, equaling $247.65 as his share of the proration. The buyer then owes $148.35 to make the total tax of $396. Thus, if the seller has already paid the taxes for the entire year, the buyer will be charged $148.35 at the close of escrow.

Usually the escrow holder computes the proration, but you should always double-check his figures.

SEGREGATION OF TAXES

When a landowner subdivides his property for sale, the taxes for the year in which he sells the land will be based on the value of the original parcel. By filing for a "segregation of taxes," the year's taxes will be proportioned among the new pieces of land according to their respective values. Do not confuse this with a "proration" of taxes, discussed above.

Here's an example of how a segregation is worked out. Assume a seller subdivides 120 acres into three 40-acre parcels. His taxes for the year of sale on 120 acres are $680. This amount must be divided among the three parcels. One of the "forties" has a house on it and the other two are unimproved land. The Tax Assessor has appraised the fair market value of the land itself at $200 per acre and the value of the house at $10,000. Therefore, the appraised value of each of the two unimproved pieces of land is $8,000. The appraised value of the 40 acres with the house on it is $8,000 plus $10,000 or $18,000. In this particular

county, the assessed value (assessment ratio) is 20 percent of the appraised value and the tax rate is 10 percent. Thus, the assessed value of each of the two unimproved "forties" is $1,600 and the tax on each of them is $160. The assessed value of the remaining "forty" with the house is $3,600 and the tax on it is $360. Adding $360, $160, and $160 gives the total $680 tax owed for the year.

Thus, when taxes become due on a parcel before a segregation takes place, the buyer and seller will prorate on the basis of an agreed amount specified in the Contract of Sale. (See Clause 12 in the Model Contract of Sale in Chapter 28.) Using our example, if you are buying the parcel with the house on it, you and the seller will prorate on the basis that your parcel represents 33⅓ percent of the land tax and the total tax on improvements, since your house is the only improvement on the 120 acres. If when the taxes are finally assessed after escrow closes the proportions by which you agree to segregate are different, then the seller and yourself are to make reimbursements accordingly.

The best way to find out how the property taxes will be segregated is to talk to the Tax Assessor before the close of escrow and get an estimate of how the taxes will probably break down after the segregation takes place. Let him know exactly what you are buying so he can segregate the values correctly. Be absolutely certain that he understands where the boundary lines are for the new parcels and which parcels contain the improvements. You could end up paying taxes on a house that is not on your land. Since his assessment will be based partly on what you are paying for the property, he will probably ask you for the figure. When you get your Tax Statement, check the assessments to see if they contradict those used under the Contract of Sale.

As stated in Clause 12, you and the seller must apply for segregation immediately on closing by filing all the necessary forms with the Tax Assessor. The reason a segregation cannot be obtained before the close of escrow is because the title must be transferred to the buyer before a legal segregation can occur. The Tax Assessor always segregates parcels automatically when he gets a copy of a newly recorded deed, but often a deed might not be sent to the Tax Assessor by the county Recorder for several months. To avoid this delay, file for segregation immediately on closing.

TAX IMPOUNDS BY LENDERS

If you give a mortgage or deed of trust when purchasing land, the lender will take the responsibility for paying your property taxes on time each year until the loan is paid off. If he left the responsibility to you and you failed to pay your taxes, the land could be sold at a tax sale and he would lose his only security for the loan. So that he can pay the taxes when they become due, he must collect the money from you in advance. This is done by having you pay "impounds" with your regular payments of principal and interest. Thus, you pay the taxes to the lender, and he pays them to the government.

Almost all commercial lenders collect impounds. However, if the seller finances the sale himself, he usually provides in the loan agreement that you are to pay the taxes yourself. Since he holds a mortgage or deed of trust, he will tell the Tax Collector to notify him if you fail to pay the taxes. If that occurs, under the terms of most loan agreements, the seller can foreclose.

TAX EXEMPTIONS

Homesteads and Homeowners

Here is the first good news in this chapter. Several states offer a Homestead or Homeowner's Exemption which allows some tax relief for the homeowner. This permits a specified amount to be deducted from the assessed value of your house. For example, assume your state has a $2,500 Homestead Exemption. If the assessed value (assessment ratio) is 50 percent of the appraised fair market value and your house is appraised at $15,000, the assessed value will be $7,500. You can then subtract the $2,500 exemption from that amount, which reduces the assessed value for tax purposes to $5,000.

Since each state's laws are different, ask the Tax Assessor if such an exemption is offered in your area, and, if so, how much it is for. The taxpayer usually must file for an exemption each year during a specified filing period. The following states have Homestead Exemptions: Alabama, Arkansas, California, Florida, Georgia, Iowa, Louisiana, Minnesota, Mississippi, Missouri, Oklahoma, South Dakota, Texas, West Virginia, and Wyoming.

Veterans

Veteran's Exemptions offer a discount on the assessed value of homes owned by veterans who were residents of the state when they were inducted. The amount of exemption may depend on the value of the home and the marital status of the veteran. For example, one state allows a married veteran to deduct $1,000 from the assessed value of his home if its appraised value is less than $10,000. Your Tax Assessor or local Veterans Administration regional office. (See addresses in Chapter 27.) They will have all the information on available Veteran's Exemptions in your state.

Timber

When the value of the standing timber is assessed on your land, your state might allow you to claim an exemption for all "immature timber," or other timber which will decrease your tax liability. Since the definition of mature timber varies, so does that for immature, or exempt timber.

For example, in California forest trees are exempt if they are on lands from which 70 percent of all trees over 16 inches in diameter have been removed. The remaining trees are exempt from taxation even though some or all of them are merchantable timber.

As with the other types of tax exemptions, the taxpayer must file an application to gain the benefits of an exemption. Once you file the forms, the assessor will then place an initial value on the total property you own. He will then allocate a separate value to the land and the timber, and finally apply the timber exemption to the resulting total.

The permissible exemptions in your area for timber, young fruit trees, and other crops, and other forms of real property can be investigated at the office of your local Tax Assessor or Farm Advisor.

Preferential Tax Assessment for Rural Land

Some states assess certain rural land on a preferential basis to help small farmers and ranchers stay in business and to preserve large areas of open land. Lands with favored tax status include vineyards, orchards, pasture lands, dairies, ranch lands, timber lands, and other large rural land holdings.

Three ways of applying preferential assessments are now in use in various parts of the country. The first method, called the Plain Preferential Assessment system, provides that land that qualifies is to be assessed on the basis of the present productivity of the land rather than on its potential value. The law often cuts the taxes in half on rural lands that qualify.

If you own raw land in a rapidly developing area, ordinarily your taxes will increase because the area's development makes your land more valuable for commercial use. But under preferential assessment, land is taxed as if there were no excessive growth in the area's development.

The second method, called the Tax Deferral system, allows part of the property taxes each year to be deferred by the landowner until the land is either sold or put into nonagricultural use. This method really only postpones your taxes until you can sell your land at a presumably healthy profit.

The third method, called the Planning and Zoning system, allows those lands that are zoned for agriculture or open space to be treated like lands under the Plain Preferential Assessment system. Farms and other open lands that are located in areas with other types of zoning, for example, residential or industrial zoning, are not allowed.

In order to receive preferential treatment, some states require that the landowner have a minimum number of acres and sign a contract with the state promising not to develop or subdivide his land for a specified length of time. Since the laws in each state are different and new laws are being introduced every year, you should check with your local Planning Commission and Tax Assessor to see if some kind of preferential tax assessment is available for your land. The last federal study found preferential tax benefits for rural land in the following states: California, Connecticut, Florida, Hawaii, Indiana, Iowa, Maryland, Massachusetts, Michigan, Minnesota, Nebraska, Nevada, New Jersey, New York, Ohio, Oregon, Pennsylvania, Rhode Island, Texas, Virginia, Washington, and Wisconsin. (See Useful Resources at the end of this chapter.)

ESTIMATING YOUR FUTURE TAXES

Although taxes on the land you are buying may be low now, they will not necessarily stay that way. The more land being sold in the area, the faster the taxes will increase.

The best way to get an idea of what your future taxes might be is to determine how much taxes have been increasing in the past few years. Go to the Tax Assessor's office, find your land on the tax parcel map, and get its parcel number. Sometimes part of the land will be included in one tax district and the rest will be in another. If so, the property will have two parcel numbers. Look up the property's Tax Statements in the Tax File or Index. Check all parcel number records that cover the property. The tax records will indicate the amount of past property taxes (county, school, city, special districts, etc.), when the property was last appraised, the breakdown of appraised value between improvements and the land itself, the ratio of assessed value to appraised value, the assessed value, the tax rate and the existence of any tax liens, tax sales, and other delinquencies. Reprinted here is a typical Tax Statement with all the information you will find in the Tax File or Tax Rolls. (See Illustration 65.)

Compare the current appraised value to the price you are planning to pay for the land. If the difference is great, you should expect a substantial increase in the taxes, because when you buy the land one of the factors the Tax Assessor will use when reappraising the property is the price you paid for it.

Trace the records back at least five years to see how much the taxes increased each year. Any changes in the appraisal of the property,

COUNTY TAX STATEMENT JULY 1 19   TO JUNE 30 19

PROPERTY ASSESSED MARCH 1, 19   AT 25% OF FULL CASH VALUE

PARCEL NO	TAX CODE AREA	ASSESSMENT NO
27-300-57	52-003	8366

FULL CASH VALUE → $ 5000   2680   8680

ASSESSED VALUE → $ 1500   670   2170

LAND   IMPROVEMENTS   PERSONAL PROP   EXEMPTIONS   TOTAL

SPECIAL AND DIRECT ASSESSMENT	RATE	AMOUNT

PLEASE MAKE CHECKS PAYABLE TO TAX COLLECTOR

TAX RATE	COUNTY TAX	EDUCATION	CITY TAX	SPECIAL DISTRICTS	TOTAL GEN TAX
8.13	71.83	101.77	.00	2.82	176.42

SOLD FOR TAXES 67 8272

ASSESSED TO →

PAY THIS AMOUNT →	FIRST INSTALLMENT	SECOND INSTALLMENT	TOTAL TAX
	88.21	88.21	176.42
6% PEN			
COST		3.00	
TOTAL			

YOUR CANCELLED CHECK IS YOUR BEST RECEIPT. IF YOU REQUIRE A RECEIPT IN ADDITION TO YOUR CANCELLED CHECK RETURN ENTIRE BILL WITH YOUR PAYMENT AND CHECK HERE — ☐

KEEP THIS UPPER PORTION OF BILL FOR YOUR RECORDS

SEE REVERSE SIDE FOR IMPORTANT INFORMATION

IMPORTANT INFORMATION

1. Examine this bill carefully. The Tax Collector cannot be responsible for payments on wrong property.
2. ASSESSED VALUATIONS are established by the County Assessor at an announced ratio of 25% of full cash value. Questions regarding valuation should be addressed to the County Assessor,   Courthouse,
3. PAYMENT OF TAXES should be made by mail by returning the appropriate stub or stubs with your payment in the return envelope.
   a. The Tax Collector acts only as the taxpayer's collecting agent and assumes no responsibility for the loss of any such items or the proceeds thereof in transit or for losses resulting from the failure of any bank used as a collection agency.
   b. IF A CHECK OR DRAFT WAS GIVEN IN PAYMENT OF A TAX BILL THE RECEIPT GIVEN SHALL BE VOID AND OF NO EFFECT SHOULD SAID CHECK OR DRAFT BE NOT PAID ON PRESENTATION. (Revenue and Taxation Code.)
4. THE FIRST INSTALLMENT IS DELINQUENT AFTER DECEMBER 10, 19 , 6% PENALTY ADDED THEREAFTER. THE SECOND INSTALLMENT IS DELINQUENT AFTER APRIL 10, 19 , 6% PENALTY PLUS $3.00 COSTS ADDED THEREAFTER.
5. If you find "SOLD FOR TAXES" on your tax bill, it is an indication of delinquent taxes for a previous year and thereafter, as provided by law, additional penalties will be charged. To ascertain the amount necessary to redeem, write directly to Treasurer-Tax Collector,   Courthouse,
6. TAXES ARE LEVIED ON BOTH REAL AND PERSONAL PROPERTY as it exists the first day of March. Subsequent removal or change of ownership does not relieve the real estate of the personal property lien, and the tax collector cannot credit payments for real property taxes unless the personal property tax has been paid or is tendered.
7. Tax Statements are mailed only to addresses appearing on the Assessment Rolls of the County Assessor as of the First of March.
8. If you no longer own this property, please return this tax bill, giving the name and address of new owner, if known.

YOUR CANCELLED CHECK IS YOUR BEST RECEIPT   Complete the following information for your records:

1st Inst. Paid By Check No._____Date_____ 2nd Inst. Paid By Check No._____Date_____ or Total Tax Paid Check No._____Date_____

65. EXAMPLE OF A REAL PROPERTY TAX STATEMENT

the ratio of assessed value to appraised value, or in the tax rate will affect the amount of the tax. Note the assessments made on improvements. Are there any improvements that have not yet been assessed? If so, you can expect a tax increase the next time the property is reappraised.

Don't be afraid of the Tax Assessor or his office. All files are open to the public, and the chances are that the person who appraised your land will be in the office and available for discussion. Ask him what factors he considered in appraising the property, including improvements, recent sales in the area, and the price being asked by the seller for the property. He can give you a rough estimate of how much your taxes will probably increase based on the amount you intend to pay for the land.

In a subtle way, ask him if he thinks the seller's asking price is reasonable. His answer and analysis of the property might give you some valuable information to use when negotiating the purchase price. (See Chapter 19: *Evaluating the Price of the Property,* and Chapter 20: *Bargaining to Get the Seller's Asking Price Down.*) Do not rely completely on the Tax Assessor's opinion, however, because these officials are often behind on current market values.

APPEALING THE TAX ASSESSOR'S VALUATION OF YOUR PROPERTY

Each Tax Assessor is responsible for appraising hundreds of parcels in a given area, and he rarely gets more than a surface glimpse of any one piece of land and its improvements. Often, significant depreciation factors in a home are overlooked. In addition, appraisals are sometimes determined on the basis of who the property owner happens to be. Political, economic, and personal friendships often play a large part in rural land tax appraisals. If you feel your taxes are unfair in any way, either because your property is appraised too high on its own standards or in relation to the surrounding land, you should not hesitate to protest and present your case for reappraisal.

Every county has a procedure for appealing the results of the Tax Assessor's valuations before a body that hears appeals, called the Board of Review, Tax Review Commission, or Assessment Appeal Board.

Grievance Period

If the appraised valuation of a parcel is increased by the assessor, he sends the landowner a card before taxes become due indicating the new appraisal for that year. This notification should include instructions on protesting the new valuation. If it doesn't, call the Tax Assessor's office and ask for instructions on appealing. A form, usually called a Notice of Protest, will be sent which you must fill out and present to the Appeals Board during an alloted grievance period, which might be only a single day. You might be required to speak to the Assessor first to see if you can come to some kind of an agreement. If you do not get satisfaction, you will be allowed to present your case in person before the board, either alone

or with a lawyer. The aid of a lawyer probably won't be necessary.

Preparing Your Case

Your case will be very strong if you can demonstrate that an inequity exists between the valuation of your property and that of other property in the area. Go to the Tax Assessor's office and look at the parcel maps of your area, noting the parcel numbers and acreage of surrounding pieces of property. If you know that some property in your area has been held by the same person for many years, make a special effort to locate those parcels.

Look up the properties in the Tax Files the same way that I told you to look up your own tax records earlier in this chapter. Note what the appraised fair market value (full cash value) is on each of the parcels you are using for comparison. Look only at the land value. If differences exist, try to figure out if there is any justification for them. For instance, land fronting a public road might be appraised higher than other land. If you can find no justification, you probably have a good case for a protest of unequal treatment.

If you know what structures exist on the neighboring lands, you can compare their appraised values to the values given for the improvements on your land. Compare the size, age, and other factors that are used in evaluating the worth of a house. You might discover inequities in the improvement valuation as well as the land valuation. This is usually where the assessor makes his mistakes, intentional or not.

Next make a list of all the factors contributing to the depreciation and "unmarketability" of your improvements, such as termite infestation, wood rot, a sagging foundation, the small size of the rooms, the lack of electricity or running water, the peculiar design, and anything else you can think of.

Then list those things about the land itself that decrease its resale value or its potential for development, such as a lack of building sites, poor roads, insufficient water to support further development or subdivision, the great distance from shopping areas, schools, or other facilities. If you have some extra money, get a professional appraisal made of the property to use as evidence on your behalf. The taxes you might save could pay for the cost of the appraisal.

Making Your Appearance

Carefully prepare your case in writing before the Appeals Board hearing. Make a detailed list of those things you think lower the value of your land and improvements. Make a chart comparing your land to similar neighboring lands, and compare the valuations made on the land and improvements to show the inequity. Refute any questionable statements the Tax Assessor made to you on how he arrived at his evaluation of your land. For instance, state that the amount of time he told you he spent examining the property was too short for a thorough evaluation of its deficiencies. If he based his figures on current asking prices given to him by local real estate agents, refute them by stating that they are inflated prices. Then state a figure that you think represents a reasonable value of the land.

Take several copies of your written statement with you when you appear so that you can give one to each member of the board and retain one for yourself. If you have had a professional appraisal made, also have copies of those results ready for distribution, assuming, of course, they are in your favor. Quote the opinions of several local real estate agents, if they are in your favor.

Your oral presentation will be a review of the information contained in your statement. If you hire a lawyer, he may charge you a percentage of the taxes he saves you if the amount is considerable or he may charge a flat fee. However, because the Tax Appeal Board re-

sembles a small claims court and the members of the board are used to hearing cases presented personally by protesting taxpayers, I don't think you will gain much by hiring an attorney.

After you present your case, the Tax Assessor may present his. When the board arrives at some decision of what your valuation should be, the results will be publicly posted on the Final Assessment Rolls in the Tax Assessor's office.

Since relatively few taxpayers ever complain, you have an advantage simply because you are willing to take the time and trouble to appear in person to protest. It doesn't hurt to protest your taxes. Don't be scared by threats that your valuation might be increased rather than decreased if you protest. This rarely happens.

KEEP THOROUGH TAX RECORDS

Generally taxes are collected in installments during the year to ease the burden on the landowner. Different taxes might be due at different times of the year. Get a list of due dates for all taxes from the local Tax Collector. There is a penalty for late payment, and some states reduce your tax as a reward for early payment.

The majority of tax delinquencies occur during the first year of property ownership. This is due to the following circumstances:

(1) A new owner not reading or not understanding the title report or escrow papers as they pertain to taxes paid and taxes "subject to."

(2) Not knowing tax due dates and delinquent dates on real property taxes.

(3) Misunderstanding who is to pay the

YEAR	TAX DATE	LAND		IMPROVEMENTS		STATE and/or COUNTY TAXES		CITY TAXES		EDUCATION (SCHOOL) and/or SPECIAL ASSESSMENTS		PERSONAL PROPERTY and/or OTHER TAXES	
		Full Cash (True) Value	Assessed Value	Full Cash (True) Value	Assessed Value	Amount Due	Date Paid	Amount Due	Date Paid	Amount Due	Date Paid	Amount Due	Date Paid

66. SAMPLE METHOD OF MAINTAINING TAX RECORDS

taxes—the property owner or his lending agency.

(4) Erroneously believing that property is not subject to taxes or penalties unless a tax bill is rendered.

(5) Not inquiring about taxes until billed.

(6) A new owner not receiving a tax bill because it is sent to the previous owner. Non-receipt of a tax bill does not prevent the imposition of penalties after the delinquent date.

Illustration 66 is an example of how you might set up your tax records. By keeping the chart up to date, you can have all your tax information readily available.

USEFUL RESOURCES

The following are free from:
U.S. Department of Agriculture
Office of Information
Washington, D.C. 20250

Timber Owner and His Federal Income Tax—AH 274
Revised Estimates of Taxes Levied on Farm Real Property—SB 441
Personal Property Taxes Levied on Farmers—SB 447

The following are available for the specified prices from:

The Superintendent of Documents
Government Printing Office
Washington, D.C. 20402

Taxation of Farmland in the Rural-Urban Fringe: A Summary of State Preferential Assessments Activity, Agricultural Economic Report No. 119, Catalog No. 93.28:119, 45¢
Forest Taxation and the Preservation of Rural Values in New York and Other States, Catalog No. A 93.28:150, 30¢
State Guides for Assessing Forest Land and Timber, Catalog No. A 1.38:1061, 50¢

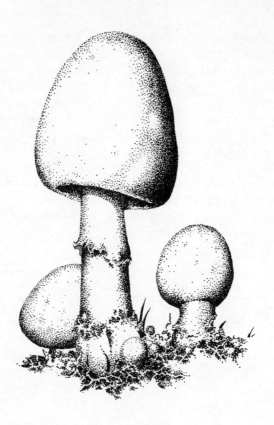

chapter 18

Insuring Your Property for Yourself and Your Creditors

Even if you don't want to pay to have your property insured, you might not have a choice. Institutional lenders always require that insurance against loss by fire be taken out by the borrower to protect a mortgaged home. Most sellers who take back a mortgage or deed of trust will also want the house insured during the payment period. These creditors are concerned that if they don't require you to insure your house, and it burns down and you default on your payments, it will be difficult to collect the money you owe them even if they fore-

close, since the value of the property will have greatly decreased.

If your property is not being held as security, your decision on whether to get insurance will depend mainly on your philosophy and pocketbook. Although throughout this book I have strongly advised that you do many things to protect yourself when buying land, I make no recommendations on whether or not to get insurance.

If you do feel the need to be insured, shop around to find the kind of coverage you want at the lowest price. Insurance premiums for the same amount of coverage differ among companies by as much as 20 percent. Never buy insurance from a mail order company or from someone who sells insurance as a side line. Avoid taking out a policy through the real estate agent who handles your deal until you have compared the cost of his coverage with similar insurance that is available through other companies. Go to reputable insurance companies and individual insurance brokers, preferably in the area of your rural home. Ask around for recommendations. Compare types of coverage being offered and the cost of premiums being charged.

FIRE INSURANCE AND THE LENDER'S INSURANCE REQUIREMENTS

If your lender requires that you get insurance, the amount and type of coverage will be dictated by his demands. The standard condition in a loan agreement states that:

The Buyer agrees to keep all buildings now on, or that may hereafter be placed on, said property, insured in the name of the Lender [or Seller] against loss by fire in an amount not less than the fair replacement value thereof, and in no event for less than ———— Dollars ($———), the policies to be in a form and in a company or companies satisfactory to the Lender [or Seller]. The Lender [or Seller] may require that the Buyer deposit said policies with him.

If you fail to get insurance according to the lender's condition or maintain the premium payments, most loan documents allow the lender to make the payments and then add the amount on to the total debt owed, making it subject to interest. If necessary, he can foreclose on you. Most creditors only require that the property be insured against loss by fire, although some might require extended coverage. A single policy covering both yourself and your creditor can often be obtained at no greater cost than if just one of you was named as the beneficiary. Both you and your creditor will keep copies of the policy.

If you are in a rural area where water is scarce and fire protection is not readily available, you should assume that in case of fire your house would suffer a total loss. Therefore, you would probably want to, and may be required to, insure it to its maximum value. When figuring its value for insurance, rather than use the price you paid for the house, you must determine the "replacement value," or the amount that would be necessary to rebuild the house. When calculating the "replacement value," do not figure in the value of the land since most policies will not cover land.

Insurance companies usually require that you get a minimum coverage of 80 percent of the replacement value of the house. The coverage can be extended upward for relatively little money above the minimum premium amount. Therefore, you should probably get the maximum coverage that you can afford up to 100 percent coverage for fire.

Insurance policies generally run for three years and are then renewed. The premium payment schedule can be arranged with the insurance agent, but the most common schedule is three annual payments. If the seller is financing your purchase, you will probably be responsible for paying the insurance premiums yourself, and your seller will order the insurance company to inform him if you do not make the required payments. If your loan is from a commercial lender, you will usually pay monthly "impounds," with your regular loan payments, which cover the cost of the insurance premiums. The lender will make the premium payments when they become due from the money you have prepaid in the impounds. (See Chapter 23: *Buying Property That Is Encumbered by a Loan Agreement*.)

Most policies include a "deductible" clause, which requires that in case of loss you must pay the deductible amount and the insurance company pays the rest up to the amount of the coverage. The deductible amount is usually $50 or $100. For example, when you have a $100-deductible clause, if your house sustains $200 worth of damages from a fire, you pay $100 and the insurer pays $100. Most policies reduce the deductible amount as the total coverage increases. Before taking out a policy, be sure you understand all the terms regarding deductible items and have the insurance agent explain anything you don't understand until it is completely clear. If the policy does not seem worth the price, go somewhere else.

EXTENDED COVERAGE

For a small additional cost you can get "extended coverage," which protects you against losses caused by hailstorms, tornados, wind, erosion, riots, aircraft damage, vehicle damage, and smoke damage from cooking or heating units. Read the policy, because smoke damage from fireplaces may not be covered. A maximum amount to be paid for broken windows, such as $50, may be specified. If you want coverage for vandalism and malicious mischief or for earthquake damage, specify that it be included in your policy. An extended policy never covers loss or damage to personal property, only to the structures. Theft must be covered by a separate policy, which I discuss later.

The pamphlet *Insurance Facts for Farmers —F-2137* is available free from the United States Department of Agriculture, Office of Information, Washington, D.C. 20250.

THE "RISK OF LOSS" RULE AND PROPERTY INSURANCE

If you take possession of your future home after the Contract of Sale is signed but before escrow closes, your insurance should cover you from the time you take possession rather than the time title is transferred to you. Consider the following possibility:

A family is buying a house in the country and is very anxious to move in. The Contract of Sale is signed and the deal looks as if it is going to go through to everybody's satisfaction. Two weeks before the closing of escrow the seller allows the buyer and his family to move into the house. A week before escrow closes, the house burns down in a fire of unknown origin while the buyer's family is away for the weekend. Does the buyer still have to complete the purchase? The seller does not want the property now that it is destroyed, and the buyer doesn't want to make payments for ten years on a pile of ashes. Most states have now adopted the standard Vendor and Purchaser Act, or Risk of Loss Rule, which places the loss on the party in possession before title is transferred. Thus, in this example, the buyer will be legally required to proceed with the deal. He did not get insurance covering him from the time he took possession, and the seller's insurance company is going to deny liability because its insured party, the seller, was not in possession of the property at the time the loss occurred.

If you are going to take over the seller's insurance policy, get him to place your name with the company as an insured beneficiary as of the date you are to take possession of the property and get a certificate from the company stating you are insured as well as a copy of the policy with your name as beneficiary. If the seller cannot put you on his policy, you must get your own. Never permit a clause in the Contract of Sale which places the burden of loss on you as soon as the Contract of Sale is signed, or makes you liable if you are not in possession of the property.

If you are not going to take possession early, your policy should insure you as of the date of the closing of escrow, whether or not you move onto the property at that time. Once you receive title to the land, the responsibility for any loss will always fall on you because you are then the owner, unless the destruction is caused by the seller's actions after you take title.

PERSONAL LIABILITY INSURANCE

Insurance covering injuries to other people while they are on your property is the most important type of coverage to have in the country, whether or not you have a house on the land. The possibilities for accidents are numerous. Someone's child could fall out of a tree, someone could slip in your creek or fall into your well, get bitten by your dog or kicked by your horse. When you invite someone onto your land, you are under a legal duty to exercise care to prevent injury to that person, and you could suffer great losses if a person were to sue you because of an injury suffered on your property.

Liability, or indemnity, insurance protects you up to the amount of coverage if legal action is taken against you for personal injury. The usual policy, costing about $90 a year, covers you up to $100,000 for injuries to each person or $300,000 damages per incident. If you intend to invite many people to your land, you might want greater coverage, because $100,000 is not much when you see the kinds of awards juries are giving to injured plaintiffs these days.

This type of policy does not cover injuries to yourself or your family. Those injuries are covered under medical insurance.

THEFT INSURANCE

If you are buying a country home you intend to occupy only part of the year, you might want theft insurance. The country, too, has burglaries, although they are not as prevalent as in the city. The type of coverage varies widely as does the maximum amount of coverage available.

A new program has been started by the federal government called the Federal Crime Insurance Program. The government provides crime insurance at a low rate in any state that does not have ready crime insurance available for homeowners. The insurance is sold through licensed insurance agents and brokers and through private insurance companies acting as servicing companies for the Federal Insurance Administration. Coverage includes loss from burglary, larceny, and robbery. A licensed insurance broker should be able to provide you with the current information on this program and the appropriate application forms. Your local office of Housing and Urban Development (HUD) will also have this information (see Chapter 27 for addresses), or write to the Federal Insurance Administration, United States Department of Housing and Urban Development, Washington, D.C. 20410.

THE HOMEOWNER'S INSURANCE POLICY

The most common type of policy today is the "Standard" or "Homeowners" policy, which combines the features of fire, personal liability, and theft insurance at a cheaper rate than they would cost if purchased individually. The policy covers the home, garage, and other structures on the land as well as personal property. The policy should state the type and the value of the property covered, the maximum amount that will be paid in case of loss, and the kinds of losses covered. Generally, damage to buildings other than the house and personal property outside the home will not be covered to their full replacement value. Find out what kind of proof you will have to provide as evidence of your loss. You should keep a list of all your personal property and its value in case of loss.

The types of coverage and costs vary greatly throughout the insurance industry, so you will have to shop around for the best deal.

THE NATIONAL FLOOD INSURANCE PROGRAM

The standard insurance policies never cover structural damage due to floods or mudslides. Because of the great losses that occur annually, the federal government decided to offer federally subsidized flood insurance, through the private insurance industry, to homeowners in areas that have met land use and flood control requirements and have been approved for this type of subsidy by the United States Department of Housing and Urban Development.

Any local property and casualty insurance agent or broker should have information regarding the availability of flood insurance in your area, or write to the Federal Insurance Administration, United States Department of Housing and Urban Development, Washington, D.C. 20410. Ask if your state is in the subsidy program and, if so, where the nearest office is that offers such coverage.

The pamphlet *The National Flood Insurance Program, HUD—283-1* is available free from HUD at the above address or any HUD office listed in Chapter 27.

MORTGAGE LIFE INSURANCE

This is a unique form of life insurance which provides that in the event of the death or disability of the head of a family, the insurance company will continue to make mortgage payments until the amount due is completely paid. The cost of the premium will depend on the age of the insured and the amount of the mortgage. Some lenders and sellers might require you to carry this type of insurance. Any reputable insurance broker can give you complete information.

ASSUMING THE SELLER'S INSURANCE POLICY

The seller may already have the property insured and you might find it to your advantage to simply take over his policy. Ask him to show you a copy of his policy with the schedule of premium payments. Sometimes an insurance company will want to increase the premium rates for the person assuming an existing policy. Find out if they intend to do so in your case. Then investigate to see if you can get a better deal elsewhere.

If you decide to assume the seller's insurance, you must agree to do so in writing. This is specified in Clause 9(b) of the Model Contract of Sale. (See Chapter 28.) The policy does not transfer automatically with the sale of the property; the insurance company must consent in writing to your assuming it. The local insurance broker or escrow holder can handle the problems involved in transferring the policy to you.

Prorating of Prepaid Insurance Premium When You Assume a Policy

If you assume the seller's insurance policy, the premium will have to be prorated according to the time you are to take possession of or title to the property. The seller will probably have paid the premium in advance, so you will have to reimburse him for the amount of the premium that will cover your ownership of the property. Sometimes the insurance company will reimburse the seller for the amount, write a new policy for you, and have you pay them immediately.

The following example illustrates how such a proration is done. Assume that the seller has a three-year extended coverage fire insurance policy and that he paid a premium of $180 on July 1, 1973, covering the next three years. The policy will expire on June 30, 1976, but the buyer is to take title to the property on May 9, 1974. We want to figure out how many days the seller will have used the insurance, and how many days the buyer will benefit from it. Dividing the premium amount by 3, we get the yearly rate of $60. Dividing $60 by 12, we get the monthly rate of $5. Figuring thirty days per month, the premium divides further into an approximate rate of 17¢ per day.

The seller was covered from July 1, 1973, to May 9, 1974, a period of ten months and nine days. Since the premium is $5 per month, he used $50 worth of insurance for the ten months. The cost for nine days comes to $1.53. Thus, $51.53 out of the $180 premium will have covered the seller. Since the buyer will be covered for the rest of the insuring period, he must reimburse the seller for the remaining amount of the premium. Subtracting $51.53 from $180 leaves $128.47, which the buyer is to pay to the seller at the closing of escrow. (See Chapter 30: *Opening and Closing of Escrow and the Role of the Escrow Holder.*) This is the method of proration specified in Clause 9(b) of the Model Contract of Sale. (See Chapter 28.)

IV

DECIDING
ON A
FAIR PRICE

chapter 19

Evaluating the Price of the Property

When you find some land that is right for you, that meets all your requirements and feels like home, you will want to evaluate what that land is worth and compare your results with the seller's asking price. Then you can begin the bargaining game described in the next chapter.

To evaluate the price of the land you want to buy, regardless of where it is located, you can do a number of things without employing a professional appraiser. This chapter will tell you how to make your own appraisal of the property and how to hire a professional if you decide you need one. Finally, I explain how the seller establishes his asking price.

WHAT DETERMINES THE VALUE OF A PIECE OF PROPERTY?

Determining the value of a piece of land is a complex and ambiguous process. If there is any such thing as a formula for finding land value, it would have to be: Value is determined by the law of supply and demand. Although the supply of land is ultimately finite, its availability is constantly fluctuating as large ranches, farms, and other land parcels are split up for sale to the public.

Large landholdings are being split up at an increasingly accelerated pace. Government reports estimate that more than one million farms will go out of business in the seventies. California alone has twenty thousand farms that will fold before 1980. Many of these farms will be absorbed by larger commercial farmers, known as "agrimonoliths," but there will also be a large amount of acreage that will be subdivided and sold to the general public. The most recent estimate is that 20 percent of the

201

land in California will be subdivided within five years after it is sold. This same pattern is developing throughout the United States.

The United States Department of Agriculture has released its study of land value increases for farm land during the year 1970. Values increased in the following areas at the following rates:

Corn Belt, Northern Plains, Pacific Regions	1%
Southeast, Delta Regions	8–10%
All other regions	4–5%

The above figures are specifically related to farm land but the value of recreational land is increasing even faster, based primarily on the increasing demand. A government study in 1972 showed that the number of second-home owners has been increasing at the rate of a quarter of a million each year.

The Bureau of Census took a special survey in 1971 to determine where the average person prefers to have his primary residence. The results are shown below:

Residential Location and Preferences, 1971

	Where do you live now? (percent)	Where would you prefer to live? (percent)
Open Country	12	34
Small Town or City	33	30
Medium-Sized City or Suburb	28	22
Larger City or Suburb	27	14
Total	100	100

Sixty-four percent of the people questioned expressed a desire to live in a non-urban setting. Only 45 percent of the interviewees now live in this type of area. If you combine the 19 percent who wish to make a permanent move away from the cities and suburbs with the increasing number of second-home land buyers, it is clear that there is a tremendous demand for rural and semi-rural property.

By 1973, there were already over 3 million second or "vacation" homes, with the number increasing by 200,000 each year. In 1972, 15 percent of the total housing construction was for vacation homes, with a total of $8 billion being invested that year.

All indications are that the rate of interested land buyers will continue to increase at a faster rate than land will become available and prices will continue to rise at varying rates in all parts of the country.

A LIST OF VALUE FACTORS

Many elements must be considered in deciding whether the price of a piece of property is "worth it." A general list of the basic factors includes the following:

—Supply.

—Demand.

—Usability, e.g., level land is more valuable.

—State of the title, e.g., what "clouds," or defects, exist?

—Location, e.g., neighbors, schools, shopping, public transportation, church, recreational facilities.

—Directional growth of the area, e.g., industrial, commercial, recreational, or residential.

—Population and economic growth in the area.

—Aesthetics, e.g., nice view, landscaping, beautiful house.

—Road frontage.

—Accessibility to the property, e.g., condition of the roads.

—Water: quality and quantity.

—Soil and drainage, e.g., for agricultural and building purposes.

—Orchards and garden, e.g., have they been well cared for?

—Amount of timber and type of vegetation.

—Availability of utilities.

—Zoning and building codes.

—Public Health measures and regulations.

—Condition and age of the house and other structures.

—Size of the parcel, e.g., the larger the parcel, the smaller the price per acre.

—Any stigma attached to the property.

—Personal property included in the sale.

—Climate.

—Exposure of the land, e.g., north slope versus south slope.

—Timing of the sale, e.g., the owner must sell quickly because he is being transferred to a different location in his job.

Each of these elements has its own effect on the value of a parcel of land. For example, the closer property is to a populated area, the more desirable and expensive it will be. If it is close to employment, if it accessible by a paved road, if utilities are supplied, if a house and other improvements are on the land, it will be more expensive than land without these features.

Potential Use

One of the main determinants of value is the land's potential for development, meaning that it is valuable not for its own qualities but as a possible site for future activities of a profitable nature. Thus, if large numbers of people are moving into the area and the land is level or nearly so, more intensive use of the land may be expected and this potential increases the value of the land considerably. This is because level land can be subdivided into more usable parcels than steep land. The real estate agent will always play up the land's suitability for subdivision to lure you with the thought of future profits and thus make the present asking price seem more reasonable. If large timber is standing on the land, the price will be higher because you can cut and sell the trees. It is irrelevant whether you actually want to do so. The fact is that the potential is there.

When you evaluate land, look at the potential uses for it and how soon the property will be in demand for such uses. How close is the nearest subdivision and how well is it selling? Are any large industries planned nearby that might foretell a growing population? These things indicate the extent of the land's potential in determining its price.

HOW THE TAX ASSESSOR EVALUATES THE LAND AND ITS IMPROVEMENTS

A good place to start when determining the value of the land and its improvements is by checking the county Tax Assessor's records for the appraised market value. (The appraisal of land for tax purposes is discussed in Chapter 17: *Taxes and Assessments.*) First you must know how current the appraisal is. Talk to a Tax Assessor to see how recently he has been to your area. Usually several assessors work in the office and you can ask to talk to the one who appraised the seller's land. He will tell you what he thinks it is worth, which is usually somewhat more than he appraises it for taxes. You can tell him what the seller's asking price is and get his opinion of it.

You can also ask his opinion of any improvements on the land, their condition and value, independent of the land itself. He will take into consideration factors of depreciation and appreciation.

The assessor will be familiar with prices of surrounding land and he can tell you what kind of prices land has been going for in your area. He will also know about developments being planned in the area and their possible effect on land values. This information is used in the most important and common of all appraisal techniques used by Tax Assessors and Land Appraisers, the Comparison Test.

The Comparison Test

A parcel of land is compared to other parcels in the area which have recently been sold to determine its current value on the market, often called the "fair market value." You must find out the purchase prices of two or three specific pieces of land nearby that have been sold recently and that are similar in size and major features to the land you are interested in. For instance, if you are looking at land along a creek, try to find out the price of creek land above and below your prospective place.

Since each parcel of land is unique, you must be careful in comparing prices. Any improvements and other features, such as buildings, orchards, ponds, and equipment, will raise the value of the property, so take these things into consideration. Two pieces of land that are basically similar except for the fact that one has a house on it and the other doesn't may be difficult to compare because of the added value of the house.

Where tax stamps are required on deeds, they can be used to find the purchase price of a piece of land. Prior to January 1, 1968, federal law required the placing of Internal Revenue Documentary Tax Stamps on every deed used to transfer property. Since that time many states have enforced their own tax stamp, or real property transfer tax, laws. If your state imposes a transfer tax, you can find out how the tax is computed from the county Recorder and look up the deed of any land parcel to find out the purchase price from either the stamps affixed to it or the stated amount of taxes which were paid. (See Chapter 33: *Deeds and Recording*.) For example, under the old federal tax, 55¢ worth of tax stamps were required for every $500 or fraction thereof of the purchase price. Thus, property that sold for $19,850 would have $22 worth of documentary stamps on the deed. To figure out the sale price from the stamps, divide the amount of the stamps by 55¢, then multiply that quotient by $500. The basic procedure can be used to determine the selling price whenever taxes are required. However, you must use some caution when doing this, because buyers frequently include more stamps than required to make the property seem more valuable when they decide to sell it. Thus take as many different samplings as you can.

After looking at recent selling prices of comparable land you will price land currently for sale. The more land you look at, the better idea you will have as to whether the land you like is priced high or low for the area. Ask other real estate agents who show you land if they are familiar with the land you are interested in. Tell them what the asking price is to see their reaction. Of course, you should not rely on their appraisal, but it will be interesting to hear what they say about it. When you compare the asking prices of other land for sale remember that asking prices are always inflated.

As you compare the price of similar parcels to the land you are interested in, try to determine if there is justification for any difference in price. If a large discrepancy exists with no justification that you can see, keep it in mind to bring up during the bargaining and negotiations with the seller when you are pointing out why the price is too high.

If the seller bought the land within the past few years, try to find out the price he paid for it. You can simply ask him, although he may be reluctant to tell you, especially if he is making a large profit. You can look up his deed and determine the purchase price by the amount of transfer taxes paid or the number of tax stamps if they are required (remembering, always, that he might have put more stamps on than was necessary.) Also compare the Tax Assessor's appraised value of his land the year before he bought the property with its appraised value after he took title. The amount of increase reflects the amount he paid for it.

You should ask everyone familiar with the property his opinion of the reasonableness of the asking price. This includes the Building Inspector, Tax Assessor, other real estate agents, people living in the area, and the Farm Advisor.

HIRING A PROFESSIONAL APPRAISER

A professional appraiser does not have access to any information you cannot get to, but experience is on his side. The appraiser who works in one section of the country for many years should be thoroughly familiar with property values in the area and how they are set. But if you do a thorough job of comparing land prices and getting the opinions of people who have been in the area a long time, I believe you can efficiently appraise the value of the land yourself. Even professional appraisals vary between 2 and 3 percent.

Unfortunately real estate appraisers are not regulated by any state laws so you must be careful whom you select. Anybody can call himself an appraiser. However, appraisers belonging to one of several national organizations are supposed to abide by a code of ethics and pass some accreditation standards. If you look in the local telephone book under "Appraisers," those with memberships in a professional organization will be so designated. The group that seems to be preferred by professional lenders is the American Institute of Real Estate Appraisers, identified as "MAS." Other groups include the Society of Real Estate Appraisers ("SRA"), the National Association of Real Estate Appraisers ("NREA"), the American Society of Appraisers ("ASA"), and the American Society of Farm Managers and Rural Appraisers, Inc. ("AFM-ARA"). In "Useful Resources" at the end of this chapter you will find the addresses of these organizations. If you write them they will send you a list of where their appraisers are located. Always use a registered appraiser if at all possible.

Appraisal fees are usually based on the amount of time needed to complete the job, and that depends on how thoroughly a job must be done. Undeveloped land will not take as long to evaluate as land that has a house on it. Costs vary throughout the country, but the minimum is usually around $50. A good report includes an evaluation of the house and other structures, the availability of utilities and other services, the value of the location, the potential for resale at a profit, present zoning and possible future rezoning, recorded restrictions, the expected economic and population growth in the community, and comparison figures on other similar sales in the area. The result of this research will be a figure that is the appraised fair market value of the property in question.

Never use the real estate broker who is selling the land as your appraiser, because his commission depends on how much money the property sells for. You must also be careful that the appraiser you hire does not have a personal friendship with the broker handling the deal, which might sway his evaluation.

If you are a veteran you can apply for a loan, and the Veterans Administration will appraise the property for a small fee as part of the loan. You must fill out a form called Request for Determination of Reasonable Value. You do not have to go through with the loan, but you will know that if it is approved, the asking price is reasonable. The Veterans Administration should also tell you what their appraisal is. (See Chapter 26: *FHA and VA Loans.*)

You can also apply for a regular commercial or FHA loan to get an inexpensive appraisal, but they generally do not tell you the results of the appraisal. They will only tell you if they accept or reject the application for the loan.

The seller might have had a professional appraisal done. If he presents you with an appraisal that equals his asking price, go to the appraiser yourself, talk to him, and try to get a sense of how honest he is.

HOW THE SELLER SETS HIS ASKING PRICE

The seller usually arrives at his asking price by combining four factors: (1) the value of the property and the improvements; (2) the costs of selling the land; (3) the bargaining margin and the profit; (4) the psychology of numbers.

The Value of the Property and the Improvements

The seller may determine the value of the property and improvements by using the same methods as those explained above. However, he naturally will tend to estimate the value higher than you, the buyer, because of his sentimental attachment to the property. He will tend to emphasize appreciation due to a greater demand to live in the area or to improvements made on the land, and overlook depreciation due to physical deterioration of the land and improvements, the obsolescence of structures because of stylistic trends and technological advances, or the decline in the demand to live in the area. The seller usually considers the price he paid for the land and adds on whatever he spent to get its actual value. But it is possible he paid too much, so don't assume you automatically have to pay him at least whatever he paid.

The Costs of Selling the Land

Once the seller determines what he believes the actual value of the property to be, he will add on the costs involved in selling the land. These could include the real estate agent's commission, attorney's fees, escrow charges, taxes, and survey, appraisal, and title insurance costs. By figuring them into the asking price, the seller passes these costs onto the buyer. This is standard procedure, and brokers generally advise sellers to set their prices in this manner.

The Bargaining Margin and the Profit

The seller then adds on a bargaining and profit margin figure, usually anywhere from 10 to 50 percent of the property's value as he sees it. Part of the purpose of this additional figure is to give the seller room to negotiate with the buyer. When the buyer offers a low figure the seller can "compromise" by coming down in his asking price and still realize a profit. He might allow the buyer to talk him down in price several times, giving the buyer the illusion that he is getting a "steal." If the seller finances the purchase himself, he will realize an additional profit in the interest over the years so he might reduce his initial profit margin by quite a bit. (See Chapter 22: *Terms of the Loan Agreement and Their Effect on the Total Price.*) You will see how this works in the negotiations in Chapter 20: *Bargaining To Get the Seller's Asking Price Down.*)

The real estate agent often plays an important role in setting the price because sellers rely on his appraisal and judgment. One common practice is for the agent to set the price high in order to convince the seller to give him an exclusive listing. He makes a few attempts to sell the property, then tells the seller the market is bad and he should lower the price. The seller almost invariably follows the agent's advice. Then the agent tries to get a quick sale and commission. He will lower the price according to how desperately he needs a sale. Competition is so cutthroat in the rural real estate business that most agents would rather sell the property and take a small commission than risk losing the seller to another agent when his contract expires. You might come along at just the right time.

However, usually the agent estimates high, hoping that a buyer will pay the inflated price, which will increase his commission since it is based on a percentage of the sale price. Especially if he knows that the seller is not in a hurry to sell, he may let the property sit on the market until the right buyer comes along to take it at the high price. In general, all the agents in an area will try to keep prices inflated because it helps them all.

The Psychology of Numbers

Often a seller, or agent, will use a figure that seems much lower than it actually is. For example, instead of setting the price at $17,000, he will ask for $16,750. This is an old device which was first used by J. C. Penney and is now widely employed as a sales technique. The psychology of the odd price gives the buyer the feeling that he is getting a bargain and that the price has been cut as far as possible.

THE APPRAISAL AS A SAFETY VALVE IN THE CONTRACT OF SALE

A common safety valve put in buyers' contracts by attorneys is the condition that the purchase may be terminated if the buyer has the property appraised and he is dissatisfied with the results. Clause 19(b) in the Model Contract of Sale in Chapter 28 allows this type of condition to be inserted. You should always write in the parenthetical part that you are having an appraisal conducted on the property. You can use anyone you want as an appraiser. If you should decide sometime after the seller has signed the contract and made it binding that you want out of the deal, all you have to do is write the seller a letter saying you do not approve the results of the appraisal you had done. You don't even have to show him these results.

USEFUL RESOURCES

The following is free from any FHA office. (All addresses are given in "Useful Resources" in Chapter 27.)

Questions and Answers on FHA Home Property Appraisals—HUD-38-F

The following are available for the specified price from:

The Superintendent of Documents
Government Printing Office
Washington, D.C. 20402

U.S. Land Prices: Directions and Dynamics Catalog No. Pr 36.8:Uri/2R31 no. 13, 75¢

Major Statistical Services of the U.S. Department of Agriculture. Vol. 6, *Land Values and Farm Finance,* 1971. Catalog No. A 1.76:365/v.6, 45¢

You can get appraisal information and a directory of appraisers throughout the United States from each of the following professional appraiser organizations:

American Society of Farm Managers and Rural Appraisers, Inc.
470 South Colorado Boulevard
Suite 8
Denver, Colorado 80222

American Society of Appraisers
Dulles International Airport
P.O. Box 17265
Washington, D. C.

National Association of Real Estate Appraisers
22 East 13th Street
New York, N.Y. 10003

Society of Real Estate Appraisers
7 South Dearborn Street
Chicago, Illinois 60603

chapter 20

Bargaining to Get the Seller's Asking Price Down

THE RULES OF THE GAME AND ORDER OF THE MOVES

The game of bargaining is an ancient one and the rules and moves are well established. Because each piece of land is unique, uniform prices cannot be set and bargaining has survived as the most common means of buying and selling land. The seller usually sets his price higher than he hopes to receive because he expects to bargain. Naturally, you and the seller will be acting in your individual self-interest. Your job is to lower the price so that it is fair to you, which means keeping the seller's profit as low as possible. Don't worry about a seller losing money on the deal. It rarely happens.

I have outlined in the previous chapter, *Evaluating the Price of the Property,* how the seller determines his asking price and how you can appraise the land to see if that price is fair. Usually it will be higher than you want to pay and you will want to negotiate the price down. Bargaining is a game of endurance and coolness. I have isolated seven factors that influence all negotiations and affect the nature of your bargaining and the final purchase price. They are: (1) the willingness of both parties to play the game; (2) the seller's anxiety to sell the property and your anxiety to find a home; (3) the length of time the property has been up for sale; (4) the current market for the property; (5) your ability to point out deficiencies of the property vs. the seller's ability to point out its desirable features; (6) your ability to come up with more cash and the seller's desire to take more than he originally asks for; (7) your ability to know when you are getting a fair deal.

The Willingness of Both Parties to Play the Game

The game is bargaining. If you and the seller are going to play you must both be willing to make compromises. Unless you and the seller are willing to change your positions the game cannot be played.

The seller always sets his asking price higher than he expects to get for the specific purpose of establishing a position from which to bargain. His expectation of bargaining is implicit in the words "asking price." In other words, he intends to play the game and he will be very surprised if you don't play along by making a low offer in return. You will then bargain back and forth until either a stalemate or common agreement is reached.

Unfortunately, every seller is not a game player. There are occasions when a seller sets his price with no intention of bringing it down regardless of the circumstances. He intends to sit and wait until he gets a buyer at his price, even if it takes four or five years. I have known such people but there are not many. You should always assume, until you find out otherwise, that the seller will come down in his price and that you will have to come up from your original offer. In other words, be prepared to play the game.

Needless to say, the real estate agent will play his part in the game. He has a vested interest in the results: his commission is based on the final selling price, but he doesn't get his commission until the property is sold. This places him in a curious position. Although he will always favor the seller because he works for him, he will attempt to get the seller and you to compromise your positions so that the property gets sold and he receives his commission. The average rural town agent dislikes a stubborn seller as much as an unwilling buyer. The longer he has to spend showing the property and dealing with buyers, the less monetary return he will get for his time. So he will be right there in the middle pushing you and the seller, trying to get you to sign a contract. This is the essence of the bargaining game.

The Seller's Anxiety to Sell the Property and Your Anxiety to Find a Home

This factor is closely related to the previous one. The less anxious a seller is to get rid of his property, the less bargaining and compromising he will do. He may be holding the land as an investment and tax shelter and thus can afford to wait until he can "make a killing." All he has to do is make the payments, pay the annual taxes, and wait as long as necessary to get a buyer at his nonnegotiable price. You cannot negotiate with this type of land-owner, and the real estate agent won't try very hard to sell his property.

However, if the owner does not live on the land and he is obviously an investor, this does not necessarily mean that he is not anxious to sell or unwilling to come down in his price. You do not know what his situation is. He might have to sell because he needs fast money for an emergency or a new investment, or land values in the area might not be increasing as fast as he thought they would.

An owner who is presently living on the land, or has recently moved from it, will usually want to sell as soon as possible. He may have a job waiting for him in another area, his family may have outgrown the house, he may not be able to make payments or keep up with the taxes, or he may be involved in a bankruptcy or divorce. Land is also sold at premium prices when an owner dies and his beneficiaries want to sell as fast as possible in order to settle the estate. The greater the pressures are on the seller to sell, the better the circumstances are for getting the price down.

It may be difficult for you to determine the seller's anxiety. One of the first things you should do is ask the owner or the real estate agent why the land is for sale. You may not get an honest answer if the truth might dissuade you from buying the land or encourage you to drive a hard bargain. You should verify what you are told by speaking to surrounding land-owners and other real estate agents in the area. Often local agents know the facts about a piece of property even if it is not listed with them. If you can discover the seller's situation, you may feel more confident when bargaining with him.

You should be conscious too of the fact that your own urgency can work to the seller's advantage. "Buyer's fever" has caused many to buy land at inflated prices simply because they were tired of looking for a place. Often a real estate agent can scare people into believing that a land boom is on, that property is going fast, and that prices are soaring. This is his job. If he can convince you that the land won't be there tomorrow and thus increase your anxiety to buy, you will not be very hardnosed when it comes to bargaining. Notice as you look at land how many times you hear the phrase "Someone else might beat you to the bargain if you delay." The real estate agent attempts to play on your insecurity in order to soften you up.

If you are unusually itchy to buy land because you have been looking for a long time, or you need to get settled quickly, do not fail to exercise your full bargaining power anyway. Be cool. Don't let on how long you have been looking and how tired and anxious you are to find a home. The seller may be willing to go much lower than you realize. You will always be in a more secure position than he is because you can usually look at a lot of land for as long as you want until you find what you like, but he has to patiently wait and hope that he gets a purchaser at his price.

If the agent and seller know that you are anxious to move out of the city or get a second home as soon as possible, they will plan their sales pitch with that in mind. For the sake of bettering your bargaining position, therefore, you should assume that any landowner who puts his property up for sale is anxious to sell, and you should never reveal your own desperation to buy.

The Length of Time the Property Has Been Up for Sale

The longer a parcel of land has been on the market, the more realistic the seller tends to become in his demands. The seller is at a disadvantage when his property does not sell for a long time because he knows that prospective buyers will wonder if something is wrong with it. It is natural to assume that if property is worth the price, it will sell reasonably quickly. If it stays on the market for an excessive amount of time, the assumption is that it's overpriced or seriously deficient.

Ask the real estate agent how long the property has been for sale, not just how long he personally has listed it. Ask if the price has been reduced since it was first put on the market and, if so, how many times and by what amounts. This is another time when you should verify the answers you get with other agents and neighboring landowners.

If the property has just been placed on the market, you will not have the bargaining advantage of time on your side. However, if the land has been listed for a long time, try to find out why it hasn't sold. It is possible that the market for such land, especially if it is very rugged, is very small. Point out the fact that something must be wrong if the land hasn't brought any acceptable offers in such a long time. Tell the seller, or agent, you are willing to pay a fair price and then make your offer. If the agent is anxious to get the owner to sell, your arguments and persistence might get him to increase his pressure on the seller to lower his demands.

I have watched the attitudes of property owners trying to sell their property over a long period of time. They always start out with tremendous demands and a great amount of optimism that they will get a buyer at their price. The longer their property stays on the market, the more nervous and malleable they become. For example, I know of 40 acres that was put up for sale at $11,000. In the first year, six offers were made in the range of $5,000–$7,000. Then six months went by with no offers. The seller and agent began to get pessimistic and decided they would take the next reasonable offer. They did, and the land sold for $6,000. The owner and agent were glad to get rid of it after two years of trying, even at that price.

The Current Market for the Property

Since the beginning of the 1900s, the demographic trend has been for most people to move from country farms to the city, although there have been a few "back to the land" movements during this time. The last one was in the late forties. The present land rush started in the late sixties and is still going on. Conditions in the cities and suburbs are getting worse and the emigration to more rural areas increases annually. In addition, the idea of a second home is increasingly more inviting to the urban resident who finds himself with more leisure time.

When looking at different areas you would like to live in, remember that the more people there are moving into an area, the higher the prices will be due to the old rule of supply and demand. You may feel more comfortable in an area where there are other people like yourself who are moving away from the city to begin a new life in the country or are discovering the pleasures of owning a vacation home. In those places, your bargaining powers will be diminished because buyer competition will be high. However, if you venture into those parts of the country that have not yet become popular (and there are many), the market will be very small and prices will be lower and negotiable.

As land buying spreads to new areas, the buyers in the first rush always get the best deals. They buy when competition is low, before the demand for land increases. We bought our land just before our area started to attract a steady stream of homesteaders. Land selling for $200 an acre when we bought is now going for two or three times that much, and will be even more expensive by the time you read this book.

Regardless of the area, the demand for extremely isolated and undeveloped land always remains small. There are still very few people willing to build their own houses, live without electricity, develop their own water systems, haul their own garbage, and live many miles from the nearest towns. Such areas will always have the cheapest land and a relatively small market of purchasers. Undeveloped backwoods land for sale is always a buyer's market.

However, you can find land with more conveniences that is not yet affected by the inflated prices of a large market if you avoid obviously popular and publicized areas. Some of the nicest areas of the country have not yet been touched by the second-home boom and if you shop wisely you can find an undiscovered area near you.

Your Ability to Point Out Deficiencies of the Property vs. the Seller's Ability to Point Out Its Desirable Features

As a prospective purchaser you are on the offensive in the bargaining game. This is a strong tactical advantage when you begin to point out the deficiencies of the property. If you have read the first part of this book, you should be an expert at this. Every piece of property has some deficiencies—your job is to find and use them to get the price down when you bargain with the seller. Certain defects will be much costlier than others and these major items are the ones you should emphasize.

For instance, when downgrading a house your first comments should be directed at structural weaknesses, such as a cracked foundation, dry rot, termites, a leaky roof or basement, poor plumbing, old wiring, and faulty electricity. Emphasize the serious and expensive items first. Then bring in the smaller items like broken windows, cracked tile, peeling paint, and torn screens.

When you point out the bad points, the seller will counter with such desirable features as a beautiful fireplace, the isolation of the house, the gardens, the redwood shake exterior, and other things that are plus factors to most people. If any of these factors are not a positive feature to you, let the seller know it. Since the real estate agent represents the seller you can be sure he will raise a vigorous defense to your criticisms.

Your complaints do not have to deal solely with the structures or land features. You can point out that the land is in a poor location or that there are no utilities available or anything else you can think of. If you can afford to get a complete house inspection and land appraisal, you can use these professional analyses in your bargaining, but you have enough information from reading this book to do these things yourself. Take notes on what you learn and get estimates of what it will cost you to correct existing defects in the property. At least try to decrease the asking price by the estimated amount needed to repair the major defects in the property. In the seller's defense, the real estate agent will tell you that all the deficiencies were taken into account when the asking price was set. You should then ask him to break down the asking price to indicate just how these deficiencies were figured into it. How do his figures compare to yours? What are his estimates to correct the existing structural and other defects of the property? He might have an appraisal and inspection for the property. This appraisal will probably be different from yours or he wouldn't show it to you. Read it carefully to find out when it was conducted and what items were covered. Was the appraiser a member of a professional organization? Even if the seller's appraisal concludes the property is worth more than your own appraisal does, yours is just as valid as his and you should continue to press its results, assuming they are in your favor. If the seller's inspection report has underestimated the defects, say so. Use your evidence for all it's worth when bargaining. Don't worry about being repetitive. Let the seller know you are a careful buyer.

There might also be "clouds," or defects, on the title, such as a reservation of an easement across the property or a reservation of a right to take minerals or water. The structure might not have been properly approved by the Building Inspector or there might be a restrictive covenant in the deed that diminishes the future uses of the property.

If you can't find any deficiencies in the land, the improvements, the location, or the title, you haven't looked hard enough.

Your Ability to Come Up with More Cash, and the Seller's Desire to Take More than He Originally Asks

After you have made several offers and have brought the price down as far as possible, there is a final move left you can make. You can offer a larger down payment or full cash in exchange for a lower price.

When a seller finances the sale he always asks for a cash down payment with monthly payments to continue until the principal and interest are paid. The requested down payment is usually 10–33 percent of the total asking price. However, the seller is often grateful to get more immediate cash than he asks for even if it means he will get less money in the long

run. If you think this doesn't seem likely, listen to our case.

When we were bargaining for our land, I got the seller down to what he claimed was his "rock-bottom" price. Then I asked him how much of a discount he would give us if we paid the entire purchase price immediately in cash. He offered to reduce the price by an additional 30 percent. We got a loan, at the same interest rate as the interest rate on our land payments would have been, and paid cash. Thus, not only did we reduce the price by 30 percent but we reached the total amount of interest we would have to pay because the amount of the principal was cut.

If you have to borrow the money at a higher interest rate, you will have to figure out if you are actually saving by paying cash. Here are two simple illustrations of how this works:

Suppose the asking price of a parcel of land is $10,000 with a $2,500 down payment and monthly installments at the rate of 6 percent on the remaining $7,500. You already have $2,500 and you can borrow another $2,500 at 9 percent interest from the bank. The seller offers to cut his price to $8,500 if you give him a $5,000 down payment. If you accept this offer you will pay 6 percent interest on the remaining $3,500 owed the seller and 9 percent on the $2,500 owed the bank. The question is whether this is cheaper than paying 6 percent on $7,500. Assuming your total monthly payments will be equal in both cases, figuring the interest for the first year you get:

> 6 percent interest on $7,500 = $450

whereas

> 6 percent interest on $3,500 = $210
> 9 percent interest on $2,500 = $225

so that

> $210 + $225 = $435 is less than $450

The interest is less even if you borrow at 9 percent interest, and the asking price is less, so you should take the offer.

Now look at this example. The asking price for some land is again $10,000 with a down payment of $2,500 and monthly installments at the rate of 6 percent on the remaining $7,500. You again offer to give the seller a $5,000 down payment since you can borrow $2,500 at 9 percent interest from the bank. The seller this time offers to cut his selling price only by $1,000, making it $9,000. Figuring the first year's interest, you get:

6 percent interest on $7,500 = $450

whereas

6 percent interest on $4,000 = $240
9 percent interest on $2,500 = $225

so that

$240 + $225 = $465 is more than $450

This time the interest is higher by $15 the first year; there will be a smaller difference in succeeding years. Even if you pay off the loan over ten years, you will pay only about $150 more in interest by taking out a loan from the bank while your purchase price has been cut by $1,000. Thus, you will save about $850 if you take out the bank loan and accept the seller's offer to cut the price by $1,000. You should do this type of analysis on your own deal if you are in the position of being able to make a higher down payment than is asked for.

The seller will have a down payment established as part of the purchase price when he places the land on the market and you should just tell him that you think you will be able to meet it if you decide to buy the land. Never reveal to the seller that you have a larger amount of cash available until the last minute because you want to get his price as low as possible by the other methods before offering him your final enticement.

Sometimes this strategy might not get you anywhere because there are landowners who don't want a larger down payment or full cash for their land because of their tax situation or because they prefer to make more money in the long run by the accrual of interest. But usually when the possibility of more cash is presented to the seller, he will make adjustments in his price to get it.

Your Ability to Know When You Are Getting a Fair Deal

This is the most subtle part of effective bargaining. You must realize when you have pushed the price down as far as it is going to go. The buyer who continues haggling beyond the point where a fair deal has been reached often loses the property because another buyer comes along and makes a better offer which the seller accepts. Don't be greedy. The price is right when the seller stands to make a little money and you get a good piece of land at a reasonable sum. You will make your profit when you decide to sell. This is not to say that the seller always makes a profit, but he usually does and you should approach the negotiations with that in mind. Bargain strongly on your own behalf but also be willing to compromise. Temper your self-interest just when the price is right and you can't go wrong. Don't hesitate to finalize the deal if you feel you have bargained wisely and you are getting a good deal.

Now that you understand the interacting elements, or "rules," affecting the bargaining process, you are ready to begin making your "moves," which consist of offers, rejections, counter offers, and finally acceptance.

YOUR FIRST MOVE— YOUR OFFER

Your first move in the bargaining process is your offer to the seller to buy his property. Your offer should be made in a Contract of Sale which states all the terms you want and the price you are offering to pay. If you are dealing through a real estate agent, he must relay your offer to the owner. Just as the asking price is set high to give the seller room to bargain, your offer should be much lower than you expect to pay. You can always go up when the seller rejects your offer, but if you start high and your offer is accepted, it is too late then to bargain for a lower price. You never know how badly the seller wants to dispose of his property. Disregard any statements by the agent that the seller does not intend to reduce his price.

How low should your first offer be? In my experience the best way for you to begin bargaining is to offer somewhere between one-half to three-quarters of the asking price. Never offer more than 75 percent initially. You might think this is ridiculous and will offend the seller. The agent may imply that you are crazy and attempt to dissuade you from "wasting everybody's time." But do not give in. Tell him you have looked at a lot of land and feel your offer is a reasonable one.

The agent cannot refuse to relay your offer

to the seller. The worst thing that can happen is that the seller will reject your offer. Since you already expect him to do so you should not feel embarrassed. It is all part of the game.

Because you start low you will have ample room to come up in later offers, giving the impression that the seller is forcing you higher. Being in this position gives you a psychological edge over the seller, particularly in the later stages of the negotiations.

THE SELLER'S REJECTION, COUNTEROFFER, OR FINAL ACCEPTANCE

The seller will respond to your offer in one of three ways. First, he might accept it and then you can move to close the deal. However, this is unlikely. Second, he might simply reject it and say it is not enough money and that he cannot afford to let the property go at your price. Or third, he might start bargaining by rejecting your offer and making a counteroffer. His counteroffer will either be a new price lower than his original one, or it will be some added or deleted terms in the Contract of Sale. This is the usual response and it means that he is willing to bargain with you. He might "split the difference" with you and go to the halfway point, but usually he will only reduce his price by 5 or 10 percent. There is usually a 15 percent difference between the asking price and final selling price.

After the seller sends this new price to you through the agent, you can bring out the various deficiencies in the property that you have been accumulating. You will then make your second offer, which will be slightly higher than your first one. He may reject it and make a new counteroffer. If you feel this is as low as he will go, then you can offer a larger down payment or full cash (if you can get it) if he will cut more off the price. Eventually you will force him to his lowest position, and he will bring you to your highest one. If your compromises are mutually satisfactory, then a deal has been made. If not, you had better start looking somewhere else.

Frequently during the bargaining process something occurs that can bring things to a head faster than anticipated. For example, an-

other interested buyer might enter the picture and force you to compete with him for the land. A well-known sales trick used by some real estate agents is to tell you that your offer has been surpassed by another prospective buyer, although this is actually not true. A variation on this trick is for the seller to arrange to have a friend or his broker telephone while he is showing the house to you. The call presumably is another interested buyer. Don't rush your decision unless you are certain you are getting what you want. Ask to meet the other buyer or see his offer.

There are a few tricks you can use yourself. Pick out a piece of property that another agent in town is handling under a completely different deal and announce to your original agent that you are preparing to buy the other property if the seller does not accept your present offer, which is your final one. This might scare the seller or make him more willing to compromise with you if he is anxious to sell and does not want to lose you as a prospective buyer.

YOUR DEPOSIT OR EARNEST MONEY BINDER WITH THE CONTRACT OF SALE

When you make your first and subsequent offers to the seller, you will do so using the Model Contract of Sale in Chapter 28, which you will adapt to your own situation. When you present him with the contract, which is also an offer to purchase, you will include a small deposit in order to show your seriousness and to whet the seller's appetite for more. This is usually called a deposit, or earnest money payment. (See Chapter 28: *The Model Contract of Sale*.)

Usually the seller or real estate agent gives the buyer a "Deposit Receipt" to be signed before the final sales contract is drawn up. This is deceptive. The Deposit Receipt becomes a legally enforceable contract for the purchase of land as soon as both you and the seller sign it, and it leaves you completely unprotected. Nothing you are told verbally is legally binding. If you agree to some condition orally with the seller and if you then make a cash deposit and sign a binder without the condition written into it, that condition is not binding on the seller, and he does not have to write it into a more complete Contract of Sale later on. One of the most frequent complaints made to the local real estate departments comes from buyers who demand the return of their deposits. The buyer usually suffers because he did not get his terms or agreements with the real estate agent or seller put in writing. Do not make the mistake of assuming, as many buyers do, that anything not called a "contract" will not be important. Often contracts for the sale and purchase of land are given such names as Conditional Sales Agreement, Offer to Purchase, Preliminary Sales Agreement, Deposit Receipt, Sales Deposit Receipt, Agreement for Sale of Real Estate, Binder, Installment Contract, and Contract of Sale.

Instead of signing the usual binder, I recommend that you submit your deposit and your offer to purchase with all the terms of the sale in a single document called the "Contract of Sale," which is explained in detail in Chapter 28.

V

FINANCING
YOUR
PURCHASE

chapter 21

Types of Financing: Land Contract, Mortgage, Deed of Trust

When you find land you want to buy, you must decide how you are going to pay for it. Unless you have enough money to pay cash, you will have to pay off your purchase gradually. Country land sales are usually financed by the seller, since it is generally difficult to get a loan from a commercial lender. If the seller extends you credit, you will pay him a down payment and pay off the rest of the purchase price gradually

under the terms of either a "land contract," "mortgage," or a "deed of trust." If you are able to borrow money from a third party to combine with your own money, you can pay the seller cash for the land and give the lender either a mortgage or a deed of trust.

Each type of financing is diagramed in Illustration 72 at the end of this chapter. As you read each of the following sections, you should refer to this illustration (pages 233–234).

THE LAND CONTRACT

Financing by land contract is the riskiest way to buy rural land. Do not confuse the land contract with the Contract of Sale. The Contract of Sale is the document that contains the terms and conditions of the sale. (See the Model Contract of Sale in Chapter 28.) The land contract only details the financial arrangements of the purchase and the rights and obligations of the seller and buyer during the payment period.

A land contract may also be called an Installment Sale Contract, Second Contract, Land Sale Contract, Land Contract of Sale, or Conditional Sales Contract. Regardless of the name used, the principle of "buying on contract" remains the same.

You give the seller a cash down payment and then make regular payments until the purchase price and interest are paid off. What makes buying on contract risky is that during the payment period the seller only gives you *possession* of the land. You will not get a deed until after all the payments have been made. (This is what differentiates this plan from a mortgage or deed of trust, as you will see below.)

The seller holds the title to the land during this entire period. He can encumber the land with easements, mortgages, and other liens that will seriously affect the title you are to eventually receive. Often a seller will convey land under a land contract while still paying for it himself. If he fails to make his payments, his loan is foreclosed, and he loses the land, and you will also lose the land. If you go to court at that time you may get your payments back, but it is very unlikely you will get the land since the seller no longer has it. The situation is similar if the seller goes bankrupt or dies and passes title to his heirs.

Sellers like land contracts because of the great advantages they offer if you are unable to make your payments. Under the "strict foreclosure action" generally used for land contracts, the seller simply asks you to leave the premises. Since he already has title to the land, he does not have to go through a regular court foreclosure. At the end of the foreclosure the seller not only has the land but he has all the money you have already paid him.

Although you can sue him for the value of improvements you made on the land, such as buildings, septic tanks, and water systems, you must hire a lawyer and initiate a costly court action. If you refuse to leave the property, the seller will be forced to go to court and obtain an "action for ejectment" against you. He might be willing to make a settlement with you out of court to avoid this expense, in which case you can demand that he reimburse you

for the improvements you have made on the land. You should also ask for the money you have paid him under the land contract. You will get at least some of your money back in this manner. Never leave the land voluntarily unless the seller makes a deal.

Because of the nature of the land contract, sellers often require an extremely small down payment and low monthly terms. This might be the only way some of you can buy a piece of country land because of your poor financial condition. I recommend that you never buy "on contract" unless you have no alternative. If you have no other choice, at least be sure you have the following essential protections written into the land contract:

—The land contract should state that the seller is to put the title to the land in trust with an escrow holder, or third party trustee, until you complete your payments or default on them.

—Have the seller write out a deed to you and place it with the trustee with instructions to give it to you upon the completion of your payments. This will help prevent him from selling or encumbering the title to the land before you receive it.

—The land contract should state that your payments are to go to the trustee, who is to use the money to pay all taxes and other liens on the land, such as the seller's mortgage, before he forwards the money to the seller. This will prevent a foreclosure by the seller's creditor or a tax sale.

—Require that the land contract be recorded immediately with the county Recorder.

—The land contract must specifically forbid the seller from encumbering the title in any way. He should not be allowed to bequeath the title to a beneficiary in his will. If he dies while you are still making payments, the land should remain under the care of his executor until you have either made all your payments or defaulted.

—Get the seller to include a clause in which he promises to convey all or part of the title to you after you have completed a certain amount of the total payments. For example, after you have made half of the payments, he will give you full title to the land and you can give him back a mortgage or trust deed for the remaining amount due. The earlier you get title to the land the better.

—Never allow the seller to put a "prepayment penalty" clause into the land contract penalizing you for paying off the balance at an earlier date than scheduled. For example, if your payments are to be $100 a month, you should be permitted to pay "$100 or more per month." (See Chapter 22 for more on this.)

—You will be required to keep the property in good repair and to pay for fire and hazard insurance on the property under terms to be approved by the seller. Be sure you are a beneficiary under the policy, as well as the seller.

—Have the seller state, in detail, the conditions under which he can force you off the land. Make sure you understand them.

—Use the information in Chapter 22 on the terms and elements of amortization to get the best financing arrangement possible.

THE MORTGAGE (PURCHASE MONEY MORTGAGE) AND DEED OF TRUST

Unlike the land contract, when you give a mortgage or deed of trust in exchange for either cash or credit, you receive title to the land immediately. The property is always held as security, or collateral, for the loan so that the lender has sufficient protection if you default on your payments.

A mortgage is technically called a purchase money mortgage when it is used for the specific purpose of buying land. (The term "mortgage" used throughout this book actually refers to a purchase money mortgage.) If the seller "finances the deal" himself, he does not actually give you money to buy the land. Instead he allows you to pay off the purchase price over a period of time. He is giving you credit, which is like lending you the money.

When you borrow money from a third party in return for a mortgage or deed of trust, you actually receive cash to give to the seller for the land. You then pay back the lender * over a period of time.

* Throughout this and subsequent chapters, when I refer to the "lender" I am talking about either the seller who finances the sale himself or a third party lender, unless I specify otherwise. It is assumed that the borrower is the buyer. A creditor is a person to whom money is owed. A debtor is the person who owes the money.

THE "TITLE THEORY" OF MORTGAGES

Seventeen states use the "title theory" of mortgages. Under this financial arrangement you do not keep the title to the land during your payment period. For example, if the seller finances the sale, he delivers title to you at the close of escrow. Because you receive title at that time you can get the standard title protections, such as a title search and title insurance. You receive a deed specifying ownership in your name. Then, when you give the mortgage to the seller, it is as if you are giving the seller back your title to the land. He then holds title until you complete your payments. During that time, you have the right to the possession of the land. When you complete the required payments of principal and interest, the seller makes a new deed and redelivers the title to you. If you default on your payments, the seller merely keeps the title to the land.

If you give a mortgage under this system to a third party lender, the seller delivers title to you and then you deliver it to the lender with a mortgage in exchange for cash, which you give to the seller. The terms of a "title theory" mortgage must specify that the creditor not alter the title in any way from the time you give it to him as security with the mortgage until he redelivers it to you on your last required payment.

The difference between this system and a land contract is that in the latter form of financing you never receive title until you have completely paid for the property. With a "title mortgage" you receive title immediately and then give it back to the seller in the form of a mortgage. You have much greater protection under a "title theory" mortgage than with a land contract.

The states that use this "title theory" of mortgages are Alabama, Arkansas, Connecticut, Illinois, Maine, Maryland, Massachusetts, Mississippi, New Hampshire, New Jersey, North Carolina, Ohio, Pennsylvania, Rhode Island, Tennessee, Vermont, and West Virginia. If your land is in any of these states you should determine whether the "title theory" is still observed at the time of your purchase. (Illustration 67 is a sample mortgage form.)

SAMPLE MORTGAGE FORM

THIS MORTGAGE, made this _____ day of _____, 19_____.
BETWEEN _____(name of borrower)_____, herein called Mortgagor,
Whose address is _____,
and _____(name of lender)_____, herein called Mortgagee;
WITNESSETH: That Mortgagor hereby mortgages to Mortgagee, all that property located in
the City of _____, County of _____, _____, described as:

(Legal Description of the Property)

TOGETHER WITH all the tenements, hereditaments, and appurtenances thereunto belonging or in any wise appertaining thereto, the reversions, remainders, rents, issues, and profits thereof, and also all the estate, right, title, and interest, homestead or other claim or demand, in law and in equity, which Mortgagor now has or may hereafter acquire, in and to said property, or any part thereof, as security for the payment of the indebtedness evidenced by a promissory note, of even date herewith, executed by Mortgagor in the sum of _____ Dollars, ($_____), in favor of Mortgagee, for any additional sums and interest thereon which may hereafter be loaned to the Mortgagor or his successors or assigns by the Mortgagee, and for the performance of each agreement herein contained. Additional loans hereafter made and interest thereon shall be secured by this Mortgage only if made to the Mortgagor while he is the owner of record of his present interest in said property, or to his successors or assigns while they are the owners of record thereof, and shall be evidenced by a promissory note reciting that it is secured by this Mortgage.

A. TO PROTECT THE SECURITY OF THIS MORTGAGE, MORTGAGOR AGREES:

Maintenance and Repair

1. To keep said property in good condition and repair; not to remove or demolish any building thereon; to complete or restore promptly and in good and workmanlike manner any building which may be constructed, damaged, or destroyed thereon and to pay when due all claims for labor performed and materials furnished therefor; to comply with all laws affecting said property or requiring any alterations or improvements to be made thereon; not to commit or permit waste thereof; not to commit, suffer, or permit any act upon said property in violation of law; to cultivate, irrigate, fertilize, fumigate, prune, and do all other acts which from the character or use of said property may be reasonably necessary, the specific enumeration herein not excluding the general.

Fire Insurance

2. To provide, maintain, and deliver to Mortgagee fire insurance satisfactory to and with loss payable to Mortgagee. The amount collected under any fire or other insurance policy may be applied by Mortgagee upon any indebtedness secured hereby and in such order as Mortgagee may determine, or at the option of Mortgagee the entire amount so collected or any part thereof may be released to Mortgagor. Such application or release shall not cure or waive any default or Notice of Default hereunder or invalidate any act done pursuant to such notice.

Defense of Security

3. To appear in and defend any action or proceeding purporting to affect the security hereof or the rights or powers of Mortgagee, and to pay all costs and expenses, including cost of evidence of title and attorney's fees in a reasonable sum, in any such action or proceeding in which Mortgagee may appear, and in any suit brought by Mortgagee to foreclose this Mortgage.

67. SAMPLE MORTGAGE FORM

Payment of Liens and Taxes

4. To pay the following: (a) all taxes and assessments affecting said property, including assessments on appurtenant water stock, at least _____ days before delinquency; (b) when due, all encumbrances, charges, and liens, with interest, on said property or any part thereof, which appear to be prior or superior hereto; and (c) all costs, fees, and expenses of this Mortgage. Should Mortgagor fail to make any payment or to do any act as herein provided, the Mortgagee, but without obligation so to do and without notice to or demand upon Mortgagor and without releasing Mortgagor from any obligation hereof, may do the following: (a) make or do the same in such manner and to such extent as he deems necessary to protect the security hereof (Mortgagee being authorized to enter upon said property for such purposes); (b) appear in and defend any action or proceeding purporting to affect the security hereof or the rights or powers of Mortgagee; (c) pay, purchase, contest, or compromise any encumbrance, charge, or lien which in the judgment of Mortgagee appears to be prior or superior hereto; and (d) in exercising any such powers, pay necessary expenses, employ counsel, and pay his reasonable fees.

Reimbursement of Costs

5. To pay immediately and without demand all sums so expended by Mortgagee, with interest from date of expenditure at the amount allowed by law in effect at the date hereof, and to pay for any statement provided for by law in effect at the date hereof regarding the obligation secured hereby any amount demanded by the Mortgagee not to exceed the maximum allowed by law at the time when said statement is demanded.

Condemnation Awards

6. That any award of damages in connection with any condemnation for public use of or injury to said property or any part thereof is hereby assigned and shall be paid to Mortgagee who may apply or release such moneys received by him in the same manner and with the same effect as above provided for disposition of proceeds of fire or other insurance.

Waiver of Late Payments

7. That by accepting payment of any sum secured hereby after its due date, Mortgagee does not waive his right either to require prompt payment when due of all other sums so secured or to declare default for failure so to pay.

Release and Subordination

8. That at any time or from time to time, without liability therefor and without affecting the personal liability of any person for payment of the indebtedness secured hereby, or the effect of this mortgage upon the remainder of said property, Mortgagee may: (a) release any part of said property from this Mortgage; (b) consent to the making of any map or plat thereof; (c) join in granting any easement thereon; or (d) join in any extension agreement or any agreement subordinating the lien or charge hereof.

Satisfaction of Mortgage

9. When all sums secured hereby have been paid in full; the lien created hereby shall cease and become void, and Mortgagee shall cause a satisfaction of mortgage to be entered of record stating that all sums secured thereby have been fully paid, satisfied, and discharged, and that said property has been released from the lien of this Mortgage. At such time, Mortgagee shall also cancel the note secured hereby and shall return this Mortgage and said note to the Mortgagor.

Assignment of Rents

10. That as additional security, Mortgagor hereby gives to and confers upon Morgagee the right, power, and authority, during the continuance of this Mortgage, to collect the rents, issues, and profits of said property, reserving unto the Mortgagor the right, prior to any default by Mortgagor in payment of any indebtedness secured hereby or in the performance of any agreement hereunder, to collect and retain such rents, issues, and profits as they become

due and payable. Upon any such default, Mortgagee may at any time without notice, either in person, by agent, or by a receiver to be appointed by a court, and without regard to the adequacy of any security for the indebtedness hereby secured, enter upon and take possession of said property or any part thereof, in his own name sue for or otherwise collect such rents, issues, and profits, including those past due and unpaid, and apply the same, less costs and expenses of operation and collection, including reasonable attorney's fees, upon any indebtedness secured hereby, and in such order as Mortgagee may determine. The entering upon and taking possession of said property, the collection of such rents, issues, and profits and the application thereof as aforesaid, shall not cure or waive any default or Notice of Default hereunder or invalidate any act done pursuant to such notice.

Default and Foreclosure

11. That upon default by Mortgagor in payment of any indebtedness secured hereby or in performance of any agreement hereunder, Mortgagee may declare all sums secured hereby immediately due and payable by instituting legal proceedings for judicial foreclosure of this Mortgage, in which case the net proceeds from the sale under the direction and decree of a court of competent jurisdiction shall be applied to the indebtedness secured hereby.

Inurement

12. That this Mortgage applies to, inures to the benefit of, and binds all parties hereto, their heirs, legatees, devisees, administrators, executors, successors, and assigns. In this Mortgage, whenever the context so requires, the masculine includes the feminine and/or neuter, and the singular number includes the plural.

The undersigned Mortgagor requests that a copy of any Notice of Default and of any Notice of Sale hereunder be mailed to him at his address hereinbefore set forth.

The promissory note secured hereby is given as a part of the purchase price of the property herein described.

Signature of Mortgagor

_____

Acknowledgment

State of _____ } ss
County of _____ }

On _____, 19___, before me, the undersigned, a Notary Public in and for said county and state, personally appeared ____(name of mortgagor)____ known to me to be the person(s) whose name(s) is(are) subscribed to the within instrument and acknowledged to me that he (she or they) executed the same.

WITNESS my hand and official seal.

_____

NOTARIAL

SEAL

Notary Public in and for said County and State

_____

Type or Print Name of Notary
My Commission expires _____

THE "LIEN THEORY" OF MORTGAGES

All of the other states follow the "lien theory" of mortgaging property. When you give a mortgage, you do not give up title to the land but simply promise, in writing, that you will repay the lender or complete payments to the seller. The mortgage becomes a lien on the property, which means that a foreclosure action can be taken if payments are not made. Title and possession rights remain with you, the buyer, during the entire period. The seller's, or lender's, lien on the land will be removed upon completion of all payments. Because you always keep the title in your possession, it is much harder to have your land taken from you if you default on your payments than under the "title theory" of mortgages where the lender already has title to the land if you default.

Under both mortgage theories, the buyer who gives the mortgage is called the "mortgagor." The lender or seller who receives the mortgage is called the "mortgagee."

THE DEED OF TRUST (TRUST DEED)

Thirteen states prefer the system where the borrower, or "trustor," delivers a deed of trust to a third party, or "trustee," rather than giving a mortgage to the lender or seller. Under this system, the lender is the "beneficiary" or the "trust." The third party trustee is usually a commercial institution such as a bank, title company, or escrow company. The trustee is basically an escrow holder for the purchase. (See Chapter 30: *Opening and Closing of Escrow and the Role of the Escrow Holder.*)

The trust is established in the following manner. The seller delivers title to you, the buyer, by giving you a deed to the land. If the seller is your creditor, you give him a down payment on the land and sign a deed of trust. If you borrow the money from a third party,

you pay the seller the entire purchase price and sign a deed of trust for the lender. You then place the deed to the land with the trustee, to whom you make payments. The trustee pays the taxes and other liens on the land and delivers payments to the seller or lender. When the loan has been completely paid, the trustee redelivers the deed to you. If you fail to make payments, the trustee has the right to sell the land and deliver the title to the new purchaser. Any money owed to the seller or lender is paid from the money received from this sale. This method of disposing of the title to the land upon default makes the deed of trust the preferred security instrument from the seller's point of view.

Do not confuse a deed with the deed of trust. A deed is evidence of ownership of the property. The deed of trust, sometimes called the trust deed, is a method of financing a sale of land. It is slowly being accepted throughout the country, although the mortgage remains the primary means of securing property for a loan.

The District of Columbia and California, Colorado, Idaho, Illinois, Mississippi, Missouri, Nevada, New Mexico, Tennessee, Texas, Virginia, West Virginia, and Utah use deeds of trust. (Illustration 68 is a sample deed of trust form.)

THE PROMISSORY NOTE OR BOND

The mortgage or deed of trust is always accompanied by a promissory note or bond, which is the document that actually specifies the debt and how it is to be paid. A mortgage and deed of trust only specify the security for the debt. In the note the borrower makes an unconditional promise in writing to the lender that he will pay the loan according to a specified plan. Illustration 69 is a sample note, titled "Installment Note," which would be used in the case of a deed of trust. (A note for a mortgage would include the same elements, only all references to the lien would be to a mortgage rather than a deed of trust.) The note or bond is signed and recorded with the county Recorder at the same time as the mortgage or trust deed, which are always recorded.

DEED OF TRUST

This Deed of Trust, made this _____(Date)_____ day of _____, 19___,
Between _____(Name of Borrower)_____

Whose address is _____(Address of Borrower)_____
_____(Number and Street)_____   (City)   (State)

herein called Trustor, _____(Name of Trustee)_____, a ___(State)___ corporation, herein called Trustee,
and _____(Name of Seller or Lender)_____

_____ herein called Beneficiary,
Witnesseth: That Trustor irrevocably GRANTS, TRANSFERS AND ASSIGNS to TRUSTEE IN
TRUST, WITH POWER OF SALE, that property in _____(City where land is located)_____
County of _____(County where located)_____, _____(State)_____, described as

(Legal Description of the Property)

TOGETHER WITH the rents, issues and profits thereof, SUBJECT, HOWEVER, to the right, power
and authority given to and conferred upon Beneficiary by Paragraph 5 of Part B of the provisions
incorporated herein by reference to collect and apply such rents, issues and profits, For the Purpose
of Securing payment of the indebtedness evidenced by a promissory note, of even date herewith,
executed by Trustor in the sum of _____(Amount of Loan)_____
_____ Dollars, ($_____).
any additional sums and interest thereon which may hereafter be loaned to the Trustor or his successors or assigns by the Beneficiary, and the performance of each agreement herein contained. Additional loans hereafter made and interest thereon shall be secured by this Deed of Trust only if made
to the Trustor while he is the owner of record of his present interest in said property, or to his successors or assigns while they are the owners of record thereof, and shall be evidenced by a promissory
note reciting that it is secured by this Deed of Trust.

By the execution and delivery of this Deed of Trust and the note secured hereby the parties hereto
agree that there are adopted and included herein for any and all purposes by reference as though the
same were written in full herein the provisions of Section A, including paragraphs 1 through 6 thereof,
and of Section B, including paragraphs 1 through 10 thereof, of that certain fictitious Deed of Trust
recorded in the official records in the offices of the County Recorders of the following counties ___
(List of counties in state)
_____

A copy of said provisions so adopted and included herein by reference is set forth on the reverse
hereof.

The undersigned Trustor requests that a copy of any notice of default and of any notice of sale
hereunder be mailed to him at his address given above.

(Name of Borrower)
_____
(Signature of Borrower)   _____

State of _____
County of _____ } ss.

On this _____ day of _____(Date this agreement is signed)_____, 19___,
before me, the undersigned, a Notary Public in and for said _____(Name of County)_____
County, personally appeared _____(Name of Borrower)_____

known to me to be the person(s) whose name(s) _____ subscribed to the within instrument, and
acknowledged that _____ executed the same.
WITNESS my hand and official seal.
(SEAL)

(Signature of Notary)
_____
Notary Public in and for said County & State
My Commission Expires: _____(Date of Expiration)_____ (Name of Notary)
_____
Type or Print Name of Notary

68. SAMPLE DEED OF TRUST

The following is a copy of the provisions of Section A, including Paragraphs 1 through 6 thereof, and of Section B, including Paragraphs 1 through 10, thereof, of that certain fictitious Deed of Trust recorded as set forth on the reverse hereof:

A. TO PROTECT THE SECURITY OF THIS DEED OF TRUST, TRUSTOR AGREES:

Maintenance and Repair

1. To keep said property in good condition and repair; not to remove or demolish any building thereon; to complete or restore promptly and in good and workmanlike manner any building which may be constructed, damaged or destroyed thereon and to pay when due all claims for labor performed and materials furnished therefor; to comply with all laws affecting said property or requiring any alterations or improvements to be made thereon; not to commit or permit waste thereof; not to commit, suffer or permit any act upon said property in violation of law; to cultivate, irrigate, fertilize, fumigate, prune and do all other acts which from the character or use of said property may be reasonably necessary, the specific enumerations herein not excluding the general.

Fire Insurance

2. To provide, maintain and deliver to Beneficiary fire insurance satisfactory to and with loss payable to Beneficiary. The amount collected under any fire or other insurance policy may be applied by Beneficiary upon any indebtedness secured hereby and in such order as Beneficiary may determine, or at the option of Beneficiary the entire amount so collected or any part thereof may be released to Trustor. Such application or release shall not cure or waive any default or notice of default hereunder or invalidate any act done pursuant to such notice.

Defense of Security

3. To appear in and defend any action or proceeding purporting to affect the security hereof or the rights or powers of Beneficiary, or Trustee; and to pay all costs and expenses, including cost of evidence of title and attorney's fees in a reasonable sum, in any such action or proceeding in which Beneficiary or Trustee may appear.

Payment of Liens and Taxes

4. To pay: at least ten days before delinquency all taxes and assessments affecting said property, including assessments on appurtenant water stock; when due, all encumbrances, charges and liens, with interest, on said property or any part thereof, which appear to be prior or superior hereto; all costs, fees and expenses of this Trust.

Reimbursement of Costs

5. To pay immediately and without demand all sums expended by Beneficiary or Trustee pursuant to the provisions hereof, with interest from date of expenditure at seven percent per annum.

Right to Protect the Security

6. Should Trustor fail to make any payment or to do any act as herein provided, then Beneficiary or Trustee, but without obligation so to do and without notice to or demand upon Trustor and without releasing Trustor from any obligation hereof, may: make or do the same in such manner and to such extent as either may deem necessary to protect the security hereof, Beneficiary or Trustee being authorized to enter upon said property for such purposes; appear in and defend any action or proceeding purporting to affect the security hereof or the right or powers of Beneficiary or Trustee; pay, purchase, contest or compromise any encumbrance, charge or lien which in the judgment of either appears to be prior or superior hereto; and, in exercising any such powers, pay necessary expenses, employ counsel and pay the reasonable fees.

B. IT IS MUTUALLY AGREED THAT:

Condemnation Award

1. Any award of damages in connection with any condemnation for public use or injury to said property or any part thereof is hereby assigned and shall be paid to Beneficiary who may apply or release such moneys received by him in the same manner and with the same effect as above provided for disposition of proceeds of fire or other insurance.

Waiver of Late Payments

2. By accepting payment of any sum secured hereby after its due date, Beneficiary does not waive his right either to require prompt payment when due of all other sums so secured or to declare default for failure so to pay.

Release and Subordination

3. At any time or from time to time, without liability therefor and without notice, upon written request of Beneficiary and presentation of this Deed and said note for endorsement, and without affecting the personal liability of any person for payment of the

227

indebtedness secured hereby, Trustee may: reconvey all or any part of said property; consent to the making of any map or plat thereof; join in granting any easement thereon; or join in any extension agreement or any agreement subordinating the lien or charge hereof.

Full Reconveyance

4. Upon written request of Beneficiary stating that all sums secured hereby have been paid, and upon surrender of this Deed and said note to Trustee for cancellation and retention and upon payment of its fees, Trustee shall reconvey, without warranty, the property then held hereunder. The recitals in any reconveyance executed under this deed of trust of any matters or facts shall be conclusive proof of the truthfulness thereof. The grantee in such reconveyance may be described as "the person or persons legally entitled thereto."

Assignment of Rents

5. As additional security, Trustor hereby gives to and confers upon Beneficiary the right, power and authority, during the continuance of these Trusts, to collect the rents, issues and profits of said property, reserving unto Trustor the right, prior to any default by Trustor in payment of any indebtedness secured hereby or in performance of any agreement hereunder, to collect and retain such rents, issues and profits as they become due and payable. Upon any such default, Beneficiary may at any time without notice, either in person, by agent, or by a receiver to be appointed by a court, and without regard to the adequacy of any security for the indebtedness hereby secured, enter upon and take possession of said property or any part thereof, in his own name sue for or otherwise collect such rents, issues and profits, including those past due and unpaid, and apply the same, less cost and expenses of operation and collection, including reasonable attorney's fees, upon any indebtedness secured hereby, and in such order as Beneficiary may determine. The entering upon and taking possession of said property, the collection of such rents, issues and profits and the application thereof as aforesaid, shall not cure or waive any default or notice of default hereunder or invalidate any act done pursuant to such notice.

Default and Foreclosure

6. Upon default by Trustor in payment of any indebtedness secured hereby or in performance of any agreement hereunder, all sums secured hereby shall immediately become due and payable at the option of the Beneficiary. In the event of default, Beneficiary shall execute or cause the Trustee to execute a written notice of such default and his election to cause to be sold the herein described property to satisfy the obligations hereof, and shall cause such notice to be recorded in the office of the recorder of each county wherein said real property or some part thereof is situated.

Notice of sale having been given as then required by law, and not less than the time then required by law having elapsed after recordation of such notice of default, Trustee, without demand on Trustor, shall sell said property at the time and place fixed by it in said notice of sale, either as a whole or in separate parcels and in such order as it may determine, at public auction to the highest bidder for cash in lawful money of the United States, payable at time of sale. Trustee may postpone sale of all or any portion of said property by public announcement at such time and place of sale, and from time to time thereafter may postpone such sale by public announcement at the time and place fixed by the preceding postponement. Trustee shall deliver to the purchaser its deed conveying the property so sold, but without any covenant or warranty, express or implied. The recitals in such deed of any matters or facts shall be conclusive proof of the truthfulness thereof. Any person, including Trustor, Trustee, or Beneficiary, may purchase at such sale.

After deducting all costs, fees and expenses of Trustee and of this Trust, including cost of evidence of title and reasonable counsel fees in connection with sale, Trustee shall apply the proceeds of sale to payment of: all sums expended under the terms hereof, not then repaid, with accrued interest at seven per cent per annum; all other sums then secured hereby; and the remainder, if any, to the person or persons legally entitled thereto.

Inurement

7. This Deed applies to, inures to the benefit of, and binds all parties hereto, their heirs, legatees, devisees, administrators, executors, successors and assigns. The term Beneficiary shall mean the holder and owner of the note secured hereby; or, if the note has been pledged, the pledgee thereof. In this Deed, whenever the context so requires, the masculine gender includes the feminine and/or neuter, and the singular number includes the plural.

Acceptance by Trustee

8. Trustee accepts this Trust when this Deed, duly executed and acknowledged, is made a public record as provided by law. Trustee is not obligated to notify any party hereto of pending sale under any other Deed of Trust or of any action or proceeding in which Trustor, Beneficiary or Trustee shall be a party unless brought by Trustee.

Substitution of Trustees

9. Beneficiary may, from time to time, as provided by statue, or by a writing, signed and acknowledged by him and recorded in the office of the county recorder of the county in which said land or such part thereof as is then affected by this deed of trust is situated, appoint another Trustee in place and stead of Trustee herein named, and thereupon, the Trustee herein named shall be discharged and Trustee so appointed shall be substituted as Trustee hereunder with the same effect as if originally named Trustee herein.

Cotrustees

10. If two or more persons be designated as Trustee herein, any, or all, powers granted herein to Trustee may be exercised by any of such persons, if the other person or persons is unable for any reason, to act, and any recital of such inability in any instrument executed by any of such persons shall be conclusive against Trustor, his heirs and assigns.

DO NOT RECORD

To obtain either a partial Reconveyance or a Subordination Agreement, this Deed of Trust, together with the note secured hereby, must be presented to the Trustee for endorsement, accompanied by either a Request for Partial Reconveyance or a Subordination Agreement, as the case may be, and Trustee's fee.

To obtain a full Reconveyance of this Deed of Trust present to the Trustee this request properly executed, the Deed of Trust, the original note secured by said Deed of Trust and any other evidence of indebtedness secured thereby, together with reconveyance fee.

REQUEST FOR FULL RECONVEYANCE

To_____(name of trustee)_____, Trustee.   Date: _____(date)_____

The undersigned is the legal owner and holder of the note in the amount of $_____(loan)_____and all other indebtedness secured by the foregoing Deed of Trust, which was recorded in Book_____Page_____of_____Official Records of the____(name of office where document recorded)____County of_____,_____(name of county)_____

_____

You are hereby notified that said note and all other sums and indebtedness secured by said Deed of Trust have been fully paid and satisfied; and you are hereby requested and directed upon surrender to you of said note, Deed of Trust, and evidence of any other indebtedness secured thereby, for cancellation and retention, and upon payment to you of any sums owing to you under the terms of said Deed of Trust, to reconvey, without warranty, to "the person or persons legally entitled thereto," the estate now held by you thereunder.

Mail reconveyance to this address:

_____(address of borrower)_____   Signed:_____(signature of lender)_____

Received reconveyance: _____   Signed:_____(signature of borrower)_____

229

Form 41

INSTALLMENT NOTE
(Combined Principal and Interest in Equal Installments)

$(Amount of Loan)   (City)   (State) _____(Date)__, 19____

FOR VALUE RECEIVED, I promise to pay in lawful money of the United States of America,

to _____(Name of Lender)_____

_____, or order at

___(Trustee or Institution which will collect the payments)_____

the principal sum of___(Amount of Loan)_____(Interest__ Dollars,

with interest in like lawful money from_(Date loan is made)___, 19_____ at__Rate)_____per cent

per annum on the amounts of principal sum remaining unpaid from time to time.

Principal and interest payable in_(monthly, quarterly, annual)_____installments of

_____(Amount of Payment to be made with each installment)_____ Dollars,

or more each, on the_(Day of Payment)_____day of each and every_(Payment Period)_

beginning (The date payments must start to be made on the loan)

Each payment shall be credited first, to the interest then due; and the remainder to the principal sum; and interest shall thereupon cease upon the amount so paid on said principal sum. AND I agree that in case of default in the payment of any installments when due, then the whole of said principal sum then remaining unpaid, together with the interest that shall have accrued thereon, shall forthwith become due and payable at the election of the holder of this note, without notice. AND, I agree, if action be instituted on this note to pay such sum as the Court may fix as Attorney's fees. THIS NOTE IS secured by a deed of trust of even date herewith to (Name of Trustee) a (State) Corporation, as TRUSTEE.

(Name of Borrower)

(Signature of Borrower)

69. SAMPLE INSTALLMENT NOTE

Most notes are negotiable, which means they are as good as money and the holder of the note can sell or transfer it to another person and "order" the debtor to make all future payments to the new holder of the note. If the note states that you are to "pay to the order of" somebody, it is negotiable. If no words to that effect are present, the note is probably nonnegotiable, and you should only pay the person named in the note.

If you give a mortgage or trust deed to your seller, try to sign a nonnegotiable note so that if you discover later that he violated the Con-tract of Sale, you can cease paying on the note. If the note has been transferred to someone other than the seller it will be difficult for you to legally justify not paying since the new holder is not the party who wronged you.

A few states use a bond rather than a note as evidence of the debt. A bond generally contains the same information as a note and has the additional protection of a formal seal by a notary public. You might also encounter a document that incorporates both the security of the debt and the evidence of the debt. That is, the elements of a mortgage or trust deed and a note or bond are combined in the same form. Read every word and thoroughly understand the provisions of any document you sign. Always keep a copy.

A SECOND, OR "JUNIOR," MORTGAGE AND DEED OF TRUST

If you have more than one mortgage on your land, one is always junior to the other, which means that under a foreclosure action, the senior lender collects first and any surplus goes to the junior lender.

For example, say you want to buy some property for $20,000, but the seller wants 75 percent cash down payment and you only have $5,000. You find you can get a loan from a bank for $10,000 to make the $15,000 down payment, but then you must give the seller a "second mortgage" on the remaining $5,000 owed for the land. The seller will have to agree to "subordinate" his mortgage to the bank's mortgage in order for the bank to make the loan. Commercial lenders always insist on

having a lien on the property that is superior to all other credit liens. If you fail to make your payments either to the bank or to the seller, the loan will be foreclosed, and the bank will get to collect its money first. Any money left over goes next to the seller holding the second mortgage up to the amount of his lien. If any money is left, it goes to you. If the seller takes a second mortgage he runs a greater risk of not being able to collect the money owed him if a foreclosure becomes necessary. Therefore, he might charge you a higher rate of interest on his mortgage. You will usually have to repay both mortgages simultaneously.

You might want a second mortgage or trust deed to obtain money to construct a house or other improvement on the land after you take title. If you give the seller a mortgage on the land, you might convince him to subordinate it to enable you to obtain a bank load to build a house. Since a house increases the value of the property and, therefore, the potential selling price of the land, the risk of losing money in the event that a foreclosure becomes necessary diminishes for both the commercial lender and the seller.

DEED OF RECONVEYANCE

_____, a corporation, as TRUSTEE under the Deed of Trust executed _____, 19___ by

and recorded in Liber _____ of Official Records of _____ County, State of _____, at page _____ (Recorder's Serial No._____) pursuant to the written request of the beneficiary, does hereby GRANT AND RECONVEY unto the PERSON OR PERSONS LEGALLY ENTITLED THERETO, without warranty, all the estate and interest derived to said TRUSTEE by or through said Deed of Trust, in the lands therein described.

_____, Trustee,   Dated _____, 19 ___

By _____   By _____
         Its Vice President   *Its Vice President*

STATE OF _____, County of _____
On _____, 19___ before me, the undersigned, a Notary Public, in and for said
County and State, personally appeared _____
known to me to be the Vice Presidents of the corporation that executed the within instrument, and
also known to me to be the persons who executed it on behalf of such corporation and acknowledged
to me that such corporation executed the same.

_____ *Notary Public*
         Type or Print Name of Notary

70. SAMPLE DEED OF RECONVEYANCE

When you have "satisfied" the loan by completing all your payments, you must request that your creditor issue you a Certificate of Satisfaction, or, if you have a "title theory" mortgage or deed of trust, a Deed of Reconveyance. (Illustration 70 is a sample Deed of Reconveyance which would be used with a deed of trust.) This document must be recorded immediately with the county Recorder. Once it is recorded, your title becomes clear of the lien against it. You should also have the original mortgage or deed of trust and the note or bond returned to you.

ILLUSTRATIONS COMPARING TYPES OF FINANCING AND WHERE THEY ARE USED

Illustration 71 shows which forms of financing are most common in each state. Illustration 72 shows the different operations of the four types of financing; Land Contract, Title Theory of Mortgage, Lien Theory of Mortgage, and Deed of Trust. By following this diagram as you read the text you will readily understand the different methods used.

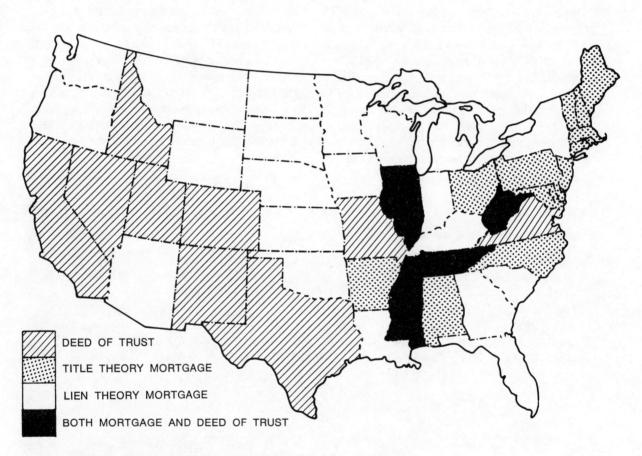

DEED OF TRUST

TITLE THEORY MORTGAGE

LIEN THEORY MORTGAGE

BOTH MORTGAGE AND DEED OF TRUST

71. COMMON FINANCING ARRANGEMENTS BY STATES

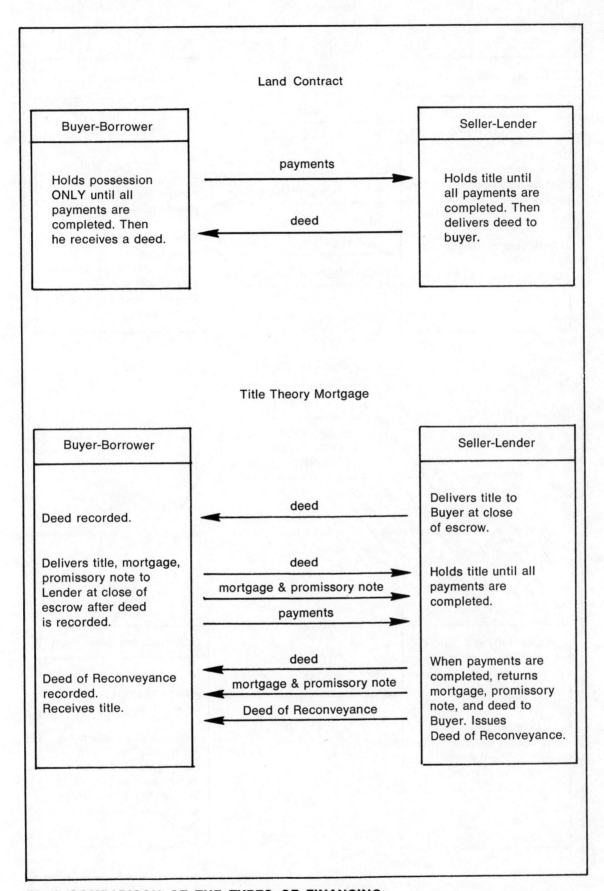

Land Contract

Buyer-Borrower

Holds possession ONLY until all payments are completed. Then he receives a deed.

payments →

← deed

Seller-Lender

Holds title until all payments are completed. Then delivers deed to buyer.

Title Theory Mortgage

Buyer-Borrower

Deed recorded.

Delivers title, mortgage, promissory note to Lender at close of escrow after deed is recorded.

Deed of Reconveyance recorded.
Receives title.

← deed

deed →
mortgage & promissory note →
payments →

← deed
← mortgage & promissory note
← Deed of Reconveyance

Seller-Lender

Delivers title to Buyer at close of escrow.

Holds title until all payments are completed.

When payments are completed, returns mortgage, promissory note, and deed to Buyer. Issues Deed of Reconveyance.

72. A COMPARISON OF THE TYPES OF FINANCING

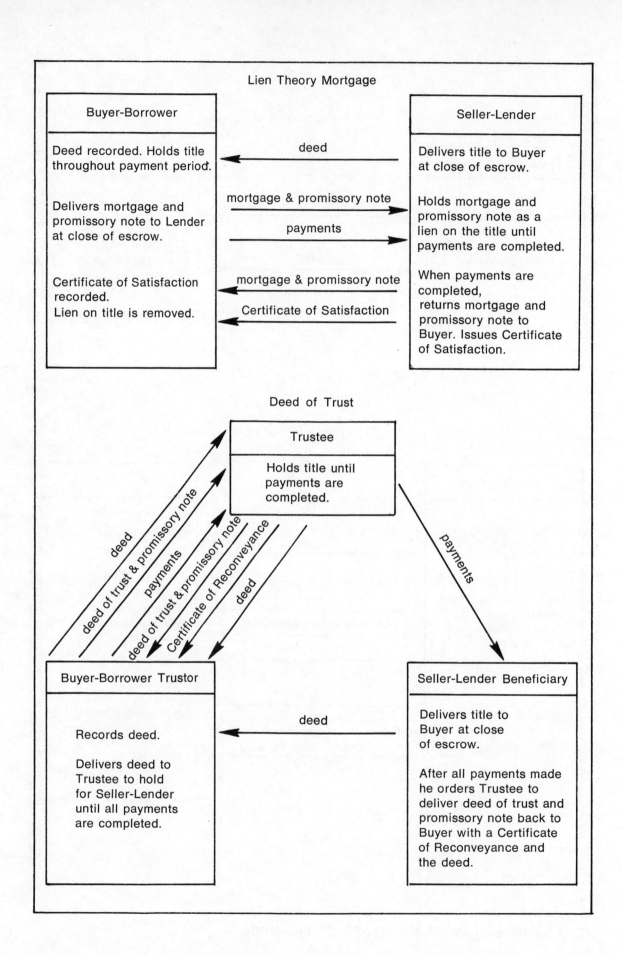

Lien Theory Mortgage

Buyer-Borrower

Deed recorded. Holds title throughout payment period.

Delivers mortgage and promissory note to Lender at close of escrow.

Certificate of Satisfaction recorded.
Lien on title is removed.

deed

mortgage & promissory note

payments

mortgage & promissory note

Certificate of Satisfaction

Seller-Lender

Delivers title to Buyer at close of escrow.

Holds mortgage and promissory note as a lien on the title until payments are completed.

When payments are completed, returns mortgage and promissory note to Buyer. Issues Certificate of Satisfaction.

Deed of Trust

Trustee

Holds title until payments are completed.

deed

deed of trust & promissory note

payments

deed of trust & promissory note

Certificate of Reconveyance

deed

payments

Buyer-Borrower Trustor

Records deed.

Delivers deed to Trustee to hold for Seller-Lender until all payments are completed.

deed

Seller-Lender Beneficiary

Delivers title to Buyer at close of escrow.

After all payments made he orders Trustee to deliver deed of trust and promissory note back to Buyer with a Certificate of Reconveyance and the deed.

chapter 22

Terms of the Loan Agreement and Their Effect on the Total Price

The terms of a loan include the amount of the loan, the interest rate being charged, the length of time in which the loan is to be paid off, the amount of each payment, and the payment plan (when each payment is to be made).

THREE DIFFERENT TYPES OF AMORTIZATION

Regardless of the type of financing you arrange, you will be making payments at regular intervals for a set length of time. This method of paying off a debt is called "amortization,"

and each installment you make will usually consist of principal and interest.

The "principal" is the amount of money you borrow or owe. The "interest" is the price you are charged for the privilege of being allowed to pay the principal over a period of time. Interest is charged as a percentage of the unpaid principal and should always be quoted to you on a per annum, or yearly, rather than monthly or quarterly basis.

The three types of loan are the unamortized, the partially amortized, and the fully amortized loan. Each type results in differing costs to the borrower. To illustrate how to figure out the different financial aspects of each kind of loan I will use one simple example. Say you are buying 40 acres of land for $10,000. You are to give the seller a down payment of 20 percent of the purchase price, or $2,000, and he will take back a note and mortgage for the remaining $8,000. The $8,000 is to be paid off in ten years with 7 percent interest due per year on the outstanding principal. Here are the figures for easy reference:

Total price	$10,000
Cash down payment	$2,000
Principal (to be paid in ten years)	$8,000
Interest rate	7 percent

Unamortized Loan

Since "amortize" means to pay off a loan in installments, under an unamortized loan the entire principal is paid in a lump sum at the end of a specified period of time. Interest on the principal is paid at regular intervals. The total amount of interest you will pay using this type of payment plan is extremely large due to the fact that the principal does not decrease as the interest is paid. Using our example, the principal of $8,000 is to be paid in one sum at the end of ten years. During those ten years, interest may be paid once a year. Seven percent of $8,000 is $560 interest due each year. Interest of $560 per year for ten years will amount to $5,600 interest for the entire period of the loan. At the end of ten years, the principal amount of $8,000 is due. The total cost of interest on the loan is $5,600.

Partially Amortized Loan

The partially amortized method of paying off a loan is rarely used but is much cheaper than the unamortized method. By this method you pay a fixed amount of the principal plus interest in regular installments. The amount of principal paid each time is always the same, but the amount of each payment changes because the amount of interest due gets progressively smaller as the debt is paid. Say the $8,000 is to be paid in annual installments of $800 for ten years. At the end of the first year the amount of interest is 7 percent of the full $8,000 since none of the loan has been paid yet. Seven percent of $8,000 is $560. Thus, the first payment will consist of $800 principal and $560 interest or a total of $1,360. Subtracting the $800 payment of principal from the total borrowed leaves $7,200 of the loan left unpaid. The interest due at the end of the next year will be 7 percent of $7,200, or $504, and that year's payment will be $800 plus $504, or $1,304. This leaves $6,400 of the principal unpaid. The interest the next year will be 7 percent of $6,400, or $448, so the payment will be $800 plus $448, or $1,248. As the amount of interest due gets smaller, each payment gets smaller, until the last year's payment will consist of only $56 interest plus $800 principal, or $856. By adding up the interest paid each time, the total amount of interest for ten years is $3,080. This is much smaller than the $5,600 interest paid on the unamortized loan.

Fully Amortized Loan

A fully amortized loan is the most common payment method used today. This loan plan, like the partially amortized method, combines paying principal and interest in each installment, but the amount of each payment is always the same. Since interest is charged as a percentage of the unpaid principal, the portion going to pay the interest is quite large in the first payments. As you pay off the loan, the portion of each payment allotted to the principal gradually increases, while the amount going to pay the interest gradually decreases. You will see how this works below.

Because payments are almost always made in monthly, rather than annual, installments, I will do the following example using a monthly payment plan. An amortization table (see Illustration 73) is very helpful in figuring out various aspects of the payment schedule.

1. Figuring the amount of each payment.

To figure the amount of each monthly payment using our example, first look at Illustration 73 under "Term of years" for 10 years. Then move to the right under the column "7%" which is the interest rate. The number there, $11.62, is the amount you must pay per month for each $1,000 due on the mortgage. Since you owe $8,000, you multiply this figure by 8. The result, $92.96, is the amount of each monthly payment to pay off a loan of $8,000 at 7 percent interest over a period of ten years. When the seller or lender tells you what his terms are, you can plug in the figures to determine what each monthly payment will be.

2. Figuring the length of the amortization period.

When dealing with money, figures are often rounded off to a figure easy to work with,

Term of years	5%	5¼%	5½%	5¾%	6%	6¼%	6½%	6.6%	6¾%	7%	7.2%	7¼%	7½%	7¾%	7.8%	8%	8.4%	8½%	9%	9½%	10%
5	18.88	18.99	19.11	19.22	19.34	19.45	19.57	19.62	19.69	19.81	19.90	19.92	20.04	20.16	20.19	20.28	20.47	20.52	20.76	21.01	21.25
6	16.11	16.23	16.34	16.46	16.58	16.70	16.81	16.86	16.93	17.05	17.15	17.17	17.30	17.42	17.44	17.54	17.73	17.78	18.03	18.28	18.53
7	14.14	14.26	14.38	14.49	14.61	14.73	14.85	14.90	14.98	15.10	15.20	15.22	15.34	15.47	15.49	15.59	15.79	15.84	16.09	16.35	16.61
8	12.66	12.78	12.90	13.03	13.15	13.27	13.39	13.44	13.51	13.64	13.74	13.76	13.89	14.01	14.04	14.14	14.35	14.40	14.66	14.92	15.18
9	11.52	11.64	11.76	11.89	12.01	12.13	12.26	12.31	12.39	12.51	12.61	12.64	12.77	12.89	12.92	13.02	13.23	13.28	13.55	13.81	14.08
10	10.61	10.73	10.86	10.98	11.11	11.23	11.36	11.41	11.49	11.62	11.72	11.75	11.88	12.01	12.03	12.14	12.35	12.40	12.67	12.94	13.22
11	9.87	9.99	10.12	10.25	10.37	10.50	10.63	10.68	10.76	10.89	10.99	11.02	11.15	11.29	11.31	11.42	11.64	11.69	11.97	12.24	12.52
12	9.25	9.38	9.51	9.63	9.76	9.89	10.02	10.08	10.16	10.29	10.40	10.42	10.56	10.69	10.72	10.83	11.05	11.11	11.39	11.67	11.96
13	8.74	8.86	8.99	9.12	9.25	9.38	9.52	9.57	9.65	9.79	9.89	9.92	10.06	10.20	10.22	10.34	10.56	10.62	10.90	11.19	11.48
14	8.29	8.42	8.55	8.68	8.82	8.95	9.09	9.14	9.22	9.36	9.47	9.50	9.64	9.78	9.80	9.92	10.15	10.20	10.49	10.79	11.09
15	7.91	8.04	8.17	8.31	8.44	8.58	8.72	8.77	8.85	8.99	9.11	9.13	9.28	9.42	9.45	9.56	9.79	9.85	10.15	10.45	10.75
16	7.58	7.71	7.85	7.98	8.12	8.26	8.40	8.45	8.54	8.63	8.79	8.82	8.96	9.11	9.14	9.25	9.49	9.55	9.85	10.15	10.46
17	7.29	7.43	7.56	7.70	7.84	7.98	8.12	8.17	8.26	8.40	8.52	8.55	8.69	8.84	8.87	8.99	9.23	9.29	9.59	9.90	10.22
18	7.04	7.17	7.31	7.45	7.59	7.73	7.87	7.93	8.01	8.16	8.28	8.31	8.45	8.60	8.63	8.75	9.00	9.06	9.37	9.68	10.00
19	6.81	6.95	7.08	7.22	7.37	7.51	7.65	7.71	7.80	7.95	8.07	8.10	8.25	8.40	8.43	8.55	8.80	8.86	9.17	9.49	9.82
20	6.60	6.74	6.88	7.03	7.17	7.31	7.46	7.52	7.61	7.76	7.88	7.91	8.06	8.21	8.25	8.37	8.62	8.68	9.00	9.33	9.66
21	6.42	6.56	6.70	6.85	6.99	7.14	7.29	7.35	7.44	7.59	7.71	7.74	7.90	8.05	8.08	8.21	8.46	8.53	8.85	9.18	9.51
22	6.26	6.40	6.54	6.69	6.84	6.98	7.13	7.19	7.29	7.44	7.56	7.59	7.75	7.91	7.94	8.07	8.32	8.39	8.72	9.05	9.39
23	6.11	6.25	6.40	6.54	6.69	6.84	7.00	7.06	7.15	7.30	7.43	7.46	7.62	7.78	7.81	7.94	8.20	8.27	8.60	8.93	9.28
24	5.97	6.12	6.27	6.41	6.56	6.72	6.87	6.93	7.03	7.18	7.31	7.34	7.50	7.66	7.70	7.83	8.09	8.16	8.49	8.83	9.18
25	5.85	6.00	6.15	6.30	6.45	6.60	6.76	6.82	6.91	7.07	7.20	7.23	7.39	7.56	7.59	7.72	7.99	8.06	8.40	8.74	9.09
26	5.74	5.89	6.04	6.19	6.34	6.50	6.65	6.72	6.81	6.97	7.10	7.14	7.30	7.46	7.50	7.63	7.90				
27	5.64	5.78	5.94	6.09	6.24	6.40	6.56	6.62	6.72	6.88	7.01	7.05	7.21	7.38	7.41	7.55	7.82				
28	5.54	5.69	5.84	6.00	6.16	6.31	6.48	6.54	6.64	6.80	6.93	6.97	7.13	7.30	7.34	7.47	7.75				
29	5.45	5.61	5.76	5.92	6.08	6.24	6.40	6.46	6.56	6.73	6.86	6.89	7.06	7.23	7.27	7.40	7.68				
30	5.37	5.53	5.68	5.84	6.00	6.16	6.33	6.39	6.49	6.66	6.79	6.83	7.00	7.17	7.20	7.34	7.62				
35	5.05	5.21	5.38	5.54	5.71	5.88	6.05	6.12	6.22	6.39	6.53	6.57	6.75	6.93	6.96	7.11	7.40				
40	4.83	4.99	5.16	5.33	5.51	5.68	5.86	5.93	6.04	6.22	6.37	6.40	6.59	6.77	6.81	6.96	7.26				

73. TABLE OF PAYMENTS TO AMORTIZE $1,000 LOAN

usually to the nearest $1 or $5. Thus, if it worked out that your monthly payment were to be $92.96 per month, this figure would probably be rounded off to $93 per month. This is the figure I will use in the following example.

If the seller or lender tells you what your monthly payments will be but not how long you will be paying, you can determine this by working backwards in Illustration 73. Using the same example, if you are told that each payment is to be $93 per month, divide that figure by 8, since your principal is $8,000 rather than $1,000. Look down the "7%" column until you find the figure closest to the result— $11.62. The chart shows that for this monthly payment you will be paying ten years.

3. Figuring the total amount of interest on the loan.

Once you know what your monthly payments will be and how long you have to pay off the loan, you can easily determine how much the total interest will be. Continuing our example: The payments will extend for ten years. Twelve monthly payments per year for ten years makes a total of 120 monthly payments. By multiplying the $93 of each monthly payment by 120 payments, you get the total amount of principal and interest you will pay on your loan over ten years, which is $11,160. Since the loan is for $8,000, subtract that amount to see how much the total interest will be. $11,160 minus $8,000 is $3,160. This is the amount of interest on the loan.

4. Figuring how much of each payment is allocated for principal and interest.

You will want to know how much of each payment goes toward paying off the principal and how much goes toward paying the interest. Using our example (see Illustration 74): At the time of the first payment the unpaid balance is the total loan amount of $8,000. Since the interest rate is 7 percent per year on the unpaid principal, 7 percent of $8,000 is $560. Since $560 is the interest for an entire year, divide this figure by 12 to get the amount due the first month: $560 divided by 12 equals $46.67. Thus, out of a $93.00 payment, $46.67 will go to pay interest and $93.00 minus $46.67, or $46.33, will go to pay off the principal.

To figure the next month's ratio between interest and principal, subtract the $46.33 of the principal already paid from $8,000, which leaves $7,953.67 to be paid. Multiply that figure by 7 percent, getting $556.76 interest for the next twelve months. Dividing that figure by 12, the amount of the second installment going to pay the interest is $46.40 and the

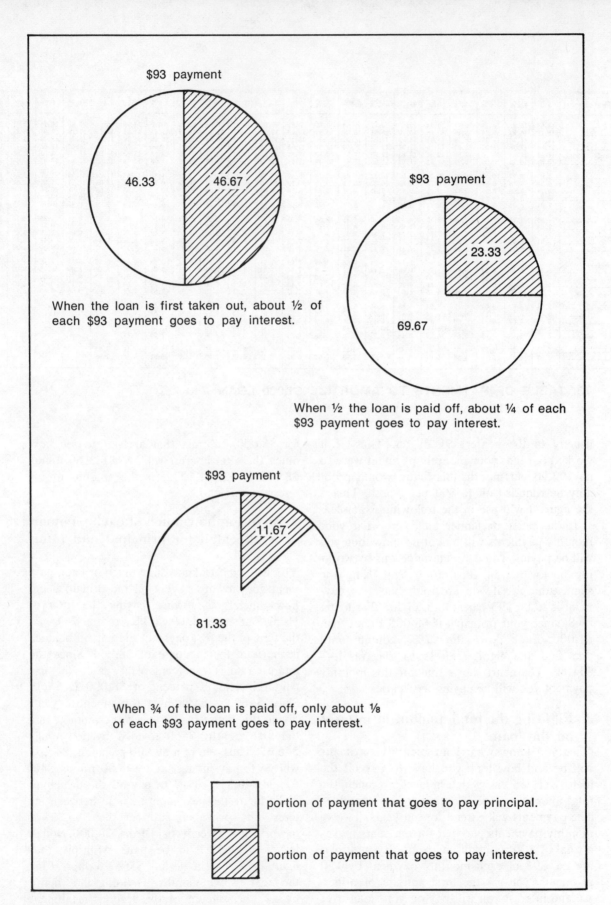

$93 payment

46.33   46.67

When the loan is first taken out, about ½ of each $93 payment goes to pay interest.

$93 payment

23.33

69.67

When ½ the loan is paid off, about ¼ of each $93 payment goes to pay interest.

$93 payment

11.67

81.33

When ¾ of the loan is paid off, only about ⅛ of each $93 payment goes to pay interest.

portion of payment that goes to pay principal.

portion of payment that goes to pay interest.

74. RELATIONSHIP BETWEEN PRINCIPAL AND INTEREST DURING PAYMENT PERIOD

amount going to pay the principal is $93.00 minus $46.40, or $46.60. Each succeeding monthly payment can be computed in this same way.

You see that the amount of interest paid when you first start to make payments is nearly the same as the amount of principal being paid. However, as the principal is paid off, the portion of the payment going to pay interest will drop steadily. By the time you have paid off half of the principal, the amount of interest in each payment will be much lower than the amount going to the principal. Figuring 7 percent of $4,000, half the principal, amounts to $280 interest for a year. Dividing this figure by 12, you get $23.33 interest due for one month. Out of the $93.00 payment now, only $23.33 goes to interest and $93.00 minus $23.33, or $69.67, goes to pay the principal, a considerable increase in the ratio of principal to interest. By the time three-quarters of the loan is paid off, the interest portion will be quite low, amounting to only $11.67 out of the $93.00 payment.

Another method of determining the portion of each monthly payment that goes toward paying the interest is by using an interest table, such as Illustration 75. This table breaks a year into 12 months of 30 days each with 360 days to a year. For this reason, the results are only close approximations rather than the exact figures you get using the above method. Remember we determined that the first month's payment of $93.00 included $46.67 interest owed on the principal. Now let's use the table in Illustration 75 to determine this amount.

Look under the column "Days" to find 30, representing one month, since the payments are made each month. Since the interest rate is 7 percent, move to the right to the "7%" column. The number there is 5.8333, called the "factor." The table is figured on the basis of $1,000. The principal amount remaining at the first payment is $8,000. Divide this amount by $1,000 to get 8. Multiply the factor by 8 to get the amount of interest due that month, in this case $46.6664 or $46.67, when rounded off, the same figure we got before. Now let's

360 Days to the Year

Days	5%	6%	7%	8%	9%	10%
1	0.1389	0.1667	0.1944	0.2222	0.2500	0.2778
2	0.2778	0.3333	0.3889	0.4444	0.5000	0.5556
3	0.4167	0.5000	0.5833	0.6666	0.7500	0.8334
4	0.5556	0.6667	0.7778	0.8888	1.0000	1.1112
5	0.6944	0.8333	0.9722	1.1111	1.2500	1.3890
6	0.8333	1.0000	1.1667	1.3333	1.5000	1.6668
7	0.9722	1.1667	1.3611	1.5555	1.7500	1.9446
8	1.1111	1.3333	1.5556	1.7777	2.0000	2.2224
9	1.2500	1.5000	1.7500	2.0000	2.2500	2.5002
10	1.3889	1.6667	1.9444	2.2222	2.5000	2.7780
11	1.5278	1.8333	2.1389	2.4444	2.7500	3.0558
12	1.6667	2.0000	2.3333	2.6666	3.0000	3.3336
13	1.8056	2.1667	2.5278	2.8888	3.2500	3.6114
14	1.9444	2.3333	2.7222	3.1111	3.5000	3.8892
15	2.0833	2.5000	2.9167	3.3333	3.7500	4.1670
16	2.2222	2.6667	3.1111	3.5555	4.0000	4.4448
17	2.3611	2.8333	3.3055	3.7777	4.2500	4.7226
18	2.5000	3.0000	3.5000	4.0000	4.5000	5.0004
19	2.6389	3.1667	3.6944	4.2222	4.7500	5.2782
20	2.7778	3.3333	3.8889	4.4444	5.0000	5.5560
21	2.9167	3.5000	4.0833	4.6666	5.2500	5.8338
22	3.0556	3.6667	4.2778	4.8888	5.5000	6.1116
23	3.1944	3.8333	4.4722	5.1111	5.7500	6.3894
24	3.2222	4.0000	4.6667	5.3333	6.0000	6.6672
25	3.4722	4.1667	4.8611	5.5555	6.2500	6.9450
26	3.6111	4.3333	5.0555	5.7777	6.5000	7.2228
27	3.7500	4.5000	5.2500	6.0000	6.7500	7.5006
28	3.8889	4.6667	5.4444	6.2222	7.0000	7.7784
29	4.0278	4.8333	5.6389	6.4444	7.2500	8.0562
30	4.1667	5.0000	5.8333	6.6666	7.5000	8.3340
31st day						

75. INTEREST TABLE FIGURED ON $1,000

figure the second monthly payment with the table. The remaining principal is $7,953.67. Dividing this by $1,000, we get 7.95367, which rounds off to 7.954. Multiply the factor, 5.8333, by this number, 7.954, to get the amount of interest due the second month, which is $46.398, or $46.40.

THE BALLOON PAYMENT

A "balloon payment" is the last payment made on the loan. It is "ballooned" because it is much larger than the regular installment amount. For example, on a $15,000 loan for fifteen years, on the last month of the fifteenth year, you might have only repaid $13,000 of the principal. Thus, you will have a balloon of slightly more than $2,000, which includes the remaining principal and interest.

THE LOAN FEES

Every financial institution charges extra money for the privilege of receiving a loan, which is in addition to the lender's charges for credit checks, property appraisal, points, and drawing up and recording the loan documents (to be discussed in Chapter 25: *Borrowing from Third Party Lenders*). The charge can be called one of the following: a "debt service fee," "origination fee," "loan installment fee," "loan brokerage fee," "new loan fee," or "placement fee." It is usually calculated as a certain percentage of the loan. The fees are not standard from lender to lender, so it is possible to save a few hundred dollars by shopping around for a low fee lender.

HOW TO GET A COMPUTERIZED LOAN AMORTIZATION SCHEDULE

Although knowing how to compute all the aspects of your loan yourself is essential, a computer company in Santa Monica, California, will compute everything for you for a slight fee. You must send the following information: the amount of the loan, the interest rate, the term

of the loan in years and months, the amount of each payment, the payment plan (monthly, quarterly, annually, etc.) You can omit either the term of the loan or the amount of each payment and they can still compute your loan. Indicate if the interest is to be paid as part of each installment. If you are to make monthly payments and escrow closes in the middle of the month, the first payment will not be for a full thirty days. Give the number of days accounted for in that first month.

Getting a Loan Amortization Schedule costs $4. It gives the terms of the loan, including the number of payments, the amount of each payment, the breakdown of how much of each payment goes toward principal and how much toward interest, the amount of the principal still unpaid at the end of each payment, and the sum of the entire loan. You can also buy a Truth in Lending Law Disclosure Statement for an additional $4. It states the full amount of any finance charges the lending institution may attach and the interest charged on the loan. The company responds to requests immediately. Send your name and address and the information you desire to: Delphi Information Sciences Corporation, P.O. Box 3066, Santa Monica, California 90403. (See "Useful Resources" in Chapter 27 for a pamphlet on Truth in Lending.) You should, however, try to get the seller or real estate agent to furnish this essential information for you.

FACTORS THAT AFFECT THE COST OF A LOAN

The Effect of the Interest Rate on the Cost of the Loan

When a loan is being paid off over a long period of time, a variation in the interest rate of even 0.5 percent can make quite a difference in the total amount you pay. The figures below show the effect of 0.5 percent increases in the interest rate on an $8,000 loan over a period of ten years:

Interest Rate (%)	Monthly Payment of Principal and Interest	Total Interest for 10 years
6	$88.88	$2,665.60
6½	90.88	2,895.60
7	92.96	3,960.00
7½	95.06	3,407.20
8	97.12	3,654.40
8½	99.20	3,904.00
9	101.36	4,163.20

Payment Period (years)	Monthly Payment of Principal and Interest	Total Interest Paid
5	$158.48	$1,508.80
7	120.80	2,147.20
9	100.08	2,808.64
10	92.96	3,160.00

The Effect of the Amount of the Down Payment on the Cost of the Loan

The more cash you can afford for a down payment, the cheaper your loan will be in the long run. The figures below show the amount of interest paid in proportion to various down payments made on a $10,000 purchase at 7 percent interest paid off in monthly installments for ten years:

Down Payment	Monthly Payment of Principal and Interest for 10 years	Total Interest for 10 years
0	$116.20	$3,944.00
500.00	111.84	3,920.80
1,000.00	104.58	3,549.60
2,000.00	92.96	3,160.00
3,000.00	81.34	2,760.80
4,000.00	69.72	2,366.40
5,000.00	58.10	1,972.00

The Effect of the Payment Period on the Cost of the Loan

Although the total amount of interest will be lower if you pay off your loan fast, most buyers like to spread their payments over a long period of time in order to keep the monthly payments at a level easy to meet. However, to give you an example of the effect of the payment period on the cost of a loan, the figures below show the size of each payment and the total amount of interest on an $8,000 loan at 7 percent interest for four different payment periods:

THE ADVANTAGES OF PREPAYMENT WITHOUT PENALTY OR PROHIBITION

You can cut down on the total amount of interest you will ultimately pay by making larger payments early in the payment schedule since interest is figured as a percentage of the unpaid principal. You can only do this if your loan agreement includes a statement that "the principal and interest are payable in installments of———dollars or more." (See Illustration 69 in Chapter 21.)

Your creditor may not want you to pay off your loan early because that would deprive him of interest. Another reason for prohibition of early payment is that the creditor does not want to take in more money than expected because it would push him into a higher income tax bracket. He might put a "prepayment penalty clause" in the note that specifies that you are to be penalized if you pay off any part of the loan in advance. This penalty makes up for the interest lost by the early payment. Always fight to have such a penalty clause removed from the loan agreement and note.

If you are permitted to make larger payments when you choose to do so, you should specify that if you pay more than the amount due for one installment, that amount can be credited later if you miss a payment. Thus, if you have some financial trouble you can use previous extra payments in place of the payments you are forced to miss.

If you decide to sell your land before it is fully paid for, you will be in a better position if you can offer your buyer title free of encumbrances. If you are allowed to prepay your debt, when your buyer pays you for the land you can pay off your creditor to get clear title. If you are not permitted to prepay your debt, you will be unable to clear the title for your buyer and you might have trouble selling the land.

Sometimes a lender will be very happy to receive a large amount of cash early and you might save some money. If you come into some money, you can offer to prepay the total remaining due if your creditor gives you a discount on the remaining unpaid balance. It might be that the lender could really use that extra cash and is anxious to have the mortgage paid off early in exchange for a discount. Such a situation occurs frequently when the seller finances the sale himself.

"ESCALATION CLAUSE" AND THE "VARIABLE INTEREST RATE"

Your creditor may have an "escalation clause" in the loan agreement which permits him to "adjust" the interest rate he is charging you at any time during the payment period. Because he decides when to adjust the rate, he will do it only when the current market interest rate rises. Do not permit the inclusion of such a clause in your agreement.

However, a loan with a "variable interest rate," whereby the interest rate increases or decreases with the movement of the money market, may be valuable if interest rates are exceedingly high at the time you take out a loan. Under the variable loan, or floating loan, the interest rate is adjusted in line with fluctuations in the general interest on the loan

market. A market "index" has been established which registers rising and falling interest rates throughout the country, and this index is the basis for the variable interest rate. Ask your lender about this optional loan plan. Just remember that interest rates go up more often than they go down.

LOAN INTEREST IS TAX DEDUCTIBLE

You are permitted to deduct any interest you pay on a loan from your state and federal income tax obligation. This, along with the right to deduct property taxes from your income taxes, makes land ownership easier for the average-income family.

MAINTAINING A PAYMENT SCHEDULE

It is important to maintain an accurate schedule of your loan payments and the terms of your loan. Illustration 76 can be used as a model when you set up your payment schedule. You can figure out what portion of each payment goes to principal and to interest by using the methods explained at the beginning of this chapter.

76. SAMPLE PAYMENT SCHEDULE

Amount of Principal Indebtedness _____

Interest Rate of _____ % Payable _____ (e.g., monthly, quarterly)

Payments Made _____ (e.g., the first day of each month) Beginning _____

Date	Amount of Full Payment	Amount of Interest Paid	Amount Going Towards Principal	Principal Balance Still Owed

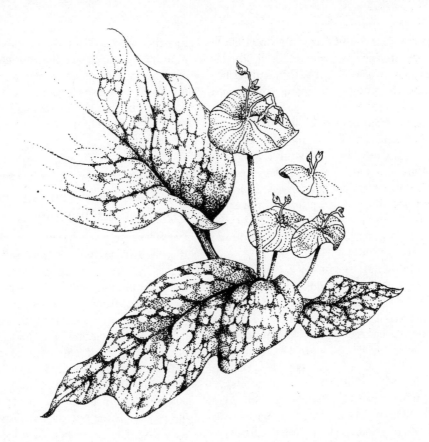

chapter 23

Buying Property That Is Encumbered by a Loan Agreement

TAKING SUBJECT TO OR ASSUMING A LOAN

When you buy land, if the seller still owes money under a loan agreement that he cannot pay off before conveying title to you, you will either take the land "subject to" the loan or you will "assume" the loan.

If you buy "subject to" a loan, the seller continues to be personally responsible for making the payments until his loan is fully paid. You make a separate loan agreement with the seller.

You then pay him and he pays his creditor. When he pays off his loan he will get clear title to the land. When you finish paying your seller he will give you good title. During this time, if the seller fails to make his payments, his creditor can foreclose on his loan and you will lose the land because your seller won't have it to convey to you.

On the other hand, if you "assume" the loan, you replace the seller and become personally liable to his creditor for the remaining debt. You pay your seller a sum of money in cash and get the property, with the remaining obligation on the loan. You are then primarily responsible for paying the loan. If you fail to make your payments, the creditor can foreclose on your loan. He can also sue your seller if he seeks a deficiency judgment, unless your seller gets the creditor to sign a document relieving him of liability under the loan once you assume it.

Most loan agreements have a clause that prohibits transferring the debt without the written approval of the lender. If you are to assume a loan, be certain that the seller has his creditor's approval to transfer the property to you. Often a creditor will only allow the debtor to transfer his obligation if the interest rate can be raised. If it will be raised before you are to assume the loan, you should shop around to see if you can get a new loan on better terms from someone else. If you can, borrow the money and pay for the land in cash, and give a mortgage to your lender under the terms you have received. If you cannot get a better deal than the loan you are to assume and you still want to purchase the land, get the seller to reduce his asking price by the amount of the increased interest you will be bound to pay.

It is usually better to assume a loan than to take subject to it. If the seller will only allow you to take title to the land subject to his loan rather than by assuming it, be careful. He may be planning to charge you a higher interest rate in his loan agreement with you than he is paying his lender so he can make a profit on the extra interest. This type of "secondary" loan agreement is called a "wrap-around" loan agreement because your mortgage with your seller "wraps around," or includes, the loan agreement the seller has with his lender. Find out what the seller's interest rate is and if he intends to overcharge you if you buy subject to his loan. Do not let him get away with this. Even if his increased interest rate is no larger than you would get under a new loan agreement, you are always better off assuming a loan than taking subject to it because you can deal directly with the creditor.

If you do take title subject to a loan agreement, be sure the seller has permission from his lender to sell the property. Many loan agreements contain an "acceleration clause," or "due-on-sale" clause, which is activated if the borrower sells or encumbers the land without permission. If the land is sold to you without permission from the lender, he can demand immediate payment of the entire remaining principal and interest. If your seller cannot pay this amount, the loan can be foreclosed on, and you could lose the land. Under these provisions the only way a seller can convey his land is by paying the remaining money due before the sale.

The Contract of Sale should specify if you are to take title subject to, or by assuming, an existing loan. Either way, you should receive an Offset Statement from the creditor specifying the amount of interest and principal remaining on the loan, the amount of each payment, and how much longer payments must be made. If you are assuming a loan held by a commercial lender, a fee will be charged for the necessary paperwork to transfer the documents.

Prorating the Loan Agreement if You Assume the Obligation

If you assume the responsibility of paying off the seller's loan on the property, you may have to prorate the seller's payment during the month that escrow closes. For instance, say escrow is to close on the thirteenth day of the month and payments are made on the first. If the monthly payments you are to assume are $150 including principal and interest, divide this figure by 30, the commonly accepted number of days in a month, to get the amount of the payment due per day, in this case $5. Multiply the $5 owed per day by the seventeen days that you will own the land that month. You will credit the seller with this amount, in this case $85, since he paid the entire month's payment on the first. To see how this fits into the pattern of closing of escrow, see Chapter 30: *Opening and Closing of Escrow and the Role of the Escrow Holder.*

Getting the Seller to Remove the Lien at the Time of Purchase

If you want title to the property free of an existing loan agreement, Clause 4 of the Model Contract of Sale (Chapter 28) takes care of this. When you place your money in escrow, you should instruct the escrow holder to pay the lender the money due him and request that a Certificate of Satisfaction or Deed of Reconveyance be recorded with the deed to the property and that you receive a copy.

Assignment of the Loan Agreement

During the time you are making payments, your creditor might "assign" his rights to receive your payments to a third party in exchange for cash. Some commercial businesses buy loan agreement notes for an amount of cash that is less than the amount due on the loan. A person who needs money might be willing to sell his note at a loss for immediate cash. This frequently occurs with sellers who finance their own sales.

When an "assignment" occurs, a document is executed between your creditor and the buyer of your note which is recorded with the county Recorder. When the recording takes place, you will be notified and bound to make all further payments to the new holder of the note. You might be required to sign a document, called an Owner's Estoppel Certificate, which certifies the amount of money you still owe on the loan and states that you are personally bound to pay the remaining amount. This document is executed to protect the person who is buying the right to receive your payments.

If you want to be able to sell your land before paying off your loan, you will also want the right to assign your obligation to your buyer. Your mortgage or trust deed and note must specify that you have the right to assign your liabilities to a purchaser who can take the property subject to your debt or assume it entirely.

PAYING THE INSURANCE, TAXES, AND ASSESSMENTS ON THE LAND—IMPOUNDS

Since the basic security for a loan is the property, your creditor wants to be certain that nothing happens to endanger his security. Therefore, he will probably require that you pay him the money for insurance, taxes, and assessments in advance and he can then pay them as they become due. These additions to your normal payments are called "impounds." Generally, in each payment you will be charged a portion of the annual insurance premiums and taxes for that year. The insurance premium and taxes are divided equally into twelve monthly installments if that is how you pay your mortgage or deed of trust.

If the seller rather than a financial institution is your creditor, you may be responsible for paying these expenses yourself. But the Tax Collector will be instructed to notify him of any lapses in tax payments so that he can have a chance to pay them before the land is subjected to a tax sale. If you fail to pay the taxes or premiums the creditor can legally foreclose on you. If there is a house on the land your creditor will probably require you to carry a basic policy of property insurance protecting the property against fire and other hazards. You will have to name the lender as beneficiary in the policy and deliver a copy of the insurance coverage to him. The loan agreement will specify the amount of insurance coverage you must buy. These impounds will increase your monthly payments by $5 to $20 per month over the principal and interest due.

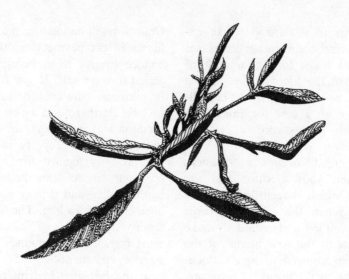

chapter 24

Foreclosure, Redemption, and What to Do if You Can't Make Payments

FORECLOSURE

If you fail to make your payments on time, your creditor under a mortgage or deed of trust can "foreclose" the loan. Foreclosure is exercised in various ways depending on the laws in the particular state but the end result is always the same. You will lose your land.

Most states require a court foreclosure, which means that a Notice of Default must first be filed with the county Recorder stating that the buyer has not made the required payments. The buyer is then given from one to three months to make up the missed payments. If the payments are not made, the creditor can

file a Petition To Foreclose in the county court. The court evaluates the creditor's claim, determines its validity, declares the amount of money that is due him, and orders a foreclosure.

Then the creditor usually publishes a notice in the local newspaper that the property is to be sold to the highest cash bidder at a public auction. The sale is supervised by the court and often handled by a court-appointed commissioner. The proceeds from the sale are used to pay the creditor any money due on the land sale. If any surplus money remains, it goes to the defaulting buyer. This may not be a bad deal for the buyer if the land sells for a good price, but often it sells for less than its actual worth and the buyer loses a great deal of money and the land.

Under other policies, such as the "foreclosure without sale," "strict foreclosure," or "foreclosure by entry and possession," the creditor takes the entire property and can do with it as he wishes. The debtor will not take any excess profits from a land sale. In some states, the creditor can only take back an amount of land equal in value to the amount of money still owed him. Thus, if half the payments have already been made, the creditor can take only half the land.

When executing a loan agreement, you should understand the type of foreclosure the creditor can use if you default. You can attempt to include a provision limiting a foreclosure on the loan to a portion of the land representing the amount of the outstanding balance and/or stating you have the right to the proceeds of a foreclosure sale in excess of the amount due the creditor.

The Dangerous Acceleration Clause

A clause creditors usually put into the loan agreement states that the creditor can immediately demand, or "accelerate," the entire amount of the remaining principal and interest if you either miss a payment, cause a lien to be placed against the property, or go bankrupt. You cannot prevent foreclosure by simply making up back payments. The entire amount due must be paid. Although this is a standard clause in most loan agreements, you should try to have it striken and replaced with a normal right-of-redemption clause.

THE RIGHT OF REDEMPTION

Most states have laws allowing the debtor a certain period of time after foreclosure proceedings have begun to make up his payments and keep the land. This grace period, which is usually one year, is referred to as the "right of redemption" or "equity of redemption." However, a penalty fee of up to 1 percent of the remaining principal and interest may be levied.

In some states, the redemption period extends until the time of the sale by foreclosure, which might be anywhere from two months to a year after the buyer defaults. If you make up your back payments during this grace period, no further action can be taken against you by the creditor, except for the collection of a penalty. If you do not make up your payments by the time the foreclosure sale is initiated, you have no further chance of keeping the land.

Some states allow a right of redemption even after a sale or repossession of the land by foreclosure. When the land is sold at a foreclosure sale, the new buyer does not take full title to it but gets an "equitable right" to the title during the period of redemption. He will get full

legal title only if the debtor does not make up his payments by the end of the redemption period. During this time, the debtor still retains the right of possession of the land.

Be certain that a right-of-redemption clause exists in your loan agreement. Although it is usually absent in a loan agreement, try to get such a right added in writing to the form, specifying that the right of redemption exists up to one year after the land is sold by foreclosure. This is a good idea, even if the state law already provides for a one-year redemption period.

THE DEFICIENCY JUDGMENT

Sometimes the lender has a right to sue the borrower to get a "deficiency judgment" if an insufficient amount of money is obtained from a foreclosure sale to make up the amount of money due him. However, most states and courts will not permit a deficiency judgment when the loan is made for the purchase of a home or land. Since the loan was made on the basis of the value of the security, the creditor cannot complain if it later results that the property is worth less than the loan. If enough money is not obtained at a resale of land, the court assumes that the buyer probably paid too much for it in the first place and should not have to suffer further because of that circumstance.

For instance, the seller sells you his land for $15,000, you make $5,000 worth of payments, and then default. You still owe $10,000. The seller forecloses the loan and resells the land for only $8,000. In most states, he cannot then obtain a deficiency judgment against you for the remaining $2,000.

ADVANTAGES OF A PARTIAL RECONVEYANCE OR PARTIAL RELEASE CLAUSE

If you can have a clause inserted that calls for a partial release of land with clear title after you make a specified number of payments, you will lose only the remaining land should you default at a later date. Also you can use the released portion of the land as security for a new loan to finance constructing of a house or meet other financial needs. Since you will have clear title to part of the land, you may be able to sell that portion not encumbered by liens if you find it necessary to sell off part of the land to finance the remaining portion.

For example, if you make a down payment of 25 percent of the purchase price at the close of escrow, you receive clear title to 25 percent of the land at that time and give back a mortgage or deed of trust on the remaining 75 percent of the land. When you complete another 25 percent of the payments, you receive clear title to another 25 percent of the land, and so on.

WHAT TO DO IF YOU ARE HAVING TROUBLE MAKING PAYMENTS

If you find after you buy your land that you are unable to keep up with the agreed upon payment schedule, immediately inform your creditor of this fact. Never let payments pass in the hope that your money will not be missed. Payment plans can often be reorganized by mutual agreement to more reasonably meet your capabilities, but you will have to convince the creditor that you will be able to meet the new obligation if he agrees to rework the payment plan. Call him and explain your predicament before he calls you demanding to know why you aren't making your payments. If he sends you notices or letters, answer them rather than ignore them.

Believe it or not, the fact is that most creditors, like their debtors, do not want to be subjected to the legal and monetary problems of a foreclosure, since they may lose money if deficiency judgments are not allowed. They usually must hire an attorney to carry through the foreclosure in the courts, which is also costly. A creditor would rather get his payments and interest without these hassles. Therefore, never try to avoid your creditor if you feel he may be amenable to changing your payments in order to facilitate your obligations.

If you know that you cannot keep up with the payments, even if the creditor agrees to lower them, always sell the land before the creditor forecloses on your loan. Don't tell the creditor that you cannot make payments regardless of how low they are. If you can keep up your payments long enough to find a buyer to assume your payments or to pay cash so that you can pay off your creditor and transfer full title to your buyer, you stand a chance of realizing a profit and need not suffer the consequences of a foreclosure and possible deficiency judgment. Try to stay on good terms with your creditor to make stalling easier if you have to resort to selling your land in order to avoid a foreclosure.

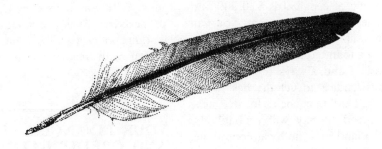

chapter 25

Borrowing from Third Party Lenders

Most commercial lenders do not loan money on rural land because they consider country property to be a speculative security. Values on such land are not easily determinable since fluctuations in the supply and demand are great. Whereas a small piece of land in the city with a $30,000 house on it is apt to sell quickly at a predictable price if a foreclosure becomes necessary, it is much harder to sell 20 acres of land 100 miles from the nearest city, which has no structures, electricity, running water, or paved access.

If you are interested in rural land that has a house and basic amenities, your chances of getting a loan are improved because the lender's risk is reduced. If your country property is to be a second home and you have a mortgage on your first home, a commercial lender assumes that if you ever get into financial difficulty, you will default on your country property before defaulting on your regular home. When second-home loans are made, the lender often prefers to insure his loan by tak-

ing a first or second mortgage on the borrower's city house. These mortgages are called "homeowner loans," and many lending agencies, particularly mortgage specialists, offer them. Since 64 percent of the householders in the United States own the houses they occupy, homeowner loans are becoming a major method of financing. The loan is based on the amount of equity the owner has in his house. Equity is calculated as the difference between the current fair market value of the house and the remaining balance owed on the first mortgage, if there is one. For example, if your house is appraised by the lender at $30,000 and you still owe $20,000 on the existing mortgage, you have an equity of $10,000 and the amount of money you can borrow for a second-home is based on this amount. Interest rates are usually higher on homeowner loans than on conventional first mortgages.

If you are buying a "working farm," the commercial lender wants assurance that the income to be derived from it is enough to pay your family and business expenses as well as your loan. As with most country land, productive farm property is usually financed by the seller.

When a commercial lender does give a loan for purchase of country property, the terms are stricter than usual. The standard loan rule is: The greater the risk to the lender, the higher will be the interest rate, the shorter the maturity date, and the lower the ratio of loan to value. The ratio of loan to value is the per-

249

centage of the appraised value of the property that will be given as a loan. For instance, if the appraised value of a parcel is $10,000 and the loan to value ratio is 75 percent, you can get a maximum loan of $7,500.

When seeking a loan, go to as many different sources as possible and always try to bargain with the various lenders to get the best terms you can. Because lending agencies located near the land you intend to buy will probably be familiar with the land and the local conditions, you should go to them first, unless you have established credit with, and are trusted by, an institution in your city.

Speak to the real estate agent handling the sale to see if he can offer some leads. Agents often have close ties with local banks and other lenders and can help you get a loan. However, be cautious. Lenders often offer kickbacks to agents who bring them business, and these are ultimately charged to the borrower indirectly through the loan fees. This problem is so rampant in the lending industry that the federal government has submitted a recent proposal to Congress to deny FHA approval to any lender engaged in such practices. See what the agent can get you, and then try to find a loan on better terms. You always have absolute discretion to choose your own lender, so never give in to pressure from the agent. Only if he has the best deal should you go through him, but get an accounting of the loan fees first (see below).

Your chances of obtaining a loan depend to a great extent on whether money is "tight" or "easy" at the time you are making your purchase. Lending agencies constantly change their loan policies depending on the national and local economic situation and on the changes in the real estate market. Every lending agency has its own policies. For example, many lenders prefer loans underwritten by the government and prefer to loan money for home purchasers. It is never easy to get financing on rural property, except from the seller, but if a commercial lender thinks your credit is very good, he might place more emphasis on this aspect than on the property value, and lend you some money. This chapter tells you what is available on the loan market. Never assume you can't get a loan without trying, particularly if the property has a house on it and your credit is good.

Each year the number of second-home buyers increases by a quarter of a million persons. With this increasing demand for country property, there is every reason to believe that lending policies will continue to become more liberal with regard to the purchase of rural land.

YOUR FINANCIAL HISTORY AND CREDIT RATING

When you apply for a loan, you will be asked to fill out an application in which you are to give complete details of your financial condition and credit history, and you will be requested to produce documents relating to this information. Although the maximum amount of your loan will never be as much as the appraised value of the property, the lender is always concerned about your ability and willingness to repay the loan. Foreclosures are an expensive and time-consuming procedure. It is much easier for a creditor to work out feasible monthly payments than to go through an expensive foreclosure and the process of advertising and selling the property in order to have the loan repaid.

When answering questions be as truthful as possible. The computerization of bank and credit accounts is becoming so thorough that any dishonest answers are likely to be uncovered when the lending institution does its independent investigation. If you have had some problems in the past repaying debts, you should explain this to the loan officer handling your case rather than misstate the facts and have the lender discover the truth in some other manner.

The following information is required by all major lending institutions:

1. How much cash and how many liquid assets do you own at the time you apply for the loan? Liquid assets are those things that can easily be converted to a known amount of cash, such as bonds and stocks, as opposed to real estate, which is a nonliquid asset. The lender will combine separate bank accounts of a married couple. He will request a copy of your bank balance, savings account balance, and an accounting of your stocks and bonds.

2. What type of employment do you have

and what is your current income? A female spouse's income will only be included if she is over the age of thirty, because lenders consider the possibility of pregnancy and loss of work to be very high prior to thirty. (Although this is a frequent rule, it should not be considered as an automatic policy of every institution.) The type of her employment is also important in this evaluation.

3. How many current debts do you have? All current debts in your family will be considered, as well as possible future debts, such as schooling and common necessities. The lender will determine whether you have too many debts for the size of your income, which would prevent you from being capable of paying further debts. A common formula used to determine the borrower's ability to repay a loan for the purpose of buying land is: The borrower's total monthly income plus a specified portion of his spouse's income minus the payments due on other loans must be at least four to four and a half times greater than the amount of the monthly payments that will be required on principal, interest, taxes, assessments, and insurance premiums.

4. What type of credit history do you have? This involves an investigation of your entire past with regard to loans and buying on credit. The lender will be looking to see whether you have always paid your bills on time, whether you borrow constantly for everything you buy, how many different persons you owe money to, whether you have ever declared bankruptcy, how often you move, whether you change jobs often, and how long you have had your present job.

5. What is your past banking experience? Here you will be asked to list your bank(s). They will be contacted for information regarding the size of your account, the length of time you have been banking with them, the average amount of money you have on hand, and any other information they can supply.

6. Do you have adequate personal and credit references? You will be required to bring in letters from creditors and acquaintances regarding your reliability and integrity. The amount of stress placed on these letters varies from lender to lender.

7. How old are you and your spouse? Age is often a relevant factor because your earning potential usually declines as you get older. A common formula used in lending institutions is the "rule of seventy," which states that the length of time you will be given to pay back the loan must not extend beyond the date when you will reach the age of seventy. Thus, if you are forty-five years old at the time you apply for a loan, the maximum time you will be permitted to repay the money is twenty-five years.

8. You will be asked to state the amount of money you wish to borrow and the repayment schedule you desire.

THE FAIR CREDIT REPORTING ACT

In investigating your credit history, prospective lenders often use the services of a Consumer Reporting Agency. This agency will issue a Consumer Report or Investigative Consumer Report showing how you pay your bills, if you have ever been sued, arrested, or declared bankrupt, what your neighbors' and employer's opinions are of your character, general reputation, and manner of living, and any other information relating to your reliability as a borrower.

Sometimes obsolete or inaccurate information is given by an agency which prevents you from obtaining a loan. Under the Federal Fair Credit Reporting Act of 1971, you can discover the type of information being distributed about you and your activities.

You have the right to be told the name and address of the agency which prepared the report that led to the denial of credit to you. Within thirty days of the denial of credit, you can approach the agency and discover the nature and sources of their information without paying a fee. You can request a reinvestigation of incomplete or incorrect information and have the revised information sent to your prospective lender. If you desire, you may include in your file your own version of any dispute with the agency and have it included in any future Consumer Reports. An agency is not permitted to report adverse information seven years after the occurrence unless it is a bankruptcy, which may be reported up to fourteen years later.

If you want more information about your rights under the Fair Credit Reporting Act, see

Useful Resources in Chapter 27 for a pamphlet on the Act, or call any field office of the Federal Trade Commission. They are located in the following cities:

Phoenix, Arizona 85002
Los Angeles, California 90057
San Diego, California 95112
San Francisco, California 94111
Denver, Colorado 80202
Washington, D.C. 20005
Miami, Florida 33100
Atlanta, Georgia 30303
Honolulu, Hawaii 96801
Chicago, Illinois 60607
New Orleans, Louisiana 70113
Boston, Massachusetts 02114
Detroit, Michigan 48226
Kansas City, Missouri 64100
St. Louis, Missouri 63101
Buffalo, New York 14202
New York, New York 10007
Charlotte, North Carolina 28200
Cleveland, Ohio 44199
Portland, Oregon 97204
Upper Darby, Pennsylvania 19082
Oak Ridge, Tennessee 37830
Dallas, Texas 75202
San Antonio, Texas 78204
Seattle, Washington 98101

THE APPRAISAL OF THE PROPERTY

All lending institutions employ their own property appraisers to evaluate the fair price of houses and land to be used as security for a loan. These appraisers use the same criteria as other property appraisers (see Chapters 19 and 20), such as the location of the neighborhood, the size of the property, the physical soundness of the structures, the desirability of the archi-

tectual design, and the sale prices of similar property in the area. However, they base their evaluation on the probable market value of the property during the entire life of the loan rather than on its value at the time you buy it, since a foreclosure may have to be made at any time during the loan repayment schedule. Inflation, the increase in the value of the land, and the decrease, or depreciation, in the value of the structures during this period are also taken into consideration.

Within thirty days of filing a loan application, the lending agency will appraise the property, review your financial and credit history, and notify you as to whether it will grant your loan. Although you will rarely be able to see the results of the appraisal, if your application is rejected, the company probably feels the asking price is too high.

THE LETTER OF COMMITMENT

If your application is accepted, the lender will issue you a Letter of Commitment detailing the terms of the loan and stating that the money will be delivered at a specific time based on certain conditions that you must meet, such as getting title cleared and having a survey completed and approved. Be sure to get this commitment in writing since lenders sometimes refuse to grant the loan at the last minute, making it impossible for the borrower to go ahead with his purchase.

Sometimes a commitment fee of 0.5 to 2 percent of the amount to be borrowed is required, which is usually refunded when you get the loan. Be sure to have a refund clause included in your Letter of Commitment, providing that

MISS PEACH - By MELL LAZARUS

© Field Enterprises, Inc., 1973

MARCIA'S KELLY SCHOOL LOAN CO.

BORROW MONEY FROM US ON A COMPLETELY CONFIDENTIAL BASIS!

NO EMBARRASSMENT! NO HUMILIATION!
Our loans are made strictly on a discreet, private basis!

OUR SATISFIED BORROWERS:
IRA BROM, 224 ELM AVE. — $2.00
LESTER LARSON, 113 Courtney Pl. 1.50
FRANCINE FOSTER, 48 Wilton St.-1.25
ARTHUR STRIMM, 391 Corbin Cir. 1.80
SHEILA SHAW, 10 Brook Lane, 2.30
(PHOTOS AND COPIES OF THEIR LOAN APPLICATIONS on REQUEST)
MELL LAZARUS. 3-27

your money will be returned in case you do not purchase the land or close the loan.

THE FINANCE CONDITION IN THE CONTRACT OF SALE

The Model Contract of Sale (Chapter 28) conditions the closing of escrow on your ability to obtain a loan under the terms you desire. (See Clause 19(e).) This is an essential contingency whereby your ability to make the purchase is dependent on obtaining a loan. Without this condition, if you sign the contract and then are unable to get a loan, you will lose your deposit or earnest money. Read the accompanying explanation to Clause 19(e) and use the information in Part V: *Financing Your Purchase* to fill in the blanks in the financing clause.

DISCLOSURE STATEMENT UNDER THE TRUTH IN LENDING LAW

The Truth in Lending Law requires that the lender supply you with a Disclosure Statement specifying the total amount of interest you will pay on the loan, the percentages of each payment going to interest and to principal, the amount of each payment, when payments are to be made, the number of payments to be made, the date of the last payment, the amount of a balloon payment, and all loan fees and other "extra" costs. You are to sign this Disclosure Statement as proof that you saw it and approved of its contents. The signed document is the lending agency's proof that it did not violate the law should a problem arise at a later date. Study the statement carefully before signing to be sure it contains all the terms you have agreed to.

PRIVATE MORTGAGE INSURANCE

Most lending institutions today will lend the buyer only between 65 and 80 percent of the appraised value of the property. Since you must come up with the rest of the purchase price as well as all of the closing costs, on a land purchase of $20,000 you might have to supply from $4,000 to $7,000 in cash.

A fairly new innovation in the lending business, however, allows lenders to obtain Private Mortgage Insurance, which enables them to lend the borrower up to 95 percent of the purchase price. The Mortgage Insurance Policy insures the lender for a certain portion of the mortgage loan, usually that amount above the normal loan amount. This is called "assuming the top of the risk."

The oldest and largest company offering this insurance is the Mortgage Guarantee Insurance Corporation, referred to as MGIC or "Magic." Its insured funds are mostly available through savings and loan associations, savings banks, and mortgage companies. Under the MGIC plan, you can borrow 90 percent of the purchase price up to a maximum of $54,000.

Before MGIC insures the lender, it evaluates your credit and appraises the property, based on the documents you and the lender supply. You must pay the insurance company a fee of $50 to $100 for processing the application.

You must also pay a premium for the insurance policy, part of which is due at the closing of the loan (when you receive the money), with the rest to be paid in installments during the payment period of the loan. If you borrow 90 percent of the purchase price of the property, your annaul MGIC premium will probably be 0.5–1 percent of the unpaid balance of the loan during the first year, and 0.25 percent of the balance remaining each year thereafter. You can also pay the entire premium at the closing of the loan, in which case it is usually 3 percent of the amount borrowed.

Although the interest rates are slightly higher than on uninsured loans, a MGIC loan might be the only way you can get enough money to make your purchase. You should discuss the possibilities of obtaining mortgage insurance with your prospective lender if you need more money than he is willing to lend.

VARIOUS LENDERS

The "primary loan market" includes institutional and noninstitutional lenders. The four primary institutional lenders and their 1973 percentage share of the residential loan market for privately owned one- to four-family homes, are savings and loan associations (53 percent), commercial banks (18 percent), mutual savings banks (13 percent), and life insurance companies (7 percent).

The noninstitutional lenders include mortgage companies, private individuals, and nonfinancial organizations. These lenders offer "conventional financing" by lending money directly to the borrower on a long-term basis and holding the land for security until the debt is discharged.

If you qualify, you can turn a conventional loan into a Veterans' Administration (VA) Guaranteed Loan or a Federal Housing Administration (FHA) Insured Loan (see Chapter 26).

The Federal Land Bank System and the Farmers Home Administration (see Chapter 26) are unique loan sources for rural property owners.

Savings and Loan Associations

The largest home lenders in the United States are the federal and state savings and loan associations which were established to promote the investing of money and the sound, economical financing of homes. The federally chartered associations are governed by the Federal Home Loan Bank Board and the state-licensed associations are regulated by the Savings and Loan Commissioner of the state.

Like most commercial lenders, savings and loan associations believe that unimproved land is not a good form of security. Loans are not usually given on active farms and are only occasionally given on unimproved land. Unless a house already exists on the land you are planning to buy, it is not likely that a savings and loan association will lend more than 10 percent of the appraised value, if that much.

However, savings and loan associations are generally more amenable to financing second homes that are within 100 miles of a lending office than other institutional lenders, particularly with a VA or FHA loan. Because of the growing demand for second homes, this re-

quirement is likely to be liberalized in the near future.

Loans for owner-occupied single-family dwellings average 70 percent of the appraised value of the house. If the purchase price is less than the appraised value, the full purchase price might be loaned. The maximum loan permitted depends upon the amount borrowed, with a maximum amortization period of thirty years. The opinions of two appraisers are required. Much importance is placed on the geographical location and age of the home.

Although the interest rate varies in different areas and at different times, it is generally higher than the interest rate on loans given by insurance companies and banks. However, savings and loan associations are generally more liberal in their lending policies. They will usually lend a higher percentage of the appraised value of the property than these other institutions and will lend to persons having fairly small incomes. In recent years, interest rates have risen from 6½ to 9 percent, and are likely to go higher with continued inflation.

Loan fees of savings and loan associations are higher than those normally charged by other lenders, ranging from 1 to 10 percent or more of the full amount of the loan. In addition, a prepayment penalty of three to six months' interest is usually charged if more than 20 percent of the loan is repaid before maturity.

Commercial Banks

Banks are "general purpose" lenders, regulated by federal law and organized under federal and state charters. Loans by both federal and state banks are fairly similar. During the Depression in the 1930s, commercial banks were hit hardest because they had invested heavily in real estate, a nonliquid asset that cannot be quickly turned into cash to meet withdrawal demands. This experience left a bad taste in the mouths of bank presidents, and therefore home loans are low on their priority list of investments.

The most common type of bank loan is for the purpose of building a home. Loans for the purpose of buying land are given only for improved land and unimproved land that is to be improved after the loan is granted. State banks are more amenable to lending for unimproved property than federal banks. Most banks will lend approximately 50 percent of the appraised value of a second home amortized for ten to twenty years. Since commercial banks are the most common financial institution outside of urban areas, they are the major source of loan funds in rural areas.

Although some banks will not make FHA and VA loans, most will do so at a higher ratio of loan to appraised value for a longer maturity period than is given on a conventional loan.

Mutual Savings Banks

Mutual savings banks are located predominently in the Atlantic and New England states where they replace the savings and loan associations. Their policies are similar to those of the latter, and they invest most of their assets in mortgages, with a heavy preference for government-underwritten loans.

Life Insurance Companies

Approximately 30 percent of the assets of life insurance companies are invested in home mortgages. Many insurance companies will only make loans that are insured by the FHA or guaranteed by the VA.

The amount and terms of life insurance company loans are regulated by each state. Loans are usually restricted to an amount not more than two and a half times the borrower's annual income with monthly payments lower than 20–25 percent of the borrower's monthly take-home pay. The normal loan has a maximum maturity of twenty-five years and a maximum of 75 percent of the appraised value of the house and land. Although financing is fairly liberal on farm property, insurance companies' appraisal policies tend to be conservative. Getting a loan on an old house is difficult unless it is in exceptionally good condition. Life insurance companies' interest rates tend to be lower than those of other financial institutions, but this is highly variable.

Most life insurance companies require the borrower to purchase a life insurance policy insuring full payment of the loan if the borrower dies during the amortization period.

Life insurance companies lend money at lower interest rates if the borrower has a life insurance policy with the company. As you pay insurance premiums you build up "cash value" in the policy which can be borrowed in the form of cash from the company. You will still need to be covered by your policy during the period of the loan if you do this. Find out the specifics from your insurance company on how you can use your life insurance policy to borrow money for the purchase of property.

Mortgage Companies or Mortgage Banks

Mortgage companies and mortgage banks are considered to be noninstitutional sources of mortgage funds, and together with other noninstitutional lenders, supply 25 percent of the loans for all property in the United States. Mortgage companies are regulated by each state, and they are generally much more liberal than other lending institutions.

In reality, mortgage companies are temporary lenders in that they give loans and then sell the notes to insurance companies, commercial banks, savings and loan associations, and other institutions. After selling the notes, they continue to serve the note buyer by collecting the payments, paying the taxes, watching over the property, keeping it insured, and foreclosing when necessary. They charge the buyer of the note a fee of 0.5 percent of the outstanding loan balance for their services.

The mortgage companies prefer government-underwritten loans and generally restrict their loans to low-risk single-family dwellings in the low price range.

Do not confuse the mortgage banker with the mortgage broker. The latter simply finds good investments for potential lenders and is paid a finder's fee for this service. Never use a mortgage broker to obtain a mortgage.

Borrowing from Individuals

The most common source of private loans is relatives and close friends. If they trust you to repay the loan, taking a mortgage is one of the best investments they can make since the interest rate is higher than they can get by placing their money in a bank or savings and loan association. In fact, they can charge up to the maximum allowed by the state's usury laws, which is commonly 10 percent per year. Obtaining a high-interest loan from a relative might be the only way you can purchase a country home.

Although your relative-lender can take back a mortgage or deed of trust, he might want the greater protection of having his name put on the deed as a co-owner of the property. In a written contract between yourselves, you can specify that he will transfer his share in the land to you upon complete payment of the loan. If you make this type of arrangement be certain that all the terms of the agreement are written in a legally binding contract between yourselves. Never agree to anything by a friendly handshake alone.

Other Nonfinancial Institutional Lenders

Title companies, realtors, and brokers lend money under certain circumstances. These non-institutional lenders are not regulated and can establish any terms they desire unless they take an FHA or VA loan. Usually they do not have as rigid a credit investigation as the institutional lenders, and they often conduct their own appraisal of the property. They are often a good source for second mortgage loans.

LOANS FROM THE FEDERAL LAND BANK SYSTEM

A recent government report gives the following statistics on sources of loans for the construction of farm buildings and purchase of farm land:

40.3 percent from individual lenders and others
23.5 percent from farmer-owned Federal Land Banks
20.2 percent from insurance companies
14.4 percent from commercial banks
 1.6 percent from the Farmers Home Administration

In 1933, Congress established an independent federal agency called the Credit Administration which supervises a Farm Credit System to make loans to farmers and prospective farmers through twelve Federal Land Banks set up around the country. These Federal Land Banks have 625 Federal Land Bank Associations scattered throughout all parts of the United States, which supply 23.5 percent of the loans on farm property.

Each Land Bank Association is owned cooperatively by the borrowers, who must become members in order to obtain a loan. When you become a Land Bank borrower, 5 percent of the amount you borrow must be used to purchase shares in the association. In the meantime, you get dividends on your shares. Sales of this stock and of federal Farm Loan Bonds are the source of the money for Land Bank loans.

You can borrow money to purchase land or to make improvements on land you already own. Loans are made for up to 70 percent of the appraised "normal agricultural" value of the farm. This "normal value" is based on the dependable farm income from the property, the advantages of the property as a home, any other steady income of the borrower, and the fair market value of the property on the current land market. This "normal value" is usually 60 percent of the "market value." Thus, you will have to come up with quite a large amount of cash to make up the difference in the purchase price.

The loan must be secured by a first lien on the property. The amortization period can extend from five to forty years, and payments can be made annually, semi-annually, quarterly, or monthly. There is no prepayment penalty. In fact, the Land Bank pays interest on money they receive in advance and early payments can be put into a future payment fund to meet later installments if you run into trouble making payments later.

The current interest rate is 7½–9 percent per year, depending on where the property is located. The Land Bank has its own version of the variable interest rate called a "floating rate." Under this system the interest rate in effect at the time the loan is closed is guaranteed for three years. Thereafter, at three-year intervals, the interest rate is readjusted to meet current loan rates on the mortgage market, which is more likely to go up than down.

If you are purchasing forest land rather than farm land, you can obtain a Federal Land Bank forest land loan, which is based on the value of the marketable timber on the land. Check into the requirements for "marketable timber" in your area. Usually a tree must be twelve inches or more in diameter. Although you must be engaged in timber growing, you do not have to cut the timber to get the loan. The Land Bank simply wants to be sure that they can cut the timber to get their money back should they have to foreclose. Forest land loans are usually not made on raw timberland, so some building, such as a house, must be on the property. This is an excellent way to finance a vacation home in the woods.

You can borrow up to 65 percent of the appraised normal value of the timber and land, and the repayment schedules are the same as those on farm loans.

To determine if there is a Federal Land Bank Association in the area where you want to buy land look in the phone book under "Federal Land Bank Association." For a packet of information on obtaining a Land Bank loan and the address of the Land Bank Association near you, see "Useful Resources" at the end of Chapter 27.

THE DISCOUNT RATE OR POINTS CHARGE

Commercial lenders have developed a tricky thing called a "discount rate," or "points" charge, in order to confuse the borrower, beat the legal interest rate ceilings, and make more on their money. The discount rate is most often applied to FHA and VA loans, which I will talk about in the next chapter.

Every state sets a maximum permissible interest rate, or ceiling, which financial institutions must adhere to. When the prevailing mortgages rates in the business world begin to rise and go higher than the state-controlled ceiling rate, loans may be "discounted" to permit the lender to make up the difference between the ceiling rate and the prevailing rate. Although the word "discount" usually connotes a savings, here the term means that the amount to be loaned will be decreased by an amount of "discount" or "points" and the borrower must pay back on a larger principal than he receives.

Each point is generally $1 for every $100 of principal. For example, if you borrow $10,000 and are being charged four points at this rate, you will only receive $9,600 in cash from the lender, but you will have to repay on the basis of a $10,000 principal. Often a higher interest rate would be preferable to paying points. Since the points charge is "paid" when the loan is given, you cannot reduce your point costs by making prepayments as you can with the interest on a loan.

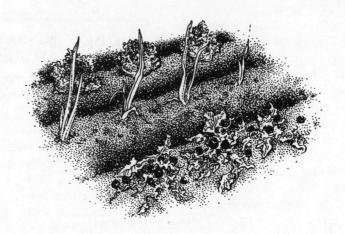

chapter 26

FHA and VA Loans

FEDERAL HOUSING ADMINISTRATION (FHA)— INSURED LOANS

To enable people to purchase their own homes, the Federal Housing Administration, commonly referred to as the FHA, a subsidiary of the Department of Housing and Urban Development (HUD), has organized a program of mortgage insurance that protects the lender, enabling him to give more liberal financing terms. The FHA insures the commercial lender against possible loss due to a defaulting borrower by allowing the lender to foreclose and give the property to the FHA in exchange for cash or to assign the defaulted mortgage to the FHA, which proceeds with the foreclosure and reimburses the lender after the foreclosure. Although most of the FHA loans are for "urban" housing and land, some "country" property is actually classified as "urban," and there are special FHA loans for purchasing property in "outlying areas" which I will describe later in this chapter.

To obtain an FHA loan, you first follow the same procedure used in obtaining a commercial loan. When you apply for a loan from a lending institution, it will order an appraisal to be made of the property, check your credit his-tory, employment, and current bank account, and send this information along with its lending terms to the local FHA office. (See "Useful Resources" in Chapter 27 for the addresses of all FHA offices.)

Using this information, the FHA examines the applicant's credit history, his motivation for wanting to buy the property, the adequacy of his income to meet future payments, the adequacy of his current assets to meet the down payment and closing costs, and his integrity and motivation to carry through on the repayment of the loan. The incomes of both spouses are considered when it is certain that their employment will continue.

The property, too, must meet certain conditions. General requirements are that the house be soundly built and suitably located. Any defects in the property must be repaired before the FHA will insure a mortgage on it. The FHA makes its own appraisal of the value of the property, to determine the amount it is willing to insure the loan for.

If both you and the property are acceptable, the FHA issues a "conditional commitment" to the lender which states the estimate of the value of the property and the maximum loan it will insure.

The maximum interest rate permitted under an FHA loan is currently 8½ percent a year. The rate can go up or down depending on the market conditions, but most of the time it is lower than the current interest rate on conventional loans. Because lenders do not like to accept the lower rates, they are allowed to "discount the loan" or charge points (discussed in Chapter 25: *Borrowing from Third Party*

Lenders) to make up the difference between the FHA interest rate and the current interest rate on the mortgage money market. The FHA prohibits the lender from collecting this discount from the buyer, because to do so would defeat the purpose of the FHA loan. Therefore, the seller is supposed to pay the points, but often he simply raises his purchase price to cover the amount he will have to pay, so the buyer ends up paying it anyway.

The borrower must pay an FHA application fee of $35, a lender's service charge of 1 percent or less of the loan, the charge for a title search and Title Insurance Policy premium, $40 for an FHA appraisal, $15 for a credit report, and the fees charged to prepare, record, and notarize the deed, mortgage, and other documents, and other standard closing costs. It is specified in the Model Contract of Sale that the seller is to share the cost of many of these charges with you. (See Chapter 28: *The Model Contract of Sale*.)

Under an FHA loan, a special charge of 0.5 percent per year, called the Mortgage Insurance Premium, is made on the outstanding balance of the mortgage during the year, which goes into the FHA fund to pay its expenses and insurance losses on defaults. This premium is collected with the monthly mortgage payment and is in addition to the monthly payment of interest and principal.

The borrower is to pay the taxes and special assessments on the property, and he will be charged for the premiums on fire and hazard insurance, taken out to protect the lender's security.

There is no prepayment penalty on an FHA loan, but the buyer must give the lender thirty days' notice if he intends to make more than one month's payment at one time.

You can purchase a home that is already under an FHA-insured mortgage. If you buy "subject to" the mortgage, no FHA approval is needed because the seller's name remains on the mortgage and he bears the responsibility for the mortgage payments if you fail to make them. If you are approved by the FHA, the lender can release the seller from his obligation on the mortgage and substitute you, whereby you "assume" the mortgage.

The FHA has several different insurance programs which you might use:

Mutual Mortgage Insurance

The most commonly used program, Mutual Mortgage Insurance, Section 203(b), provides for the purchase of family homes. You can borrow up to $33,000 for a term of thirty years. The loan to value ratio varies depending on the age of the house and whether it was built under FHA approval. For example, a borrower purchasing a home over one year old or built under FHA inspection can get a maximum insured mortgage of 97 percent of the value up to $15,000 plus 90 percent of the value between $15,000 and $25,000 plus 80 percent of the value over $25,000 to a maximum loan of $33,000.

Outlying Area Properties Loan

The FHA plan that will probably be applicable to most of you is the Outlying Area Properties Loan, Section 203(i). Under this plan, FHA approval is given for mortgages on nonfarm, or new farm, housing on five or more acres adjacent to a highway in small communities. Many of the requirements on the standards of construction and the condition of the house are much less rigid than those for mortgage insurance on housing in built-up urban areas. The maximum loan permitted is 97 percent of the appraised value of the property up to a maximum of $16,200. If the purchase price is higher than the FHA estimate of the value of the property plus closing costs, the buyer must pay the difference in cash. You can choose between ten-, fifteen-, twenty-, twenty-five-, or thirty-year maturity periods.

FHA Unsubsidized Cooperative Housing Loan Insurance

An unusual loan insurance plan that can be utilized by a group of people purchasing land together is the FHA Unsubsidized Cooperative Housing Loan Insurance, Section 213 and 221 (d)(3). The FHA will insure financing for cooperative housing projects that will belong to, and provide housing for, members of a nonprofit cooperative cooperation. Five or more dwellings must be purchased by individual members of the cooperative. Each purchaser may obtain FHA insurance. Although the most common use of this program is by large developers building low-cost cooperative housing, there is no reason why a commune or group of people could not get together and form their own nonprofit cooperative and apply for loan insurance to finance construction of their homes. This program does not insure loans for the purchase of land, only for the construction of dwellings. Thus, your group could purchase some inexpensive land and then borrow under the FHA plan to build your houses. The first thing to do if you are considering such a project is to discuss your plan with the local HUD/FHA insuring office. For more information on cooperative, see Chapter 32: *Types of Co-Ownership.*

Experimental Housing Mortgage Insurance

Experimental Housing Mortgage Insurance, Section 233, provides insurance on loans for housing that incorporates new or untried construction concepts aimed at reducing housing costs, raising living standards, and improving neighborhood design. If you can afford to pay for the land itself, you could attempt to get the FHA to insure a loan to build domes, modular design houses, ferro-cement houses, or other "experimental" buildings. Try to talk the FHA into the idea that your designs are incorporating new and improved construction concepts with the aim of improving conventional construction methods.

Condominium Housing Insurance

Condominium Housing Insurance, Section 234, presents another loan possibility for a group or commune to obtain money for financing the construction of their dwellings on land they have purchased. The program was initiated to help "investors" develop condominiums, but you can organize a group of "nonprofit investors" seeking insured financing to build four or more dwelling units. After the housing is built, each unit is sold to an individual in the group. His payments go to pay off the insured loan

given to construct the dwellings. Each owner has complete title to his dwelling unit and has an undivided interest with the remaining owners in common areas and facilities serving the group. (See Chapter 32: *Types of Co-Ownership.*)

Home Ownership Loans for Lower-Income Families

The Home Ownership Loans for Lower-Income Families, Section 235, provide help for people who would otherwise never be able to purchase a home. The maximum mortgage is $21,000–$24,000, depending on the size of your family and the dwelling. There is a variable maximum interest rate. The buyer must make a minimum down payment of $200. Thereafter, he pays 20 percent of his adjusted monthly income toward the monthly mortgage payment on the home. Each area of the country has its own independent family-income limits which determine eligibility under this program. You will have to check with your local FHA office or FHA-approved lending institution for your area's requirements. The term of the mortgage can run as long as forty years. Since the buyer's income will likely change during that time, his payments are adjusted accordingly so that he always pays 20 percent of his monthly income. The borrower must make periodic income reports to the lender during the payment period.

President Nixon suspended this loan program in 1973, so you will need to check with the FHA to see if it has been reactivated.

Insured Title 1 Mobile Home Loans Program

If you want to buy a mobile home after purchasing, you can get an insured loan through the Insured Title 1 Mobile Home Loans Program. You can borrow up to $15,000 for a two or more unit mobile home which you intend to use as your principal residence. The interest rate varies, as does the down payment you must make, and the home must meet FHA standards of construction for a single- or multiple-unit home.

Property Improvement Loans

Once you own your land you can get FHA Property Improvement Loans to finance repairs and improvements of existing structures and to build small nonresidential structures, such as agricultural buildings.

See "Useful Resources" in Chapter 27 for a list of pamphlets about the FHA and the various programs listed above.

VETERANS ADMINISTRATION (VA)—GUARANTEED LOANS (GI LOANS)

Since World War II, the federal government has been guaranteeing loans made by commercial lenders to honorably discharged veterans. Loans may be obtained for purchasing homes and farms, constructing homes, and improving existing dwellings. These loans are called VA- or GI-guaranteed loans.

To be eligible, the borrower must be a World War II veteran who served in active military service for at least ninety days between September 16, 1940, and July 25, 1947, or a Korean War veteran who served on active duty for at least ninety days between June 27, 1950, and January 31, 1955, or a veteran who served on active duty for a period of 181 days, any part of which occurred after January 31, 1955. Also eligible are persons now on active duty who have not been discharged since January 31, 1955, and have been on active duty for a period of two years or more.

When the veteran becomes eligible he receives a $12,500 "entitlement," which means he can borrow that much from a financial institution and have it guaranteed by the Veterans Administration. A loan guarantee from the VA means that if you default on the loan, the VA will repay the lender for you. You then become liable for payment to the Veterans Administration.

If you are a World War II or Korean War Veteran, your entitlement is valid until used. If you are a veteran discharged after 1955, you can take advantage of a GI Loan only up to twenty years from your discharge date. Two or more veterans can put their entitlements to- gether and purchase property as a group. A veteran may also use this entitlement with a nonveteran to purchase a farm or home.

The first thing a veteran must do is obtain a Certificate of Eligibility by filling out VA Form 1880 and submitting it with separation papers (DD214) to the local VA office or financial institution.

Before the VA will guarantee a loan it appraises the property in the same way as the FHA does. The appraisal report indicates the current fair market value at the time the appraisal is made. It does not indicate whether the purchase is a good one or what the resale value will be at a future date. After completion of the appraisal, the VA sends a Certificate of Reasonable Value to the prospective lender. Although the total loan can be for any amount, the VA only guarantees the first $12,500 of any loan. The maximum maturity allowed is thirty years for a house, and forty years for a farm. There is usually no prepayment penalty. As of this writing, the maximum interest allowed under a VA loan is 8½ percent, but this could go higher in line with general money market changes.

First you must find the property you want to buy. Then make a deposit and sign a Contract of Sale which conditions the sale on your ability to obtain a GI loan. (See Clause 19(e) in the Model Contract of Sale, Chapter 28.) A legal description of the property and a survey or sketch of its boundaries must be presented with your Certificate of Eligibility to the lending institution where you apply for a loan. The lender will run a credit history check and employment report on you and the VA will conduct their appraisal of the property. The VA sends the Certificate of Reasonable Value to the lender. If the lender decides to lend you the money, he gets a guarantee from the regional VA office, then gives you the money.

You will have to pay certain fees on a VA-guaranteed loan. The application fee includes $30 for the appraisal and $15 for the credit report. You must also pay a 1 percent processing fee, or point fee, to the lender, although this fee can vary. If extra points are charged, the seller is supposed to pay them rather than the buyer. All the other standard closing costs are divided between the buyer and the seller.

Under certain circumstances, the Veterans

Administration makes direct loans, called Housing Credit Shortage Loans, to veteran purchasers. In areas where loans are difficult to to obtain, such as rural areas and small towns far from a major city, the veteran can apply for a direct loan from the VA. All requirements are the same as for any other GI loan, but on a direct loan the veteran can obtain a maximum of $21,000 under an interest rate that varies with the mortgage market. If you cannot get a GI loan from a financial institution, you should write or visit the regional VA office and ask for a direct loan.

In addition to the VA loans, which are federally funded, many states have their own programs that make funds available to veterans through state bond issues. These state programs feature direct loans to veterans, who repay them at a low interest rate. You can obtain information on these loans at the Veterans Administration regional office in your area. See "Useful Resources" in Chapter 27 for the addresses of all VA regional offices and a list of available pamphlets on GI Loans.

LOANS FROM THE FARMERS HOME ADMINISTRATION (FHA-USDA)

Leave it to the federal government to create two separate financial agencies with the initials "FHA." The Farmers Home Administration is not the same organization as the Federal Housing Administration. The former is operated by the United States Department of Agriculture (USDA), the latter by the Department of Housing and Urban Development (HUD). When I speak about the FHA in other parts of this book, I refer to the Federal Housing Administration that operates under HUD unless I specify otherwise.

The Farmers Home Administration, which I will refer to in this section as the FHA-USDA to distinguish it from the HUD FHA, makes housing loans available to farm families and other people in rural areas and small communities of 10,000 persons or less. Their intent is to develop the resources of rural areas

and upgrade the standard of living of people wishing to live in these places. You can use money obtained from an FHA-USDA housing loan to buy an existing house, to buy a parcel of land and build a house on it, or to build or repair a house on land you already own. Purchasing forest land is permitted if you can show that it will produce income as a commercial or recreational enterprise. After the loan is made, the FHA-USDA will give you technical advice for making profitable use of the land and its resources and help you manage your finances in general.

Another purpose of the FHA-USDA loan is to assist people who are unable to get reasonable credit elsewhere. You must agree to refinance your loan with a commercial lender as soon as you can after you build up equity in your property. Although special provisions are made for low-income families, usually the borrower is expected to have sufficient income to pay the installments, insurance premiums, taxes, and other debts and living expenses. If your income is not sufficient, a co-signer might be necessary.

If you purchase a family farm there is a maximum amortization period of forty years with a current interest rate of 5 percent per year. The interest rate is 7¾ percent on a loan for the purchase of a non-farm dwelling. Prepayments are allowed without penalty and may be kept in reserve to use in periods of low income when payments cannot be met.

To qualify for an FHA-USDA loan you must be certified by a local committee and loan supervisor. You must have had recent farm experience or training and be capable of conducting a farm operation. If you have a dependable off-farm income, you can obtain a loan for a small farm without meeting all these qualifications. A standard credit and employment check is conducted, and veterans get preferential treatment for any FHA-USDA loan.

A separate program which might be useful if you are a commune or group of people buying land is the FHA-USDA Self-Help Housing Loan, whereby funds are loaned to a group of people to buy building sites and materials. The majority of the construction is then done by the families themselves under a FHA-USDA construction expert. The houses are expected to be modest in size and cost. You are encouraged to submit your own building plans but are advised to keep the house size around 1,100 square feet.

The best way to find out about the FHA-USDA programs available in your area is to write to your local office. See "Useful Reserves" in Chapter 27 for the address of the main office and a list of FHA-USDA pamphlets.

chapter 27

Glossary of Financing Terms, Checklist for Evaluating a Loan, and Useful Resources

GLOSSARY OF FINANCING TERMS

Acceleration Clause—a clause in the mortgage or trust deed which gives the lender the right to receive the entire principal and interest owed to him by the buyer upon the happening of a certain event such as a missed payment, attempt to sell, or disrepair of the property. They are common but should be avoided by a buyer whenever possible.

Amortization—paying off a debt by means of installment payments. As each payment toward the principal and interest due is made, the loan amount is reduced or amortized by the amount of that payment.

Assignment—a creditor sells or gives his rights under note to another party.

Assumption of a Loan—the buyer takes title to the property and assumes the liability for payment of a note for which the property has been given as security. The buyer does not become personally liable for payment of the debt if he takes title "subject to" a loan.

Balloon Payment—an extra-large installment payment made at the end of the amortization period.

Beneficiary—under a Deed of Trust the seller or lender is called the "beneficiary" of the trust.

Bond—another name for a note.

Closing the Loan—usually done at the same time escrow is closed. It occurs when the money is actually given to the buyer who gives a mortgage or deed of trust and a note in return.

Commitment—also called a "Letter of Commitment." A pledge or promise by the lender that you will receive the loan you desire.

Conventional Loan—any loan other than an FHA-insured or VA-guaranteed loan.

Credit Check—this is performed by a lender when you apply for a loan. Your credit and employment history are evaluated, along with your present financial condition, to determine the likelihood that you will repay the loan on time.

Creditor—the person to whom money is owed.

Deed of Trust (Trust Deed or Trust Indenture)—used in a minority of states in place of a mortgage. The buyer receives title to the property and gives it to a trustee, or neutral third party, as security for the loan. When the debt is paid, the title is reconveyed to the borrower. If the debt is not paid, the trustee can foreclose or sell the property to satisfy the debt to the lender, or beneficiary.

Debtor—the person who owes the money.

Default—a debtor's failure to make his loan payments. (He is said to default on the loan or mortgage or deed of trust.)

Discount Rate ("Points")—usually charged by a lender, under an FHA loan. The FHA sets a maximum permissible interest rate which is often lower than the current conventional loan mortgage interest rate. The lender makes the loan but "discounts," or subtracts, an amount of money from it to make up the difference lost by charging the lower interest rate. Each point is 1 percent, or $1 for every $100 of loan money. The seller is supposed to pay the points under an FHA loan. Lenders also charge points to get more money than permitted under current interest ceilings.

Due-on-Sale Clause—similar to an acceleration clause. It means that if the borrower desires to sell his property before the loan is repaid he must pay off the entire amount due on the loan before he can convey title to a purchaser.

Easy Money—means that loans are readily available and interest rates are fairly low or at an average level.

Equity—a buyer's ownership rights or investment in his property, excluding the debt liens against it. When the down payment is made, his equity is the amount of the payment. When the loan is fully paid off the buyer has 100 percent equity in the property. If the house has a fair market value of $30,000,

and the buyer owes $20,000 on an existing mortgage, he has an equity of $10,000.

Escalation Clause (Escalator Clause)—permits the lender, or seller, to raise the interest rate on the loan during the period of the mortgage or deed of trust. The buyer should always attempt to keep such a clause out of the loan document.

Farmers Home Administration (FHA-USDA)—a government agency under the U.S. Department of Agriculture (USDA) which makes loans to farmers and rural residents who cannot obtain loans elsewhere.

Federal Housing Administration (FHA)—a government agency under the U.S. Department of Housing and Urban Development (HUD) which insures loans made to borrowers by institutional lenders. The FHA insures the lender that he will receive full payment if the buyer defaults. Loans can be for home building, purchase, and improvement. Although they are primarily concerned with "urban" areas they do have certain loans that can benefit rural purchasers, such as their "Outlying Areas" loan program.

Federal Land Bank—an organization owned by the rural residents who borrow from it. It is regulated by the Federal Farm Credit Administration. The Land Bank lends money, through local Land Bank Associations, to owners and purchasers of farm and timber land. A borrower must purchase shares of stock in the Land Bank as part of his loan and he has a vote in selecting the local Board of Directors who administer the Land Bank in his area.

Fixed Interest Loan—means that the interest rate on the loan at the time it is borrowed will remain constant throughout the entire amortization period.

Floating Interest Rate—the opposite of a fixed interest loan. Under a floating interest rate, the interest on the loan goes up or down in line with the current mortgage interest rate on the money market. If you borrow under this type of interest rate you will probably see your interest go up rather than down.

Foreclosure—the procedure used to sell property given as security for a debt when the borrower defaults in payments. The lender attempts to get his money through a foreclosure sale. In some cases, he might keep the property rather than sell it.

Homeowner Loan—a mortgage or deed of trust on one's present home given in order to borrow money to buy a second-home. Also called a second-home loan. This loan is based on the amount of equity the owner has in his present home. Interest rates for it are often higher than on a conventional first mortgage or deed of trust.

Installment Note—a document that specifies the amount of payment due on specified dates for the repayment of a loan.

Interest Rate—a percentage of the principal amount of the loan which the lender charges the borrower for the loan. The borrower should always determine what the interest rate is "per annum," or per year, for the entire amortization period.

Land Contract—a device used to finance the purchase of property. A Land Contract should never be confused with a Contract of Sale or other purchase agreement. The Seller does not convey title to the land until the buyer has completely paid off the purchase price. This can be a dangerous means of purchasing land and is tempting to the buyer who does not have much cash available for a down payment. It should be used with extreme caution.

Maturity—the end of the length of time for which a loan is made. If a loan is to be repaid in ten years, it has a ten-year maturity.

Mortgage—a document that places a lien on the borrower's property as security for a loan. The borrower keeps title to the property, but the lender has a lien against it until the loan is repaid.

Mortgagee—the seller or lender who receives a mortgage from a mortgagor.

Mortgage Insurance Premium—the payment made by a borrower under an FHA loan which helps the FHA defray the cost of its loan insurance program and provides a reserve fund to use for the protection of lenders if the borrower defaults in payments. The current mortgage insurance premium is 0.5 percent of the loan paid on a monthly basis to the FHA.

Mortgagor—the person who borrows the money, or purchases the land, under a mortgage agreement. The mortgagor gives a mortgage to the seller or lender, who is called the "mortgagee."

Note (Promissory Note)—given with a mortgage or deed of trust. It is a signed document wherein the buyer acknowledges the debt and promises to repay it in full. The terms of repayment are specified in the note.

Partial Reconveyance Clause (Release Clause) —in a loan instrument specifies that the seller or lender is to convey to the buyer a specified portion of the land title free and clear from the overall lien, after a certain amount of the debt is repaid.

Payments—are made monthly, quarterly, semi-annually, or annually under the amortization schedule. A payment should include part of the principal and interest due on the loan.

Points—see Discount Rate.

Prepayment Clause—in a mortgage, deed of trust or Land Contract permits the buyer to pay off the debt in advance of the maturity date. It also permits the buyer to make a larger installment than what is due and may allow him later to credit this advance to payments he is unable to make.

Prepayment Penalty—a clause that specifies that the buyer will pay a penalty for paying off any part of the loan at a greater rate than that called for in the loan instrument. The penalty is usually a percentage of the amount due.

Principal—the amount of money owed by the purchaser to a lender or seller of land. For example, if the selling price is $15,000 and you pay a $3,000 down payment and give a mortgage for the remainder, the principal on the loan is $12,000. The interest due will be calculated on the basis of this principal amount.

Purchase Money Mortgage—any mortgage given for the specific purpose of purchasing a piece of property.

Reconveyance—of the title to the borrower-trustor is made after the debt is repaid in full under a deed of trust.

Redemption—the right of the borrower to regain his property after a foreclosure has occurred. You always want to have a right of redemption in your loan instrument.

Refinance—means that the buyer gets a new loan to pay off his original loan. This is commonly done when interest rates drop and a cheaper loan can be obtained. The borrower gives a new mortgage or deed of trust for the new loan.

Release Clause—see Partial Reconveyance Clause

Satisfaction—when a debt is paid in full, a satisfaction is signed by the lender, recorded, and given to the borrower as evidence that the lien against his property has been removed.

Second Home—a vacation home or part-time residence, usually in the country.

Second Home Loan—same as a Homeowner Loan.

Second Mortgage—a mortgage against the property given for a loan after the buyer has already given a first mortgage to a lender. A holder of a second mortgage can only get his money on a foreclosure after the holder of the first mortgage has received what is due him. There can be third and fourth mortgages. All commercial lenders require a first mortgage when the loan is for the purchase of property.

Subject to a Mortgage or Deed of Trust—when a buyer purchases the land subject to a pre-existing lien against the property he is not personally responsible for the payment of the existing amount which is due. If there is a foreclosure later, he will lose the land. Do not take title subject to a mortgage if you can assume it. See Assumption of a Loan.

Term—refers to the amortization period or maturity date on a loan.

Tight Money—means that loans are hard to get and interest rates are higher than normal.

Trust Deed—same as deed of trust.

Trust Indenture—same as deed of trust.

Trustee—the neutral third person who holds title during the period of a deed of trust is held against the property.

Trustor—the person who deeds his property to a trustee under a deed of trust. This person is the purchaser of the property who is paying for it over a period of time or who is repaying a loan.

Unamortized Loan—refers to a loan that must be repaid in one large payment at the end of a specified period of time. It is not usually used for the purchase of land.

Usury Rate—the permissible rate of interest allowed under state law.

VA (GI) Guaranteed Loan—qualified veterans can obtain a loan that is guaranteed by the Veterans Administration. This makes it easier to obtain a loan with more liberal terms.

Variable Interest Rate—same as a Floating Interest Rate.

Wrap-Around Loan—a loan that includes another loan. When a seller conveys the title to the buyer who takes it "subject to" an existing encumbrance, the seller might make the buyer pay a higher interest rate on his mortgage than the seller pays himself on his mortgage to his creditor. Thus, the buyer's mortgage "wraps around" the seller's mortgage.

CHECKLIST FOR EVALUATING A LOAN

—How much will the lender give you? (What is the loan to value ratio?)

—How soon can you get the loan?

—Do you need a co-signer or security other than the land you intend to buy?

Interest Rate

—What is the annual interest rate?

—Is the interest rate under a variable interest plan?

—What will be the total amount of interest on the loan?

—Is there an escalation clause that permits the lender to increase the interest rate in the future?

Payment Plan

—How long is the amortization period (maturity date)?

—When are the installments to be paid: monthly, quarterly, annually, etc?

—How much is each installment to be?

—Is there a prepayment clause which allows you to make payments in advance and have them credited in the future if you cannot make a payment?

—Are there any other prepayment privileges?

—Is there a prepayment penalty? If so, what does it specify?

—Is there a provision for a balloon payment? If so, how much is it?

—Does the loan include an acceleration clause which permits the lender to force you to pay the entire amount due if you miss a payment, fail to pay taxes or assessments, attempt to sell the land, or let the property fall into disrepair?

—Are you supposed to make impound payments for taxes and assessments with your loan payments?

Foreclosure

—What rights does the lender have if you get behind in your payments?

—What procedure does he have to follow to foreclose your loan? Does he have to go to court first in order to foreclose?

—Do you have a period of redemption? If so, how long is it and what period does it cover?

—Does the loan specify that you are to be reimbursed for all money you have put into the land for improvements if there is a foreclosure?

—Is it stated that you are to receive any surplus money from a foreclosure sale?

—If the lender only has the right to take back the property rather than conduct a foreclosure sale, is it specified that he can only retake an amount of land equal in value to the unpaid balance on the debt?

—If an insufficient amount of money is received from a foreclosure to meet the debt, can the lender get a deficiency judgment against you?

Assignment Rights

—Is the note negotiable or nonnegotiable?

—Is the lender permitted to assign his interest under the loan?

—Can you sell or assign your interest in the property and have the buyer assume your debt? If so, are there any conditions, such as lender approval?

—Can you place a second mortgage or deed of trust on the property?

—Can you put other liens on the property during the loan period?

—Will you be allowed to borrow on your property and give a second mortgage to the same or another lender?

Extra Fees

—Will you be charged for preliminary costs other than interest, for example, points, extras, origination fees? If so, how much will the charge be for each one?

—When do these fees have to be paid? Can they be included in the loan installments over a period of time?

—How much will you have to pay for having the loan documents drawn up?

—What type of insurance and how much coverage are you bound to carry on the property?

—How do you pay for the insurance?

—How much do you have to pay for a credit and employment report?

—How much do you have to pay for a property appraisal?

—Taking everything into account, how much will it cost you to borrow the money?

USEFUL RESOURCES

Federal Land Bank Loans

For a free packet of information on obtaining a Federal Land Bank Loan and the address of the Land Bank Association near you, write to:

Information Division
Farm Credit Administration
Washington, D.C. 20578

Federal Housing Administration (FHA) Insured Loans

The following is a list of area offices of the Department of Housing and Urban Development (HUD), and insuring offices of the Federal Housing Administration (FHA). These offices can supply you with information on lending policies in your area. The other source of FHA information is any FHA-approved financial instiution. A list of these approved lenders is available from any HUD or FHA office.

HUD Area Offices and FHA Insuring Offices

* HUD Area Office.

ALABAMA
Daniel Building
15 South 20th Street
*Birmingham 35233

ALASKA
Federal Building
Room 228
P.O. Box 480
Anchorage 99501

ARIZONA
244 West Osborne Road
P.O. Box 13468
Phoenix 85002

ARKANSAS
No. 1 Union National Plaza
*Little Rock 72201

CALIFORNIA
2500 Wilshire Boulevard
*Los Angeles 90057

801 I Street
P.O. Box 1978
Sacramento 95809

110 West "C" Street
P.O. Box 2648
San Diego 92112

1 Embarcadero Center
Suite 1600
*San Francisco 94111

Santa Ana Freeway Center Building
1440 E. First Street
Santa Ana 92701

COLORADO
Railway Exchange Building
Fourth Floor
909 17th Street
Denver 80202

CONNECTICUT
999 Asylum Avenue
*Hartford 06105

DELAWARE
536 Wilmington Trust Building
Wilmington 19801

DISTRICT OF COLUMBIA
1310 L Street, N.W.
Washington, D.C. 20005

FLORIDA
3001 Ponce de Leon Boulevard
Coral Gables 33134

400 West Bay Street
Box 35009
Jacksonville 32202

4224-28 Henderson Boulevard
P.O. Box 18165
Tampa 33609

GEORGIA
Peachtree Center Building
Third Floor
230 Peachtree Street, N.W.
Atlanta 30303

HAWAII
333 Queen Street
P.O. Box 3377
Honolulu 96801

IDAHO
331 Idaho Street
Boise 83701

ILLINOIS
22 West Madison, 12th Floor
Chicago 60602

628 East Adams Street
P.O. Box 1628
Springfield 62705

INDIANA
Architects and Builders Building
333 North Pennsylvania Street
Indianapolis 46204

IOWA
Room 259
Federal Building
210 Walnut Street
Des Moines 50309

KANSAS
1 Gateway Center
*Kansas City 66117

700 Kansas Avenue
Topeka 66603

KENTUCKY
New Federal Building
Room 1058
P.O. Box 1044
Louisville 40202

LOUISIANA
Plaza Towers Building
1001 Howard Avenue
*New Orleans 70113

Ricou-Brewster Building
Fifth Floor
425 Milam Street
Shreveport 71101

MAINE
U.S. Federal Building
 & Post Office
202 Harlow Street
Bangor 04401

MARYLAND
Federal Building
Room G-13
31 Hopkins Plaza
Baltimore 21201

MASSACHUSETTS
Bullfinch Building
15 New Chardon Street
*Boston 02114

MICHIGAN
Book Building
1249 Washington Boulevard
*Detroit 48226

921 Division Avenue, North
Grand Rapids 49503

MINNESOTA
256 Federal Building
 & U.S. Court House
110 South 4th Street
Minneapolis 55401

MISSISSIPPI
301 Building
301 North Lamar Street
Jackson 39201

MISSOURI
210 North 12th Street
*St. Louis 63101

MONTANA
Steamboat Block
616 Helena Avenue
Helena 59601

NEBRASKA
Univac Building
7100 West Center Road
*Omaha 68106

NEVADA
70 Linden Street
P.O. Box 4700
Reno 89505

NEW HAMPSHIRE
Davison Building
1230 Elm Street
*Manchester 03101

NEW JERSEY
The Parkade Building
519 Federal Street
*Camden 08103

Gateway Building No. 1
Raymond Plaza
*Newark 07102

NEW MEXICO
625 Truman Street, N.E.
Albuquerque 87110

NEW YORK
Westgate North
30 Russell Road
Albany 12206

Grant Building
560 Main Street
*Buffalo 14202

175 Fulton Avenue
Hempstead 11550

120 Church Street
*New York 10007

NORTH CAROLINA
324 West Market Street
Greensboro 27401

NORTH DAKOTA
Federal Building
653 2nd Avenue North
P.O. Box 2483
Fargo 58102

270

OHIO
Federal Office Building
Room 9009
550 Main Street
Cincinnati 45202

Federal Building
Room 907
1240 East 9th Street
Cleveland 44199

Tenth Floor
100 East Broad Street
Columbus Center Building
Columbus 43215

OKLAHOMA
301 North Hudson
*Oklahoma City 73102

1708 Utica Square
P.O. Box 4054
Tulsa 74152

OREGON
Cascade Building
520 Southwest 6th Avenue
*Portland 97204

PENNSYLVANIA
Curtis Building
625 Walnut Street
Philadelphia 19106

1000 Liberty Avenue
*Pittsburgh 15222

PUERTO RICO
New Pan Am Building
255 Ponce de Leon Avenue
P.O. Box 3869 GPO
*San Juan 00936

RHODE ISLAND
Post Office Annex
Providence 02903

SOUTH CAROLINA
1515 Lady Street
Columbia 29201

SOUTH DAKOTA
Federal Building
U.S. Court House
Room 119
400 S. Phillips Avenue
Sioux Falls 57102

TENNESSEE
725 Gay Street, S.W.
Knoxville 37902

Federal Office Building
Room 447
167 North Main Street
Memphis 38103

TEXAS
1100 Commerce Street
14th Floor
*Dallas 75202

Federal Building
819 Taylor Street
Fort Worth 76102

Federal Building
Room 7419
515 Rusk Avenue
Houston 77002

1601 Avenue North
Lubbock 79401

410 South Main Avenue
*San Antonio 78204

UTAH
125 South State Street
P.O. Box 11009
Salt Lake City 84111

VERMONT
Federal Building
Room 630
Elmwood Avenue
Burlington 05402

VIRGINIA
Federal Building
Eighth Floor
Richmond 23240

WASHINGTON
Arcade Plaza Building
1321 Second Avenue
*Seattle 98101

746 U.S. Court House Building
West 920 Riverside Avenue
Spokane 99201

WEST VIRGINIA
New Federal Office Building
500 Quarrier Street
Charleston 25301

744 North 4th Street
Milwaukee 53203

Federal Office Building
Room 4227
100 East B Street
P.O. Box 580
Casper 82601

The following pamphlets are available free from any HUD or FHA office listed above:

Let's Consider Cooperatives—HUD-17-F(2)

Homeownership for Lower Income Families—HUD-36-F(3)

Questions and Answers on FHA Home Property Appraisals—HUD-38-F

Home Mortgage Insurance—HUD-43-F(2)

Financing Condominium Housing—HUD-77-F

HUD-FHA Assisted Program for Houses Built for Sale to Lower Income Families—HUD-89-F(4)

HUD-FHA Program for Home Mortgage Insurance—HUD-97-F(3)

HUD-FHA Program for Unsubsidized Cooperative Housing—HUD-256-F

Mobile Home Financing Through HUD—HUD-265-F

Wise Home Buying—HUD-267-F

Veterans Administration (VA) Guaranteed Loans (GI Loans)

The following is a list of Veterans Administration (VA) Guaranty Service Regional Offices. You can obtain information and necessary loan forms by sending a note to the Director of any of these offices.

ALABAMA
VA Regional Office
Aronov Building
474 South Court Street
Montgomery, Alabama 36104

ARIZONA
VA Regional Office
Federal Building
230 North First Avenue
Phoenix, Arizona 85025

ARKANSAS
VA Regional Office
Federal Office Building
700 West Capitol Avenue
Little Rock, Arkansas 72201

CALIFORNIA
VA Regional Office
Federal Building
1100 Wilshire Boulevard
Los Angeles, California 90024

VA Regional Office
49 Fourth Street
San Francisco, California 94103

COLORADO
VA Regional Office
Denver Federal Center
Denver, Colorado 80225

CONNECTICUT
VA Regional Office
450 Main Street
Hartford, Connecticut 06103

DELAWARE
VA Center
1601 Kirkwood Highway
Wilmington, Delaware 19805

WASHINGTON, D.C.
Veterans Benefits Office
Veterans Administration
2033 M Street NW.
Washington, D.C. 20421

FLORIDA
VA Regional Office
P.O. Box 1437
1144 First Avenue, South
St. Petersburg, Florida 33731

GEORGIA
VA Regional Office
730 Peachtree Street NE.
Atlanta, Georgia 30308

HAWAII
VA Regional Office
P.O. Box 3198
680 Ala Moana Boulevard
Honolulu, Hawaii 96801

IDAHO
VA Center
Fifth and Fort Street
Boise, Idaho 83707

ILLINOIS
VA Regional Office
2030 West Taylor Street
Chicago, Illinois 60612

INDIANA
VA Regional Office
36 South Pennsylvania Street
Indianapolis, Indiana 46204

IOWA
VA Regional Office
210 Walnut Street
Des Moines, Iowa 50309

KANSAS
VA Center
5500 East Kellogg
Wichita, Kansas 67218

KENTUCKY
VA Regional Office
600 Federal Place
Louisville, Kentucky 40202

LOUISIANA
VA Regional Office
701 Loyola Avenue
New Orleans, Louisiana 70113

MAINE
VA Center
Togus, Maine 04330

MARYLAND
VA Regional Office
Federal Building—Charles Center
31 Hopkins Plaza
Baltimore, Maryland 21201

MASSACHUSETTS
VA Regional Office
John Fitzgerald Kennedy
    Federal Building
Government Center
Boston, Massachusetts 02203

MICHIGAN
VA Regional Office
801 West Baltimore at Third
P.O. Box 1117—A
Detroit, Michigan 48232

MINNESOTA
VA Center
Federal Building
Fort Snelling
St. Paul, Minnesota 55111

MISSISSIPPI
VA Center
1500 East Woodrow Wilson Drive
Jackson, Mississippi 39216

MISSOURI
VA Regional Office
Room 4705 Federal Building
1520 Market Street
St. Louis, Missouri 63103

MONTANA
VA Center
Fort Harrison, Montana 59636

NEBRASKA
VA Regional Office
220 South 17th Street
Lincoln, Nebraska 68508

NEVADA
VA Center
1000 Locust Street
Reno, Nevada 89502

NEW HAMPSHIRE
VA Regional Office
497 Silver Street
Manchester, New Hampshire 03103

NEW JERSEY
VA Regional Office
20 Washington Place
Newark, New Jersey 07102

NEW MEXICO
VA Regional Office
500 Gold Avenue South West
Albuquerque, New Mexico 87101

NEW YORK
VA Regional Office
1021 Main Street
Buffalo, New York 14203

VA Regional Office
252 Seventh Avenue
New York, New York 10001

NORTH CAROLINA
VA Regional Office
Wachovia Building
301 North Main Street
Winston-Salem, North Carolina 27102

NORTH DAKOTA
VA Center
Fargo, North Dakota 58102

OHIO
    VA Regional Office
    Federal Office Building
    1240 East Ninth Street
    Cleveland, Ohio 44199

OKLAHOMA
    VA Regional Office
    Second and Court Streets
    Muskogee, Oklahoma 74401

OREGON
    VA Regional Office
    426 Southwest Stark Street
    Portland, Oregon 97204

PENNSYLVANIA
    VA Center
    P.O. Box 8079
    5000 Wissahickon Avenue
    Philadelphia, Pennsylvania 19101

    VA Regional Office
    Federal Building
    1000 Liberty Avenue
    Pittsburgh, Pennsylvania 15222

PUERTO RICO
    VA Center
    Barrio Monacillos
    GPO Box 4867
    Rio Piedras, Puerto Rico 00936

RHODE ISLAND
    VA Regional Office
    Federal Building, Kennedy Plaza
    Providence, Rhode Island 02903

SOUTH CAROLINA
    VA Regional Office
    1801 Assembly Street
    Columbia, South Carolina 29201

SOUTH DAKOTA
    VA Center
    Sioux Falls, South Dakota 57101

TENNESSEE
    VA Regional Office
    U.S. Courthouse
    801 Broadway
    Nashville, Tennessee 37203

TEXAS
    VA Regional Office
    515 Rusk Avenue
    Houston, Texas 77061

VA Regional Office
1400 North Valley Mills Drive
Waco, Texas 76710

UTAH
    VA Regional Office
    125 South State Street
    Salt Lake City, Utah 84111

VERMONT
    VA Center
    White River Junction, Vermont 05001

VIRGINIA
    VA Regional Office
    211 West Campbell Avenue
    Roanoke, Viginia 24011

WASHINGTON
    VA Regional Office
    Sixth and Lenora Building
    Seattle, Washington 98121

WEST VIRGINIA
    VA Regional Office
    502 Eighth Street
    Huntington, West Virginia 25701

WISCONSIN
    VA Regional Office
    342 North Water Street
    Milwaukee, Wisconsin 53202

WYOMING
    NOTE: Wyoming loans are handled out of the Denver, Colorado, office. See above.

The following pamphlets on VA loans are available free from any VA regional office listed above:

> *Questions and Answers on Guaranteed and Direct Loans for Veterans*—VA Pamphlet 26-4
> *Pointers for the Veteran Homeowner*—VA Pamphlet 26-5
> *To the Home-Buying Vet*—VA Pamphlet 26-6

Farmers Home Administration (FHA-USDA)

For information on FHA-USDA programs available in your area write to your local FHA-USDA office. To get the address of your local office write to:

274

The Farmers Home Administration
U.S. Department of Agriculture
Washington, D.C. 20250

The following pamphlets are available free from any local Farmers Home Administration office or the main office listed above:

Farmer Co-Operatives in the United States—FCS B 1
Farm Ownership Loans—PA 62
Rural Housing Loans—PA 476
Loans for Forestry Purposes—PA 624
Loans to Co-Operatives Servicing Rural Families with Low Incomes—PA 662
Opportunity Loans to Rural Families with Low Incomes—PA 663
Farmers Home Administration—PA 705
Need a Little Financial Help?—PA 706
Loans for Recreation Enterprises—PA 723
Rental and Co-Op Housing in Rural Areas—PA 800
Self-Help Housing for Low Income Rural Families—PA 822
Investors Opportunity in Farmers Home Insured Notes—PA 926
Building Rural America Through Farmers Home Insured Notes—PA 927
Soil and Water Loans—PA 972
This Is FHA—PA 973
Home Ownership—PA 977

General Information

In addition to the lenders and federal agencies mentioned above, you can get financial advice from your local Farm Advisor and from your local Agricultural Experiment Station. (See addresses in "Useful Resources" at the end of Chapter 5: *The Earth-Soil, Vegetation, Topography*.)

The following are available free from:

Consumer Product Information
Public Documents Distribution Center
Pueblo, Colorado 81009

The Fair Credit Reporting Act-046A
Truth in Lending-059A
Buying and Financing a Mobile Home-127A
Cooperatives vs. Condominiums-129A

The following is available free from any savings and loan association office:

Your Guide to a Savings and Loan Mortgage

The following is available for 15¢ from:

Small Homes Council-Building Research Council
University of Illinois
Urbana-Champaign
One East Saint Mary's Road
Champaign, Illinois 61820

Financing the Home—A 1.3

The following are available for the specified cost from:

The Superintendent of Documents
Government Printing Office
Washington, D.C. 20402

Selecting and Financing a Home, Catalog No. A 1.77:182/2, 15¢
Condominiums-Their Development and Management, Catalog Number HH 1.2:C 75/3 S/N 2300-00202, $1.25
Advice on the Purchase and Sale of a Home by Military Personnel, 11 AF JAG L. Rev. (No. 1), Winter 1969 AFRP-110-1, Catalog No. D 302.9: Winter 1969, 70¢

VI

THE
CONTRACT
OF SALE

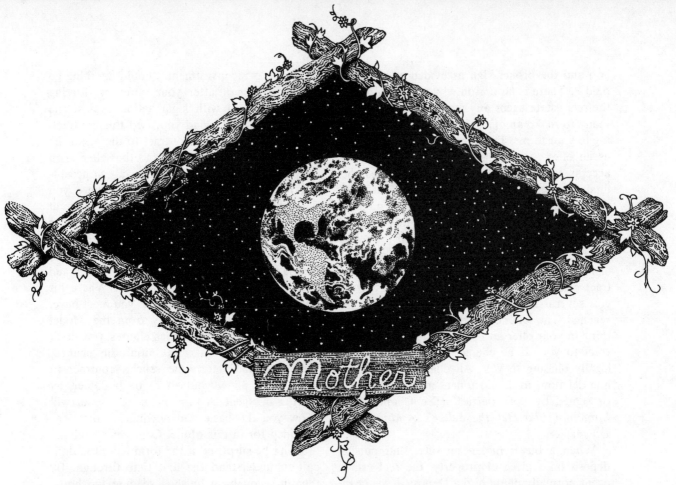

chapter 28

The Model Contract of Sale

This chapter is the heart of the book. It contains a Model Contract of Sale which can be used in your land purchase. Every landowner I have met who did not hire a lawyer to handle his deal signed a contract submitted to him by the real estate agent. Many of these buyers have since regretted such action. It is a plain and simple fact that any contract supplied by the agent is written to protect the seller, not the buyer. This is true whether the contract is endorsed by the state Real Estate Commissioner or drawn up by the seller's attorney.

As stated previously, many times real estate agents will give documents to buyers to sign without making it clear that they potentially are contracts. The Deposit Receipt is the most infamous example of this practice throughout the United States. Any document that is dated, contains the name of the parties, states what is being sold and for how much, and is signed by the parties is a legally binding contract, regardless of what it is called.

Each section of the Model Contract is accompanied by an explanation of what the terms mean, why they are included, and how you should fill in the blank spaces. Where applicable you are referred to the other parts of the book that have more information on that section of the Model Contract. First, read the entire contract, then go back over each section while reading the explanation that goes with it. If you have read the rest of this book, you will then have an understanding of how to use this Model Contract in your purchase to protect yourself.

You will not use every clause contained in this contract. Many sections will be deleted for your purchases, as explained in the discussion of each section. For example, if there is no house on the land, you will delete each section of the contract that relates to the purchase of a house.

This contract serves three purposes. First, it is a receipt for your deposit money, which you and the broker sign as evidence you have paid it. There is no reason why you should give the real estate agent any money unless you are ready to make an offer to buy the land according to your terms. Thus, the contract also serves as an offer to purchase the land. If the seller accepts your offer, the contract becomes the final agreement between the parties. That is its third function. When you fill in the amount of money to be paid for the property, this is really the amount you are offering to pay. If the seller rejects your offer, he will return the contract unsigned. It will not be surprising if this contract passes back and forth between the two of you several times before a final agreement is reached. The seller can cross out or change anything in your offer and sign and return the contract to you. If he changes anything, it is not legally binding to you. All changes, additions, and deletions in the document must be initialed or signed by both parties. (See Chapter 20: *Bargaining To Get the Seller's Asking Price Down.*)

When a buyer makes an offer and puts a deposit on a piece of property, the real estate agent normally offers him a Deposit Receipt or Contract of Sale to fill out and sign. But, you can tell him that you wish to use your own form. Get all the information from him that you need to complete this contract. Then, go through the contract and delete and add whatever is necessary. Type the resulting contract on regular typing paper, fill in the blanks and sign it, and give it to the agent or seller, whichever party you are dealing with. He will probably be shocked. Compared to the simple form that the agent usually gives a buyer, your Contract of Sale will look like a manifesto. Don't worry about a thing. The purpose of all this is

to protect your investment. Should anything go wrong during or after your purchase, forcing you to proceed with legal action against the seller, you will be glad you used this contract.

When you give this contract to the agent, he is bound by law to deliver it to the seller. You may get resistance from the seller about accepting it. However, I mention areas where you can make compromises with the seller without jeopardizing your basic protections. If the seller absolutely refuses to deal with this contract, you can ask him to give you a contract form that is acceptable to him. Take his contract and compare it to the Model Contract. Where his contract has omitted protections you must have, write in the clauses directly from the Model Contract. If his contract has clauses you don't like, cross them out and initial the change. Then you can return the seller's contract to him. Never allow yourself to be buffaloed by a seller or agent. A fair and honest seller will allow you the basic and adequate protections provided for in this Model Contract of Sale.

Don't be surprised if the form is a little difficult to understand the first time through. By the time you have finished reading the book, looked at some land, talked to some real estate agents and public officials, everything will fit into place. Even if you decide to retain the services of an attorney, this chapter will give you a good understanding of what he should be doing for you. It provides you with the information you need to ask him intelligent questions about the transaction. You should compare this Model Contract with the contract your lawyer prepares for you. If you find anything omitted from his contract or if any clauses are in conflict, point this out to him. Lawyers are not infallible.

MODEL CONTRACT OF SALE

City of _____, County of _____, State of _____,
_____, 19___
        (date)

Received from _____ (herein called Buyer), the sum
of _____ Dollars ($_____) evidenced by _____
                                                        (personal check or cashier's check)
as deposit on account of purchase price of _____ Dollars ($_____) for the pur-
chase of property, situated in City of _____, County of _____,
State of _____, described as follows: _____
_____
_____.

Said deposit will be placed in the following account: _____.
Buyer will deposit in escrow with _____ the balance of purchase price as
follows:

The sum of _____ Dollars ($_____.___) to be deposited in escrow on, or before,
_____, 19___ as a down payment, which shall include the above deposit;
                                                                    (note and mortgage
The sum of _____ Dollars ($_____.___) to be represented by a or deed of trust),
    to be payable _____ Dollars ($_____.___) or more on the first day of each
    and every month, beginning _____, 19___ with interest on all unpaid principal
    beginning _____, 19___.

Interest on deferred payments will be _____% per annum, from _____, 19___
    payable with each monthly payment as part of the same.

1. Buyer's signature hereon constitutes an offer to Seller to purchase the real estate and personal property described above. Unless acceptance hereof is signed by Seller and the signed
copy delivered to Buyer, either in person or by mail to the address shown below within
_____ days hereof, this offer shall be deemed revoked and the deposit shall be returned
to Buyer within 48 hours.

2. The price of said property is _____ Dollars ($_____.___) per acre. The total num-
ber of acres is _____.

3. The total acreage on which the purchase price is computed shall be based on a legal survey completed by a licensed surveyor or registered civil engineer. The results of the survey
are to be approved by Buyer before the close of escrow. The expense of the survey is to be
paid by the Seller.

4. Title is to be free of liens, encumbrances, easements, covenants, reservations, restrictions,
rights and conditions other than the following: _____
_____
_____.

5. Within _____ days of the Seller's acceptance hereof, escrow instructions signed by
Buyer and Seller shall be delivered to _____. Either
                                        (name and address of escrow holder)
party failing to open and sign as provided shall be guilty of a breach of this agreement. If
both parties fail to sign within the time prescribed, the agreement shall be deemed rescinded,
and all money and documents shall be returned to the party from whom derived.
    Escrow instructions signed by both parties shall provide for closing within _____ days
from the opening of escrow, subject to written extensions signed by Buyer and Seller.
    Close of escrow means the time when the documents transferring title are recorded.
    It is mutually agreed between Buyer and Seller that this agreement shall become an in-
tegral part of the escrow proceedings in which the transfer of the property is finalized and
this agreement shall be binding on both parties even if these provisions are not specifically
recorded or mentioned in escrow proceedings.
    Any inconsistency between the escrow instructions and this agreement is to be resolved
in a manner consistent with this agreement unless the inconsistent provision of this agreement is expressly waived by a writing specifically referring to the inconsistent provision in
this agreement.

6. Unless otherwise designated in the escrow instructions of Buyer, title shall vest as follows:
_____ .

7. Seller shall by Full Covenant and Warranty Deed convey to Buyer a marketable fee simple title as approved by Buyer in the following manner: Within _____ days of the Seller's acceptance hereof, Seller shall cause to be delivered to Buyer a Preliminary Title Report issued by _____(title company)_____ describing the property, and copies of all documents referred to in it. Within _____ days after Buyer's receipt of the Preliminary Title Report and all documents referred to in it, Buyer shall give Seller notice specifying the matters disapproved by Buyer. If these matters are not corrected by the Seller to the satisfaction and approval of the Buyer before the close of escrow, the Buyer may, at his election, terminate this agreement and any deposit and other money placed in escrow and paid under this agreement shall immediately be returned to him.

8. Seller shall furnish to Buyer a marketable fee simple title as evidenced by a ____(standard or extended)____ Owner's Title Insurance Policy insuring title in Buyer for at least the amount of the purchase price of said property. The Seller shall furnish the Buyer with a copy of a ____(standard or extended)____ Owner's Title Insurance Policy on close of escrow. Said Policy shall be issued by _____(title company)_____ and shall be subject only to liens, encumbrances, easements, covenants, reservations, restrictions, rights and conditions of record as set forth in this agreement and in the Policy. If Seller fails to deliver title as herein provided, Buyer at his election may terminate this agreement and any deposit and other money placed in escrow and paid under this agreement shall immediately be returned to him.

9. The following prorations shall be made in escrow on the basis of a 30-day month and shall be prorated as of (1) the date of recordation of the deed or (2) _____:

(a) Real property taxes based on the most recent official information applicable to the fiscal year in which the proration date occurs, and obtainable in the office of the particular taxing authority;

(b) Premiums on existing transferable insurance policies approved by Buyer by notice delivered to escrow before _____ 19___, covering damage to or destruction of the property transferred to Buyer through escrow. The policies are listed in Exhibit _____, attached hereto; they are to be assigned to Buyer and delivered through escrow, with a loss payable clause in favor of creditors whose obligations are secured by encumbrances on the property as specified in this agreement;

(c) Interest on obligations secured by encumbrances to which the property will remain subject after close of escrow. All new notes shall be dated as of close of escrow; if any new notes are dated before closing, they shall be endorsed: "Interest to run only from _____, 19___."

(d) Installments of principal and interest on the following personal property: _____ _____ which are to be included with this transaction.

10. If impounded funds are held by the lender in connection with a mortgage, deed of trust, or other encumbrance remaining of record at close of escrow, Buyer shall be charged and Seller credited with the full amount.

11. If, at the close of escrow, all or any part of the property is affected by any liens, assessment liens, or bonds, all or part of which are or may become payable, all the unpaid installments of these, including those that are to become due after close of escrow shall, for purposes of this agreement, be considered due and liens on the property, and except for _____, Seller shall pay and discharge them before close of escrow or, at Buyer's election, allow them as a credit against the _____(cash or note)_____ due at closing for the unpaid balance of the purchase price.

12. At close of escrow the parties shall apply for segregation of taxes on said property and shall sign and deposit in escrow any affidavits, applications, or other papers necessary for that purpose. If after close of escrow and before segregation, any tax for tax years following 19___–19___ or any installment becomes due, it will be prorated between the parties and paid by each of them before delinquency on the following basis:

(a) Taxes for land: _____% shall be allocated to said property.

(b) Taxes for improvements to land (excluding special assessments for improvements): in the proportion the assessed valuation of improvements on each party's land bears to the total assessed valuation of all improvements assessed.

(c) Taxes for personal property: in the proportion the assessed valuation of each party's personal property bears to the total assessed valuation of all personal property.

(d) If the assessed valuations on the land on subsequent segregation are different from those stated, adjustments will be made between the parties on the basis of the assessed values of each parcel instead of the percentage stated in (a) above.

13. Buyer shall pay _____% of the escrow fee; the escrow holder's customary charges to Buyer for document-drafting, recording, and miscellaneous charges; and the title insurance premium to the extent that it exceeds the premium for standard coverage with a liability equal to the purchase price.

Seller shall pay _____% of the escrow fee; the escrow holder's customary charges to Seller for document-drafting, recording, and miscellaneous charges (including local transfer taxes); and the title insurance premium to the extent that it does not exceed the premium for standard coverage with a liability equal to the purchase price.

In addition, each party will pay reasonable compensation to the escrow holder for extraordinary or unusual services rendered to or for that party, if any, plus costs and expenses incurred in connection with those services.

14. Seller shall deliver possession of the property, all improvements thereon, and all personal property if any, to Buyer in substantially the same condition, reasonable wear and tear excepted, as on the date of this agreement: (strike out inapplicable alternatives below)

(a) on close of escrow: or

(b) not later than _____ days after closing escrow: or

(c) _____

(d) If the Seller has not vacated the property by the date Buyer is to take possession, the Seller shall be liable to the Buyer for a daily rental equal to the sum of _____ Dollars ($_____.___) per day for each and every day the Seller remains on the property as a holdover Seller in possession; or the Buyer, at his option, may terminate this agreement and any deposit and other money deposited in escrow shall thereupon be returned to him.

15. If, when neither legal title nor possession of the property has been transferred to the Buyer, any part of the property is destroyed, materially damaged, or taken by eminent domain, the Buyer, at his option, may be relieved of his obligation to complete the purchase, or he may obtain a reduction of the purchase price to the extent of the cost of repairing or replacing the damage from destruction or the diminution in value resulting from eminent domain.

16. Seller recognizes that Buyer will spend time and effort preparing for the acquisition of this property, and Buyer recognizes that Seller's property will be removed from the market during the existence of this agreement. Both parties agree that if either fails to perform under this contract, the other should be entitled to compensation for the detriment described above, but that it is extremely difficult and impractical to ascertain the extent of the detriment. To avoid these problems, the parties agree to liquidate damages as follows:

If Seller fails to perform for any reason, Buyer shall be entitled to recover his deposit and any other money he has deposited into escrow or paid to or for Seller's account and shall also recover from Seller the sum of _____ Dollars ($_____.___) as liquidated damages.

If Buyer fails to perform for any reason, Seller shall be entitled to recover the sum of _____ Dollars ($_____.___) as liquidated damages and shall be entitled
(amount of deposit or less)
to obtain the sum out of any deposit made by Buyer to Seller or his agent or into escrow and out of any other money Buyer has deposited into escrow or paid to or for Seller's account.

Both parties agree that these sums stated as liquidated damages shall be in lieu of any other monetary relief to which the parties might otherwise be entitled by virtue of this contract or by operation of law.

17. The Seller, for himself, and his heirs, representatives, and assignees, covenants with the Buyer and his heirs, representatives, and assignees as follows:

(a) That the Seller is lawfully seised of the described property in fee simple, and has the right to convey the same;

(b) That the property is free from all liens and encumbrances, except as aforesaid;

(c) That the Buyer shall quietly enjoy the property;

(d) That the Seller will do any further acts or procure any further necessary assurance of the title for the purpose of perfecting the title to the property;

(e) That the Seller forever warrants and will defend the title of the property against the lawful claims and demands of all persons.

(f) All of the above covenants shall survive delivery of the deed.

18. The Seller warrants and represents the following:

(a) That the land title conveyed to the Buyer contains legal access rights from the most accessible public road to the building sites on the conveyed land which is the subject of this agreement. These access roads shall include, but not be limited to, the existing access roads to the building sites on the conveyed land if any are in existence at the time of this conveyance.

(b) That as of the closing of escrow the property will have a legal survey completed by a licensed surveyor or registered civil engineer with all corners staked on the ground and all boundaries marked and visible on the ground; and will include within its boundaries the following structures and land features: _____.

(c) That as of the closing of escrow the property will include a spring, well, creek, or other water supply with a year-round output of, at least, _____ gallons per _____.

(d) That at this time and as of the close of escrow the property is and will be zoned _____, under the laws of the city of _____, the county of _____, and the state of _____.

(e) That as of the closing of escrow the structures will be free of any damage from infestation by wood-destroying pests and organisms, including but not limited to termites, dry rot, and fungi.

(f) That at present and as of close of escrow no violation exists or will exist with respect to the property or any improvements, of any statute, ordinance, regulation, or administrative or judicial order or holding, whether or not appearing in public records.

(g) That the property is not, and at the close of escrow shall not, be the subject of any proposed liens, assessment liens, or bonds other than those excepted in Clause 11 above, by reason of any work or improvement completed or installed at or before the close of escrow, or to be completed after the close of escrow.

(h) That at present and as of close of escrow the Seller has no knowledge of any intent to take any part of the property by condemnation or eminent domain.

(i) That at present and as of close of escrow the Seller owns, in full, those items listed as personal property to be conveyed to the Buyer according to this agreement. The following such items are not owned, in full, by the Seller: _____

(j) That no poisonous sprays, insecticides, pesticides, or herbicides have been used in any way on said property or applied to any vegetation growing on said property.

(k) All of the above warranties and representations shall survive delivery of the deed.

19. Buyer's obligation to perform this agreement is subject to the following terms and conditions:

(a) If Buyer notifies Seller that Buyer disapproves any matter set out in this Clause, or if there is a breach of Seller's warranties and representations set out in this agreement discovered by Buyer before close of escrow, Seller shall diligently attempt to correct these matters at his own expense within _____ days after Buyer's notice of objection. If all these matters are not corrected within that time, Buyer has the election within _____ days after Seller's time for correction has expired of:

   (1) Terminating the agreement without liability on his part; or

   (2) Completing the purchase, in which event the purchase price shall be reduced by an amount equal to the reduction in market value resulting from the uncorrected matters; or

   (3) Removing the defect, in which event the purchase price shall be reduced by an amount equal to his cost of correcting those matters.

   (4) If Buyer makes no election, his silence shall be deemed an election of option **(1)**. If the agreement is terminated by Buyer's election or failure to elect under this paragraph, all funds or other things deposited by him shall be returned to him immediately on demand, and Seller shall pay all title company and escrow charges.

(5) If Buyer elects option **(2)**, the reduction in market value caused by a lien or encumbrance securing a liquidated dollar amount shall be deemed to be the unpaid principal balance of that amount plus accrued interest not charged to Seller in escrow. Other reductions in market value should be mutually agreed upon by Buyer and Seller. The reduction in price shall first be applied to the down payment and second to the purchase money note.

(6) If Buyer elects option **(3)**, the closing shall be extended for no more than _____ days. If Buyer does not remove the defects within that time, he shall still be entitled to exercise option **(1)** or option **(2)** within that time. If he does not remove the defects within that time and fails to elect either of the other two options, his silence shall be deemed an election of option **(1)**.

(b) Buyer's approval, within _____ days after the date of this agreement, of _____
(survey, soil tests, termite and house inspection, appraisal of land and improvements, etc.)

Buyer and his representatives shall have the right from this date to enter on the property to obtain the pertinent information and for any other purposes reasonably related to carrying out the provisions of this agreement. If the condition is not satisfied, Buyer has the right at his election to terminate the agreement or waive the condition. Buyer's termination or waiver shall be evidence by notice to Seller within _____ days after execution of this agreement. If he gives no notice, his silence shall waive the condition.

(c) Buyer's ability to secure the right, under applicable zoning and land use laws, regulations, and ordinances, to _____ (zoning or use designation being sought, building permits, etc.) _____.

Buyer shall file the documents and pay the fees necessary to obtain the change. If Buyer has proceeded with reasonable diligence but has not obtained a final determination by the time scheduled for closing, on Buyer's written election the closing shall be extended until final determination, provided Buyer is diligently pursuing a determination. Seller may terminate this agreement on _____ days notice if Buyer is not diligent in pursuing a determination. If the final determination is adverse, Buyer alone shall have the election either to terminate this agreement or to waive this condition. Buyer shall make his election within _____ days after final determination.

(d) Seller's deposit in escrow, within _____ days after execution of this agreement, of a report as of a date after the date of this agreement from _____ (name of company) _____, a licensed structural pest control operator, selected by the Buyer, certifying that normally accessible areas of the property are free from infestation by wood-destroying pests and organisms, including but not limited to termites, dry rot, and fungi, and that no corrective work is required, the cost of the report to be borne _____ (equally by Buyer and Seller, by Seller, or by Buyer).

Buyer shall notify Seller by _____, 19__, if the condition is not satisfied, and Buyer may, at his election, terminate the agreement or waive the condition. If he gives no notice, his silence shall waive the condition.

(e) Buyer's obtaining from a lender of his choice within __ days of execution of this agreement a loan of not less than _____ Dollars ($_____.__) secured by (first deed of trust, mortgage) _____ on the property on terms no less favorable to the Buyer than the following: Interest at _____% per year, principal and interest payable in equal monthly installments of _____ Dollars ($_____.__) per month, term of _____ years, privilege of prepayment at any time without penalty, loan fees and costs of not more than _____%, acceleration provisions to be approved by Buyer, (guaranteed by VA or insured by FHA) and the deposit in escrow of documents by Buyer and lender that will permit the recordation, concurrently with the recordation of the deed from Seller to Buyer under this agreement, of the security instrument for the loan.

Buyer shall give Seller notice within _____ days after execution of this agreement if the condition is satisfied. If he fails to give notice, his silence shall waive the condition; if he gives notice that the condition is not satisfied, the agreement shall be terminated, and all funds and other things deposited by either party shall be returned to each of them.

Buyer shall make diligent application to at least two lending institutions and execute and furnish documents and supply all information reasonably requested by the lending institutions in connection with his applications. Within _____ days after notice from Buyer to Seller of Buyer's inability to satisfy this condition or after the expiration of the period provided for Buyer to obtain it, without notice from the Buyer that he has obtained it, the Seller may obtain the financing for Buyer according to the terms set forth herein, and Buyer agrees to supply all information and execute all documents reasonably required by the lender to apply for and close the loan.

(f) The Seller shall make a diligent effort to locate and develop a year-round adequate water supply for the Buyer's needs on the property. If necessary, the Seller shall drill a well to a maximum depth of _____. The water supply must have a year-round output of at least _____ gallons per minute. If the Seller cannot locate and develop an adequate water supply, then this agreement shall be terminated immediately and all funds deposited and paid by the Buyer shall be returned immediately and the Buyer shall suffer no further liability under this agreement.

20. The prevailing party in any action or proceeding between the parties shall be entitled to reasonable attorney's fees in addition to all other relief to which he may be entitled.

21. As used in this agreement, the masculine, feminine, or neuter gender, and the singular or plural number shall each be deemed to include the others whenever the context so indicates, and the words Buyer and Seller shall include the respective successors in interest of each, whenever the context so requires.

22. All Exhibits to which reference is made are deemed incorporated in the agreement, whether or not actually attached.

23. The waiver by one party of the performance of any covenant, condition, or promise shall not invalidate this agreement nor shall it be considered a waiver by him of any other covenant, condition, or promise. The waiver by either or both parties of the time for performing any act shall not constitute a waiver of the time for performing any other act or an identical act required to be performed at a later time. The exercise of any remedy provided in this agreement shall not be a waiver of any consistent remedy provided by law, and the provision in this agreement for any remedy shall not exclude other consistent remedies unless they are expressly excluded.

24. All notices and demands shall be given in writing by registered or certified mail, postage prepaid, and return receipt requested. Notice shall be considered given when mailed. Notices shall be addressed as appears below for the respective person, provided that if any party gives notice of a change of name or address, notices to the giver of that notice shall thereafter be given as demanded in that notice. Notices to any party of the transaction, sent after escrow is opened, shall also be sent to the escrow holder.

25. This agreement shall apply to and bind the heirs, executors, administrators, successors, and assignees of the respective parties.

26. Any change in or modification of this agreement must be in writing and signed by the parties thereto.

27. Time is of the essence in this agreement.

Name of Escrow Holder

Name of Agent

Address

Address

Telephone

Telephone

The undersigned Buyer offers and agrees to buy the above described property on the terms and conditions above stated and acknowledges receipt of a copy hereof. Upon acceptance by the Seller and delivery to the Buyer of the signed copy, this instrument becomes a binding contract on the Buyer's part.

Dated

Address

Telephone

Name of Buyer

Buyer's signature

EXPLANATION OF CLAUSES IN MODEL CONTRACT OF SALE

Where appropriate, an explanation will be followed by an example showing you how the blanks on the contract can be filled in. Reference will be made to other chapters that include more details and information on the subject of each clause.

Place and Date of Signing

Write in the city, county, and state, in which this transaction occurs and the date you sign this contract. This date is important because it starts the time period in which the seller must accept your offer, according to Clause 3 below.

Buyer's Name and Type of Ownership

Your name and the type of ownership by which you will take title to the property are inserted here. Each buyer must indicate his or her marital status. If there are two or more buyers, you must state how you are taking title, whether as joint tenants, tenants-in-common, a partnership, or some other form of ownership. (See Chapter 32: *Types of Co-Ownership*.)

Example: Brian Wilcox, a single person, and Daniel and Louise Varre both married persons, as joint tenants.

Amount and Form of Deposit (Earnest Money)

Next you specify the amount of your deposit. Any time money amounts are given in the contract, they should first be written out and then given numerically. (For example: Two Hundred Dollars; $200.00) This avoids any possibility of confusion due to a typographical error since the amount written out always takes priority over the numerical figure. Although the deposit can be for any amount, it is generally 1–5 percent of the purchase price. The seller will want the amount to be as large as possible, at least enough to cover the broker's commission, since the seller gets to keep it as a forfeiture penalty if you break the contract and back out of the deal later. Naturally, you as buyer will want to make it a small amount in case of such eventuality. Never deposit more than 5 percent. On a $20,000 offer, I would deposit $200, which is 1 percent of the total purchase price.

You should pay the deposit in the form of a personal check rather than cash. If the seller won't accept a personal check, use a cashier's check. Make the check payable to the escrow holder. Give it to the real estate agent to hold in his separate business trust account until the seller accepts your offer and escrow is opened. Since the check is made out to the escrow holder, neither the agent nor the seller can cash and misuse it before the agreement becomes final. When escrow opens, the deposit will go in with the down payment, or the remainder of the purchase price if you are paying cash.

If the seller rejects your offer or at any time breaches the contract, the deposit will be returned to you, as indicated in Clause 1 and Clause 16. If the seller accepts your offer and the deal terminates before closing for any reason other than your breach of the contract, you will get the deposit back. Since you did not submit cash or endorse the check to the seller or agent, you should have no problem getting your deposit back. You can instruct your bank, at any time, to stop payment on the check. If you default on the agreement, the deposit will go to the seller, as indicated in Clause 16. (See Chapter 20: *Bargaining to Get the Seller's Asking Price Down*.)

Amount of Full Purchase Price (Your Offer to the Seller)

You must also fill in the purchase price here, which is really only an offer until the seller accepts and signs this contract without changing any of its terms. Once he accepts the contract, this figure becomes the final purchase price. (See Chapter 20: *Bargaining to Get the Seller's Asking Price Down*.)

Location and Description of the Property

Write in the name of the city, county, and state in which the land is located. After "described as follows," you must give the description of the property as it is to appear in the deed. The real estate agent will give you a copy of this description, which you can copy into the contract. The description is usually by metes and bounds or by reference to the United States Rectangular Survey, to adjoining lands, to a subdivision map, a deed or other instrument, or to a licensed survey. The description must identify the land so that it cannot be confused with any other piece of land. If the property has not yet been surveyed, this can be done after you sign the contract and before the close of escrow. This is provided for in Clause 3, Clause 18(b), and Clause 19(b). (See Chapter 8: *Land Descriptions and Surveys*.)

This description should include what will be excluded from the title to the property, such as mineral and timber rights. (See Chapter 11: *Oil, Gas, Mineral, Timber, Soil, and Other Rights*.)

Describe any easements you will receive with the property, since an easement is a property right. (See Chapter 9: *Easement Rights*.) If you are being given a right to take water or anything else from another person's property, it should also be included here. (See Chapter 10: *Water Rights*.)

List all personal property to be included in the deal. This is everything except the "real property," which is the land and the things permanently attached to the land, such as structures and vegetation. Personal property can include such things as machinery, tools, furniture, rugs, appliances, and animals. Make this list complete because if you omit an item that you expect to receive, this could be construed to mean that it is not included in the sale. This list should be an inventory of everything you are buying that could be removed and taken by the seller. If you wish, you can list the property on a separate piece of paper and attach it to the contract. You would refer to it here. See Clause 22.

Example: (This is a property description by reference to the United States Rectangular Survey. Mineral rights are excluded from the title to the land. An easement across the neighbor's land is included as are several items of personal property.)

PARCEL ONE: The South Half of the Northwest Quarter of Section 21, Township 4 South, Range 2 East, New Mexico Meridian.

EXCEPTING therefrom all coal and other mineral rights in said land together with the right to prospect for, mine, and remove the same as reserved by the United States of America in Patent recorded June 8, 1928 in Book 24, Page 214, of Patents in the office of the County Recorder of said County.

PARCEL TWO: A nonexclusive easement in the Southerly portion of the Northeast Quarter of the Northeast Quarter of Section 21, in Township 4 South, Range 2 East, New Mexico Meridian, and extending Easterly to the West line of the County Road, together with the right to convey said easement to others.

PERSONAL PROPERTY included in this purchase shall include:

One (1) Homelite Chain Saw, Model 14, Serial Number A246415.

One (1) Servel Propane Refrigerator.

Fifteen (15) Rhode Island Red Chickens: four (4) roosters, eleven (11) hens.

Location of the Real Estate Agent's Business (Trust) Account

By law, a real estate agent must have a separate account, called a special trust account, in which he must keep funds of persons involved in negotiations through his office to prevent their misuse. Ask the agent in which bank his account is located and insert that information here.

Example: Account Number 431 OL 104 in the Bank of America, Bronwood, Georgia.

As the contract indicates, the deposit will go into escrow once the agreement has been finalized and escrow opens.

Name and Location of the Escrow Holder

You should locate a reputable escrow company to manage the escrow proceedings. Every real estate agent has one or two companies that handle his deals, but you do not have to use his company. Often a title company acts as the escrow holder for the agent and if the agent is good friends with the title officer, you might not get the objective advice you need about your purchase and title. In addition, escrow fees vary and you might be able to find a better deal than the agent's company can offer. It is best for the buyer to pick out the escrow holder. Find a properly licensed and reputable escrow or title company or bank and insert its name and location here. (See Chapter 30: *Opening and Closing of Escrow and the Role of the Escrow Holder*.)

Example: Home Land Title Company of Bronwood, Georgia.

Details of the Purchase Price and Financing

Detail here how you will pay the purchase price. This is actually the amount of your offer and the terms you are offering to pay. State the down payment you are offering to pay the seller. This is usually 10–30 percent of the total price. (For example, it could be $4,000 down on a total price of $20,000.) It is paid at the closing of escrow. Insert the closing date. You must use this same date throughout the rest of the contract. The down payment will include the deposit money you are making with this offer.

After the down payment is made, the rest of the purchase price will be paid in cash or under some kind of financing arrangement. If you will pay cash at the closing of escrow, you will have to rewrite this section to specify an all-cash deal. Change "down payment" to "full payment" and omit the rest of the section. Usually, however, a buyer pays the seller for the land over a period of time. After you fill in the amount of the down payment, state the remaining amount of the purchase price you are offering to pay.

You then state the payment plan to be used. For example: "a Note and Purchase Money Mortgage," "a Note and Deed of Trust," or "a Land Contract."

Then specify the amount of money you want to make with each payment, when the payment is to be made (usually monthly), when payments and interest on the principal are to begin (usually the first month after escrow closes).

Then give the rate of interest paid on the principal on a yearly, "per annum," basis. The date it will commence should be the same date your payments are to begin.

This section gives you the right of prepayment without penalty. It also specifies that each payment will include both principal and interest.

If you are assuming an existing mortgage or deed of trust with the purchase, that should be specified here as well as in Clause 4. (See Chapter 21: *Types of Financing: Land Contract, Mortgage, Deed of Trust.*)

Example:

the balance of purchase price as follows:
The sum of *Twenty Five Hundred and No/100* Dollars (*$2,500.00*) to be deposited in escrow on, or before, *June 1, 1974* as a down payment, which shall include the above deposit;
The sum of *Eight Thousand and No/100* Dollars (*$8,000.00*) to be represented by a *Note and Mortgage* to be payable *One Hundred and Fifty and No/100* Dollars (*$150.00*) or more on the first day of each and every month, beginning *June 1, 1974* with interest on all unpaid principal beginning *June 1, 1974.*
Interest on deferred payments will be *7%* per annum, from *June 1, 1974* payable with each monthly payment as part of the same.

Clause 1—Buyer's Offer and Seller's Procedure for Accepting

This contract is not binding on either party unless the seller signs it without making any changes and returns it within the specified time limit. If you decide to withdraw your offer, you can do so without penalty until you receive the signed contract from the seller. If you want to revoke your offer, you must notify the seller in writing that your offer is no longer open and that your deposit should be returned to you.

You will write your address at the end of the contract. You must state the amount of time the seller has to accept or reject your offer. You do not want to give him too much time because he may stall around waiting for other buyers. Seven to fourteen days is a standard time limit for a response. If you are really

anxious to know where you stand, you can make the time limit shorter.

Clause 2—Price per Acre and Number of Acres

Sometimes land is advertised and sold on the basis of a specified amount of money per acre rather than a price for the total piece of land. If this is true of your deal, leave this clause in the contract. Otherwise, omit it. Most sellers are reluctant to state an exact acreage figure because they often don't know how much it is themselves. This is why you will sometimes see a figure like "40+ acres" or "40− acres." The advantage of the clause is that if you have the land surveyed during escrow and find that the number of acres actually included in the parcel is less than the amount advertised, you can terminate the deal or get the price reduced accordingly. This relates to Clause 18(b). (See Chapter 8: *Land Descriptions and Surveys.*)

Clause 3—Requirement of a Survey to Be Approved by the Buyer

Here is a protective clause that should not be removed from the contract. It provides that a legal survey must be furnished with the land and that the purchase is contingent on your approval of it. If the survey shows that the land does not include what you thought it did, you will notify the seller in writing that you disapprove of the results and you can terminate the deal.

This clause states that the seller is to pay for the cost of a survey. In some cases, a survey will already have been done and there will not be a problem. But if the land has not been surveyed, this can be a point of conflict between you and the seller. He will not want to pay the added expense of a survey. This is a point where you can compromise if you wish, by offering to pay half of the cost. In some cases, the real estate agent will pay for it in order to make the sale. If you cannot afford to pay for a survey and the seller refuses to supply one, you can tell him to increase the purchase price by the cost of a survey and that you will pay for it over a period of time, should the deal be finalized. However you work it out, get the land surveyed before you buy. (See Chapter 8: *Land Descriptions and Surveys.*)

Clause 4—Conditions and Limitations of the Title

Title indicates legal ownership. Many things can interfere with your absolute ownership of of piece of property. Before you give this contract to the seller to sign, the real estate agent should list for you all the items that will limit your title to the land. You should already have investigated these limitations before offering to buy the land because many of them could make the deal undesirable for you. The seller must be honest in enumerating these things because if he signs the contract as you submit it to him, he will be liable for breach of contract if everything is not listed.

—Liens include any taxes, bonds, assessments, insurance premiums, mortgages, and judgments that have not yet been paid and which could lead to a forced sale of the land in order to obtain money for their payment. (See Chapter 17: *Taxes and Assessments;* Chapter 18: *Insuring Your Property for Yourself and Your Creditor;* Chapter 23: *Buying Property That Is Encumbered by a Loan Agreement.*)

—Encumbrances can include many of the same things as liens but are more general. An encumbrance can be anything that affects or limits your title to the property.

—An easement is a legal right of way belonging to other persons over your land. (See Chapter 9: *Easement Rights.*)

—Covenants are usually included in the deed as "restrictive covenants" which specify what uses will be permitted or prohibited on the land. (See Chapter 33: *Deeds and Recording.*)

—Reservations are rights held by the seller or other persons to do certain things on your land, such as remove minerals or trees from the property. (See Chapter 11: *Mineral, Oil, Gas, Timber, Soil, and Other Rights.*)

—Restrictions, like covenants, include any-

thing that limits what you can do with or on your land.

—Rights and conditions is a catchall for anything that can't be included under the other terms.

All of these items are considered defects in the title. If they are recorded, they will be uncovered and indicated by a title search or Abstract of Title. However, the seller must list all defects whether or not they are recorded in the public records or are included in writing in any type of form, because this clause is all-inclusive. This is important because certain defects, like prescriptive easements, are not recorded but are still legally binding. (See Chapter 31: *The Title Search, Abstract of Title, and Title Insurance Policy.*)

The seller must deliver a copy of every document that contains a defect in title as noted in this clause, so that you can inspect its contents. This is provided in Clause 7.

Example: An easement over the property would state that the title is subject to:

a nonexclusive easement 60 feet in width for ingress and egress and public utilities over the existing road located in the Northeast Quarter of the Southeast Quarter of the Northwest Quarter of said Section 21 as granted to Sheila M. Eisenberg by deed recorded June 19, 1970, in Book 4710 of Official Records, page 122, Elk County Official Records.

Clause 5—Escrow Instructions and Opening and Closing of Escrow

First Paragraph: This provides for delivery of escrow instructions. After the seller accepts this offer to purchase and signs the contract, both of you will submit written escrow instructions to the escrow holder on how to go about closing the deal. A ten-day time limit for submission of instructions is reasonable. Fill in the name and address of the escrow holder as given in the beginning of this contract.

Second Paragraph: You can set any closing date you desire. You should provide enough time for any condition that must be completed, such as a loan arrangement, pest report, and survey. Usually thirty to sixty days is sufficient time to complete necessary arrangements for the closing of escrow. If you need more time, both parties can mutually agree to an extension.

Third Paragraph: The purchase is final when the deed is recorded and escrow closes.

Fourth Paragraph: Escrow instructions will be given in a separate document. This contract should be submitted with the escrow instructions so that the escrow holder understands the terms of the agreement.

Fifth Paragraph: Since there might be an unintentional contradiction between the terms of the contract and the escrow instructions, it is specified that the contract takes precedence. (See Chapter 30: *Opening and Closing of Escrow and the Role of the Escrow Holder.*)

Clause 6—How Title Shall Vest

Vesting title refers to the form of ownership by which the buyers will take the property; e.g., as husband and wife, joint tenants, tenants-in-common, a corporation, a church, etc. The method used is important for legal reasons. You should give the buyers' names and the same form of co-ownership specified at the beginning of this contract. (See Chapter 32: *Types of Co-Ownership.*)

Example: Brian Wilcox, a single person, and Daniel and Louise Varre both married persons, as joint tenants.

Clause 7—Type of Deed, Preliminary Title Report, and Buyer Approval

The full covenant and warranty deed gives the buyer the maximum protection. (See Chapter 33: *Deeds and Recording.*) You must know what your deed will convey before escrow closes. The best way to get this information is by a Preliminary Title Report, which is usually included free as part of the Policy of Title Insurance. The report will indicate all recorded defects of title. If you want a defect removed, you can ask the seller to clear it up before the purchase is finalized and escrow closes. A seller can remove defects, or "clouds" on a title, more easily than the buyer because he knows the parties involved. You should be able to get a Preliminary Title Report within a week of the opening of escrow, but you can fill in the blank with any time period amount. You should

give yourself a week or two to notify the seller of those things you want cleared, and that time limit is stated in the third blank space.

You must state the name of the title company that is to conduct the title search and issue the report and policy. You can choose any title company you desire.

An important part of this clause is the fact that the seller must provide you with copies of each document referred to in the Preliminary Title Report. For example, if the land is subject to an existing mortgage you must receive a copy of the mortgage so that you can see what its terms are, how much is left to be paid, and who holds the note.

In some areas of the country, title reports are replaced by Abstracts of Title. In that case, substitute "Abstract of Title" for "Preliminary Title Report" and fill in the name of the abstract company or lawyer who is to prepare the abstract. (See Chapter 31: *The Title Search, Abstract of Title, and Title Insurance Policy.*)

Clause 8—The Title Insurance Policy

Marketable fee simple title means that the seller owns the property and there is no question about his rights of ownership. A Policy of Title Insurance is to be delivered to you by the seller guaranteeing marketable fee simple title. Although a standard policy has limited coverage, it is the most common buyer's policy. For more money you can get extended coverage offering greater protection. You can specify that the seller is to provide an extended policy but you are likely to meet resistance to this demand. (See Clause 13.)

The usual amount of coverage of the standard policy is equal to the purchase price of the property. Thus, if you build a house after escrow closes, and a title problem later develops, the title company is only liable to reimburse you for the price of the land. The value of the house is not included. If you want greater coverage, you will usually have to pay for it. (See Clause 13.)

State which company is to issue the Title Insurance Policy. It should be the same company named in Clause 7. The seller must deliver the title to you in the form agreed upon or you can terminate the entire deal and have all of your money returned. (See Chapter 31: *The Title Search, Abstract of Title, and Title Insurance Policy.*)

Clause 9—Prorations

This clause specifies the proportionate breakdown between the seller and yourself of taxes, insurance premiums, interest on existing loans, and installment payments on personal property. The amount each party pays depends on their respective periods of ownership or possession. Proration usually occurs at the closing of escrow because that is the date on which the property is transferred to the buyer. In cases where the buyer moves onto the property before escrow closes, the date he takes possession might be used as the proration date. In that case, cross out (1) and write the date in (2).

(a) Since property taxes are calculated on an annual basis, under the proration you should only pay taxes for that part of the year you own the land. (See Chapter 17: *Taxes and Assessments.*)

(b) The proration of insurance premiums only occurs when you take over insurance held by the seller. If he is not transferring his policy to you, omit this section. State a date several days before escrow closes so that the escrow holder will know whether or not to prorate insurance premiums, and the seller will have time to cancel his insurance if you decide not to take it over.

The insurance policy should be included with this contract as an exhibit attached at the end. An "exhibit" is a document or list of items on a separate sheet of paper which is included as part of a contract. If a copy of the policy cannot be obtained at the time you submit this contract to the seller, you can obtain a copy at a later date.

If you decide to take over the seller's insurance policy, he must have your name placed on it as the insured. If the seller or a third party lender is taking a mortgage or trust deed, it is usually required that the creditor be named as a beneficiary of the policy. Since the property is the creditor's only form of security for the loan, as a beneficiary under the policy he will be protected should the property be destroyed. (See Chapter 18: *Insuring Your Property for Yourself and Your Creditor.*)

(c) If you are taking title subject to a pre-existing encumbrance, such as a mortgage or deed of trust, you should prorate the interest to be paid by you and the seller, since you do not want to pay interest on the loan for the period before you take title to the land. If you sign a new note for the existing loan before the close of escrow, write in the date from which the interest on the loan will be charged to you. If you are taking title to the land free of any existing encumbrance, omit this section. (See Chapter 23: *Buying Property That Is Encumbered by a Loan Agreement.*)

(d) If the sale includes personal property, such as appliances and machinery, which is not fully paid for, you should prorate the installment payments so that you will begin to take over payments as of the close of escrow. If you are not taking over payments on any personal property as part of the purchase, omit this section.

Any other item that you want to prorate with the seller can be included in Clause 9 by a statement identifying what is to be prorated. (See Chapter 30: *Opening and Closing of Escrow and the Role of the Escrow Holder.*)

Clause 10—Credit for Impounded Funds

When land is bought under a mortgage or deed of trust, the party who holds the land as security usually continues to pay the taxes, assessments, and insurance premiums so that he can be certain the property won't become subject to a lien that would interfere with his security interest. To pay these expenses, the lender takes payments from the buyer called "impounds." These impounds are prepaid by the buyer in order to be available for upcoming payments. For instance, the buyer might pay the lender for taxes a year in advance.

When escrow closes, some funds which the seller has already paid will be in this account. He will be credited with this amount and proration will determine the breakdown of payments between the buyer and seller. When you see a copy of the existing mortgage or deed of trust, it will include a list of impounded funds.

If you are not assuming or taking title subject to an existing loan, this clause should be deleted from the contract. (See Chapter 23: *Buying Property That Is Encumbered by a Loan Agreement.*)

Clause 11—Payment of Liens, Assessments, and Bonds

It is indicated here that the seller is to pay all money due on liens, assessments, and bonds before the close of escrow. This clause is used when the county has enacted a special assessment against the property. This is commonly done by local governments to pay for roads, sewer plants, and other major improvements.

It is always best to get the seller to pay these assessments before you take title to the land or to allow you to subtract the amount due from the purchase price. Since this cuts into the seller's profits, he will resist clearing the state of these liens. If he absolutely refuses to pay off the entire amount due, you should prorate these assessments and liens as part of Clause 9. State what assessments exist and the date that is to be used for proration.

Often these debts are prorated between the parties, with the seller paying for assessments made on work actually started before the date the Contract of Sale is signed. The buyer then pays for assessments on work begun after that date. I think this is unfair for the buyer and explain why in great detail in Chapter 17: *Taxes and Assessments.*

Clause 12—Segregation of Taxes

Use this clause only if you are buying land that is part of a land split or subdivision that has not yet been segregated. When the original parcel of land, which has been taxed as one parcel, is split, future taxes will have to be reallocated according to the assessment of each new parcel's value. This is called segregation of taxes.

For example, if a single 40-acre parcel of unimproved land is taxed $400 a year, and the owner splits it into four 10-acre parcels, each

parcel will then be taxed separately. To do this, the owner must file for a segregation of taxes, but often this is not done until the parcels are sold. Presumably each parcel will be taxed $100 after segregation. Thus, in 12(a) you would write in 25%. If for any reason the Tax Assessor does not divide the taxes in this manner after segregation, an adjustment is to be made between the parties, as specified in 12(d).

12(b) includes improvements in the segregation if any structures are on the property. 12(c) includes personal property that is taxed.

The tax year stated here should be the current taxable year at the signing of this contract.

Proper segregation is important for your protection, and this condition must be included in the contract if a subdivision is involved. If no segregation is necessary, omit this entire clause. Do not confuse segregation of taxes with proration of taxes, which is covered in Clause 9. (See Chapter 17: *Taxes and Assessments.*)

Clause 13—Apportionment of Escrow Charges and Title Insurance Premium

Usually, the buyer and seller each pay half of escrow charges, in which case 50% would be inserted in both spaces here. When you first submit this contract to the seller, you can state that he is to pay 100% of the fee. Later, you can "compromise" and offer to pay half.

The real estate agent may tell you that these charges are apportioned according to local custom, but you can come to any agreement with the seller that you want. For example, you and the seller can split the fees of escrow and title insurance premium equally or you can pay the recording and drafting fees and the seller can pay the insurance premium. I feel that the seller should always pay the premium on a standard coverage Title Insurance Policy. That is what is specified in this clause. But if you desire the extra coverage of an extended policy, you will probably have to pay the added cost. (See Chapter 30: *Opening and Closing of Escrow and the Role of the Escrow Holder,* and Chapter 31: *The Title Search, Abstract of Title, and Title Insurance Policy.*)

Clause 14—Delivering Possession of the Property and Penalty for Holdover

Possession is "delivered" when the buyer moves onto the property or when he has the right to do so. The seller can give the buyer the right to possession at any time, even before the buyer takes title to the land. The importance of fixing a date for possession stems from the fact that liability for property damage usually follows possession.

The person in possession bears the risk of property destruction because he is the only person in a position to protect the property. Many states have laws, called Risk of Loss Acts, which expressly state this rule. Once title has passed to the buyer, he will always be the one to bear the loss, regardless of who is in possession, unless specified otherwise in the contract.

If you move into a house before title is transferred to you and the house burns down, you are still legally required to go ahead with the purchase. I don't think it is wise to take possession before the close of escrow, but sometimes this can't be avoided when the buyer is desperate for a place to live. Specify here when you are to take possession.

If you are going to take over the seller's property insurance, have him add your name to his policy as an insured person as of the date you take possession and adjust the proration of the premium accordingly in Clause 9. Never permit the seller to insert a clause that states that you are to assume the burden of insuring the land before you take possession of the property. (See Chapter 18: *Insuring Your Property for Yourself and Your Creditor.*)

The second part of this clause provides that a penalty will be levied on the seller if he does not deliver possession of the property on the specified date. A fine of $20 per day is usually considered a reasonable amount to be paid by a "holdover seller." If you choose, you can terminate the entire deal and have your money returned. To insure that money will be available for the fine or refund, instruct the escrow holder to keep all money paid into escrow until you have notified him that the seller has vacated. If you are buying land that is already vacant, you can delete this part of this clause.

(See Chapter 30: *Opening and Closing of Escrow and the Role of the Escrow Holder.*)

Clause 15—Buyer's Options if Property Is Destroyed or Taken by Eminent Domain

This section permits you to terminate the deal or have the purchase price reduced if anything happens to the property before you receive possession or title. It is important that you have both of these choices. (See Clause 14, Chapter 15: *Eminent Domain and Condemnation,* and Chapter 30: *Opening and Closing of Escrow and the Role of the Escrow Holder.*)

Clause 16—Default and Liquidated Damages

When the seller accepts the terms of your offer by signing this contract, each of you has specified obligations to perform as stated in the contract. This clause states the damages that will be levied if one party breaks the agreement. Because the amount of damages is specified before any damages actually occur, this is referred to as a "liquidated damages" clause.

If the seller fails to carry through on the contract, you get the deposit and any other money returned in addition to a penalty amount which is to be inserted here. You can make this any figure you wish but it should approximate what your actual damages will probably be. For example, if you are paying for an appraisal of the property, you would insert the amount you pay here so that you can get your money back if the seller later backs out. If you have no expenses and the return of your deposit is sufficient, you can leave this space blank.

If you default, the seller can keep the amount specified in the blank. You should fill in the amount of your deposit, or less if you put down a large amount. It is standard procedure that if a buyer defaults he loses his entire deposit, but you should not permit the seller to take any more than that, and in no case should you make this figure larger than $200.

Most courts will overlook this clause if the stated amounts do not represent the actual damages that do occur later. The courts can always adjust the amount up or down if a party protests that an inequity exists. Because court costs are so high, however, it is unlikely that either you or the seller will want to go to court and that is the purpose of this clause. Try to keep the figure as reasonable as possible.

This clause only offers monetary damages for breach of contract. In another type of remedy, called "specific performance," the court can force a party to go through with the deal, or perform the contract. Thus, if the seller refuses to sell you the land after this agreement has been signed and you have met all the conditions, you do not have to accept money if it is really the land you want. But you will have to get a court order to force the seller to give you the land. Also the seller can force you to complete the purchase if he feels monetary damages are not sufficient. These legal options are available despite their exclusion from the liquidated damages clause.

Clause 17—Comprehensive Title Covenant and Warranty

Paragraphs (a) through (e) state that the seller owns the land he is selling, that he has the right to sell it, that no liens or encumbrances exist other than those stated in the contract, that your ownership will not be disturbed by any other person with a valid title to the land, that he will fulfill any other condition you require in order to clear the title to the land, and that he will pay for costs involved if you have to defend your right to the land.

If you get title insurance, the same warranties will be covered and insured by the title company. The title company will defend you if your title is challenged. In states where title insurance is available, the type of clause is often excluded from the contract. But I see no reason why the seller should not warrant these things regardless of whether you are insured. Thus, I have included them.

If the seller is vehemently opposed to including this clause, and he intends to give you a full covenant and warranty deed and you can obtain title insurance, then you can remove this clause from the contract and still be adequately protected. The reason for his opposition is that he will be liable to pay for your

defense if anybody challenges your ownership.

Paragraph (f), that these covenants will survive delivery of the deed, means that they will still be binding on the seller after you accept the deed for the property. Usually once the deed is accepted, the terms of the Contract of Sale are superceded by the terms of the deed and are no longer binding. The court assumes that if you accept the deed you cannot complain later that the terms of the contract have been violated. But the warranty negates the assumption that you intend to let the seller "off the hook" by accepting his deed. (See Chapter 33: *Deeds and Recording.*)

Clause 18—Warranties and Representations by the Seller

In this clause you should insert any elements of the sale for which you want the seller to give a warranty. If you insert a provision which he refuses to warrant, find out why he is reluctant to do so. You might discover something that should discourage you from making the purchase. I have included here a list of the most common warranties used in sales agreements. If the seller accepts the contract and an item that is included as a warranty is later discovered to be untrue, this clause will be extremely useful to you in a court action. If you want the seller to warrant something that is not included here, write out the details of your warranty, using these as a model, and insert it into your contract. If any of the warranties are irrelevant in your case, simply omit them from your contract.

18(a) This is a warranty that you have a legal right of way to your building site from the public road. You may very likely have trouble getting a seller to agree to this because many pieces of land are sold with inadequate access. Do not purchase one of these parcels. If you don't have good access, you cannot use the land. Make sure this warranty stays in the Contract. (See Chapter 9: *Easement Rights.*)

18(b) The only part of this warranty you might allow the seller to modify is that specifying surveyed boundaries. On a small parcel or on a flat piece of land you will be fairly safe if only the corners of the property are marked by a licensed surveyor because you can often estimate from them where the boundary lines run.

However, if you have any doubt about whether an item, such as a spring, a house, or a creek, is on the property or not, you will definitely want the entire boundary lines marked by a licensed surveyor. You gain additional protection by listing those things that are essential to your purchase, like structures, waterfalls, springs, creeks, etc. (See Chapter 8: *Land Descriptions and Surveys.*)

18(c) This is your guarantee that there is a year-round water supply on the land. Estimate the amount of water you will need for anything you plan to do on the land or use the figures the seller gives you. If he says a well produces 25 gallons a minute every day of the year, then he must be willing to allow this warranty in the contract. This is a warranty that must be included without compromise, especially where wells are used. (See Chapter 4: *Is There Enough Water on the Land?*)

18(d) If the zoning of the area is changed before the close of escrow, this warranty makes the seller, rather than you, bear the risk that the change might prohibit your intended use of the land. (See Chapter 12: *Zoning Laws.*)

18(e) If there is a house or other structure on the land, this warranty should be inserted for your protection, especially where the structure represents a large portion of the purchase price. Because it does not require freedom from pests until the closing of escrow, the seller has time to get the house sprayed or fumigated before you buy it. (Chapter 6: *Evaluating the House and Other Structures.*)

18(f) This warranty will be important if there are structures or sewage facilities on the land since it insures that these conform to the local building and health codes and zoning ordinances. Violations that have not yet been cited by the local authorities are also covered. (See Chapter 13: *Building and Health Codes.*)

18(g) This warranty insures that there are no liens on the property, including assessments and bonds levied for past and future improvements, mechanic's liens for work completed and not paid for, or notes given for personal debts secured by a mortgage or Deed of Trust on the land. A title search or abstract will not cover unrecorded items. But the seller might know of liens, assessments, or bonds that will be levied against the land and are not yet part of the public records, and he is supposed to insert these here. (See Chapter 17: *Taxes*

and Assessments, and Chapter 31: *The Title Search, Abstract of Title, and Title Insurance Policy.*)

18(h) Often if a seller discovers that the government has plans to take all or part of his land by eminent domain, he will try to sell his property quickly at a higher price than he expects to get from the government. The ignorant buyer then suffers the consequences of the condemnation. This warranty is excellent protection should such circumstances arise after you take title. If you had to go to court, you would have the burden of proving the seller knew that condemnation was imminent. But at least you will be able to get to court with this warranty in the contract. (See Chapter 15: *Eminent Domain and Condemnation.*)

18(i) This warranty refers to the complete list of personal property included above with the description of the property to be conveyed. The seller is to list those items that will not be fully paid for by the time escrow closes. If personal property is not included in the sale, omit this warranty.

18(j) For those who are interested in back-to-nature or "organic" living, this warranty will be very important. It is self-explanatory. (See Chapter 5: *The Earth—Soil, Vegetation, Topography.*)

18(k) See Clause 17(e) above.

Clause 19—Conditions to the Agreement

This clause, in which you list all conditions or contingencies which you want met before being bound by this agreement, is one of the most important in the contract. You can specify essential elements for your protection, as well as any aspect of the deal you are unsure of, and wait to approve before escrow closes.

Some lawyers prefer to list these conditions in a separate document called a Contingency Contract. However, to avoid possible misunderstandings, I list these items in the Contract of Sale. When the seller signs the Contract of Sale he agrees to these conditions. If he crosses out anything, according to the law of contracts, he rejects the entire offer.

In this Model Contract I include the most common conditions used for the protection of the buyer. You can insert any conditions you like in your contract and hope the seller accepts them. If he won't, you will have to decide whether they are absolutely essential for your protection or whether you should compromise on them. If the conditions he will not accept are necessary for your protection, you had best not buy the land. Irrelevant conditions here listed should be omitted from your contract. If you have a condition you want that is not here, write it up in the same manner as those here and insert it into your contract.

19(a) If you do not approve of any matters specified in the following conditions, or you discover that a warranty in Clause 18 is untrue, it is stated here that you are to tell the seller of your objections and give him a certain amount of time to correct the conditions. The time limit you are to insert here will depend on the amount of time allowed for the close of escrow. Giving the seller fourteen days to correct the faults is reasonable. You should give yourself about five days in which to choose your option of (1), (2), or (3) if the seller does not meet his obligations.

19(a) (1), (2), and (3) are the options you have if the seller fails to meet the condition or satisfy the warranty. You can terminate the deal and get your money back. You can go ahead with the purchase and pay a reduced price. Or you can correct the deficiency yourself before escrow closes and have the purchase price reduced accordingly.

For example: The seller has a mortgage on the land which he has agreed to remove two weeks before escrow closes. If he has not done so, you can refuse to go ahead with the deal, 19(a)(1), or you can buy the land with the price reduced by the amount of the outstanding mortgage and interest, 19(a)(2), or you can pay off the mortgage yourself before escrow closes and pay a reduced price, 19(a)(3).

If the seller has warranted that the land will be surveyed and he does not get the survey done, you can get the survey yourself, pay for it, and reduce your purchase price accordingly under 19(a)(3). If you need more time to have the survey done before escrow closes, you can have the amount of time that you insert in the blank in 19(a)(6). To be on the safe side, you should write in at least thirty days in 19(a)(6). If you do not get the survey done in that time, you can then terminate the deal or buy the land at a reduced purchase price.

19(b) State any report you want made on the property, such as a survey, soil test, pest report, termite and structural inspection, potability test, or property appraisal. You can choose who will do these reports and set your own standards for approval. The only rule generally followed in the law is that you cannot disapprove a survey, test, or report unreasonably. If the seller is to have a survey run before closing and it does not include something you want on the property, you can send your disapproval to the seller in writing and you can terminate the deal.

If you pay for a test or report yourself, you do not have to show the result to the seller. If he desires to see them, you should ask him to help pay the cost of obtaining the information. The time limit you allow should be inserted in both blanks in 19(b). The time will depend on what is to be done. A survey takes longer than a termite inspection usually. Give yourself at least thirty days to be on the safe side.

If you get cold feet after you sign the contract, you can have a friend appraise the property for you and you can then tell the seller you do not approve of the results of the appraisal. You can legally terminate the deal within the terms of the contract. (See Chapter 8: *Land Descriptions and Surveys,* Chapter 6: *Evaluating the House and Other Structures,* and Chapter 19: *Evaluating the Price of the Property.*)

19(c). This condition protects you if you need to get the land rezoned or if you need a permit for something you intend to do or build on the property. For example, some areas only permit one dwelling for each 20 acres of land. If you know that you want to build two houses on your 20-acre parcel, you may extend the close of escrow to give you time to seek a variance. If you cannot get the variance and permit you seek, you have the option to terminate the deal or waive the condition. Even if no regulation affecting you is in force at the time you sign this agreement, a new law might be passed before the close of escrow which does affect you and this condition would then be vital. I have stated that you are to pay the costs of getting a permit or whatever you are after. Of course, you should try to get the seller to help with the fees. You must proceed with haste and diligence or the seller can terminate this contract. (See Chapter 13: *Building and Health Codes,* and Chapter 12: *Zoning Laws.*)

19(d) You need this condition if there are buildings on the land. The pest report must be taken after the date the contract is signed so that the seller won't attempt to show you an old report. You can write in the name of the company you want to do the report if you have selected one by the time you sign the contract. Otherwise, leave the space blank. You should try to get the seller to pay for it. You may also offer to share the cost with him or pay it entirely yourself. I have written in all three options and you can choose whichever you want. But first submit the contract with the seller specified as having to pay for the test. If he objects you can offer to pay half, or you can try to get the real estate agent to pay for it. (See Chapter 6: *Evaluating the House and Other Structures.*)

19(e) If your purchase is dependent on getting a loan from a party other than the seller, you should have this condition in the contract. If the seller is taking back a mortgage or Deed of Trust, the payment provision at the beginning of the contract will be sufficient, and you do not need this lending clause. The condition states that you must obtain the loan rather than just a commitment for one since the lender could change his mind before the papers are signed. The date inserted as a time limit for obtaining the loan should be the date of escrow closing, since you can only be positive you will get the loan at that time. If the lender decides at the last minute not to lend you the money, you can still get out of the contract. The loan itself can't be made before closing since you must have title to give as security for the loan.

Specify the terms under which you are willing to take a loan. Keep them low for your initial attempt to obtain financing, you can always raise them later. If you are seeking an FHA-insured or VA-guaranteed loan you should insert this as part of the condition.

If you cannot get a loan, you must notify the seller in writing within the specified time period or you waive the condition. The time period for notice should be the date of closing of escrow for the same reasons as given above. If it is obvious you cannot get the financing, inform the seller of that fact, and give him an opportunity to obtain a loan for you on your terms.

If you cannot get one, you will get your deposit back. Never let the seller omit this clause from the contract if your purchase is dependent on obtaining a loan. You should investigate your loan possibilities before signing the contract so that you don't waste your time. For example, it is almost impossible to get a loan for undeveloped "raw" land. (See Part V: *Financing Your Purchase.*)

19(f) If the seller does not want to give the warranty specified above in Clause 18(c), this condition must be included in the agreement. One or the other is absolutely essential. Under this clause, he must make a "diligent effort" to search for water, meaning that he must dig a well, if necessary, to a depth not greater than that which you insert here. If you don't obtain the minimum rate of flow you specify, the agreement will be terminated and you should get any money back you have paid the seller. This condition must be met before escrow closes. The problem is that you will not know whether the flow of water will be adequate in the driest time of year until that time. You will have to decide whether you want to go ahead and risk the chance that it will be sufficient. (The well-driller might have a well log that indicates the flow during the dry season.) Since the condition and warranty specify "year-round" supply, if it develops that it is insufficient, you can always attempt to rescind the contract and get your money back. Of course, the seller will put up a fight. The figures you use here for maximum depth should be the average depth for your area and the output should be the amount you will need.

Often sellers are reluctant to allow this condition in a contract for obvious reasons. Regardless of how beautiful the land is and how good the price is, if no visible means of water supply exist, do not purchase the property without a condition of this type. Even if 90 percent of the landowners in the area have located adequate water by drilling a well, you could be in the unlucky 10 percent, in which case the land will be worthless to you. If the seller will not allow this condition in the contract he is out to cheat you. Your only compromise should be that you will either pay half or all of the costs of water development. I don't think you should pay more than half, but if you are hooked on the land go ahead and get a well drilled. If no water develops, you can still get out of the contract and you will only lose the cost of drilling, which is better than losing the entire purchase price. (See Chapter 4: *Is There Enough Water on the Land?*)

Clause 20—Liability for Attorney's Fees in Case of Lawsuit

If you ever have to sue the seller because of a breach of this agreement, you will get your attorney's fees paid for as part of the damages. Of course, the same thing applies if the seller sues you and wins. This is a standard clause in a Contract of Sale.

Clause 21—Explanation of Terms in This Agreement

This is a standard clause in any Contract of Sale.

Clause 22—Incorporation of Exhibits

Insurance policies, copies of a mortgage or deed of trust, surveys, lists of personal property, and anything else specified in the agreement and included on separate sheets of paper or in other documents are called "exhibits" and, according to this clause, are part of the contract whether or not they are directly attached. Label attached forms as "Exhibit A, B, C," and so on. This is a standard clause in any Contract of Sale.

Clause 23—Waiver of Performance, Time for Performance, and Remedies

This is a standard clause in any Contract of Sale.

Clause 24—Requirements of Valid Notice

You must give notice by the means specified here if you want it to be valid. Clause 1 specifies that notice of acceptance is not considered "given" until received by the buyer. It is an exception to this clause. This is a standard clause in any Contract of Sale.

Clause 25—Other Persons Bound by This Agreement

This is a standard clause in any Contract of Sale. It protects both you and the seller in the event either of you dies or assigns his rights under the contract after it becomes binding. At that time your successors or assignees will also be bound by the contract.

Clause 26—Requirements for Change or Modification of This Contract

This is a standard clause in any Contract of Sale. If you submit this contract to the seller and he deletes or adds anything, you must sign your name next to the change before it becomes binding.

Clause 27—Time Is of the Essence

Each time limit specified in this agreement is to be strictly enforced. Any extensions must be agreed to by all parties in writing. If a provision has no time limit indicated, the period allowed is to be a "reasonable" amount of time. It is always preferable to specify exact time limits wherever possible. This is a standard clause in any Contract of Sale.

Identification of Escrow Holder and Real Estate Agent

Insert the names, addresses, and phone numbers of the escrow holder and the agent. These are needed in case any of the parties must get in contact with them regarding an element of the transaction.

Buyer Signs the Contract of Sale and States Form of Acceptance by Seller

You, the buyer, sign here. Be sure to keep a copy of this agreement for yourself and give a signed copy to the seller. The seller's acceptance is not valid until you receive the returned contract signed by him.

Before you sign this contract, or any other document, be absolutely certain that everything you want has been expressed in writing, including all conditions of purchase and warranties by the seller. No oral statements made to or by the real estate agent or seller are binding in any way. All the buyers should sign here.

Acceptance—Details of Real Estate Agent's Commission

Here the seller will fill in the commission he has agreed to pay the real estate agent, if any. The commission will be paid only if the deal closes, if the seller breaks the contract, or if the seller recovers money from you because you default.

Seller Signs the Contract and Accepts Your Offer

Finally the seller signs his name in acceptance of your offer and the Contract of Sale. Once he signs, the contract becomes legally enforceable, and you and the seller are bound by its terms. If all conditions and terms of the agreement are met by both parties, the transaction will close as scheduled on the day escrow closes.

If the seller alters the document in any way, it is invalid until the changes have been approved and initialed by you. If he makes changes and sends the altered contract back to you, he is making a counteroffer for you to purchase the land on the basis of the contract as he has changed it. Or he might return your offer unsigned and submit his own contract to you for acceptance. You will have to decide whether his new terms are acceptable. This Contract of Sale may be sent back and forth several times before a final agreement is reached, if one is reached. So many alterations may be made during the course of your bargaining that you might have to type up a new contract three or four times. But usually you will have negotiated enough verbally with the seller before you submit your contract that it will merely put in writing what you have already agreed to verbally. (See Chapter 20: *Bargaining to Get the Seller's Asking Price Down.*)

If the seller signs the contract, the real estate agent signs below the seller's name as evidence of his consent to the amount of commission stated, and then he returns the contract to you as a representative of the seller. If you are buying directly from the seller, you should omit all reference in this section to a real estate agent and a sales commission.

chapter 29

Option Agreements

THE LEASE OPTION
TO PURCHASE

The Lease Option is an excellent way to buy land for the person who is unsure of whether he really wants to live in the country. This option allows you to move onto the property and pay rent for an agreed upon time. If you decide to buy the property during that time, you can exercise the option and form a binding Contract of Sale, and all of the rent money you have paid will be credited toward payment of the total purchase price. If you do not exercise the option during the period of your lease, you lose nothing.

Since your lease might run for as long as a year, the owner is going to resist setting a price on the property because it will be worth more at the end of the year than at the be-

ginning. The purchase price is often determined as of the date the option is exercised and is based on a stated appraisal formula. However, you should get him to establish a final price when you sign the Lease Option.

Since a binding contract occurs when the option is exercised, the original Lease Option agreement must contain all the essential items of a Contract of Sale. You should use the Model Contract of Sale in Chapter 28 with the lease agreement. Most options that are handled on a standard preprinted form by landlords are not sufficient and you would be wise to obtain legal advice if you have any questions about the validity of yours. All terms of the Lease Option must be in writing and recorded with the county Recorder in order to give the public notice of your rights.

Occasionally a Lease Option might only give the tenant the "first right of refusal." A "first right of refusal" means that if the landlord-owner decides to sell his property during the terms of your lease, you, as holder of the option, will have the first chance to purchase it or refuse to purchase it. This is not worth paying extra money for. In the normal Lease Option, the landlord-owner agrees to sell the tenant the land when he signs the Lease Option and the final sale is dependent solely on whether the tenant exercises the option, not on whether the seller offers to sell the property during the lease period. If it is a regular Lease Option that you want, be sure you don't get a First Right of Refusal Option instead. Read the agreement carefully.

OPTION TO PURCHASE

The Option to Purchase is an alternative to the earnest money, land deposit, or binder. Its purpose is to get the land off the market while you decide if you want to buy it. This option is created when the buyer gives an amount of money, called the "consideration," to the seller who promises, in return, not to sell his property until the end of the specified option period. The amount of consideration can be for any amount of money. For instance, suppose you are interested in buying a certain piece of land but cannot decide if you really want it, and you don't want to commit yourself to the extent of offering the seller a Contract of Sale. You know that several other prospective buyers are also very interested in the land, so you want the seller to take the land off the market for awhile. You offer to pay him $100 if he doesn't sell the land for three months, and he gives you an Option to Purchase the land. The seller, or "optioner," gives the option to you, the buyer, or "optionee," and you sign an Option to Purchase Contract.

During the next ninety days, you can exercise that option by offering to buy the land at any time. The seller must not sell his property during that time to anyone but you. If he breaches the option, you can successfully sue him for damages. If you do exercise the option and buy the land within the time period, the Contract of Sale becomes binding as of the date the option agreement was signed and the option payment of $100 is credited toward the purchase price. If you do not exercise the option by the time ninety days pass, the seller keeps your consideration of $100 and puts the property back on the market.

Since the Option to Purchase is a contract, it should contain all essential elements in writing: the names and addresses of the seller and potential buyer, the date the option goes into effect (usually upon signing), the amount of payment, or consideration, given by the potential buyer to the seller, the express statement that an option has been created, the period the option is for and the date of expiration, how the option is to be exercised (usually by written notice to the seller), the full purchase price and terms of the sale, a statement that the option money is lost if the option is not exercised, the right for you to give, or sell, your rights under the option to someone else during the option period, and the signatures of the parties.

The option should be stated in a short contract with all the required details attached to it in the unsigned Contract of Sale, which is signed if and when the option is exercised. Personally, I do not recommend the use of an Option to Purchase in the standard land purchase because it is often a waste of money and it destroys much of the flexibility needed for negotiation. An option is almost always taken out on the basis of the seller's asking price.

If you use a Contract of Sale in the beginning, your conditions in the Contract will be a sufficient escape device if you decide to get out of the deal before the close of escrow. You can get your deposit back and get the same benefits of an Option to Purchase.

It is very important to get notice of the option, if you use one, in the public records. If, during your option period, the seller sells the property, the buyer will have a greater right to the land than you will unless you have filed the Option to Purchase document with the county Recorder's office. (See Chapter 33: *Deeds and Recording.*)

An Option to Purchase is a separate transaction from the signing of a Contract of Sale. Be sure you are not signing a Contract of Sale under a different name or some other type of sales contract under the pretext that what you are signing is an option. Because of its binding nature, you may want to check the whole deal out with your lawyer before signing or promising anything, since I am not giving you a Model Option to Purchase agreement here.

VII

GOING
THROUGH
ESCROW

chapter 30

Opening and Closing of Escrow and the Role of the Escrow Holder

One of the most important aspects of your land purchase is the function of "escrow." The "escrow holder" is a disinterested "go-between" for the parties involved in the transaction who safeguards the interests of everyone involved. Although an escrow may be used for many kinds of business transactions, it is primarily used in the sale of real estate. Through escrow, title to land is transferred from the seller to the buyer according to the written Escrow Instructions of each party. These Escrow Instructions constitute the Escrow Agreement and are submitted to the escrow holder, also called the escrow agent, escrow officer, or escrowee, who is bound to carry them out before the deed can be transferred to the buyer, the purchase price conveyed to the seller, and the sale consummated. Escrow is "opened" when the instructions are given to the escrow holder and is "closed" when the deed is transferred to the buyer.

The most commonly used escrow agents are title insurance and abstract companies, trust companies, banks, savings and loan associations, and escrow companies. The function of any escrow agent is the same, although the specific procedures might differ. Lawyers are sometimes used as escrow holders, but the institutional agents can perform the necessary escrow services at a lower fee than an attorney usually can, because they have escrow departments which specialize in these services.

It is best to use a different escrow agent than the one normally used by the real estate agent handling the sale since he and the escrow holder have probably become close friends after working together over a long period of time, and the necessary element of "disinterest" on the part of the escrow holder might be lacking. Fees charged by escrow agents vary considerably. You should look for the most reputable and professional escrow holder you can find who charges a reasonable fee.

There Must Be a Valid Contract of Sale Before Escrow Can Open

You and the seller must complete your negotiations and sign a valid Contract of Sale before going into escrow. The contract will state when escrow is to open by the submission of instructions, when escrow is to close, and who the escrow holder shall be, giving the name and address of the individual or institution involved. See Clause 5 of the Model Contract of Sale in Chapter 28, for where these items are to be included.

Parties Submit Escrow Instructions and Buyer Includes His Deposit

Instructions to the escrow holder are submitted by both the buyer and the seller, as well as the lender if a third party loan is involved. These instructions must be in writing and signed by each party who submits them. They are legally binding on the parties, and once they are submitted, they cannot be revoked. Escrow opens and remains open until the transaction is terminated according to the terms of the Contract of Sale and the Instructions. Therefore, you must be certain that the instructions contain everything you expect to receive in the purchase. In some areas, both the buyer's and the seller's instructions are included on a single form, but usually both parties submit separate documents.

Escrow holders generally have standard preprinted forms which the parties are supposed to fill in with the necessary information. However, the best way to protect your interests is to write your own Escrow Instructions, just as you will write your own Contract of Sale. In Chapter 28, I gave you a Model Contract of Sale which you can copy and use in your transaction by inserting appropriate information. I am including in this chapter a Model Form for Buyer's Escrow Instructions, which is meant to be used in conjunction with the Model Contract of Sale. The information you give in these two forms should never be contradictory. As a safety measure, both documents specify that an inconsistency is to be interpreted in favor of the Contract of Sale. (See Clause 5 of the Model Contract of Sale and Clause 9 of the Model Escrow Instructions.) Although it is not required, I think it is advisable to submit a copy of the Contract of Sale with your Escrow Instructions so that the escrow holder will have both documents at his disposal for clarification of the terms of the transaction.

MODEL FORM FOR BUYER'S ESCROW INSTRUCTIONS

To _____ Escrow No. _____
　　　　　(name of escrow holder)
_____ Escrow Officer _____
　　　　　(address of escrow holder)
　　　　　　　　　　　　　　　　　　　　　　　Date: _____,19___

These Escrow Instructions constitute part of an agreement by which _____,
called Buyer, agrees to buy, and _____, called Seller, agrees to sell the real property described in Exhibit A, attached hereto and made a part hereof.
Buyer delivers to you with these instructions _____ Dollars, ($_____.___)
　　　　　　　　　　　　　　　　　　　　　　(amount of deposit)
by _____ to your order as part of the total purchase price of
　　　　(cashier's or personal check)
_____ Dollars, ($_____.___).

Buyer will also hand to you or cause to be handed to you, on or before _____:
　　　　　　　　　　　　　　　　　　　　　　　　　　　　　　　　　(date escrow closes)
(Describe how the remaining purchase money is to be paid. For example, "Balance of the purchase price in Buyer's promissory note and mortgage in the form attached, or placed in your hands before the close of escrow, bearing interest at _____% per year, principal in _____ equal _____ installments
　　　　　(number of payments)　　　　　　　　　(monthly, etc.)
including interest on the unpaid balance, beginning on or before _____,
19___."
At the end of these instructions you should attach a copy of the mortgage or deed of trust and promissory note. If you don't have these at this time, give them to the escrow holder as soon as you have them. For samples of these documents, see Chapter 21: *Types of Financing: Land Contract, Mortgage, Deed of Trust.*)

Buyer will also hand to you or cause to be handed to you, on or before _____ (date escrow closes)
all additional funds and documents necessary on the part of Buyer to enable you to comply
with these instructions.

1. You are authorized to use the foregoing money and documents when each of the following conditions have been fulfilled:

   (a) You have received notice of approval of all conditions in this transaction, as called
   for in Exhibit B, attached hereto and made a part hereof, or the time for notice of
   approval has expired without notice of disapproval of the conditions. Each requirement of notice to a party in Exhibit B and the Contract of Sale shall be construed
   also as a requirement of notice to the escrow holder.

   (b) You can issue or obtain at _____ (Buyer's or Seller's) expense a _____ (standard or extended coverage)
   Policy of Title Insurance with liability equal to _____ Dollars, ($_____.___)
   showing title to the described property vested in _____
   _____
   (Buyer's name and marital status, and manner by which title is taken, e.g.,
   _____
   joint tenancy, husband and wife, tenants-in-common, etc.)
   _____
   _____ ,

   subject only to exceptions approved by Buyer in writing. You are authorized to record
   any instruments delivered through this escrow if necessary or proper for issuance of
   the Policy of Title Insurance called for above.

2. Prorate as of _____ (date escrow closes or date of possession) _____ on the basis of a 30-day month:

   (a) Real property taxes based on the most recent official information applicable to the
   fiscal year in which the proration date occurs, and obtainable in the office of the
   particular taxing authority.

   (b) Premiums on existing transferable insurance policies approved by Buyer by notice delivered to escrow covering damage to or destruction of the property transferred to
   Buyer through escrow.

   (c) Interest on obligations secured by encumbrances to which the property will remain
   subject after close of escrow. All new notes shall be dated as of close of escrow. If
   any new notes are dated before closing, they shall be endorsed; "Interest to run only
   from _____, 19___."

   (d) Installments of principal and interest on the following personal property: _____ (List any personal
   property that will be transferred to you with the sale that you will continue to make payments on.) _____
   _____

   which are to be included with this transaction.

3. If impounded funds are held by the lender in connection with a mortgage, deed or trust,
   or other encumbrance remaining of record at close of escrow, Buyer shall be charged
   and Seller credited with the full amount.

4. Buyer shall pay _____% of the escrow fee; the escrow holder's customary charges to
   Buyer for document-drafting, recording, and miscellaneous charges; and the title insurance premium to the extent that it exceeds the premium for standard coverage with a
   liability equal to the purchase price.

5. Seller shall pay _____% of the escrow fee; and the escrow holder's customary charges to
   Seller for document-drafting, recording, and miscellaneous charges, including local real
   property transfer taxes; and the title insurance premium to the extent that it does not exceed the premium for standard coverage with a liability equal to the purchase price.
   (In the above two clauses, it is assumed that the Seller will pay for the Policy of Title Insurance. If this is not the case you can change the statement to apply to your situation.)

6. In addition each party shall pay reasonable compensation to the escrow holder for extraordinary or unusual services rendered to or for that party, if any, plus costs and expenses incurred in connection with these services.

7. These Escrow Instructions are to be construed with the instructions of Seller placed in
   this escrow with you.

8. If conflicting demands are made or notices served on you, you may, at your election, withhold and stop all further proceedings in this escrow without liability and without determining the merits of the demands, notices, or litigation.

9. As a matter of agreement between the parties, with which you are not to be concerned, any inconsistency between these Escrow Instructions and the Contract of Sale is to be resolved in a manner consistent with the Contract of Sale unless the inconsistent provision of the agreement is expressly waived by a writing specifically referring to the inconsistent provision in the Contract of Sale.

10. Time is of the essence for these instructions. If for any reason other than my failure to comply with the foregoing instructions this escrow cannot be closed by _____,19__, I may, by written notice to you, demand the return of all money and/or documents that I have placed herein. If both parties fail to comply within the said time limit, then neither party shall be entitled to the return of money and/or documents until, after demand, a five-day notice shall have been given to the other party by ordinary mail at address given you. If no demand for the return of money and/or documents is given, close this escrow as soon as possible.

11. Any provision requiring an act to be performed or a condition to be satisfied at or before close of escrow refers to the date above; provided that the time for closing shall be extended if and to the extent that any time limit expressly given in the Escrow Instructions or the Contract of Sale between the parties has not expired on the above date.

12. Close of escrow means the time when the documents transferring title are recorded.

13. As soon after close of escrow as possible, deliver funds and documents to the parties respectively entitled to receive them. Make delivery to the address given below.

(Here list what money and documents are to be given to each party. For example: "Seller gets purchase money or down payment, mortgage, promissory note. Buyer gets deed, Title Insurance Policy, Fire Insurance Policy.")

_____
_____
_____

14. Buyer is to pay the following charges: ___ (For example: "drawing up and recording the deed.")
_____

I acknowledge receipt of a copy of these instructions.
Buyer, as referred to in these instructions, consists of the undersigned:

(signature of Buyer)
_____
(typed name of Buyer)
_____
(signature of Buyer)
_____
(typed name of Buyer)
_____

Buyer's address for notice is the following:

(City and State)
_____
(Zip Code)
_____
(Telephone Number)
_____

CLOSING OF ESCROW

The Model Escrow Instructions are meant to be a guide to protect you. You may use a preprinted form given to you by the escrow holder if you make changes and additions to it which specify all of the necessary information that is included in the Model Instructions. The most important fact to remember about the instructions to the escrow holder is that all the facts of the purchase must be made known to him so that he can carry out the expectations of both parties to their satisfaction.

If you decide to use the escrow holder's preprinted form, beware of clauses that relieve the escrow holder of liability, such as a clause specifying that the escrow holder is not bound to inform the parties regarding facts within his knowledge. Also beware of any clauses that might be against your interests, such as a clause specifying that the buyer is to "take title subject to all covenants, conditions, and restrictions of record" without giving you a detailed list of what these are, or that the escrow holder is to assume that the buyer automatically approves of the seller's insurance policies.

The seller's instructions will basically require that before the close of escrow you must deposit the amount of money you and he have agreed upon, either the full purchase price or a down payment and mortgage or deed of trust. The Contract of Sale specified that if you gave the real estate agent any earnest money as a deposit on the land when you signed the Contract of Sale, he must submit that money into escrow when the Escrow Instructions are submitted. This money is to be held until the terms of the Contract of Sale are met and escrow closes. The seller's instructions should not be in conflict with your instructions or the terms of the Contract of Sale. Any conflict must be resolved before escrow can close.

If you are borrowing money from a third party, such as a commercial bank, the lender will submit separate Lender's Instructions to the escrow holder explaining his role in the transaction and what the escrow holder is to do for the lender.

When you submit your instructions, an escrow number will be issued which will be written at the top of the instructions, and if an institution is to be the escrow holder it will assign an escrow officer who will personally handle your transaction. Ask for this escrow

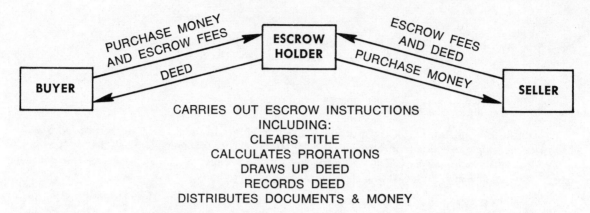

CARRIES OUT ESCROW INSTRUCTIONS
INCLUDING:
CLEARS TITLE
CALCULATES PRORATIONS
DRAWS UP DEED
RECORDS DEED
DISTRIBUTES DOCUMENTS & MONEY

77. DIAGRAM OF HOW ESCROW WORKS

officer and use your escrow number whenever you need to discuss your transaction with the escrow holder.

In some states, the parties submit their instructions in person and meet with the escrow holder to discuss what is to be done before the closing of escrow. It is becoming common, however, for the parties to give their instructions to the real estate agent who delivers them to the escrow holder and orders the opening of escrow. The buyer and seller may never meet the escrow holder. To protect your interests to the fullest extent, I think you should maintain personal contact with your escrow holder throughout the entire escrow process. Illustration 77 is a simple diagram of how escrow works and what the duties of each party are.

Summary of Things You Must Check Prior to Closing of Escrow

Before escrow closes, you want to be certain that you have examined every aspect of the purchase and that everything meets your approval. Once you accept the deed, it will be difficult to complain later about anything that has not been performed according to the Contract of Sale, since accepting the document implies you approve of the transaction. Therefore, be sure you have checked each one of the following points before the day escrow is to close. Each of these things is discussed in detail in its respective chapter.

1. Make a complete inspection of the land and structures and give your approval or disapproval of any aspects you find to the seller. If someone is living on the land, determine his status and have the seller ask him to leave before escrow closes. Look for and investigate any roads or paths across the land which could be unrecorded easements. Find out if the sale of the land creates an implied easement for the seller or anyone else. Match the description of the easement that will be in your deed with its physical location on the ground to be sure you have access to your building site. If you notice recent repairs or construction when you examine the structures, be sure all costs for the work have been paid by the seller so that future liens cannot be brought against the title. If the closing is contingent upon your approval of an appraisal or report of any kind, be sure the report covers the subject to your satisfaction. Check the water source to determine if it supplies the quantity of water as warranted by the seller.

2. Check the survey to be sure it was done recently enough to be legal. Use a legal survey to locate the land's boundaries on the ground and be sure that all the structures and physical features you expect to get are within them. Also use the survey to check the location of easements.

3. Examine any personal property that goes with the real estate. If you are buying machinery or tools, operate them to see if they are in working condition. Ask the seller to show you records that all the personal property

is paid for. If any payments are still due, find out how much is owed and whether you are to assume them.

4. Check building, health, and zoning codes to be sure no violations of ordinances or regulations exist regarding the land. Find out whether these permits have all been paid.

5. Examine the title and order the seller to clear any defects you object to. The Escrow Instructions state that the title must be searched, cleared and insured before the close of escrow. The seller must furnish you with a Preliminary Title Report, Abstract of Title, or similar document showing the results of a title search along with all documents representing encumbrances on the title, such as easements, reservations, mortgages, or other liens. When escrow opens, the first thing the escrow holder will do is order a title search and Preliminary Title Report. He will charge this search to the seller according to your instructions. The title search will be done by the escrow holder if the escrow holder is a title company.

If you have any objections to the state of the title as shown by the Preliminary Title Report or Abstract, you are to inform the escrow holder that the seller is to have the encumbrances removed before escrow closes. For example, if back taxes are due on the land, you want them paid; if money is still owed on a mortgage, you want it satisfied; or if a judgment exists against the seller's land, it should be paid off. The escrow holder will usually obtain the money from the seller to pay and clear these liens. If the seller does not have sufficient funds to remove existing encumbrances but is willing to do so as soon as he obtains the purchase money from you, the escrow holder can take your purchase money on closing day and pay off the liens before closing escrow and delivering the purchase money to the seller. He will then be able to convey a satisfactory title to you with documents that show the encumbrances have been removed. For example, these documents might include a receipt for taxes paid to the Tax Collector, or a Satisfaction of Mortgage from the seller's creditor.

Regardless of what encumbrances exist, escrow should never be closed as long as you have objections to the title you are to receive. Provisions for making objections to the title are contained in Clause 7 of the Model Contract of Sale and in Exhibit B, Clause 2, of the Model

Escrow Instructions. If all defects in the title that you object to are not cleared within a specified time, you are entitled to have your money returned and the transaction terminated.

When all terms and conditions of escrow have been performed and the title is ready to be transferred, the escrow holder will order the title insurance company to issue a Policy of Title Insurance which insures your title up to the exact minute that the deed is recorded. The policy must show that your title is free of any defects that you have previously disapproved of. If you cannot get title insurance in your state, you will have to determine from the Abstract and Certificate of Title or similar document that the title is satisfactory. (See Chapter 31: *The Title Search, Abstract of Title, and Title Insurance Policy.*)

Escrow Holder Transfers the Insurance Policy to the Buyer

If the seller has his property insured and you agree to assume the insurance policy, the seller will give a copy of the policy to the escrow holder. If he obtains permission from the insurance company to assign it to you, he then draws up the document of assignment and gets the insurance policy and assignment form ready to be delivered to you at the close of escrow. Sometimes, the insurance company will draw up a new policy in your name and deliver it to the escrow holder. (See Chapter 18: *Insuring Your Property for Yourself and Your Creditor.*)

Escrow Holder Makes Prorations and Adjustments

Prorations between you and the seller of property taxes and assessments, insurance premiums, and interest on an existing mortgage are usually made by the escrow holder according to the date escrow closes. The method used in prorating each obligation is explained in the following chapters: Chapter 17: *Taxes and Assessments,* Chapter 18: *Insuring Your Property for Yourself and Your Creditor,* and Chapter 23: *Buying Property That Is Encumbered by a Loan Agreement.*

Buyer Pays Purchase Price or Down Payment and Submits Loan Agreement and Note

The escrow holder will receive your deposit when escrow opens. You can submit into escrow any other cash you are to pay the seller at any time after escrow opens. However, you should wait until after you receive a Preliminary Title Report or Abstract of Title and after all other conditions to the Contract of Sale and the Escrow Instructions have been met. It is best to submit purchase money on the day escrow is to close.

When the escrow holder receives your funds for the purchase, he will use them to clear up any encumbrances on the title as specified in his instructions, pay the charges owed by the seller, and deliver the rest to the seller after closing.

I caution you against giving the seller any money outside of escrow. The purpose of escrow is to protect you in your dealings with the seller. The seller should not receive your money until you receive what you are paying for. The escrow holder can see that both sides meet their obligations before he disburses the money, deed, and other documents.

If you have arranged a loan from a commercial lender, he will not want to pay you until you have received clear title because he wants to be sure to receive good security for his loan. The seller, on the other hand, does not want to give up his title to the land until, and unless, he is certain of receiving the full purchase price. An escrow holder handles this situation to everybody's satisfaction in the following manner.

Before closing, the escrow holder receives the deed from the seller, a signed mortgage or deed of trust and note from you, and the money from the lender. If all the terms and conditions of the sale have been satisfied, the escrow holder records the deed and delivers it to the buyer. He also records the signed mortgage and note and delivers it to the lender. He then delivers the purchase money to the seller. Thus, all parties are protected during the period of escrow and everything is managed by the disinterested escrow holder without the pos-

sibility of fraud or violation of any terms of the agreement.

Be sure all financial documents are prepared and ready to be signed before escrow closes. If you are getting an FHA or VA loan, finalize all arrangments with the appropriate agency. If the seller is financing the sale, be sure the mortgage of deed of trust and the note or bond are prepared and approved by you before the closing.

CLOSING COSTS

The "closing costs" are the expenses in addition to the purchase price which must be paid before you take title. You should be fully aware before escrow closes how much you will be expected to pay and that you will actually receive what you are paying for. Believe it or not, I have met buyers who paid for title insurance and never received a copy of the policy. This should never be allowed to happen.

Your closing costs can be anywhere from $50 to $1,000. Illustration 78 lists all the items that can be included in closing costs. Your transaction probably won't include all of them. With each item, it is stated what party most often pays the charges involved. In many instances, this will be a matter of negotiation between you and the seller, and it is your goal to keep your costs as low as possible. I don't indicate the amount each will cost because prices are never standard.

A Warning Regarding Closing Costs

A Congressional Subcommittee on Housing has just completed a study comparing closing costs for similarly priced houses in various parts of the United States. Although they primarily sampled urban housing their findings are interesting for any real estate buyer, since the same problems arise on the rural land market.

For a house sold in the $20,000 to $24,000 price range, depending on what area of the country the house was located in, closing costs varied from less than $50 to nearly $2,000. Similar inequities were found to exist even

78. POSSIBLE CLOSING COSTS

PAID BY (B = Buyer) (S = Seller)

1. Fees for a title search, title examination, or Abstract of Title (seller pays to clear existing liens on demand of buyer) — B or S or shared
2. Premium for the Policy of Title Insurance — B or S or shared
3. Escrow fee — Usually shared
4. Fee to draw up and notarize the deed — S
5. Fee to record the deed — B
6. Real property transfer tax — S or shared
7. Termite and structural inspection fee — S or shared
8. Cost of survey — B or S or shared
9. Cost for water drilling and water quality test — B or S or shared
10. Buyer's attorney's fees — B
11. Seller's attorney's fees — S
12. Real estate agent's commission — S
13. Prorations (see 14(h) below)
14. Possible loan costs
    (a) Fees charged by the escrow holder or the lawyer representing the seller or lending institution to draw up, notarize, and record the mortgage or deed of trust and note or bond — B
    (b) Amount of an existing loan to be paid off before closing with possible prepayment penalty fee — S
    (c) Credit report fee — B
    (d) Appraisal fee — B
    (e) "Point" charge — S
    (f) Assumption fee charged by the lender, if you are assuming a loan — B
    (g) State mortgage tax, in some states, based on the amount of the mortgage (usually 0.5–1 percent of the mortgage amount) — B
    (h) Prorations to seller for prepaid taxes, assessments, insurance, and loan impounds — B
    (i) First impound installment for taxes, assessments, and insurance to a third party lender — B
    (j) FHA insurance premium — B

within the same county. For example, in Ramsey County, Minnesota, the costs for the same closing and escrow services for the sale of similarly priced homes ranged from about $200 to $621. In Cook County, Illinois, they went from a low of $102 to a high of $723. In Los Angeles County, California, they ranged from about $200 to nearly $1,000. Similar disparities were found in all the areas of the country studied by the subcommittee.

How do you protect yourself against excessive closing cost charges? Before hiring anybody, shop around and ask what charges will be levied. Even after you have an escrow holder, before escrow closes, ask him for an itemized accounting of every single charge that is to be levied against you and make sure you receive a complete Closing Statement.

THE CLOSING STATEMENT

The Closing Statement shows the facts and figures of the closing of escrow for both the buyer and the seller. This document is usually prepared by the escrow holder, although the real estate agent or the seller's attorney might do it in some areas.

A separate Closing Statement may be used for each party or both parties may be included on one statement. If separate statements are used, be sure that you and the seller are not both charged for a single service. This unfair practice is especially prevalent when closing is conducted by mail. For example, if drawing up and recording the deed costs $15, the buyer and seller might each be charged $15 and the escrow holder gets paid double the amount due him. Since neither party knows what the other is paying, duplicate charges are undetectable on the surface. I recommend using a single Closing Statement that enumerates the charges for each party on one sheet of paper with the buyer and seller receiving duplicate copies. All parties should have a complete knowledge of the costs involved, what services are provided, and who is expected to pay for each service.

Illustration 79 is a sample Closing Statement that includes many of the typical charges and credits for a buyer and seller. Study the sample and read the accompanying explanation so you will be fully prepared to examine your own Closing Statement for accuracy and understand how the itemization system of "charges" and "credits" functions.

EXPLANATION OF SAMPLE CLOSING STATEMENT (ILLUSTRATION 79)

The buyer and seller each have a column of charges and credits. Amounts that must be paid into escrow by each party are "charged" against them. Amounts that have already been paid into, or that are to be paid out of, escrow

STATEMENT OF ESCROW NO. _____   OFFICE _____
TO _____   DATE _____

Seller		Item	Buyer	
Charge	Credit		Charge	Credit
	$15,000.00	PURCHASE PRICE	$15,000.00	
		Deposit (3/5/74)		$ 200.00
		Deposit (5/1/74)		3,300.00
$11,500.00		By First Mortgage		11,500.00
		PRORATIONS AS OF 5/1/74		
	28.00	Taxes	28.00	
84.00		Pay Current Taxes		
	110.50	Insurance (Premium $153.00)	110.50	
190.00		POLICY OF TITLE INSURANCE		
5.00		DRAWING DEED		
16.50		REAL PROPERTY TRANSFER TAX		
		RECORDING DEED	2.00	
		DRAWING MORTGAGE	5.00	
		RECORDING MORTGAGE	2.00	
		NOTARY	1.00	
37.50		ESCROW FEE (½ Each)	37.50	
1,200.00		REALTOR'S COMMISSION (8%)		
		BUYER OWES AT CLOSING		186.00
2,105.50		DUE SELLER AT CLOSING		
$15,138.50	$15,138.50		$15,186.00	$15,186.00

79. SAMPLE CLOSING STATEMENT

are "credited" to each party. The amount charged to each party must equal the amount credited to him. This accounting method is the one most commonly used. It may not make complete sense to a nonaccountant, but it works.

Purchase Price

In our example, the buyer is paying $15,000 for the property. This amount is charged against the buyer and credited to the seller. The buyer made an initial earnest money deposit of $200, which was submitted into escrow when escrow opened, and he has since submitted into escrow a down payment of $3,300. Thus, he is credited for having already paid $3,500 into escrow. He has arranged to pay the remainder of the purchase price by giving the seller a mortgage and note for $11,500. Although no cash actually changes hands, the seller is "charged" for "lending" the $11,500 to the buyer. In return, the buyer signs the mortgage and note and is credited with having agreed to "pay back" this amount to the seller.

Prorations

Prorations are to be made as of the date of closing, which is May 1, 1974. The property taxes for the year of sale, from July 1, 1973, to June 30, 1974, are $168, to be paid in two equal installments of $84 each. The seller has already paid the first installment, covering the time from July 1, 1973, to December 30, 1973. Although the second installment is not due until June 1, 1974, the buyer wants all the taxes paid before he takes title. Since the closing date is May 1, 1974, the seller will be paying taxes for two months (May and June) during which the buyer will own the property. Thus, the taxes must be prorated. Since the second tax installment is $84, by dividing this amount by 6 (months), we find that the taxes are $14 per month. Thus, on the Closing Statement the seller is charged the amount of $84 needed to pay off the second tax installment, but is credited the $28 worth of taxes he will have paid for months during which he will not own the land. The buyer is charged this $28.

A similar proration is performed for a fire insurance policy which the buyer is assuming. The policy extends for a three-year period, dating from July 1, 1973, to June 30, 1976. The seller has already paid the three-year premium of $153. At the closing date, he will have been covered under the policy for ten months, from July 1, 1973, to May 1, 1974. Since the policy extends for a total of thirty-six months, the buyer will be covered for twenty-six months. The entire premium must be divided into monthly amounts in order to prorate it: $153 divided by 36 equals $4.25. The buyer owes $4.25 times 26 (months), or $110.50, for the period he will own the land under the policy. He is charged this amount on the Closing Statement, and the seller is credited this amount.

Remaining Fees

The remaining fees are divided between the seller and buyer according to the terms agreed to in the Contract of Sale and specified in the Escrow Instructions. The charges shown here are the average fees charged for these services. Separate fees are usually charged for drawing up, notarizing, and recording documents, as in done in this statement. The escrow fee is usually based either on the amount of money passing through escrow or on the total price of the transaction. In this example, the escrow fee is 0.5 percent of the purchase price and is shared by the buyer and the seller. The state in which this sale occurs has a real property transfer tax. This tax is levied by requiring that for each $500 of the purchase price, 55¢ in taxes must be paid to the state. This item will be written on the deed or evidenced by tax stamps on the deed. The $16.50 transfer taxes required in this purchase is charged to the seller. These taxes vary among the states. Of course, the seller is charged for the real estate agent's commission, given here as 8 percent of the purchase price.

Since the buyer must pay his charges into escrow at closing, all the items from the prorations down to the escrow fee are added to get $186 which he is credited with paying at the close of escrow. The seller must pay all his charges out of the money *due him* that the buyer pays into escrow, in this case the $3,500 down payment and $28 and $110.50 from the two prorations. Since the seller's charges equal $1,533, the escrow holder deducts this amount from the money paid in by the buyer ($3,638.50), leaving $2,105.50 to be distributed to the seller by the escrow holder after closing.

CHECKING THE STATEMENT

You can personally check the mathematics of the Closing Statement by using the same system that the escrow holder uses. This check is done by balancing the money he takes in with the money he will pay out. Using our Sample Closing Statement, you see that the escrow holder will receive $3,500 in cash from the buyer as part of the purchase price and $186 for the various fees charged to him. Thus, his total receipts from the buyer on closing day equal $3,686.

Now the escrow holder adds up the total amount of disbursements that he will have to make according to the Closing Statement. I list them in the accompanying table.

Escrow Holder's Balance Sheet

Pay Current Taxes	$ 84.00
Policy of Title Insurance	190.00
Drawing up deed	5.00
Real Property Transfer Tax	16.50
Recording deed	2.00
Drawing up mortgage	5.00
Recording mortgage	2.00
Notary	1.00
Escrow Fee	75.00
Realtor's commission	1,200.00
Seller to receive	2,105.50
	$3,686.00

Thus, he takes in $3,686 and pays out $3,686, and the figures balance as they should. Never leave the job of calculating your costs and totaling up your money to the escrow holder or anyone else without double-checking all the figures yourself.

PREPARATION OF DOCUMENTS FOR CLOSING

When the title has been cleared to your satisfaction and all other conditions of the sale have been met, the escrow holder will prepare the forms necessary to complete your purchase. He, or possibly the seller's attorney or title company, will prepare a new deed in your name. If the Contract of Sale calls for a Full Covenant and Warranty Deed he must draw up that type of deed. If the title cannot be cleared as specified in the contract, which prevents the delivery of a proper deed, escrow cannot close. The deed should be signed by the seller and ready to be recorded before the day of closing arrives. Many states impose a tax on the transfer of all real estate. Evidence of the payment of this tax is shown by having tax stamps placed on the deed or writing the amount paid somewhere on the deed. The escrow holder pays the tax and affixes the stamps, if required. (See Chapter 33: *Deeds and Recording.*) If the seller is financing your loan, the escrow holder or the seller's attorney prepares the mortgage or deed of trust and note. All forms are sent to the parties for proper signatures and acknowledgments before escrow closes, unless the parties all meet together on closing day.

THE CLOSING DAY (SETTLEMENT DAY)

The "close of escrow" is the last of the "closings" during your land purchase. The first, the "closing of the sale," occurs when you and the seller sign a legally binding Contract of Sale. The "financial closing" occurs when you have negotiated a loan and signed all the necessary documents. The "close of escrow," or "legal closing," occurs when all terms and conditions of the sale have been met by both parties and the title to the land is officially transferred to you by recording the deed with the county Recorder. You then own the land, although you may still be obligated to pay off a mortgage or deed of trust for many years to come.

The day of legal closing, also called "settlement day" or "paper signing day," is the day on which the deed and other documents are recorded. This will happen anywhere from a few weeks to a few months after both parties sign the Contract of Sale. Although the contract will specify a closing date, this date can be, and often is, postponed or extended, if both parties agree to an extension. (See Clause 5 of Model

Contract of Sale in Chapter 28.) Occasionally the party granting a requested extension might penalize the other. If the seller has not met all your conditions specified in the Contract of Sale by the closing date, you have several options. You can grant him an extension or you can terminate the deal if you desire since the Contract of Sale specifies that "time is of the essence." If you incur any expenses caused by the seller's delay in closing and transferring possession to you, he should be charged for this.

The closing is generally handled either by mail or in person. If it is to be done by mail, the escrow holder draws up and sends each party the documents to be signed, completes his other duties according to the Escrow Instructions, such as clearing the title and making the various prorations. Each party returns the documents and pays the money charged against him. On closing day, the escrow holder records the documents with the county Recorder, returns copies to each of the parties, and delivers the money due the seller.

If the closing is to be done in person, all parties, including the buyer, the seller, the real estate agent, the escrow holder, any attorneys, and, if a loan is involved, the lender's representative, meet to sign the documents. This meeting usually occurs at the escrow holder's office. However, the office of the real estate agent, the seller's attorney, or the lender, if the buyer is borrowing money from a financial institution, may be used. The person handling the closing will present a Closing Statement to each person. The buyer submits the money he is obligated to give the seller at closing for the purchase price and other expenses. These payments are usually made by personal check, with each check marked as to what it is to cover. If the seller is financing the purchase, the buyer will sign and give him a mortgage or deed of trust and a promissory note. If a third party lender is involved, he will deliver the loan money at closing, and take back a mortgage or deed of trust and promissory note from the buyer. The lender will want to see the Policy of Title Insurance and get copies of the fire and other insurance before handing over the money. The buyer will pay any money due the lender at this time, such as loan fees and impounds. When all documents have been signed and all money has been submitted into escrow,

the documents will be brought to the county Recorder to be recorded, after which time all parties will be paid and will receive their documents according to the escrow instructions.

REVIEW THE DOCUMENTS FOR THE CLOSE OF ESCROW

At the closing you must be certain that everything is done exactly right and that the terms are as you have negotiated them. You should receive copies of all documents involved in the purchase. Read every word of these documents. Look for clerical errors and double-check all mathematical figuring. Never let yourself be rushed through these procedures. There is a great temptation to just sign the papers, pay your money, and "get the thing over with." Never become casual about any part of your purchase, particularly these final and extremely important details. You are to receive the following items and assure yourself that they are in order:

1. The seller gives you a deed to the property which should be signed by him and notarized. The description of the property and encumbrances in the deed must conform to the Contract of Sale. Check every word in the deed to see that it is exactly as it should be. A mistake in the property description or a misspelling of any names can cause complications in the future. The deed is recorded with the county Recorder, who will make a copy of it and return the original to you.

2. You should receive a copy of the final Title Report or Abstract of Title and the Policy of Title Insurance. Check the date and time on which the policy is to take effect to be sure the title insurance covers you up to the exact moment that the deed is recorded. If you are to receive other evidence of title, such as a Certificate of Title, you will get it at the closing. Your lender will also want a copy of the policy and he might want to be named as a co-beneficiary in the policy. You should postpone closing until all liens, or potential liens, on the title have been cleared as specified in the Contract of Sale.

3. If you are receiving personal property in the sale, get a bill of sale signed by the seller

listing everything. Generally personal property is not included in the deed, so it must be provided for separately. Get all available instructions and warranties for appliances, machinery, and equipment and get a list of the people who have been servicing them. You should get all keys for locks on the property.

4. You should receive a copy of the survey of the property, and copies of any blueprints of the buildings.

5. If you are borrowing money, you will sign a mortgage or deed of trust and a promissory note to the lender, who will give you a check for the loan amount. You will endorse it and deliver it to the seller with your own cash contribution to the purchase price. If the seller is financing the purchase, you will give the escrow holder the down payment, less the amount of earnest money already paid. He should give you a receipt for this payment. You will then sign a mortgage or deed of trust and promissory note to him. These documents will be recorded with the county Recorder and remain as a lien against your title until all payments have been completed.

6. If you are to assume an existing mortgage or deed of trust, you must get all pertinent documents, including the seller's receipts for payments he has made already, since you will need these to receive a Release Deed or Reconveyance of Title after all payments have been completed. You also want a statement, called a Certificate of Reduction of Mortgage or Estoppel Certificate, signed and notarized by the seller's lender specifying the amount still due on the existing mortgage or deed of trust, so the lender cannot later claim that more is due him than is actually the case. This statement should contain all the terms of the loan that you are to accept, and the nature of the lien on the property, such as a first mortgage. Examine the document carefully, checking all the figures to see that they are correct according to your Contract of Sale. I think it is also advisable to ask the lender for a written statement that he is aware of the fact that you are to take over payment on the loan and that this arrangement is satisfactory to him.

7. If you are borrowing under an FHA or VA plan, you will have to fill out government forms on, or just before, closing day as part of the loan.

8. Get receipts showing the disposition of all liens that you have asked the seller to remove before you take title. For example, you might want the current receipts as evidence that taxes, special assessments, utilities, and propane have been paid for. If you are to pay any bills, you should get a copy of the bill indicating what is due and the final date payment can be made. The bills should be computed to the date of closing in line with the prorations that are to be made by the escrow holder, according to the Contract of Sale and Escrow Instructions.

9. Double-check the prorations made on the taxes, insurance premiums, interest on assumed mortgages, utilities, and other items to see that the escrow holder has done his figuring properly.

10. If you are borrowing money from a commercial lender who is going to take impounds, you will have to sign an Authorization to Tax Collector which instructs the Tax Collector to have all tax bills on your property sent to the lender for payment. Your lender may have you sign a similar document covering premium payments on your insurance policies.

11. If you are taking over the seller's insurance policy, you will want to get a legal copy of the policy on closing day. The seller should assign this policy to you in writing and the insurer should give written recognition that he is aware of this transfer and approves of it. A cover note from the insurance company should state that your property will be protected by the insurance policy from the time of closing until your new policy is prepared and delivered to you. The seller or your lender will probably want to be named as a co-beneficiary. Your lender, if you have one, will also want a copy of this document.

12. If the seller has paid for and received any permits or certificates such as building and sanitation permits, road encroachment permits, or certificates of occupancy, have him give you his copies of these documents. If he does not have copies in his possession, it is his responsibility to go to the appropriate agencies and have copies made.

13. If you are purchasing a subdivided parcel, you and the seller must complete tax segregation forms at the closing so that you can proceed with the segregation of your land for purposes of proper taxation as quickly as possible. If it is possible, the seller should have

the segregation completed before the closing and should give you a statement from the Tax Collector that the segregation has been completed with a breakdown of how it was computed.

THE ROLE OF THE LENDER'S ESCROW DEPARTMENT WHEN MONEY IS BORROWED—LOAN PAYMENTS AND IMPOUNDS

If the seller is financing your purchase, a third party escrow holder will generally not be utilized for the purpose of collecting impounds and land payments. You will make your payments to a bank or the seller, and you or the seller will take care of paying taxes and insurance premiums.

However, if you borrow from a commercial lender, you will make your payments to the lender's special escrow department. These payments will not only include principal and interest on the loan but will also include the property taxes, assessments, and insurance premiums that will become due during the year. These impounds are usually divided up equally into the number of payments you will make each year and will be added into those payments. The lender's escrow officer pays the taxes, assessments, and insurance bills, thus insuring the protection of the lender's security. The lending institution often acts as the escrow holder throughout the entire purchase and is responsible for preparing all closing documents. (On impounds, see Chapter 23: *Buying Property That Is Encumbered by a Loan Agreement*.)

LONG-TERM ESCROWS AND LAND CONTRACTS

As explained earlier, in the section on land contracts in Chapter 21: *Types of Financing: Land Contract, Mortgage, Deed of Trust,* you must be certain to have title held in escrow during the entire payment period if you are buying land under a land contract. Since the seller keeps the title to the land until you complete all of your payments, you must protect yourself against the seller's transferring title to someone else or otherwise encumbering the title before your payments are completed. You should require the seller to make out a deed in your name to give to the escrow holder with instructions to deliver it to you when you make your final payment. If you are to have part of the title conveyed to you after a specified number of payments have been made, this should be written in the Escrow Instructions.

You should also instruct the escrow holder to record the land contract in the County Records so that public notice is given that the seller is not free to encumber the title. Nevertheless, because the title to the land does remain with the seller during the payment period, he could have a judgment rendered against the title in a lawsuit, a federal income tax lien could be placed against the title, or he could go bankrupt, in which case his creditors would be able to attach the title. For these reasons, among others, it is risky and foolish to buy property under a land contract. Always demand a mortgage or deed of trust.

PRECAUTIONS FOR THE BUYER IF AN ESCROW IS NOT USED

I strongly recommend that you use an escrow in your purchase. However, if you and the seller decide not to, you should do certain things to protect yourself. Do not pay any money to the seller until the deed is recorded in your name. Go with the seller to the county Recorder with a check in hand. When the deed is recorded, you can hand him the money. Be sure your Title Insurance Policy covers the title up to the second that the deed is recorded. If you are not receiving title insurance, then you must receive some other kind of legal protection that the title is being delivered to you as specified in the Contract of Sale. (See Chapter 31: *The Title Search, Abstract of Title, and Title Insurance Policy*.) Never avoid using an escrow to save a little money on escrow fees. A reputable and intelligent escrow holder can be of tremendous assistance to you through all stages of your purchase and you should maintain close personal contact with your escrow holder at all times.

chapter 31

The Title Search, Abstract of Title, and Title Insurance Policy

When you buy a parcel of land, you are purchasing "title," or legal ownership, to the land. The deed is the instrument by which title is passed from one person to another. It is similar to a "pink slip" on a car which is evidence of, and passes, legal ownership of the car referred to in it. However, a person can have a "pink slip" for his car but not have full and clear title to it: a creditor might have placed a lien on his car for debts owed by the owner.

Similarly, an owner of land might not have clear title even though he has a deed and a right to legally possess the land. A "defect," or "cloud," on his title might exist, because someone has a legal right to claim all or part of the property or to make demands on the owner. For example, if the owner has mortgaged the property, he still owns it, but the mortgagee has a lien against the title and can take the property if the mortgage is not paid off; or if a landowner does not pay his property taxes, the county will bring a lien against the land for the collection of back taxes.

The terms "marketable" or "merchantable" title mean that the seller has the legal right to sell the land. As you will see, any defects that make the title unmarketable must be removed before you buy the land. To find the defects that exist against a seller's title, and to determine the title's marketability, you must look at its history by searching the public records.

This chapter tells how to do this in order to protect yourself as much as possible when buying title to a piece of land. First, there is a list of the types of defects that can cloud a title. Then there is a description of how a title is searched, going back through the chain of title. The types of documents that you need to determine the state of the title—the Abstract of Title or Title Report—are described. Finally the importance of obtaining a Policy of Title Insurance or the other title coverage is discussed.

LIENS AND ENCUMBRANCES

Liens and encumbrances are the two most common defects on a land title. They do not make the title unmarketable, because the seller has the legal right to sell the land subject to the liens and encumbrances. Encumbrances include anything that limits or affects the title, such as the following:

—*Mineral, timber, or water rights* held, or "reserved," by the seller or a third party. These can be in writing or by prescription. (See Chapter 11: *Mineral, Oil, Gas, Timber, Soil, and Other Rights,* and Chapter 10: *Water Rights.*)

—*Easement rights* permitting others to cross your property. These can be in writing, by implication and necessity, or by prescription. (See Chapter 9: *Easement Rights.*)

—*Restrictive covenants* in the deed limiting what the property can be used for. (See Chapter 33: *Deeds and Recording.*)

Liens are also encumbrances, but a lien arises only when the property becomes a security for the payment of a debt or obligation as in the following situations:

—When the owner gives a *mortgage or deed of trust* using the land as security. The title will have a lien on it until the debt is paid. If the debt is not paid, the creditor can foreclose the loan. (See Chapter 21: *Types of Financing: Land Contract, Mortgage, Deed of Trust.*)

—*Federal, state, and local taxes* can become liens against the property when they have not been paid. *Special assessments* remain liens against the land until they are paid. The property can be sold for nonpayment of taxes and assessments. (Chapter 17: *Taxes and Assessments.*)

—A *mechanic's lien* can be held against the property by anybody who furnished labor or materials for improvements to the property and was not paid by the owner. This lien could force the sale of the land to satisfy the debts if they remain unpaid.

—A plaintiff initiating a lawsuit against the owner can attach the property, by an *attachment,* to prevent the owner from disposing of the property for the duration of the lawsuit. If the plaintiff wins a *judgment* against the owner,

he can force him to sell the property to satisfy the judgment.

—*Liens for debts of the decedent* can exist against his property if they remain unpaid. If the creditors cannot get their money from the personal property, then the real estate can be sold to satisfy their liens.

—*Federal and state inheritance tax liens* can exist against the property of deceased persons. The property can be sold by court order to meet these taxes.

Clause 4 of the Model Contract of Sale (See Chapter 28) states that the title conveyed to the buyer is to be free of any defects, including liens, encumbrances, easements, covenants, reservations, restrictions, and rights and conditions of the title. If the seller knows that there are defects in the title, he is to list those "clouds" in this clause. In addition to this protection, you must always search the title and receive an Abstract of Title or Policy of Title Insurance.

SEARCHING BACK THROUGH THE "CHAIN OF TITLE"

All land in this country was originally in the possession of the Native Americans. Their various conquerors took their lands from them, divided them up, and kept records of who took ownership of each parcel. The transfer of title from owner to owner, eventually to your seller, established a "chain of title" from the present back to the first recorded document of ownership.

The history of New Mexico is a good example of how far back records were kept in this country and how a chain of title develops. In 1539, the area around the present city of Gallup, New Mexico, was claimed by a Franciscan friar for Spain. The fact that American Indians lived on this land already did not deter the "missionaries" from taking it and extending the boundaries of the huge Spanish colony of Mexico. The King of Spain offered large parcels of property to those who would colonize the new land. These gifts were recorded in documents called the Crown Land Grant Records. Spanish immigrants began to move into the area, and the province of New Mexico was established.

Mexico gained its independence from Spain in 1831, and in 1846 the Mexican War began between the United States and Mexico. That war ended in 1848 with the Treaty of Guadalupe Hidalgo, which passed sovereign control of the northern part of Mexico, including the province of New Mexico, to the United States. Spanish and Mexican land records were transferred with the land. In 1912, the territory of New Mexico became a state. At that time, the federal and state governments traced land ownerships back as far as they were recorded to settle all existing claims to title and took control of the rest of the "public lands," which were eventually sold to private owners or retained as government lands. Accurate records of all land transfers have been kept since that time, and make up the chain of title.

After you sign the Contract of Sale you will hire an abstract of title company, a title insurance company, or a lawyer to "search," or trace back, the ownership of the land through the chain of title to determine whether the current owner has legal ownership with the right to sell the land, and to discover what, if any, defects exist on the title.

The title does not have to be searched back to the first colonizers. Each state has its own laws (statutes of limitations) specifying how far back a title search must extend to be legally "sound." This period ranges from twenty-two years in Nebraska to fifty years in Minnesota.

The primary sources of information that form the links in the chain are the documents recorded with the county Recorder or Clerk, the Tax Collector, the various courts, and other government agencies. The person doing the search will trace all of these documents back for the specified number of years to locate anything affecting the title to the land. Since all these records are public, you can do your own title search. However, because of its importance I don't recommend that you rely solely on your own examination. You must obtain a professional title search before the close of escrow, which I discussed in the previous chapter. Nevertheless I will tell you how a title search is performed so that you will understand this vital aspect of your purchase, and hopefully you will do your own search even

though you have a professional examination to confirm it. This is one of the most interesting aspects of your investigation because you will learn the history of the land you are preparing to buy.

The deed is the basic instrument for transferring ownership of land and it includes a description of the title being conveyed. Every state has recording statutes which require that valid deeds be publicly recorded with the county Recorder or similar official. When escrow closes on a property transaction, the deed is photocopied by the county Recorder who places it in the Deed Index, which is arranged chronologically. (See Chapter 33: *Deeds and Recording*.) Other documents affecting the land are similarly recorded in separate indexes. Each index consists of a set of books or microfilms which together form the "official records."

There are two systems of recording and indexing documents affecting real estate. These are the Grantor-Grantee Index and the Tract Index.

GRANTOR-GRANTEE INDEX

The most common system used for indexing recorded documents is the Grantor-Grantee Index. The Grantor Index alphabetically lists the name of every seller, or grantor, according to the year of the land sale and the Grantee Index lists every buyer, or grantee, in a similar manner. Leases, mortgages, trust deeds, assignments, wills, liens, "lis pendens" (i.e., pending legal actions involving the property), and judgments may also be indexed in this general Grantor-Grantee Index. Never hesitate to ask the county Recorder to describe the indexing system used in the office.

As an example of how to do a title search using the Grantor-Grantee Index, let's assume that you are buying a parcel of land from a seller by the name of Daniel Lawrence.

Names are listed in the indexes alphabetically for the year the document was recorded. Before you can look up Lawrence's name in the Grantee Index, you must know the year in which he bought the land. Ask the real estate agent or Lawrence himself for the date. The Tax Assessor also has this information in the tax rolls.

In the county Recorder's office, locate the Grantee Index for the year in which your seller bought the land and look under the section containing last names beginning with "L." Entries within this section are made according to the date the documents are received for recording during the year and thus are not alphabetical. The first thing you want to locate is the seller's deed. If Lawrence took title on May 9, 1970, the page on which you will find Daniel Lawrence's name as it was recorded when he received his deed might look like this:

GRANTEE	GRANTOR	DATE	BOOK (LIBER)	PAGE
Leifer, William	Brown, Lewis	May 2	308	89
Leland, Donald	Jones, Orpha	May 4	309	95
Lutz, Dewey	Oliver, Richard	May 4	309	120
Ladrini, Duncan	Herbert, Gerald	May 8	309	142
Lawrence, Daniel	Charles, Edward	May 9	310	3
Lambert, Damon	Howard, Robert	May 12	311	54
Lytle, Drew	Glickman, Raymond	May 20	312	122
Lund, David	Grandjean, James	May 20	312	132

The book and page numbers refer you to the location of Lawrence's deed. This index will also refer you to the location of other documents in Lawrence's name that have been recorded, such as mortgages. The county Recorder can show you where to find the book referred to in the index and how to use it. The book might be a general index of all the county records, or it might only contain copies of deeds.

Look up Lawrence's deed in Book 310 on page 3. Read the deed in its entirety. Does it include a description of the land you are planning to buy from Lawrence? The description might be of a larger parcel which has been subdivided but it should definitely include the entire parcel you are buying. If it doesn't, then he does not own the land. Note what kind of deed was given, whether it was a quit-claim deed, a full covenant and warranty deed, or some other kind. (See Chapter 33: *Deeds and Recording.*) Are there any easements, reservations of mineral, timber, water or other rights, restrictive covenants, or other "clouds" written into the deed? Write down the names of the sellers who signed the deed to Lawrence.

If there is any indication that the property was conveyed by an administrator or executor after the death of the owner, you must examine the Probate Court records (ask the county Recorder to tell you where they are located) to determine whether the property was properly distributed to the heirs. Keep notes on everything in the deed, including notations referring to the location of other documents.

Next look up all these other documents and copy their contents. For example, there might be a copy of a mortgage Lawrence gave a lender. If so, you want to see a copy of a Satisfaction of Mortgage to determine if the loan was paid off.

After you have examined the deed and all other documents referred to in it, you must search the records to be sure Lawrence hasn't already sold the land to some other party. This part of the title search is very tedious. It involves looking in the Grantor Index to see if Lawrence has ever sold the land he is selling you. Go to the Grantor Index for the current year and look for Daniel Lawrence's name as a grantor. This index will be arranged in the same manner as the Grantee Index except that the grantor and grantee columns will be reversed. If you find Lawrence's name listed in the grantor column, look up the document referred to and see whether it is a deed selling the same parcel you intend to buy. If it is, you cannot get title since he no longer has title to pass to you. If this is the case, you are being defrauded. However, he may have owned and sold a different parcel of land, so read the description to see if the deed is for another piece of property. If it is, go back to the Grantor Index and continue looking for Lawrence's name by going backwards until you reach the date he received title, which is May 9, 1970.

If you determine that Lawrence has not sold the land to anyone else and that he still owns it, you must then carry your search back another link in the chain of title by repeating the entire process for Lawrence's seller, Edward Charles. Hopefully, Lawrence's deed in some way referred you to the location of Charles' deed. If not, you must go through the Grantee Index starting with the year in which Charles sold the land to Lawrence and search backwards through each year's list looking for reference to his deed. Or you can get the date from the Tax Assessor. When you find Edward Charles' name in the Grantee Index, his seller's name will be given, with the date the deed was recorded and the book and page number of its location in the index. Look up his deed and check all those things that you checked in Lawrence's deed. Remember to take notes and to examine all other documents referred to in the deed. Then go backwards through the Grantor Index looking for Charles' name, from the time he sold the land to Lawrence to the time he bought the land, to be sure he did not sell the land to anyone other than Lawrence. Repeat this procedure for each owner of the land back as far as is required by the law of your state.

Usually the Grantor-Grantee Index will include indexing of recorded leases, assignments, mortgages, deeds of trust, attachments, and judgments. The grantor column might include the names of defendants in legal actions involving real property, assignors of loans, mortgagors, and trustors. The Grantee Index thus includes plaintiffs, assignees, mortgagees, and beneficiaries of deeds of trust.

Instead of a general all-inclusive Grantor-Grantee Index that refers to the location of all the documents, the county Recorder might use a multiple index system, in which case you must check through each type of index to uncover relevant documents. This makes the general title search much more difficult. For example, there will be a Mortgagor-Mortgagee Index, which you must examine to determine whether anyone who ever owned the land gave a mortgage on the property and, if so, whether any mortgage still exists as a lien against the title. Let's assume that Edward Charles gave a mortgage on the property during the period of his ownership. By checking through the Mortgagor Index, you find that he gave a mortgage to a savings and loan company on July 2, 1964. Note the book and page numbers where a copy of the mortgage can be found and look it up. If it has been paid off, you will be referred to a book and page number where you will find a copy of the Satisfaction of Mortgage. Sometimes the satisfaction will be attached to the copy of the mortgage. If you can't find any evidence that the mortgage has been paid off, then it is a lien on the title.

Often these counties have a separate Lis Pendens Index which lists all pending legal actions initiated in the county according to plaintiffs and defendants and refers you to the location of the documents filed in those actions. If such an index exists, check to see whether any previous owner of the land has an action pending against him, such as a foreclosure, mechanic's lien, or civil suit. If a name shows up, check the files to be sure that the property has been cleared of any connection with the legal action. Do not buy land with a lis pendens filed against it since you must take the property subject to that pending action.

There may also be a separate Judgment Roll or Judgment Index which lists creditors and debtors named in judgments resulting from lawsuits. The index will usually name the attorney of the creditor and will indicate whether the debt has been paid off. Look for the name of any previous owner of the property in the column of debtors for the years he owned the property. If a former owner is listed, you must examine the recorded document to determine the status of the debt. You should never purchase land subject to a judgment lien. In some areas, you might have to ask the clerk of the local courts to check for proceedings affecting the property if court records aren't kept in the county Recorder's office.

There will also be separate indexes for Federal Tax Liens, Lessors-Lessees, Assignors-Assignees, Wills, and Deeds.

Finally you must examine the County Tax Rolls located in the Tax Collector's office to see if any back taxes are due on the land. These tax liens are indexed according to the parcel number, which can be found in the tax books. Ask the Tax Assessor to show you how to use the books.

When you have finished examining all the public records, ask the Recorder to check to see if any documents have been recorded since the last index entry, that have not yet been placed in the indexes.

The above description of how a title search is conducted probably has you rather confused. Don't worry about it. You will have it done by a professional anyway. But if you go to the County Records and start looking through them you will become familiar with the system of indexing for your area, and everything in this chapter will begin to make sense. The records are always open to the public, and there is no substitute for actually going and investigating yourself. If you are confused, the clerks are public servants and are there to assist you.

TRACT INDEX

A much simpler system used to index recorded documents affecting a piece of land is the Tract Index. Unfortunately it is found only in a few states: Iowa, Louisiana, Nebraska, North Dakota, Oklahoma, South Dakota, Utah, Wisconsin, and Wyoming. This system has a page for every single parcel, or tract, of land in the county. Every transaction affecting each particular parcel is indexed on its page with the locations of the recorded documents referred to. For example, if you look up the parcel you are buying, the index page will state the location of every deed used to convey the land since it was first sold by the government. Every mortgage and other recorded instrument affecting the title will also be referred to.

Thus, the entire chain of title papers in one spot, unlike in the Grantor-Grantee Index system where you must trace every transaction yourself. As land is subdivided, the new parcels are added to the Tract Index.

UNRECORDED ITEMS THAT AFFECT THE TITLE

Some things that affect land title will not be found in the indexes: building and health code regulations, zoning restrictions, renters leasing the land, persons with a legal right to title by adverse possession, prescriptive easements or prescriptive profits, changes in the boundaries due to erosion or accretion, water rights laws, and work that has been done on the land that could lead to a mechanic's lien being filed after you buy the land.

Therefore an important aspect of your investigation will be to determine the laws that apply to your land and to personally inspect the property to see what is happening to it. How to do these things is explained in previous chapters.

TYPES OF TITLE PROOF

A professional title search must be conducted before you can receive proof of good title by an Abstract of Title, a Title Insurance Policy, or a title certificate by an attorney. Illustration 80 shows which form of title proof is mainly used in each state.

THE ABSTRACT OF TITLE

In many parts of the United States, particularly in rural parts of the Midwest, land buyers commonly get an Abstract of Title after signing a Contract of Sale. An abstract is a summary of the title history of a parcel of land based on recorded documents for as far back as is required by the state or the buyer. It is prepared by an abstract company using its own records of all the transactions in that area. These private files, called "title plants," are often better organized and more up to date than the public records in the county Recorder's office. An Abstract of Title tells the effect on the title of all deeds, mortgages, trust deeds, release deeds, satisfactions, recorded leases, mechanic's liens, foreclosure actions, special assessments, wills, attachments and judgments, tax sales, encumbrances, and other items of record. The contents of each document affecting title are summarized in chronological order in the abstract, and any irregularities in them will be pointed out by the abstractor.

An entry in the abstract will look like this example:

	Warranty Deed
Pahky M. Berman and	dated July 23, 1970
Deborah R. Berman,	ack. July 23, 1970
husband and wife,	rec. July 26, 1970
to	Liber 43, p. 92

Katherine C. Hackett
Conveys Lot #43 of the Map of Happy Acres Development Company.

When the abstract company delivers the complete abstract, it issues a Certificate of Title, which states that the property title is held by the seller, subject to the encumbrances of record shown in the abstract. This certificate is the abstractor's guarantee that his research

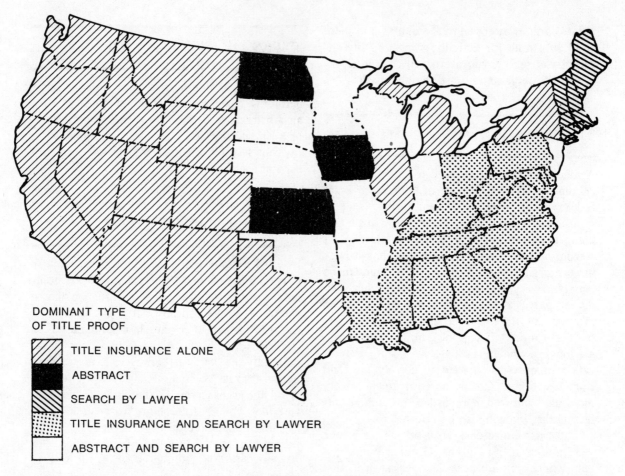

DOMINANT TYPE
OF TITLE PROOF

TITLE INSURANCE ALONE

ABSTRACT

SEARCH BY LAWYER

TITLE INSURANCE AND SEARCH BY LAWYER

ABSTRACT AND SEARCH BY LAWYER

80. TYPE OF TITLE PROOF USED BY EACH STATE

and examination of the public records are correct. However, the abstract company is liable for a mistake only to the person who contracts for the abstract. Therefore, if the seller has the abstract done and shows it to you as evidence of his title, you have no protection if you later discover that an error was made in it. If you must use an Abstract of Title, have it performed in your name even if the seller pays for it so that the company will be liable to you.

Unless you are buying a newly subdivided parcel, an Abstract of Title probably already exists for the property, completed when an earlier buyer purchased the land. If this is the case, you do not have to get a complete abstract done. Simply have the abstract company bring the existing one up to date. They will examine the title from the time the last abstract was completed and show any new encumbrances. The company will then give you a certificate called a "reissue" or "recertification" which guarantees that the entire abstract, in-

cluding the former and the newly completed section, is correct. This will be much cheaper than getting an entire abstract done and the recertification makes the company liable to you if it is done in your name. Never accept an old abstract as proof of good title from the seller unless it has been brought up to date and recertified. Be sure the abstract company is bonded with the state or federal government and is licensed and reputable. Although abstract companies are usually regulated by state agencies, if you must use one, exercise care in choosing.

PRELIMINARY TITLE REPORT AND THE POLICY OF TITLE INSURANCE

An Abstract of Title only informs you about the contents of documents in the public records exactly as they appear there and guarantees you that their search is complete. But the title to the land you are buying is not guaranteed or insured. You are not protected against title defects not shown by the records nor are you protected against documents that are part of the records but improperly executed. Only the owner's Policy of Title Insurance insures the title you are being sold and protects you if there are defects not shown in the records. I strongly recommend that you get title insurance if it is available rather than an Abstract of Title.

Many kinds of defects are so serious that they can render your title unmarketable. Title insurance protects you if any such defects exist. Some of these defects not shown by examining the public records are:

—*Clerical Errors:* A clerk in any of the public offices responsible for recording the documents in the chain of title could have made an error in transcription or filing, or a document could be misstated, incomplete, or misplaced. E.g., if a lien appears after you take title which was misfiled by the Recorder, the title insurance company will pay your losses up to its coverage if the lien results in your losing title to the land.

—*Forgery:* The deed, or any other document, might be a forged instrument or fraudulent in some other way.

—*Incorrectly Given Marital Status:* A former owner may have been a married person whose spouse was not named in a transaction conveying title to the property during the marriage. The unnamed spouse might later claim an interest in the property under a state law. (See Chapter 32: *Types of Co-Ownership.*)

—*Undisclosed Heirs:* If a former owner had died while he owned the property and all of his heirs did not execute the deed conveying title, the title could be disturbed later by a legal action brought by an undisclosed heir.

—*Post-Death Deed Delivery:* A deed might have been signed by the seller but not legally delivered to the buyer before his death. The date of delivery on the deed in the records would not indicate a prior death of the seller, and a suit could be brought at a later time by an heir claiming title or by the government claiming estate taxes.

—*Lack of Capacity of a Party to a Transaction:* If a deed or other document affecting title was executed by a person who was a minor, insane, intoxicated or drugged, or acting without the authority of the owner although otherwise a proper agent-employee of his, the deed does not properly convey a valid title to the property.

—*Improper Interpretation of Wills:* Most lands have been conveyed by a will at least once in their history, which may have been improperly interpreted so that title was not conveyed correctly, leaving open the possibility that someone might contest the transaction after you take title to the land.

The possibility of any of the above events occurring might not be very great, but anyone can bring a court action against your title, causing you much grief and expense, even if he does not have a valid and proper claim to make. Title insurance will pay for court costs and legal fees in the event this should happen. Besides insuring you for any possible claims that might arise hostile to your claim of title, the title company insures you against errors made in their title search.

Before issuing insurance, the title company conducts a title search to determine the soundness of the title it will be insuring and the existence of liens and encumbrances. Just as a life insurance company will not insure a man without giving him a thorough physical examination, a title insurance company won't issue a policy without doing a thorough search. Thus, if the title company issues you an insurance policy, you know that they are convinced that the seller has valid marketable title to give to you. They exclude from the policy any liens or encumbrances on the title which they list in the policy.

Preliminary Title Report

Before issuing the insurance policy, the title company will give you, at your request, a Preliminary Title Report showing the status of the seller's title to the land. Often this report is included as part of the final Title Insurance Policy and both are covered by a single fee or premium. All encumbrances and liens on the land will be indicated and the title company will inform you if they are willing to issue you a final policy. They will indicate which encumbrances must be removed in order to make the title eligible for insurance. The Preliminary Title Report does not insure the title. It simply describes the condition of the title as of the date the report is issued. Never rely solely on this report without getting an insurance policy.

Clause 7 in the Model Contract of Sale (see Chapter 28) specifies that the seller is to have a Preliminary Title Report made and delivered to you. If a defect, such as a lien or encumbrance, is shown by the report and you want it removed before the close of escrow, you are to notify the seller of your disapproval. If the seller has not removed the defect by the closing date, you can terminate your purchase and have any money you have paid returned to you.

In those areas where an Abstract of Title is used rather than a Title Report and Title Insurance Policy, Clause 7 of the Contract of Sale should be changed to state when you are to get the abstract for inspection. The Abstract of Title, as well as the Preliminary Title Report, should cover the title up to the date you receive it. After examining the abstract you should notify the seller of any objections you have and he should clear the defects before closing. At the time you get the abstract or Preliminary Title Report, Clause 7 states that the seller must include copies of all documents that are listed as encumbrances on the title so that you can examine them in their entirety before the close of escrow.

The Policy of Title Insurance

Unlike other insurance policies, a Policy of Title Insurance is paid for at one time only and continues as long as you and your legal successors hold title to the property. The premium for a policy is based on the amount of coverage, which is usually the amount paid for the property. Each title company has its own fee schedule. Generally, a $20,000 policy will cost about $150.

Clause 8 of the Model Contract of Sale states that the seller is to furnish and pay for the insurance policy, which is to be issued in your name, with you as beneficiary. Sometimes the seller might object to paying the entire premium and if you choose you can compro-

mise and split the costs with him. I do not think you should pay the entire amount, since the seller has a duty to provide you with a valid and insured title.

A Title Insurance Policy issued in your name is never assignable or transferable to subsequent purchasers of the property. For instance, the seller cannot transfer his policy to you. Each new buyer of a piece of land must purchase a completely new policy regardless of how recent the seller had a title search conducted. A title company only needs to search back to the date that the seller's policy was issued in order to bring the title up to date for the buyer. Despite the amount of work involved in a search, the premiums always remain the same.

A Standard Coverage Title Insurance Policy usually insures the buyer for the price he pays for the land. This means that if the title company has to defend you in a court action it will only be responsible for bearing costs up to the amount paid for the property. After you have owned the land for a period of time and have made improvements on it, its value will increase. You can then pay the title company to increase its liability to you based on the increased market value.

EXAMPLE OF A TITLE INSURANCE POLICY AND AN EXPLANATION OF ITS CONTENTS

The type of title insurance usually taken by a buyer is the Standard Coverage Policy of Title Insurance. (I discuss Extended Coverage later in the chapter.) Although each state has its own policy form, the type of coverage granted is basically the same. Illustration 81 is a copy of a Standard Coverage Policy. The policy you will receive will be very similar to this one. The following is an explanation of the terms of the policy:

The amount of coverage, the cost of the premium, and the names of the buyers taking title and being insured by the policy are inserted in Schedule A, later in the policy.

The policy first states that anyone other than a purchaser who takes title from the parties insured by the policy will have coverage trans-

POLICY OF TITLE INSURANCE

ISSUED BY

Title Insurance Company

TITLE INSURANCE COMPANY, a California corporation, herein called the Company, for a valuable consideration paid for this policy, the number, the effective date, and amount of which are shown in Schedule A, hereby insures the parties named as Insured in Schedule A, the heirs, devisees, personal representatives of such Insured, or if a corporation, its successors by dissolution, merger or consolidation, against loss or damage not exceeding the amount stated in Schedule A, together with costs, attorney's fees and expenses which the Company may become obligated to pay as provided in the Conditions and Stipulations hereof, which the Insured shall sustain by reason of:

1. Any defect in or lien or encumbrance on the title to the estate or interest covered hereby in the land described or referred to in Schedule C, existing at the date hereof, not shown or referred to in Schedule B or excluded from coverage in Schedule B or in the Conditions and Stipulations; or

2. Unmarketability of such title; or

3. Any defect in the execution of any mortgage shown in Schedule B securing an indebtedness, the owner of which is named as Insured in Schedule A, but only insofar as such defect affects the lien or charge of said mortgage upon the estate or interest referred to in this policy; or

4. Priority over said mortgage, at the date hereof, of any lien or encumbrance not shown or referred to in Schedule B, or excluded from coverage in Schedule B or in the Conditions and Stipulations, said mortgage being shown in Schedule B in the order of its priority.

    all subject, however, to the Conditions and Stipulations hereto annexed, which Conditions and Stipulations, together with Schedules A, B, and C are hereby made a part of this policy.

In Witness Whereof, Title Insurance Company has caused its corporate name and seal to be hereunto affixed by its duly authorized officers, on the date shown in Schedule A.

Title Insurance Company

BY   PRESIDENT

ATTEST   SECRETARY

81. EXAMPLE OF POLICY OF TITLE INSURANCE

SCHEDULE A

Total Fee for Title Search, Examination

and Title Insurance $

Amount $ Policy No.

Effective Date

Insured

1.   Title to the estate or interest covered by this policy at the date hereof is vested in:

2.   The estate or interest in the land described or referred to in Schedule C covered by this policy is:

SCHEDULE B

This policy does not insure against loss or damage by reason of the matters shown in parts one and two following:
Part One:

    1.   Taxes or assessments which are not shown as existing liens by the records of any taxing authority that levies taxes or assessments on real property or by the public records.

    2.   Any facts, rights, interests, or claims which are not shown by the public records but which could be ascertained by an inspection of said land or by making inquiry of persons in possession thereof.

    3.   Easements, claims of easement or encumbrances which are not shown by the public records.

    4.   Discrepancies, conflicts in boundary lines, shortage in area, encroachments, or any other facts which a correct survey would disclose.

    5.   Unpatented mining claims; reservations or exceptions in patents or in Acts authorizing the issuance thereof, water rights, claims or title to water.

Part Two:

SCHEDULE C

The land referred to in this policy is situated in the State of   County
of   and is described as follows:

332

CONDITIONS AND STIPULATIONS

1. Definition of Terms

The following terms when used in this policy mean:

(a) "land": the land described, specifically or by reference, in Schedule A and improvements affixed thereto which by law constitute real property;

(b) "public records": those records which impart constructive notice of matters relating to said land;

(c) "knowledge": actual knowledge, not constructive knowledge or notice which may be imputed to the Insured by reason of any public records;

(d) "date": the effective date;

(e) "mortgage": mortgage, deed of trust, trust deed, or other security instrument; and

(f) "insured": the party or parties named as Insured, and if the owner of the indebtedness secured by a mortgage shown in Schedule B is named as an Insured in Schedule A, the Insured shall include (1) each successor in interest in ownership of such indebtedness, (2) any such owner who acquires the estate or interest referred to in this policy by foreclosure, trustee's sale, or other legal manner in satisfaction of said indebtedness, and (3) any federal agency or instrumentality which is an insurer or guarantor under an insurance contract or guaranty insuring or guaranteeing said indebtedness, or any part thereof, whether named as an insured herein or not, subject otherwise to the provisions hereof.

2. Benefits after Acquisition of Title

If an insured owner of the indebtedness secured by a mortgage described in Schedule B acquires said estate or interest, or any part thereof, by foreclosure, trustee's sale, or other legal manner in satisfaction of said indebtedness, or any part thereof, or if a federal agency or instrumentality acquires said estate or interest, or any part thereof, as a consequence of an insurance contract or guaranty insuring or guaranteeing the indebtedness secured by a mortgage covered by this policy, or any part thereof, this policy shall continue in force in favor of such Insured, agency or instrumentality, subject to all of the conditions and stipulations hereof.

3. Exclusions from the Coverage of this Policy

This policy does not insure against loss or damage by reason of the following:

(a) Any law, ordinance or governmental regulation (including but not limited to building and zoning ordinances) restricting or regulating or prohibiting the occupancy, use or enjoyment of the land, or regulating the character, dimensions, or location of any improvement now or hereafter erected on said land, or prohibiting a separation in ownership or a reduction in the dimensions or area of any lot or parcel of land.

(b) Governmental rights of police power or eminent domain unless notice of the exercise of such rights appears in the public records at the date hereof.

(c) Title to any property beyond the lines of the land expressly described in Schedule A, or title to streets, roads, avenues, lanes, ways or waterways on which such land abuts, or the right to maintain therein vaults, tunnels, ramps or any other structure or improvement; or any rights or easements therein unless this policy specifically provides that such property, rights or easements are insured, except that if the land abuts upon one or more physically open streets or highways this policy insures the ordinary rights of abutting owners for access to one of such streets or highways, unless otherwise excepted or excluded herein.

(d) Defects, liens, encumbrances, adverse claims against the title as insured or other matters (1) created, suffered, assumed or agreed to by the Insured claiming loss or damage; or (2) known to the Insured Claimant either at the date of this policy or at the date such Insured Claimant acquired an estate or interest insured by this policy and not shown by the public records, unless dis-

closure thereof in writing by the Insured shall have been made to the Company prior to the date of this policy; or (3) resulting in no loss to the Insured Claimant; or (4) attaching or created subsequent to the date hereof.

(e) Loss or damage which would not have been sustained if the Insured were a purchaser or encumbrancer for value without knowledge.

(f) Consumer credit protection, truth in lending or similar law.

4. Defense and Prosecution of Actions—Notice of Claim to be Given by the Insured

(a) The Company, at its own cost and without undue delay shall provide (1) for the defense of the Insured in all litigation consisting of actions or proceedings commenced against the Insured, or defenses, restraining orders, or injunctions interposed against a foreclosure or sale of the mortgage and indebtedness covered by this policy or a sale of the estate or interest in said land; or (2) for such action as may be appropriate to establish the title of the estate or interest or the lien of the mortgage as insured, which litigation or action in any of such events is founded upon an alleged defect, lien or encumbrance insured against by this policy, and may pursue any litigation to final determination in the court of last resort.

(b) In any case any such action or proceeding shall be begun, or defense interposed, or in case knowledge shall come to the Insured of any claim of title or interest which is adverse to the title of the estate or interest or lien of the mortgage as insured, or which might cause loss or damage for which the Company shall or may be liable by virtue of this policy, or if the Insured shall in good faith contract to sell the indebtedness secured by a mortgage covered by this policy, or, if an Insured in good faith leases or contracts to sell, lease or mortgage the same, or if the successful bidder at a foreclosure sale under a mortgage covered by this policy refuses to purchase and in any such event the title to said estate or interest is rejected as unmarketable, the Insured shall notify the Company thereof in writing. If such notice shall not be given to the Company within ten days of the receipt of process or pleadings or if the Insured shall not, in writing, promptly notify the Company of any defect, lien or encumbrance insured against which shall come to the knowledge of the Insured, of if the Insured shall not, in writing, promptly notify the Company of any such rejection by reason of claimed unmarketability of title, then all liability of the Company in regard to the subject matter of such action, proceeding or matter shall cease and terminate, provided, however, that failure to notify shall in no case prejudice the claim of any Insured unless the Company shall be actually prejudiced by such failure and then only to the extent of such prejudice.

(c) The Company shall have the right at its own cost to institute and prosecute any action or proceeding or do any other act which in its opinion may be necessary or desirable to establish the title of the estate or interest or the lien of the mortgage as insured; and the Company may take any appropriate action under the terms of this policy whether or not it shall be liable thereunder and shall not thereby concede liability or waive any provision of this policy.

(d) In all cases where this policy permits or requires the Company to prosecute or provide for the defense of any action or proceeding, the Insured shall secure to it the right to so prosecute or provide defense in such action or proceeding, and all appeals therein, and permit it to use, at its option, the name of the Insured for such purpose. Whenever requested by the Company the Insured shall give the Company all reasonable aid in any such action or proceeding, in effecting settlement, securing evidence, obtaining witnesses, or prosecuting or defending such action or proceeding, and the Company shall reimburse the Insured for any expense so incurred.

5. Notice of Loss—Limitation of Action

In addition to the notices required under paragraph 4(b), a statement in writing of any loss or damage for which it is claimed the Company is liable under this policy shall be furnished to the Company within sixty days after such loss or damage shall have been determined and no right of action shall accrue to the Insured under this policy until thirty days after such statement shall have been furnished, and no recovery shall be had by the Insured under this policy unless action shall be commenced thereon within five years after expiration of said thirty day period. Failure to furnish such statement of loss or damage, or to commence such action within the time hereinbefore specified, shall be a conclusive bar against maintenance by the Insured of any action under this policy.

6. Option to Pay, Settle or Compromise Claims

The Company shall have the option to pay or settle or compromise for or in the name of the Insured any claim insured against or to pay the full amount of this policy, or, in case loss is claimed under this policy by the owner of the indebtedness secured by a mortgage covered by this policy, the Company shall have the option to purchase said indebtedness; such purchase, payment or tender of payment of the full amount of this policy, together with all costs, attorneys' fees and expenses which the Company is obligated hereunder to pay, shall terminate all liability of the Company hereunder. In the event, after notice of claim has been given to the Company by the Insured, the Company offers to purchase said indebtedness, the owner of such indebtedness shall transfer and assign said indebtedness and the mortgage securing the same to the Company upon payment of the purchase price.

7. Payment of Loss

(a) The liability of the Company under this policy shall in no case exceed, in all, the actual loss of the Insured and costs and attorneys' fees which the Company may be obligated hereunder to pay.

(b) The Company will pay, in addition to any loss insured against by this policy, all costs imposed upon the Insured in litigation carried on by the Company for the Insured, and all costs and attorneys' fees in litigation carried on by the Insured with the written authorization of the Company.

(c) No claim for damages shall arise or be maintainable under this policy (1) if the Company, after having received notice of an alleged defect, lien or encumbrance not excepted or excluded herein removes such defect, lien or encumbrance within a reasonable time after receipt of such notice, or (2) for liability voluntarily assumed by the Insured in settling any claim or suit without written consent of the Company, or (3) in the event the title is rejected as unmarketable because of a defect, lien or encumbrance not excepted or excluded in this policy, until there has been a final determination by a court of competent jurisdiction sustaining such rejection.

(d) All payments under this policy, except payments made for costs, attorneys' fees and expenses, shall reduce the amount of the insurance pro tanto and no payment shall be made without producing this policy for endorsement of such payment unless the policy be lost or destroyed, in which case proof of such loss or destruction shall be furnished to the satisfaction of the Company; provided, however, if the owner of an indebtedness secured by a mortgage shown in Schedule B is an Insured herein then such payments shall not reduce pro tanto the amount of the insurance afforded hereunder as to such Insured, except to the extent that such payments reduce the amount of the indebtedness secured by such mortgage. Payment in full by any person or voluntary satisfaction or release by the Insured of a mortgage covered by this policy shall terminate all liability of the Company to the insured owner of the indebtedness secured by such mortgage, except as provided in paragraph 2 hereof.

(e) When liability has been definitely fixed in accordance with the conditions of this policy the loss or damage shall be payable within thirty days thereafter.

8. Liability Noncumulative

It is expressly understood that the amount of this policy is reduced by any amount the Company may pay under any policy insuring the validity or priority of any mortgage shown or referred to in Schedule B hereof or any mortgage hereafter executed by the Insured which is a charge or lien on the estate or interest described or referred to in Schedule A, and the amount so paid shall be deemed a payment to the Insured under this policy. The provisions of this paragraph numbered 8 shall not apply to an Insured owner of an indebtedness secured by a mortgage shown in Schedule B unless such Insured acquires title to said estate or interest in satisfaction of said indebtedness or any part thereof.

9. Subrogation upon Payment or Settlement:

Whenever the Company shall have settled a claim under this policy, all right of subrogation shall vest in the Company unaffected by any act of the Insured, and it shall be subrogated to and be entitled to all rights and remedies which the Insured would have had against any person or property in respect to such claim had this policy not been issued. If the payment does not cover the loss of the Insured, the Company shall be subrogated to such rights and remedies in the proportion which said payment bears to the amount of said loss. If loss should result from any act of the Insured such act shall not void this policy, but the Company, in that event, shall be required to pay only that part of any losses insured against hereunder which shall exceed the amount, if any, lost to the Company by reason of the impairment of the right of subrogation. The Insured, if requested by the Company, shall transfer to the Company all rights and remedies against any person or property necessary in order to perfect such right of subrogation, and shall permit the Company to use the name of the Insured in any transaction or litigation involving such rights or remedies.

If the Insured is the owner of the indebtedness secured by a mortgage covered by this policy, such Insured may release or substitute the personal liability of any debtor or guarantor, or extend or otherwise modify the terms of payment, or release a portion of the estate or interest from the lien of the mortgage, or release any collateral security for the indebtedness, provided such act does not result in any loss of priority of the lien of the mortgage.

10. Policy Entire Contract

Any action or actions or rights of action that the Insured may have or may bring against the Company arising out of the status of the lien of the mortgage covered by this policy or the title of the estate or interest insured herein must be based on the provisions of this policy.

No provision or condition of this policy can be waived or changed except by writing endorsed hereon or attached hereto signed by the President, a Vice President, the Secretary, an Assistant Secretary or other validating officer of the Company.

11. Notices, Where Sent

All notices required to be given the Company and any statement in writing required to be furnished the Company shall be addressed to Home Office of

12. THE PREMIUM SPECIFIED ON THE FIRST PAGE OF THIS POLICY IS THE ENTIRE CHARGE FOR TITLE SEARCH, TITLE EXAMINATION AND TITLE INSURANCE.

ferred to him. For example, if the insured parties die, their heirs to the property will continue to be insured. The title company agrees to pay all costs of fighting a challenge to the title up to the amount of coverage as provided in Conditions and Stipulations, Clause 4(a) at the end of this policy.

Liability

The policy then lists the four instances in which the company will be liable for loss or damage to the insured.

1. Protects the insured if the title company makes any mistakes in searching the title. If defects are later found to exist that are not specified in the policy, the damages caused by them are covered. Defects that have been found and thus excluded from coverage are listed in Schedule B. Other items not covered are listed in the Conditions and Stipulations.

2. Protects you against the existence of a defect that would make the title unmarketable, which means the seller did not have a right to sell the land. These are such things as forgeries, undisclosed heirs, and the other defects listed earlier in this chapter. Never accept any policy that does not insure that the title is marketable.

3. Protects the lender, named as an insured, who has a lien on the buyer's title as security for the loan. This could be the seller who has taken back a mortgage from the buyer, both he and the buyer are insured under this policy. The company is liable for a defect in the execution of a mortgage or deed of trust which adversely affects the resulting lien on the property. Before insuring the lender, the company examines the executed mortgage or deed of trust for completeness. If you borrow from a bank or other lending institution, a different type of policy, called a Mortgage or Lender's Policy, is often used. (See below in this chapter.)

4. Insures against the existence of any prior lien or encumbrance, such as a mortgage, not excepted in Schedule B, which would adversely affect the mortgage held by the lender or seller who is insured by the policy. For example, if a lender makes a loan to the buyer and he thinks it is the only mortgage on the property, under this policy if another mortgage exists that is superior and not excepted by this policy, any losses suffered by the insured lender will be paid.

Schedule A

First, the cost of the policy, the amount of the coverage, and the policy number are inserted at the top.

Next are spaces that must be filled in with the date and exact time, to the second, that the deed to you is recorded. This is the "Effective Date" of the policy. You want to be covered for any defects arising up to the time you take title. Any defect arising after this time will not be covered in the policy. When you get your deed, check the recording time stamped on it with the time and date written into the policy to see if they correspond. If they do not, make an immediate complaint to the title company and have them change the policy to the proper time.

The names of the parties being covered by the policy, the "Insured," are inserted next.

1. Each buyer's name must be inserted and his marital status must be given. The type of ownership by which the buyers are taking title is then given, e.g., tenants-in-common, joint tenants, or husband and wife.

2. Indicates the form of title to be given to the buyers, their names, and the type of ownership to be transferred to them. The type of "estate or interest" you should get is called a "fee estate" or "fee simple" title, which means you will have complete ownership of the land to sell, give away, or encumber as you wish, subject to the terms of your mortgage or deed of trust.

Schedule B

Part One. Lists the five common exceptions from coverage in Standard Coverage Policies. These are:

1. Any taxes or assessments levied against the property before the close of escrow, but not indicated on the public, or tax authority, records, are not insured against by this policy. Thus, it is very important to make the seller liable for such liens in the Contract of Sale,

as stated in Clause 11 of the Model Contract of Sale. (See Chapter 28.)

2. Encumbrances that can only be discovered by physically inspecting the property and by asking questions of people living on it are not covered by the policy. For example, you could discover an adverse possessor only by inspecting the land. You will not be insured against a claim for adverse possession after you purchase the property. (See Chapter 16: *Adverse Possession.*) Another common unrecorded defect is a lease held by a renter which is not recorded but which would be binding on a purchaser of the land. Thus, you must talk to the people living on the land to ascertain if they have a lease. The policy will not cover any legal claims made by such persons in possession after you take title.

3. The seller of the property may have granted easement rights to an adjoining landowner or other person without recording this grant in the public records, or a person might have gained a prescriptive easement by meeting the requirements for obtaining this right. (See Chapter 9: *Easement Rights.*) This policy does not insure against easements which could not be discovered by searching the public records. It is your responsibility to determine the status of any right-of-way crossing the property that is not a recorded easement to insure yourself against future claims against the land. The seller is supposed to list all existing easements in Clause 4 of the Model Contract of Sale. (See Chapter 28.)

4. This policy does not require the existence of a legal survey and thus only insures that you will receive the seller's title to the property described in this policy and the deed. It does not insure the exact location of that property on the ground. Thus, if you buy land without a survey and later discover that the boundary lines are not where you thought they were, the policy does not protect you. The amount of acreage you will receive is not insured nor are "boundary line agreements" made between an owner and an adjoining landowner which are not recorded. Thus, you should get a survey as provided in Clauses 18(b) and 19(b) of the Model Contract of Sale.

5. Here the policy excludes from coverage one of the most complicated areas of land ownership, water rights. Since many rights to take water are based on the riparian nature of the property rather than on the recording of any documents, the policy does not take any liability for future water disputes. (See Chapter 10: *Water Rights.*) Mining claims and mineral rights in existence against the property which would not show up in a title search are also excluded from coverage. (See Chapter 11: *Mineral, Oil Gas, Timber, Soil, and Other Rights.*)

Part Two. Any encumbrances against the title that the title company found during its title search are listed here, including tax, assessment, and mechanic's liens; mortgages or deeds of trust on the property; easements on the land; covenants, conditions, and restrictions of ownership binding on the owner; attachments and judgments. These are defects in the title, but they do not make the title "unmarketable." If an encumbrance did make the title unmarketable, the title company would not issue a Policy of Title Insurance since it insures the marketability of the title.

Schedule C

A complete description of the property is given. This description should specify any easements, water rights, or other property rights to be included in your purchase to that they will be insured by the policy. If any parts of the property are to be excluded from the conveyance, such as mineral or timber rights, they should also be specified here.

Conditions and Stipulations

These conditions are common to most Standard Coverage Title Insurance Policies:

1. (a)–(f) The terms used in the policy are defined.

2. The policy covers an insured lender who acquires title to the property to satisfy an obligation owed to him by the insured buyer. For example, if the mortgagee (lender) is one of the insured parties named at the beginning of the policy and he forecloses on the loan at a later date, the mortgagee will be covered by the policy in place of the buyer. But the policy does not continue in favor of another person

who purchases the property from the insured party.

3. Further exclusions from the coverage of this policy are listed here. The policy does not insure the buyer for any losses that he might suffer because of:

(a) Government regulations and laws, such as building codes and zoning regulations, that restrict the use of the property. (See Chapter 13: *Building and Health Codes,* and Chapter 12: *Zoning Laws.*)

(b) Unrecorded police power rights, such as an eminent domain action of condemnation against the property, unless the condemnation has been recorded before the policy goes into effect. (See Chapter 15: *Eminent Domain and Condemnation.*)

(c) Anything not within the boundaries of the property as described in the policy, except rights of way onto adjoining public roads if the property abuts such a public road.

(d) Unrecorded defects known about or agreed to by the buyer but not reported to the title company, or defects which do not result in loss to the insured or which were created after the date the policy was issued.

(e) For example, if the seller sells the land to someone else before he sells it to you, and the first buyer does not record his deed, if you record your deed before he does and you don't know that the land has already been sold, you are the only person with a legal right to the land because you are a "purchaser without knowledge," and if the first buyer sues you, the policy pays for your defense. But if you buy the land knowing it has already been sold, even if the first buyer does not record his deed, you do not have a legal right to the property because you are a "purchaser with knowledge" and if you are sued, this policy does not cover you.

(f) You are not insured if you are a lender and suffer losses because you violate consumer protection laws, such as the truth in lending law.

4. (a)–(d) This clause establishes the obligation of the title company to protect your title by bringing and defending actions. An interesting part of the defense obligation stipulates that if you make a contract to sell the property and your prospective buyer terminates his purchase because he discovers a defect in your title not excluded from coverage in this policy, the company will cover your damages from the loss of the sale up to the amount of the policy coverage. It is stated that the insured must "promptly notify" the title company of any claim it must fight. The title company also has the right to commence an action to clear title on its own initiative. Finally, the policy states that the company shall be allowed to use the insured's name in the prosecution or defense of a case and that the insured shall give the company full cooperation should it have to meet a challenge to the title it is insuring.

5. Additional requirements of notice to the company of its liability are given here. The insured has sixty days after any loss or damage to notify the company in writing of his claim under the policy.

6. The company has the option to meet its obligations to the insured by either paying his loss up to the amount of coverage or securing his title for him so that he does not suffer a loss.

7. (a)–(e) This section specifies the elements involved in determining and paying for any losses covered by the policy: (a) and (b) deal with the determination of loss—the title company is liable for the actual loss of the insured plus court costs and legal fees up to the amount of coverage; (c) states the limitation of liability—the company has the right to obtain the removal of a defect, if possible, to prevent the insured from suffering a loss. The insured cannot initiate any type of action relating to any matter covered in the policy without the consent of the company. The company is not bound to pay for a loss covered by the policy until all legal proceedings have terminated and resulted in a judgment against the insured; (d) deals with the reduction of the company's liability—if the company makes any payment to the insured for a partial loss due to a defect in title, the amount of liability under the policy decreases by that amount; (e) specifies the time for payment of loss—the company must render payment within thirty days after liability has definitely been determined.

8. If you have given a mortgage on the land and a judgment later renders your title unmarketable or it is discovered that a lien or encumbrance exists which is covered by the policy, the company must first pay any money

to the lender-mortgagee before it can pay you, the insured. If the defect results in a partial loss only, the amount paid, whether to the lender or to you, will reduce the future liability of the company by that amount in order to prevent the accumulation of liabilities beyond the amount of the policy.

9. To subrogate means to substitute. For example, assume that the seller did not reveal in the Contract of Sale an unrecorded defect in the title when he sold the land to the insured buyer, and the insured buyer suffers a loss because of the defect. After the title company pays the insured for his loss, if it is covered by the policy, the company then has the right to subrogate, or substitute, itself in the place of the insured and sue the seller for his breach of the Contract of Sale. The company can sue in its own name and in the name of the insured, and if any damages are awarded, the title company keeps the money.

The second paragraph of this section applies only to a lender who is insured under the policy and will not affect you.

10. All the terms of the insurance agreement between the company and the insured persons are expressed only in the policy. Any changes made in the policy must be approved in writing by a valid representative of the title company.

11. The address given here should be used if you have to make a claim or notify the company for any reason.

WHY YOU NEED TITLE INSURANCE IN ADDITION TO THE CONTRACT OF SALE

The Model Contract of Sale includes every protection that you receive in the Policy of Title Insurance. Under the Contract the seller is liable to you for your damages, while under the Policy of Title Insurance, the title company assumes liability. Therefore, it might appear that getting a Policy of Title Insurance is an unnecessary expense. However, if you are not insured and you have to proceed against the seller for any defect in title and breach of the Contract of Sale, you will have to pay the legal expenses prior to a judgment, you might not be able to locate the seller to collect a judgment

from him, and he might not have any money to pay a judgment. A Title Insurance Policy pays your legal costs and insures you coverage for any losses included in the policy. At this time, it is the best insurance you can have when buying land. It should be an essential part of your purchase, and must always include a Preliminary Title Report so that you will know what defects exist in the title to the land.

THE LOAN POLICY OF TITLE INSURANCE

If the seller takes back a Purchase Money Mortgage or deed of trust and note when he sells you the land, usually he is included as an insured party in your Standard Coverage Owner's Policy of Title Insurance. But if a commercial lender extends a loan to you for the purchase and takes back a mortgage or deed of trust with the land as security, you will be charged the expense of obtaining a more inclusive form of title insurance called a Loan Policy or Lender's Policy, which was established by the American Land Title Association (ALTA) for the protection of lenders.

All those items excluded from coverage in the Owner's Policy are included in the Loan Policy, which includes a legal survey and physical inspection by the insurer before a policy will be issued. The cost of this type of coverage is much greater than that of a Standard Coverage Policy, but since a lender usually wants as much protection for his security as possible, he will demand an ALTA Policy.

Usually the buyer pays for the Loan Policy as part of the loan. This policy only insures the lender-mortgagee and does not protect the buyer. Thus you must also get your own Policy of Title Insurance. The amount of coverage is for the amount of the debt owed to the lender, since that would be the extent of his loss should there be a defect in the title to the land. As the amount of the debt is paid off by the buyer, the amount of coverage decreases by an equal amount. When the debt is totally paid, the Loan Policy terminates since there is no longer anything to insure the lender for.

If you order a Loan Policy at the same time you order an Owner's Policy, a discount is usually given by the title company. A few states combine the Owner's Policy and the Loan Policy in a Joint Protection Policy, issued in the amount of the purchase price. As the buyer pays off his loan, the company's liability to the lender decreases and its liability to the buyer increases. When the loan is completely paid, the buyer remains as the only party insured by the policy.

THE EXTENDED COVERAGE OWNER'S POLICY OF TITLE INSURANCE

The greater protection given to a lender by the Loan Policy can be obtained by a buyer if he "extends" the Standard Owner's Policy to cover these possible defects. The Extended Coverage Owner's Policy generally gives buyers what the ALTA Policy gives lenders, except that insured access rights are usually not included. The main advantage of Extended Coverage is that it insures a survey and everything that can be found by a physical inspection of the property. But the survey taken by the title company is usually more expensive than any survey you can have done elsewhere. Therefore, because it is easy to inspect the property for unrecorded easements and to determine the state of persons in possession of the land, if you get your own legal survey done, you will get adequate coverage with a Standard Owner's Policy of Title Insurance. Of course, if the seller is willing to pay for it, get the Extended Coverage Policy.

In the Model Contract of Sale, Clause 13 covers charges to the parties and specifies that the seller pays the premium up to the amount of a Standard Coverage Policy and the buyer pays any additional premium for an Extended Policy if he demands one. I think this is an equitable agreement, but if you desire you can specify that the seller is to pay the entire amount of an Extended Policy. It is very easy to change the clause in the Contract of Sale if you want to provide for this. (See Chapter 28: *The Model Contract of Sale*.)

If you want any information about title insurance in your state, write to your state Insurance Commissioner or Land Title Association.

ATTORNEY'S CERTIFICATE OF TITLE

In a few states in the East (see Illustration 80 earlier in this chapter), Abstracts of Title by abstract companies and Title Insurance Policies are not commonly used. Instead, an attorney is hired to examine all of the recorded documents relating to the title and he makes up the Abstract of Title. He issues the results of his title search in a Certificate of Title which details what records were examined and what encumbrances exist against the title, if any. This certificate is basically the same as an Abstracts of Title Certificate. It is not insurance of marketable title and does not insure against undisclosed defects, such as forgery and the others listed earlier. Thus, like an Abstract of Title, it is not an adequate form of protection for the buyer.

If the attorney makes a negligent mistake in his title search, you will have to sue him for any losses you suffer due to his negligence. In contract, under a Title Insurance Policy you will be compensated if the company is negligent and for unknown defects in the title subject to any exception in the policy.

Always insist on a Policy of Title Insurance. If the real estate agent or seller tells you that they are not issued in your area, do some investigating on your own to determine the location of the nearest title company. Title insurance is becoming more widespread every year. Look in the Yellow Pages under "Title Companies." If you can't locate a title company send an inquiry to: The American Land Title Association (ALTA), 1828 L Street, N.W., Washington, D.C. 20036.

THE TORRENS TITLE SYSTEM AND TORRENS CERTIFICATE

Less than 1 percent of the country uses a completely different method of guaranteeing title to land, called the Torrens Title System. In this system, the county Recorder maintains a record of all encumbrances that exist on the title to each piece of property in the county. Before a parcel of land can be sold or mortgaged, the buyer and seller must go to court for a hearing. The county Recorder sends a notice of the hearing to anybody who he determines could have a claim against the title according to the County Records. Anybody with a claim must sue to have his claim settled before title is passed to the buyer. The court dismisses or settles all the claims, orders the title to be registered in the buyer's name, and issues the new owner a Torren's Certificate, which lists any liens and encumbrances against the title. If a Torren's Certificate is issued, the title is declared marketable and no undisclosed defects can be used later to cause a loss of title.

chapter 32

Types of Co-Ownership

In this chapter, I describe the advantages and disadvantages of the various types of co-ownership by which a married couple or a group can take title to a parcel of land. Today more and more people are joining together with others willing and able to share the costs of owning country land and are buying as a group. Generally the larger the parcel of land, the cheaper it is per acre. As a group the individuals can pool their funds to buy a larger parcel. Even if you do not want to share ownership of your land with anyone else, you might agree to buy a large parcel of land with some other people and then subdivide the property among yourselves with each of you taking separate title to your individual parcel. However, you must check the local zoning regulations first to be sure that you will be allowed to subdivide, or partition, your land after purchasing it. Some areas have minimum acreage laws for parcel splits and limits to the number of residences per parcel. (See Chapter 12: *Zoning Laws*.)

Whenever two or more people plan to buy land together, before signing the Contract of Sale all the buyers should understand what each person's goals and desires are regarding the land. It is often useful to draw up an Owner's Agreement specifying the group's goals and desires on paper. I have included a Model Owner's Agreement at the end of this chapter which your group can use as a basis for drawing up your own contract. Then the group should decide on the form of co-ownership best suited to it.

The two most common forms of land co-ownership are the tenancy-in-common and joint tenancy. People can also join together in a corporation, nonprofit association, or cooperative. Since all the legal aspects of these legal entities could fill another book of this size, I will merely summarize their advantages and disadvantages to give you a basic idea of the possibilities available to your group.

I also include some information pertaining to property ownership by a husband and wife, specifically tenancy by the entireties, dower and curtesy, and community property rights. There is also a section on how to declare a Homestead Exemption.

OWNING LAND AS TENANTS-IN-COMMON

When buying land as tenants-in-common, each purchaser shares an undivided interest in the total parcel of land. This means that one party cannot claim any specific portion of the land as his alone unless it is so specified in a contract among all the owners. Each co-tenant does not necessarily have to own an equal share. For instance, one person might have a quarter interest, another a half interest, and two others might each have a one-eighth interest in the land. Usually each person is financially responsible only to the extent of his ownership.

The only way one tenant can destroy the tenancy-in-common, or co-tenancy, without the other owners' approval is by going to court and filing an action to "partition" the land among the owners. If the court feels there are justifiable reasons to end the co-tenancy, the judge will appoint a commissioner, or referee, who will equitably divide the land into separate parcels according to the amount of interest held by each tenant. Each person then becomes the sole owner of his respective portion. If, for geographical or other reasons, the land cannot be split up in this manner, the court may order that the entire piece of land be sold and the proceeds split up among the owners according to their respective interests. If all the owners are willing, of course, they can par-

tition the land themselves without initiating a court action, although getting everyone to agree on a fair division of the land is usually difficult. The owners can also mutually agree in writing to replace the co-tenancy with another form of co-ownership.

Each individual co-tenant can sell or mortgage his interest in the land, but he acts only for his own share and cannot bind anyone else's interest. Thus, if a person's mortgage on his share were to be foreclosed, his lender would take his share as a tenant-in-common with the other owners. Because the lender would then have to either sell his interest in the land, or file for a partition in order to sell the land and get the money owed him, a commercial lender will not likely grant a loan to just one co-tenant in a tenancy-in-common.

To avoid possible problems with lenders or a purchaser of a co-tenant's interest, the owners can specify in a contract among themselves that no tenant may sell or mortgage his share, or that the remaining owners have the "right of first refusal" if one tenant wants to sell his interest. The right of first refusal means that the tenant who wants to sell his interest must first offer to sell it to the other owners before he can offer it to anyone else. The Model Owner's Agreement at the conclusion of this chapter illustrates how such an agreement can be written.

If a co-tenant fails to make his payments on the land and other expenses, the other co-owners can foreclose on his interest in the property. If a co-tenant dies, his interest in the property goes to his heirs, who take his place as tenants-in-common with the other owners. This inheritance rule is the most important legal aspect of a tenancy-in-common differentiating it from other forms of co-ownership. Under a joint tenancy (see next section), if an owner dies, his interest in the property goes to the surviving owners. Because most people want their property to go to their heirs, unrelated land buyers usually buy as tenants-in-common rather than joint tenants. Most states assume that, unless stated otherwise, title to property will be under a tenancy-in-common. Nevertheless, you should specify in your Contract of Sale, in your Escrow Instructions, and in your deed that you are to take the property as "tenants-in-common" if that is your choice.

OWNING LAND AS JOINT TENANTS

Whereas tenants-in-common may hold undivided unequal interests in the land, joint tenants always share an undivided equal interest in the land. The major legal difference between these two types of co-ownership is that under a joint tenancy the co-owners have the right of survivorship, which means that if one of the parties dies, his interest automatically passes to the surviving owners. A joint tenant cannot will his interest to his heirs or anyone else, and his interest does not become part of his estate on his death. The surviving co-tenants inherit the deceased's interest free from personal debts and liens. Since no will is involved, an expensive and lengthy probate proceeding is unnecessary. Depending on the state, an inheritance tax may be levied, based on the value of the deceased person's interest in the land.

Since each person owns an equal interest in the land, all expenses, including land payments, taxes, repairs, insurance, and other items, must be shared equally. If one party fails to contribute his share, the other tenants can place a lien against his interest in the property and eventually foreclose.

Once a joint tenancy has been created, no joint tenant can get out of it without destroying that form of co-ownership. If a party sells his interest, his buyer comes in as a tenant-in-common rather than a joint tenant to the others. For example, if X, Y, and Z hold a piece of land as joint tenants and Z sells his interest to A, A buys in as a tenant-in-common. If A dies, his share goes to his heirs, rather than to X and Y. X and Y remain joint tenants and each has a right of survivorship to the other's interest. Upon death, their interests never go to A. If X and Y choose, they can change their arrangement to become tenants-in-common with A. If only two people are joint tenants and one sells his interest, the joint tenancy is terminated and transformed into a tenancy-in-common when the new owner takes title. (See Illustration 82.) If a joint tenant chooses to sell his interest, he can do so without the consent of the other owners, unless the owners specify otherwise in a contract among themselves.

If a joint tenant, like a tenant-in-common, wants to borrow money for a private loan, he can mortgage his interest in the property. However, if his loan is foreclosed, his lender will take his interest as a tenant-in-common and the remaining tenants then automatically become tenants-in-common. A joint tenant, like a tenant-in-common, would probably have a hard time finding a lender willing to lend him money solely on the security of his joint tenancy interest.

If a money judgment is rendered against one tenant for personal debts, his interest can be split off from the others and used to pay his obligations.

Any owner, or creditor, can go to court to file an action for partition of the individual interests just as in a tenancy-in-common, or the owners can mutually agree in writing to change the arrangement.

If you choose to take ownership under a joint tenancy, you must specify in your Contract of Sale, Escrow Instructions, and deed that you are to take title as "joint tenants" or as "joint tenant with the right of survivorship." A few states, Alabama, Florida, Georgia, Kentucky, North Carolina, Ohio, Oregon, Pennsylvania, South Carolina, Tennessee, Texas, Virginia, Washington, and West Virginia, have abolished the right of survivorship in joint tenancy and title passes to the heirs on the death of a joint tenant as if he were a tenant-in-common.

OWNING LAND AS TENANTS BY THE ENTIRETIES

This type of ownership applies only to a husband and wife. In a few states, Arkansas, Delaware, Florida, Indiana, Kentucky, Maryland, Massachusetts, Michigan, Missouri, New Jersey, New York, North Carolina, Oklahoma, Oregon, Pennsylvania, Rhode Island, Tennessee, Vermont, Virginia, West Virginia, Wisconsin, and Wyoming, a sale to a married couple automatically creates a tenancy by the entireties between the spouses, unless specified otherwise. Under a tenancy by the entireties,

343

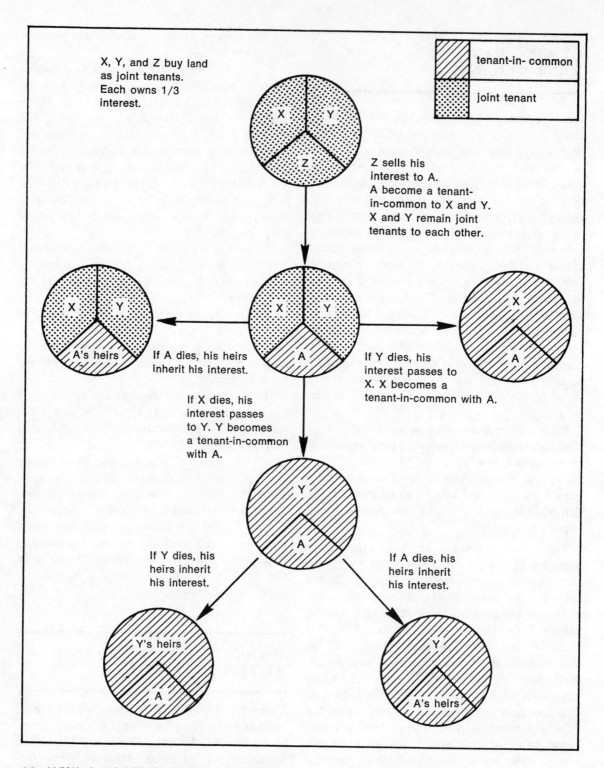

X, Y, and Z buy land as joint tenants. Each owns 1/3 interest.

tenant-in-common

joint tenant

Z sells his interest to A. A become a tenant-in-common to X and Y. X and Y remain joint tenants to each other.

If A dies, his heirs inherit his interest.

If Y dies, his interest passes to X. X becomes a tenant-in-common with A.

If X dies, his interest passes to Y. Y becomes a tenant-in-common with A.

If Y dies, his heirs inherit his interest.

If A dies, his heirs inherit his interest.

82. HOW A JOINT TENANCY OPERATES

title is held by both persons as if they were one owner. Each has complete ownership of the property, and when one dies the other keeps full ownership rights. Thus, like joint tenants, they have the right of survivorship. If the deceased spouse had individual debts, his creditors cannot get a lien against the property. However, if the debtor spouse is the one who survives or if the husband and wife had common debts, the creditors can attach the property.

If a married couple buys land with a single

person, another couple, or a group of people, each married couple will be considered as tenants by the entireties within a group of joint tenants. For instance, if X and Y, a husband and wife, buy land with Z, a single person, X and Y can be considered one person under the law of tenancy by the entireties and own an undivided half interest in the property as a joint tenant with Z, who also owns an undivided half interest in the land. Compare this with a strict joint tenancy under which X, Y, and Z would each own an undivided one-third interest in the land. If a divorce occurs, X and Y split their half interest and become tenants-in-common with Z and the right of survivorship terminates.

No action for partition can be forced by only one of the spouses in a tenancy by the entireties, and no sale of the property can be made by one spouse without the written consent of the other.

DOWER AND CURTESY RIGHTS AND COMMUNITY PROPERTY

Several states recognize either dower and curtesy rights or community property rights of a husband and wife, which, like a tenancy by the entireties, require that both spouses consent to a sale of their mutual property. Although these rights are not a type of ownership, strictly speaking, they will affect your title if you are a married couple, and they could affect the title of the land you are buying if the sellers include a married couple.

Dower and Curtesy Rights

Where recognized, dower rights give a widow one-third of her husband's real estate upon his death. Some states have increased this to a half interest. On the other hand, curtesy is the husband's right to one-third of his wife's real estate upon her death, but he only obtains the right if a child was born during the marriage.

Dower and curtesy rights cannot be cut off by one spouse selling the land without the permission of the other. Both parties must consent to the sale in writing and must sign the

deed. For instance, in a dower and curtesy state, if you buy land from a husband and the wife does not sign the deed, you run the risk that if her husband dies before she does, she can collect her share of her husband's estate from you, since she never signed away her dower interests in the land. To be sure that both parties will agree to sign the deed, you should get both the husband and wife to sign the Contract of Sale. If both parties do not sign the Contract of Sale, the one who didn't can later claim not to have agreed to the sale and can refuse to sign the deed. However, if both sign the Contract of Sale, neither party can refuse to sign the deed without legal liability.

The states that still recognize dower and curtesy rights are Alabama, Alaska, Arkansas, Delaware, Georgia, Hawaii, Kentucky, Maryland, Massachusetts, New Jersey, Ohio, Oregon, Rhode Island, Tennessee, Virginia, West Virginia, and Wisconsin.

Community Property

Eight states, Arizona, California, Idaho, Louisiana, Nevada, New Mexico, Texas, and Washington, regard any property purchased during a marriage as "community property." Both husband and wife have an equal right to possess the property during marriage and upon the death of either spouse the survivor automatically receives half of the community property and the other half passes to the lawful heirs. In some states, the survivor automatically receives the entire amount of community property. Of course, the deceased partner may will the other half to the surviving spouse regardless of the state law. In a divorce, the community property is always split in half between the spouses. Community property laws, like dower and curtesy laws and tenancy by the entireties, were enacted to prevent a surviving spouse from being totally deprived of property under the will of the deceased.

You must be sure that both the husband and wife sign the Contract of Sale and the deed when conveying any community property to you. Regardless of the state law, it is always advisable to have both spouses sign a Contract of Sale and deed if you are purchasing land from a married couple.

THE HOMESTEAD EXEMPTION

In some states, Homestead Exemption laws protect your family's home against possible attachment by creditors up to a certain amount of the value of the home. The amount of protection varies among the states that have enacted such laws. If no homestead protection exists in your state and you are unable to pay a debt, such as a personal loan or judgment lien resulting from a lawsuit, your home can be attached along with your personal property. After attachment an order of execution can be obtained and your home may be forceably sold to raise enough money to pay your debts.

If a Homestead Exemption exists, however, your home will be protected up to the amount of the exemption. Suppose your state has a $10,000 Homestead Exemption, and you have a personal debt of $8,000 which you cannot pay. Your creditor cannot attach your family home and sell it to make up your debts if it is worth $10,000 or less because the first $10,000 of home value is exempt under the law. If your home is worth more than $10,000, your creditor can get a court order to sell it. Say it sells for $15,000. You will keep $10,000 and your creditor will get $5,000. Even though you still owe him $3,000, most states will not allow the creditor to collect any more of the money you received from the home sale. However, you must use the funds to purchase a new home within a specified period of time, usually six months to a year. If you have not bought a home in that time, your creditor can go after the rest of the money you owe him.

In most states, the Homestead Exemption law applies only to married couples and their families who occupy the land as their permanent home. A few states also have a "head of household exemption" for two or more people living together as a family unit with one person supporting the other members of the "family." The head of the family must own the property, or have an interest in it. Thus, in these states, a commune or other group together can take advantage of the Homestead Exemption.

If the family sells the homestead property, the exemption rights terminate. If one spouse dies, the survivor and any children can live on the property under an exemption until the survivor dies and the youngest child reaches age twenty-one.

Exemptions are not automatic in every state that grants them. Sometimes you must file a Declaration of Homestead document which must be recorded in the County Records as notice to possible creditors of your limited liability. The husband or wife or the "head of household," depending on the state's law, files the declaration and in it states that he or she is married or is the head of household, describes the land, and estimates the land's value. The document is signed, notarized, and given to the county Recorder. To see what a form looks like, go the Recorder's office. If a Homestead Exemption exists, the public files will be full of them.

Some types of debts are superior to the Homestead Exemption. Unpaid property taxes and special assessments can be collected from exempt property. If you don't pay a person whom you hired to make an improvement on your land, that person can place a mechanic's lien on your property and have it sold to collect his money, despite a Homestead Exemption, because you had the work done on your own initiative for the purpose of increasing the value of your property. If you give a mortgage or deed of trust using the property as security, you cannot then hide behind a Homestead Exemption to avoid paying the debt. Land under a Homestead Exemption law can never be given as security for a loan unless both spouses consent in writing to give up the exemption. The mortgage or deed of trust also will usually have a clause which both parties must sign waiving all homestead rights. Thus, the exemption is usually only good against "unsecured" debts, those created without using the property as security in any way. Such things as unsecured loans, credit on the purchase of consumer goods, and gambling debts fall within most exemption regulations.

The amount of exemption permitted and the requirements to qualify vary greatly among the states that offer a Homestead Exemption. You should find out the exact information for your state in order to be fully protected. Any local bank, finance company, realtor, or legal aid office can tell you what, if any, exemptions exist. Your county Recorder will tell you how to file for an exemption. It is very easy to do and does not require the services of a lawyer. The states that offer some kind of Homestead Exemption are: Alabama, Arizona, Arkansas, California, Florida, Georgia, Idaho, Illinois, Kansas, Louisiana, Michigan, Minnesota, Mississippi, Missouri, Montana, North Carolina, North Dakota, Ohio, Oklahoma, Oregon, South Dakota, Texas, Vermont, Washington, West Virginia, Wisconsin, and Wyoming.

FORMING A CORPORATION TO BUY LAND

If you have a fairly large group which wants to purchase land together, you might consider corporate ownership. Its unique feature is that a corporation has all of the legal aspects of a single person. When a corporation is formed, each person puts in a sum of money in return for shares of stock and becomes a shareholder in the corporation. This money goes to make the down payment for the land. The shares are issued as in any other type of corporation and entitle the shareholder to live on the land and obligate him to pay assessments to the corporation to cover its costs of owning the property.

The shareholders must draw up Articles of Incorporation, by-laws, and a Shareholders' Agreement. Each state has its own requirements regarding the proper legal form of these documents, but every state requires the filing of the articles and by-laws with the Secretary of State for approval. A filing fee is required and, in most states, an annual corporation tax.

The corporation is managed by a Board of Directors. Each shareholder can be a member of the board and thus take part in all the decision-making. The voting power of each member will depend on the number of shares of stock he owns. For simplicity, it is preferable in a large group to keep things equal. The group will specify in the by-laws the number of votes required to approve an action taken by the board. For instance, the group might decide that 75 percent of the board members must agree on any decision. The board passes resolutions authorizing its officers, including a president, vice president, secretary, and trea-

surer, to handle particular problems involving the land, such as paying taxes and insurance premiums, hiring someone to do road work, and paying off the mortgage. Each board member can take turns being an officer.

The Shareholders' Agreement specifies any terms the group wants binding on the shareholders. It must be in writing, but it does not have to be filed with the Secretary of State. The agreement is a contract signed by all the shareholders which states their rights and obligations. For example, the agreement can specify that no shares can be sold or transferred by a shareholder without the approval of the board or that the use or occupancy of the land by any person other than a shareholder is prohibited unless approval is granted.

To form a corporation, it is not necessary to have an income-producing business. I have had Articles of Incorporation approved which state that "the specific business in which the corporation is primarily to engage is to own and occupy certain real property." This type of corporation will have no income and, therefore, will be charged no federal income tax. Of course, a profit will be made when the land is sold, and a tax will be levied at that time. Although the corporation has no regular income, it will have regular expenses, such as mortgage payments, property taxes, and maintenance costs, which the individual shareholders must pay according to the terms in the Shareholders' Agreement. Thus, the corporation operates at a loss each year.

Some states permit each shareholder to deduct from his annual personal income tax return the amount of the corporation's net loss in proportion to the number of shares of stock he owns. Thus, the shareholder receives an annual tax benefit because the corporation "loses" money. If the shareholder lives on the land, an amount equal to the appraised rental value of the land must be subtracted from the above allowed deduction unless he can show that he is living on the land to perform duties for the corporation, such as maintenance and care of the property.

If a shareholder fails to pay his obligations as specified in the Shareholders' Agreement, the Board of Directors can vote to sell his shares to recoup the money owed to the corporation. When a buyer is found and approved, the transfer of ownership merely necessitates changing the name of the shareholder in the corporate books instead of the usual foreclosure procedure. A reserve "slush" fund is always maintained by the corporation to use if a shareholder falls behind in his payments in order to prevent a default on the mortgage payments.

If the shareholders vote to sell the entire corporate land, the profits will be divided according to the amount of stock each shareholder owns.

An advantage of a corporation is that the shareholders do not have personal liability for the acts of the corporation, and conversely the corporation does not have liability for the acts of the individual shareholders. Thus, land owned by a corporation cannot be attached for personal debts or judgments rendered against any of its shareholders. A creditor can only attach the person's shares in the corporation. He then becomes a shareholder and must abide by the rules of the corporation. In this way, the other landowners are protected from having their ownership disrupted by an unwelcome stranger. If the Board of Directors must approve the sale of any stock, the creditor might find it difficult to collect his money.

On the other hand, if the corporation cannot pay its debts, none of the shareholders can individually be forced to pay a creditor, although the corporation's assets, such as its land, can be reached and sold to make up a debt. If the land is worth less than the amount of debts, the creditors cannot get a deficiency judgment against the shareholders.

The major disadvantage of a corporation is the cost involved in incorporating, since you will probably need an attorney to draw up the documents and you will have to pay state filing fees and state corporation taxes. But the corporate form of ownership has many advantages for a group that wants to own a large undivided parcel of land.

Cooperative Corporation

If your group plans to buy land primarily for the purpose of living on it rather than for the purpose of investment, you might see whether your state recognizes a specific corporation called the "cooperative corporation."

Under a cooperative corporation the corporate organization is seen as a "landlord" and the individual shareholding members are viewed as "tenants." Because this arrangement is more a type of property ownership rather than a true corporation, some states have placed the cooperative corporation under the supervision of the Real Estate Commissioner rather than the Secretary of State, who normally oversees corporations. Instead of issuing shares of stock, the cooperative corporation issues a "certificate" entitling the holders to a vote in the corporation's management and the right to live on the land. Everything else in this type of corporation is arranged in basically the same way as the profit-type corporation. Each state has its own laws on cooperatives, particularly with regard to their tax status.

The Nonprofit Corporation

Another type of corporation you might investigate if you are not planning to make money on the land is the "nonprofit corporation." Your group must fit into one of the special nonprofit and nonpolitical categories, such as religious, educational, scientific, or charitable. If you qualify, the nonprofit corporation may not have to pay income taxes, and, in many states, will also be exempt from paying property taxes. However, you will have to maintain thorough financial records and file detailed tax returns covering the nature of your nonprofit operation.

Instead of issuing stock, the nonprofit corporation may sell or give "memberships" to the individuals, who elect a Board of Directors and vote on the operation of the corporation. Like a profit-oriented corporation, Articles of Incorporation and by-laws are required, and an additional application for nonprofit status must be made to the Internal Revenue Service and to the appropriate state agency, which determine whether the corporation is truly nonprofit and, therefore, eligible for tax exemptions.

Once formed, the nonprofit corporation remains in existence until it is "dissolved." This dissolution process could present problems to the individual owners of the corporation because the Secretary of State or state corporations official may determine that the corporation's assets were held in trust for the nonprofit purpose which the corporation claims to represent. This causes delays and legal problems when you try to sell the property and divide the profits among yourselves because the Secretary might attempt to prevent the profits from going to private individuals. If your group is now, or wants to become, a church or other nonprofit organization and buy land you will probably need a lawyer to get you through the legal paperwork involved in setting up the corporation in the best manner possible to meet your needs.

FORMING AN UNINCORPORATED NONPROFIT ASSOCIATION

A religious, social, educational, or other nonprofit group can also form an unincorporated nonprofit association to buy land. Although the group must appoint one of its members as a trustee who takes the title to the land in his name, the organization, rather than the trustee or other members of the group, retains liability for its own debts. The trustee only acts according to the charter and by-laws of the organization.

In a nonprofit association, no single person owns any part of the land. The members of the group usually agree to pay rent to the association for living on the land, which can be used by the association to pay its mortgage and other expenses without making a profit. This type of purchase appeals primarily to communes, ecological groups interested in preserving open space, and people interested in forming some type of community in the country without actually being personal landowners.

Arrangements must be made in writing at the time the association is formed as to how the funds from a future sale of the property will be disbursed. Each state has its own rules regarding the formation of an unincorporated nonprofit association, and you can get all the necessary information from your Secretary of State or Commissioner of Corporations. Forming such as association is usually easy and you may not require the services of an attorney. Associations are easier to form because the regulations for corporations are avoided.

A MODEL OWNERS' AGREEMENT

If you are going to buy land with other people, you should get together to discuss and write out in detail the terms of the co-ownership before making your purchase. The entire group should understand as completely as possible the intentions and desires of each person. The best of friends one year can become bitter enemies the following year over conflicts involving such things as mate switching, being a vegetarian versus being a meat eater, whether to hunt or not, nudity versus modesty, religious fervor versus atheism, or basic personality clashes. The best-intentioned people cannot possibly predict what will happen to them when they become co-owners of land, with all the responsibilities that that entails, particularly if they are living in the country for the first time.

Often people who have never lived together in the city think they will automatically be able to commune together in the country. Actually, life in the country is more difficult because you must rely to a much greater extent on yourselves, not only for the basic necessities of survival, such as providing water, heat, shelter, but also for more subtle psychological reinforcements. The distractions of the city, which help relieve the pressures of living and working together with the same people day after day, are gone, and individual levels of awareness and personal conflicts are, therefore, emphasized. Although you cannot prevent problems from arising, you can eliminate basic misunderstandings and decide how to deal with potential future problems in an Owners' Agreement.

Each buyer signs the agreement, which should state in writing all the details of the purchase, including such items as each person's rights and obligations regarding the property and its use, the construction of improvements, future resale of the property, financing, decision-making, the sale of one person's interest, individual personal liability, and what happens in the event of a death, divorce, separation, or insolvency.

All financial aspects of the purchase should be specified. Some people might want to live on the land year-round while others might only want to use the property as a vacation home. Are you all going to want to pay an equal share? Each person should understand what his financial obligations will entail, including mortgage payments and maintenance costs, and must be willing and able to meet them.

The group must decide how the members want to live on the land. For instance, is the group going to build one communal house and share the rest of all the land without dividing it up? Are the members of the group going to build houses on separate building sites and share the rest of the land communally? Or is the group going to divide up the entire land into proportionate sections for each person with none of the land shared by the group? Regardless of how it is done, be sure that adequate building sites exist for everyone who wants to construct his own house. Every site is not equally inviting so decide who gets what before you take title to the property.

The Model Owners' Agreement I am including at the end of this chapter is the one my two land partners and I drew up among ourselves at the time we decided to buy land together. It covers the two basic areas required in any co-owner's agreement. First it details each buyer's ownership rights and obligations, and second it states the rules to be observed in relating to the land. We bought as tenants-in-common with each person having an equal one third interest in the land, and we agreed to make all decisions on the basis of a simple majority. You can use any figure you want for approval of co-owner decisions.

You should have no problem understanding the agreement. Notice how we stated the means by which we would handle potential situations.

Each owner is responsible for building his or her own house and the amount of money put into the house will be returned upon the sale of the property. We provide for the possibility that one owner might want to sell his interest and get out of the agreement, in which case the remaining owners have "the right of first refusal." We specify the terms under which the remaining owners can buy the seller's interest, or if they decide not to buy it, that they have the right to approve a new buyer. Because we are interested in preserving the natural environment as much as possible, we have specified in great detail what we can and cannot do on the land.

You can use this agreement as a guide to your specific group needs, whether there are two or twenty of you. You can insert and omit specific clauses depending on your situation. Whatever agreement you make, it must be in writing, dated, and signed by all the owners. It is always adviseable to notarize all the signatures. This is a simple and inexpensive process. The agreement should also be drawn up and signed before you buy the land so that you can iron out basic problems in advance. Some group members might come to realize that they do not see eye-to-eye with the other members on major issues and will decide to drop out of the deal before it's too late. I have seen this happen many times. Our agreement is very formal and legal sounding, but yours can be expressed in any manner you choose. Informality or choice of language is irrelevant, as long as you express clearly and thoroughly what each individual's rights, obligations, and expectations will be after the group takes title to the property.

MODEL OWNERS' AGREEMENT

This Owners' Agreement is made this _____ day of _____, 19___, by and between _____, _____, _____, whereby it is agreed as follows:

1. The purpose of this Owners' Agreement is to specify the rights and obligations of the undersigned Owners with regard to that certain real property situated in the County of _____ _____, State of _____, described as the _____.

2. The purpose of this Owners' Agreement is also to specify the rules and regulations regarding the use and enjoyment of said property.

3. Each Owner shall have one vote in any decision regarding said property or any condition specified in this Agreement.

4. Each Owner shall pay an equal amount of the principal and interest on the existing mortgage; and each Owner shall pay an equal amount of the property taxes, assessments, and maintenance costs, including road repair.

5. If any owner is in default in any obligation under the terms of this Agreement, the Owners, by a majority vote, may then sell the defaulting Owner's interest without his or her consent after 30 days written notice to said Owner, provided that his or her interest shall be sold for the best price and upon the best terms obtainable from a person acceptable to the remaining Owners. In any such sale, the Owners may recoup from the proceeds of said sale any funds owed by the defaulting Owner.

6. In the event any Owner should desire to sell his or her interest in the said property, or in the event of a sale after default, the first opportunity for rejection shall be accorded to the remaining Owners. The option vested in the remaining Owners shall entitle them to purchase all rights and liabilities of the interest of the selling, or defaulting, Owner at a price equivalent to the total investment to date made by the selling, or defaulting, Owner in the said property, plus interest on that investment. The interest shall be computed at a rate of 5% per annum from the date of investment. The term "investment" shall include all money paid in the form of mortgage payments, including that portion of the payment which is accorded to principal and that portion of the payment which is accorded to interest.

The selling, or defaulting, Owner shall also be entitled to reimbursement for his or her portion of the investment in any improvements made on said property. The term "improvement" shall include structures, orchards and gardens, development of water systems, sewage systems, and drainage systems, and any other construction or development on said property which increases its value for sale. For this Agreement, the term "improvements" shall also include any items which will remain on said property, such as machinery, tools, and animals. The term "investment," with regard to improvements, shall include all money paid for the improvement. The value of an Owner's labor shall not be included in the computation of said Owner's investment.

The selling, or defaulting, Owner shall be entitled to all reimbursements to be paid him in a period not to exceed five years at a rate of one-fifth (1/5) of the principal amount due, or more, per year.

Reimbursements and payments to the selling, or defaulting, Owner for his portion of investment in improvements shall include interest on the money invested in the improvements from the date of the sale to the date of the reimbursement payment. There shall be no interest for investment to the date of sale.

7. Any Owner desiring to sell his or her interest as a tenant-in-common in said property shall so advise the other Owners in writing and all Owners shall use their best efforts to locate a buyer for the interest. No interest shall be sold to any person without the written consent and approval of a majority of all the Owners.

8. No Owner shall encumber or permit the encumbrance of his or her interest as a tenant-in-common of said property by any person or legal entity without the written consent of a majority of Owners.

9. No Owner may make a gift or donation of his or her interest in said property without the written approval and consent of a majority of all the Owners.

10. No Owner shall split or divide his or her interest in said property with any other persons for any reason. Should an Owner attempt to do so, such action will be interpreted as a desire to sell his or her interest in said property, and the rules of this Agreement regarding the sale of an interest shall apply.

11. In the event of the death of an Owner, the heir to his or her interest shall be bound by the terms of this Agreement.

12. This Agreement secures for each Owner the right, should he or she choose, to construct a habitation on said property. A majority approval is required with regard to the exercise of said right to the extent that the Owners may consider aesthetic, environmental, and other considerations relevant to the location and construction of said habitation.

13. Any physical alterations of said property must be approved by a majority of the Owners. "Physical alterations" shall include, among other things, the construction of any structures, such as houses, barns, garages, greenhouses, roads, dams, wells, water tanks and other forms of land development. The term "physical alteration" shall also include the cutting of any trees and vegetation and the clearing of any part of said property.

14. There must be approval by a majority of the Owners before any gas water or sewage pipes or electrical lines can be installed on said property from outside sources.

15. There shall be no use of pesticides, herbicides, or other poisons at any time or any place on said property without the approval of all the Owners.

16. The hunting and killing of wildlife shall be absolutely and strictly prohibited on said property at all times and during all seasons, except that killing of wildlife will be permitted for the protection of dwellings. The wildlife in the category of animals that threaten dwellings shall include mice, rats, and skunks. Under no circumstances shall bears, wildcats, deer, or birds be killed. The taking of any fish from the creeks on said property shall be in accordance with state and local regulations.

17. The keeping of all domestic and farm animals shall be subject to approval by a majority of the Owners.

18. There shall be no unnecessary discharge of firearms at any time or place on said property. The term "unnecessary discharge" shall include the use of firearms for target or practice shooting.

19. If, at any time, none of the Owners is willing or able to live on said property, then the Owners will allow one or more persons to act as caretakers of said property. The caretakers must be approved by a majority of said Owners. If any caretakers operate to the dissatisfaction of the majority of Owners they shall be asked to leave. Under no circumstances may an Owner permit a non-Owner to live on said property without the approval of all Owners living on said property.

20. The entire amount of said property may be sold if approval for such sale is given by a majority of the Owners in writing. In the event the entire parcel of said property is sold, a majority of the Owners shall agree on a selling price. The Owners may hire a licensed appraiser to determine the fair market value of said property and improvements. The fees and costs of said appraisal, and the fees and costs of any other expenses involved in the selling of said property, shall be borne equally by each Owner.

21. In the event the entire parcel of said property is sold, after reimbursement of each Owner according to the terms in Paragraph 6 of this Agreement, all remaining proceeds shall be divided equally among the Owners.

22. In exercising the majority approval and vote rule of this Agreement, the Owners shall make all reasonable efforts to contact and consult with an absentee Owner and accord to him or her the right to exercise a vote whenever any matter subject to approval should arise. "Reasonable efforts" shall include, but not be limited to, special delivery letters and telegrams. Should the absentee Owner be unavailable after the expenditure of a reasonable amount of time and effort to locate him or her, then the remaining Owners shall proceed with the granting or denying of approval.

23. A majority of the Owners shall have the right to initiate legal action against any Owner who violates the terms of this Agreement.

24. If a majority of the Owners initiate any legal action against another Owner due to a violation of the terms of this Agreement, the defendant Owner shall be liable for reasonable court costs and attorney fees.

25. Any amendments or additions to this Agreement must be approved in writing by a majority of the Owners of said property.

26. This Agreement is written and approved in the spirit of fairness to all the Owners in the hope that no Owner shall derive any benefit at the unfair expense of any other Owner.

(Owner's Signature)
_____

(Owner's Signature)
_____

(Owner's Signature)
_____

chapter 33

Deeds and Recording

The development of the deed as a method of transferring title is perhaps the most important element to evolve during the history of private land ownership. Not until 1676, when the Statute of Frauds was enacted in England, were written documents required and widely used as evidence of land ownership. Prior to that time, the tranfer of land titles was mainly done orally and symbolically. A seller would simply hand the buyer a stick, an acorn, a rock, or a handful of dirt from his land and pronounce that he was passing title to the land. Many problems arose under this system,

the most common of which was the lack of evidence of the conveyance. Nothing prevented the seller from returning to his land and claiming he never sold it. Buyers, demanding greater protection, began to call on neighbors to witness land transactions. The seller, standing on his land, would make a public statement to the buyer and the witnesses who stood a short distance off the land. After stating that he was selling his land to the buyer, the seller would walk off the land and the buyer would walk onto it. Thus, many witnesses heard and saw the seller convey his land to the buyer. But witnesses eventually die or move away, and a better system had to be found.

The first written documents showing land transfers eventually evolved into what we now call "deeds." A deed is not the title to the land being conveyed. "Title" represents ownership. A deed is the instrument used to transfer the title or ownership of property from one person to another. A person holding a deed to a parcel of land holds the title as represented by the writing in the deed, which states that title was transferred by the former owner to the party now holding the deed.

A deed is not a contract between the buyer and seller and should never be used as one. The terms and conditions of the sale are stated in the formal Contract of Sale. (See Chapter 28: *The Model of Contract Sale.*) Do not confuse a deed, which transfers title, with a deed of trust, which is a means of financing a land purchase in some states. (See Chapter 21: *Types of Financing: Land Contract, Mortgage, Deed of Trust.*)

BASIC PROVISIONS OF ANY LEGAL DEED

Although various types of deeds are used to convey property, any deed must contain certain basic elements to be legally valid.

1. A deed must be in writing and all of its terms must be contained within it. The seller, who must be legally and mentally competent, is responsible for having the deed drawn up and delivered to the buyer.

2. The date of the conveyance must be stated.

3. The name of each person who owns the land, including both spouses, must be given in full.

4. The names of all the buyers must be given in full and their marital status specified. Also the deed must state how title is to be taken, e.g., joint tenants or tenants-in-common. (See Chapter 32: *Types of Co-Ownership.*) If the buyers are dividing their interests in the property into unequal portions, the division should be specified; e.g., "to A, B, and C as tenants in common. A with an undivided half interest, B with an undivided two-sixths interests, and C with an undivided one-sixth interest."

5. All owners, including both spouses, must sign the deed, as sellers, using the same names by which they took title to the property. Some states require witnesses to also sign the deed. The buyer does not usually sign it, unless he is assuming a mortgage or deed of trust.

6. Words of conveyance must be used in a "granting clause" which states that the seller is conveying, or transferring, his title to the buyer. For example, the seller does hereby "bargain and sell," "grant and convey," or "quitclaim and release" his title.

7. Although most states do not require that the purchase price be given, the deed must state that something of value was given. The phrase "good and valuable consideration" is often used in place of an actual monetary figure.

8. The property being conveyed must be described in full, including easements, water rights, and other property rights that the buyer is getting. The description must also include reservations, exceptions, and restrictive covenants in the title. For example, if mineral rights will not be included in the conveyance, the deed must state that they are excepted from the title and must identify the person in whose name the rights are reserved.

9. Depending on the type of deed, various warranties and covenants of title might be included. These are described later in this chapter.

10. If the title is being conveyed "subject to" an existing encumbrance, such as a mortgage, deed of trust, tax or other lien, the encumbrance might be stated and fully described in a "subject to clause." This is not a legal requirement for a valid deed.

11. The deed must be authenticated by an "acknowledgment," whereby the seller declares before a public official, usually a notary public, that his act of delivering title is voluntary. The notary signs the deed and stamps it with his official notarization.

12. Real property transfer tax stamps must be placed on the deed or the amount of taxes must be written on the deed in states that levy such a tax. (See Chapter 19: *Evaluating the Price of the Property.*)

13. Before the transfer of title is valid, the deed must be delivered to the buyer, or escrow holder. Acceptance of the delivery is considered complete when the deed is recorded in the County Records, whereby notice is given to the world that the seller has transferred his title to the buyer.

14. Some states require the buyer to state his address on the deed to facilitate communication with him.

RESTRICTIVE COVENANTS
IN A DEED

Restrictions are often placed in a deed to a piece of land which are binding on anybody who purchases the land thereafter. A restrictive covenant limits what you can do on the property. For example, a covenant might specify that the land can be used "only for residential purposes," or only during certain times of the year. Only "private dwellings" or "one building per parcel, might be permitted. A line might be established, called a "building line restriction," beyond which no buildings can be constructed. These are not government restrictions, like zoning, building, and health codes. Restrictive covenants are established and enforced by private parties to a transaction, usually a subdivider or seller.

If any restrictions exist, they should be listed in the Model Contract of Sale in Clause 4. (See Chapter 28.) The real estate agent should show you what restrictions exist and you can also look them up in the seller's deed in the County Records. Chapter 31: *The Title Search, Abstract of Title, and Title Insurance Policy* tells how to look up deeds.

Restrictive convenants might be written in a Declaration of Restrictions, which is a form used when land is being subdivided and all the parcels are to be bound by the same restrictions. The Declaration of Restriction is filed with the Subdivision Public Report and Plat (see Chapter 14: *Subdivisions*) and may not appear in your deed. Instead the deed will refer to the location of the recorded restrictive covenants. For example, the deed might state that "title is conveyed subject to the restrictions listed in The Declaration of Restrictions recorded in the Office of the County Recorder, Case 5, Drawer 12, Page 68." You should locate and examine this document thoroughly to see what restrictions exist.

How will existing restrictions affect your intended use of the land? The seller will usually try to include a condition in the contract that if you violate any restrictions, the land will automatically revert back to the seller and you will not be reimbursed. If a subdivision was formed with the same restriction included in each buyer's deed, any land-owner in the subdivision can bring a legal action against any other owner who is violating the restrictions.

If the restriction will hinder your use, ask the seller to either release the restriction himself or get it released by whoever initially placed it on the land before you agree to purchase it. If that can't be done and you will be prevented from using the land as you wish, you had better look elsewhere.

A restriction might not be to your disadvantage. Particularly in a subdivision, you may want restrictions prohibiting commercial development or placing a minimum size on subdivided parcels. If another landowner in the subdivision violates a restriction, you can take legal action against him if the restriction has been established for the entire subdivision as shown in the plat and report. If the restriction is made only in each individual purchaser's deed or Contract of Sale, the seller alone can take action for violations. For example, if you want a restriction on commercial development in the subdivision, it must be so stated in the plat and report and not individually in each buyer's deed.

FULL COVENANT
AND WARRANTY DEED

In Clause 7 of the Model Contract of Sale (Chapter 28) I specify that the seller shall convey title by a Full Covenant and Warranty Deed because this deed offers the best protection to the buyer. You might be told by the real estate agent or title company that a local custom favors the use of a different kind of deed but you need not be bound by this preference.

The advantage of the Full Covenant and Warranty Deed (also called Warranty Deed with Full Covenants or General Warranty Deed) is that when the seller gives the title to the land, he includes five specific warranties, called Covenants of Title. These warranties must be written into the deed as the: Covenant of Seizin, Covenant Against Encumbrances, Covenant of Quiet Enjoyment, Covenant of Further Assurance, and Covenant of Warranty of Title.

1. The *Covenant of Seizin* guarantees that the seller is "seised" of the full title to the land, which means he has possession of a "fee simple estate." In this covenant the seller also warrants that he has a legal right to sell the land and that he has not previously sold it to any other person.

2. The *Covenant Against Encumbrances* assures the buyer that the only encumbrances existing against the title are listed in the deed. Encumbrances include mortgages, deeds of trust, tax and assessment liens, judgment liens, restrictions, easements, rights of spouses, and all other liens. If you should find out later that a lien does exist against the property which is not included in the deed, the covenant is breached, and you can take legal action against the seller.

3. The *Covenant of Quiet Enjoyment* assures the buyer that neither the seller nor any other person will have a better title to the land than the buyer himself and that his "quiet enjoyment" of the land will not be disturbed by the actions of anyone after he receives the deed to the property. If the buyer is forced to lease the property because of a court order, he can take legal action against the seller for breach of this covenant. Furthermore, if the buyer sells the property, his buyers will also be covered by this covenant.

4. The *Covenant of Further Assurance* guarantees that the seller will do anything necessary to give the buyer the title promised in the deed. For example, if the seller is to pay off an existing mortgage before the deed is delivered and later it is discovered that a mistake was made and the mortgage was not legally paid, the seller must clear the defect on the title. Or if there is a mistake in the deed, the seller must rewrite the deed to correct the error. Regardless of when a mistake is discovered in the title, the seller must do whatever is necessary to put the title to the land in the condition in which he promised to deliver it to you.

5. The *Covenant of Warranty of Title* guarantees the buyer good title and possession of the land forever. If a third party presents a rightful claim to the title of the land, the seller must defend the buyer's title. If the buyer loses his title, the seller must pay him damages for the loss.

These five warranties give basically the same protection as the Standard Owner's Policy of Title Insurance. But title insurance places liability for a defective title on the title company whereas a Full Covenant and Warranty Deed makes the seller responsible to you. Thus, you get double protection if you have both, and it is always desirable to get as much protection as possible. In an area where title insurance is not available, a Full Covenant and Warranty Deed is essential.

You will notice that Clause 17 in the Model Contract of Sale also includes the five covenants of title. A sixth provision states that the covenants survive delivery of the deed, thus protecting the buyer after he receives title to the land. (See Chapter 28.) If the seller wants to delete the warranties from the contract, he probably will not be willing to give you a Full Covenant and Warranty Deed. If he is not, there might be some question in his mind regarding the state of the title, and if you detect this in his actions, you must proceed with extreme caution and determine the cause of his reluctance.

GRANT DEED

A few state legislatures have established a special warranty deed called a Grant Deed. The law states that a Grant Deed automatically includes certain warranties that do not have to be written into the document. You should find out from the title company or escrow holder what warranties are included in the deed by state law. Usually a Grant Deed includes only a few of the five warranties I have discussed above. Although the Grant Deed is used, you can still ask the seller to use a Full Covenant and Warranty Deed.

BARGAIN AND SALE DEED

Most Bargain and Sale Deeds make two warranties. First, the seller warrants that he owns the land he is conveying. The second guarantee is "that the seller has not done or suffered anything whereby the said premises have been encumbered in any way." Under this warranty, called a Covenant against Grantor's Acts, the seller is liable only if he has caused a defect to be placed on the title, whereas in a Full Covenant and Warranty Deed the seller is also liable if any other person, including his seller, has placed an encumbrance on the title to the land.

For example, if your seller intends to use a Bargain and Sale Deed and he has given a mortgage on the property, he must pay off that mortgage before conveying title to you. However, if your seller's seller had mortgaged the property during his ownership, your seller would not be liable under a Bargain and Sale Deed for giving you the title subject to the mortgage, whereas under a Warranty Deed he would. This type of deed is also called a Bargain and Sale Deed with Covenant Against Grantor's Acts, a Grant, Bargain, and Sale Deed with Covenant Against Grantor's Acts, or, because the protection is less than a Warranty Deed, a Special Warranty Deed or Limited Warranty Deed.

There can also be a Bargain and Sale Deed Without Covenant Against Grantor's Acts. The only warranty in this deed is that the seller owns the land he is conveying. No guarantees are made against liens and encumbrances on the title.

THE QUITCLAIM DEED

In the Quitclaim Deed, the seller makes no warranties or guarantees about anything. Whenever you see the word "quitclaim" in a deed, such as "the seller does hereby quitclaim and release," or "remise, release, and forever quitclaim," that deed only transfers to the buyer whatever interest the seller has in the land. If he has full title, the buyer will get full title. If the seller has nothing, the buyer will get nothing. When you are buying land never, under any circumstances, accept a Quitclaim Deed. Somebody could legally sell you the Grand Canyon with such a deed. Regardless of what the title search shows and despite the fact that the seller is willing to give you a

Policy of Title Insurance, don't buy land under a Quitclaim Deed.

PATENTS

When the federal or a state government transfers or sells land it owns, a patent rather than a deed is used. A patent serves the same function as a deed and also gives notice that the land was formerly owned by the government. Almost every parcel of land in the United States has a patent in its chain of title since most land was originally owned by the government. If you buy land that has oil, mineral, timber, or other rights reserved by the government, your deed will state that those rights are reserved in a patent recorded in a Patent Record Book in the county Recorder's office. Ask the county Recorder how to look up this patent so you can read it.

RECORDING YOUR DEED AND OTHER DOCUMENTS

The deed to your land must be recorded as soon as you receive title to the property. Only recording it protects you against the possibility that the seller will convey the title to another person after selling it to you. For instance, suppose escrow closes and you receive a Full Covenant and Warranty Deed to the land on May 1 and you do not record it. On May 2 the seller sells the same land to another person and gives him a Full Covenant and Warranty Deed. The second buyer knows nothing about the sale to you the day before, and since you are not living on the property, he cannot tell by inspecting it that the land has already been sold to you. On that same day, May 2, he records his deed with the county Recorder. On May 3, you record your deed. Under every law regarding title to land, you will not have legal title to the property because you did not have your deed recorded first. If you and the second buyer were to go to court, the judge would undoubtedly declare that the other purchaser holds the only legal title to the land.

The first person to record a deed to a parcel of land is the owner. Once a deed is recorded, the law declares that everybody in the world has full knowledge, or has "constructive knowledge," of the deed. Thus, if you had recorded your deed first, the second buyer could not claim that he did not know the land had already been sold, since the deed would be part of the public record. The recording system was established to show the chronological sequence of land transfers and other actions affecting the title to land.

A deed is recorded in the Recorder's office of the county where the land is located. The county Recorder will either photograph, photocopy, xerox, or microfilm the deed and the original will be returned to you. The copy is filed with the other documents and indexed in the Grantor-Grantee Index or the Tract Index. (These indexes are discussed in detail in Chapter 31: *The Title Search, Abstract of Title, and Title Insurance Policy*.) A recording fee, which is usually $10 or less, will always be charged, usually to the buyer.

The escrow holder usually records the deed as a routine part of escrow. Be sure your escrow holder is to do this and that your Policy of Title Insurance goes into effect at exactly the same time. The burden of making sure the deed is recorded is on the buyer. If, for any reason, the deed is returned to you before it is recorded, you must take it to the county Recorder and have it recorded immediately. Generally, the title insurance company will also be watching to be sure the deed is recorded since the Policy of Title Insurance insures the title up until the moment the deed is recorded.

Most deeds contain a space in which the buyer is to write an address where all the tax statements and other official notices are to be sent. Be sure to give a current address where you are certain to receive your mail, and keep the county informed of any changes. Non-receipt of mail is not a good defense for failure to pay property taxes.

Any other document affecting title to land is also recorded and open to public inspection in the county Recorder's office. Some of these documents include mortgages, deeds of trust, release deeds, satisfactions of mortgages or deeds of trust, and assignments of mortgages or deeds of trust.

A FINAL NOTE AND WARNING

I have not included a copy of a deed in this chapter because you can see hundreds of them along with other land documents by looking through any of the record books in your local county Recorder's office. I cannot encourage you strongly enough to become familiar with these records. Look up the seller's deed to the land you are planning to buy. (I tell you how to do this in Chapter 31: *The Title Search, Abstract of Title, and Title Insurance Policy*.) What kind of deed did he receive and what is included in it?

You must specify in your Contract of Sale the type of deed you want the seller to give you. Your Escrow Instructions should also specify the same type of deed. I recommend that you state you want a Full Covenant and Warranty Deed, and this is what I have used in the Model Contract of Sale. If the seller tells you he cannot give you such a deed, find out why. What is he afraid of? Does he doubt that he has full and clear title to the land or does he have good title but simply want to avoid liability by giving you a Policy of Title Insurance which places liability on the title company? If you do not specify what type of deed you are to receive, the seller might deliver you a Quitclaim Deed. Maybe he'll sell you part of Yosemite National Park while he's at it.

VIII

USING
A LAWYER

chapter 34

Do You Need a Lawyer?

If you follow the course I outline in this book, you should have no problems handling your land deal with the minimal assistance of an attorney. Every transaction, however, is unique, and you might have an unusual problem involving complicated legal questions I do not cover. If there is any matter you do not fully understand, do not sign anything at any stage until you see a lawyer.

Because laws and practices vary throughout the country and are constantly being revised, you will have to investigate which laws apply to your area. Some of you will not have the time or inclination to do a thorough job of investigation and negotiation yourselves and will want a lawyer to do some of this for you. Although a lawyer cannot tell you if the property is satisfactory with reference to location, water, soil, climate, amenities, and condition of the structures, or if the price is reasonable, he can help you write the Contract of Sale, negotiate with the seller, or decide whether you have the necessary easements, water rights, and other legal rights.

If you retain a lawyer to handle your real estate deal, he will be working exclusively on your behalf, doing everything he can to see that you receive what you expect to get. All other parties, such as the title company, mortgagee, lending institution, local and state government officials, the seller, and the real estate agent, will have interests contrary to your own. As explained in Chapter 2: *Real Estate Agents, Realtors, and Salesmen,* the real estate agent works for the seller. He cannot give you legal advice and may, in fact, give you false advice due to ignorance or intent. Beware of the agent who discourages you from obtaining an attorney or who asks you to rely on his own attorney's advice. A broker's interest is in making a quick and easy sale so that he can collect his commission. A lawyer's interest is in protecting the client who employs him.

WHAT A LAWYER CAN DO FOR YOU

You can retain a lawyer to do anything from double-checking your Contract of Sale to handling all the legal aspects of the purchase from start to finish.

By the time you start negotiating to get the price down, you might be too friendly with the agent to become a hard bargainer. Sometimes it is to your advantage to have an attorney negotiate on your behalf with the real estate agent and seller. When the agent tells you that your demands are unreasonable, you can blame your lawyer for insisting on them. A lawyer also might have good connections with a bank or finance company and be able to help you obtain a loan.

Drawing up contracts and examining forms you are asked to sign are important functions of a lawyer. In many states, a real estate agent is permitted to write contracts, but these contracts will not give you sufficient protection. The Model Contract of Sale in this book gives complete protection to the buyer, but its details must be carefully studied and adjusted to fit your situation. If you cannot spend the necessary time, retain a lawyer to write your contract. If you have doubts about any document involved in the transaction, a lawyer can determine its legality and explain its contents.

You can have an attorney investigate the zoning and other ordinances that affect your property and tell you whether your intended use will be permissible. An attorney can do a title search or obtain one for you. He can personally examine the land for any constructive defects of title that would not be recorded in the County Records such as prescriptive easements or adverse possession claims. (See Chapter 9: *Easement Rights* and Chapter 16: *Adverse Possession*.) Then he can help you get the seller to clear any defects of title before you buy, such as an unwanted easement or tax lien.

The means by which you take title and the financial terms of the purchase have tax consequences which can be to your benefit or detriment, and you might want to ask an attorney's advice on these matters if you have an unusual situation. The retention of a lawyer is mandatory if you are a group planning to incorporate or form a nonprofit organization such as a church or foundation. Certain state regulations must be satisfied and the legal problems involved can be complex.

CHOOSING YOUR LAWYER

You must decide whether to use a city or a country lawyer. Then you must choose between a general practitioner or a real estate specialist.

If you already have a lawyer in the city who has handled other matters for you, you may want him to handle your land deal. Most attorneys are reluctant to oversee a real estate transaction more than 100 miles away because it is difficult to inspect the land and speak with the parties involved. Your regular attorney will probably recommend that you retain local counsel. A local lawyer not only knows the land, or can easily reach it, he knows everybody in town and has established a working relationship with surveyors, well-diggers, appraisers, inspectors, government officials, title company officials, bankers and other lending institution officials, escrow holders, sellers, and real estate agents. Your city lawyer may be able to refer you to a local attorney he knows personally or by reputation. If you still want your regular attorney's aid, you can make an arrangement whereby he will double-check the local country lawyer's work and advice.

You must be careful that the lawyer's association with the local residents does not interfere with his work on your behalf. For example, some lawyers will try to work out the deal in the real estate agent's interest by recommending that you make the purchase without researching certain matters that could complicate the deal. Be careful to recognize when, and if, the lawyer is trying to talk you out of necessary protections such as surveys, appraisals, and contingencies in the contract. If you read anything in this book that your lawyer does not mention to you, question him on the matter and try to determine if he has any ties with the real estate agent, seller, or other party which might be a conflict of interest.

Many lawyers in the country specialize in real estate law because the majority of their cases involve land problems. Often such a specialist will charge less than a general practitioner. He is more familiar with the problems and laws involved and will have to do less research and spend less time on the case than the lawyer who handles such deals only occasionally. You should compare the estimated fee of the local specialist with that of the local general practitioner.

In most rural areas, your choice of attorneys will be limited because of the scarcity of lawyers practicing in the country. Usually several lawyers practice in the county seat, and the farther you go from that base, the fewer lawyers you will encounter. If a local, state, or federal Legal Assistance Office is located in the area, ask for recommendations and information on who are the most trustworthy and reasonable lawyers in the area. Call the county Bar Association and ask for a list of real estate specialists. If you know a lawyer in the city, ask if he can recommend a good lawyer in the area in which you intend to purchase land. Talk to local people and try to get an idea of the reputation of the local attorneys. You may find that one lawyer will be consistently referred to as being the most honest lawyer in town.

Sometimes a large real estate agency will have an attorney who works for the office drawing up papers and overseeing the legalities of sales. Do not rely on him to represent you. If he draws up any documents, you should examine them yourself very carefully, and if you hire an attorney, he must also inspect them.

HOW TO RELATE TO YOUR LAWYER

Good feelings between you and your lawyer are essential. If you don't feel comfortable with him after you retain him, you should fire him and go to someone else. Since your lawyer needs to be able to contact you, keep him informed of your whereabouts at all times. Keep him up to date regarding all conversations you have with the real estate agent or seller, give him copies of every document you receive, and inform him of any other matters relating to your purchase. When giving him information, don't tell him only what you think is relevant. Tell him everything. He should also keep you informed about everything he is doing for you.

Sometimes a lawyer will put you off when you try to contact him or will seem to be very slow in getting his job done for you. This is probably because he has many clients, but if you do not think he is giving your case enough attention, do not hesitate to stay on his back and prod him along at a reasonable pace.

HOW TO KNOW WHETHER YOUR LAWYER IS DOING A GOOD JOB

Check everything the lawyer does against the information contained in this book. If his advice or information conflicts with what I say, bring it to his attention and resolve the problem. He does not necessarily have to agree with everything I say, but he should give you an adequate explanation of why he disagrees. New laws may have been passed or practices may be different in your area.

If your lawyer uses "standard forms," which are preprinted forms containing blank spaces for inserting the necessary information, be certain that they protect you adequately. Forms drawn up specifically for your individual situation are much better, since preprinted forms often do not satisfactorily deal with your individual circumstances. Nevertheless, most lawyers will use them to save time. Check the forms used by your attorney against those which I include in this book for completeness. After any forms are drawn up, carefully review them with your attorney to be sure they include everything you expect to get out of the deal, particularly regarding conditions of the sale and financing. Show my Model Contract of Sale to your attorney so he can use it, making the appropriate changes. (Of course, the purpose of including it is to enable you to draw up your own contract, but you might want to have it double-checked by an attorney if you are uncertain about something.)

HOW MUCH WILL A LAWYER COST?

A lawyer's fee is based on several factors, including the time and labor which he estimates will be required, the difficulty of the problems involved, the amount of skill involved and the level of his expertise, the standard fees of lawyers in his community, the amount of money and benefits which you will receive from his services, and whether you are an established or a new client.

When you see a lawyer, after explaining

365

what you want him to do, ask him what his fee is. Depending on the situation, he will either quote you a single fee as a "package" price, or an hourly fee with an estimate of the time involved. The method he chooses will largely depend on what you hire him to do. If you want him to handle the whole purchase, including all the negotiations, execution and examination of documents, he will probably give you a package rate. If you simply want to come to him whenever a problem arises that you think you cannot deal with, he will charge by the hour, and he will probably keep track of every letter he writes, every phone call he makes, and every minute he spends talking to you, in person or on the phone. If you run into any time-consuming problems in the middle of the transaction the amount of the fee could easily be as much as, or more than, it would be if the lawyer handled the entire purchase for a package price. In a legally complicated land deal you might find that it is cheaper to pay a set fee and let the lawyer handle it entirely.

If a lawyer charges a single fee, he usually bases it on the purchase price of the property since that is the value of the item which he is making "safe" for you. The common fee is 1 to 3 percent of the purchase price with a minimum of $100. Thus, on a $10,000 purchase price, the lawyer's fee would probably be between $100 and $300, but it could go higher. All fees are negotiable and you can offer goods or services as part or all of the fee. Hourly fees usually start at a minimum of $10–$25. If the lawyer has a good reputation he could charge $50 per hour or more.

If you draw up your own Contract of Sale based on the Model Contract in this book, you can take it to an attorney for an "examination and opinion." The average minimum fee for this service is $25–$75. If you have the lawyer draw up the Contract of Sale, the average minimum fee is $75–$150. Thus, even if you are uncertain about some aspects of the contract, you can save money by executing it yourself and having it double-checked by an attorney.

If you are buying as a group and want to form a corporation or nonprofit entity, you will have to retain an attorney to draw up and file the proper documents. This service could cost several hundred dollars, although if it is combined with other aspects of the purchase, such as examining and executing other documents, you can get a deal on the total price.

Whatever your decision is regarding the use of a lawyer, one thing is certain: It will cost you more time and money to go to court after the transaction is completed than to pay a lawyer to oversee your purchase from the beginning or to double-check your own legal work.

By considering your responses to the following questions you will be able to better determine whether or not you need to retain an attorney: What is your business experience in general and your prior experience in land transactions? How large is your purchase and what could you lose if something goes wrong? Is a good lawyer available? What are his fees? What do you want a lawyer to do for you? After reading this book, do you feel confident that you can handle the entire deal on your own? If you do retain an attorney, this book can be used to help you understand what is involved in the purchase and to enable you to oversee his work.

chapter 35

Some Final Words

I hope that the information in this book has not only made you more aware of the complexities involved in finding and buying your place in the country, but has also given you the confidence to handle many aspects of your purchase yourself. By referring to this book, you should be able to find the answers to any questions and the solutions to any problems that might arise. If you encounter a unique problem or an example of a fraudulent real estate practice I have not discussed, I will be interested to read about it. Your information might be useful to include in future revisions. You can write to me in care of the publisher.

Even after you buy your land, you will find that much of the information herein will continue to be useful. When you decide to sell your property, you can take this book from the shelf and refresh your memory on the many aspects of buying and selling real property. You will find that by having been a wise land buyer, you will also be a successful land seller.

Appendix A.

Land Catalogues and Other Advertising Sources

Strout Realty

Franchises in forty-one states. Catalogues issued three times a year, available at any local office (see your telephone directory Yellow Pages) or from:

P.O. Box 2757
Springfield, Missouri 65803

Box 690
Arcadia, California 91106

311 Springfield Avenue
Summit, New Jersey 07901

United Farm Agency

Franchises in thirty-three states. Catalogues issued four times a year, available at any local office (see your telephone directory Yellow Pages) or from:

612 W. 47th Street
Kansas City, Missouri 64112

Safe-Buy Real Estate Agency

Franchises in eleven states: Arkansas, Colorado, Florida, Minnesota, Missouri, New York, Oklahoma, Oregon, Pennsylvania, Tennessee, Texas. Catalogues issued four times a year, available at local office or from:

2405 Gaines Street
P.O. Box 589
Little Rock, Arkansas 72203

Ozark Land

Catalogue available from:

Owensby and Sons
Home office
South Side of Public Square
Buffalo, Missouri 65022

The Market Bulletin

Lists land for sale in West Virginia:

Department of Agriculture
Charleston, West Virginia 25300

Arkansas Land Catalogue

State Wide Realty Company
200 Highway 62 East
Mountain Home, Arkansas 72653

The Farm Market

A regular section in *Organic Gardening and Farming Magazine* (a monthly publication, $5.85 per year) advertises organic farms for sale. Available on local news stands or from:

Organic Gardening and Farming Magazine
33 East Minor Street
Emmaus, Pennsylvania 18049

Lifestyles

A regular Mother Earth News publication (bi-monthly, $6 per year). Advertises places for rent, for sale, and to trade. Available on local news stands, in bookstores, or from:

Lifestyle
Editorial and Subscription Offices
P.O. Box 1
Unionville, Ohio 44088

Mother Earth News

Similar to the above publication (bi-monthly, $8 per year). Available on local news stands, in bookstores, or from:

The Mother Earth News
Editorial and Subscription Offices
P.O. Box 70
Hendersonville, North Carolina 28739

Appendix B. The Bureau of Land Management (BLM) and District Offices

The following offices are the main branches of the BLM. They will have the information you need about present and future uses of federal land adjoining or near the land you wish to buy. Look at their maps and studies of projected multiple uses.

Alaska
  Southern Alaska
    Anchorage Land Office
    555 Cordova Street
    Anchorage, Alaska 99501

  Northern Alaska
    Fairbanks District & Land Office
    516 Second Avenue
    Fairbanks, Alaska 99701

Arizona
  Arizona
    Arizona Land Office
    Federal Building, Room 3022
    Phoenix, Arizona 85025

  Lower Colorado River Area
    Lower Colorado River Office
    Crescent Building
    2450 Fourth Avenue
    Yuma, Arizona 85364

California
  Bakersfield Area
    Bakersfield District Office
    U.S. Federal Building, Room 311
    800 Truxtun Avenue
    Bakersfield, California 93301

  Folsom Area
    Folsom District Office
    63 Natoma Street
    Folsom, California 95630

Redding Area
Redding District Office
2460 Athens Avenue
Redding, California 96001

Southern California
Riverside District & Land Office
1414 University Avenue, Box 723
Riverside, California 92502

Northern California
Sacramento Land Office
Federal Office Building
2800 Cottage Way, E-2841
Sacramento, California 95825

Susanville Area
Susanville District Office
P.O. Box 1090
Susanville, California 96130

Ukiah Area
Ukiah District Office
168 Washington Avenue
Ukiah, California 95482

Colorado
Colorado Land Office
Colorado State Bank Building
1600 Broadway, Room 700
Denver, Colorado 80202

Idaho
Idaho Land Office
Federal Building, Room 224
550 West Fort Street
Boise, Idaho 83702

Montana, North Dakota, and South Dakota
Montana Land Office
Federal Building and
U.S. Courthouse
316 North 26th Street
Billings, Montana 59101

Nevada
Nevada Land Office
Federal Building, Room 3008
300 Booth Street
Reno, Nevada 89502

New Mexico, Oklahoma, and Texas
New Mexico Land Office
U.S. Post Office and
Federal Building
South Federal Place
P.O. Box 1449
Santa Fe, New Mexico 87501

Oregon and Washington
Oregon Land Office
729 Northeast Oregon Street
P.O. Box 2965
Portland, Oregon 97208

Utah
Utah Land Office
Federal Building
125 South State
P.O. Box 11505
Salt Lake City, Utah 84111

Wyoming, Kansas, and Nebraska
Wyoming Land Office
U.S. Post Office and
Courthouse Building
2120 Capitol Avenue
P.O. Box 1828
Cheyenne, Wyoming 82001

Eastern States
Arkansas, Iowa, Louisiana, Minnesota (minerals only), Missouri, and all states east of the Mississippi River
Eastern States Land Office
7981 Eastern Avenue
Silver Spring, Maryland 20910

Main Office
Director, Department of the Interior
Bureau of Land Management
Eighteenth and C Streets N.W.
Washington, D.C. 20240

Appendix C.
Federal Lands
for Sale

The following pamphlets are available free from the Bureau of Land Management (BLM addresses are listed in Appendix B).

What Are "The Public Lands"? Information
Bulletin No. 1 (0-241-847)
How To Buy Public Lands, Information
Bulletin No. 4 (0-265-484)

The Bureau of Land Management issues *Our Public Lands* four times a year for $1. It contains a "Public Sale Bulletin Board" indicating federal land for sale under the BLM. See it at your public library or write to:

Superintendent of Documents
United States Government Printing Office
Washington, D.C. 20402

For information on federal reclaimed land for sale, write to:

The Bureau of Reclamation (Region 1)
United States Department of the Interior
Washington, D.C. 20240

Bureau of Reclamation (Region 2)
2800 Cottage Way
Sacramento, California 95825

Bureau of Reclamation (Region 3)
Administration Building
Boulder City, Nevada 89005

Yuma Projects Office
Bureau of Reclamation (Region 3)
P.O. Bin 5569
Yuma, Arizona 85364

For information on the Small Tract Act, which involves leasing and selling federal lands, write to any BLM office for:

Sales and Exchanges of Public Lands, Circular No. 2151
Public Lands Information, Pamphlet No. 703

and for any pamphlets on available Small Tracts in the particular state you are interested in.

Appendix D.
Homesteading

For information on homesteading in each state, contact the Bureau of Land Management (BLM) Land Office in that state. These offices are listed above in Appendix B.

Write for the following free BLM pamphlets:

Homesteading
Regulations Pertaining to Occupancy on the Public Lands–Homesteads, Circular No. 2171

Homesteading Past and Present
Establishing a Farm in Alaska
The Hard Facts of Homesteading

Appendix E.
Mining Claims

Get the following free pamphlets from any Bureau of Land Management (BLM) office. BLM addresses are listed above in Appendix B.

Regulations Pertaining to Mining Claims under the General Mining Laws of 1872, Circular No. 2289
Mineral Patents—Basic Procedure for Obtaining Patent to a Mining Claim
Questions and Answers Concerning Mining Claims under the General Mining Laws, Circular No. 04912.2
Patenting a Mining Claim on Federal Lands —Basic Procedure
Staking a Mining Claim on Federal Lands —Questions and Answers

The pamphlet *Basic Placer Mining* is free from:

California Division of Mines and Geology
P.O. Box 2980
Sacramento, California 59801

Appendix F. Special Uses of the National Forests, Including Habitation for Summer Homes and Sale to the Public

The following are free from:

Forest Service
United States Department of Agriculture
Washington, D.C. 20250

Special Uses of the National Forests.
Field Offices of the Forest Service, FS-13.
National Forest Lands.

For information on leasing summer homes in National Forests in each state, write to the United States Forest Service Regional Field Office for your state. All addresses are given in "Useful Resources" in Chapter 5; *The Earth—Soil, Vegetation, Topography.*

Appendix G. State Lands for Sale

For information on state lands for sale, write to:

Alaska
State Division of Lands
Anchorage

Alabama
Secretary of State
Montgomery 36104

Arizona
State Land Commissioner
Phoenix 85025

Arkansas
Commissioner of State Lands
Little Rock 72201

California
Division of State Lands
Sacramento 95801

Colorado
State Board of Land Commissioners
Denver 80225

Connecticut
State Treasurer
Hartford 06103

Delaware
Chairman, State Park Commission
Dover 19901

Florida
Commissioner of Agriculture
Tallahassee 32301

Georgia
Secretary of State
Atlanta 30308

Idaho
State Land Commissioner
Boise 83707

Illinois
Auditor of Public Accounts
Springfield 62700

Indiana
Auditor of State
Indianapolis 46204

Iowa
State Highway Commissioner
Ames 50010

Kansas
Auditor of State and Register of State Lands
Topeka 66600

Kentucky
Auditor of State
Frankfort 40601

Louisiana
Register, State Land Office
Baton Rouge 70800

Maine
  State Land Agent and Forest Commissioner
  Augusta 04330

Maryland
  Land Commissioner
  Annapolis 21400

Massachusetts
  Department of Conservation
  Boston 02203

Michigan
  Director, Department of Conservation
  Lansing 48900

Minnesota
  Director, Division of Lands and Minerals
  St. Paul 55111

Mississippi
  Land Commissioner
  Jackson 39216

Missouri
  Secretary of State
  Jefferson City 65101

Montana
  Commissioner of State Lands and Investments
  Helena 59601

Nebraska
  Board of Educational Lands and Funds
  Lincoln 68508

Nevada
  State Land Register
  Carson City 89701

New Hampshire
  State Forester
  Concord 03301

New Jersey
  Department of Conservation and Economic
    Development
  Trenton 08600

New Mexico
  Commissioner of Public Lands
  Santa Fe 87501

New York
  State Department of Conservation
  Albany 12200

North Carolina
  Secretary of State
  Raleigh 27600

North Dakota
  State Land Commissioner
  Bismarck 58501

Ohio
  Auditor of State
  Columbus 43200

Oklahoma
  Secretary, Commissioner of Land Office
  Oklahoma City 73100

Oregon
  Clerk of State Land Board
  Salem 97301

Pennsylvania
  Secretary of Internal Affairs
  Harrisburg 17101

Rhode Island
  (No state land office)

South Carolina
  Secretary, Sinking Fund Commission
  Columbia 29201

South Dakota
  Commissioner of School and Public Lands
  Pierre 57501

Tennessee
  State Property Administration
  Nashville 37203

Texas
  Commissioner, General Land Office
  Austin 78700

Utah
  Executive Secretary, State Land Board
  Salt Lake City 84111

Vermont
  State Forester
  Montpelier 05602

Virginia
  State Librarian, Virginia State Library
  Richmond 23200

Washington
  Commissioner, Department of Public Lands
  Olympia 98501

West Virginia
  State Tax Commissioner, or State Auditor
  Charleston 25300

Wisconsin
  The Commissioners of the Public Lands
  Madison 53700

Wyoming
  Commissioner of Public Lands
  Cheyenne 82001

Appendix H. Alaska

For information on federal land use, including homesteading, write for:

Circular No. 2297—Regulations Pertaining to Disposition Occupancy and Use: Alaska Occupancy and Use—Homesteads
Information Bulletin No. 2—What About Land in Alaska?
Yearbook Separate No. 2923—Seward's Folly Can Be a Great Land (a BLM reprint from *Yearbook of Agriculture*)
Establishing a Farm in Alaska

from:
  Bureau of Land Management
  Department of the Interior
  Washington, D.C. 20240

  Manager, Land Office
  344 6th Avenue
  Anchorage, Alaska 99501

  Anchorage Land Office
  555 Cordova Street
  Anchorage, Alaska 99051

  Manager, Land Office
  2nd Avenue
  Fairbanks, Alaska 99701

  Manager, Land Office
  Box 1481
  Juneau, Alaska 99801

For information on state lands for lease and sale, write to:
  State of Alaska
  Department of Lands and Minerals
  Fairbanks Land Office
  State Office Building
  Barnette and Sixth
  Fairbanks, Alaska 99701

  State of Alaska
  Department of Lands and Minerals
  Juneau, Alaska, 99801

The following pamphlets on homesteading state land are free from:

Alaska Department of Natural Resources
Division of Lands
323 E. 4th Avenue
Anchorage, Alaska 99501

Alaska Land Lines Magazine
Facts About Alaska Lands

For information on climate, farming conditions, and markets for produce, write to:

Director
Alaska Agricultural Experiment Station
Palmer, Alaska 99645

For maps, write to:

United States Geological Survey
Fairbanks Office
1st Avenue
Fairbanks, Alaska 99701

For a good magazine on life in Alaska, write for:

Alaska Magazine
Alaska Northwest Publishing Company
Box 4-EEE
Anchorage, Alaska 99503

Appendix I. Canada

Although most of the legal problems in buying land are the same in Canada and the United States, there are a few areas of major importance which are unique to Canada. Thus, I advise you to retain an attorney in Canada if you intend to purchase land there. The information in this Appendix is to help get you started in your search for land in Canada.

General Information on Canada

The following pamphlets and general information on climate in Canada are available from:

The Director
Meteorological Branch
Department of Public Transport
315 Bloor Street West
Toronto 5, Ontario, Canada

Precipitation Normals for (the province you want), 10¢
Temperature Normals of (the province you want), 10¢

A list of maps and aerial photographs for every region in Canada can be obtained free from:

National Geodetic Survey and Mining Office
Ottawa, Ontario, Canada

An index and list of topographic maps showing the agricultural value of the land and the grade of the terrain in every region in Canada is available free from:

Map Distribution Office
Department of Mining and Technical Surveys
615 Booth Street
Ottawa 4, Ontario, Canada

Information on soil, water, agriculture, and other land-related matters can be obtained from:

Agricultural Economics Research Council of Canada
55 Parkdale Avenue
Ottawa 3, Ontario, Canada

Queen's Printer
Daly Bldg., Corner MacKenzie-Rideau
Ottawa, Ontario, Canada

The *Research Centers Directory* lists all agencies in Canada involved in land-related research. (See "Useful Resources" at the end of Chapter 5: *The Earth-Soil, Vegetation, Topography.*)

Information on buying land in Canada and a listing of licensed real estate agents and realtors can be obtained from:

Canadian Association of Real Estate Boards
20 Eglinton Avenue East
Toronto 12, Ontario, Canada

Canadian Institute of Realtors
20 Eglinton Avenue East
Toronto 12, Ontario, Canada

Tax sales are held each year by the government to make up unpaid back taxes. You can acquire information regarding these sales from the agencies listed throughout this appendix. However, there is one company which buys up land in tax sales for the purpose of reselling it themselves. Their catalogs list this land which is priced in order for them to realize a profit on their investment. Land catalogs are issued four times a year at an annual subscription price of $1. They will send you one issue as a sample on request. As much care should be used in purchasing this land as any other real estate. For a sample issue or subscription, write to:

H. M. Dignam Corporation Ltd.
85 Bloor Street East
Toronto 5, Ontario, Canada

For information on immigration to Canada, write to:

The Department of Citizenship and Immigration
Ottawa, Ontario, Canada

Alberta

Maps showing available public lands and geographic features of the area are available from the address below. Information on climate, soil, water, and land conditions is also available on request. The following pamphlets are also available free from:

Director of Lands
Department of Lands and Forests
Natural Resources Building
109th Street and 99th Avenue
Edmonton, Alberta, Canada

General Information Concerning Acquisition of Recreational Land and the Sale or Leasing of Land in Alberta, Department of Lands and Forests Leaflet
Information Regarding Homestead Sales in the Government of the Province of Alberta—Form LH 48

A list of real estate agents who can send you their land listings is available free with other general information on purchasing land in Alberta from:

Secretary-Treasurer
Alberta Real Estate Association
503-7th Street S.W.
Calgary 1, Alberta, Canada

British Columbia

A list of available maps of British Columbia is available free from:

Director, Surveys and Mapping Branch
Geographic Division
Department of Lands, Forests, and Water
    Resources
Victoria, British Columbia, Canada

Maps and nautical charts of British Columbia are also available from:

Dominion Map Limited
626 Howe Street
Vancouver 1, British Columbia, Canada

Geographic Bulletins 1 through 10 on geographic materials for British Columbia are available free from:

Province of British Columbia Lands Service
Department of Lands, Forests, and Water
    Resources
Victoria, British Columbia, Canada

Information on climate, soil, water, land use, and agriculture is available from both of the following agencies:

Canadian Agriculture Research Station
University of British Columbia
6660 Northwest Marine Drive
Vancouver 8, British Columbia, Canada

Department of Agriculture
Government of British Columbia
Victoria, British Columbia, Canada

For information on the availability and requirements to buy Crown Lands, write to:

British Columbia Lands Branch
Victoria, British Columbia, Canada

The following pamphlet is free from:

Government Printing Bureau
Victoria, British Columbia, Canada

The Acquisition of Crown Lands in British Columbia, Land Series Bulletin No. 11

For homestead and general land information, write to:

Director, Surveys and Mapping Branch
Geographic Division
Department of Lands, Forests, and Water
    Resources
Victoria, British Columbia, Canada

The following pamphlets are available free, as well as any other necessary information on homesteading and purchasing land next to, or on, the Queen Charlotte Islands from:

Director of Lands
British Columbia Lands Service
Parliament Building
Victoria, British Columbia, Canada

Land Bulletin No. 8
Status Map 103F of Available Land

For information on leasing or buying land in British Columbia, write to any of the following:

Land Commissioner
Burns Lake, British Columbia, Canada

Land Commissioner
1600 Third Street
Prince George, British Columbia, Canada

Land Inspector
British Columbia Lands Service
1300 Third Street
Prince George, British Columbia, Canada

Director of Lands
British Columbia Lands Service
Department of Lands, Forest, and Water
    Resources
Victoria, British Columbia, Canada

For information on buying land and for listings of land for sale, write to any of the following:

Mr. P. J. Humphreys, Secretary
Chilliwack & District Real Estate Board
46225 Larch Street
Chilliwack, British Columbia, Canada

Mr. C. H. Williams, Secretary-Manager
Okanagan-Mainline Real Estate Board
General Delivery
Kelowna, British Columbia, Canada

Mr. D. C. Lawford, Secretary
Vancouver Island Real Estate Board
80 Commercial Street
Nanaimo, British Columbia, Canada

Mr. Reg. B. Dixon, Secretary
Kootenay Real Estate Board, Box 590
Nelson, British Columbia, Canada

Mr. David F. Stacey, Secretary Manager
Cariboo Real Estate Board
30-444 Victoria Street
Prince George, British Columbia, Canada

Mr. S. R. Parker, Secretary
Real Estate Board of Northwestern British
  Columbia
612 West Third Avenue
Prince Rupert, British Columbia, Canada

Mr. W. R. Bennett, Executive Secretary
Westminster County Real Estate Board
15483-104th Avenue
Surrey, British Columbia, Canada

Mr. A. G. Creer, R. I. (B. C.), Secretary
The Real Estate Board of Greater Vancouver
1101 West Broadway
Vancouver 9, British Columbia, Canada

Mr. J. Hicks, N. P., Secretary
The Victoria Real Estate Board
1216 Broad Street
Victoria, British Columbia, Canada

British Columbia Association of Real Estate
  Boards
475 Howe Street, Room 502
Vancouver 1, British Columbia, Canada

Real Estate Institute of British Columbia
608-626 West Pender Street
Vancouver 2, British Columbia, Canada

Manitoba

Information on Crown Land for sale and the free pamphlet *Available Crown Land in Manitoba* can be obtained from:

Lands Branch
Department of Mines and Natural Resources
810 Norquay Building
Winnipeg 1, Manitoba, Canada

Information on maps and available homestead land can be obtained from the Director of Surveys at the same address.

Information on soil, water, agriculture, and other land-related matters can be obtained from:

Canada Agriculture Research Station
University of Manitoba
25 Dafoe Road
Winnipeg 19, Manitoba, Canada

Information on buying land and land for sale in Manitoba can be obtained from:

Executive Secretary
Manitoba Real Estate Association
1315 Portage Avenue
Winnipeg 10, Manitoba, Canada

New Brunswick

Information on Crown Lands and other lands for sale in New Brunswick can be obtained from:

Director of Lands Branch
Department of Natural Resources
Fredericton, New Brunswick, Canada

Information on buying land and land for sale in New Brunswick can be obtained from:

Secretary Treasurer
Association of New Brunswick Real Estate
  Brokers
P.O. Box 681
Saint John, New Brunswick, Canada

Newfoundland and Labrador

Information on Crown Lands and other lands for sale can be obtained from:

Director, Crown Lands and Surveys
Department of Mines, Agriculture, and Resources
Confederation Building
St. Johns, New Brunswick, Canada

Information on buying land and land for sale can be obtained from:

Secretary
Newfoundland and Labrador Real Estate Board
P.O. Box E-5476
St. Johns, New Brunswick, Canada

Northwest Territory

Information on Crown Lands and other lands for sale can be obtained from:

Water, Forest and Lands Division
Development Branch of the Department of Indian Affairs and Northern Development
Ottawa, Ontario, Canada

Nova Scotia

Information on Crown Lands and other lands for sale can be obtained from:

Director of Immigration and Land Settlement
Truro, Nova Scotia, Canada

Information on buying land and land for sale can be obtained from:

Executive Secretary
Nova Scotia Real Estate Association
1553 Granville Street
P.O. Box 2255
Halifax, Nova Scotia, Canada

Ontario

Information on Crown Lands and other lands for sale can be obtained from:

Director, Lands and Surveys Branch
Department of Lands and Forests
Parliament Buildings
Toronto 5, Ontario, Canada

Information on buying land and land for sale can be obtained from:

Reed & Zelsman Ltd.
3768 Bathurst Street
Downsview
Toronto, Ontario, Canada

H. Keith Ltd.
181 Eglinton Ave. E.
Toronto, Ontario, Canada

Tax Sale Lands
Queen's Printer
Parliament Bldgs.
Toronto, Ontario, Canada

Director
Tourist Industry Development Branch
Department of Tourism and Information
Parliament Buildings
Toronto 5, Ontario, Canada

Prince Edward Island

Information on Crown Lands and other lands for sale can be obtained from:

Commissioner of Public Lands
Department of the Attorney General
Province House
Charlottetown, Prince Edward Island, Canada

Information on buying land and land for sale can be obtained from:

Secretary
Prince Edward Island Real Estate Brokers Association
c/o Mr. John Ives
92 Kent Street
Charlottetown, Prince Edward Island, Canada

Quebec

Information on Crown Lands for sale, and the free pamphlet *Canada Land* can be obtained from:

Deputy Minister
Department of Lands and Forests
Parliament Buildings
200 St. Foi Street
Quebec City, Quebec, Canada

Information on agriculture can be obtained from:

Deputy Minister
Department of Agriculture and Colonization
Parliament Buildings
200 St. Foi Street
Quebec City, Quebec, Canada

Information on soil, water, and other land-related matters can be obtained from:

Geographical Branch
Department of Mines and Technical Surveys
Parliament Buildings
200 St. Foi Street
Quebec City, Quebec, Canada

Information on buying land and land for sale can be obtained from.

Executive Secretary
Corporation of Real Estate Brokers of Quebec
1080 Beaver Hall Hill-Room 802
Montreal 128, Quebec, Canada

Saskatchewan

Information on Crown Lands and other lands for sale, and the pamphlet *Available Crown Land in Saskatchewan* can be obtained from:

Controller of Surveys
Department of Natural Resources
Administration Building
Regina, Saskatchewan, Canada

Information on soil, water, agriculture, and other land-related matters can be obtained from:

Canada Agriculture Research Station
University of Saskatchewan
University Campus
Saskatoon, Saskatchewan, Canada

Information on buying land and on land for sale can be obtained from:

General Manager
Saskatchewan Real Estate Association
100 Ross Block
116 Third Avenue South
Saskatoon, Saskatchewan, Canada

Yukon Territory

Maps and other information on buying land can be obtained from:

Map Distribution Office
Department of Mines and Technical Surveys
Ottawa, Ontario, Canada

Information on Crown Lands and other lands lands for sale can be obtained from:

Supervisor of Lands
P.O. Box 1767
Whitehorse, Yukon Territory

Appendix J. United States Government Printing Office Bookstores

In addition to the mail order service provided by the Office of the Superintendent of Documents, Government Printing Office, there are also thirteen retail bookstores outside of Washington, D.C. The locations of these stores are shown below:

Atlanta Bookstore
Room 100, Federal Building
275 Peachtree Street NE.
Atlanta, Georgia 30303

Birmingham Bookstore
Room 102A, 2121 Building
2121 Eighth Avenue North
Birmingham, Alabama 35203

Boston Bookstore
Room G25, John F. Kennedy Federal Building
Sudbury Street
Boston, Massachusetts 02203

Canton Bookstore
Federal Office Building
201 Cleveland Avenue SW.
Canton, Ohio 44702

Chicago Bookstore
Room 1463—14th floor
Everett McKinley Dirksen Building
219 South Dearborn Street
Chicago, Illinois 60604

Dallas Bookstore
Room 1C46
Federal Building—U.S. Courthouse
1100 Commerce Street
Dallas, Texas 75202

Denver Bookstore
Room 1421
Federal Building—U.S. Courthouse
1961 Stout Street
Denver, Colorado 80202

Detroit Bookstore
Room 229, Federal Building
231 W. Lafayette Blvd.
Detroit, Michigan 48226

Kansas City Bookstore
Room 135, Federal Office Building
601 East 12th Street
Kansas City, Missouri 64106

Los Angeles Bookstore
Room 1015, Federal Office Building
300 North Los Angeles Street
Los Angeles, California 90012

New York Bookstore
Room 110
26 Federal Plaza
New York, New York 10007

Philadelphia Bookstore
U.S. Post Office and Courthouse
Main Lobby
Ninth and Chestnut Streets
Philadelphia, Pennsylvania 19107

San Francisco Bookstore
Room 1023, Federal Office Building
450 Golden Gate Avenue
San Franicsco, California 94102

index

Note: Boldface page numbers refer to illustrations.